DATE DUE

MAY 11

Money,
Debt and
Economic
Activity

19, 30, 33

Money, Debt and Economic Activity

Fourth Edition

Albert Gailord Hart
Professor of Economics

Peter B. Kenen
Professor of Economics

Alan D. Entine
Assistant Professor of Economics

PRENTICE-HALL, INC., *Englewood Cliffs, New Jersey*

PRENTICE-HALL, INTERNATIONAL, INC., *London*
PRENTICE-HALL OF AUSTRALIA, PTY. LTD., *Sydney*
PRENTICE-HALL OF CANADA, LTD., *Toronto*
PRENTICE-HALL OF INDIA PRIVATE LTD., *New Delhi*
PRENTICE-HALL OF JAPAN, INC., *Tokyo*

In memory of
HASTINGS HORNELL HART

Preface

When my good friend and colleague, Albert Hart, asked me to join him in writing the third edition of his book, I had many reservations. Could two economists agree on enough of the controversial issues in monetary economics to put forth a consistent textbook that would deal with those issues—not creep around them? Could the junior partner work within the fixed framework, intellectual and expositional, set forth by his senior partner's previous efforts? Experience furnished happy answers to both of these questions, and the endeavor was exciting. As is so often the case, I learned by trying to teach others and came away from the project with a better grasp of the subject than I had before. Albert Hart and I hope that our new colleague, Alan Entine, has had the same happy experience. We are, for our part, delighted with the huge contribution he has made in this fourth edition. He has done much more than routine revision. More than trimming and bringing the story up to date, he has added new ideas and brought new perspectives to bear on familiar materials.

Here, as in previous revisions, we have tried to concentrate on recent developments. Current events and new data in the monetary field have been used to illustrate policy problems and to judge the relevance of monetary theory. Nonetheless, older materials have been retained, for history remains the friend and teacher of anyone who seeks to understand the present. Interwar experience with monetary policy, domestic and international, are discussed in some detail, as they were in previous editions. Much of this material may seem slightly irrelevant to a college student born during or after the Second World War, but that is all the more reason to introduce it; economics is a cumulative subject, and economic theory cannot have meaning unless it illuminates economic behavior under a wide range of conditions. Macroeconomic theory and fiscal policy are not discussed so thoroughly as before, due chiefly to limitations of space, but also because separate courses and texts on these two subjects have become much more abundant in the last few years.

Several things are new in this fourth edition. The discussion of deposit creation has been recast to focus on owned reserves (on which we have valuable new data in the *Federal Reserve Bulletin*). Further, the exposition of this vital material has been simplified. The discussion of fiscal policy has been revised in the light of American experience during the first half of the 1960's—to draw lessons from the tax cuts of 1962 and 1964 and the failure to raise taxes in 1966–67. Hart's early discussion of built-in stabilizers, one of the first to appear in a textbook, has been recast. The monetary analysis has been restructured to measure Federal Reserve responses to changing economic conditions and to examine key monetary-link variables as transmitters of Federal Reserve policy. The international chapters look closely at current and emerging problems, providing the student with background he will need to analyze the many drastic changes looming ahead.

The basic intellectual influences on this book are those mentioned by Albert Hart in prefaces to earlier editions. His acknowledgments to Lord Keynes, John Hicks, Henry Simons, Lloyd Mints, and Gardiner Means, among others, are supplemented by our additional debts recorded in the notes appended to most chapters. Finally, we are most grateful to Jerald Rothstein, Columbia College '67, for providing invaluable statistical help, and to Frederick Dahl at Prentice-Hall for his most cooperative editorial assistance.

PBK

New York

Table of Contents

Part I

Banking and the Debt Structure

Part II

Money, Output, and Prices

8. The Varieties of Monetary Theory, 143

9. The Stream of Payments, 155

Part IV

Stabilization Policy

19. The Framework for Stabilization Policy, 377

20. The Economic Annals: 1919–1951, 399

Money,
Debt and
Economic
Activity

Introduction

Why Study Money?

Money, employment, and prices. Is it healthy to focus on the study of money? Is this subject anything more than a desert of technicalities; a part of economics where we never talk about human beings; a study of empty symbols when we might be studying underlying realities? Is there any reason beyond force of habit for keeping money on the active list of economic problems?

The answer is another series of questions. Does it matter whether workers can get jobs readily or are forced to stand idle? Does it matter whether the buying power of your dollars is eaten away by rising price levels? Does it matter whether public policies toward jobs and toward price levels are practical and effective? Does it matter whether these policies put private decisions in a strait jacket of governmental "directives," or whether government influence can be kept fairly limited and impersonal?

If you care about these questions—which are thoroughly human questions, and not mere technicalities—you need to study money. Recent history is full of episodes where money was crucial. It is generally agreed that the Great Depression of the 1930's was so severe largely because bankers felt forced to collect old loans without making new ones, because of bank failures, and because the international monetary machinery made the depression in each country compound the depression in others. Some analysts think that premature tightening

1

of money broke off recovery from the depression far below full employment in 1937. The postwar inflation of 1945–47 rested largely on the "excess liquidity" resulting from wartime debt financing of the federal government—reinforced by postwar bank loan expansion. The 1950's and 1960's provide a multitude of instances and issues for the student of money. Some say that a tightening of monetary controls brought on the recessions of 1953–54 and 1957–58. Others credit the recovery of 1958–59 and the expansion of 1961–65 to monetary ease.

Since the importance of money grows out of policy issues, this book is policy-oriented. This does *not* mean that it aims to sell a specific line of policy measures. (We will indicate some policy preferences, but whether you agree or disagree need not affect the usefulness of the book.) By "policy-oriented" we mean that we regard relevance to public policy as the test of what belongs in the book and what can be omitted.

Monetary versus "real" analysis.   Among noneconomists, the monetary side of economic life is often taken to be all-important. Economists are forever struggling against a popular tendency to take things at face value and ignore what we call in economics "real" considerations. For instance, we have to deny, loud and often, the proposition that whatever raises prices of real estate and stock exchange securities enriches the nation, whereas whatever lowers these prices impoverishes the nation. We have to insist on the importance of "real wages" as against money wages. While the economist's traditional skirmishes with "money cranks—who proposed to bring in the millennium on very short notice by introducing a new type of money—seem to be a thing of the past, we now have to struggle perpetually with a neo-orthodoxy which is ready to sacrifice everything else to "maintaining the international value of the dollar" (or pound, or peso).

In reaction to this muddled thinking economists for generations sternly insisted on analyzing the economy in "real" terms. Using "real" terms means stressing the actual physical quantities produced and consumed, not merely their dollar value; the value of a commodity in terms of other commodities; the purchasing power of incomes, not their nominal size. Economists pictured money merely as a veil that shrouds the true nature of the economic system. To sweep away the monetary implications of the word *price,* the theory of prices was labeled the theory of *value;* and that theory was often treated as a theory of exchange under barter, which it emphatically is not.

This reaction went dangerously far, so that economists have recently felt compelled to correct its excesses. Of course, money values are not identical with social welfare, and money measures must always be accepted with something more than a grain of salt. But we also insist that the way our economy works depends very much on its monetary system and on our people's attitudes toward money. Few economic problems can be solved without monetary analysis.

When economists were preoccupied with "real" problems, they felt that monetary analysis need only explain the general price level. They were prepared to leave all other problems to the other branches of economics. This view is no longer accepted. We now feel that almost every branch of economics has monetary aspects. The study of money involves us in studies of public finance, the capital market and debt system, and even the problems of labor and monopoly, besides the traditional sphere of "money and banking."

Plan of the book. As the goal of this book is the analysis of policy, the choice and arrangement of material will point toward the study of policy.

The rest of the introduction develops the concepts that are strategic to the study of money: money, unit of account, debt, near-moneys, credit institutions, and payments.

Part I deals with *institutions*—those that deal in debt and so determine the "debt structure." The focus is on banking because the banks are especially important dealers in debt and manufacture a species of debt that makes up a large part of our money supply. We shall describe the mechanics of banking, but will stress the standards bankers use to choose their assets, and the mystery of "liquidity." These standards not only explain the way the banking system behaves, but they also give a clue to the way other people choose *their* assets—a clue that will be useful in Part II.

Part II deals with *monetary theory*—with economists' views of the relations of the liquid holdings of the public to money payments, output, employment, and prices. This second part will start with a survey of business fluctuations in the United States to help us define the impact of money upon economic activity. It will then examine some of the primitive monetary theories that focused entirely on prices, and will go on to present the modern theories that consider putput and employment as well.

Part III deals with *international monetary relations*. A nation's "balance of international payments" can affect domestic activity and will probably influence its policy makers. The international ramifications of monetary policy have long been a dominant concern of Britain's government and have played an increasingly important part in American thinking in recent years. Monetary mechanics come up again here.

Part IV deals with *monetary policy*. We begin by surveying the objectives a government may pursue when managing money, and the instruments it may use. We then describe and appraise monetary-fiscal policy in the United States since World War I. Finally, we scan some alternative instruments for economic stabilization—taxation and government spending—and conclude with a prescription for the "monetary constitution."

Money and The Unit of Account

Money defined. *Money* is a word of many overtones, without any definite and universally accepted meaning in common usage. At one extreme of coverage, we use the word loosely to mean wealth in general, as when we say that the Ford Foundation has lots of money. At the other extreme, we find official figures on *money in circulation* restricted to small change and paper money—what we will call *currency*. Consequently, we must either do without money as a technical term, or set up a working definition that limits it to one of its many conversational meanings.

TABLE I-1

LIQUID ASSETS OF THE NONBANK PUBLIC, DECEMBER 31, 1966,

BY DEGREE OF MONEYNESS

(dollar amounts in billion: data without seasonal adjustment)

```
Metallic small    ⎫ Currency
   change ..  4.0 ⎬  .. 39.1 ⎫ Money
Paper bills  35.1 ⎭          ⎬ ....175.2 ⎫ "Money-a-la-
Checking deposits  ..136.1  ⎭            ⎬  Friedman"  ⎫ Cash
Time deposits in commercial banks 156.3 ⎭  ......331.5 ⎬  assets   ⎫ Liquid
Time deposits in savings banks................. 55.2 ⎭           ⎬ ..386.7 ⎬ assets,
Savings and loan "savings capital" ......................113.9 ⎭         ⎬ Federal  ⎫ Liquid
U.S. government securities:                                              ⎬ Reserve  ⎬ assets,
   Redeemable ............................. 50.2 ⎫                        ⎬ concept  ⎬ broader
   Marketable:                                  ⎬                        ⎬ ..650.5  ⎬ concept
      Maturing within 1 year ............ 49.3 ⎫ 98.5 ⎬ ..149.9         ⎭         ⎬ ..771.0
      Longer maturities ................ 49.2 ⎭      ⎬                            ⎭
   Other .................................... 1.2 ⎭
Net cash values of life insurance, roughly ...........................120.5 ⎭
```

Source: Federal Reserve Bulletin, except for life insurance. For life insurance, *Survey of Current Business* and *Life Insurance Fact Book.*

The definition we use in this book is that *money is property with which the owner can pay off a definite amount of debt with certainty and without delay.* This is plainly a "handsome is as handsome does" definition: what is money depends on community usage. An ordinary American dollar bill is money in Buffalo but not in Tibet; most of the time it is money in Niagara Falls, Ontario, but may cease to be money there when American-Canadian exchange rates are in flux. Within the United States, however, the definition will safely cover *currency* (metallic small change plus paper bills) plus bank deposits subject to check.[1]

The law gives currency a special relation to debt settlement when it makes that currency "legal tender." Obviously, a creditor cannot reasonably be required to accept whatever the debtor takes it into his head to offer in settlement

---

[1] Checking deposits are perhaps not quite so completely money as is currency, since checks are not always acceptable from people whose identity or credit rating is open to doubt. In the first edition of this book, resting a good deal of weight on this rather small difference in customs, the author included a clause about acceptability among strangers in the definition, and treated checking deposits as a *near-money*. But most users of the book seem to find this bothersome; and since the object of setting up a list of technical terms is to communicate with readers rather than to "differentiate the product," including checking deposits as money seems preferable [AGH].

of debt. If the creditor does not want the used auto the debtor wants to part with, does not need to have the debtor mow his lawn this week, or doubts that the debtor has enough funds on deposit to cover a check, he is entitled to refuse payment in these forms. On the other hand, the creditor cannot be allowed to keep a sword hanging over the debtor's head; he cannot be allowed to refuse settlement of any kind when the debt is due, or wait deliberately for an inconvenient time to demand payment. The law, therefore, designates certain instruments as "legal tender," declaring that if the debtor offers "legal tender" the creditor may not balk at taking it. The debtor is thereby protected against further interest charges, penalties for late payment, tying up of property pledged as collateral, and so forth.[2] Whatever is legal tender is bound to be money under this definition. But not all money need be legal tender. During the 1920's, for example, most United States paper money in denominations larger than $1 consisted of Federal Reserve notes, which were not legal tender; but it never occurred to creditors to refuse settlement in Federal Reserve notes. We can paraphrase our definition, then: *Money is property that community custom treats as if it were legal tender.*

Moneyness. Whichever way we put the definition, one can easily think of things that are almost, but not quite, money. Many things are available for the quick settlement of a debt, but not with equal certainty. We cannot be as sure of their market prices, nor as sure that they will be accepted in settlement of debts. So moneyness is not a yes-or-no affair, but a more-or-less affair. Wherever you draw the line between money and other things, something is always just outside the line that has almost as much moneyness as the last item you included. This may be seen by drawing up a classification of assets somewhat similar to money, in order of moneyness. Such a classification (with the amounts held by the nonbank public in December 1966) is shown in Table I-1, building up into more and more inclusive groupings.

If we chose to apply the term "money" only to metallic and paper currency, we would have to remember that checking deposits were almost as suitable for face-to-face settlements-and actually more available for settlements by mail. Even when we draw the line, as we have above, between checking and time deposits, we must remember that the holder of a savings account can ordinarily cash it any time in banking hours.[3] If we expanded the term "money" to cover

---

[2] On legal tender, see Arthur Nussbaum, *Money in the Law,* 2nd ed. (Brooklyn: Foundation Press, 1950).

Under the Legal Tender Act of 1933, *all* American coin and paper money is now legal tender. Incidentally, this Act did not carry forward the old rules limiting the sums for which small coins are legal tender, so that we sometimes hear of debtors paying large sums in pennies purely to annoy their creditors.

[3] Milton Friedman, with whom a number of other monetary economists concur, prefers to include time deposits *in commercial banks* (but not in mutual savings banks) in his definition of "money." Especially for historical studies, the Friedman practice has the advantage that it evades problems of the comparability of deposit-classifications by commercial banks, which at times have been highly arbitrary. Friedman would also contend (with many others dissent-

all cash assets (including time deposits), we would have to remember that holders of Savings bonds and of savings and loan shares also can get cash any time in banking hours, and that holders of some other government securities can rely on a fairly stable market for instant sale. If we expanded the term to cover all of what we have labeled liquid assets (following Federal Reserve usage), we would still have to remember that the holder of a life insurance policy can obtain the "cash loan or surrender value" of his policy on a few days' notice, or can borrow at his bank on life insurance collateral, that the holder of a top-grade privately issued bond has a firm market on which to sell, and so forth.[4]

Debt. A "debt," formally speaking, is an obligation to pay money—in a definite amount at a definite time and place. But because we have just defined money in terms of the ability to settle debt, this definition starts us into a logical circle.[5] A closer look shows a more useful definition of debt.

More fundamentally, *"debt" is negative wealth, stated in a unit of account*. Negative wealth is a matter of everyday experience. If you have a pound of sugar in the cupboard, that is a piece of wealth. If you borrowed a pound of sugar from next door yesterday, to be returned today, however, *your* sugar is zero—you have

---

ing) that behavior of cash-holders is more readily "explained" by statistical analysis based on the hypothesis that they view checking deposits and commercial-bank time deposits as convertible rather than on the hypothesis that they view them as distinct. The recent shift of funds on the part of large corporations into "time certificates of deposit" (which by the end of 1967 accounted for over 10 per cent of all commercial-bank time deposits) suggests that substantial amounts may now be held as time deposits which under the arrangements of a few years ago would have been held as demand deposits, without any substantial change in their actual availability.

[4] To remind us of the importance of near-moneys, there is some merit in a definition (like that used in the first edition of this book) that is obviously too narrow to cover everything of monetary importance. But after a good deal of thought, the system of terminology indicated in Table I-1 strikes the author as the best we can do while keeping in touch with Federal Reserve statistical terminology and (so far as possible) with the rather inconsistent usages of textbooks and conversation.

Federal Reserve terminology defines "liquid assets" to include savings and loan shares but to exclude life insurance cash values. For reasons that will appear in Part I, this strikes the author as an awkward boundary. At the other end of the scale, the Federal Reserve uses "currency" for small change plus paper bills, and the author follows this usage. The Federal Reserve also uses "money" as a synonym for "currency." To do so, however, wastes this useful term on a terminological notch that is already well filled, and reduces the Federal Reserve to saying "demand deposits adjusted and currency" where the author says "money." What the author calls "cash assets" has also an inconvenient label ("deposits adjusted and currency") in Federal Reserve terminology. While "cash" has a somewhat variable coverage in business accounting, a term for a defined category more inclusive than money but less inclusive than liquid assets is so useful that it seems worth trying to freeze the meaning of the term. As will appear later, "cash assets" is the most inclusive category for which a mere addition of dollar amounts at face value is very useful [AGH].

[5] Such a circle in a set of definitions should not worry us too much, however, even if we cannot get out of it. Philosophers often classify some terms in a discussion as "indefinable," meaning that in the set of terms there are fewer *independent* definitions than there are terms. But this fact does not prevent us (or excuse us) from saying comprehensibly what our terms mean.

sugar, but it is your neighbor's. Suppose that when you go to the cupboard, you find that the children have mixed all the sugar into their mud pies. Then *your* sugar is less than nothing—you have to scurry around and get a pound before your sugar will be zero. You have to get two pounds before you own one pound, because the borrowed sugar counts as minus one pound. Similarly, a debt is something you have to subtract from the amount of property in your hands to find out how much *your* wealth is.

The difference between "owing" a pound of sugar and owing a debt is that the unit of debt is not physically concrete. When you borrow physical goods, you may be pledged to hand back a physical object which somebody else owns but has let you use, such as a borrowed umbrella.[6] If not that, then you are pledged to hand back a quantity of something measured in cubic feet, pounds, bushels, or gallons—units that are defined by reference to museum specimens actually on hand at the Bureau of Standards in Washington. But the Bureau of Standards has no specimen of a unit of account. No way exists to make a specimen because the modern unit of account is abstract.

The unit of account defined.   A *"unit of account" is a unit* (such as the dollar) *in which people value commodities and services sold, reckon up wealth, and calculate debts.* All civilized societies have such units. So do most of the societies we choose to brand "primitive." The whole economic thinking of Western peoples is permeated by units of account; one doubts whether men could think "economically" without their help.

Under our definition of money, the units in which money is counted are necessarily units of account. But there may be other units of account. A few centuries ago, it could and did happen that most of the coins in circulation would come to be thin and underweight. When this happened, valuations were sometimes made by the actual number of coins, sometimes by the equivalent number of full-weight coins. This practice meant having more than one unit of account. During the American Civil War, some accounts were kept in gold dollars which did not circulate, although most accounts were kept in current dollars, corresponding to the circulating greenbacks. There were two units of account, only one of which had a form of money attached.[7] During the great inflations in Germany and Austria in the early 1920's, many accounts were

---

[6] In such cases, though, the sense of obligation to repay sometimes wears thin. As a poet we cannot identify has put it:

> The rain falls on the just
> And on the unjust fella,
> But mostly on the just, because
> The unjust has the just's umbrella.

[7] After the American devaluation of 1933–34, some holders of "gold bonds" claimed that their bonds should be valued in a unit-of-account "gold dollar" which was worth more than the dollar proper. This claim was held by the courts to be invalid—not so much incorrect as impracticable to enforce—and was disallowed.

kept in Swiss francs or American dollars, although these currencies were not in actual circulation there.

Tendency toward a single unit. Logically, many units of account could exist side by side at any one time and place. Shoes or ships or sealing-wax may serve as units, and purely abstract units are common. We have just looked at several historical cases of side-by-side units of account in which there was *only one* type of money. Besides these, there have been side-by-side units each linked to a *separate* type of money. Foreign money is often used in frontier regions and in very small countries overshadowed by their neighbors, and it sometimes circulates alongside domestic money, both units being used in accounting. This happened in the United States in the early days of the federal Constitution.[8] For centuries, both gold and silver served as money in most Western countries, with varying relative values.

Side-by-side units of account are always a nuisance, so modern governments have worked for standardization. Each national government has set up its own official unit and tried to prevent use of side-by-side units. Commonly the courts have construed contracts using other units so as to push the contracting parties back into the use of official units.[9] There have even been international efforts to cut down differences between units of account—notably the Latin Monetary Union before World War I, under which the currency units and coins of France, Italy, Belgium, Switzerland, and Greece were made substantially interchangeable.

Abstract units. Monetary evolution has not only standardized units of account, but has made them more and more abstract. Most of the oldest names for units of account are also names for units of weight, conspicuously the British "pound."[10] Many units were initially related to weights of *metals,* commonly gold and silver. But units of account have sometimes been tied to other commodities. The word *pecuniary* (from Latin *pecus*—a cow-critter) suggests that the early Romans reckoned in cattle; and scriptural and other sources imply similar valuation elsewhere in ancient times. Americans should not forget, moreover, that tobacco provided a unit of account in colonial Virginia.

---

[8] The expression "two bits" is a relic of the use of Spanish (that is, Mexican) currency and accounting units. Thoreau kept accounts in shillings and pence.

[9] Compare the "gold clause" cases in the United States, cited above. Another instance was the handling of life insurance and bank accounts in Austria during the 1930's. In Austria, people's confidence in the new "schilling" established after the great inflation of the 1920's was so weak that many insisted on having life insurance, bank balances, and the like, payable in foreign-currency units. But in 1931 it became hard to keep up the value of the Austrian schilling relative to other currencies, and the government forced reconversion of these claims to schillings at standard rates.

[10] Once corresponding to a pound ("Troy weight") of silver. The pound was once a unit used over most of Western Europe. The conventional symbol for the British pound (a modified L) is the initial of the Latin term *Librum* (corresponding to French *livre*—do you remember reading *The Three Musketeers?*). But reckoning in pounds has died out on the Continent except for the Italian *lira.*

The unit of account was gradually separated from concrete quantities of goods by the medieval practice of "debasing the currency"—deciding that a "pound" should contain only half as much silver as it used to, and changing the coins to correspond.[11] In the Middle Ages, however, the unit of account had to be hitched back on to the metals, silver or gold, at once, because people thought of money as metallic. Only after paper money came into wide use in the eighteenth century could purely abstract units seem natural.

Paper money, when it first appeared, was expressed in a familiar unit of account and was convertible into metallic money expressed in the same unit. But breakdowns of convertibility were common; and when they happened, there were side-by-side units because the paper-money unit was worth less than its supposed metallic equivalent. If the paper was only a small part of the community's circulation, accounting was not much affected.[12] But if paper was the bulk of the circulation, as it often came to be, many accounting records were kept in the paper-money unit. This unit was obviously abstract.

Abstract units of account, then, often grew out of traditional concrete units. Furthermore, they were generally expected to get back into touch with the concrete units; it was assumed that redemption of paper notes in gold or silver would resume (whether at or below the traditional ratio of values). In a few conspicuous cases before the twentieth century, hopes of redemption lapsed (the Continental currency of the American Revolution and the assignats of the French Revolution are examples). The commodity value of the abstract unit involved sank so rapidly as to drive it largely out of accounting use. On the other hand, eventual resumption was taken for granted in the classic cases—the British "restriction" period during the Napoleonic Wars, the American Civil War "greenback" era, and most of the World War I suspensions of redemption. Thus, experience down to 1920 or so suggested that purely abstract units could not stand up for long.

During the interwar period, however, several further steps toward abstractness were taken. The prewar habit of using large-denomination coins was not renewed, so that dealings in monetary metals ceased to be commonplace[13] and the linkage of accounting units with precious metals could no longer give units of account concreteness. Indeed, it would be more nearly true to say that linkage

---

[11]The motive for doing this was commonly profit for the money-issuing authority, which called in existing coins and repaid the owners with *the same number* of lighter coins, retaining the difference in weight of metal. On account of this practice the metallic equivalent of European units had a marked downward drift.

[12]Thus, in nineteenth-century American banking, if one bank stopped giving gold and silver for its notes, these notes went at a discount compared with notes of other banks. But instead of quoting prices, and so forth, in depreciated notes, merchants had standard quotations which they puffed up if payment was to be made in such notes. On the other hand, at times when few banks were converting their notes into silver or gold on demand but notes of many banks were at par with each other, reckoning of prices and debts on a paper basis was common.

[13]Most Americans, for example, met with gold coins during the 1920's and the early 1930's merely as prizes and gifts.

with accounting units has made the money metals mere abstractions to most people. From 1931 on, the more mechanical relations of the various units of account with gold and silver were successively broken and they have not been fully restored. Psychological ties, of course, remain. Most people would probably be shocked were they told that gold and silver would henceforth have no relation to the nation's money.[14] But the present connection is extremely tenuous, and few people expect a restoration of redemption in coin.

Money and Near-Moneys

Monetary evolution.   As may be seen from Table I-1, money in the United States today consists chiefly of checking deposits. These are supplemented by paper currency and, for small transactions, by metallic small change. Nonmonetary liquid assets (or "near-moneys") consist chiefly of the debts of credit institutions (commercial and savings banks, savings and loan associations, life insurance companies) and of the federal government. The situation in other countries is much the same, except that paper currency often plays a larger part than in the United States.[15]

Three hundred years ago, the situation was very different. Money then consisted primarily of gold and silver coins, supplemented by coppers and, here and there, by bank notes. The role of near-money was also taken largely by gold and silver—in the form of jewelry and of "plate."[16] "Bills" upon private merchants and financiers were used as liquid reserves and to make some payments—but only by special agreement, so that they were not strictly money.

During the eighteenth and nineteenth centuries, bank notes became sufficiently standardized and familiar to become acceptable without question as a means of payment, and thus to become money in the strict sense. For large transactions, notes proved more practical than coins—easier to count, carry, and protect, and not subject to a discount for wear and tear. For small transactions, "full-bodied" coins—with enough silver or gold to be worth as much as metal as they were as money—tended to be replaced by "token" coins. This was partly because full-bodied coins were melted down in times of high silver

---

[14]It is interesting that Hitler's Germany went to a good deal of inconvenience to pretend that the relation of the mark to gold was "normal" long after the Western countries had given up the pretense for their currencies. Only after a year of World War II did the Nazis openly announce plans for a goldless future.

[15]Another important difference, behind the scenes of the official statistics, is the existence in many countries of substantial private hoards of gold and foreign currency—which under present conditions would classify as near-moneys for the holders.

[16]While much of the value of silver cups, platters, candlesticks, and so forth, lay in the workmanship, the possibility of melting such objects down in case of a sudden need of money was often in the owner's mind. For revealing comment on "plate," see the celebrated seventeenth-century *Diary* of Samuel Pepys.

prices,[17] partly because such coins as a silver five-cent piece were inconveniently small and handier to use if diluted or replaced by other metal. Down to World War I, however, there was still some hand-to-hand circulation of full-bodied coins such as the British sovereign and the American $20 gold piece—partly from habit, partly for convenience when traveling away from home, and partly (in the case of the sovereign) because of a prohibition on bank notes smaller than five pounds. After World War I, most governments as a matter of policy discouraged gold-coin circulation. In the 1930's the United States and other governments actually set up prohibitions on private ownership of monetary gold.[18]

During the nineteenth century, bank notes were everywhere regulated and standardized by governments, and the notes of ordinary banks were gradually replaced by those of semiofficial central banks or of the government itself. At the same time that the issue of notes was becoming a semigovernmental function, more and more people were getting used to holding bank accounts, and to handling checks. By the beginning of the twentieth century, checking deposits were effective money in the United States.[19]

Present composition of American money. Checking deposits, as may be seen from Table I-1, outweigh the public's currency holdings by about three to one in dollar amount. Before the Great Depression, this ratio was a good deal higher (over six to one in 1929). Perhaps the ratio is higher than it looks today, since part of the currency reported in circulation in the United States is undoubtedly held abroad.[20]

---

[17]This happened, for instance, during the American Civil War of 1861–65. The public fell back on the use of postage stamps. But even when special stamps without gum were put out for this purpose ("shinplasters"), they proved highly inconvenient, and the public was glad to see them replaced by token coins.

[18]Given a choice between coin and paper in the $5–20 range, almost everybody regards paper as safer and handier. In fact, since World War I, the bias has been toward letting paper go too far into the range of small change, as the value has been sucked out of lower denominations by inflation. In France in the 1950's, ten-franc notes printed during the war (and worth under three cents in 1952) were still in circulation, and no coin of over fifty francs was available. In the United States, at recent levels of prices and incomes, the dollar is perhaps too small for a first paper unit. If the experiment were tried of offering a $1 coin less destructive to pocketbooks than the massive silver dollar, many people might prefer it to paper.

[19]In many countries, passing a check is still a matter for special agreement. American students should be aware, however, that in many countries much business is done by "giro" transactions, which amount to having a debtor make a deposit on behalf of his creditor and send him the deposit slip as evidence of payment. Such transactions, and the funds—often described as "postal savings"—usable in giro payments must be taken into account in monetary analyses, especially of European countries.

[20]The currency figure in Table I-1 represents the excess of "currency outside Treasury and Federal Reserve Banks" over estimated commercial-bank holdings. American currency sent abroad *through banks* (less return flow through banks) is subtracted out. But currency taken abroad by tourists and other individuals is not reported. One suspects that a good part of the American currency spent abroad during and since World War II by American soldiers and tourists has gone into unreported holdings of foreigners.

Putting some stress on the hetereogeneity of types of paper currency used to make sense; but today these type-differences seem of no practical importance. The only type-difference of currency that deserves any attention is between paper and metallic small change, which in recent years has sometimes run short and commanded a premium—presumably because part of what is supposed to be in circulation has been melted down to realize the value of metallic silver content.

For many purposes, checking deposits should be regarded as made up of a number of distinct types. In the course of the book, we will see some differences among deposit-types classified by ownership (corporations, individuals, state and local governments), size of balance of the holder, size of city where the bank is located, and so forth. But we need not go into detail in this introductory view.

Evolution of near-moneys. While bank notes and bank deposits were replacing gold and silver coin, the obligations of credit institutions and governments were replacing "bills" and gold and silver plate and jewelry as near-moneys. On both sides, debts receivable were coming to the fore as liquid assets at the expense of "real" assets.

The declining importance of plate resulted partly from improvements in substitute products; candlesticks, mugs, and platters of silver were largely displaced by modern lighting, glass, and porcelain. In addition, the popularity of plate was diminished by the sharpening distinction between business and personal assets; a business corporation is reluctant to put wealth in merely ornamental form.

The declining importance of "trade bills" as liquid assets of the nonbank public is a by-product of banking. Part I will show that bankers regard a medium-term debt of a widely known business firm as an ideal asset. But a private person is not apt to find such a debt a satisfactory asset. He may not be able to pass it on to his own creditors because its size is unlikely to match that of the payments he must make. Bank notes in round amounts, or checks tailored to the size of the payment, are more handy. Consequently bankers can outbid others for the ownership of private debt instruments that might otherwise become liquid assets of the nonbank public.

The rising importance of credit-institution debts is also largely a consequence of the rise of banks—both directly and indirectly. Time-deposit facilities at banks have become available and familiar everywhere. The habit of banking has also probably made the use of savings and loan facilities more natural, and put people in a frame of mind to consider such complicated financial dealings as are involved in life insurance. (The insurance salesman has greatly contributed to credit-institution development, but he makes noticeably less headway in countries that make less use of banks.)

The use of government debt as a near-money, which may be observed in many countries, is a by-product of war. War not only runs governments into debt, but gives them incentives to make their debts effective near-moneys.

There once was an American tradition of retiring war debts completely when peace lasted long enough. But the continuation of defense spending and the way we have built government debt into our monetary structure suggest that we may confidently expect government debt to loom large for generations ahead.

The Payment System

Creation of debts by transactions. Many people think of money chiefly as a "means of payment" for goods and services. Emphasis on this aspect of money can be overdone. To understand the crucial relation of money to debt, we need a picture of the payment system.[21]

Our society has an elaborate division of labor; an enormous number of separate firms, households, and government bodies is involved in production and consumption. There is an incessant flow of "transactions" in which the ownership of goods and services changes hands. Every such transaction is a "purchase" for the person or firm getting the goods, a "sale" for the person or firm parting with them. Every transaction, moreover, creates a *debt*: the buyer owes the seller the agreed monetary value of the item sold. In "cash and carry" dealings, the debt is extinguished at once by cash payment. But the great bulk of the debts arising from each day's transactions are still on the books at the end of the day—often, much longer.

Debt settlement by offset. Some debts are settled by offset between pairs of people each in debt to the other. If a farmer sells eggs to a storekeeper and gets his canned goods at the store, such an offset is simple. Offest also works well between stockbrokers and their customers. The broker may sell stock for his customer in the morning and buy in the afternoon; then only the difference between the two debts need be settled in cash.

Occasionally offset extends to more than two dealers and becomes *clearing*. The New York stockbrokers pile up debts to each other for stocks and bonds exchanged in the course of a day's dealings. But since only "members" of the Exchange transfer securities on its floor, every debt owed *by* a stockbroker for securities transferred into his office is simultaneously a debt owed *to* some other broker for securities transferred from his office. Furthermore, each broker is both buyer and seller, and for most brokers, debts payable and debts receivable as a result of the day's transactions are about equal. Instead of sending thousands of checks to each other, the brokers "clear" their debts. Each broker who is a net debtor pays a central agency a sum equal to the excess of his debts payable over his debts receivable. The central agency in turn pays each broker who is a net creditor the excess of his debts receivable over his debts payable. By this device all interbroker debts are settled with a minimum of bother.

---

[21]For a more detailed picture, see Chapter 9.

Debt settlement by transfer of bank debt. The most common form of debt settlement in our economy is payment by check. This is a way of discharging one debt by transferring another. When we write a check, we tell our banker to pay the "money" he owes us at the direction of the person to whom the check is made out. In order to draw a valid check, we must have a checking account with a sufficient balance "on deposit"—that is, the banker must owe us at least as much as the face value of the check.[22]

The process of check settlement creates interbank debts, for the person receiving the check is rarely a depositor at the same bank as the drawer. When the receiver of the check endorses it and sends it to his bank for deposit to his account, he transfers to his banker the claim the check represents. The bank on which the check is drawn thus comes to be in debt to the bank at which the check is deposited. This interbank debt could be settled in currency. But the huge number of individual items makes this difficult. At the same time, bankers in a given locality find themselves in the same situation that makes clearing convenient for the New York stock brokers:[23] their debts on account of checks deposited are chiefly to each other, and each individual bank has debts payable and debts receivable on this account of roughly equal size.[24] Most

---

[22]In the last few years, there has been a rapid growth of the use of "privilege checking accounts," which permit a depositor to draw more than he has on deposit under an agreement where the banker takes the arrival of the check as the signal to "lend" the depositor enough to cover the check. This development, like the use of overdrafts in Britain and Scandinavia, makes it somewhat doubtful how much "money" the public has at its disposal.

[23]Clearing is in fact an invention of the bankers which the stock brokers have imitated. The New York Clearing House of the bankers, the oldest in this country, dates from 1853; the Stock Exchange Clearing House is much younger.

[24]The logic of the clearing operation is easily seen by setting up a simplified version of a day's record, showing the to-whom-from-whom of a batch of checks. A five-bank clearing-house, for example, might trace the following record (dollar amounts in thousands):

| Bank on which check is drawn | Bank presenting check for clearing | | | | | |
	First National Bank	Aboriginal Trust Co.	Nearest National Bank	Steady State Bank	Enterprise Trust Co.	Total presented
First National	...	$102	$ 58	$ 43	$ 29	$232
Aboriginal Trust	$ 94	...	51	33	28	206
Nearest National	63	54	...	30	22	169
Steady State	44	31	29	...	16	120
Enterprise Trust	34	30	21	18	...	103
Total presented	$235	$217	$159	$124	$ 95	$830
—Total to be met	−232	−206	−169	−120	−103	−830
Net receivable from clearing house	$ 3	$ 11	$−10	$ 4	$−8	$ 0

major financial centers, therefore, have clearinghouses where member banks send checks on other members once or twice daily and settle for net balances.[25]

Another way to settle interbank debts is through correspondent relationships. For a number of reasons, most commercial banks own checking accounts at one or more other banks, and the downtown banks in great centers like New York and Chicago specialize in such banker's business. If a bank gets a check on another bank outside its own clearinghouse, it can deposit the check with a correspondent, thereby transferring the collection problem to the correspondent. By a chain of these transactions, the check can be routed home— either to the bank on which it is drawn, or by way of another bank in that bank's clearinghouse. This is the basic process for collecting out-of-town checks.

Before we had the Federal Reserve System, check collection often involved long chains of correspondents, and might take weeks for some checks. But under the Federal Reserve System, most of our banks are "on the par list." They guarantee to accept checks for collection through one of the twelve Federal Reserve banks. Each Federal Reserve bank, moreover, accepts checks for collection from each of the other eleven, as well as from commercial banks. In consequence, intercity collections can be made through Federal Reserve channels, with no intermediaries except one or two of the Federal Reserve banks.

Settlement by clearing could conceivably be made universal. The debt of a canning factory to its workers, for example, might be offset against debts of the workers to the canning factory (through their grocers). But direct clearing works well only on a two-way market, like a stock exchange, where dealers in a narrow class of articles form a closed circle. Most dealings, by contrast, are on one-way markets, where each dealer sells one sort of thing to one group of persons, and buys another sort of thing from another group. Our canning factory sells canned goods to grocers but buys nothing from grocers; it buys labor services from its workers, but sells nothing directly to its workers. To get a closed circle of transactions a vast number of dealers would have to be represented at the clearings; check settlement is simpler.[26] For the present, the transmutation of private debt into negotiable bank debt by drawing a check is our smoothest way of handling payments.

---

[25]Besides their clearing functions, clearinghouses serve as trade associations of bankers. Some organizations under this title, in fact, have entirely given up clearing functions.

[26]One student at Columbia pointed out several years ago that once the telephone dial system became nationwide, the machinery needed to calculate phone bills could be adapted to instant transfer of funds by telephone dial. Very recently banking institutions have experimented with instantaneous credit transfer systems for individuals and businesses anywhere in the country (see the *New York Times,* May 21, 1967, Section 3, page 1). In any event, it is most unlikely that monetary evolution is at an end.

NOTES ON
ALTERNATIVE POINTS OF VIEW
AND SUPPLEMENTARY READINGS

We have deliberately avoided the traditional discussion of the "functions of money" as "medium of exchange," "standard of value," "standard of deferred payments," and "store of value." This nomenclature strikes us as confusing, because the various "functions" are not coordinate. The unit of account, not money, is the standard of value; debt, not money, is the ordinary medium of exchange; all wealth, not only money, is a store of value. But this is a minority judgment; if it bothers you, compare it with other standard textbooks.

The approach in this introduction rests largely on D. H. Robertson, *Money,* 4th ed., (London: Nisbet & Co., 1948) and R. G. Hawtrey, *Currency and Credit,* 3rd ed. (London: Longmans, 1928). It has also been influenced by A. Nussbaum, *Money in the Law,* 2nd ed. (Brooklyn: Foundation Press, 1950).

Part I

Banking and the Debt Structure

Chapter 1

Dealers in Debt

Money and debt. As the introduction indicated, many connections exist between money and debt. First, there is the definitional connection: money is property that can be used to pay off a given amount of debt promptly and with certainty. Second, money itself is often a form of debt: a checking account, for example, is a debt owed by a bank to its depositor. Third, money may sometimes be substituted for other varieties of debt, and vice versa: an individual may hold many forms of property and is constantly obliged to contemplate exchanging one for another. He may hold a bank account, a Savings bond, an insurance policy, or real estate, and will often sell one asset to buy another, as his personal circumstances and the quality of each asset dictate. Some forms of debt may be close substitutes for money in the portfolios of property-holders; others may be less perfect substitutes. How much money each household or company will hold must depend in part upon the supply and the quality of the other forms of debt available to it.

As the study of money is intimately connected to the study of debt, it requires a study of dealers in debt—institutions that create, exchange, and extinguish it. In particular, it is linked to the study of *credit institutions*—those that exist in order to deal in debt.

The variety of credit institutions. There are many species of dealers in debt. The stockbroker is one, the commercial bank a second, the life insurance company a third. All do business in debts, but each has unique characteristics.

The stockbroker is a simple intermediary. He may carry a portfolio of securities, but as a broker it is his function to bring buyers and sellers together, not to deal in debts for his own account. He merely assists in the transfer of debts from one investor to another, and does not alter the debts in which he deals, nor issue new debt.[1]

Most of the other dealers in debt perform additional functions. Their operations create debt, or transform it in some significant fashion. The mutual fund or investment does something more than transfer debt. It creates debt; it sells shares to investors and uses the money these shares bring in to buy securities. Similarly, a savings bank buys securities and makes loans with the funds depositors place at its disposal. A life insurance company does much the same thing, though its debts are a bit different from those a savings bank or mutual fund generates. They are not marketable, like those of the mutual fund, nor redeemable on demand, like those of the savings bank. They are promises to pay stated sums of money under special circumstances.

The credit institution is distinguished from the simple intermediary by the character of its operations. The credit institution creates debt in the course of its operations. It is a dealer in debt with assets consisting chiefly of cash and debts receivable and with debts of its own almost as large as its total assets. Credit institutions may differ as regards the assets they hold. Some may acquire real property as well as debts, or may hold common stocks rather than bonds. Others will purchase mainly mortgages, or may make loans to consumers. They may also differ as to their liabilities. Some are prepared to redeem their debts on demand. Others may issue marketable debt. Still others, like insurance companies, may discharge their debts only upon the death of the creditor or in other special circumstances. Finally, some credit institutions are privately owned, while others are government agencies.

The special role of commercial banks.   Though we shall have to examine many credit institutions in our study of money, we shall give special emphasis to commercial banks because the debts they create are money. This gives them a particular importance that may be illustrated by a simple example.

Suppose that you are asked to lend a businessman a thousand dollars so that he may expand his factory. Clearly, you must have a thousand dollars at your disposal in order to make the loan. You cannot simply give him an IOU because he cannot use it to buy building materials and machinery. If you are a producer of the things he needs, you can give him a thousand dollars worth of bricks and mortar, but this would be a special coincidence. Ordinarily, you must offer him an asset that he may exchange for the goods he requires.

---

[1] Strictly speaking, common stocks are not evidence of debt, but evidence of ownership. For the present purpose, however, and for many others, they are indistinguishable from debt.

The same limitation applies to most of the credit institutions we shall consider. They cannot acquire debt—they cannot lend—unless they have money on hand. They cannot simply write an IOU and hand it to a borrower because that IOU cannot be exchanged for goods and services. The commercial banks, however, are in a special position. Their IOU's are checking deposits. When they buy debt, they create a deposit to the credit of the businessman or consumer who is borrowing from them. This deposit, we have seen, is money. *The commercial banks are the only private dealers in debt whose own debts are generally accepted as a means of payment.*

We can put the same point differently: The typical credit institution is limited in its ability to acquire debt by its ability to acquire money. It must persuade the holders of money to exchange that money for an IOU issued by the credit institution. The commercial banks are limited in their capacity to acquire debt only by their ability to create money.[2] To be sure, this power is itself limited—partly by law and institutional arrangements, and partly by the pervasive and familiar principles of economic behavior that we shall explore in this book. But the difference between commercial banks and other credit institutions is sufficient to require that we study them first and in greater detail. All other credit institutions are dependent upon the commercial banks, because the banks are the main source of money in a modern economy and the other credit institutions must have money to acquire debt.

NOTES ON
ALTERNATIVE POINTS OF VIEW
AND SUPPLEMENTARY READINGS

Some recent writers would have us treat commercial banks on a par with other credit institutions. The leading exponents of this view are John G. Gurley and Edward S. Shaw, *Money in a Theory of Finance* (Washington, D.C.: The Brookings Institution, 1960). Raymond Goldsmith also takes this view in his distinguished study of financial institutions, *Financial Intermediaries in the American Economy Since 1900* (Princeton: National Bureau of Economic Research, 1958). Traditional money and banking texts, by contrast, devote relatively little attention to credit institutions other than commercial banks. We shall have more to say on this issue in later chapters.

---

[2] Note that we are speaking here of commercial banks, not a single commercial bank. In Chapter 6, we shall see that the individual bank is in much the same position as the individual savings bank. It is the system of commercial banks, as a whole, which is in a favored position compared to other credit institutions or to groups of other credit institutions.

Chapter 2

The Development of
Commercial Banking

Types of commercial banks. The discussion to this point provides us with a working definition of the commercial bank. It is a *credit institution that allows its creditors* (depositors) *to transfer claims by check.*[1] When you draw a check, you are getting rid of a debt you owe, by putting your banker in debt to your former creditor. In exchange, the bank's debt to you is diminished.

Two useful ways exist to classify commercial banks: (1) by type of government supervision; (2) by the class of city in which they operate. The relative importance of the different groups of banks (as measured by deposits) is shown in Chart 2–1.

The classification by supervision has three aspects. It will affect: (1) the kinds of business banks can do; (2) the cash reserve requirements to which they are subject; (3) the frequency and rigor of bank examination.[2] These controls are

---

[1] Other agencies used to provide checking facilities; for example, stockbrokers gave some of their customers checkbooks in the 1920's. There was a time, besides, when the ancestors of our present commercial banks did not give their customers checkbooks, but issued transferable debts only in the form of bank notes. But for the United States since the Civil War, at least, letting check facilities define the commercial bank is at no point seriously misleading. Even now, of course, Federal Reserve banks also provide checking facilities, but only for banks and the federal government.

[2] This means inspection of the bank's books now and then by an examiner, to make sure that: (1) the books are correct, without errors or falsifications; (2) reserve requirements and charter provisions are followed; (3) rules for the selection of assets are obeyed.

22

handled differently by the various states and by the federal government. Broadly speaking, the controls stiffen as banks become more involved with the federal government.

The classification of banks by the control situation may be shown as a sort of totem pole (Chart 2–1, left-hand column). At the top of the pole are the banks on which controls sit lightest—the group (*A*) of "noninsured commercial banks." These banks are subject only to the rather mild charter provisions, reserve requirements, and examinations that are established by state laws.

The next group down are (*B*) "insured nonmember commercial banks." These are subject to the same state controls as group *A*, but they have protected their depositors by joining the Federal Deposit Insurance Corporation and are consequently subject to FDIC examinations and FDIC rules for the selection of assets. FDIC controls are stiffer than those of many states.

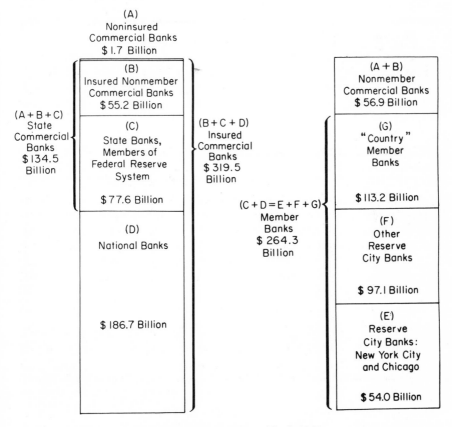

Source: Federal Reserve Bulletin, March, 1967.

Chart 2-1: Types of commercial banks. Heights on the diagram measure deposits (other than interbank) in June 1966. Detail may not add precisely to totals because of rounding to nearest $0.1 billion.

The next group are (C) "state member banks." To secure the conveniences of Federal Reserve membership (and to some extent for prestige), these banks have chosen to join the Federal Reserve System. Membership subjects them to Federal Reserve examinations, and to reserve requirements a good deal higher than those imposed by the states.

The bottom group are (D) "national banks." These banks are incorporated under federal rather than under state law. They are examined by the office of the Comptroller of the Currency—a bureau of the Treasury. His standards are much the same as those of the Federal Reserve, but national-bank charters are usually more restrictive than state charters. National banks are required to belong to the Federal Reserve System, so that, going up the totem pole, groups D and C are all "member banks." By amount of deposits in 1966, national banks were 59 per cent of the commercial banking system and state member banks 24 per cent, so that member banks were 83 per cent.[3]

All member banks of the Federal Reserve System are required to belong to the Federal Deposit Insurance Corporation. So groups D, C, and B are all "insured banks." Noninsured banks hold less than 1 per cent of deposits, so it is fairly accurate to talk as though all commercial banks were insured.[4]

Groups C, B, and A are called "state banks." At one time, they could be classified by legal status as "state commercial banks," "trust companies," and "private (unincorporated) banks." But the differences between "state commercial banks" and trust companies have faded, and private banks are now of trifling importance, so that this basis of classification is now only of historical significance.

The other classification is shown on the righthand side of Chart 2-1. Here, "member banks" are classified on a different basis. At the bottom are (E) "reserve city banks: New York and Chicago."[5] These are the downtown banks of New York and Chicago and are tabulated separately because they are located in the nation's major financial centers. Next come (F) "reserve city banks." These are the downtown banks of the other important metropolitan areas. Other member banks (whether or not in cities) are called "country banks" (G) in Federal Reserve jargon. Nonmember banks (A + B), with the lightest reserve requirements of all, are at the top of the column. This classification corresponds to a falling scale of cash reserve requirements.

Origins of commercial banking.   Though banking was well established in Europe, and had blossomed sporadically in the American colonies prior to 1776, commercial banking did not begin to grow rapidly here until after the

---

[3] By *number of banks,* however, national banks were only 35 per cent and all member banks only 45 per cent.

[4] By number, noninsured banks are nearly 2 per cent of all commercial banks.

[5] All reserve city banks are subject to the same reserve requirements; prior to 1960 downtown banks in New York and Chicago were called central reserve city banks and were subject to higher reserve requirements than the reserve city banks.

Revolution. The first important bank in the United States was the Bank of North America, set up in Philadelphia in 1781. Commercial banks were also established in Boston and in New York in 1784 (although a regular charter for the Bank of New York was not secured until 1791).

The Continental Congress subscribed part of the capital for the Bank of North America and used the Bank as its financial agent. The new federal government had a hand in starting the First Bank of the United States (1791–1811), and again put in some capital. This Bank stood in much the same relation to the American government as the Bank of England to the British, although in England the government held no shares.

Before 1833 each of the banks incorporated in the United States was chartered by a special legislative act. The federal government issued no charters except for the First Bank of the United States (1791–1811) and for the Second Bank (1816–36), which replaced it after a five-year hiatus. But the states passed acts to incorporate a number of banks. There were also many "private banks" which operated as partnerships, without corporate charters.

In 1838, New York State adopted an act for "free banking." This act allowed any person or group to go into the banking business provided they could satisfy certain standard requirements. The main requirement was the posting of collateral (bonds of New York or of the United States)[6] for all bank notes issued. Other states followed suit, and would-be bankers no longer had to persuade state legislatures to pass special acts for their benefit.[7]

Before the Civil War, the debts ("liabilities") of banks in the United States were largely bank notes. These were ostensibly convertible on demand into gold or silver. Often, however, they were not redeemable, and were consequently accepted by the business world only at a discount. Banks also had debts in the form of deposits. Deposits, indeed, grew faster than bank notes, and were considerably larger in dollar amount by 1860. Checks were gradually coming into use—as is evidenced by the establishment of the first American clearinghouse in New York in 1853. But the bulk of the deposits were probably not payable on demand. In this country, it would seem, people felt that you could not run a bank without issuing notes.[8]

The assets of banks in the United States before the Civil War were mainly loans to private individuals and unincorporated firms. American bankers gave lip service to the English "real bills" tradition—that loans should only be made to firms in production and commerce and should be secured by goods that would soon be ready for sale and whose sale would finance repayment of the loan. But in practice many banks made long-term loans. Loans that were

---

[6] At first, other types of collateral were accepted; but bank failures led to shortening of the list.

[7] This New York act was a major step in the development of "general incorporation laws" for business in general.

[8] In England, however, no London banks except the Bank of England were allowed to issue notes. Modern deposit banking developed there much earlier than in the United States.

short term in form were effectively long-term loans because they were repeatedly renewed. Real estate was a favorite security. "Investments" held by banks were comparatively small.[9] Banks reported large "cash" holdings but these consisted chiefly of interbank debts.

The form of banking just described worked pretty well part of the time. The Second Bank of the United States policed the bank notes of the state banks during the 1820's by insisting on prompt redemption. But its charter lapsed in 1836, just in time to unleash the banks during the land-boom frenzy of 1836–37 and to allow a rash of incautious lending. The 1837 crash involved wholesale bank failures. Another crash occurred in 1841, and still another in 1857. Some areas had banking systems that worked fairly smoothly between major crises—New England, under the "Suffolk Bank System," New York, under its often-amended bank laws, Louisiana, under its Act of 1842, and Indiana and Ohio, with state banks modeled on the Bank of the United States. Through most of the West and South, however, bank failures caused by rash management or downright fraud were frequent. The holders of bank notes and bank deposits were continuously exposed to loss in most parts of the country.

Banking from the Civil War to World War I. The Civil War brought sharp changes in American banking. The national-bank system and the elimination of bank notes issued by state-chartered banks were by-products of war finance. The federal government began to issue national bank charters on the "free-banking" priniciple to all applicants who fulfilled stated requirements. These new national banks were allowed to issue bank notes upon pledging United States bonds with the Comptroller of the Currency. Bank notes of state-chartered banks were subjected to a heavy tax, and vanished about 1870. Most of the existing incorporated banks apparently gave up their state charters and took out new charters as national banks. By 1866, there were 1,600 national banks, and the number of state banks was much smaller. But bankers soon realized that the main advantages of a national bank charter were the income arising from bank-note issues[10] and a certain prestige. They also saw that a bank did not need to issue bank notes in order to operate at a profit and that state charters gave banks many advantages, offering lower cash-reserve requirements

---

[9] This fact is testimony to the slowness with which the states enforced their bond-collateral requirements for bank notes. Even by 1860, reporting banks showed only $70 million of investments for over $200 million of note circulation, and some of these investments were not even eligible as bank-note collateral.

[10] In effect, a national bank could buy government bonds by issuing bank notes and could pocket the interest on the bonds. For banks which were "in on the ground floor," this interest was a substantial contribution to income. Bonds that were eligible as bank-note collateral ("had the circulation privilege") were priced above other bonds on the market, showing that it was worthwhile to issue notes. At the same time, however, the fact that these bonds sold at a premium (and could be used as bank-note collateral only up to par) limited the marginal profitability of note issue. The premium, of course, had to be paid with funds other than the bank notes that the bonds secured, and was "amortized" out of the interest received.

and fewer restrictions on loans.[11] "Trust companies" under state charter could carry on general banking with low reserves, and could add to income by acting as agents for corporations, handling estates, and the like. Banking under state charter revived very quickly. By the early 1870's, deposits in state commercial banks, trust companies, and private (unincorporated) banks were roughly as large as in national banks.[12] Although state banks suffered more than national banks during the "hard times" of 1873–78 and 1893–98, state banks outgrew national banks in prosperity years. By 1914, national banks comprised a good deal less than half of the commercial banking system.

National-bank notes solved the problem of safety for the note-holder because the national banks had to meet severe collateral requirements. People no longer had to worry about the soundness of the banks whose notes they held. One bank note was as good as another—or as good as a United States note ("greenback") issued by the Treasury. A businessman who held enough bank notes to pay off his debts could no longer be forced into bankruptcy for lack of "legal tender," as many had been in the panics of 1837 and 1857. Under the national-bank system, bank notes *were* legal tender; and from 1879 onward they were also convertible into gold. But in the panics of 1873, 1884, 1893, and 1907, the old trouble took a new form. By this time, deposit balances were far larger than the bank-note issue. In a panic, businessmen could still be forced into bankruptcy because checks were not legal tender and banks ceased to cash checks. A way had to be found to make the note issue more "flexible" so that the banks could obtain currency and would not have to cease cashing checks in a crisis. The search for a solution was accelerated by the panic of 1907 and the outcome was the Federal Reserve Act of 1913—of which more later.

From the Civil War to World War I, the banks' main assets were loans to customers. The national banks also held bonds to secure their bank notes and some other United States government securities, and banks took to buying the bonds of state and local governments and of railways. But in 1914, the securities held by national banks, other than United States government bonds, were only one-sixth as large as their loans. The commercial banks under state charter bought bonds more heavily, but even their bondholdings were only one-fourth as large as their loans in 1914.

---

[11]A sore point for national banks was the long-lasting prohibition of loans on real estate, which barred many attractive loans.

[12]The widely used compilations of the Comptroller of the Currency show the low ebb of state banking around 1870 and suggest that state banking expanded rapidly during the 1870's. All the way from 1870 to 1914, they show state banks outgrowing national banks by a wide margin. The Comptroller's figures, however, are totally unreliable for dates before 1914. They cover simply what was reported to the Comptroller by state authorities; whole blocks of states are omitted for the early years. Moreover, they take no account of "private banks," which were very important in the early years but failed to grow much, so that their relative importance fell. A much more accurate picture for the early years is given by figures based on the federal tax on bank deposits, levied from 1865 to 1883. (See Federal Deposit Insurance Corporation, *Annual Report for 1934*, p. 103. An estimate of the Comptroller's errors of omission is given, *ibid.*, p. 105.)

Although the *character* of banking was changing slowly, its *scale* changed rather quickly. The public's deposit balances at commercial banks were about $25 per capita in 1873, and nearly $150 per capita in 1914.[13] These figures understate the importance of this growth, since prices in 1914 were lower than in 1873. The "real" equivalent of the public's per capita deposit holdings grew by roughly 5 per cent per annum, a rate of growth about double the speed of growth of real national wealth per capita.

Banking from World War I to World War II.   The Federal Reserve System was set up just at the opening of World War I. It put the desired "flexibility" into the nation's paper money by enabling "member banks" to borrow from the Federal Reserve banks which, in turn, could issue notes. All of the national banks were *required* to become members; other banks were *allowed* to do so. Most of the large state-chartered banks and trust companies also joined. By 1923, when the country had settled down to peacetime living,[14] "state member banks" had about as much in deposits as "nonmember commercial banks." Hence the national and state member banks combined accounted for over two-thirds of the *dollar amount* of commercial-bank deposits (excluding interbank deposits). Two-thirds of the *number of banks,* however, stayed outside the Federal Reserve System.

Loans were still the major commercial-bank assets during the interwar prosperity. But during World War I, banks had bought government bonds on a large scale; and after the war, their holdings of bonds of other types outgrew their loans. Within the loan portfolio, the most rapid growth was in loans on securities (helping to finance the great stock-market boom of the 1920's) and on real estate. By 1929, when production, employment, and prices made their sharp downturn, old-fashioned loans were no longer dominant. At member banks, only about $13 billion out of $36 billion of "loans and investments" was apparently in business loans. Ten billion dollars was in "investments," $10 billion in loans on securities, and $3 billion in loans an real estate.[15]

During the great economic collapse of 1930–1932, the commercial banks

---

[13]This is the author's own estimate, arrived at by using the tax data referred to in footnote 12 for 1873, and correcting roughly for duplication because of checks in process of collection. In "1929 dollars" per capita (obtained by using the Bureau of Labor Statistics wholesale-price index to give a rough adjustment), the corresponding figures are $28 for 1873 and $204 for 1914 [AGH].

[14]The years 1919–20 were disturbed by a lively inflationary boom; after the break in 1920, the depression lasted through most of 1922. See Chapter 20.

[15]Since the classification of bank assets in official statistics kept changing, it is hard to guess how quickly this change from nineteenth-century banking came about. Doubtless many loans in 1873 or 1914 were secured by real estate and securities—or would have been if 1929 rules for collateral on loans had been in force. Perhaps tradition exaggerates the importance of business loans in the old days. In any case, we must clearly understand that by the end of the 1920's—if not before—banking rested chiefly on investments and on loans whose collateral was not created by current production.

were at the storm center.[16] Banks failed right and left—on a scale the country had not experienced since the days of "wildcat banking" before the Civil War. Although the Federal Reserve System had been established to prevent bank panics, an old-fashioned bank panic occurred early in 1933. Banks were closed for a week everywhere in March 1933, and for several weeks in some parts of the country. Apart from deposits in banks that reopened promptly after the "banking holiday," $8 billion of customer's deposit balances was tied up by bank failures between the middle of 1929 and March 1933; and, of this, $4 billion was still tied up in June 1933. This was a significant slice of the public's money stock; the public's total deposits in operating commercial banks were $43 billion in 1929 and $27 billion in June 1933.

To rebuild public confidence in the safety of banks, the federal government helped them in several ways from 1933 onward.[17] Most important, it set up the Federal Deposit Insurance Corporation to guarantee depositors prompt repayment up to $5,000 in case of failure.[18] This measure made deposits as safe from the owner's standpoint as bank notes had been under the national-bank system. Many small banks stayed out of the system, out of choice or because the FDIC felt that they were poor risks. But the banks that joined the insurance system held the overwhelming bulk of deposits. Once the banks were reopened, they rapidly expanded operations again. Deposits rose to within 10 per cent of the 1929 level by 1936, and passed the 1929 level in 1939.

The great slump carried the banks another stage away from reliance on loans. From the middle of 1929 to the depression low of 1935, total loans of commercial banks fell from $36 to $15 billion; and at the end of the interwar period (1939) they had risen only to $17 billion. Something like $5 billion of the shrinkage was sheer evaporation—losses written off by banks when debtors could not pay. But another $14 billion represented collections from debtors in excess of new loans made. Obviously, many debtors found it very painful to pay off loans in depression times. But the contraction of loans also hurt the banks badly. Many of the business firms and banks that had been most active in the predepression loan business were killed off by the depression. The surviving borrowers and lenders were both more cautious about bank loans. At the end of 1939, investments at commercial banks were about one-and-a-third times as large as loans.

World War II brought a further change in the composition of bank assets. Although the banks' loans grew rapidly, their holdings of government securities

---

[16]For an account of the bank crisis of the 1930's, see A. G. Hart, *Debts and Recovery* (New York: 20th Century Fund, 1938), Chapter 3 and Appendix, Tables 2–9. The figures in the text are from this source. The depression shrinkage hit nonmember banks much harder than member banks, raising the member banks' proportion of the banking business.

[17]See Chapters 6, 7, and 20.

[18]The amount has since been raised to $15,000 and to $30,000 on joint accounts.

grew faster, and at the end of 1945 investments, at $97.9 billion, were 3.8 times the loan total of $26.1 billion.

In the postwar period, the apparent trend toward a decline of lending in relation to other bank activities reversed itself rather dramatically. During the immediate postwar inflation, investments actually fell rather sharply while loans rose, and by the end of 1948 investments were only 1.7 times loans.[19] In the ensuing years, loans rose almost without interruption; while investments showed a more gradual uptrend with some setbacks. By the end of 1966, commercial-bank investments were only half as great as loans, and well toward half of investments consisted of corporate and "municipal" bonds rather than United States government securities.

Concentration and competition in banking.　Although banks are many, a few giant banks do much of the business. Out of 13,366 commercial banks insured by the Federal Deposit Insurance Corporation in 1965, only 392 had deposits of more than $100 million each. At the other extreme, 6,612 banks (nearly one-half of the total number) had deposits smaller than $5 million each. The small group of large banks had nearly two-thirds of the total assets; the large group of small banks had less than 6 per cent.

Despite the postwar prosperity and population growth, the total number of commercial banks has been declining until quite recently. From 1947 to 1962 the number steadily diminished from 14,181 to 13,427. Since then, the number of banks increased slightly and reached 13,784 by the end of 1966.[20] Virtually all of the postwar decline has been the result of mergers and acquisitions which absorbed independent banks.[21]

Concentration in banking would be still greater if it were not for our traditional hostility toward "branch banking." In most other countries, a handful of giant banks, each with hundreds of branch offices, does almost all the banking business. In the United States, no commercial bank may open offices outside its home state. In many states, branch banking is entirely prohibited; in others it is limited to the bank's head office city. Sixteen states, located primarily in the western half of the nation, permit statewide branch banking.

This limitation of branch banking is sharply criticized by many bankers and economists. It does help to limit the concentration of economic power—a generally accepted objective in the United States. But our restraints on branch banking interfere with the flow of savings from city to countryside and from

---

[19]Part of the wartime increase and 1946–48 decrease in investments was caused by the prudence of the Treasury in floating more bonds for wartime financing than in the end proved necessary, so that after the war some redundant Treasury cash was used to retire some bonds.

[20]Figures computed from Federal Deposit Insurance Corporation, *Annual Report for 1966*.

[21]There has been, however, a large increase in the number of banking offices. In 1950 there were approximately 19,000 bank offices throughout the nation; by the end of 1965 there were nearly 30,000.

east to south and west.[22] They also bar the provision of banking facilities to towns too small to support independent banks. And they contributed to the destructive wave of bank failures in the early 1930's.[23] Balancing advantages and disadvantages, we might be better off if we were to permit the increased centralization of power implied by branch banking and were still vigilant against its abuse.

Interest in competition within the commercial banking industry has intensified in recent years. The growing number of mergers has raised the issue whether the industry should be subject to exisiting national anti-trust legislation. The Bank Merger Act of 1960 set "the public interest" as the primary criteria by which bank merger applications should by judged by federal bank regulatory agencies. In 1963 and 1964 the Supreme Court ruled, however, that bank mergers could not take place if they violated the Clayton and Sherman Anti-trust Acts. Congress responded with the Bank Merger Act of 1966 which authorized federal banking agencies and the courts to approve bank mergers which may threaten to lessen competition if the anti-competitive effects of such mergers are "clearly outweighed in the public interest by the probable effect of the transaction in meeting the convenience and needs of the community to be served."

In March 1967 the Supreme Court ruled that bank mergers are subject to the Clayton Act despite the provisions of the 1966 Bank Merger Act. This decision did not nullify existing legislation and left room for further clarification of the criteria by which bank mergers should be evaluated.

NOTES ON

ALTERNATIVE POINTS OF VIEW

AND SUPPLEMENTARY READINGS

On banking in the United States before World War I, Horace White, *Money and Banking,* 4th ed. (Boston: Ginn and Company, 1911) is lively and fairly detailed.

Banking since World War I is viewed in two articles which appear in Deane Carson's volume of readings, *Banking and Monetary Studies* (Homewood, Ill.: Richard

---

[22]In countries with branch banking (in Canada, for instance), some offices have deposits far in excess of loans, while others have loans equaling or exceeding deposits. The transfer of funds from offices rich in depositors to offices rich in loan opportunities has helped narrow the spread between interest rates charged farmers and those charged city-dwellers.

[23]The failure of a bank with branches is not impossible. But rescue operations by government are much easier than if all the bank offices involved are under separate ownership. The virtual certainty that government will rescue a bank with branches rather than let it collapse wards off panic. In none of the branch-banking countries was there any heavy loss to bank depositors through failures in the 1930's, such as we experienced in this country. (See Jacob Viner, "Recent Legislation and the Banking Situation," *American Economic Review,* Supplement, March 1936, pp. 106 ff.)

D. Irwin, 1963): "Dual Banking Between Two World Wars" by Raymond B. Kent (pp. 43–63), and "The Federal Reserve System—Working Partner of the National Banking System for Half a Century" by Allan Sproul (pp. 64–79).

A comprehensive review of the structure and function of the banking industry is found in the American Bankers Association monograph prepared for the Commission on Money and Credit, *The Commercial Banking Industry* (Englewood Cliffs, N.J.: Prentice-Hall, Inc., 1962).

For an excellent discussion of the relevant issues concerning bank mergers see Almarin Phillips, "Competition, Confusion, and Commercial Banking," *The Journal of Finance,* March 1964, pp. 32–45.

Chapter 3

The Banking Business

The Banker's Point of View

The banker's profits. Banking is studied in this book because of its relation to money. We will examine banking as it affects the public interest—as a source of money and near-moneys, and as an influence on the way the public uses these liquid assets. To understand how banks work, we start by taking the banker's point of view, and asking why he does what he does.

First, remember that a commercial bank is a profit-making business corporation. Banking has a strong flavor of public service about it, and is hedged about by restrictions imposed by law and by supervisory authorities. The banker is less free than most businessmen to take every profit opportunity that may appear. But regulation does not extend to the rate of profit, as it does with public utilities, and the banker is mainly motivated by the search for higher revenues to cover his costs, to perpetuate the business, and to yield dividends for his stockholders.

This profit motive is somewhat obscured by the way people talk about banking, and by the bankers' "conservatism." Banking is analyzed, more than any other business, in terms of its *balance sheet* as opposed to its *income account;* we will adopt a balance-sheet approach in this chapter. Banking is a very polite business, and it is not considered polite to talk openly about profits or appear to bargain closely. Conservatism implies a willingness to reject glittering

33

prospects of a quick profit. But the profit motive is there, however subdued it may seem. As businesses go, a bank has a phenomenally long expectation of life, so it is neither cowardly nor unbusinesslike for the banker to reject chances for quick profits which come linked with a slight danger of heavy losses. "He who fights and runs away lives to fight another day." Over a long series of "other days," the banker can be confident of ample earnings. He is motivated by profit, but by long-run rather than immediate gain.

Sources of bank revenue. The banker must count on getting most of his revenue in the form of interest on "earning assets"—loans and bonds. Out of $19.5 billion earned by the insured commercial banks in 1966, $16.9 billion (87 per cent) came from these sources.[1] Service charges on deposit accounts yielded about $0.9 billion and all other sources of earnings about $1.7 billion.

Much the most important single item is income on loans. They provided $13.3 billion. Investments were a poor second at $3.8 billion. This was partly because loans are larger than investments, but also because loans are much more profitable. Loans brought in $6.32 of interest and fees per $100 outstanding, as against $3.69 per $100 outstanding from investments.

Offsetting expenses. Commercial banks are expensive to run. Insured banks paid their employees $4.70 billion in 1966. They paid $6.26 billion interest on savings and time deposits. Miscellaneous expenses brought the total up to $14.6 billion, leaving $4.95 billion of "net operating earnings." After loss provision and income taxes, "net profits after taxes" were $2.68 billion.

The major item—interest on savings and time deposits—has increased from 25 per cent of bank expenses in 1960 to 42.2 per cent in 1966. This growth reflects the several increases in the levels of interest payments on savings and time deposits during the sixties and the consequent growth of these deposits from $73 billion in 1960 to $159 billion in 1966. Another significant proportion of the expenses results from handling deposit accounts. Most bank employees and most of the supplies are used to handle dealings with depositors over the counter and to process checks and depositors' bank statements; it is for these dealings that banks require large ground-floor offices. The officers (as distinct from junior employees) are largely concerned with loans and investments, but it is hard to allocate nearly one-third of the $14.6 billion of operating expenses to the handling of earning assets and deposit accounts. Investments are presumably much cheaper to handle than loans—at least for large banks.

The paradox of bank operations. The upshot of this analysis seems to conflict with the idea that banks are businesslike. It would certainly be disconcerting to find a bus company, for example, carrying passengers at a cost of

---

[1] *Annual Report of the Federal Deposit Insurance Corporation, 1966*, pp. 158–60.

ten cents a trip, charging only a penny as fare, and covering most of its costs out of interest on securities owned. We would expect such a company to suspend its bus service and thereby to cut its costs, and pocket its interest income. How can we explain the banker's behavior—his willingness to handle deposits that cost him much more than they bring in as service charges, and to cover the deficit out of revenue from earning assets?

This apparent paradox is not quite real. If a banker told his depositors that he could no longer be bothered with their accounts, he could indeed cut his costs. He could discharge most of the bank's help, sell the bank building, and move upstairs to a quiet office suite, but he would thereby drive himself out of the loan business. To pay off the depositors, he would have to sell off more than nine-tenths of the bank's earning assets.[2] Even if he kept the most remunerative assets, he would have parted with a good four-fifths of his gross income.

In short, the bank incurs expenses to induce depositors to carry balances at the bank, and thus to enable the bank to have large earning assets. Savings depositors get interest on their balances—roughly 4 per cent on the average. Demand depositors do not receive interest; since 1935, bankers have been prohibited by law from paying cash interest on demand deposits. But demand deposits which are large and stable are handled without charge. Sometimes the banker calculates what the account costs him, credits the customer with an interest equivalent on his balance, and bills the customer for service if the costs exceed the credit. Sometimes the arrangement is more informal, no service charge is made if the customer carries a certain minimum balance and does not have too "active" an account. In any case, the bank compensates the depositors (in a mixture of cash interest and "free" services) for enhancing the bank's power to hold earning assets.

Basis of bank earnings. What makes banking profitable? Is the banker simply a passenger on the economic ship, or does he help to make it go?

On the whole, the banks do useful work. The accounting job they do is clearly necessary. Perhaps bank customers use facilities wastefully, since they are sometimes able to put the bank to avoidable extra work without being penalized. But the banker gains if he can locate these situations and persuade the customers in question to change their practices. The banker also gains if he can invent procedures for doing the accounting job with less work. This suggests that the banker is rewarded for economizing on manpower and supplies, which is all to the good. On the other hand, the fact that banks engage in "nonprice competition" rather than "price competition" makes it likely that

---

[2] At the end of 1966, according to Federal Reserve figures, all insured commercial banks had total assets of $402.9 billion, and liabilities of $371.2 billion. To pay off all these liabilities would leave only $31.7 billion of assets (assuming securities, buildings, and so forth at book value). This is less than 10 per cent of the $334.2 billion of earning assets held at the end of 1966 and some of this remainder would have to be held as a working cash balance.

they are providing many services that customers would cheerfully do without if billed for them separately.[3]

On the side of asset management, the banker who profits most is the one most successful at sifting assets that will pay off on schedule from those that will not. There is a reward for the banker who will back productive enterprises that are not recognized by other financiers—who will see that business opportunities do not go to waste for lack of funds. This reward puts the banker's skills to work placing capital where it is needed. To some extent, however, the successful banker may merely be guessing shrewdly which bonds will rise in price in advance of maturity. To this extent, his contribution to the productiveness of the economic system is more doubtful.

Earnings versus liquidity.   Bank management is a tug of war between immediate earnings and "liquidity." Because the bank gets its profit primarily out of interest on its "earning assets," it must continue to ask whether it can increase its earning assets, or can swap a low-interest asset for a high-interest asset. But in choosing its assets, a bank has also to guard its "liquidity." A bank that chose only the assets that bore a high interest rate would be likely to have trouble paying off depositors who wished to withdraw their funds, and could not hold its depositors. Its reputation would suffer, and without a reputation for "soundness," a bank cannot survive.

The conflict of liquidity and earnings must not be exaggerated. When deciding whether to make a particular loan or to buy a particular security, the banker is deciding between liquidity and earnings. But this year's interest earnings *and* this year's liquidity *both* contribute to the bank's long-run earning power. The banker must administer his *whole* portfolio to obtain earnings and liquidity.

The "real-bills" tradition; "self-liquidating assets."   Traditionally, the liquidity of a bank[4] was thought to depend upon having individual assets that were "self-liquidating." Bank loans commonly grow out of customers'

---

[3] The gentlemanly atmosphere of banking and the fact that the other banks to which depositors might turn ordinarily belong to the same clearinghouse association make it very unusual for any bank to attract depositors by offering identical services cheaper. But it is often possible to offer additional services without extra charge. In such a competitive pattern, extra services may be offered that are worth only a fraction of their cost to customers. To take an example from an unrelated field, suppose neither the Waldorf Astoria nor the Americana is full. One way for the hotels to compete is to offer better room service. If the room service can be made one dollar's worth more attractive at a cost of two dollars, this is well worth the while of either of the competing hotels for by taking a larger loss on service the successful competitor can gain hundreds a day in revenues.

[4] *Note on terminology:* In this book, we avoid applying the term *liquidity* to an individual piece of property, because the term *moneyness* seems more clear-cut, and because there is another job for the term *liquidity*. This other job is to describe the *balance-sheet and income position* of a bank, a business, or a person—the degree of assurance that debts can be met and cash found for unexpected payments. This assurance rests not on the moneyness of single assets, but on the relation of assets to liabilities and of the balance sheet to revenue and expenses. The adjective *liquid* is applied both to assets high in moneyness and to business positions high in liquidity.

business dealings. The feeling was that if a loan grew out of a transaction which in itself would help the borrower get funds to repay the loan, all was well. Thus, the most liquid bank assets were thought to be loans to businessmen secured by physical goods in the process of orderly marketing (or in shipment, or in production in a factory). The loan could be repaid out of the price the goods would fetch when sold. This was the so-called "real-bills" doctrine.[5] In the United States it has always been honored more in the breach than in the observance, but until recently, a breach of the doctrine called for excuses.

This doctrine of "self-liquidating" loans sounds plausible—all the more so because it has a tinge of unattainable moral beauty about it. But it hides a fallacy. Suppose that all bank loans are "real" in this sense and that one bank needing cash starts to reduce its loans. As old loans fall due, the bank insists on payment; as new loans are applied for, the bank refuses to grant them. What happens? Unless other banks are also trying to reduce their loans, the customers of the single bank that is trying to retrench may be able to borrow elsewhere. Even if they cannot, other merchants may be able to do so and can thereby purchase the goods that the first bank's debtors must sell to pay off their debts. If, however, the other commercial banks are also striving to reduce their loans, the first bank's debtors may not be able to liquidate their "self-liquidating" loans. The merchants to whom these debtors must sell their goods would themselves have trouble obtaining loans and so would have difficulty financing their purchases. The first bank's debtors would have trouble raising cash to pay off their loans.

One part of the banking community could succeed in reducing its outstanding loans by this process only if other bankers stepped up their lending. A *universal* attempt to reduce outstanding loans, in a thoroughgoing "real-bills" system, would cripple the buying power of disappointed borrowers. This would, in turn, cripple the loan-repaying power of other debtors. The result would inevitably be a general freezing of credit.

"Shiftability" of assets. Shrewd observers of American banking decided

---

[5] This is an English rather than an American term. In England (and on the European Continent), immediate payment for goods sold was often made in *trade bills.* That is, the seller drew a "bill" calling on the buyer to pay (just as a department store does when a woman buys a dress). But instead of simply sending the bill to the buyer for cash settlement, the seller would pass the bill on to his suppliers, or "discount" it with his banker. Such bills were commonly "accepted" by the buyers on whom they were drawn—that is, payment was guaranteed as of the future date specified in the bill. Then they became *trade acceptances.* Where the buyer's name was not widely known but his local credit standing was good, essentially the same transaction could be carried on with a "banker's bill," by making an agreement under which the seller of goods could draw the "bill" against the buyer's banker, and the buyer would later reimburse the banker.

With a little ingenuity, capital could be raised through "bills" that had no direct linkage with commodity transactions. Such bills were known as *accommodation paper,* and were viewed with suspicion—for the very good reason that their issue was likely to show that the debtor was trying to do business with inadequate capital and might go bankrupt.

many years ago that the self-liquidity of assets was a delusion. From the standpoint of a bank, they argued, an asset is "liquid" only if it is shiftable.

A shiftable asset is one that directly or indirectly will find another holder in case the present holder decides to part with it. On this principle loans that can be sold on an open market are directly shiftable.[6] Loans that are based on goods in process are indirectly shiftable only if other banks are willing to make such loans, as those other banks will thereby provide funds to buy the goods that the first bank's customer has to sell.

Securities for which there is a strong and active market are also directly shiftable. This is true of all federal securities, and of the bonds of well-known corporations and local governments. Bonds of small local concerns and local governments whose credit rating is doubtful may not be as shiftable. Finally, shiftability is at a minimum for loans based on the personal relationship of banker and borrower. If the banker would lose valuable good will by handing the borrower over to another creditor, the loan would not be very shiftable. Old-fashioned mortgages were not very shiftable—except indirectly, at maturity, when the customer could sometimes be sent elsewhere for a renewal. Present-day amortized mortgages are more easily transferred without creating a crisis for the debtor.

Shiftability and moneyness. "Shiftability" may be useless without *price certainty*. Corporation stocks, if listed on a stock exchange, are highly shiftable. There is always a market, but at a price which no one can accurately predict in advance. Consequently, stocks are shiftable but not very liquid. In the terms used in this book, they are low in moneyness because the amount of debt that can be paid off by selling them is not certain.[7]

It is for this reason that our account of bank assets will stress both the sort of market available and the certainty of price. We shall regard Treasury bills as very liquid because a bank that holds them can readily shift its burden onto the Treasury by waiting a few weeks till the bill matures, or can shift it onto some other bank by selling the bill or borrowing against it. We shall regard corporation stocks as less liquid for the reasons just cited—shiftability does not offset price uncertainty.

Any asset can be given moneyness artificially if somebody chooses to create a ready market for it with a reasonably certain price. Much of the activity of

---

[6] This is true of acceptances. Such a market also exists for "open-market commercial paper"—promissory notes that are made out for round sums and payable to bearer, issued by certain rather well-known business firms to raise capital for short periods. Open-market commercial paper is, therefore, similar to corporate bonds, except that it is issued for short instead of long periods and that it is not usually backed by pledges of real estate or other assets.

[7] If holders of stocks close their eyes to the record of stock-price gyrations, and come to have unreasoning confidence in the stability of stock prices, odd results may follow. So long as this attitude holds, corporation stocks are a "near-money," whose holders feel their need for other "near-moneys" to be reduced. When some shock breaks down this unreasoning confidence, the "moneyness" of stock evaporates. Something of this sort seems to have happened around the business downturn of 1929.

central banks (in the United States, of the Federal Reserve banks) consists of creating markets for assets so as to influence bank policy.

Selection of "sound" assets; credit rationing. Even though his liquidity may not be at issue in an individual case, the banker has to decide whether a loan or a bond is "sound"—whether it is reasonably free from risk of loss. He must, therefore, appraise the prospects of the firm or household whose debt is in question. The banker wants to be sure that the firm's earning power is sufficient to cover interest and eventually retire the debt or, as a minimum, that the debtor will be able to borrow from somebody else to pay off what the bank lends. Assurance of these results depends upon the composition of the borrower's assets, the prospects of the industry to which the borrower belongs, and alert and thrifty management.

Study of the prospects of loan applicants and of firms whose bonds may be bought is always going on at the banks; it is for such study that they need high-salaried executives. But the bank's officers cannot take the time to think themselves fully into the borrower's problems. To do that, they would have to duplicate policy-thinking within the borrowing firms—and then sit down to criticize it.

The banker must reduce the job of credit analysis to manageable proportions; he must take short cuts and content himself with a study of key items. Rules of thumb are applied, and are supplemented by detailed study only where the sum of money involved is important or where the borrower has a special claim to attention as an old customer. The banker insists that the borrower show signs of reasonable prudence. For instance, he checks to see that the borrower carries adequate cash balances and adequate insurance against various risks, and steers clear of speculation unrelated to his business. He insists on a reasonable ratio (varying from industry to industry) of "current assets" (cash, receivables, and inventories) to "current liabilities." Where any doubt exists about the safety of the loan, the banker asks to be protected by a pledge of collateral (securities, real estate, accounts receivable from the borrower's customers, or claims on commodities) with a greater value than the amount of the loan.

Where possible, the bank also uses "credit ratings" for borrowers, established by outside agencies. There are a number of specialists (such as Dun and Bradstreet) whose "ratings" help both bankers and business firms to decide whether a would-be borrower can safely be given a cash loan or goods on credit. The banks give special attention to ratings of bonds—not only because banks value the opinion of the rating agencies (like Moody's), but also because bond ratings may affect bank examinations. A bond rated as high grade will pass muster without question from a bank examiner. But if the bond is rated as low grade (or is not rated by these agencies), the banker may have to argue about his investment with the supervising authority. At best, this is a nuisance; if the banker loses the argument, his own standing suffers.

The banker's notions of "soundness" in earning assets have two important consequences: (a) They contribute to business fluctuations; (b) they subject borrowers to "credit rationing"—which affects the whole attitude of the nonbank public toward cash assets and "liquidity."

The effect on fluctuations goes back to the fact that standards of "soundness" unavoidably vary with business activity. A firm that has good business prospects on a business upswing may have very bad prospects on a downswing. Its loan application may be rated as "sound" on the upswing and "unsound" on the downswing, even though the firm's balance sheet shows just the same assets and liabilities. Thus, it is easier to get loans on an upswing than on a downswing, which helps to intensify the expansion or contraction of business, whichever is in progress. Bond ratings also vary somewhat in business fluctuations, more bonds being rated high grade in prosperity. This shift in bond ratings probably makes less difference than the shift in the "soundness" of loan applicants, for the banks that hesitate to buy corporation bonds are still free to buy government bonds. But the shifts in bond ratings as well as in loan standards doubtless add something to business fluctuations.

The effect on "credit rationing" is more pervasive. A borrower's access to bank credit depends largely on the degree to which the banker's rules of thumb fit his case. Most firms in the United States probably feel that they are entitled to borrow more than banks would lend them; many would be willing to borrow more than they do, at the interest rates they now pay. We must beware of assuming that the interest rates banks charge effectively limit the amount borrowed. This is the case with some borrowers, but there is always an "unsatisfied fringe" of would-be borrowers who are not allowed to borrow, and of actual borrowers who want more. Even those borrowers who now can borrow all they want have to reckon on the limits that banking rules set to their "lines of credit," and on the fact that those limits may tighten in the future.

Balance-Sheet Structure

Uses of balance-sheet analysis. As we said above, banking situations are commonly analyzed in terms of balance sheets or "statements of condition" listing assets and liabilities. Here, we aim to give you a feel for this kind of analysis by examining the combined balance sheet of all insured commercial banks.

General structure. The broad outlines of the asset-liability structure of commercial banks are shown in Table 3-1. For each of the groups of banks shown, earning assets (loans plus investments) make up 75.7 to 87.5 per cent of total assets. The proportion in earning assets rises somewhat as we move from left to right in the table—that is, as we shift our attention from banks at the financial focus of the country to outlying banks. As will appear shortly,

TABLE 3-1

PRINCIPAL ASSETS AND LIABILITIES OF COMMERCIAL BANKS, JUNE 30, 1966

(dollar amounts in billions, rounded to nearest $0.1 billion)*

Banks in Federal Deposit Insurance System

Balance-Sheet Item	Members of Federal Reserve System			Insured Nonmember Banks	Non-insured Commercial Banks	All Commercial Banks
	Reserve City Banks: New York and Chicago	Other Reserve City Banks	"Country" Banks			
Number of banks	23	170	6,001	7,359	249	13,802
Assets:						
1. Cash assets	$15.3	$ 20.8	$ 16.8	$ 6.6	$0.5	$ 60.0
2. Investments	13.8	26.1	39.7	21.9	0.8	102.3
3. Loans	44.4	67.8	66.1	32.5	1.5	212.3
4. All other assets**	3.4	3.5	2.7	1.2	0.3	11.1
Total assets	$76.9	$118.2	$125.3	$62.2	$3.1	$385.7
Liabilities and capital accounts:						
5. Personal and business deposits	$51.1	$ 84.3	$ 96.7	$48.6	$1.5	$282.2
6. Government deposits	5.3	12.6	14.0	6.7	0.2	38.8
7. Interbank deposits	7.7	7.4	2.0	0.7	0.3	18.1
Total deposits	$64.1	$104.3	$112.7	$56.0	$2.0	$339.1
8. Miscellaneous liabilities**	6.5	4.6	2.5	1.0	0.7	15.3
Total liabilities:	$70.6	$108.9	$115.2	$57.0	$2.7	$354.4
9. Capital accounts	6.3	9.3	10.1	5.2	0.4	31.3
Total liabilities plus capital accounts	$76.9	$118.2	$125.3	$62.2	$3.1	$385.7

Source: Federal Reserve Bulletin, March 1967, pp. 408–13.

*Detail may not add to total because of rounding.
**Not separately published; estimates may err by as much as $0.2 billion.

this difference reflects chiefly differences in reserve requirements. The relative weight of loans is greatest in the left-hand columns of the table—a fact which testifies to the initiative of giant banks in big cities in the postwar revival of bank lending activity.

All of the classes of insured banks have liabilities from 91.6 to 92.1 per cent of assets, and have almost all their liabilities in deposits. Interbank deposits are mostly in the big downtown banks in the central reserve city and reserve city classifications; government deposits are spread more evenly (outside New York and Chicago); in each group of banks, three-fourths or more of the deposits are owned by individuals and businesses.

Capital accounts. Banks, like other credit institutions, owe almost as much as they own. Total deposits plus miscellaneous liabilities add up to 92 per cent of total assets. The remaining 8 per cent represents the banks' book value from the standpoint of their stockholders—their "capital accounts."

In more detail, the capital accounts for insured banks work out as follows:

9a. "Capital stock, notes and debentures"—recording
amounts paid in by bank owners when the bank was
organized or since[8] . . . . $10.6 billion

9b. "Surplus"—recording amounts that bank directors have
resolved to add to capital funds permanently rather than
pay out as dividends[9] . . . . $14.0 billion

9c. "Undivided profits"—earnings not yet allocated either to
permanent surplus or to dividends . . . . $ 6.2 billion

9d. "Reserves" . . . . $ 0.9 billion

In principle, any change in a bank's assets which is not fully offset by changes in its debts (liabilities) affects the capital account. If the market price of a bond held by a bank falls below its book value, the bank will usually reduce its value on the books and make an equal reduction in "reserves" (item 9d) or undivided profits (item 9c). If a loan has been written off as a bad debt and the debtor subsequently pays it off with a check drawn on another bank, that check is treated as an unexpected addition to cash assets, and undivided profits are increased by this amount.[10]

---

[8] In recent years potential tax advantages have encouraged banks to issue notes and debentures. In 1966 notes and debentures were $1.7 billion compared to $8.9 billion of common stock.

[9] Some banks started business with a "paid-in surplus" to escape disabilities imposed on banks with surplus below a certain minimum. In some banks, a surplus has been created by a downward revaluation of capital stock. But the bulk of surplus represents earnings plowed back into the business. Since 1934, the surplus of all insured commercial banks has climbed from $2.0 to $14.0 billion; surplus plus undivided profits from $2.5 to $20.2 billion.

[10] This account has to be qualified because of "valuation reserves" that are treated as negative assets rather than as capital accounts. The total of loans shown for insured banks in Table 3-1 is estimated by subtracting a valuation reserve from the gross total of loans. When a loan is determined to be a bad debt, the bank may write it off from the gross-loans figure and from the loan-valuation reserve, leaving capital account unaffected. If the debtor proves able to pay at a later date and the loan is reinstated with a deferred maturity, the "recovery" may again affect the gross-loans total and loan-valuation reserve without going through capital account.

The capital account also reflects the bank's income. The growth of net worth through interest on loans, for example, shows up as an increase in undivided profits.[11] In the other direction, when dividends are paid to stockholders, undivided profits shrink.

The Debts of Commercial Banks : Deposits

Classification of deposits.   The deposit figures from Table 3-1 are shown in more detail in Table 3-2. The deposit classification is set up on two different principles—by type of depositor and by type of debt contract between the bank and its deposit creditor. Later in the book we will be more concerned with the type-of-depositor classification. But here we are trying to view the landscape through the banker's eyes, so that the stress is on the type-of-contract classification.

A major part of commercial bank deposits are "demand deposits"—payable at any moment the depositor chooses, and transferable by check. The demand-deposit items of Table 3-2 are self-explanatory, save, perhaps, for item 5a, the full name of which is "certified and officers' checks, cash letters of credit and traveler's checks outstanding, and amounts due to Federal Reserve banks."[12] This item consists of bank debt outstanding in the form of checks drawn on the

---

[11]Interest on loans and on bonds is ordinarily received in lump sums; but bank accounting spreads it smoothly over the period during which it is earned, by the use of an account called "income accrued but not collected" among the miscellaneous assets and an account called "income collected but not earned" among the miscellaneous liabilities.

Income accrued but not collected consists chiefly of bond interest. Suppose a bank holds a $10,000 Treasury bond which pays $150 of interest on March 15 and $150 on September 15. Then on May 15, the bank's assets include $50 of accrued interest on this bond (since one-third of the period from March 15 to September 15 has elapsed); on June 15, $75 (since half the period has elapsed). When the bank gets its $150 on September 15, the cash received replaces accrued interest among the assets, and this bond's contribution to "income accrued but not collected" drops to zero. As this asset account builds up through interest accruals, the double-entry bookkeeping of the bank adds equal increments to "undivided profits" on the liability side of the books.

Loans on which interest is collected at maturity also contribute to "income accrued but not collected." When (as is more common) the loan is "discounted," a note for $100,000 payable in three months at a rate of 4 per cent per annum provides only $99,000 for the borrower. The bank deducts $1,000 of interest when it makes the loan. But the note goes on the books at $100,000. The bank's accountants will not show the $1,000 difference as a gain in the bank's net worth at the moment the note is discounted, for it will only be earned over the next three months. So they add $1,000 to the liability account for "income collected but not earned." Then over the three months, they gradually scale down this amount until at maturity this note's contribution to that account is zero. As they scale down the $1,000, they add equal amounts to undivided profits.

[12]Certified checks are customers' checks that are presented to the bank on which they are drawn *before* they are used in payment; they are deducted at once from the customer's balance, and bear a stamp showing that the bank guarantees payment. Officers' checks (ordinarily "cashiers' checks") are drawn by a bank upon itself. (Bank drafts, which serve similar purposes, are checks drawn by one bank upon another bank where it has an account; these are not included in item 5a.)

TABLE 3-2

CLASSIFICATION OF DEPOSITS IN COMMERCIAL BANKS, JUNE 30, 1966

(dollar amounts in billions, rounded to nearest $0.1 billion)*

	Banks in Federal Deposit Insurance System					All Commercial Banks
	Members of Federal Reserve System			Insured Nonmember Banks	Non-insured Commercial Banks	
Balance-Sheet Item	*Reserve City Banks: New York and Chicago*	*Other Reserve City Banks*	*"Country" Banks*			
Deposits owned by individuals, partnerships, and corporations:						
5a. Certified and officers checks, etc.	$ 3.8	$ 1.2	$ 1.1	$ 0.5	$0.1	$ 6.7
5b. Other demand deposits (subject to check)	24.3	39.8	44.9	22.4	0.8	132.2
5c. Time and savings deposits	23.0	43.3	50.7	25.7	0.6	143.3
5. Total	$51.1	$84.3	$96.7	$48.6	$ 1.5	$282.2
Deposits owned by government bodies:						
6a. United States government, demand	$ 2.9	$ 4.0	$ 3.1	$ 1.0	†	$ 11.0
6b. United States government time and savings**	0.1	0.1	0.1	†	†	0.3

6c. State and local, demand	1.1	3.5	6.8	3.4	0.1	14.9
6d. State and local, time and savings	1.1	5.1	4.0	2.3	0.1	12.6
6. Total	$ 5.3	$ 12.6	$ 14.0	$ 6.7	$0.2	$ 38.8
Interbank deposits:						
7a. Domestic banks, demand	$ 6.0	$ 6.8	$ 1.9	$ 0.6	$0.2	$ 15.5
7b. Foreign banks, demand	1.0	0.3	0.1	†	0.1	1.5
7c. Domestic and foreign, time and savings	0.7	0.2	0.1	0.1	†	1.1
7. Total	$ 7.7	$ 7.4	$ 2.0	$ 0.7	$0.3	$ 18.1
Total demand (5a + 5b + 6a + 6c + 7a + 7b)	$39.1	$ 55.6	$ 57.9	$27.9	$1.3	$181.8
Total time and savings (5c + 6b + 6d + 7c)	24.9	48.7	54.9	28.1	0.7	157.3
Total deposits	$64.1	$104.3	$112.7	$56.0	$2.0	$339.1

Source: Federal Reserve Bulletin, March 1967, pp. 408–13.

* Detail may not add to total because of rounding.

**Includes Postal Savings.

† Less than $0.05 billion.

bank's responsibility—either to make a payment on behalf of the bank itself, or to make a payment on behalf of a customer for which his ordinary personal check will not serve.[13] These checks can be cashed at any moment; indeed, most of those on the books at the end of any business day have already been cashed and are on their way home through the collection machinery, placing them in the demand-deposit group.

We should mention that there is a difference between the $153.8 billion of demand deposits attributed to the nonbank public—that is, "IPC's" (individuals, partnerships, and corporations) plus state and local governments—as of June 1966 and the $131.5 of such deposits included in the money supply as of the same date. This difference reflects an element of double-counting in the figure of $153.8 billion. When a check is deposited to the account of the drawee, the statement which the bank keeps for him has this amount added the same day; but commonly the check is not subtracted on the bank statement of the drawer until a day or two later after completion of the clearing process. The amount of these unallocated "cash items" in June 1966 was over $20 billion —about a sixth of the "adjusted demand deposits" figured after subtraction of such items from the amounts shown on bank statements and in Table 3-2.[14]

Time deposits consist largely of individual savings balances. Each savings depositor has a passbook in which the bank enters the amounts deposited and withdrawn, and keeps a record of the balance. Formally, the time depositor is not entitled to withdraw cash without giving thirty days' notice. In practice, unannounced withdrawals are ordinarily permitted, but at some loss of interest. Included here are corporate time deposits which include the large denomination short-term negotiable certificates of deposit.

Government accounts have some peculiarities. Banks are commonly required to set aside or "earmark" holdings of government securities as a pledge to

---

[13]The unquestioned and widely known credit standing of a bank makes its check acceptable where a personal check will not be accepted. This holds especially for people who need to cash checks far from home—hence the popularity of the traveler's check, which is a bank check in a round amount, requiring the customer's duplicated signature to activate it.

[14]In addition, of course, there are checks which have been drawn and are still in the mail between drawer and drawee, or between the drawee and his bank. Both these sets of checks have been allowed for on the *checkbooks* of drawers; the first group also on those of drawees.

The total amount of funds represented by checks in transit cannot be precisely estimated. But as of June 1966, we must include the $20.3 billion subtracted in calculating "adjusted demand deposits," plus the $6.7 billion of "certified and officers' checks," plus the "inter-customer float," which must be of about the same size as the $20.3 billion of "interbank float"—in total, some $45–50 billion, or about a third of the adjusted demand deposits.

This image of the proportion of demand deposits which is actually in motion can be checked roughly by statistics for "bank debits"—that is, the total of checks charged against customers' balances on bank books, excluding interbank and United States government accounts. Such debits totalled in 1966 some $5,942 billion, or about 45 times the average "adjusted demand deposits." Since there were about 250 business days in the year, the average dollar of deposits was called up for use about every 5-1/2 business days. If about a third of deposits were in motion on the average, we conclude that the average time from drawing to adjustment of the drawer's bank statement was (5-1/2)/(3) or about two business days—which is clearly a reasonable order of magnitude.

insure the repayment of these deposits. Over $15 billion of assets are so pledged. The federal government's handling of its accounts is also distinctive. The total amount on deposit fluctuates rather sharply with tax collections, public debt transactions, and the like. To avoid any appearance of playing favorites and to make its operations more predictable, the Treasury puts much of its funds into special accounts and draws upon these accounts by "calls" that take a uniform proportion from each bank in a broad grouping of banks.

Traditions of the stability of deposits. In planning his business, the banker has to allow for deposit instability. If a bank's deposits shrink, the bank has to pay out cash and may have to sell investments or call in loans to raise cash. The extent of deposit stability helps to determine the bank's choice of assets.

The banker has traditionally regarded his time deposits as the most stable and his interbank deposits as least stable, with the general public's checking deposits and government deposits in between. The behavior of large masses of deposits does not square with this tradition, but it probably holds true for individual accounts.

Time depositors, to begin with, think of their accounts as "savings" to provide for long-run goals or emergencies, not as funds for everyday use. Bankers, moreover, try to avoid instability in individual savings accounts by rejecting accounts which are likely to be unstable and by offering individual depositors incentives to keep stable balances. They often pay interest only on the *smallest* amount which the depositor has to his credit in a half-year. The banker's right to demand thirty day's notice is almost never exercised,[15] but the knowledge that this right exists may have a sobering effect on depositors.

Interest-sensitive corporate time deposits—especially in the form of large denomination certificates of deposit—are of all deposits perhaps the least tied to a particular bank. On the other hand, a bank of good reputation can be confident of its ability to attract such deposits if it sets an interest rate that slightly outshines the competition. The interest ceiling on savings and time deposits enforced by the Federal Reserve through Regulation Q can create a special hazard, however: if a bank's rate is at the ceiling and market rates on competing assets rise, the bank has no effective way to avoid a drain of such deposits. A general pinch of this sort was experienced by the banks offering CD's in the latter half of 1966, when in a three-month period of rising interest rates, the volume of outstanding large-denomination CD's fell from $18.3 billion to $15.5 billion.

Interbank accounts have traditionally been regarded as highly unstable.

[15]Banks do not require notice before payment as a matter of daily routine; the bother, expense, and loss of good will involved are prohibitive. But a bank cannot *suddenly* start requiring notice without alarming its customers. Any effort to check an outflow of cash from the bank by requiring notice is likely to boomerang; depositors who would otherwise have left their money on deposit are likely to give notice in order to "be on the safe side."

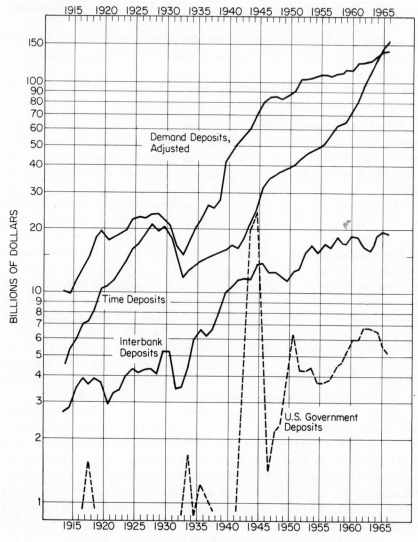

Source: *Federal Reserve Bulletin* and *Banking and Monetary Statistics*.

Chart 3-1: Deposits at commercial banks, 1914–66.

They are held largely in the major downtown banks of New York and Chicago, and the owners are predominantly smaller banks in the hinterland. Before the Federal Reserve System was established, any pressure applied to country banks by withdrawals of currency over their counters tended to amplify itself as a pressure on "reserve city banks" as country banks drew on interbank accounts to replenish currency; and the big-city banks looked on the holding of such balances as a risky but profitable part of their business.

Instability in practice. The record tends to confirm some aspects of the tradition of deposit stability and to cast doubt upon others. The history since 1914 (at the beginning of Federal Reserve operations) is shown in Chart 3-1. This chart—like most of the historical charts of this book—is drawn upon a semilogarithmic scale (sometimes called a "ratio scale"), with vertical distances proportional to the logarithms of the quantities. The effect is to make equal *percentage rates of growth* as between different series over the same time-span, or for a given series over different time-spans of the same length, appear as equal *slopes*. A 50 per cent rise is measured by a rise of about one centimeter (on the scale used in printing this chart), whether it is a rise from 2 to 3, from 10 to 15, or from 60 to 90.

As will be seen at a glance, time deposits have never shown any substantial decline except on the downswing of the Great Depression in 1929-33, while demand deposits, United States government deposits, and interbank deposits all have shown several important setbacks in their total quantity. (For demand deposits since World War II, however, setbacks have been interruptions of growth rather than appreciable absolute declines.) Of all these classes of deposits, interbank deposits have shown the most abrupt postwar gyrations. The course of time deposits may be no more *predictable* than that of demand deposits: the sharp acceleration of time-deposit growth from 1960 onward shows powerful new forces at work. But, of course, bank management can more easily adapt to unpredictable changes in growth rates than to unpredictable absolute declines.

One cannot emphasize too much that these curves show *national aggregates*. There may be a great deal of gyration in individual demand-deposit accounts, or in subaggregates for different types of such accounts, without any appreciable wobble of the curve, if declines for one type of depositor are made up by gains for another type. Furthermore, many individual banks may suffer from instability, with gains for one cancelling in the aggregate losses for another. But in fact and on the whole, work with more fine-grained data confirms the general impression as to relative stability that one gets from the aggregate curves.

On the whole, we are probably right in assuming that bankers rely upon the traditions about deposit stability under "normal conditions," and use them to guide asset management. But as the experience of the 1930's shows, these traditions are not correct for all situations, and changes in bank attitudes are possible.

The Assets of Commercial Banks

Major classes of assets. The main classes of bank assets, as we saw in Table 3-1, are investments, loans, and cash assets. The history of the main asset classes is traced in Chart 3-2. For a long time, the drift in asset structure

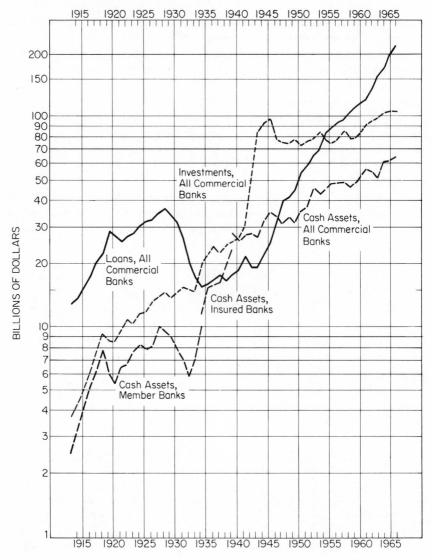

Source: Federal Reserve Bulletin and *Banking and Monetary Statistics.*

Chart 3-2: Major classes of commercial bank assets, 1916–66.

was largely from loans toward investments. Investments grew at a much
greater percentage rate than loans during World War I, and slightly faster than
loans during the 1920's; at the same time, loans came to be based more largely
on securities. In the Great Depression, loans were radically deflated—from
$36 to $15 billion between 1929 and 1935—and investments held roughly level
till 1934, then expanded rapidly.

During World War II, bank loans grew fast, but purchases of government securities raised investments even faster. By 1946, investments were up to nearly $100 billion—well over three times the amount of loans. But after the war, loans began to grow very fast; they came to exceed investments about the end of 1954, and were more than twice as great as investments by the end of 1966.

Cash assets and reserve requirements. Among the cash assets of commercial banks (inventoried in Table 3-3), the most important are the checking balances at the Federal Reserve banks (item 1b), which make up the bulk of the legal reserves of the member banks. Deposits at other banks (item 1c) are very important for banks that do not belong to the Federal Reserve System (and therefore do not hold reserves at Federal Reserve banks) and of some importance for "country" member banks. Checks in collection (item 1e) bulk very large statistically. But each bank must reckon that checks returning to it through the clearings offset the checks it has sent to other banks, so this item does not strengthen a bank against emergencies as do coin and paper money (item 1a) or deposits at the Federal Reserve.[16]

Prudent bankers have always held cash reserves so that they could convert as many customers' deposits into cash as would normally be withdrawn. In the United States,[17] the reserve tradition has crystallized into legal *required minimum* ratios of reserves to customers' balances. For member banks of the Federal Reserve System, these ratios are set (within statutory limits) by the Federal Reserve Board and are met by the member banks with balances deposited at the Federal Reserve banks and to a minor extent with vault cash. The requirements effective at the end of June 1966 are shown as item M2 of Table 3-3.[18] Note that the size of the reserve required depends mainly on demand deposits.

Banks are free to hold more than the required minimum of reserves. Through most of the 1930's, excess reserves were a large fraction of the total—for a few months, they were actually greater than required reserves. But during the postwar period, excess reserves have been relatively small, often smaller than member-bank borrowings from the Federal Reserve banks. Free reserves—the difference between excess reserves and borrowed reserves—have often been negative for the system as a whole. To put the same point differently, the banks'

---

[16]For monetary analysis, it is commonly better to treat checks in collection as a subtraction from deposit liabilities rather than an addition to cash assets. "Adjusted demand deposits" are calculated by taking the gross total of demand deposits payable to individuals, partnerships, corporations, and state and local governments (including cashiers' checks and so forth), and subtracting checks in collection as shown on the banks' asset accounts. The result is a picture of the balances that depositors would own *if nobody drew any more checks until those lately drawn had been collected.*

[17]In some other countries, the concentration of banking in the great branch-banking systems makes informal control more effective, and legal minimum ratios are not employed.

[18]These requirements have recently changed fairly often. The requirements for central reserve city banks and reserve city banks have been equalized by recent changes, and both will be treated as one group from now on.

TABLE 3-3

CASH ASSETS OF COMMERCIAL BANKS, JUNE 30, 1966

(dollar amounts in billions, rounded to nearest $0.1 billion)*

| Balance-Sheet Item | Banks in Federal Deposit Insurance System | | | | | |
| | Members of Federal Reserve System | | | | | |
	Reserve City Banks: New York and Chicago	*Other Reserve City Banks*	*"Country" Banks*	*Insured Non-member Banks*	*Non-insured Commercial Banks*	*All Commercial Banks*
1a. "Cash in vault" (currency on hand)	$ 0.4	$ 1.2	$ 2.4	$1.2	†	$ 5.2
1b. Reserve balances with Federal Reserve banks	4.3	8.1	5.7	†	†	18.1
1c. Balances at other domestic banks	0.5	2.2	5.5	4.9	0.4	13.5
1d. Balances with foreign banks**	0.7	0.3	0.2	0.1	0.1	1.4
1e. Cash items in process of collection	9.4	9.0	3.0	0.4	†	21.8
1. Total cash assets	$15.3	$20.8	$16.8	$6.6	$0.5	$ 60.0
Memoranda: Deposits subject to reserve:						
M1a. Net demand	$26.4	$41.8	$47.7	—	—	$115.9
M1b. Time	24.8	48.1	54.2	—	—	127.1
Reserve percentage required by Federal Reserve:						
M2a. Net demand	16½%	16½%	12%	—	—	—
M2b. Time	4%	4%	4%	—	—	—
Amount of reserves:						
M3a. Required	$ 5.4	$ 8.8	$ 7.9	—	—	$ 22.1
M3b. Excess	†	†	0.3	—	—	0.3
M3. Total reserve deposits	$ 5.4	$ 8.8	$ 8.2	—	—	$122.4
M4. Borrowing from Federal Reserve banks	$ 1.8	$ 1.8	$ 0.4	—	—	$ 4.0
M5. Free reserve (excess reserves less borrowing)	−1.8	−1.8	−0.1	—	—	−3.7

Source: Federal Reserve Bulletin, March 1967, pp. 408–13.

* Detail may not add to total because of rounding.

**Not separately published; estimates may err as much as $0.2 billion.

† Less than $0.05 billion.

owned reserves have frequently been smaller than those they were required to hold, forcing the banks to borrow.

Coin and paper money held by commercial banks are also small relative to reserve requirements. The amounts held are chiefly determined by what is needed to make change and to take up fluctuations in the flow of paper money over the counter without wasteful shipments to and from the reserve banks.

For nonmember banks, interbank deposits are often treated by state law as reserve funds. For "country member banks," moreover, interbank deposits have a similar role in fact, although the law does not recognize them as reserves. But the lower reserve ratio to which country banks are subject reflects the fact that country banks do habitually treat balances with big-city banks as reserves, whereas the latter have an extra responsibility because their country correspondents expect to draw on them in emergencies.[19] The base for reserve requirements ("net deposits") includes deposits of the general public and of government bodies plus the *excess* of deposits belonging to other banks over those the bank in question has in other commercial banks.

Bank holdings of securities. Securities at commercial banks shade off from near-moneys of almost perfect moneyness (Treasury bills) to securities with almost no moneyness at all (Federal Reserve stock). The order of the items in Table 3-4 corresponds roughly to the degree of moneyness.

Treasury bills and certificates (item 2a.i) mature in three or twelve months from the date of issue and are redeemed at face value by the Treasury, with checks on the Federal Reserve banks. On the average, those held by banks are about halfway between issue and maturity.[20] These securities are forever turning into cash, and a bank that holds them can quickly build up its cash reserves by "letting them run off"—that is, by failing to buy new ones as old ones mature. There is also an active market for these securities if a holder wants to sell before maturity.

During World War II the Federal Reserve established a fixed "buying rate" for bills; it agreed to buy all that were offered at a discount from face value of three-eighths of 1 per cent per annum. Certificates also could be sold to the Federal Reserve at five-eighths of 1 per cent, and these assets became nearly the

---

[19]This extra responsibility is concentrated most sharply on the reserve city banks in New York and Chicago, which hold interbank deposits for many other reserve city banks as well as for "country" banks. Under the national-bank system, "country" banks had a 15 per cent reserve requirement (and could satisfy two-thirds of this requirement with deposits in reserve city banks). Both reserve city banks and central reserve city banks had 25 per cent reserve requirements. But the former could, and the latter could not, apply deposits in central reserve city banks toward half the requirement.

[20]Bills are issued weekly and generally mature in three months. They are sold "on a discount basis"—that is, for slightly below face value. Certificates are issued less regularly and ordinarily mature in a year. At maturity they pay par plus a slight addition for interest.

TABLE 3-4

INVESTMENTS HELD BY COMMERCIAL BANKS, JUNE 30, 1966

(dollar amounts in billions, rounded to nearest $0.1 billion)*

Balance-Sheet Item	Banks in Federal Deposit Insurance System					
	Members of Federal Reserve System					
	Reserve CityBanks: New York and Chicago	*Other Reserve City Banks*	*"Country" Banks*	*Insured Non-member Banks*	*Non-insured Commercial Banks ***	*All Commercial Banks*
2a. U.S. government obligations						
i. Treasury bills and certificates	$ 1.9	$ 1.7	$ 2.8	$ 2.8	$ 0.1	$ 9.3
ii. Notes	1.0	2.5	5.6	3.3	0.1	12.5
iii. Bonds	3.4	8.3	13.7	7.3	0.2	32.9
2a. Total†	$ 6.1	$12.2	$21.7	$13.1	$ 0.4	$ 53.5
2b. Other securities	$ 7.7	$13.9	$18.0	$ 8.8	$ 0.4	$ 48.8
2. Total investments	$13.8	$26.1	$39.7	$21.9	$ 0.8	$102.3

Source: Federal Reserve Bulletin, March 1967, pp. 408–13.

*Detail may not add to total because of rounding.
**Not separately published; estimates may err by as much as $0.2 billion.
†Components shown at par rather than at book value; they do not add precisely to the total (shown at book value).

same as cash. A bank holding bills or certificates had almost all the advantages of holding reserve funds, plus a little interest, for it could always convert bills and certificates into cash almost instantly. The Federal Reserve dropped the rigid buying rate of three-eighths of 1 per cent in the middle of 1947, and thus introduced uncertainty into the price of bills.

Treasury notes (item 2a.ii) are close substitutes for bills and certificates. They pay more interest, but subject the holder to more uncertainty as to the price he can get if he sells. Treasury notes have sometimes been issued on a five-year basis, sometimes on a three-year. A good proportion of those held by banks normally have more than a year to run. But the market will ordinarily provide a price near par should the holder of notes want to sell them.

Federal bonds (item 2a.iii), like short-term Treasury securities, are certain to pay off in full. But many have remote maturities—as much as twenty years in the future—and sometimes uncertainty exists as to when repayment will occur. The Treasury often reserves the right to redeem its bonds two or three years ahead of final maturity. This right is ordinarily exercised when money is easy and bonds are selling at prices above par, but not when money is tight and bonds are selling at a discount.[21]

Bonds with many years to run are susceptible to sharp price changes, despite the certainty of repayment. The price of a twenty-year $100 bond, paying $4 of interest per annum, fluctuated from $92.80 in September 1965 to $82.60 in September 1966. This was because other interest rates were rising. Once the annual interest payment on a bond is fixed, its price in the market will vary inversely with market rates of interest, in order to align its effective yield with other interest rates. The fall in the price of the 4 per cent bond mentioned above brought its yield above $5\frac{1}{2}$ per cent, as other yields rose.[22] A bank that buys very long-term bonds is taking an appreciable risk; if it has to sell the bonds, it may lose heavily. On the other hand, long-term bonds yield somewhat more income than the more secure short-term issues.

Securities of state and local governments (included in item 2b) are a step further from money. During the Great Depression, a number of local governments (chiefly school districts, but also some important cities) failed to pay principal and interest on their bonds. In 1933, fears of default depressed their prices very sharply.[23] While such defaults have almost never happened since World War II, there have at times been serious misgivings about bonds of turnpike authorities and the like, and default risks cannot be completely ignored as they are for federal issues. These bonds, therefore, yield somewhat more than federals. They have the added attraction that the income they yield is exempt from federal income taxes.

The corporate bonds that are included in item 2b are of many "grades." Some are virtually sure to pay principal and interest when due. With those of "low grade," however, the risk of default is considered serious, and some corporate bonds (notably of railways) are always in default. In serious depressions, corporate bonds previously rated as high grade have often slipped into lower ratings. Here the price risk is much heavier than with government bonds, and the yield is higher.[24]

At the low end of the scale in moneyness are some $0.2 billion of stock in

---

[21]As a technical matter, when an issue of bonds is selling above par, the Treasury can sell at par securities of the same maturity with a lower interest rate. Thus early redemption permits a saving of interest, which is not available when bonds are selling below par. More broadly, when bond prices are high, the Treasury has a strong market, and is apt to prefer to sell refunding securities immediately rather than to wait and risk a weakening of the market.

[22]We shall have more to say on the recent course of interest rates and bond prices in Part IV.

[23]The Standard Statistics index of municipal bond prices stood at 93.3 in January 1933 (which was close to the levels of the 1920's), and fell to 80.4 in May—a drop of 12.9 points in four months.

[24]A list of sixty corporate bonds kept by the Standard Statistics Company had an average price of 101.6 in September 1930, and reached a depression low of 60.6 in June 1932. They dropped *from month to month* by nearly 5 per cent from August to September 1931, $7^1/_2$ per cent from September to October, and 11 per cent from November to December—falling in four months from 92.9 to 73.1, or by one-fifth. In 1937–38 there was another sharp drop.

Federal Reserve banks and about $0.1 billion of other corporate stocks held by banks—chiefly in affiliated banks and bank subsidiaries. These assets are much like bank buildings: to part with them, the bank that holds them would have radically to change its way of doing business. To cash its Federal Reserve stock, it would have to abandon membership in the Federal Reserve System; to cash its other stocks, it would have to give up partial ownership of affiliated banks or sell off its separately incorporated safe-deposit business.

Bank loans. The main types of bank loans are listed in Table 3-5. The item with most moneyness, brokers' loans (item 3a.i), heads the table. These

TABLE 3-5

LOANS OUTSTANDING AT COMMERCIAL BANKS, JUNE 30, 1966
(dollar amounts in billions, rounded to nearest $0.1 billion)*

| | Banks in Federal Deposit Insurance System | | | | | |
| | Members of Federal Reserve System | | | | | |
Balance-Sheet Item	*Reserve City Banks: New York and Chicago*	*Other Reserve City Banks*	*"Country" Banks*	*Insured Non-member Banks*	*Non-insured Commercial Banks***	*All Commercial Banks*
3a. Loans for purchasing or carrying securities:						
i. To brokers, etc.	$ 3.7	$ 0.9	$ 0.4	$ 0.2	$ 0.2	$ 5.4
ii. To others	0.9	1.1	0.7	0.5	0.1	3.3
3b. Commercial loans, including open market paper	24.8	26.9	17.7	7.3	0.5	77.2
3c. Agricultural loans	†	1.3	3.9	3.3	†	8.5
3d. Loans to financial institutions:						
i. Banks	1.1	0.6	0.2	†	0.1	2.0
ii. Others	5.2	5.9	2.0	0.7	0.1	13.9
3e. Real estate loans (mortgages)	4.0	15.6	21.2	10.7	0.3	51.9
3f. Consumer loans	3.7	14.7	19.6	9.6	0.2	47.7
3g. Other loans	1.7	1.9	1.3	0.4	†	5.2
Total loans, gross	$45.1	$68.9	$67.0	$32.7	$ 1.5	$215.1
3h. Valuation reserves	1.0	1.3	1.4	0.5	†	4.1
3. Total loans, net	$44.1	$67.6	$65.6	$32.2	$ 1.5	$211.0

Source: Federal Reserve Bulletin, March 1967, pp. 408–13.

*Detail may not add to total because of rounding.
**Not separately published; estimates may err by as much as $0.2 billion.
†Less than $0.05 billion.

loans are concentrated at central reserve city banks because the only important stock exchange is in New York. They are mostly "call loans," on which the bank can demand repayment any day. Losses on such loans are very rare. The broker borrows on behalf of a customer, and if the loan is called, the broker can get funds for repayment from his customer or from the sale of the customer's securities which are held by the broker as collateral. Besides, the broker whose loan is called is usually able to borrow at another bank—directly or through a stock exchange "money desk"—unless the collateral becomes inadequate.[25] Thus a bank which calls such a loan rarely squeezes an individual broker in a way that will cost the bank good will.

Security loans other than those to brokers (item 3a.ii) are fairly high in moneyness. They are largely short term and are backed by stock-exchange collateral which ordinarily guarantees that the debtor can pay off if pressed (by selling his securities if not otherwise). But the banker cannot always call them without injuring and offending his customer, so in practice the bank gains more safety than liquidity by insisting on such collateral.[26]

The bulk of the bank loans which serve to finance ordinary business are found in item 3b. The loans that make up this category vary sharply in moneyness. Some are short-term loans, others provide for repayment in installments over several years. Some are loans that borrowers could pay off quickly by selling assets or by borrowing elsewhere, others could not be repaid without the liquidation of the borrower's business. The banker's ability to raise cash by reducing these loans—by collecting those outstanding and making few new ones—is limited by their personal character. The borrowers are his "customers." They feel they have a claim upon the bank's lending power. Sometimes they have established "lines of credit" which they regard as options to borrow when they wish, up to an agreed limit. Refusal of an expected loan is a blow to their businesses and to their dignity. The banker's good will is involved. The same holds for farm loans (item 3c), for interbank loans (item 3d), and in less degree for consumer loans (item 3f).

Loans on real estate security (item 3e) were long regarded as improper for banks. In the great slump of the 1930's, they saddled the banks with heavy losses. Since then, however, they have gained in safety and in moneyness. Present-day mortgages are "fully amortized." The debtor pays frequent installments on the principal along with his interest. This reduces the danger that the debtor may be obliged to make a lump-sum payment that he cannot meet. Besides, many mortgages are now "insured" by the Federal Housing Admin-

---

[25]The proportion of the value of securities bought on credit which a customer must put up in cash—the "margin"—is fixed by regulation of the Federal Reserve Board. This requirement applies to brokers' loans and to bank loans "to others for the purpose of purchasing or carrying securities."

[26]Perhaps a good part of the miscellaneous business loans and consumer loans in items 3b, 3f, and 3g are the same kind of loan in substance—granted without the formality of posting stock-exchange collateral in cases where the banker is sure that his customer is "good for it."

istration. With the risk of loss thus reduced, mortgages are more shiftable than they once were.

Consumer loans by banks (item 3f) have been rising rapidly in importance since the Great Depression. The bulk of these loans are installment-payment contracts—made directly with individual borrowers, or purchased from auto dealers and other sellers of durable goods. Some are small single-payment loans to consumers. (If single-payment loans exceed $3,000, they go into item 3g.)

The terms of bank lending. A bank attaches several conditions to its loans. First, of course, it requires that the borrower show evidence that he can repay the loan when it falls due. It examines his assets and his prospective income, and may ask him to pledge some of his assets as collateral for the loan or to take out insurance on the loan, as with FHA mortgages. Second, it sets down the method of repayment. It may call for several payments, as is usual with consumer loans, or one lump-sum payment at a specified date. In some cases, it may reserve the right to call the loan at will, as with brokers' loans. Third, the bank sets a rate of interest on the loan. This sum may be paid gradually, at maturity, or may be deducted from the amount of the loan when it is made. In the latter case, the stated rate of interest is below the effective rate. If a bank charges 5 per cent on a one-year $1,000 loan, and requires a prepayment of interest, the borrower receives only $950 for his $1,000 IOU. Hence he is really paying $50/$950 in interest, or 5.26 per cent. If, in addition, the bank requires that the borrower keep a balance at the bank larger than he would otherwise maintain, the real cost of credit may be even higher than 5.26 per cent.

Although we know much less about the terms of bank loans than we should, one thing is clear: The stated rate of interest is but one of several costs that a borrower must pay to secure bank credit.

Other assets. Other bank assets (item 4 in Table 3-1) are small in proportion to the major classes just examined—less than 3 per cent of total assets. These consist of bank premises, furniture and fixtures, "income accrued but not collected," which is really a valuation adjustment for investments and loans,[27] and "customers' liability on acceptances,"[28] which goes to offset a "miscellaneous liability" item for "acceptances outstanding."

---

[27]See footnote 11.

[28]When a bank's customer has to buy raw materials in Latin America, the bank sometimes issues a "letter of credit," which authorizes the seller of the raw materials to draw a "bill" ordering our bank to pay the price of the goods in American dollars. This bill is "discounted" with a South American bank (enabling the seller to collect in his own currency) and sent by that bank to New York. Our bank then "accepts" the bill—that is, stamps it to guarantee that it will be paid when due—and the bill is added to the stock of "open-market paper" on the New York market. The accepted bill appears as a liability of our bank. But the customer who has bought the materials is pledged to pay the bank when the bill falls due; his obligation goes into item 4.

NOTES ON
ALTERNATIVE POINTS OF VIEW
AND SUPPLEMENTARY READINGS

Additional information on the structure of bank balance sheets can be found in the Federal Deposit Insurance Corporation *Annual Reports* (Washington, D.C.: U.S. Government Printing Office).

Chapter 4

The Creation
of Deposits

Commercial banks and the supply of money. Today, bank deposits are our chief variety of money. Save for small transactions, they have taken the place of currency. The way in which money is created, then, must be connected to the operations of commercial banks.

At one time, bankers denied that the banks could create cash. They argued that deposits came into existence simply by people "putting money in the bank" and that banking was essentially passive. Recently, however, the bankers have come to recognize that they have great powers and may aggravate inflations and deflations. They no longer feel forced to argue that they can never do damage by expanding credit, though they believe that their activities on the whole do much more good than harm. Economists no longer feel bound to display their cleverness in observing that deposits can be created. They are more concerned with the consequences and control of the process.

The following discussion begins with the mechanics of the lending process. It then proceeds to the general logic of deposit creation, and considers the relation of deposit creation or contraction to bank reserves, and other factors that set limits to the process. Finally, it contrasts deposit creation by commercial banks with the activities of other credit institutions.

Deposit-creation mechanics. The simplest way to grasp the process of deposit creation is to look at the changes in bank balance sheets. Fix your eye on the Nearest National Bank. It is subject to reserve requirements (the ratio of cash reserves to deposits) of 20 per cent. On Day Zero it was all "loaned up"—it had no margin of excess cash reserves with which to buy more earning assets.

Nearest National Bank: Close of Business, Day Zero

Cash reserves	$ 20,000		Deposits:	
(Required $20,000)			Mr. Newaire	$ 1,000
(Excess 0)			Local Grocery	2,000
			All others	97,000
Loans	30,000			
Investments	50,000			
Total assets	$100,000		Total liabilities	$100,000

But on Day One Mr. Newaire walks in and deposits $10,000 in paper currency which was found under the carpet in the house of his late lamented aunt. As only $2,000 is needed to meet reserve requirements on Mr. Newaire's enlarged balance, the Nearest National Bank now has $8,000 of excess reserves:

Nearest National Bank: Close of Business, Day One

Cash reserves	$ 30,000		Deposits:	
(Required $22,000)			Mr. Newaire	$ 11,000
(Excess 8,000)			Local Grocery	2,000
			All others	97,000
Loans	30,000			
Investments	50,000			
Total assets	$110,000		Total liabilities	$110,000

On Day Two Mr. Smith of Local Grocery comes in with a loan application. He wants an $8,000 loan to buy a new meat cooler. Agreed! The vice-president at the loan desk hands Mr. Smith a check.[1] At that moment the bank's balance sheet looks like this:

Nearest National Bank: 10:59AM, Day Two

Cash reserves	$ 30,000		Deposits:	
(Required $23,600)			Mr. Newaire	$ 11,000
(Excess 6,400)			Local Grocery	2,000
			All others	97,000
Loans	38,000		Officers' checks, etc.	8,000
(Others 30,000)				
(Grocery 8,000)				
Investments	50,000			
Total assets	$118,000		Total liabilities	$118,000

[1] This will be a cashier's check—an order *on the bank by the bank* to pay $8,000. Alternatively, the loan officer may bypass the drawing and deposit of the check by handing Mr. Smith a *deposit slip,* made out: "Proceeds of loan, $8,000." The "creation" of a deposit stands out very clearly in the deposit-slip procedure.

Mr. Smith then steps over to the receiving teller and deposits this sum ($8,000) in the Local Grocery account. Naturally, the bank's balance sheet changes to reflect this transaction:

Nearest National Bank: 11:01AM, Day Two

Cash reserves	$ 30,000	Deposits:	
(Required $23,600)		Mr. Newaire	$ 11,000
(Excess 6,400)		Local Grocery	10,000
		All others	97,000
Loans	38,000		
(Others 30,000)			
(Grocery 8,000)			
Investments	50,000		
Total assets	$118,000	Total liabilities	$118,000

We may now analyze the effects of these operations on the bank's balance sheet. (To keep things simple, suppose that no other loans are made or repaid and that other depositors are not making deposits or withdrawals.) You will observe that the expansion of Mr. Newaire's balance and of the Local Grocery's balance takes place without a depletion of anybody else's balance. Mr. Newaire's windfall consisted of paper currency that had not seen the inside of a bank for years. Although the bank may be said to have lent Mr. Newaire's money to the Local Grocery, Mr. Newaire still has the right to draw his $10,000 and, *in addition,* the Local Grocery has the right to draw $8,000. Mr. Newaire has merely changed the form of his money holding, not its amount; but Local Grocery's deposit has been *created* by the bank's loan.

Next, let us extend our chain of transactions. Suppose that the Local Grocery pays the Deepchill Company for the cooler, drawing a check for this payment on Day Two soon after the loan proceeds were deposited. Deepchill has an account in the Aboriginal Trust Company. Also subject to a 20 per cent reserve requirement, Aboriginal's balance sheet looked like this on Day Two:

Aboriginal Trust Company: Day Two

Cash reserves	$ 10,000	Deposits:	
(Required $10,000)		Deepchill	$ 2,000
(Excess 0)		Stuffed Panda	3,000
		All others	45,000
Loans	20,000		
Investments	20,000		
Total assets	$ 50,000	Total liabilities	$ 50,000

After this check has been cleared (say on Day Four), the newly created deposits will be found in the Aboriginal Trust and the Nearest National will have transferred $8,000 of cash reserves to the Aboriginal Trust. The Aboriginal Trust Company now has $8,000 of additional deposits and $8,000 of additional reserves, of which $1,600 must be earmarked to satisfy increased reserve requirements. The balance sheets of the two banks will stand as follows:

Nearest National Bank: Day Four

Cash reserves	$ 22,000		Deposits:	
(Required $22,000)			Mr. Newaire	$ 11,000
(Excess 0)			Local Grocery	2,000
			All others	97,000
Loans	38,000			
(Others $30,000)				
(Grocery 8,000)				
Investments	50,000			
Total assets	$110,000		Total liabilities	$110,000

Aboriginal Trust Co.: Day Four

Cash reserves	$ 18,000		Deposits:	
(Required $11,600)			Deepchill	$ 10,000
(Excess 6,400)			Stuffed Panda	3,000
Loans	20,000		All others	45,000
Investments	20,000			
Total assets	$ 58,000		Total liabilities	$ 58,000

In short, when Local Grocery spends the borrowed funds, the deposit position of Nearest National is restored to its preloan condition (Day Four looks the same as Day One). But on the asset side, Nearest National has more loans and less cash. The relation between Mr. Newaire's deposit and the loan to the Local Grocery is now clear: the deposit gave the bank excess reserves with which it could face the drain on its reserves that would follow when Local Grocery disbursed the borrowed funds.

Let us now turn our attention to the Aboriginal Trust Company. The bulge of deposits created by the Local Grocery loan now appears in the Deepchill account. Since this transfer of deposits brought an equal transfer of cash reserves, Aboriginal Trust on Day Four has the $6,400 of excess reserves that existed on Day Two at Nearest National. If Aboriginal Trust can assume that Deepchill's deposit will be stable at $10,000 because the Deepchill account was abnormally low on Day Two, Aboriginal Trust now has additional lending power.[2]

---

[2] In this pattern of exposition, economists often describe the initial cash arriving in the first bank (Mr. Newaire's deposit) as a "primary deposit" for the first bank, and the funds created by the loan (the $8,000 going into the Local Grocery account) as a "secondary deposit." Then when the borrowed funds are transferred (the $8,000 appearing in the Deepchill account), they become a "primary deposit" for the second bank. This terminology does not seem very helpful, since the sum of the primary and secondary deposits arising from the operation adds up to more than the increase of deposits—most of the primary deposits arising simply from the transfer of secondary deposits.

Suppose that Aboriginal Trust uses its gain in lending power to lend $6,400 to another depositor—the Stuffed Panda Company which is producing toys for the Christmas trade. This will create a further $6,400 of deposits that will appear on Day Five alongside the added loan on the Aboriginal Trust balance sheet:

Aboriginal Trust Company: Day Five

Cash reserves	$ 18,000		Deposits:	
(Required $12,880)			Deepchill	$ 10,000
(Excess 5,120)			Stuffed Panda	9,400
			All others	45,000
Loans	26,400			
(Others $20,000)				
(Stuffed Panda 6,400)				
Investments	20,000			
Total assets	$ 64,400		Total liabilities	$ 64,400

Stuffed Panda is borrowing in order to pay its suppliers—say to buy an order for $6,400 of materials from the Fur and Stuffing Company which banks at the First American (also subject to 20 per cent reserve requirements). On Day Five, First American's balance sheet looked like this:

First American Bank: Day Five

Cash reserves	$ 40,000		Deposits:	
(Required $40,000)			Fur and Stuffing	$ 20,000
(Excess 0)			All others	180,000
Loans	100,000			
Investments	60,000			
Total assets	$200,000		Total liabilities	$200,000

Allowing two days for Stuffed Panda's check to clear, the transaction will raise deposits and reserves at American National. The balance sheets of the two banks will look like this:

Aboriginal Trust: Day Seven

Cash reserves	$ 11,600		Deposits:	
(Required $11,600)			Deepchill	$ 10,000
(Excess 0)	.		Stuffed Panda	3,000
			Others	45,000
Loans	26,400			
(Others $20,000)				
(Stuffed Panda 6,400)				
Investments	20,000			
Total assets	$ 58,000		Total liabilities	$ 58,000

First American Bank: Day Seven

Cash reserves	$ 46,400	Deposits:	
(Required $41,280)		Fur and Stuffing	$ 26,400
(Excess 5,120)		Others	180,000
Loans	$100,000		
Investments	60,000		
Total assets	$206,400	Total liabilities	$206,400

We may obtain a broader picture by adding up the balance sheet of all three banks:

COMBINED CONDITION STATEMENT OF NEAREST NATIONAL BANK,
ABORIGINAL TRUST CO., AND FIRST AMERICAN BANK

Day Zero

Cash reserves	$ 70,000	Deposits:	
(Required $70,000)			$350,000
(Excess 0)			
Loans	150,000		
Investments	130,000		
Total assets	$350,000	Total liabilities	$350,000

Day One

Cash reserves	$ 80,000	Deposits:	
(Required $72,000)			$360,000
(Excess 8,000)			
Loans	150,000		
Investments	130,000		
Total assets	$360,000	Total liabilities	$360,000

Days Two–Four

Cash reserves	$ 80,000	Deposits:	
(Required $73,600)			$368,000
(Excess 6,400)			
Loans	158,000		
Investments	130,000		
Total assets	$368,000	Total liabilities	$368,000

Days Five–Seven

Cash reserves	$ 80,000	Deposits:	
(Required $74,880)			$374,400
(Excess 5,120)			
Loans	164,400		
Investments	130,000		
Total assets	$374,400	Total liabilities	$374,400

Events between Days Two and Four, and also between Days Five and Seven, are mere shifts among banks, leaving combined totals unaffected. The total of cash reserves changes only when new cash comes in from outside the group of banks we are looking at (the Newaire deposit of Day One). The total of deposits, however, also changes when the total of loans changes. Each successive loan expansion brings not only an increase in the loan total for the group of banks, but an equal increase in the deposit total. Furthermore, the loan expansion based on an inflow of excess reserves into the group of banks is not limited to the amount of the inflow. In this illustration, the Local Grocery and Stuffed Panda loans add up to $14,400 while the Newaire deposit added only $8,000 to excess reserves. And at Day Seven, the First American retains $5,120 of excess reserves, indicating further unused lending power.

The maximum amount of additional loans which can be supported by the three banks is $26,600. After these loans are made, the group of banks will have no excess reserves and their combined balance sheet will appear as follows:

COMBINED STATEMENT OF NEAREST NATIONAL BANK,
ABORIGINAL TRUST CO., AND FIRST AMERICAN BANK

Day N

Cash reserves	$ 80,000	Deposits:	
(Required $80,000)			$400,000
(Excess 0)			
Loans	190,000		
Investments	130,000		
Total assets	$400,000	Total liabilities	$400,000

Note that cash reserves are 20 per cent of deposits and that the initial $10,000 increase in reserves can ultimately support a maximum of $40,000 in new loans and $50,000 in additional deposits.

Deposits can also be created by security purchases. When the Nearest National Bank found itself with additional reserves because of the Newaire deposit, it could have bought $8,000 worth of bonds, paying with a cashier's check. Suppose it purchased them from the Pluto Mutual Fund, which sold the bonds to obtain funds for stock purchases. Pluto Mutual is a depositor at the Colossal Bank and Trust. On Day One, before the transaction, the balance sheets at each bank looked like this:

Nearest National Bank: Day One

Cash reserves	$ 30,000	Deposits:	
(Required $22,000)		Mr. Newaire	$ 11,000
(Excess 8,000)		Local Grocery	2,000
		Others	97,000
Loans	30,000		
Investments	50,000		
Total assets	$110,000	Total liabilities	$110,000

Colossal Bank and Trust: Day One

		Deposits:	
Cash reserves	$ 50,000	Pluto Mutual	$ 50,000
(Required $50,000)		Others	200,000
(Excess 0)			
Loans	100,000		
Investments	100,000		
Total assets	$250,000	Total liabilities	$250,000

After the bonds were sold, the initial bulge in deposits would be at the Colossal Bank and Trust Company where the cashier's check was deposited—and that bank would also get an equal amount of reserves when the check cleared. In terms of bank statements, the outcome would be as follows:

Nearest National Bank: Day Three

		Deposits:	
Cash reserves	$ 22,000	Mr. Newaire	$ 11,000
(Required $22,000)		Local Grocery	2,000
(Excess 0)		Others	97,000
Loans	30,000		
Investments	58,000		
Total assets	$110,000	Total liabilities	$110,000

Colossal Bank and Trust: Day Three

		Deposits:	
Cash reserves	$ 58,000	Pluto Mutual	$ 58,000
(Required $51,600)		Others	200,000
(Excess 6,400)			
Loans	100,000		
Investments	100,000		
Total assets	$258,000	Total liabilities	$258,000

On Day Three the Colossal Bank and Trust would have reached the position attained by the Aboriginal Trust on Day Four in the previous illustration—with deposits up by $8,000 and excess reserves up by $6,400.

Deposit creation is reversed when loans are repaid or when members of the nonbank public buy securities from banks. When the Local Grocery repays its loan, for example, its check will be canceled against part of the Local Grocery's bank balance—which must be built up for this purpose before the repayment date. Thus the deposits created by a loan have only a temporary existence. But this fact does not prevent a long-continued deposit expansion, since new loans may be granted faster than old ones are repaid.

Underlying logic of deposit creation. An example like that just presented proves very little. It can illustrate the existence of a field of possibilities, but it cannot bound the field. Can we describe the limits of deposit creation?

A straightforward way to generalize our example is to ask what happens when an increase occurs in total balances of all depositors at one bank. Plainly, this cannot be the result of payments by one depositor to another; such payments subtract as much from one customer's account as they add to another. It can only occur if customers as a group deposit more *currency* than they withdraw by cashing checks, or if they deposit more *checks* drawn on outside banks than they draw to the credit of other nonmembers.

These things do happen. There is, for example, a net inflow of currency each year after Christmas, when the currency requirements of households and shops fall off and the currency deposits of business outrun withdrawals for payrolls and the like. One can similarly imagine a net inflow of checks drawn on other banks.

We can just as easily imagine events to account for an increase in the total of deposits within a city or a state. Customers may deposit checks drawn on out-of-town banks, thereby transferring deposits and reserves from one community to another. But when we turn to the nation as a whole, these possibilities are excluded. We must look to a different species of dealings—transactions as between the banks and their customers, between the banks and the government, or between the banks and foreigners. These also supply the banks with reserves and permit an increase of lending.

We have already seen how banks can create deposits by expanding loans or buying bonds. This process affects not merely the aggregate deposit balances of the banks immediately involved, but the aggregate balances of the entire nonbank public. The expansive effect of new loans and bond purchases must, of course, be set against the deposit-creation-in-reverse that happens as loans are repaid and as banks sell bonds. But if there is a *net* expansion of the loans and investments held by a country's banking system, there is a corresponding *net* creation of deposits.

Deposits are also created and retired by other bank operations. For example, banks have to draw checks to pay salaries to their officers and other employees, to remit dividends to stockholders, and to buy stationery and supplies; checks drawn for this purpose get credited to the personal bank accounts of the officers, employees, and stockholders and to the business accounts of the stationers, but of course cannot be debited to any other account belonging to the nonbank public. Hence the issue of these checks constitutes deposit creation. In the other direction, deposit-creation-in-reverse (deposit retirement) takes place when a corporation draws a check to pay interest on a long-term bank loan, or when the bank cancels part of a customer's balance to cover a service charge. In such cases there are debits to the accounts of the persons or firms involved, but the checks do not flow into the accounts of any other members of the nonbank public.

Another set of transactions that affects aggregate balances of the nonbank public is carried out by the federal government. Because we frame our concepts of the stock of money so as to illuminate the incentives and decisions of the firms and households that make up the private sector of the economic system (and of state and local governments, which in economics are also treated as a mass phenomenon), while the federal government is looked at as a decision-center which is capable of changing the domestic monetary situation, we do not count the federal government as part of the "nonbank public." Hence when the government draws a paycheck or a check for goods delivered by a supplier, the effect on the aggregate balances of the nonbank public is the same as that when a bank draws a paycheck or a check for supplies. The check will be deposited to build up the balance of some member of the nonbank public, but will not be debited against any account of the nonbank public; thus it constitutes deposit creation. In the other direction, money is retired when a citizen sends in a check to cover his income tax liability: the debit against his account is not offset by a credit to any other account belonging to the nonbank public. This effect of government payments and receipts on the aggregate stock of bank deposits (money) held by the nonbank public is one of the main links between the monetary system and what is called "fiscal policy," which will be examined later in this book.

From the standpoint of any given country, transactions across its borders also create and retire deposits. When exported goods fron the United States are sold to a foreigner, the buyer has to arrange for payment in the United States, although he probably has no funds on deposit in this country. He will get his bank abroad to "purchase dollars," and places himself in a position to pay by sending the American exporter a "bank draft" on some New York bank. So far as monetary arrangements within the United States go, the deposit of such a "draft" is exactly like the deposit of an "officer's check" drawn by the same New York bank, and constitutes deposit creation. In the opposite direction, an importer in the United States has to draw on his bank account to pay for his imports. But his check will not flow into some other account of a member of the nonbank public in the United States, but will be used to pay for a transfer of funds to some banker who represents the foreign seller of the imported goods. Hence payment for imports retires deposits. The same rules apply to international transactions which involve purchase of securities rather than goods, tourist expenditures, remittances to relatives abroad, and the like.

Limits of deposit creation.   As we saw in the illustrative chain of deposit-creating transactions involving the Nearest National Bank, Aboriginal Trust, and the others, unused lending power exists in the banking system whenever some bank holds excess reserves.[3] Suppose that there is an injection of additional

---

[3] A bank can also expand its loans even though its reserves do not exceed requirements. The result will be a drain on this bank's reserves which will pull them below requirements. But the rules require the maintenance of the legal percentages not from moment to moment but *on the average* as of the close of business over a week or a two-week period. Hence the bank can keep within the rules by *borrowing* additional reserves as soon as the drain is apparent.

Such borrowing of reserves may be from some other bank which has excess reserves (through the federal funds market, which will be examined in Chapter 5) or directly from a Federal Reserve Bank. For the present we will get a clearer line of argument if we suppose that only the first type of borrowing is used; the second type will be discussed presently.

excess reserves—perhaps by some such event as Mr. Newaire's deposit of currency, perhaps by one of the other processes we will examine in Chapter 5. Can we set quantitative bounds to the corresponding addition to the aggregate lending power of the banking system?

The amount by which new lending can increase deposits, starting from (say) a newly injected million dollars of excess reserves, depends on reserve requirements and on another factor we have not so far considered—namely, the "overflow" of new money into currency circulation outside banks. Let us suppose that reserve requirements are r per cent of deposits and q is the ratio of currency to deposits that holders of cash prefer. If we define the initial injection of excess reserves as E, the increase of currency as C, and the increase of deposits as D, we may say that reserves will be fully committed when:

$$E - C = rD.$$

But by assumption:

$$C = qD.$$

Thus:

$$E = rD + qD = D(r + q), \text{ or}$$
$$D = E\left(\frac{1}{r + q}\right).$$

But:

$$D + C = D + qD = D(1 + q)$$
$$= E\left(\frac{1 + q}{r + q}\right).$$

But this means that:

$$\frac{D + C}{E} = \frac{1 + q}{r + q}.$$

Each dollar of excess reserves can generate $(1 + q)/(r + q)$ dollars of additional money—of deposits plus currency. If, for example, q is $1/10$ and reserve requirements are at 20 per cent, the cash-creating power of a dollar of excess reserves is 3 2/3. If the proportion taking the form of currency were negligible, it would come to $1/.20$ or 5.

How does this ratio work out in concrete terms? To get an impression, suppose that an extra million dollars of money[4] is created, and distributed in the proportions which existed in June 1966. To begin with, the total of currency plus demand and time deposits in commercial banks was held 11.5 per cent in currency and 88.5 per cent in deposits; so the ratio q is $\frac{11.5}{88.5} = 0.1306$. The ratio r has to be seen as an average of requirements for the various types of deposits; we have:

Type of Deposit	Per Cent of Total Deposits in Commercial Banks	Reserve Percentage	Contribution to Average
Demand deposits:			
Reserve city banks	19.28%	16.5%	3.18%
Country banks	17.35%	12.0%	2.08%
Nonmember banks	9.39%	say: 5.0%	0.47%
Time deposits:			
Member banks	44.11%	4.0%	1.76%
Nonmember banks	9.87%	say: 2.0%	0.20%
			7.69%

Looking at the two ingredients of our formula, the numerator $(1 + q)$ is 1.1306 and the denominator $(r + q)$ is $0.1306 + 0.0769 = 0.2075$. This gives a cash-creating ratio of $\frac{1.1306}{0.2075}$ or rather above 5.[5]

When credit expansion is widespread, some individual banks can expand without taking any active steps to increase their reserves. A bank that lags behind the average rate of earning-asset expansion will nevertheless obtain its share of the general growth in deposits, as its customers will get *their* share in the course of business. Such a bank will find its deposits and reserves increasing by equal dollar amounts if it holds its earning assets level. If the reserve needed against added deposits is 20 per cent, a million dollar growth of deposits will give the bank $800,000 of excess reserves. The bank is consequently free

---

[4] This is a case where it is convenient to work with the Friedman definition of "money," including time deposits in *commercial* banks, since a decision by money-holders to transform part of their balances into this form does not entail any "leakage" of reserves out of commercial banks.

We assume implicitly that if part of the funds "created" are placed as time deposits in *savings* banks, or as "savings capital" in savings and loan associations, the savings institutions involved will put the "money" back into the commercial-bank circuit by making an equal amount of loans at once; thus the funds get back into the form of currency-plus-commercial-bank-deposits, and despite the intervention of the savings bank or savings and loan association there is still a million dollars of additional "money" in the Friedman sense.

[5] This indicates a great decline from the 1920's, when economists put the ratio about 10. In the 1920's, reserve ratios were lower and currency was smaller relative to deposits. Economists who today produce ratios similar to those of the 1920's are assuming that the leakage into currency can be ignored.

to expand its earning assets by 80 per cent of the growth in its deposits without ever needing to borrow reserves, or to sell off one type of earning asset (say, Treasury bills) to buy another. Only the banks that are expanding earning assets faster than the average rate need take such active steps.[6]

The profit motive and deposit creation. Deposits are created when bankers have incentives to expand earning assets. The profit incentive ordinarily pulls toward expansion. Contraction, or a cessation of expansion, ordinarily reflects a counterincentive—a shortage of reserves. But there are times when the profit motive for expansion relaxes. The creation of deposits may be limited by a shortage of "bankable assets." From this viewpoint, we may say that credit will expand up to the limit permitted by reserves or by bankable assets, whichever is less.

Plainly an expansion of reserves cannot *force* credit expansion in the sense that a contraction of reserves can force credit contraction. The law sets a minimum reserve position that banks must maintain, but it cannot set a maximum reserve proportion and require banks to invest any excess! A shortage of bankable assets can, therefore, check credit expansion even in the face of large excess reserves, as in the 1930's.

Banks may find that they have bought up *all* the existing assets of certain classes, such as brokers' loans, Treasury bills, bankers' acceptances, and open-market commercial paper. They may also have made *all* the loans for which they had applications from "sound" borrowers. And, as in the 1930's, they may still have an unsatisfied appetite for such assets. But an absolute shortage of *all* types of assets is hard to imagine, as there are some which bankers can always acquire at a price.[7]

Some bankable bonds are always held by nonbankers who would sell if the price were to rise enough. Until bond prices go so high that yields approach zero, banks are not faced with an absolute shortage of bonds. If they choose to hold excess reserves, leaving part of their deposit-creating power unused, it must be because they suspect that bond prices will fall, and are too "bearish" to be willing to risk more funds on the bond market.

It is only moderately true that deposit creation rests on the cooperation of borrowers as well as the reserve position of bank lenders. Even though new

---

[6] It is even possible for *all* banks to be relieved of pressure to take active steps. During the postwar years of great building activity (1947–50), such organizations as life insurance companies were selling government bonds to get funds with which to buy mortgages. Federal Reserve purchases to "support the market" for the classes of bonds in question created reserves for commercial banks just as much as would purchases corresponding to bank sales.

[7] Even the classes of assets listed earlier are not strictly rigid in supply. Loans could have been expanded somewhat in the 1930's if bankers had been less scrupulous about safety and prompt payment. In fact, bankers put a great deal of ingenuity into finding ways to extend the field of bankable assets with no great increase of risk (and into discovering low-risk assets previously overlooked). The great growth of banks' consumer loans, amortized mortgages, and "term loans" to business in the years just before and since World War II was the result of this search for assets.

borrowers do not come forward, banks can expand deposits by buying up outstanding bonds that represent past borrowing. But apparently bankers are more willing to stretch their lending power for new borrowers then to buy bonds.

Deposit creation and the public's balance sheet. Bankers do not create deposits to give them away, but to buy assets. If a bank has bought more government bonds, somebody must have sold those bonds. On the seller's balance sheet, therefore, cash (bank deposits) is now larger and bonds (a near-money) are smaller. Whatever moneyness he attributed to the bonds is gone, offsetting part of the moneyness of the deposits. His liquidity has not risen nearly so much as if somebody had made him a gift of the bank deposits and left the bonds in his possession. Similarly, if a business firm gets bank deposits by borrowing at the bank, it gains liquidity by having more cash, but loses liquidity somewhat by being in debt to the bank. Debts, especially short-term debts, must be regarded as having *negative* moneyness to the debtor. Thus, the actual transactions by which deposits are created always involve losses as well as gains of liquidity for the people with whom the banks do business— although the loss in liquidity is always smaller than the gain.

Someone has to go into debt or to reduce his debts receivable in order that banks can create deposits. But this somebody need not be a household or business firm. It may be the government. During most of World War II, deposit creation rested on growth of government debt; the same was true from 1933 to the outbreak of war. When it is government that is going in debt, the negative liquidity of added debt does not weigh on private business decisions.

On the other hand, we cannot afford to look only at *transactions*. If banks are enabled to lend more freely, they are able to *offer to lend* more freely, and "credit rationing" is relaxed. The actual loans they make are not the only things that matter. In business, *being able to borrow* contributes to liquidity even though one does not actually borrow. The ability to borrow is itself a substitute for having cash on hand as a safeguard against emergencies, and gives the potential borrower more freedom of action.

The sort of changes that lead banks to lend and buy bonds have monetary effects on nonborrowers that reinforce actual lending. When credit tightens and businessmen who have enjoyed ample "lines of credit" are told they are no longer free to borrow, there are deflationary effects over and above those due to actual loan repayments.

All in all, deposit creation is probably rather less inflationary than successful counterfeiting, per dollar of money or near-money created. Deposit retirement by a contraction of bank earning assets is clearly less deflationary than an evaporation of bank deposits through bank failures, such as happened in the early 1930's. But it is still roughly true that the creation or retirement of "invisible greenbacks" through changes in bank earning assets is equivalent to the creation or retirement of paper money.

NOTES ON
ALTERNATIVE POINTS OF VIEW
AND SUPPLEMENTARY READINGS

The standard account of the credit-creation ratio is in a pair of articles by J. W. Angell and F. K. Ficek: "Expansion of Bank Credit," *Journal of Political Economy,* 1933, pp. 1–32, 152–93.

A handy work book for students to explain the money-creation process is *Modern Money Mechanics,* published at no change by the Federal Reserve Bank of Chicago.

Chapter 5

Control of Bank Reserves: Central Banking

Control through reserves. The Federal Reserve System is at the core of bank control because it manages bank reserves to influence the process of deposit creation.[1] If commercial banks have more reserves than they need, they are *free* to acquire assets and thereby to create deposits. If they have less reserves than they need, they are *forced* to dispose of assets and to retire deposits—or else to borrow additional reserves, on terms the Federal Reserve can set.

The management of bank reserves to control bank credit is the main job of "central banks" today. But central banking has not always been seen in that light, and even today there are other points of view. The first job of this chapter, therefore, is to sketch the origins of central banking and the evolution of attitudes toward it. After that, we shall examine the ways in which a central bank may alter the banks' reserve position.

Origins of central banking. All important countries have central banks. Ours is the Federal Reserve System, Britain's the Bank of England, and so forth. These banks have the same relationship to commercial banks that the commercial banks have to the public. The commercial banks are the major depositors at the central banks, and the asset decisions of central banks influence the deposits of the commercial banks in the same way that the asset decisions of commercial banks affect the deposits of the public.

---

[1] On the relation of bank reserves to deposit creation, see Chapter 4, "The Creation of Deposits."

75

The oldest central banks grew up *before* modern commercial banking—the Bank of England, the Bank of France, and the First and Second Banks of the United States. Set up as semiofficial institutions with close government ties, these were regarded in the early 1800's merely as monster concerns in general banking,[2] although they sometimes had special prerogatives. No commercial banks of comparable size existed, and these institutions did a large part of the banking business. In the United States, the expiration of the charter of the Second Bank in 1836 ended this situation. But in Britain and France, the monsters flourished and a system of giant commercial banks grew up around them. The central banks, in turn, gradually abandoned their roles as ordinary banks and came to concentrate on the work of control and management. The precise dates at which the Bank of England and Bank of France became true central banks would be hard to determine.

In the other major countries, central banks were superimposed upon full-blown or rapidly developing commercial banking systems. The German Reichsbank, the Bank of Italy, the Federal Reserve Banks, and the central banks of the British dominions and Latin American countries were of this sort. Only the oldest of these (the Reichsbank and Bank of Italy) did any general banking business. The others were expressly designed as central banks—to concentrate on business with the commercial banks and the government.

In every country, the central bank is the focus of banking. Central banks have long been the main holders of gold—the chief means of international settlement, and the traditional basis of monetary reserves. The reserves of commercial banks, in turn, are chiefly the debts of central banks—deposit liabilities or central bank notes. In addition, the commercial banks look to their central banks for help in time of trouble, especially for emergency loans. Commonly, central banks have supervisory power over commercial banks. Often, they are empowered to change commercial bank reserve requirements. These characteristics are widely regarded as essential to central banking, but may be merely customary and useful.

Origin of the Federal Reserve System.   Before 1913, the monetary system of the United States centered on the national banks and the Independent Treasury System. This system worked in fair weather but produced frequent crises.[3] Discontent came to a head after the financial crisis of 1907, and the Federal Reserve Act of 1913 was adopted as a remedy.

The chief charge against the old system had been the lack of "elasticity" in the nation's paper currency and in bank reserves. If people became frightened and started turning even a small percentage of their deposits into coin and paper

---

[2] A rather picturesque comment on international relations in the eighteenth century is that George Washington was a stockholder and depositor in the Bank of England, which took care of his funds while he was fighting British armies.

[3] See the discussion in Chapter 2 on banking during the period from the Civil War to World War I.

money, the whole banking system suffered an immediate shortage of reserves.[4] This shortage led to "tight money," and, when it went very far, to a suspension of cash payments at the banks. Even the seasonal demand for coin and paper outside banks in the autumn "crop-moving season" played hob with bank reserves.

The Federal Reserve System was set up to give our currency the desired "elasticity." Commercial banks that became "members" were required to hold only one form of reserves—"reserve balances" at the Federal Reserve.[5] To obtain these reserve balances, member banks deposited their gold, greenbacks, and so forth, giving the Federal Reserve Banks cash reserves equal to the amount deposited. The first year-end balance sheet of the Reserve banks (1914) showed $268 million of cash reserves ($227 million of it in gold) against $265 million of member-bank reserve deposits. If a bank ran short of reserves, it could obtain additional cash by "rediscount." It could sell to its Federal Reserve bank either its own promissory note or any notes of customers that passed certain tests as "eligible paper." Thus the banks had access to extra reserves and could convert these into currency when customers wished to withdraw their deposits. The Federal Reserve Banks were allowed to issue paper money in the form of Federal Reserve Notes secured jointly by discounted paper and gold or gold certificates,[6] but with not less than 40 per cent in gold. Rediscounting could be used to meet a shortage of cash at member banks, as it would provide the Federal Reserve Banks with assets against which more notes could be issued. An incipient crisis or a seasonal drain of currency into circulation could be met by this elasticity of note issue, without reducing member-bank reserves, *provided the Federal Reserve Banks had enough slack in their gold reserve to set up the required 40 per cent reserve for the additional notes*. The resulting system was not quite crisis-proof—witness the bank holiday of 1933—but it came triumphantly through financial upsets in 1920 and 1929 that would have produced financial panics under the old system.

Federal Reserve organization. To allay nationwide fears of "Wall Street domination," the founders of the Federal Reserve System set up not a single bank in New York or Washington with branches over the country, but a chain

---

[4] The tightening effect was made sharper by the "pyramiding" of reserves—the reserves of country banks consisting largely of deposits with city banks. A country bank that deposited a million dollars of greenbacks with a city correspondent could still claim it had a million dollars of reserves. But the city bank now had an extra million of reserves with only 25 per cent (its reserve ratio) of the million added to its reserve requirement; so that excess reserves of the system grew by three-quarters of a million. In the reverse direction, a country bank that decided to hold its own million dollars again in coin and paper money for fear of a run produced a three-quarter million reserve shortage.

[5] During a transitional period, until June 1917, banks were allowed to hold part of their legal reserves in their own vaults. Under recent legislation, they are again allowed to do so.

[6] This requirement of collateral for Federal Reserve notes in the form of gold or discounted paper made trouble in 1932. At that time, the law was changed by the Glass-Steagall Act to make government securities eligible as collateral in lieu of discounted paper. Later, the gold requirement was lowered to 25 per cent.

of twelve regional banks,[7] each with its own officers and directors. The stock of each Federal Reserve Bank is owned by its member commercial banks, which elect six of the nine directors. The other three directors are named by the Board of Governors of the Federal Reserve System, which is appointed by the President to supervise the System from Washington.[8]

Formally, the Federal Reserve System still looks much as it did at the outset —a sort of bankers' co-operative supervised from Washington. But in substance, it is fairly centralized, and works much more like a single central bank with branches and subbranches. Officers of the twelve banks are elected for moderate terms, and their appointments are subject to veto by the Board of Governors. The most important operating decisions are made by the Federal Open-market Committee. This was originally an informal group made up of the executive heads of the Reserve banks, but the seven members of the Board of Governors are now members *ex officio* and constitute a majority of the committee. While the individual banks were once free to ignore the recommendations of this committee, they are now required to accept them. The banks retain a good deal of autonomy; men of stature serve as their officers, and carry weight on the Open-market Committee. But the authority of the Board of Governors is paramount.

This change in the locus of power has been accompanied by a change in the focus of policy. At the outset, the central objective was "elasticity of note circulation." "Rediscount" was regarded as the way to bring it about and the rate of interest charged on member-bank borrowings, or "rediscount rate," was regarded as the main instrument of policy—corresponding to the "bank rate" of the Bank of England. Apart from setting the "rediscount rate," the Federal Reserve System was meant to be passive, with the member banks taking the initiative in altering the reserve base of our monetary system. Today, however, the System takes the initiative. It sets out to change reserves deliberately, so that reserve requirements and "open-market policy" matter much more than rediscounting. In fact, rediscounting is now important chiefly as a loophole in open-market policy.

Minimum reserve requirements and banks' demand for owned reserves. Legal minimum reserve ratios for commercial banks have long been

---

[7] The Federal Reserve Banks are located in (1) Boston, (2) New York, (3) Philadelphia, (4) Cleveland, (5) Richmond, (6) Atlanta, (7) Chicago, (8) St. Louis, (9) Minneapolis, (10) Kansas City, (11) Dallas, and (12) San Francisco. A map showing district boundaries and the location of branches is published in the monthly *Federal Reserve Bulletin*.

[8] The original governing body was called the Federal Reserve Board, and for convenience this shorter name is still much used. The original Federal Reserve Board was replaced by the new Board of Governors by the Banking Act of 1935. Members of the new Board have fourteen-year appointments, one expiring every two years, so that their tenure and continuity of policy are very secure—unless Congress some day follows the 1935 precedent and abolishes the Board of Governors in favor of a successor body.

part of the United States tradition.[9] Until recently, these requirements were rarely changed. But the Banking Act of 1935 gave the Board of Governors the power to vary requirements between the then-existing level and up to double that level. Several changes in requirements—both increases and decreases— have been made under this authority.[10]

Reserve requirements apply for averages of from three days to two weeks, not every day or merely at call dates. A bank may have less than required on some days, if it has correspondingly more than required on other days. Even on this average basis, a deficiency of reserves is not exactly *prohibited,* but is *subject to penalty.* A bank with deficient reserves may not make new loans or pay dividends, and fines are levied for deficiencies. Most important of all, a bank that persistently fails to maintain reserves at the required level may be closed by the Comptroller of the Currency or state authority. Bank reserves do occasionally fall below required levels—enough to bring in fines that average several hundred thousand dollars a year—but, for practical purposes, we may assume that requirements are obeyed.

We should not assume that commercial banks always regard the required minimum as a guide to their reserve holdings. They have some freedom in both directions. As in the 1930's, they may choose to hold excess reserves over and above requirements. In 1937 they sought to contract credit even though their owned reserves were 10 per cent higher than requirements. On the other hand, they may seek to acquire earning assets at the expense of reserves, and may *borrow* reserves to make good the deficiency; they may rediscount or borrow from other banks that have reserves to spare. During the 1920's and late 1950's, *owned reserves* (reserve balances less rediscounts) ran several hundred million dollars below required reserves.

A change of reserve requirements may be nullified by the banks' own private standards for reserves. An unexpected increase in required minimum ratios is bound to cause a shortage of reserves, but a *foreseen* increase may simply absorb

---

[9] Abroad, such requirements for commercial banks are less common. This American peculiarity partly reflects our need to deal with thousands of "unit banks" rather than a few large branch-bank systems, and partly the American predilection for definite detailed rules rather than informal and possibly irresponsible "administration."

[10] The current levels of reserve requirements and their history for several recent years are published in the *Federal Reserve Bulletin.* As this book went to press they stood as follows:

For demand deposits at reserve city banks: up to \$5 million, 16½ per cent; on other demand deposits in excess of \$5 million, 17 per cent; range, 10–22 per cent.

For demand deposits at country banks: up to \$5 million, 12 per cent; on other demand deposits in excess of \$5 million, 12½ per cent; range, 7–14 per cent.

For time deposits: up to \$5 million, 3 per cent; on other time deposits in excess of \$5 million, 6 per cent; range, 3–10 per cent.

For savings deposits: 3 per cent; range, 3–10 per cent.

excess reserves that banks have been holding in order to meet the increase. A decrease in requirements that the banks view as temporary may not cause the banks to enlarge their earning assets. They may simply decide to hold the reserves that the change releases, to meet a later reversal of the change. Reserve policy has to work by influencing the banks' own reserve standards as well as legal requirements.

Open-market operations. We have seen that the founders of the Federal Reserve System had intended that the initiative in cash creation would lie with the commercial banks. The Federal Reserve Banks were empowered to affect the terms on which commercial banks might acquire additional reserves. They could set rediscount rates, but the commercial banks would be left to determine the volume of rediscounting. Many years ago, however, the Federal Reserve System took up active control over the process of cash creation. It set out to determine the volume of bank reserves, using open-market operations. The System has since sustained its initiative in monetary management, save during the 1940's when the initiative passed back to the banks and the public because the Reserve Banks were committed to support bond prices. Open-market operations are the chief weapon of most modern central banks.

The Federal Reserve System, through the "manager of the System open-market account," who works under "directives" formulated by the Open-market Committee, deals from day to day in United States government securities on the open market. This market (which functions chiefly over the telephone rather than at a visible meeting place like the New York Stock Exchange) is run by a small number of "dealers," who hold some government securities on their own account, and who are in continuous touch with banks, other financial institutions, and large nonfinancial companies interested in buying and selling such securities. If instructed to find buyers or sellers for a stated volume of securities "at the market," they can place a few million dollars within a few minutes, and considerably larger amounts in a few hours—though the price of a given type of securities may move appreciably up if the Federal Reserve suddenly offers to buy a large amount, or down if the Federal Reserve suddenly offers to sell a large amount. The Federal Reserve's dealings are concentrated largely on issues which will mature within a few months, however, and the market for such issues will absorb large transactions in either direction without much change in price.[11]

---

[11]At times the Federal Reserve has taken the stance that it was a matter of principle to deal in "bills only"—bills being securities sold in weekly "auctions" by the Treasury at whatever discount below face value is necessary to find buyers for the amount offered. (No interest-coupons are attached, so that interest on bills takes the form of appreciation from the original discount to a price equal to face value at maturity.) Bills never are offered with maturities over a year, and a large proportion (sometimes all) are ninety-one-day bills.

The Federal Reserve's transactions through the dealers on the "open market" consist more of purchases than of sales. This is not so much because the Federal Reserve portfolio gradually grows through time as because the Federal Reserve is continually receiving large sums from the United States Treasury in repayment of securities that mature.[12] If the portfolio is allowed to "run off" by buying less than would be necessary to replace maturing securities, pressure is applied to the market even though the Federal Reserve sells no securities. This pressure is applied directly by the Treasury, which must "refinance" virtually all of its maturing issues by selling new ones (thus "borrowing from Peter to pay Paul"); ordinarily most or all of this Treasury pressure on the market is offset by Federal Reserve purchases.

Discount. Another process by which Federal Reserve Banks acquire assets is that of *discount* of notes offered to them by member banks. When the Federal Reserve System was set up, it was expected that this would be the main source of assets for the Federal Reserve, and furthermore that the discount operation would be carried out chiefly through *re*discount of promissory notes of customers, offered to the Federal Reserve by commercial banks which had originally

---

At other times the Federal Reserve has operated also in Treasury certificates and notes (with maturities ranging up to five years) and even in bonds (which may run twenty years and more). But it is always possible on such markets that a large selling-order may move the price by a percentage point or more (as against the small fractions of 1 per cent by which bill-prices move); and the Federal Reserve is always uneasy about permitting "disorderly markets" on which the quoted market price does not give a reliable impression of the price at which a moderate amount could actually be bought or sold. Furthermore, it would be very embarrassing to everybody if sharp market fluctuations happened to bankrupt one of the dealers who "make the market," and who often hold large amounts of securities financed by bank loans. We may safely predict that the emphasis of open-market operations will be on short-dated securities in the future as it has been in the past.

[12]A table of "maturity distribution" for government securities in Federal Reserve hands is published every month in the *Federal Reserve Bulletin*. To take figures which happen to be next to the typewriter as this is written, the distribution as of the end of the first quarter (March 31) 1967 was as follows:

Period from March 31, 1967 to maturity	Millions of dollars held (par value)	Per cent of holdings
Within 15 days	$ 928	2.1%
16 days to 90 days.................	13,183	29.3
91 days to 1 year	19,401	43.2
Over 1 year to 5 years	10,133	22.6
Over 5 years to 10 years	866	1.9
Over 10 years.....................	410	0.9
	$44,921	100.0%

Since the Federal Reserve virtually never takes any newly issued Treasury securities (except in wartime), the size of the portfolio could only be kept from shrinking by buying $14.1 billion from dealers before the end of June, in addition to any amount that might be sold through dealers.

made the loans to customers.[13] Actually, the ordinary form of discount is the placing by a member bank with the Federal Reserve of the member bank's own promissory note, with government securities posted as collateral.[14] The initiative in such transactions is taken by the member bank. But the Federal Reserve sets up obstacles to borrowing—partly by charging a discount rate which is high enough to be bothersome, partly by passing the word that "continuous indebtedness" of a specific member bank at the Federal Reserve is disapproved, and continued accommodation is not guaranteed.

Incidental dealings. The Federal Reserve also carries on certain operations which are halfway-houses between rediscount and open-market operations. One such operation is to buy government securities from dealers with an explicit agreement that the dealers will buy them back a week or so later. These purchases expand member-bank reserves just like regular open-market purchases; but like rediscounts they provide in advance for a reversal of the change within a few days.

Another halfway-house operation is Federal Reserve purchase of *acceptances*. These are promissory notes whose repayment has been guaranteed in advance by commercial banks. The Federal Reserve—which has for decades tried without prodigious success to foster this kind of credit instrument—"posts a buying rate" at which it stands ready to buy all acceptances offered. These transactions are like open-market operations in that they are impersonal, and do not involve good will as between commercial banks and their customers, commercial banks and the Federal Reserve, or customers and the Federal Reserve. But they are like rediscount in that the initiative for transactions lies outside the Federal Reserve: the "Fed" sets the rate and takes the somewhat unpredictable consequences as to the volume of dealings. In contrast, in open-market operations the "Fed" decides how much to buy or sell and takes the somewhat unpredictable consequences as to security prices and open-market interest rates.

---

[13]Technically, any note taken by a commercial bank from its customer is *discounted*. This means simply that the customer contracts to repay in some such period as thirty or sixty or ninety days *more* than the amount he got from the banker at the outset, the shortfall of original loan proceeds against repayment being the discount. (This is true of a loan contract whether the customer gets $100,000 and promises to repay it "with interest at 6 per cent per annum" in sixty days— that is, to repay $101,000— or whether he promises simply to pay a lump sum of $100,000 sixty days hence and receives a discounted value of about $99,000.)

The rediscount system was expected not only to make it simple for commercial banks to replenish reserves when they got into difficulties, but also to exert a salutory influence on the *quality* of bank loans, by giving bankers an incentive to apply to lending Federal Reserve standards for "eligible paper." But it turned out to be awkward for all parties involved to have the Federal Reserve engaged in credit-ratings of customers and scrutiny of loan terms; and the normal practice soon came to be for the bank to shortcut the process and get funds by discounting its own promissory note to the Federal Reserve.

[14]Discount operations are extremely short term. The same "maturity distribution table" cited in footnote 12 has a section for discounts. As of April 12, 1967, $1,840 million were outstanding, of which $920 million were due within fifteen days and another $898 million in sixteen to ninety days. A week later (on April 19), only $426 million were outstanding, of which $213 million were due within fifteen days. Thus, the great bulk of the amount outstanding on April 12 had actually been retired within a week

During World War II, the Federal Reserve "supported" Treasury bills and certificates by posting low buying rates on the same footing as buying rates for acceptances. Thus the market took as much as it chose to hold at those rates, and any bills or certificates which did not find holders were passed on to the Federal Reserve. These wartime arrangements, however, were terminated within a few years after the end of hostilities.

Reserve-creation machinery. Just as commercial banks "create money" for the nonbank public through the deposit-creation machinery we examined in Chapter 4, central banks create what many economists (following Milton Friedman) call "high-powered money"—bank reserves or equivalent—through similar machinery. The creation of "high-powered money," like that of deposits at commercial banks, is best understood by analysis of balance sheets. But since the key actors in the process are few, and since the logic of the process is the same as what we have already presented, it is best to use concrete real data to illustrate the process, rather than to start as we did in Chapter 4 with hypothetical examples.

The best starting-point for analysis is the balance sheet of the twelve Federal Reserve Banks taken together. With a few very minor rearrangements, this balance sheet stood at mid-1966 as shown in Table 5–1.

To give an accurate account of the creation of "high-powered money, we

TABLE 5–1

CONSOLIDATED STATEMENT OF CONDITION OF ALL FEDERAL RESERVE BANKS
(billions of dollars, June 30, 1966)

Assets			*Liabilities and Capital Accounts*		
1. Gold certificate reserve		13.0	6. Federal Reserve notes (excluding those held by Federal Reserve banks)		37.4
2. Cash (excluding F.R. notes)		0.3	Deposits:		
Items making up "Federal Reserve Bank Credit":			7. Member-bank reserves	18.6	
3. U.S. gov't securities	42.2		8. U.S. Treasury	0.8	
4. Discounts and advances	0.3		9. Foreign and other	0.7	
5. Float and other*	2.1				20.1
		44.6	10. Other F.R. accounts**		0.4
Total assets (adjusted†)		57.9	Total liabilities (adjusted†)		57.9

Source: Federal Reserve Bulletin.

*Excess of asset-item, "cash items in process of collection" ($6.7 billion), over liability-item, "deferred availability cash items" ($4.7 billion), gives the net amount of credit extended by the Federal Reserve banks because they credit checks in interbank-collection on the average somewhat earlier than collection is completed. Besides this item of $2.0 billion, called *float,* item 5 includes a small holding of acceptances.

**Excess of "other liabilities" plus "capital accounts" over "bank premises" plus "other assets."

†Smaller than the published balance-sheet total of $63.7 billion because of the netting-out operations indicated in notes * and **.

must take into account along with Federal Reserve operations the monetary aspects of United States Treasury operations. For while the Treasury is only incidentally a monetary agency, it is assigned by law several crucial monetary functions. In particular, (a) the Treasury monopolizes the legal right to hold monetary gold in the United States; against its ownership of the gold stock, it has liabilities in the form of "gold certificates," owned exclusively by the Federal Reserve banks, and constituting their legal reserves.[15] In addition, (b) the Treasury is the issuer of all the public's stock of metallic small change and part of its paper currency (including until the mid-1960's all one-dollar bills). Still further, (c) the Treasury holds in its vaults part of the currency which is "outstanding"; and (d) the Treasury holds checking-account funds on deposit at Federal Reserve banks (item 8 of the statement in Table 5–1) and can switch its funds between these accounts at the Federal Reserve and Treasury accounts held with commercial banks.

The simplest way to tie in these monetary operations of the Treasury with those of the Federal Reserve is to start with the preceding statement (Table 5–1) and carry out a number of accounting "adjustments" to arrive at a statement of combined operations of "the monetary authorities"—to use a convenient term for the Treasury and Federal Reserve viewed as partners in monetary responsibility.[16] Some of these adjustments are simply regroupings of items

---

[15]Over and above the gold-certificate liability, the Treasury holds a small amount of "free gold." About $1.8 billion of "free gold" was set up in 1934, when gold was nationalized. The Federal Reserve was credited with gold turned over to Treasury ownership at the old price of $20.67 per ounce, while the new Treasury assets were valued at the new price of $35.00. Various operations have gradually whittled free gold down to about a quarter of its initial amount.

When additional gold is imported or delivered from mines in United States, its sale to the Treasury is obligatory. It can be paid for in the first instance by drawing checks on the Treasury's checking accounts at the Federal Reserve. But it is Treasury practice to replenish these accounts (item 8 on the Federal Reserve statement in Table 5–1) by a deposit of gold certificates. When gold is released for export, the Treasury's checking accounts are built up by payments for the exported gold; and the funds to the credit of the Treasury at the Federal Reserve are then used to retire gold-certificate liability.

Perhaps we should add that since gold certificates "circulate" only between the Federal Reserve banks and the Treasury, an auditor of the Federal Reserve would not find this asset represented by a bundle of engraved paper notes in a safe-deposit vault. Many of them are shown in the statement of "United States Currency Outstanding" as "held in the Treasury for F.R. banks and agents": that is, they have not been printed, but exist as bookkeeping entries. By the same token, while part of the gold which may not be owned by the Federal Reserve banks is held in government vaults at Fort Knox, a substantial share may be seen by privileged sightseers in the below-sea-level vaults of the Federal Reserve Bank of New York, where it is held in safekeeping by the Bank as Treasury agent (along with gold "earmarked" to show ownership by foreign central banks). Thus there is an element of legal fiction in the gold arrangements; and the payments, deposits of gold certificates and the like described in the previous paragraph, are *what is deemed to have happened* rather than what would appear in a moving-picture recording of events.

[16]Logically, it might be neater to set up a Treasury balance sheet and "consolidate" it with the Federal Reserve balance sheet. But such a format is not used in published accounts; so that this manner of arriving at the combined statement would not put the reader in touch with the figures which are used in practice in analyzing the bank-reserve situation.

on the statement; others are additions and subtractions on both sides of the statement which take advantage of the rule we all learned in elementary-mathematics: "When equals are added to equals, the sums are equal." Since the Federal Reserve statement from which we start can be viewed as an equation (assets =liabilities plus capital accounts), it remains an equation as we make these adjustments.

A first round of adjustments can be made as follows (using, of course, figures of the same date as the balance sheet):

Adjustments to Assets	*Adjustments to Liabilities*

Add:
  11. Monetary gold stock   +13.4
	Add:
	   1. Gold-certificate liability* +13.0
	  12. Free gold 0.4

*Note that we use for this adjustment-item the same item-number (1) as for a Federal Reserve asset on the previous statement— for the reason that the items are simply different views of the same claim. We introduce new item-numbers in the adjustments only where the items entered are not the same as some items previously used.

The sum of adjustment-items 1 and 12 on the right has to equal item 11 because *by definition* free gold is the excess of the total monetary gold stock (all owned by the United States Treasury) over the Treasury's gold-certificate liabilities. To continue the first-round adjustments:

Add:
  13. Treasury currency out-
     standing
  14. Treasury cash holdings,
     excluding gold
Subtract:
   1. F.R. gold-certificate
     reserve
	+6.0
	
	+0.6
	
	−13.0
		Add:
		  13. Treasury currency out-
		     standing
		  14. Treasury cash holdings,
		     excluding gold
		Subtract:
		   1. Treasury gold-certificate
		     liability
			+6.0
			
			+0.6
			
			−13.0

Total first-round adjust- ments, net	+7.0	Total first-round adjust- ments, net	+7.0

It may seem like a rather empty operation to add in identical terms on both sides in this manner; but to do so sets the stage for some interesting rearrangements within the lists of assets and liabilities.

Giving effect to the first-round arrangements, and adopting a sequence and grouping of assets and liabilities which is close to those of the final statement we aim at, we can restate our balance sheet (Table 5–2).

Two further adjustments are needed to reach the basis generally used for monetary analysis. Both these adjustments apply to the currency accounts. The first is a transformation of the figure for currency "outstanding" into one

TABLE 5-2

FEDERAL RESERVE STATEMENT WITH FIRST-ROUND ADJUSTMENTS
(billions of dollars, June 30, 1966)

Assets			*Liabilities*		
Federal Reserve bank credit:			Currency "outstanding":		
3. U.S. gov't securities	42.2		6. Federal Reserve notes		
4. Discounts, etc.	0.3		(outside F.R. Banks)	37.4	
5. Float, etc.	2.1		13. Treasury currency	6.0	
		44.6			43.4
Currency held by monetary authorities:			Treasury cash holdings:		
			12. Free gold	0.4	
2. Federal Reserve (excluding F.R. notes)	0.3		14. Other	0.6	
14. Treasury (excluding gold)	0.6		F.R. deposits other than member-bank reserves:		1.0
		0.9	8. U.S. Treasury	0.8	
11. Monetary gold stock	13.4		9. Foreign and other	0.7	
					1.5
13. Treasury currency outstanding		6.0	10. Other F.R. accounts	0.4	
			7. Member-bank reserve deposits		18.6
Total assets, adjusted		64.9	Total liabilities, adjusted		64.9

for currency "in circulation outside United States Treasury and Federal Reserve banks." This is done as follows:

Subtract:		Subtract:	
Currency held by monetary authorities:		Currency held by the monetary authorities:	−0.9
2. Federal Reserve	−0.3		
14. Treasury	−0.6		

The second adjustment registers the fact that part of the currency "in circulation" is actually held by commercial-bank members of the Federal Reserve System, and under recent legislation counts as part of their legal reserve. Hence we need to reallocate currency, as follows:

$$
\begin{array}{ll}
\text{Subtract:} & \\
\quad\text{Currency in circulation} & -42.5 \\
\text{Add:} & \\
\quad\text{15. "Outside circulation"} & +38.2 \\
\quad\text{16. Member-bank vault cash} & +4.3 \\
\hline
& +42.5
\end{array}
$$

With these adjustments, we arrive at almost exactly the form of statement which is published every month in the *Federal Reserve Bulletin* (Table 5–3.)

TABLE 5-3

MEMBER-BANK RESERVES, FEDERAL RESERVE BANK CREDIT,

AND RELATED ITEMS

(billions of dollars, June 30, 1966)

Factors Supplying Reserve Funds		*Factors Absorbing Reserve Funds*	
F.R. bank credit outstanding:		15. "Outside circulation"	38.2
3. U.S. gov't securities	42.2	12 + 14. Treasury cash	1.0
4. Discounts, etc.	0.3		
5. Float, etc.	2.1	F.R. deposits other than	
	44.6	member-bank reserves:	
		8. U.S. Treasury	0.8
11. Monetary gold stock	13.4	9. Foreign and other	0.7
			1.5
13. Treasury currency		Member-bank reserves:	
outstanding	6.0	1. Reserve deposits	18.6
		16. Vault cash	4.3
			22.9
Total sources of potential		Total uses of potential	
reserves	64.0	reserves	64.0

Source: Federal Reserve Bulletin. As published in the source, the table includes total currency in circulation rather than "outside circulation," and then duplicates the vault-cash component in calculating member-bank reserves. A hasty examination of the published table might thus seem to show "uses" exceeding "sources" of potential reserve funds, so that our treatment of item 15 registers a modest improvement over Federal Reserve treatment.

Note that most of the figures published in *Federal Reserve Bulletin are averages of daily figures.* For "end-of-month" figures such as those used in our illustrative figures, look at the foot of the published tables. Analytically, averages of daily figures have the decisive advantage that they obviate freaks in specific-day figures (which because of "window-dressing" in bank statements are particularly acute for dates like June 30 and December 31); but to describe the accounting operations underlying the statement, data for a specific day are more serviceable.

Controllability of reserve-determining factors: "owned reserves" as focus. If we think of the Federal Reserve as trying to control member-bank operations through the reserve position of the member banks, it is interesting to note that of the items listed in the final statement, only one is subject to unconditional Federal Reserve control. That one is the "open-market portfolio," or Federal Reserve holding of government securities.[17] All the other

---

[17]Even here, as will prove important when we come to study monetary policy, the Federal Reserve can strictly control the quantity only if it will accept the consequences for another variable of importance— the *interest yield* on government securities. If the Federal Reserve moves to reduce its holdings, it must do so by selling on the market (or by failing to replace Treasury securities that mature, thus forcing the Treasury to sell more securities than it otherwise would). To find holders for securities that would not otherwise be in private hands, the monetary authorities must push the price of those securities lower than it would otherwise go; and since the yield is a relation between contractual interest and price, they will be pushing the yield up. How far they must go to place a given amount of securities is somewhat unpredictable— particularly since a rise of yield may cause potential holders to revise upward their expectations of future yield.

items are either determined by forces outside the control of the Federal Reserve, or at best are subject to Federal Reserve *influence*. Running down the list, we can see that discounts are set by the initiative of member banks in asking for loans (affected but not strictly controlled by the Federal Reserve discount rate, and by Federal Reserve "moral suasion"). The float changes from time to time with the more or less accidental forces that determine what proportion of checks in collection have to be cleared in remote parts of the country. The gold stock (and on the liability side, foreign deposits with Federal Reserve Banks) is governed by the foreign-trade position and international-capital-movements position of the United States, and by decisions of foreign central banks as to whether to hold reserves in gold or in United States funds. Treasury currency outstanding depends on the public's demand for small change.[18] The same factor of public demand for hand-to-hand currency dominates the "outside circulation" item that heads the liability side. Since the Federal Reserve cannot let a dollar of paper currency be worth more or less than a dollar of "checkbook money," it has to let more currency flow into circulation when checks cashed by the nonbank public exceed currency inflow over commercial-bank counters.

Two items on the statement, though outside Treasury control, can be viewed as controlled by "the monetary authorities," when we look at the Federal Reserve and Treasury as a joint concern. These are "Treasury cash" and Treasury deposits at Federal Reserve Banks. In the ordinary course of Treasury operations, disbursements flow out of deposit balances at the Federal Reserve, while proceeds of taxes and security issues flow into Treasury accounts at commercial banks. The Treasury keeps up its working balances at the Federal Reserve by making "calls" from time to time for stated proportions of its balances at commercial banks. The Treasury member of the monetary-authority partnership thus wields the power to build up item 8 of the statement by accelerating its "calls"; if it does so, it puts pressure on member-bank reserves much like that applied if the Federal Reserve reduces its portfolio. But ordinarily the Treasury maintains its working balance at the Federal Reserve Banks (and also its stock of small change and paper currency) within a rather narrow range.

For purposes of analysis, monetary economists often offset the advances of

---

As an *alternative* to deciding what volume of government securities shall be in the Federal Reserve portfolio (and thus what residual volume shall be in private hands), the monetary authorities can decide on the level of interest yields, and enforce their decision by Federal Reserve offers to buy and sell. But to do this leaves it to the market to decide upon the quantity; *both* yield and quantity cannot be imposed *simultaneously* by Federal Reserve decision.

[18]During the period of transition from use as one-dollar bills exclusively of "silver certificates" to use exclusively of Federal Reserve notes, the Federal Reserve has been able to regulate "Treasury currency outstanding" by decisions to retire or to return to circulation silver certificates received in currency deposits by banks which enjoyed an excess of over-the-counter inflow of paper currency over corresponding outflow. But this has been an unusual and transitory instrument of monetary control.

the Federal Reserve to member banks (appearing in item 4 of the statement) against reserves (items 1 + 16). The excess of reserves over borrowings constitutes *owned reserves*. (Federal Reserve terminology says *unborrowed reserves*; but any gain in precision from the change of adjectives seems to be offset by the use of a rather sloppy polysyllable.) Despite the number and variety of factors that affect owned reserves, it is proper to regard the course of owned reserves as governed by Federal Reserve policy. For among the determining factors, Federal Reserve holdings of government securities are prominent; and with rare exceptions, it has been possible to move them enough to swamp movements in the other factors.

The history since the foundation of the Federal Reserve System of member banks' owned reserves and their chief determinants can now be described. Except during the 1930's, the greater part of "potential reserve funds" has been absorbed by currency in circulation. During the postwar period, the power of a dollar of bank reserves to support bank deposits has been increased steadily by a rise in the proportion of total deposits on low-reserve time deposits, and intermittently by reductions in required reserve percentages, so that the currency use of potential reserve funds has outgrown the bank-reserve use. On the asset side the course of total "monetary-reserve assets" is, of course, the mirror image of "potential reserve funds," as reflected in movements through time in the two sides of the balancesheet statement of Table 5–3.[19] Until World War II, the predominant asset was monetary gold stock; since then, it has been "Federal Reserve Credit, net," which consists almost entirely of government securities in Federal Reserve hands.

Actual effect of reserve-creation on deposit-creation. The argument of Chapter 5 implies that we should expect creation of owned reserves to induce parallel changes in bank deposits, by providing incentives to banks to expand credit. But this relationship is not automatic. Commercial banks have scope to hold "excess reserves" (declining to use some of the lending power represented by their owned reserves), and also to expand beyond what their owned reserves would support, through use of borrowed reserves obtained by discounting at the Federal Reserve. Their "free reserves" (excess reserves minus rediscounts, which is the same thing as owned reserves minus required reserves) may be either positive or negative. In practice, free reserves stated as a percentage of required reserves have varied since 1952 in a range between −3 per cent and +4 per cent. This element of slack might be used so as largely to offset the effects of Federal Reserve operations—or at least to force the Federal Reserve to carry on

---

[19]The third edition of this book pictured reserve fund creation from 1915–59 in chart form.
See third edition, p. 100.

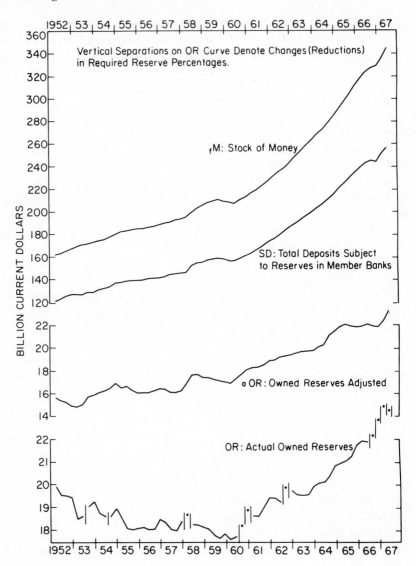

Sources: ₜM: "Money supply" plus "time deposits adjusted" from *Federal Reserve Bulletin,* August 1967, pp. 1307–1308; for 1952–1958, *ibid.,* June 1967, pp. 685–89.

SD and OR: Federal Reserve release G.10, "Aggregate Reserves and Member Bank Deposits."

*a*OR: Contemporary numbers of *Federal Reserve Bulletin.*

Chart 5-1: Levels of money stock (including time deposits in commercial banks), total deposits subject to reserve requirements, and adjusted and unadjusted owned reserves of member banks.

operations or change reserve requirements on a scale so large as to be very disturbing.

Accordingly, an interesting question of fact is whether credit expansion by commercial banks does or does not conform closely to the pattern set by creation of owned reserves. We shall examine this question with the aid of a series of charts. The first of these (Chart 5–1) traces *levels* of reserves and deposits in quarter-year averages from 1952 (when the Federal Reserve had more or less regained its freedom of action after its servitude to the Treasury during and after World War II) till mid-1967. The scale is semilogarithmic. Working upward from the bottom of the chart, the curves show successively actual owned reserves of all member banks, a series of "adjusted" owned reserves to which we will return in a moment, total deposits subject to reserve requirements at member banks, and the stock of money (in the Friedman version, including time deposits at commercial banks, for comparability with "total deposits subject to reserve requirements").

A hasty look at Chart 5–1 might suggest that contrary to expectation almost no relation exists between the course of owned reserves and that of deposits; the bottom and next-to-top curves look very unlike each other. But note the numerous places where the bottom curve is interrupted and a thin vertical line drawn through it. Each of these represents a point at which the Federal Reserve reduced reserve requirements on some or all of the classes of deposits held by member banks. The deposit-supporting power of a dollar of member-bank reserves was thus greater to the right of each of these breaks than it had been to the left. While the general drift of the actual-reserves curve seems to be horizontal, there was actually a strong upward movement of the deposit-supporting power of total reserves, corresponding to the upward movement of the next-to-top curve, over the period as a whole.

Whenever such a reduction of reserve requirements occurs, it has become customary to publish in the *Federal Reserve Bulletin* an estimate of the amount of reserves "released" by the change.[20] To show reserves across the date of such a change in a form which would reflect the actual change in their reserve-supporting power, we would have to use a virtual figure for prechange reserves, scaled down in proportion to the reduction of reserve requirements at the moment of change. The Federal Reserve has obliged bankers and economists by refiguring such a virtual series from 1967 back to 1947. The resulting figures for "adjusted required reserves" represent roughly what requirements *would have been* had the spring-1967 requirements been in force at any earlier date

---

[20]Such estimates are readily made by applying the requirement-changes to the amounts of different types of deposits. For example, suppose requirements are dropped from 16 per cent to 15 per cent on demand deposits of reserve city banks and from 12 per cent to 11 1/2 per cent on demand deposits of country banks; in this case, the amount "released" will be equal to 1 per cent of reserve-city demand deposits plus 0.5 per cent of country-bank demand deposits.

instead of the higher actual requirements.[21] The resulting adjusted curve for owned reserves is the second from the bottom on the chart (marked $_aOR$). It agrees with the curve marked SD for total deposits subject to reserve requirements in showing a general upward drift over the period—faster after mid-1960 than in the 1950's in each case. But as can be seen, the adjusted-reserve curve shows absolute declines at several points (1952–53, 1954–55, 1958–60) where the deposit curve only slackens its growth; and the general growth-rate of adjusted owned reserves falls behind that of deposits. We shall come shortly to the question of the short-term declines. For the present, let us deal only with the discrepancy in growth rates. This results from the strong growth over the period of observation in the proportion of time deposits ($31.9 billion out of $124.3 billion subject to reserves, or 25.7 per cent, in mid-1952; $140.8 out of $259.2 billion subject to reserves, or 54.3 per cent, in mid-1967). Even though the Federal Reserve calculation applies the same (1967) reserve-requirement percentages to each *class* of deposits, the increase of the share in time deposits (with the lowest required percentage) pulls down the average ratio of adjusted required reserves to total deposits subject to reserve requirements (from 12.9 per cent in mid-1952 to 9.1 per cent in mid-1967). This is an additional source of deposit-supporting power in bank reserves of which we will have to take account.

The curve (marked $_fM$) at the top of the chart is included to show that when we explain the "creation of deposits," we are also in fact explaining the quantity of money. Some items included in the stock of money (hand-to-hand currency plus checking deposits in commercial banks not members of the Federal Reserve System) are not included in "total deposits subject to reserve requirements"; on the other hand, some (deposits of the United States government and a few interbank deposits) are included in the deposits subject to reserve but excluded from the stock of money. (By adopting for the moment the Friedman definition, we include time deposits at member banks in both series although those in commercial banks not members of the Federal Reserve System enter the list of discrepancies.) But it happens that the items of difference between the two series do not show any changes in the 1952–67 period that disturb the parallelism of

---

[21]This series appears monthly in the *Federal Reserve Bulletin* on the page devoted to "Money Supply: Bank Reserves." The adjustment was made in the first instance to required reserves. The Federal Reserve then calculated figures for "unborrowed" (owned) reserves by *adding* free reserves to required reserves. Since the lending power represented by free reserves per dollar of reserves must be viewed as expanding in proportion to that represented by required reserves, it would be more logical to estimate the "adjusted" series of owned reserves by multiplication (using the actual ratio of owned to required reserves). But this refinement would not appreciably affect the month-to-month or quarter-to-quarter *changes* in owned reserves which we use in the analysis of this chapter. Lack of this refinement means, however, that if we calculated the ratio of free to required reserves from the Federal Reserve's adjusted series, we would overrate the *percentage* excess or shortfall of owned as against required reserves; so we have calculated the free-reserve ratio from original (unadjusted) data.

the $_rM$ and SD curves. Hence we do not have to worry lest our account of the "creation of deposits" leave out aspects that are highly important in the more broadly conceived "creation of money."

Analysis of changes in total deposits and in reserves. For a closer analysis, it is better to replace a chart of *levels* such as Chart 5–1 with a chart which registers *changes* in the variables under study. Since the rate of growth of each variable is reflected by the *steepness* of its curve on Chart 5–1, this chart is good enough to show a general resemblance, and also to show us that points exist at which the course of total deposits and that of adjusted reserves diverge. But comparison of slopes on Chart 5–1 is an ineffective tool for analyzing these divergencies.

An alternative chart which measures changes is Chart 5–2. Here each of the top three curves shows a *percentage rate of change,* figured within a half-year period.[22] Working down from the top, we have first curve $a\dot{OR}$, which shows the percentage rate of change in adjusted owned reserves.[23] Next we have curve $(\dot{SD})$, which shows the rate of change in the sum of demand and time deposits subject to reserve requirements. The third is the $(a\dot{OR} + \dot{R})$ curve, to which we will turn in a moment. A horizontal line is drawn through each curve at its average level for 1952–67, to guide the eye in making comparisons.

Comparing the top two curves, we can see that each of the episodes of unusually fast growth in deposits (flagged on the $\dot{SD}$ curve by letters B, D, F, and H) has some sort of counterpart on the $a\dot{OR}$ curve; and the same is true of the episodes of unusually slow growth or absolute decline (flagged by letters A, C, E, and G). But the similarity is very crude. In particular, the deposit-growth curve shows a continuous series of growth-rates above average from mid-1960 to mid-1967 (punctuated only by the interruption in the second half of 1966), while the reserve-change curve is not so consistently above average, and shows a deceleration which the deposit-growth curve does not share.

The explanation for these discrepancies lies primarily in the shift toward time deposits to which we referred above. We correct for this in the third curve, labelled $(a\dot{OR} + \dot{R})$. To the reserve-growth-rate $a\dot{OR}$ we add a correction-factor $\dot{R}$

---

[22]Following the system which has become conventional in measuring growth of the money stock, we calculate the change in average level from month to month as a per cent of the level of the first month, and then sum the monthly percentage changes for the half-year. The result is approximately to show the rate of change *within* the half-year. More strictly, we show for a January-June half-year the change to the June level from the previous December, divided by the average level of the six-month period December-May. Data are presented in half-yearly rather than monthly or quarterly form in order to reduce the prominence of "saw-teeth." Half-yearly rather than yearly intervals are preferred because many of the most interesting changes happen within calendar years. The same logic would suggest going on to quarterly figures; but we prefer to avoid the "smoothing" which *this would* necessitate.

[23]The dots over the letter R and other symbols follow the convention, which is becoming widespread in economics, to show that the variable in question is measured as a percentage rate of change.

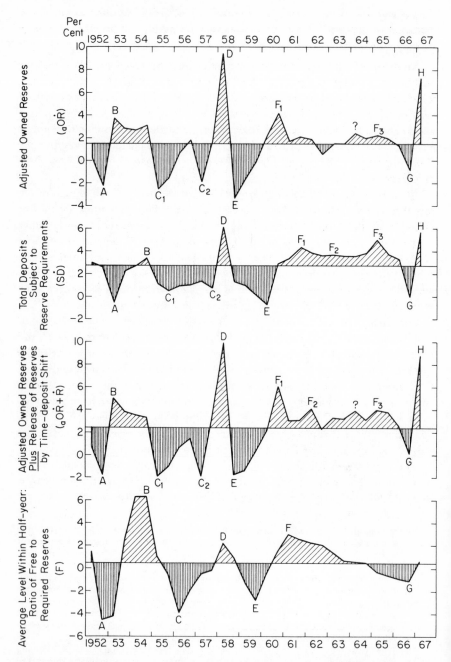

Chart 5-2: Percentage rates of change in owned reserves (with and without adjustment for time-deposit shift) and in total deposits subject to reserves, with level of free-reserve ratio.

which represents the *release of reserves through the time-deposit shift*.[24] The $(a O\dot{R} + \dot{R})$ series expresses growth in *deposit-supporting power* of reserves. Since the relative growth of time deposits accelerated in the 1960's, this adjustment raises the right-hand part of the curve more than the left-hand part. Thus the $(a O\dot{R} + \dot{R})$ curve agrees with the $(S\dot{D})$ curve in showing the 1961–67 period as one of above-average expansion, although with more irregularity in the growth of deposit-supporting power than in the growth of deposits.

Besides the similarities between the second and third curves, we should note two highly strategic differences. In the first place, corresponding episodes on the curve which shows growth in deposit-supporting power of reserves seem to come somewhat earlier in time than their counterparts on the deposit-growth curve. And in the second place, the high and low points on the $(a O\dot{R} + \dot{R})$ curve lie further above and below average than corresponding points on the deposit-growth curve; the $(a O\dot{R} + \dot{R})$ curve fluctuates with *greater amplitude*. Both these differences match very well with the hypothesis that the growth of the deposit-supporting power of reserves causes growth of deposits—but has its effect tempered through bank discretion in changing excess reserves and discounts. The fact that the reserve situation changes first may be taken as an indication that banks move in the direction indicated by reserves only after taking a little time to verify that the reserve-change is not ephemeral, and perhaps to change their stance toward would-be borrowers and broaden their search for suitable investment securities. The lesser amplitude of the deposit-creation response corresponds very well to this interpretation: if it takes a little while for member banks to accelerate or decelerate their credit expansion in response to an acceleration or deceleration in reserve-creation, part of the initial impact of a reserve-growth acceleration will be taken up in expansion of excess reserves or in reduction of rediscounts. Furthermore, if accelerations and decelerations of reserve-growth follow each other quickly (as they often do), the commercial banks may have an undigested bulge of excess reserves or of rediscounts to work off, so that part of the effect of the new direction of reserve-creation will be to complete the adjustment to the previous move.

"Reserves available for demand deposits." An interesting question is whether we would get essentially the same results if we focused our attention on the narrower definition of "money" (excluding commercial-bank time deposits) and correspondingly dealt only with growth in *demand* deposits at member banks. A chart to answer this question, designed on the same system as Chart

---

[24]This correction-factor is calculated from the Federal Reserve's data compiled to work out the adjusted-reserve series. For each month, there is, of course, a specific ratio of required reserves to total deposits subject to reserves—dropping gradually as we noted above from 12.9 per cent to 9.1 per cent. For any given half-year, the R factor is calculated by taking the drop in the ratio as a per cent of the average ratio. For example, consider a half-year when the ratio averaged 10.0 per cent. If at the end of the half-year the ratio stands at 9.8 per cent while at the end of the previous half-year it stood at 10.1 per cent, the drop is 0.3 per cent. The $\dot{R}$ factor for the half-year is then $(0.3/10.0) = 3.0$ per cent.

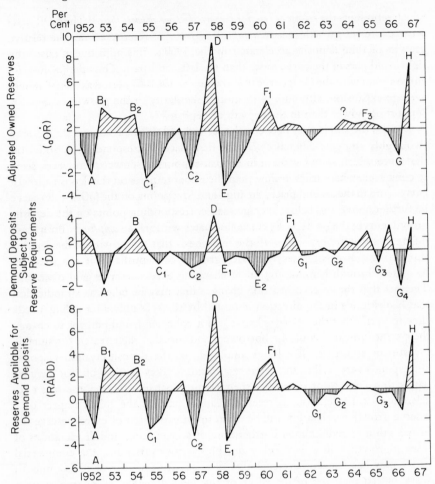

Chart 5-3: Percentage rates of change in owned reserves, demand deposits subject to reserve requirements, and reserves available for demand deposits, by half-years, 1952–1967.

5–2, is offered as Chart 5–3. Here the top curve $(a\dot{O}R)$ is the same as before. But the second curve $(\dot{D}D)$ shows the rate of change in the half-year of *demand* deposits subject to reserve, and the third curve shows the rate of change in "reserves available for demand deposits."[25]

---

[25]The measurement of "reserves available for demand deposits" has been developed by the research staff of the Federal Reserve Bank of St. Louis, under leadership of Homer Jones. But for comparability with the Federal Reserve Board's series of "adjusted reserves," we have made the adjustment simply by subtracting from total and required "adjusted reserves" a rough estimate of the part of "adjusted reserves" attributable to time deposits. Since the average requirement against time deposits in spring-1967 was about 4.1 per cent, the estimated time-deposit requirement is taken simply as 4.0 per cent of time deposits. A more refined adjustment would allow for growth through time of time deposits in banks holding over $5 million

As on Chart 5–2, comparing deposit-growth with the reserve-growth curve that allows for changes in time deposits yields a strong resemblance in shape—with a tendency as before for reserve-growth to accelerate earlier in time than deposit-growth, and to show greater amplitude of fluctuation. Since so much of the deposit growth in the 1960's has been in time deposits, the period 1960–67 no longer shows an almost continuous above-average growth—neither of reserves nor of deposits; the minor fluctuations in this period match fairly well as between the two curves.

The main difference between Chart 5–2 and Chart 5–3 is that on Chart 5–3 the correction for time deposits produces only very modest changes in the reserve-growth curve. Consequently, we would have reached almost the same conclusions if we had simply compared demand-deposit growth with the growth of adjusted reserves. But on close inspection you will find that toward the end of the period of observation (notably in 1962–63 and in 1966–67) the time-deposit shift was irregular enough to make the curve of growth in "reserves available for demand deposits" match perceptibly better with that for demand deposits than does the simple owned-reserve-growth curve.

Free reserves and deposit expansion. Many accounts of bank incentives for deposit expansion make them hinge on the level of free reserves rather than on the growth of owned deserves. To permit sizing up this view, we have included at the foot of Chart 5–2 a curve which shows free reserves (positive or negative as the case may be) as a per cent of required reserves. If the free-reserve approach is realistic, we should expect to find a high rate of deposit-growth where the free-reserve ratio is large and positive, a low rate of deposit-growth where the free-reserve ratio is large and negative, and an acceleration of deposit-growth when the free-reserve ratio rises.

These expectations for the relation between the F-curve and the $S\dot{D}$-curve are borne out reasonably well by the experience of 1952–60. But the steady decline of the F-ratio from 1961 onward has no counterpart in the $S\dot{D}$-curve—which on the contrary shows on the whole an acceleration of growth.[26] Furthermore, a closer comparison shows a number of discrepancies in particular episodes. It is noticeable, for example, that according to the behavior of the F-ratio, the expansion-episode B should have shown faster expansion than episode D, while the contrary is the case. Furthermore, the dates of fastest expansion and contraction in deposits come unduly early relative to the dates of peak positive and negative free reserves.

Apparently, therefore, the explanatory power of the F-ratio is not very high, and the free-reserve interpretation of deposit creation has not worked as well recently as it has in the past. Very likely, then, there have been institutional

of such deposits (subject to a 6 per cent requirement as opposed to 3 per cent in banks with under $5 million); but since this refinement could scarcely have a perceptible effect on percentage rates of growth of "reserves available for demand deposits," we have ignored it.

[26]If we had put the F-ratio curve also on Chart 5-3, we would have found similarly that there was a major discrepancy from 1961 onward: although demand-deposit growth does not accelerate like the growth of total deposits, it clearly does not decelerate.

changes in banking that affect free reserves. In the first place, net free reserves for all member banks can be positive only when some banks hold substantial free reserves. But the evolution of the "federal funds market" has made it more and more easy for any bank with excess reserves to lend them out profitably on a day-to-day basis to other member banks, so that the holding of substantial excess reserves grows rarer. In addition, the large banks which of recent years have been particularly aggressive in expanding loans have also developed the sale of "time certificates of deposit." This probably makes these banks more willing to expand earning assets when the overall level of free reserves is low, since, if their expansion threatens to get them into a bad reserve position, they can attract funds by selling more "CD's." These two changes in banking practice mean that a given rate of expansion is attractive to the banks at a lower level of the free-reserve ratio than a few years ago. But insofar as these changes affect the reaction of banks to a given rate of growth of owned reserves, the differential effect can be pretty adequately measured by one of the devices used in the owned-reserve analysis we have just presented. Since the time-deposit shift can be very precisely measured as it takes place, and can be forecast with reasonable accuracy for a few months in advance, it would seem that the owned-reserve analysis can give a fairly accurate picture of the intensity of expansion incentives at a given time, while the free-reserve analysis is much more flabby.

Reserve requirements at the central bank level. Central banks, like commercial banks, can have legal minimum reserve ratios. Until 1945, the Federal Reserve had to comply with a gold-reserve ratio of 40 per cent against Federal Reserve notes and 35 per cent against deposits (member-bank reserve, Treasury, and nonmember bank). A wartime act reduced the requirements to 25 per cent for notes and deposits. The gold reserve requirement was eliminated for Federal Reserve deposits in 1965 and for Federal Reserve notes in 1968. At present the Federal Reserve holds "gold certificates," which are a peculiar kind of semi-fictitious money that only circulates between the Federal Reserve banks and the Treasury.[27] The country's monetary gold stock is legally owned by he Treasury, but most of it is held in trust for the Federal Reserve banks, which hold gold certificates issued against the gold. Those certificates constitute the reserve against Federal Reserve liabilities.

Through most of its history, the Federal Reserve System has had a comfortable margin of reserves over requirements, and its policy has probably not been much influenced from month to month by fears of falling below requirements. Its reserve margin nearly disappeared in 1919–20, and a "tight money" policy developed; but the inventory boom would probably have led to the same credit policy if reserves had been much higher. From mid-1921 until 1931, the margin of reserves over requirements ranged between $1 and $2 billion.

The Federal Reserve banks came closest to a crisis on account of their reserve requirements in 1931–32. At that time, the law required that they post "col-

---

[27] See footnote 15 in this chapter.

lateral" against their notes, consisting of discounted paper plus gold or gold certificates. The wave of paper-money hoarding that resulted from bank failures in the early 1930's had caused a great expansion in the issue of Federal Reserve notes—from $1.7 billion in July 1930 to $2.2 billion in July 1931, and to $2.9 billion in December. To obtain this currency for the public, the commercial banks had been forced to rediscount. They were heavily in debt to the Federal Reserve banks and under pressure to reduce their outstanding loans. As a contraction of bank credit would worsen the depression, the Federal Reserve banks would have liked to buy securities on the open market as a way to help the banks out of debt. But this would have reduced rediscounts (which counted as collateral) while raising the System's holdings of government securities (which did not count as collateral). The Federal Reserve would then have been caught short of collateral. To make matters worse, our gold losses to other countries had cut back the gold stock, so that the Federal Reserve banks had only a small margin of "surplus" gold (gold in excess of the 40 per cent gold-collateral requirement). The Federal Reserve was, therefore, afraid to engage in the open-market purchases that were needed. This crisis was relieved by the Glass-Steagall Act of February 1932 which allowed the Federal Reserve banks to count their holdings of government securities as collateral.[28]

After 1933 and well into World War II, gold flowed in from Europe, and the Federal Reserve always had a wide margin over requirements. From mid-1935 to mid-1943, in fact, reserves were double the required amount. In the later war years, gold flowed out, and by June 1945, required reserves were up to $15 billion as compared with actual reserves of $18 billion. At this point, reserves on both notes and deposits were reduced to 25 per cent, reducing required reserves to $10 billion and again establishing a comfortable margin.

The United States monetary gold stock began to decline in the late 1950's. A sharp rise in reserve requirements was avoided by reducing member-bank reserve requirements from time to time, so that despite the growth of the public's deposits with commercial bank, member-bank deposits at Federal Reserve Banks had no strong uptrend. But with the growth of note circulation and the decline of gold stocks, the margin of gold reserves over Federal Reserve requirements shrank until in early 1965 the total gold reserve of $14.7 billion exceeded by only $1.2 billion the 25 per cent requirement against notes and deposits combined: the actual reserve ratio was barely over 27 per cent. Congress again stepped in with an act which removed the reserve requirement against deposits, so that the only requirement was 25 per cent against the $34.6 billion of notes, or $8.7 billion, and the margin was again comfortable. Against notes alone, the gold reserve was then over 42 per cent.

A further loss of gold and rise of note circulation (augmented by the use of Federal Reserve Notes to replace silver certificates in the $1 denomination)

---

[28]The provisions of the Glass–Steagal Act, at first temporary, were made permanent by later legislation; effectively, they nullified the collateral requirement. For the official view of the crisis at the time, see Federal Reserve Board, *Annual Report* for 1932, pp. 16–19.

brought the Federal Reserve at the end of February 1968 to a position where the actual ratio of gold to notes alone was only $11.4/$41.2 billion or 27.6 per cent. An act of Congress in March 1968 removed the last vestige of the gold-reserve requirement, placing the Federal Reserve in a position where, if necessary, it could release for export the equivalent of its entire $10.1 billion of "gold certificate reserve." But since in the meantime the amount of dollar bank accounts and short-term government securities held for foreign banks and governments had climbed to some $27 billion, even this change did not make the reserve position completely secure.

While for most of its history, the Federal Reserve had had strong enough reserves to be able to base its monetary policy almost purely on domestic considerations, the weakening of the reserve stock and international monetary position during the 1960's has increased the weight of the international position and foreign monetary situation.[29] Through much of the 1960's Federal Reserve policy has been more restrictive than the leaders of the system would have set it on purely domestic grounds.

Open-market operations and asset-preferences. Our discussion thus far has assumed that the task of the central bank is to control the quantity of money. This can be done without too much difficulty because the central bank can vary commercial-bank reserves with reserve ratios fixed or can alter reserve ratios against a given total of reserves. In later chapters, we shall argue that control over cash-creation may not suffice to produce stability in the American economy. If households and businesses cannot lay their hands on cash, they cannot spend beyond their incomes. Yet when the total stock of money is fixed, those households and firms that need more cash in order to execute spending plans may still be able to obtain it.

If a businessman approaches his bank for a loan, the bank may be able to satisfy him by disposing of investments—for example, government bonds. The commercial banks' capacity to switch from investments to loans is huge because they hold a great quantity of government securities. Similarly, a "deficit" business may be able to obtain cash from another that has a surplus of cash. Finally, credit institutions like savings banks may be able to satisfy the demand for loans by persuading the holders of demand deposits to exchange their money holdings for savings deposits or other money substitutes.

To the extent that consumers and businesses can lay their hands on cash, their spending may proceed unabated, although the Federal Reserve System has limited the total stock of cash. The Federal Reserve may have difficulty combating inflation unless it can make it difficult for "deficit" consumers and firms to secure the cash they desire. The central bank may have to influence the moneyness of cash-substitutes as well as to control the stock of money.

This problem has been given much attention by economists, and while they

---

[29]Our liabilities to foreigners have also increased the sensitivity of interest rates in USA to those abroad. This problem will be considered in Chapter 18.

have not reached a consensus, many now argue that the central bank can affect the "turnover" or "velocity of circulation" of the money supply, in addition to its size. We shall discuss this issue at other places in this book. Here, however, we shall illustrate the argument with reference to commercial banks.

When the Federal Reserve System sells securities in the open market, it usually depresses bond prices and may set up expectations of a further decline in securities prices. The change in prices that it causes and the further change that it threatens may deter banks from the sale of government bonds and thereby prevent them from making new loans. If a bank holds a $4\frac{1}{2}$ per cent bond and the price drops $1\frac{1}{2}$ points on account of Federal Reserve open-market sales, the bank may be reluctant to sell the bond. First, it will realize a capital loss if the price decline has carried the bond below the bank's book valuation. This is unpleasant because it puts a seal of finality on an apparent mistake, and it may be difficult to explain the loss to the bank's directors. Second, a $5\frac{1}{2}$ per cent $100 loan will be no bargain if the bank must take a $1\frac{1}{2}$ point loss on a $4\frac{1}{2}$ per cent bond in order to make the loan. On a one-year loan the bank would lose money. Open-market sales by the Federal Reserve may "lock in" the banks at the same time that they reduce bank reserves.

Treasury open-market operations. The account of open-market operations given above relates to the Federal Reserve bank, but this is a game the Treasury must also play. It has Treasury bills coming due for payment every week; certificates every few weeks; notes every few months; and every now and then, an issue of bonds that has reached the date at which the Treasury must pay it off. It must issue new securities to Peter to raise cash to pay Paul.

These Treasury operations can pose problems for the Federal Reserve. Suppose that the Federal Reserve sells Treasury notes to reduce bank reserves and stop an unhealthy expansion of credit. The commercial banks may simply pass the pressure on to the Treasury. All they have to do is take cash for the Treasury bills and certificates they hold, as these come due, and avoid buying new bills or certificates. If they do this, the funds that the Federal Reserve has absorbed must be provided by the Treasury; the commercial banks' reserves will not be impaired and they can continue with credit expansion. To prevent this outcome, the Treasury must offer its new securities on terms that are irresistibly attractive—either to banks or to members of the nonbank public. It must offer interest rates high enough in relation to other yields to persuade the banks that they cannot afford to reject the Treasury securities offered.

The effectiveness of open-market operations is unavoidably a *joint* concern of the Treasury and the Reserve banks. At a given moment, there is a certain stock of government securities in existence. What banks and nonbank holders do not elect to hold, the central authorities must hold. If they fix the interest rate, they must absorb whatever the banks choose to shift to them. If they wish to fix their own holdings, they have to make the interest rates attractive enough to find buyers.

On central banking in general. Treasury security dealings must be looked at as part of central banking. Is this the end of the matter—or must we broaden our notions of central banking still further? Is central-bankingness, like moneyness, a matter of degree?

Yes, it is. For one thing, government taxes and spending are analogous to central-bank operations. If the government spends more than it takes in as taxes, it puts cash into people's pockets just as it does when it redeems more Treasury bills than it sells. Taxes and expenditure may be viewed as especially potent species of open-market operations. When a man pays taxes, his canceled check is a mere accounting record—not a liquid asset which he can regard as a near-money. Similarly, a man who gets a government paycheck has sold services that would not have been a liquid asset for anyone else if the government had not bought them. Revenue and expenditure changes are consequently stronger influences on people's private operations per dollar received or spent than open-market operations in securities.

The "exchange stabilization funds" that were set up in many countries in the 1930's also carry on central banking. Their open-market operations are purchases and sales of debts payable abroad in foreign currency, or of nonmonetary gold. These operations affect bank reserves just like dealings in governmental securities. The United States Stabilization Fund operated on rather a small scale in the 1930's.[30] But the British Exchange Equalization Account operated on a large scale in the 1930's and continues to do so.

Commercial banks can even act as central banks. Before the Federal Reserve System was set up, the big New York banks shared with the Treasury some sense of central-bank responsibility, in default of any regular organization. If a commercial bank piles up excess reserves not because it lacks profitable chances to acquire loans and investments but because it is trying to combat an undesirable credit expansion in banking as a whole, it is acting as a central bank. This is just a possibility, however; actually, banks normally decide their reserve policy for their own business reasons, and leave central banking to the authorities.[31] Central banking, in practice, is an activity of the official central banks (in this country, the Federal Reserve), the Treasury, and official foreign-exchange funds.

---

[30]Out of the $2.0 billion fund set up in 1934, only $0.2 billion went into active use. The $1.8 billion was eventually used to finance our subscription to the International Monetary Fund.

[31]As Professor Lloyd W. Mints points out, nonbank firms or even households could carry on central banking. If the Rockefellers, for example, determined at a family council to turn all their assets into cash to resist an inflationary boom—and later to turn all the cash back into other assets to help correct a depression—they would be acting as a central bank. But even the largest private groupings do not swing enough weight to change monetary events much. Besides, they have to look out for their own business.

NOTES ON
ALTERNATIVE POINTS OF VIEW
AND SUPPLEMENTARY READINGS

On bank control, Federal Reserve Board publications designed for student use are very convenient; these are listed in the back of each *Federal Reserve Bulletin.* They include *The Federal Reserve System: Its Purposes and Functions* (Washington, D.C.: U.S. Goverment Printing Office, 1963), and *The Federal Reserve Act as Amended* (reissued at intervals to take account of new legislation).

Current banking statistics and comments on developments make up much of the monthly *Federal Reserve Bulletin;* a rich mine of back statistics is found in *Banking and Monetary Statistics* (Washington, D.C.: U.S. Government Printing Office, 1960), and in subsequent supplements. Policy rulings and official reasons are published in the Board's *Annual Report.*

For a survey and evaluation of the tools of the Federal Reserve System see Warren L. Smith, "The Instruments of General Monetary Control," *National Banking Review,* September 1963, pp. 47–76.

Open-market operations are described in detail in the booklet of the same name by Paul Meek (New York: Federal Reserve Bank of New York, 1963).

The discount rate and bank reserve requirements are examined in two adjoining articles in Deane Carson, ed., *Banking and Monetary Studies* (Homewood, Ill.: Richard D. Irwin, Inc., 1963): Murray E. Polakoff, "Federal Reserve Discount Policy and Its Critics," pp. 196–212, and Neil Jacoby, "The Structure and Use of Variable Bank Reserve Requirements," pp. 213–33.

Chapter 6

Credit Institutions and the Liquidity of the Public

Nonbank Credit Institutions

An inventory of credit institutions. Because the commercial banks enjoy a special place in our financial system, we have devoted several chapters to their operations and to the controls that have been developed to regulate them. Now we must turn to the other credit institutions. Like the banks, these institutions supply credit to business, consumers, and the government, and create liquid assets for the public to hold. Unlike commercial banks, they do not create a means of payment in the course of their operations and are not directly subject to central bank control.

The major nonbank credit institutions are:

1. Mutual savings banks
2. Savings and loan associations
3. Life insurance companies

Several other institutions will be mentioned in the discussion—pension funds, installment finance companies, and credit co-operatives. We shall focus upon the three listed above because they are the largest and are broadly representative of the group as a whole. Our survey will stress the two functions of credit institutions—to make loans and to generate liquid assets that may serve investors as money substitutes. These functions are connected because the credit institutions issue debt (create liquid assets) in order to mobilize the cash they need to make new loans.

Mutual savings banks. Of the three groups of institutions, the mutual savings banks are most nearly like commercial banks. For many purposes of analysis we may treat them as banks, but they have peculiarities that deserve special study.

The nation's 500 mutual savings banks are concentrated in the northeastern part of the country (in New England, New York, New Jersey, Pennsylvania, and Maryland), where they first took root more than a hundred years ago. Many of these banks, including several of the largest, were founded before the Civil War. They are organized without capital stock. Earnings are either paid to depositors or put into surplus, and control is in the hands of self-perpetuating boards of trustees which trace back to the groups that founded the banks.[1] All deposits in these banks are "savings deposits," not subject to check. Commonly, the banks refuse to accept deposits from any one person beyond a maximum such as $15,000.

Deposits at mutual savings banks have shown a remarkably steady rate of growth. As Chart 6–1 indicates, their increase has been similar to that of demand deposits at commercial banks, but has been much smoother. It slowed down at the crisis of 1907 and at the beginning of World War II, and declined only once—in the Great Depression—and then very slightly.[2]

On the asset side, mutual savings banks have traditionally carried very low cash reserves—from 3 to 5 per cent of deposits, kept chiefly in the form of balances at commercial banks. Their largest single asset has been loans—almost entirely mortgage loans—which averaged 56 per cent of their earning assets in the 1920's (see Table 6–1). Their loans dropped during the upswing of the late 1930's and during World War II, so that loans were a mere quarter of earning assets at the end of World War II, while government securities rose to be two-thirds of earning assets. A postwar expansion of mortgage loans brought loans back to 76.2 per cent of earning assets at the end of 1966.

As this list of assets suggests, mutual savings banks have been less concerned than commercial banks have been with the "liquidity" of their assets. This is shown also by the composition of federal securities they have held. At the end of 1966, 28 per cent of the government securities held by mutual banks were bonds maturing after 1976, against only 2 per cent for commercial banks.[3]

---

[1] In getting such a bank under way, a group of founders put in funds which they agreed not to withdraw or convert to regular deposits until the bank had accumulated enough surplus to make it secure.

[2] There were no important failures of mutual savings banks during the Great Depression. This is because of their known conservatism and careful management. They gained greatly, however, from the inflow of deposits early in the Depression, which piled on top of their portfolio a layer of assets bought at deflated prices after the Depression had started.

[3] *Federal Reserve Bulletin.*

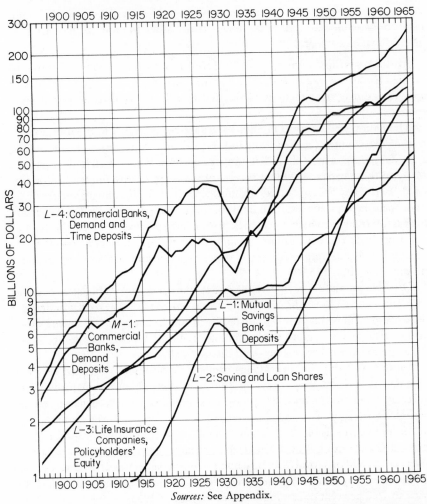

Sources: See Appendix.

Chart 6-1: Growth of credit institutions, measured by liabilities to the public, 1896–1966.

Savings and loan associations.   Savings and loan associations[4] are another group of credit institutions concerned with mortgages. Their main business has been home financing.

The "members" who have invested in these associations hold "shares" which the associations are pledged to repay at face value. But repayment is guaranteed only as funds become available from loan repayment or new investments by others. During the 1920's, many associations actually paid on demand, and some accepted deposits. In the early 1930's long delays occurred, and many associations fell into bankruptcy. The moneyness of claims on the associations

---

[4] Also called "building and loan associations"—more rarely, "co-operative banks."

TABLE 6-1

LOANS AND INVESTMENTS OF MAJOR CREDIT

INSTITUTIONS, 1920–29 AND 1950–65

(dollar amounts in billions, rounded to nearest $0.1 billion)*

Asset by Type of Institution	Dollar Amounts, Year-End Averages		Per Cent of Total Loans and Investments	
	1920–29	*1950–65*	*1920–29*	*1950–65*
1. Total loans and investments:‡				
a. Commercial banks	$41.7	$175.7	100.0	100.0
b. Mutual savings banks	7.5	35.8	100.0	100.0
c. Savings and loan associations	5.0	54.6	100.0	100.0
d. Life insurance companies	10.8	100.4	100.0	100.0
2. Real estate loans:				
a. Commercial banks	$5.0	$26.5	11.9	15.1
b. Mutual savings banks	3.9	23.2	52.0	64.7
c. Savings and loan associations	4.8	50.7	96.0	92.9
d. Life insurance companies	4.7	37.7	43.5	37.6
3. Other loans:				
a. Commercial banks	$25.4	$66.7	60.9	38.0
b. Mutual savings banks	0.3	0.4	4.0	1.0
c. Savings and loan associations	0.2	0.1	4.0	0.1
d. Life insurance companies**	1.5	4.5	13.9	4.5
4. Securities:				
a. Commercial banks	$11.4	$82.5	27.3	46.9
b. Mutual savings banks	3.3	12.3	44.0	34.3
c. Savings and loan associations	†	3.8	†	7.0
d. Life insurance companies	4.6	58.2	42.7	57.9

Sources: For 1920's, Raymond W. Goldsmith, *A Study of Savings in the United States,* Vol. I (Princeton: Princeton University Press, 1955); for 1950's and 1960's, *Federal Reserve Bulletin.*

*Detail may not add to total because of rounding.
**Policy and collateral loans for the 1920's, policy loans only for the 1950's.
†Less than $0.05 billion.
‡Excludes holdings of real estate and miscellaneous assets. These classes of assets are substantial for the life insurance companies and were large in other instances during the 1930's.

fell slightly. On the upswing from the Great Depression, associations were again able to pay with reasonable promptness, and confidence in their shares was strengthened by government backing.[5] By the 1950's, many people again looked

---

[5] The federal government supported these associations during the depression: (1) by refinancing about $800 million of their mortgages through the Home Owners Loan Corporation; (2) by setting up a system of Federal Home Loan Banks through which associations can borrow; (3) by investing directly in their "shares"; (4) by setting up a Federal Savings and Loan Insurance Corporation. The effect of this insurance is to guarantee repayment within three years if an association fails, but not immediate repayment; it insures solvency but not liquidity.

on savings and loan shares as combining full liquidity with relatively high interest, and most societies again repaid shareholders on demand.

The growth of savings and loan associations, as Chart 6–1 shows, has been erratic, but in recent years it has been phenomenal. The Great Depression carried the amount of redeemable shares down from a 1930 peak of $6.6 billion to a 1938 trough of $4.0 billion, reflecting the close linkage of savings and loan operations with the building cycle. The long depression of construction left little scope for new mortgage loans, while old ones were paid off, and low real estate values imposed losses on the associations so that they could not attract funds, or even hold those they had.[6] Since World War II, the savings and loan associations have grown faster than the other institutions described in Chart 6–1. From 1945 to 1966, their shares outstanding increased fifteenfold.

On the asset side, savings and loan associations have traditionally held almost nothing but mortgages—plus real estate coming into the hands of associations when debtors could not pay. Most of these mortgages were fully amortized—a sensible arrangement which savings and loan associations pioneered. Cash, as at mutual banks, has run from 3 per cent to 5 per cent of liabilities. Investments have usually been small. During World War II, funds came in faster than they could be placed in mortgages, and the excess went into United States government securities. But the associations used these excess liquid assets to finance part of their postwar expansion of mortgage loans. They also employed a continued inflow of savings, and received help from the Federal National Mortgage Association ("Fannie Mae").

Life insurance companies. When people think of the life insurance business as a whole, they naturally emphasize its insurance operations—payments to beneficiaries when policyholders die, and collection of premiums to finance these payments. It may then come as a surprise to find life insurance companies listed here as credit institutions, along with savings banks.

The notion of savings, however, is relevant here. Think back to the last time you talked with a life insurance salesman. In all likelihood, he did not try to sell you "term insurance," under which you would pay a premium each year covering the risk of your death that year (plus a margin for the company's expenses).[7] Under such a term-insurance contract, premiums would rise each year as the risk of your death rises as you grow older. The salesman probably urged you to buy some type of "level-premium" policy—such as "ordinary

---

[6] Since the scale of Chart 6–1 does not permit including figures below $1 billion, the history of savings and loan shares before 1910 does not appear. But the record from 1896 to 1910 confirms the interpretation in the text. From 1896 to 1901, there was a slight decline (from $436 to $419 million) in the amount of repurchasable shares outstanding. This apparently was the aftermath of the great depression of the 1890's. As in the 1930's, the upturn of savings and loan activity came only several years after the trough of general business. After 1901, as after 1938, there was a gradual acceleration of growth.

[7] Other types of insurance (automobile liability, fire and theft, and so forth) are normally sold on a term basis; this is why insurance companies other than lefe do not enter the list of credit institutions.

life," "twenty-payment life," "twenty-year endowment," or "family income." Under any level-premium policy, premiums are set *higher* than term-insurance premiums would be at the age of the policyholder when he bought the policy, but *lower* than term-insurance premiums would be in the late years of the contract. The excess premiums paid in the early years are *savings* made through the insurance company; these savings (plus interest) are used to make up the deficiency of premiums in the later years.[8]

The salesman undoubtedly pointed out that if you should change your mind about life insurance you would be able to surrender your policy and draw out your savings in cash. If you should need funds but still want insurance, you could "borrow" up to the cash-surrender value of your policy. In practice, these cash-surrender values can be drawn out within a few days—either as a whole by "surrender" or in part by "borrowing." Besides, it is easy to borrow at the bank on the security of a life insurance policy. As an asset for the policyholder, therefore, high-premium insurance policies are not radically different from savings deposits at a commercial bank or mutual savings bank.

Of all credit institutions, life insurance companies have the most remarkable record of steady growth. As Chart 6–1 shows, the growth of life insurance cash values[9] has marched on through world wars and business fluctuations. The Great Depression shows up only in a momentary leveling of the curve of cash values. The inflations of two World Wars leave no clear traces in this curve. This steadiness of growth reflects the momentum of premium payments under policies already outstanding and the steady sales efforts of the companies. While the establishment of a higher price level after each war doubtless led to a readjustment of people's insurance programs, the smoothness of the curve suggests that this readjustment was spread out over several years.

The asset management of life insurance companies resembles that of mutual savings banks.[10] Cash is held down to 2 or 3 per cent of the policies' cash values, which correspond to the deposit liabilities of savings banks. This low ratio

---

[8] The savings element is substantially the whole premium under "single-payment life policies," and the whole premium under annuity contracts which provide retirement income rather than life insurance.

[9] Roughly, cash-surrender values available to policyholders may be calculated by taking the life insurance "reserve," adding "dividends unpaid and left to accumulate," and subtracting "policy loans" and "deferred and unpaid premiums." A further deduction (for which we lack statistics) is the "surrender charge," the amount that the company would keep to compensate it for expenses, if the policy were surrendered within three or five years of the time it was bought. This deduction probably amounts to several hundred million dollars.

Current statistics for the bulk of the life insurance business are compiled by the Life Insurance Association of America and published monthly in the *Survey of Current Business;* complete annual figures are compiled by the Institute of Life Insurance.

[10]Incidentally, there is also much similarity in organization. Most of the major life insurance companies are "mutuals," like savings banks—that is, their property is held on behalf of policyholders (depositors) by trustees. Unlike mutual savings banks, life insurance companies hold elections among their policyholders. In both organizations, though, the governing boards are in practice self-perpetuating. Since they never dissolve and distribute their assets, it is difficult to say who really owns the surplus.

is safe because premiums due under outstanding contracts have recently outrun payments to policyholders by a margin exceeding 300 million monthly. The life insurance companies, as investors, have behaved in very much the same way as mutual savings banks. In the 1920's, they invested chiefly in mortgages and in bonds of railways, power companies, and local governments. During the 1930's, and even more during World War II, they invested heavily in government securities. Since the war, they have invested most of their new funds, and some funds previously invested in governments, in mortgages. Insurance companies have also expanded their holdings of industrial bonds and medium-term loans. In many cases, they have bought whole issues at "private placement," emancipating borrowers from the need to go through Securities and Exchange Commission procedures which apply to new issues publicly sold. In the fifties and mid-sixties, their securities holdings accounted for a higher proportion of total loans and investments than they did in the 1920's,[11] but they held fewer government bonds and more corporate issues than they did in the 1940's and early 1950's.

Minor credit institutions. The other credit institutions in the United States are somewhat smaller than mutual savings bank, savings and loan associations, and life insurance companies and need only brief examination. They include:

1. Stockbrokers
2. Credit unions
3. Pension funds
4. Installment loan companies
5. Sales finance companies

The first two in this list are the most like those we have already considered. They directly provide the public with liquid assets. The last three are significantly different from the rest.

Stock brokers operate as small-scale credit institutions. Their debts payable consist partly of "customers' credit balances," partly of debts to banks ("loans to brokers for purchasing and carrying securities' in bank statistics). Customers' credit balances arise when an investor sells securities and does not immediately call on his broker for payment, or when a customer sends funds to a broker but does not immediately order that the broker use them to buy securities. From the customer's standpoint, these claims are much the same as bank deposits, although he cannot draw checks upon them. Since late 1931—when the statistics begin—customers' "free" credit balances have ranged from $0.3 to $1.6

---

[11]The percentages in Table 6-1 somewhat overstate the insurance companies' relative holdings of securities because the total (1d) on which the percentages are based excludes holdings of real estate and miscellaneous assets. These are especially large in the case of insurance companies.

billion. Thus they are small as compared with bank deposits, and the like. The cash and receivables of brokers consist of bank deposits (ranging from $0.2 to $0.6 billion) and loans to customers. In the 1920's and early 1930's, when brokers operated on a larger scale, they served as intermediaries between banks and security speculators, making loans to customers to finance their dealings, and acquiring the funds by borrowing at banks. Banks in turn acted as middlemen in making brokers' loans "on account of others"—a practice since abandoned.

Credit unions are consumers' co-operatives devoted to the loan business. They operate rather like savings and loan associations, except that their debts receivable and their debts payable (repurchasable shares) are short term. For a long time, their operations were very small; outstanding loans never much exceeded $0.2 billion until after World War II. Recently they have grown at a very rapid rate, so that, by 1966, their installment loans outstanding exceeded $8.6 billion. Credit unions are still small compared to the other institutions we have surveyed, but they are gaining in absolute and relative importance.

Pension funds are a heterogeneous collection of credit institutions that have been growing rather rapidly since World War II. The majority are directly connected to companies or to labor unions and serve a limited clientele. Some extend over a broader range. The insurance companies are active in this area, selling annuities to provide retirement income instead of policies that furnish death benefits. Even the United States government is involved. The social security program (Old Age and Survivors Insurance), for example, is a pension scheme and operates a pension fund. Our social security taxes are deposited in a government "trust fund" and social security benefits are drawn from that fund. The fund's receipts are invested in government bonds.

The pension funds resemble life insurance companies in that their liabilities consist of promises to pay stated sums under fixed circumstances and their assets consist of securities and similar financial assets. They differ from insurance companies in one important respect. A worker who has contributed to a pension fund (or whose employer has done so on his behalf) cannot draw out his savings at will. The liabilities of pension funds are not really liquid assets from the standpoint of the worker, although they do represent his accumulated savings.

Unfortunately, we do not have a long series of statistics on the assets and activities of pension funds. We do know that their assets are large and that some union funds have actually acquired so much stock in the companies with which they deal that they may be able to affect company policies.

Personal finance companies and similar organizations are chiefly credit middlemen. They make loans to individuals to help them buy automobiles and household goods or to meet household deficits; they finance themselves largely by borrowing at banks. The personal finance companies may increase the liquidity of households by enhancing their borrowing power, but have practically no debts payable that can serve as liquid assets for households or for other business firms.

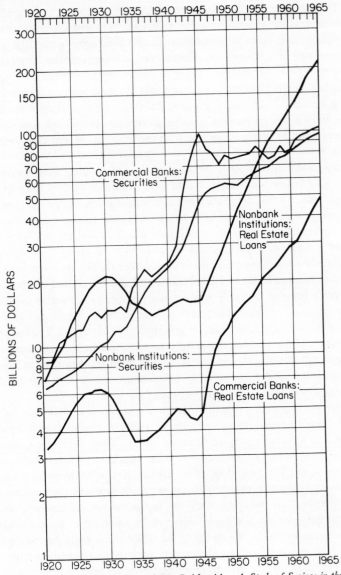

Sources: For 1920's, Raymond W. Goldsmith, *A Study of Savings in the United States,* Vol. I (Princeton: Princeton University Press, 1955; for 1950's and 1960's, *Federal Reserve Bulletin*).

Chart 6-2: Securities and real-estate loans of commercial banks and major nonbank credit institutions (mutual savings banks, savings and loan associations, and life insurance companies), 1920–1965.

Sales finance companies deal with other businesses, not with the public. They buy (rediscount) consumers' installment contracts from auto and appliance dealers to provide these merchants with cash. They thereby increase the liquidity of the dealers. Sales finance companies acquire the funds they need to purchase consumers' IOU's by borrowing from banks or by issuing their own IOU's in the money market. These IOU's are popular with large corporations that have a temporary surplus of cash and would like to put that cash to work. They are a species of cash substitute, but in lumps too large to be popular with the general public.

Specialization in the financial system.   Each of the nonbank institutions we have discussed tends to specialize in a particular type of lending. The credit unions and sales finance companies mainly finance consumer purchases of durable goods—automobiles and appliances. This helps to explain their rapid postwar growth; the 1950's and 1960's have witnessed an enormous expansion of consumer credit. The major nonbank institutions tend to specialize in mortgage lending. They share this specialty with the commercial banks, but the statistics in Table 6-1 suggest that they are more heavily committed to mortgage lending than the banks. Their mortgage loans are a much larger fraction of their total earning assets.

The tendency toward specialization among the major lenders is comparatively recent. The data in Chart 6-2 indicate that the mortgage loans of the nonbank institutions moved parallel to those of the commercial banks until World War II. Only in the postwar years did the real-estate loans of the banks lag behind.

The same chart indicates another difference between the major nonbank credit institutions and the commercial banks. In the 1920's and 1930's, the two groups' securities holdings moved together. In the 1950's, the securities holdings of commercial banks declined, while those of the nonbank institutions continued to rise. From 1960 to 1965 the two series again moved together as both commercial banks and nonbank institutions increased their holdings of securities.

The commercial banks reduced their holdings of government bonds by more than they increased their holdings of corporate securities, while the nonbank institutions increased their holdings of private securities by more than they reduced their holdings of governments. From the end of 1947 to the end of 1966, the commercial banks ran down their holdings of governments by some $15 billion, and increased their holdings of other securities by only $14 billion. The nonbank institutions, by contrast, cut their holdings of governments by $15 billion, as they increased their holdings of other securities by $58 billion.

In effect, the commercial banks have served the financial needs of business mainly by lending, while the nonbank credit institutions have done so mainly by purchasing securities. The nonbank credit institutions have not neglected business needs in their concentration upon mortgage finance, but have preferred to finance business indirectly via securities purchases.

These differences in asset structure are reflected in the several institutions' attitudes toward asset maturity. The commercial banks concentrate more upon short-term government securities primarily because their liabilities are more volatile, but also because the banks' lending to business provides the banks with assets that are not as easily marketed as are the business obligations held by the nonbank credit institutions. The banks compensate for this loss of liquidity by holding more short-term government securities.

Nonbank credit institutions and deposit creation. The nonbank credit institutions can supply consumers and business with additional funds and so may give an additional fillip to inflationary trends. In addition, they may increase the liquidity of the public, for the debts they issue can serve some households and businesses as money substitutes. This can promote consumer and business spending and may thereby add to inflationary pressures.

In Chapter 1, we segregated commercial banks from other credit institutions precisely because they can, as a group, create deposits. We are now in a position to see why other credit institutions cannot do so.

Suppose that the Mr. Newaire of our earlier example in Chapter 4 were to transfer $1,000 from his checking account to a savings account at the Thrifty Savings Bank. He would draw a check upon his account at the Nearest National and deposit that check at the savings bank. The Thrifty Savings Bank, in turn, would deposit Mr. Newaire's check in its account at a commercial bank.

At this point, the Thrifty Savings Bank would be in possession of additional reserves—its deposit of $1,000 in a commercial bank. Moreover, it would have excess reserves; neither law nor custom require that it hold $1,000 as a reserve against Mr. Newaire's enlarged account. If, for example, it normally held a reserve equal to 10 per cent of its deposit liabilities, Thrifty Savings would have $900 to lend.

When, therefore, a Mr. Jones comes in to borrow $900 with which to renovate his house, Thrifty Savings can lend him money. It will draw a check upon its account at the commercial bank and Mr. Jones will use that check to buy building materials for his house. The building supplies company, in turn, will deposit the check in its account at another commercial bank. At this point, the total of loans outstanding, by commercial and savings banks combined, has risen by $900. But there has been no increase in the total of demand deposits. Mr. Newaire's checking account is lower by $1,000, but Thrifty Savings' has risen by $100 and the building supplies dealer has an additional $900. There has been an increase of savings accounts (time deposits), but no multiple expansion. This is because Thrifty Savings has no more reserves to lend, nor has any other savings bank.

What distinguishes this case from the one we considered in Chapter 4? In the previous example, there was a multiple expansion of deposits because the deposits created by each loan were passed along to another commercial bank, along with an equal amount of reserves. In this example, there was no chain of lending because the proceeds of the first loan were deposited in a commercial bank, not in a savings bank. Hence the excess reserves of savings banks, as a group, were dissipated.[12]

Had the building supplies dealer deposited Thrifty Savings' check at another savings bank, that savings bank would have obtained Thrifty Savings' balance at the commercial bank and would have lent out another $810 ($900 less $90 as a reserve against its new deposit liability). But the building supplies dealer would not normally put its cash into a savings bank, for it must rebuild its inventories of building materials, and for this purpose it needs a checking account from which it can make payments.

We return to the statement made in Chapter 1. The commercial banks differ from other credit institutions because their deposit liabilities are a means of payment—they are money. In consequence, the deposits they create remain within the commercial banking system; apart from a small leakage into currency, they merely circulate from one commercial bank to another. The liabilities of savings banks and other credit institutions are not used as money. When a savings bank makes a loan, the savings banks as a group must lose reserves to virtually the full amount lent.

If Mr. Newaire had deposited his late aunt's nest egg directly into a savings bank, a multiple creation of deposits might have ensued, but not among the savings banks! The savings bank would have deposited that currency at a commercial bank, and the commercial bank would have begun the chain of lending we described before. At the very first step, the savings bank would have dropped out of the process.

To summarize, the savings banks can supply credit to business, but only in an amount equal to the increase of their deposit liabilities (less additional required reserves). The commercial banks can supply credit and create deposits in a multiple of any initial injection of reserves. If the central bank did not control the supply of money, the commercial banks might be prepared to "manufacture" it in whatever quantities the nonbank credit institutions desired. Because the central bank *does* control the quantity of money, it does have indirect control over the supply of funds to nonbank lenders. With the stock of money fixed, the nonbank credit institutions can secure extra funds only by persuading the holders of cash to accept money substitutes.

Furthermore, an increase in the resources of the nonbank credit institutions does not permit a large expansion of total lending. In a 1959 article, Warren L. Smith has shown that if the financial system is "loaned up" to start, a shift

---

[12]This case is analogous to a 100 per cent leakage of currency from the commercial banks. Were there such a leakage, q in our formula would approach infinity, as q is C/D and D would approach zero. But q appears in the numerator and denominator of our deposit-creation ratio. Hence that ratio would approach unity.

of $100 from a demand deposit at a commercial bank to an insurance policy or savings and loan share can only cause $68 of extra lending. A shift from a time deposit at a commercial bank to a savings and loan share can only cause a $13 increase of lending.[13]

Despite these arguments, the question of control is not yet closed. We may still have need for direct controls over the nonbank lenders, and must return to this issue later on.

Credit Institutions, Financial Markets, and Claims on Wealth

Direct and indirect ownership. The "real wealth" of the United States consists of buildings, machinery, railways, stocks of finished and unfinished goods, houses, automobiles, clothes, and so forth. These goods have owners— and by owners we mean *people*. But if you examine an inventory of the real wealth in a particular town or state, you will find that title to most of it is held by business corporations rather than by individuals. If you ask people what they own, you will find that their most important forms of property are "paper wealth"—stocks, bonds, and other *claims*. This pattern indicates that people own things indirectly—*through* the corporations whose stocks or bonds they own. Corporations are not *ultimate* owners of wealth. When we set up an accounting system to measure national wealth,[14] we treat corporations as having zero net wealth—offsetting their physical wealth and claims against the claims of their owners and creditors. We treat all wealth as directly or indirectly owned by individuals, except wealth owned by government bodies and nonprofit organizations—on which particular individuals do not have distinguishable claims.

The layering of claims. The structure of claims upon wealth is *layered:* claims rest not only on physical wealth but also on other claims. This is conspicuously true of credit institutions, which have claims (chiefly debts) as their assets, supporting a roughly equal amount of debts owned by bank depositors and other creditors.

This is not the only example of layering. A large proportion of bank deposits (of debt claims upon banks) is owned by business corporations—introducing at least one more layer between the banker and the individuals who "ultimately" own corporations. Furthermore, corporations own each other in various patterns.

---

[13]Warren L. Smith, "Financial Intermediaries and Monetary Controls," *Quarterly Journal of Economics,* LXXIII, no. 4 (November 1959), p. 540. Smith assumes that demand deposits are subject to an 18 per cent reserve requirement, that time deposits are subject to a 4 per cent requirement, and that nonbank credit institutions are also subject to a 4 per cent requirement. He assumes a currency drain of 10 per cent.

[14]See A. G. Hart, "The Structure of Claims" in *Studies in Income and Wealth,* Vol. XIV (New York: National Bureau of Economic Research, 1951).

Some corporations are wholly owned by other corporations; some corporations have as assets nothing but claims on other corporations.[15]

Layering takes forms that make it hard to use any simple image. One is tempted to describe the claims structure as a "superstructure" on physical wealth taken as "base," but the interplay of claims is so complex that even this is awkward. Both debt and stock-ownership claims can be traced around circles— Company *A* being partly owned by Company *B*, which is partly owned by Company *C*, which, in turn, is partly owned by Company *A*. Individuals are also involved in several ways. A person cannot be owned by a corporation, since slavery is prohibited, but he can be in debt to a corporation. The structure of debts is a series of criss-cross threads linking all types of economic units (households, business firms, credit institutions, and federal, state, and local governments) in all possible combinations. The structure of residual-ownership claims is almost as complex.

Markets in assets.   The layering of claims enables claims on wealth to take on values separate from the wealth itself. The market value of the bonds and shares of a corporation may be larger or smaller than the value of the actual productive wealth (plus claims on others) held by that corporation. These separate valuations are developed in the markets for claims, which are distinct from the markets for physical assets and are often more perfect. Both bonds (debt claims) and stocks ("equity," or residual-ownership claims) may have such markets, and are in fact traded on the New York Stock Exchange and on secondary stock exchanges in other leading cities.

Such a market adds to the moneyness of debts in the balance sheet of the creditor. The holder of bonds with a strong market has two strings to his bow where the holder of unlisted bonds has only one: he has the possibility of selling the bonds before payment comes due, in addition to the debtor's promise of eventual repayment.

The same is true of stocks, albeit in lesser degree. They also take on "shiftability" when there is an active market. Moneyness, however, also calls for confidence about future prices—and the prices of shares of stock are uncertain.

At the very least, presence of an organized market gives the security-holder assured borrowing power, which is nearly as good as cash in the bank. If he owns listed securities, he can count on being able to borrow a good fraction of their market value.[16] A market always gives moneyness to assets in this indirect way.

---

[15]It would even be possible—but not very useful—to set up a cluster of corporations that would own each other reciprocally without any real persons owning claims on any of the cluster. (A few individuals would of course have to own "qualifying shares" to make them eligible as directors, but such holdings can be trifles.) This would make trouble in tracing the ownership of real wealth to "ultimate" owners.

[16]Federal Reserve regulations may limit (or reduce to zero) the owner's ability to borrow "for the purpose of purchasing or carrying securities." But his securities are still available to reinforce his claim to borrow for other "purposes." Actually, most loans based on stock-exchange collateral are apparently for other "purposes."

Whether this added liquidity for stockholders is good or bad is debatable. Marketability makes people more willing to hold shares in corporations and thus smooths the way for the financing of new business. However, this kind of liquidity is artificial and unstable and may make the economic system vulnerable to financial shocks. There is sense in both arguments.

Financing the growth of wealth: investment banking. The structure of claims has a great deal to do with the way a country finances the growth of wealth. The producers of new machinery, factories, transport equipment, office buildings, and housing depend on financing for their markets.

Commercial banking has a hand in this process. An expanding firm can get bank loans to help it grow. A builder can borrow to finance the buildings he has under construction. But the traditions of commercial banking in the English-speaking countries[17] bar commercial banks from putting funds permanently into business, except to a limited extent by taking its bonds.

Economic growth can also be financed by the nonbank credit institutions, notably by life insurance companies. An insurance company can make large permanent investments in bonds, and may also invest in housing projects on its own account. But even today there are large areas that these institutions do not reach: they do not provide "equity money" through purchases of stock,[18] and every business sets limits of prudence to its borrowing.

This "equity" gap has been filled by "investment banking." Certain financial firms have specialized in "underwriting" new securities. A company that wants to get funds for a new plant by selling bonds or stocks can sell them to an investment banker or to a "syndicate" of investment bankers acting jointly. The investment banker then sends out salesmen and retails the issue to individuals and companies with funds to invest.[19] The Stock Exchange also figures in this process of "floating" an issue. Securities that are listed on the Exchange attract the retail buyers, for they can more easily sell an issue if it is listed. If some investors change their minds about the securities while they are being marketed, the "underwriters" buy up the reflux.

Finally, the financing of growth has traditionally depended on individual investors and, to some extent, investment trusts who offer "risk capital." The rank and file of security-holders always prefer "seasoned" securities—securities which have been outstanding long enough to accumulate a good price and earnings record. The buyers of the more risky new issues have mainly been a specialized group of wealthy men with wide business connections, willing to bet

---

[17]On the Continent of Europe, and especially in Germany, bankers did not feel so limited. They were free to make large permanent investments and exercise continuing control. Thus, "commercial banking" and "investment banking" did not split apart as they did in the United States.

[18]Life insurance companies are now authorized to buy limited amounts of stocks, but have begun cautiously.

[19]Companies with very good reputations can often put out new securities by way of the stock market by the device of issuing "rights" to holders of their securities already outstanding. This device was very popular in the 1920's, and has been again since World War II.

heavily on their business judgment. When the business behind a security issue succeeds and the securities rise in price, there is a process of "secondary distribution"—the specialized holders pass the now seasoned securities along to rank-and-file investors. Financiers can also profit by backing new and small firms that are not at the stage where they could get capital by floating securities, until they reach the stage for an open-market flotation.

Debts and liquidity.   Our discussion of economic growth and of new securities issues should again remind us that the growth of debt is a counterpart of economic growth. An increase of business borrowing often brings about an increase of consumer and business liquidity. It is this aspect of debt that really matters.

Alarmists about debt often point out that our total debts exceed our real wealth and suggest that we are "bankrupt." This is a statistical mirage produced by layering. The mere volume of debt is a meaningless aggregate. Yet we cannot cancel each debt against the assets that match it. The effect of a debt on the creditor cannot be measured simply by putting a minus sign in front of the effect on the debtor. The importance of debt lies not in its amount but in its *structure*—who owes whom, how much, and on what terms.

When debtor and creditor are the same sort of economic unit—both households, both business firms, or both banks—the existence of marketable debt may slightly increase the liquidity of the community. The prospect of collecting from the debtor will have a favorable effect on the creditor's liquidity that will be about as intense as the unfavorable effect on the debtor's liquidity.[20] But the creditor enjoys another dimension of liquidity: he can sell his bond on the market.

When a credit institution is the lender, the liquidity of the general public (excluding credit institutions) is even more markedly affected. If a bank buys part of a new bond issue, the negative effect of new long-term debt on the liquidity of the issuing firm is far outweighed by the positive effect of the newly created bank deposits the firm gets in exchange. If an individual saver buys savings and loan shares and the savings and loan association buys a mortgage, the saver is more liquid (and the mortgage borrower no less liquid) than if the saver had bought the mortgage directly. When a loan is short term, the borrower's loss of liquidity goes further toward offsetting his gain. Even here, a net increase of liquidity may be expected.

Transactions between governments and households can also change the public's liquidity. If the public's holdings of government debt are changed by a surplus or deficit in the budget, there will be a strong effect on the public's liquidity.[21] As the government debt rises in a period of deficits, alarmists try to frighten us by quoting the surprisingly large government debt per person or

---

[20]This assumes that both creditor and debtor take for granted that the debtor can and will pay.

[21]On government surplus or deficit as an open-market operation, see Chapter 5, "Treasury Open-Market Operations."

per family. Here again they wrongly emphasize the sheer size of debt. Private households, or firms, do not have to pay the government debt. At most, they may have to pay higher taxes to cover debt service. What worries the economist about the national debt is not that it makes the nation poor, but that it makes individuals more liquid and thereby gives an inflationary stimulus to spending.

Liquidity effects of makeup and prices of government debt. The moneyness of various types of government debt varies along a scale running from almost complete moneyness downward. Savings bonds and short-term marketable issues (Treasury bills and certificates) are at the money end of the scale. Long-term nonmarketable Treasury bonds are at the nonmoney end.

The moneyness of these assets—our ability to use them to pay off debts when we want to do so—depends on their terms of redemption and also on their market. Savings bonds can be redeemed as readily as time deposits can be withdrawn, and have the same degree of moneyness as time deposits. Short-term marketable issues will be redeemed by the Treasury in the near future, and, in addition, can be sold immediately at prices that do not vary widely. Long-term bonds gain little moneyness from their eventual repayment dates (which may be decades ahead), but a good deal from their markets, on which sudden fluctuations rarely exceed 5 per cent.

The contribution of these assets to the liquidity of investors may be low, despite their moneyness.[22] These assets offer prospects of interest income and sometimes of capital gains. In addition, they may be earmarked for specific future uses. A household may have an envelope of savings bonds held specifically for a child's college education, or as the nucleus of a home-building fund.[23] A firm may hold Treasury bills specifically to meet corporation income taxes when they become payable. A company-union trust fund for employees' retirement may work under rules which require that all its assets be in federal securities. These reasons for holding liquid assets often submerge the desire for liquidity itself, and the net contribution to liquidity of privately held government securities may be much smaller than one might suppose from the fact that the total mass held nearly equals the stock of money.

Liquid asset creation. Liquid asset creation depends upon the distribution of surpluses and deficits among spending units—households, firms, and government in its capacity as a buyer of goods and services—and upon the activities

---

[22]*Note on terminology:* This fact, we have said before, is one of the main reasons for using *both* "moneyness" and "liquidity" as technical terms in this book. The test of an asset's moneyness is the holder's confidence that he can cash it at a predictable value if he needs to pay off debts. The test of an asset's contribution to liquidity is whether its possession has much the same effects on the holder's *willingness to spend* as would possession of the same amount of checking deposits or currency. As among assets, moneyness and contribution to liquidity seem ordinarily to differ in the same direction, but not in the same degree.

[23]Paper money is also earmarked sometimes for near-future uses. A wage-earning family is apt to have an inviolable envelope of "rent money." But long-term earmarked funds are normally in time deposits, savings bonds, and the like.

of credit institutions and the government in its capacity as a monetary institution. In a simple economy consisting of two households with a fixed stock of money, the creation of liquid assets would depend upon the distribution of income between them as compared with their spending plans. If one household wished to spend a dollar more than it earned and the other wished to spend a dollar less than it earned, the "deficit" household could borrow from the "surplus" household. One dollar of debt would be created for each dollar of "excess spending" by the deficit household (or for each dollar of "saving" by the surplus household). This debt might be a long-term bond or a liquid asset.

In a more complex economy, the creation of debt might exceed the total of "excess spending." If the deficit household borrowed from a savings bank which, in turn, obtained loanable funds by persuading the surplus household to deposit its savings in the savings bank, two dollars of debt would be created for every dollar of excess spending. A dollar of consumer debt would be created by each dollar of "excess spending," and a dollar of savings-bank debts (savings deposits) would also be created. A dollar's worth of liquid assets would be generated by each dollar of "excess spending," along with each dollar's worth of long-term consumer debt. We could extend this argument by layering debt still more. The deficit household could borrow from a consumer finance company which, in turn, could borrow from the savings bank, which, in its turn, could raise funds from the surplus household. Three species of debt would now be generated—the long-term debt of the deficit household, the IOU of the consumer finance company, and the debts (deposit liabilities) of the savings bank. The savings bank and finance company debts might both qualify as liquid assets.[24]

The arithmetic of liquid-asset creation, like the arithmetic of deposit creation, can be expressed in terms of "sources and uses." But we may be hard pressed to interpret a sum of heterogeneous liquid assets, each taken at face value. The effect of debt creation on the public's liquidity will depend on the composition and prices of the liquid assets involved. Besides, the debts that make negative contributions to liquidity must also be taken into account.

The arithmetic of liquid-asset creation can be seen very clearly in war experience. Figures are given in Table 6–2. From June 1939 to June 1945, the public's liquid assets grew by $175 billion—including $78 billion of cash, $81 billion of United States government securities, and $16 billion of claims of life insurance companies and savings and loan associations. Down to the end of 1941—before we entered the war—only half of the growth of liquid assets arose from the cash deficit. A quarter came from expansion of earning assets at credit institutions; a quarter, from gold imports and shifts in Treasury currency accounts. During the war, *all* of the growth in liquid assets derived from

---

[24]Even more elaborate models of this kind are developed by John G. Gurley and Edward S. Shaw in *Money in a Theory of Finance* (Washington, D.C.: The Brookings Institution, 1960), Ch. IV.

TABLE 6-2

CREATION OF LIQUID ASSETS DURING WORLD WAR II

(billions, rounded to nearest $0.1 billion)*

Sources and Types of Liquid Assets	Amounts on the Books		
	June 30, 1939	Dec. 31, 1941	June 30, 1945
Sources of liquid assets			
1. Federal government finances:			
a. Initial debt to credit institutions and the public	$36.9	$36.9	$36.9
b. Cumulative excess of Treasury cash outgo over cash income**	0.0	14.4	171.4
	$36.9	$51.3	$208.3
2. Credit-institution assets other than United States securities:			
a. Commercial banks, net†	$17.0	$20.9	$19.4
b. Mutual savings banks	7.2	6.7	5.6
c. Life-insurance, net‡	16.8	19.3	17.0
d. Savings and loan associations, net^a	4.3	4.9	4.9
	$45.3	$51.8	$46.9
3. Monetary sources proper:			
a. Gold stock	$16.1	$22.7	$20.3
b. Treasury currency, net^b	0.3	1.0	1.9
	$16.4	$23.7	$22.2
Total sources	$98.6	$126.8	$277.4
Holdings of liquid assets by individuals, state and local governments, and corporations other than credit institutions			
4. Currency outside banks plus commercial-bank deposits:			
a. Total	$48.5	$64.5	$121.3
b. *Less* life insurance and savings and loan cash^c	−1.1	−1.2	−1.1
	$47.4	$63.3	$120.2
5. Deposits in mutual savings banks and Postal Savings	$11.7	$11.9	$17.1
6. United States government securities^d	13.6	20.1	94.5
7. Life insurance cash values^e	21.7	26.1	35.2
8. Savings and loan shares, net^f	4.0	4.6	6.8
Total liquid assets, face value	$98.4	$126.0	$273.8

*Discrepancy of totals reflects use of divergent sources of figures, and omission of some minor sources.

**From *Treasury Bulletin*.

†Loans, nongovernment bonds, miscellaneous assets, *less* miscellaneous liabilities and bank capital funds. From *Federal Reserve Bulletin*.

‡Bonds other than United States government, *plus* stocks owned, mortgages and real estate, miscellaneous assets, *less* surplus. December 31 figures of the Spectator Company, interpolated for June 30 with aid of monthly figures for major companies in *Survey of Current Business*.

the Treasury's $171 billion cash deficit. The other influences that had acted to generate liquid assets worked in reverse so that the growth of liquid assets was slightly smaller than the cash deficit itself. At the end of the war, the credit institutions' earning-asset account was near its 1939 level. Since this account is a mirror image of the public's debts to credit institutions, there was virtually no increase in negative liquidity (debts of households and firms) to offset the growth of positive liquidity.

The proportions in which the public bought the different types of assets represented the free choice of investors, under a "pattern" of prices set by Treasury policy. If the public had chosen to hold fewer government securities and more cash, it could have done so, but the Federal Reserve System and the commercial banks would have had to buy more government securities.

A longer history of liquid-asset creation was presented in Chart 6–1. Chart 6–3 attempts to collate those materials and adds data on government debt to present a composite history of gross liquidity.

The bottom-most series in Chart 6–3 (M-2) is an estimate of the public's money holdings (currency outside banks *plus* net demand deposits). This series rose in each of the two world wars, but especially during World War II. It was the basis for an enormous expansion of liquidity during that war. The next series (L-5) adds the public's holdings of certain near-moneys (time deposits at commercial and mutual savings banks *plus* savings and loan shares). These additional assets varied in moneyness during the years described. In the 1920's the savings and loan associations redeemed shares on demand; during the 1930's there were long delays before redemption. On the whole, the items added by series L-5 are the liquid assets nearet to cash in moneyness. Series L-5A attaches the government's savings bonds to our liquid assets estimate. These bonds, issued after 1934, are as near to money as time deposits; they can be redeemed at will. Note that this addition gives the liquid assets series a considerable fillip during the war.

During the 1920's and the 1930's, the cash series (M-2) and the cash-plus-near-moneys series (L-5) moved together; fluctuations in cash holdings dominated changes in gross liquidity. After World War II, the increase of near moneys was faster, raising L-5 and L-5A at a more rapid clip than M-2. This faster growth of L-5 reflects the extraordinary expansion of savings and loan associations (see Chart 6–1).

---

[a]Mortgage loans, net of pledged shares, *plus* miscellaneous assets, *less* "general reserves and surplus." December 31 figures from series for "all operating associations" in *Statistical Abstract of the United States,* interpolated for June 30.

[b]Treasury currency outstanding *less* money in Treasury, from *Federal Reserve Bulletin.*

[c]Same sources indicated in notes ‡ and *a*.

[d]*Treasury Bulletin* estimate of holdings by "individuals," "state and local governments," and "other corporations and associations," *less* an estimate of savings and loan holdings and *plus* an estimate for holdings of insurance companies other than life.

[e]Reserves *plus* dividends left to accumulate, *less* policy loans and deferred premiums. Same source indicated in note ‡.

[f]"Free shares" only, not including pledged shares. Same source indicated in note *a*.

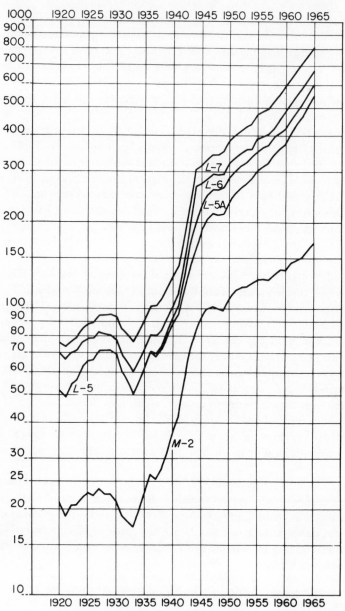

GROWTH OF THE PUBLIC'S GROSS LIQUIDITY, 1920–65
Sources: See Appendix.
Chart 6-3: Growth of the public's gross liquidity, 1920–1965.

The next two series, *L*–6 and *L*–7, add additional liquid assets to the total. *L*–6 includes marketable government bonds; *L*–7 includes government bonds and savings through life insurance. Note that these series move parallel to *L*–5 and *L*–5*A* after World War II. Apparently the increase of government debt and of life insurance policies outstanding did not accelerate the growth of gross liquidity.

The estimates of gross liquidity in Chart 6–3 are far from perfect. First, they treat each asset as having the same moneyness per dollar outstanding. An accurate estimate of liquidity would weight each asset by some index of its contribution to liquidity, given the highest weight to currency and demand deposits, somewhat lower weights to the other series in *L*–5*A*, and the lowest weight to marketable government bonds and life insurance policies. A weighted estimate, moreover, would probably split government bonds into short-term and long-term issues, assigning a greater weight to the former. Finally, it would probably include other assets that have somewhat less moneyness—corporate bonds and common stock.[25] It is difficult to choose the right weights, because certain assets deserve more weight at one time than at others. Savings and loan shares, for example, should receive a smaller weight in the 1930's than in the 1920's, and government securities a higher weight in the 1940's than in the 1950's and 1960's because their prices were fixed in the 1940's but free to fluctuate in the 1950's and 1960's.

An additional difficulty arises with the series in Chart 6–3. These are estimates of gross liquidity; they make no allowance for the negative effects of business and consumer debt. Yet growth in that debt is one cause of the increase in gross liquidity. The increase of liquidity has generated its own partial counterweight. This has been especially true of peacetime periods when private borrowing generated much of the increase in cash and near moneys. Again it is difficult to decide what weights we should give each species of debt. We have already argued that private borrowing has a positive net effect on liquidity—the increase of liquid assets raises liquidity more than the increase of debt that is its counterpart. But it is difficult to know by how much.

NOTES ON

ALTERNATIVE POINTS OF VIEW

AND SUPPLEMENTARY READINGS

On the growth of credit institutions in the twentieth century, see Raymond W. Goldsmith, *Financial Intermediaries in the American Economy Since 1900* (Princeton: Princeton University Press, 1958). For a theoretical analysis that assigns much importance to them, see John G. Gurley and Edward S. Shaw, *Money in a Theory of Finance* (Washington, D.C.: The Brookings Institution, 1960).

---

[25]An earlier edition of this book made an attempt at weighting (2nd ed., pp. 135–37).

A comparison between the credit-creation functions of banks and other financial intermediaries is found in James Tobin's article "Commercial Banks as Creators of Money," *Banking and Monetary Studies,* Deane Carson, ed. (Homewood, Ill.: Richard D. Irwin, Inc., 1963), pp. 408–19.

The following monographs prepared for the Commission on Money and Credit are studies of the structure and function of the major financial intermediaries: *Mutual Savings Banking, The Savings and Loan Business, and Life Insurance Companies as Financial Institutions.* All were published by Prentice-Hall, Inc. (Englewood Cliffs, N.J., 1962). Additional up-to-date information can be found in the annually published *Mutual Savings Banking National Fact Book* (National Association of Mutual Savings Banks, New York), *Savings and Loan Fact Book* (United States Savings and Loan League, Chicago), and the *Life Insurance Fact Book* (Institute of Life Insurance, New York).

Chapter 7

The Structure of
Credit Controls

The Quantity and Quality of Credit

The controls we have imposed on financial institutions have evolved over a century and bear witness to the wide range of monetary problems the United States has encountered. In essence they are of two kinds. First, we have controls over the quantity of money. They are based upon the attempts to make money behave so as to promote prosperity and limit economic instability. Administered by the Federal Reserve System through its efforts to affect commercial bank reserves, these controls were studied in Chapter 5.[1]

Second, we have controls over the quality of money and credit. These attempt to protect the holders of bank deposits and other liquid assets against a collapse of the institution to which they have entrusted their deposits. These controls are examined in this chapter.

---

[1] As we have seen in Chapter 5, the debts which the nonbank institutions issue are imperfect substitutes for money. They cannot be used as a means of payment and cannot always be exchanged for money as quickly (and cheaply) as the public desires. As a consequence, the nonbank institutions cannot acquire unlimited amounts of funds to lend, and their lending may be curtailed. Because the Federal Reserve controls the quantity of money, it does have indirect control over the supply of funds to nonbank lenders.

Origins of Control Agencies

The method of control.   Bank control does not consist in bossing banks around. Government agencies do not tell a bank to name Mr. X. Y. Z. Smith as vice-president,[2] how much to pay the first teller, or whether to make a loan to the Marginal Machine Works. Banks are left to decide all of their individual business transactions.

Bank control is influence, not dictatorship. Banks are usually subject to general prohibitions: they must not pay interest on checking deposits; they must not lend heavily to their own officers and directors; they must not buy speculative corporation stocks; they must not lend more to speculators on securities than allowed by the Federal Reserve "margin" rules; they must not engage in any branch of business apart from banking;[3] and so forth. Banks are also subject to general rules of positive action—notably the requirement that they keep minimum reserves. They are sometimes offered special incentives to do things that public policy desires. If, for example, they make loans to home-owners in a specified form, these loans will be "insured" by the Federal Housing Administration.

Early stages of control.   There have always been rules for banking and agencies to enforce them. Rules were laid down in bank charters, bank legislation, and court decisions from the beginning of banking in this country. These rules were chiefly reserve requirements and prohibitions on some types of transactions. The government enforced them by making bank examinations and by requiring banks to submit and publish statements of condition several times a year.

Until the Federal Reserve System was established in 1913, the law was merely concerned with guarding the "soundness" of bank loans, the legality of bank-note issues, and so forth. No one was empowered to ask whether banks were creating deposits on an excessive scale, or whether they were retiring deposits when that might accentuate a depression. From 1836 to 1913 the United States had no central bank. Furthermore, the "Independent Treasury System," es-

---

[2] During the middle 1930's, however, the Reconstruction Finance Corporation held large amounts of bank stocks and sometimes used its voting power at stockholders' meetings to choose bank directors and bank officers. Furthermore, the licensing of a bank to reopen after the "bank holiday" of 1933 was sometimes made conditional on the bank's willingness to replace officers whom the state or federal authorities thought unsatisfactory. Today, the Federal Deposit Insurance Corporation sometimes makes similar conditions for financial aid to shaky banks.

[3] Thus, a bank may rent safe-deposit boxes, but may not go into the business of insuring valuables that people keep in their own houses. If it has more space than it needs in the buildings where it does its deposit and loan business, it may rent offices to others; but it cannot simply build office buildings to rent. It should be mentioned, however, that a "one-bank holding company" seems legally to be able to own additional nonbank subsidiaries in a variety of activities.

tablished in 1846, was designed to disentangle government finance from banking. The Treasury was supposed to keep its own funds in Subtreasuries in gold (later, in greenbacks or silver), and to avoid contact with banks. But the "Independent Treasury System" actually forced the Treasury to worry about banking. The Treasury's receipts and outlays came in spurts, and when its cash went up, bank reserves of coin and paper money went down. The Treasury had to manage its affairs carefully to keep from wrecking the banks by jerking their reserves up and down. At crises, deputations of bankers were always on hand to suggest remedial measures to the Treasury. At best, however, the Treasury was only able to improvise remedies for the series of emergencies generated by this clumsy system.[4]

Control under the Federal Reserve, 1913–32. The founding of the Federal Reserve System put an end to the fiction that general monetary conditions were nobody's business. The Reserve Banks were made responsible for "sound credit conditions" and were supposed to work in co-operation with the Treasury. During World War I and into 1919, the Treasury dominated the partnership because of its need to float war loans, but after that the Federal Reserve System was the source of banking policy.

The Federal Reserve continued to use the old-fashioned controls—reserve requirements, taboos on certain types of assets, "calls" for statements of condition, and bank examinations. In addition, it began consciously to encourage the expansion or restriction of bank credit and to steer credit in desired directions. Still further, it attempted control by "moral suasion" and publicity—as when it tried to persuade banks not to finance the stock market boom in 1929.

New control agencies, 1932 onward. The Great Depression of the 1930's brought a further change in the extent and nature of controls over banking. Because it undermined the "soundness" of debts by lowering the prices of the underlying property and debtors' incomes, it precipitated a series of debt crises that led the government into rescue operations. New government agencies were created and old ones expanded, so that the system of bank control changed. The Reconstruction Finance Corporation (now defunct), farm loan agencies, and home loan agencies worked to strengthen bank assets. The Federal Deposit Insurance Corporation was established to guarantee the banks deposit liabilities, and combined with the RFC to restore public confidence in banking by rescuing many banks in difficulty.

Bank controls were not greatly affected by World War II. The partnership between Federal Reserve and Treasury remained at the center of the control system. The Treasury overshadowed the Federal Reserve during World War

---

[4] The law was forever placing the Treasury in a false position, and much of what it did to meet emergencies was of doubtful legality. On this side of monetary history, see Margaret G. Myers, *New York Money Market* (New York: Columbia University Press, 1931), Vol. I, chaps. IX and XVII.

II (as during World War I) because of the overwhelming importance of war finance; and through 1950, the Treasury's interest in a strong market for government securities took precedence over the Federal Reserve's desire to check credit expansion. But in 1951, the Federal Reserve regained pre-eminence in the partnership.

Controls over Bank Assets and Liabilities

Evolution of examination standards. Our system of bank examination evolved in response to sad experience in the early days of American banking. A banker who is immune from outside scrutiny of his books is open to temptations to which no individual should be subjected. Before supervision was effective, many bank failures arose from fraud or gross carelessness in bank management. Bank examination is meant to protect the depositor against such failures, by denying the banker temptation.

At the same time, bank examiners seek to keep banks "sound" in a broader sense. Even though no loss is imminent, an examiner may object to certain banking practices that deviate from accepted standards. This aspect of examination began as the mere application of traditional rules of thumb and of legal standards. It has developed as a way to promote prosperity and stability.

Examination machinery. Most of the work of bank examination is now done by three federal agencies. The Comptroller's office examines national banks, the Federal Reserve Banks examine state member banks, and the FDIC examines insured nonmember banks. These agencies confer once in a while to align their standards, and are increasingly inclined to talk openly about those standards.[5]

A "call date" is set at least four times a year on which banks have to turn in detailed statements of their assets and liabilities. In addition, examiners visit the individual banks at irregular intervals. These visits may last several days. The examiners check to see that the assets shown in the balance sheet really exist and correspond reasonably well to the balance sheet descriptions, and that the bank has obeyed the laws. They also "appraise" assets—that is, they classify them by type and quality and compare the bank's book value with standard valuations. Finally they draw up a report on the bank (including notes on the quality of management), which is sent to the supervisory agency and to the bank's officers and directors.[6] The examiners' visits are deliberately unpredict-

---

[5] During the deflation years of 1930–32, the framing of examination standards was a hush-hush affair. But a conference that was called in September 1934 to standardize procedures of examination at the birth of the FDIC led to public statements; and a 1938 conference led to a detailed public explanation of changes in standards in that year's FDIC, *Annual Report*.

[6] Bank examination procedure is sketched in more detail in Federal Reserve Board, *Banking Studies* (Washington, D.C.: U.S. Government Printing Office, 1941), pp. 219–27.

able in timing so as to find the bank operating normally. Ordinarily, however, an insured bank can expect to be examined at least once a year.

If the examiner's report shows anything out of order, the bank is expected to take corrective steps. If it does not act, the supervisory agency will make "recommendations for corrective action." A bank which has received such recommendations is put under surveillance; if it does not try to conform, it may lose its membership in the FDIC.

Appraisal of assets. Until shortly before World War II, the examiners were mainly interested in the liquidity of the individual bank. Loans which did not seem highly liquid were classified as "slow" or "doubtful." Bonds were chiefly judged by their "grade" as evaluated by the private companies that publish rating lists, and were usually valued "at cost or market, whichever is lower."

The 1938 agreement among the examining authorities involved a change of emphasis. The Board of Governors of the Federal Reserve System commented officially:

> The principle is clearly recognized that in making loans, whether for working capital or fixed capital purposes, the banks should be encouraged to place the emphasis upon intrinsic value rather than upon liquidity or quick maturity.
>
> Similarly, the revised examination procedure recognizes the principle that bank investments should be considered in the light of inherent soundness rather than on a basis of day-to-day market fluctuations.

Long-term loans are no longer discouraged, and loans are not criticized unless they involve a "substantial and unreasonable degree of risk to the bank." Bond grading continues, but, for all bonds rated as high as BAA, the bank's book value is accepted.[7] Low-grade bonds not in default are valued at market price—but at the average of prices in the last eighteen months rather than the day's price. Current market prices are used only for corporate stocks and bonds in default.

These changes serve to make banks less "cycle sensitive." They reflect the economists' belief that banks in the past have accentuated the ups and downs of production and prices. A business downswing downgraded assets, according to traditional examination standards, making them less "bankable." If business fell off, some outstanding loans became "slow," and banks were called upon to make special efforts to collect them and to avoid new loans that might prove "slow." If bond prices fell, and the rating agencies reclassified them, banks were called upon to sell bonds. Thus, a downswing of business put banks under pressure to contract credit and made a bad situation worse. On the other hand, an upswing of business made assets more "bankable" and encouraged the banks to expand credit, accentuating the upswing. The reform of bank examination

---

[7] If the bank has bought bonds at a premium over their face value, it must "amortize" the premium by writing off a uniform amount each year.

has largely removed these pressures insofar as they stemmed from standards used in bank supervision.

The bulk of bank assets are immune to criticism by the new standards. In 1939, only 5 per cent of assets of insured banks visited by bank examiners were criticized. In 1951, after several years of high income had improved the position of debtors and enabled banks to write down asset values, only $^4/_{10}$ of 1 per cent were criticized. In 1939, the examiners thought that a proper appraisal fell short of book value by only 0.6 per cent of total assets. By 1951, it was only 0.001 per cent.[8]

Selective asset controls. The great stock-market boom of the 1920's touched off a discussion of the need for "qualitative credit control" to keep bank loans from financing the boom. At that time the authorities merely applied "moral suasion" to inhibit such loans. But during the 1930's, the Federal Reserve Board was empowered to regulate "margin requirements" on security loans;[9] and during World War II, the Board was also empowered to regulate the terms of consumer installment buying. Both these powers were used to check inflation during the war. The installment-control powers, which had expired some years after the war, were revived to help combat the post-Korea inflation, but were allowed to lapse thereafter. In 1950, the Federal Reserve was authorized to regulate mortgages on new homes and used this power briefly.

These regulations do not directly affect the *amount* of loans extended, but rather the *terms* given to a borrower. The regulations on security loans fix the "down payment" an investor must make on securities, setting that minimum cash "margin" as a percentage of the value of the securities that are to be bought or carried with the aid of loans. When the margin required is 100 per cent, new security loans are, in effect, prohibited. These controls apply to nonbank lenders as well as to banks, but do not apply to loans on government securities. The consumer credit controls also fixed a minimum "down payment," and specified the maximum number of months over which the remainder of the price might be spread, and how soon department stores must stop giving credit to customers who did not pay past bills. These sets of requirements applied chiefly to nonbank lenders and only incidentally to banks. Mortgage controls also fixed the minimum down payment and the time allowed to retire the loan, and applied to all classes of lenders.

When we appraise selective controls, we should include the weak but broad influence that examination standards and "moral suasion" exert upon the banks' choice of assets, as well as the firm but narrow influence of direct controls. We must also remember that a particular loan may be extended under any one of many labels and that the seepage of funds from one part of the credit market

---

[8] Data from FDIC, *Annual Report* (for 1945, pp. 122–23; for 1951, pp. 154–55).
[9] See above, Chapter 3, footnote 25.

to another can be large.[10] Selective controls may be unable to limit the scale of lending and may be equally impotent in diverting bank funds from specific areas.[11]

Early controls over bank liabilities. As we have seen, the Great Depression eroded the quality of many debts that had been considered sound in 1929. Because debtors could not pay them off out of income, nor settle them by selling off property pledged as security, bank credit was "frozen." Banks could not collect from many of their debtors, and the corporate bonds they held (the long-term debts of railways, electric power companies, and so forth) fell in market price.

When depositors tried to withdraw funds from a bank, the bank could not always get enough cash from its bond holdings and loans to meet the withdrawals. The bank had to "suspend payments": it closed its doors and ceased to pay checks over the counter or through the clearinghouse.[12] Bank suspensions began on a serious scale late in 1929, and continued with occasional breathing spells into 1933.

Chiefly in hopes of stopping the bank crisis, the federal government established the Reconstruction Finance Corporation early in 1932. The RFC was to help the banks directly by lending them needed cash, and indirectly by safeguarding their railway bonds.[13]

The RFC took hold hard. By the end of 1932, it had outstanding loans of nearly $600 million to banks and $275 million to railways. Its direct loans helped banks face "runs" and doubtless dissuaded many depositors from turning their bank balances into hoarded paper money.[14] Its loans to railways enabled them to pay interest and principal on their bonds as they came due. This eased

---

[10]For example, a loan to finance stock-market speculation may be "secured" by real estate.

[11]The apparent success of installment credit control in sharply reducing consumer loans during World War II needs careful interpretation. One should remember that the supply of new consumer durables (especially automobiles and electrical appliances) was cut off, so that, as consumers paid off their existing debts, they were not taking on new ones in the normal way.

[12]After suspension, a bank was sometimes able to rally its forces and reopen—often with help from stockholders or from other banks. Sometimes the suspended bank (or a bank threatened with suspension) would be absorbed by another bank that would take over its deposit liabilities and its assets. If it could not reopen or arrange a merger, a suspended bank had to go into liquidation. A receiver was appointed, who had the job of getting cash for the bank's assets and paying it out to depositors in the form of "dividends" on deposits tied up.

[13]The operations described here were by no means the whole job of the RFC, which was the financial Pooh-Bah of the Depression and World War II. The RFC distributed $500 million of relief money to the states in 1932–33, for instance, and had an important voice in locating new factories during World War II. It is now defunct.

[14]The characteristic attitude of the bank depositor in a panic is summed up in the story of the depositor who got a bank vice-president on the phone, one morning when the lines at the tellers' windows were so long they stretched out the doors onto the sidewalk. What the depositor wanted to know was this: "Can I get my money if I come in for it? Because if I can I don't want it, but if I can't, then I do!" Assurance that the bank had plenty of currency on hand could ordinarily stop a run.

the panic that was pushing down bond prices on the New York Stock Exchange, so that railway bonds were more "liquid" in the eyes of bankers and bank examiners.

On the upswing after the bank holiday, the RFC helped clear away the wreckage. It made large loans to bank receivers with which they could speed up payments to depositors in closed banks. At their peak, late in 1934, these loans were over $400 million.

The Federal Deposit Insurance Corporation. The RFC was mainly occupied with remedial work. It did not prevent the banking crisis, nor was it designed to do so. The government had decided on a different way to prevent the recurrence of "runs" on banks. The Banking Act passed in June 1933 set up the Federal Deposit Insurance Corporation with government capital. A "temporary insurance fund" went into operation at the beginning of 1934, and was superseded in September 1935 by a permanent fund.

If an insured bank is forced to suspend payments, the FDIC provides for a quick repayment of insured deposits. Each depositor is insured up to $15,000, and joint accounts to $30,000. The FDIC also acts as the receiver for insured banks in liquidation. The claims of depositors, in excess of their insurance, and the claims of the FDIC on account of insured deposits paid are both met to the highest percentage possible by a sale of the failed bank's assets.[15] The banks must pay for deposit insurance, $1/12$ of 1 per cent of insured deposits. The FDIC's receipts from this assessment have very much exceeded its small losses.[16] Under the Federal Deposit Insurance Act of 1950, therefore, provision was made for returning to the banks 60 per cent of each year's *net* assessment—that is, the excess of the assessment over losses and administrative costs.

The main importance of the FDIC is the assurance against loss it has given to depositors, not the losses it has absorbed. The very existence of the FDIC gives almost complete moneyness to deposits in insured banks. Only very large depositors need to worry at all about the danger of loss through bank failures, and they have had practically no losses. The FDIC does not make bank failures technically impossible. A few banks have failed under it, and more will do so. Failures could conceivably be so heavy as to tie up the FDIC's surplus in its claims against banks in receivership. The FDIC would then be unable to pay depositors without help from the Treasury or Federal Reserve banks. But it is a moral certainty that any help which the FDIC needs from the Treasury or Federal Reserve will be forthcoming. The law does not require the Treasury

---

[15]The Banking Act of 1935 set up the general pattern under which the FDIC has operated since then. The FDIC's supervisory functions were discussed earlier in this chapter.

[16]Over the period from the organization of FDIC through 1965, deposit insurance assessments have added up to a cumulative total of over $2.1 billion—even after "crediting" back to insured banks over half of the amount assessed since 1950. The cumulative total of FDIC losses (including expenses of receiverships and contributions where weakened banks were taken over by others) was only $42 million, and the cumulative total of administrative and operating expenses (including bank examinations) was only $234 million. See FDIC, *Annual Report*, 1965, p. 30.

or the Federal Reserve to act in such a crisis, but they could not stand aside. Our commercial banking system is, therefore, failure-proof from the standpoint of depositors with balances below the $15,000 insurance limit.[17]

Regulations to enhance bank earnings. At one time, no one worried about bank profits except the banker, but deposit insurance gives the government a stake in the banking business. If banks earn substantial profits and add them to their capital funds, the danger of losses to the FDIC is reduced. Hence the FDIC is anxious to sustain bank earnings at reasonable levels. This has become all the more urgent as the rapid growth of assets has reduced the ratio of bank capital to assets at risk from 26.0 per cent in 1942 to 11.2 per cent in 1965.

The most important restriction that is aimed to strengthen bank income is the regulation of interest paid to depositors. The Banking Act of 1933 forbade interest payments on demand deposits by insured commercial banks (with minor exceptions for the benefit of savings banks and local governments owning demand deposits). The Federal Reserve Board, under Regulation Q, and the FDIC are also empowered to set maximum rates of interest on time deposits.

Although Regulation Q was established in 1936, it was inoperative for twenty-one years because money market interest rates remained below the $2^1/_2$ per cent interest ceiling on time deposits which was in effect from 1936 to 1957. During the tight money period of 1955–57, commercial banks were under great pressure to meet credit demands. They were unable to attract substantial amounts of new deposits because they were offering lower returns on savings deposits than the nonbank financial institutions. Consequently, Regulation Q ceilings were lifted in 1957, and continued to be raised during the early sixties as the competition for funds among financial institutions remained intense.[18] In 1966 the ceilings were lowered for the first time since 1936 in an effort to prevent the rate competition from getting out of hand. At the same time the Federal Home Loan Bank Board (see next section) and the FDIC were given authority by Congress to set ceilings on savings and loan shares and savings bank deposits.

Controls over Nonbank Financial Institutions

A wide variety of state and federal controls affect the assets and liabilities of the major nonbank financial institutions. The nation's 506 savings banks

---

[17]It has been argued that the FDIC would not lose appreciably by insuring *all* deposits, and this seems to be borne out by the record. When a bank closes, the larger depositors seem to get wind of the trouble and draw out their funds in time. In "deposit assumption cases," no distinction can be made by size of deposit, and the FDIC in effect assumes all losses. In "deposit payoff cases" (receiverships), over the years 1934–65, $204 million out of $234 million of deposits was insured; and at the end of 1965, only $1.8 million remained unpaid.

[18]After the December 1965 increase the savings-deposit interest ceiling was 4 per cent and the time-deposit interest ceiling was $5^1/_2$ per cent.

are state-chartered institutions and are regulated by the laws of the states in which they are located. State laws prescribe the quality and quantity of assets which banks may hold; the banks have rarely been hamstrung by these regulations because savings bankers traditionally have been conservative investors. Three hundred and thirty-two savings banks with 84 per cent of the industry's assets belong to the FDIC which, along with state banking agencies, may set interest ceilings on savings bank deposits.

Savings and loan associations may receive charters from state or federal agencies. In 1965 there were 4,221 state-chartered associations which were supervised by state banking or savings and loan departments and 2,011 federally chartered associations which were regulated by the Federal Home Loan Bank System.

The FHLB System was established in 1932 to prevent savings and loan association failures and to establish a national credit system for mortgage lending institutions. The FHLB System supplements the resources of member institutions through a central credit facility which extends advances to individual associations. These advances are subject to a wide range of terms; they are controlled by statute, by the lending policies of the twelve regional Federal Home Loan banks, and by the policy objectives of a governing three-man FHLB Board.[19]

The Federal Savings and Loan Insurance Corporation was established in 1934 and is similar in purpose and structure to the FDIC. In 1965 the FSLIC insured savings accounts up to $15,000 against loss at all federally chartered associations and 2,497 state-charted associations. FSLIC member associations held 96 per cent of the assets of the industry in 1965.

State governments are wholly responsible for the regulation and supervision of life insurance companies. In each state, investment laws spell out appropriate areas and standards for company investments to protect policy-holders against improper practices or speculative excess. The investment laws are administered by state banking or insurance departments.

Enhancing Asset Quality

In addition to maintaining controls over asset selection, the government operates to enhance the "bankability" of certain assets—especially to make farm and homeowner debt more thoroughly bankable. These operations grew out of the Great Depression, when a deterioration in the quality of farm and mortgage debt impaired the liquidity of banks and threatened a wholesale dispossession of farmers and homeowners.

---

[19]All federal associations and 2,497 state associations were FHLB members in 1965. Since 1966 the FHLB may establish interest ceilings on savings and loan shares offered to the public by member associations.

Farm loan agencies. The farm loan agencies had a pre-Depression history. For generations, farmers had paid higher interest rates than other people both on mortgages and on short-term loans, reflecting the fact that country banks were rich in loan opportunities but poor in deposits, while city banks were rich in deposits but relatively poor in loan opportunities. The taboo on branch banking prevented merging of the two, and kept the interest spread much wider than in Canada, where each bank has offices in city and country. In addition, farm loans tended to be small and to involve the banker in more costs per dollar lent than did larger loans to business. To reduce this disparity, in 1917 the government established the Federal Land banks (for mortgages) and the Federal Intermediate Credit banks (for working-capital loans). The Treasury supplied most of the capital.

The Land Banks raised money by issuing Land Bank bonds, which banks found acceptable as assets. They lent this money to farmers for the purchase of land. The mortgage debts that farmers owed the Land Banks were repayable in installments, due in from fifteen to forty years. By pre-Depression banking standards, such long-term mortgages were not "bankable." In effect, the Land Banks' operations transmuted nonbankable assets (farm mortgages) into bankable assets (Land bank bonds).

During the deflation of 1929–33, commercial banks and other credit institutions (notably life insurance companies) found their farm mortgages "frozen," because the farmers' cash income fell to less than half its 1929 level by 1932, and farm land prices had fallen sharply. Many farm debtors could not pay off their debts out of income, nor could they sell their farms for enough to pay the mortgage. About 45 per cent of the farmers with mortgages—owing 52 per cent of the mortgage debt—were in default at the beginning of 1933. But when creditors foreclosed, they merely exchanged an illiquid mortgage for unsalable real estate; the farms they acquired would fetch so little at forced sale that creditors felt obliged to hold the land. The foreclosure process, although very hard on farmers, was not of much help to creditors. Many states passed "moratorium laws" to stop foreclosures for several years, and the courts everywhere tried to give debtors more time.

In the spring of 1933, the federal government stepped in. The Land banks were authorized to make loans on the "normal" value of a farm as compared with "market" value, used previously. In addition, a Federal Farm Mortgage Corporation was established to make loans equaling 75 per cent of the value of the farm, compared with the 50 per cent covered by Land bank loans. Where a farmer could not pay his debt to a private creditor, the federal farm loan agencies would offer a mutually acceptable arrangement. The farmer's mortgage would be taken over by the Federal Land bank (or partly by the Land bank and partly by the FFMC) and put on a long-term amortized basis. This took care of the debtor. The creditor, in turn, received FFMC bonds guaranteed by the United States Treasury in place of his mortgage—converting a frozen asset into a liquid asset. In 1933–36, about $2 billion of mortgages (a quarter of the farm mortgage debt) were refinanced in this way. In the process, about 20 per cent of the farmer debtors got their debts scaled down; the bonds that went to the creditor were less than the face value of the old mortgage. Federal farm debt relief also included federal farm mortgage moratorium laws in 1933 and 1935.

During World War II, farmers paid off much of their mortgage debt, including debt to government agencies. But at the end of 1965, the farmers still owed the government $7.9 billion, apart from crop loans extended by the Commodity Credit Corporation in connection with our price-support program. Of this $7.9 billion, $3.8 billion was owed to the Rural Electrification Administration.[20]

In recent years, the focus of federal operations in farm debt has changed. Instead of lending directly to farmers or taking over the debts owed by individual farmers, the government has been making loans to credit institutions that lend to farmers. It has also provided a market for farmers' IOU's so that these institutions may sell off their assets to acquire cash and make new loans. These operations are conducted mainly by the Federal Intermediate Credit banks and by the Rural Electrification Administration, which make loans to local farm co-operatives. These agencies may be regarded as a means of increasing the liquidity of the private credit institutions that serve the farmer.

Home loan agencies.   In the trough of the Great Depression the home mortgage situation was much like the farm mortgage situation, except that there was no equivalent of the Federal Land banks. Between a third and a half of the homeowners with mortgages were in default, and banks and other credit institutions found their loans "frozen."

In 1933, the Home Owners' Loan Corporation was set up as a rescue operation, intervening between debtor and creditor much as did the farm loan agencies. It gave the creditor government-guaranteed bonds in exchange for his mortgage, and put the debtor under contract to pay off his debt to the HOLC over a term of years. Out of about $3.1 billion loaned, about $0.5 billion went to refinance mortgages held by commercial banks. By the end of 1950, the HOLC had recovered its funds by payments from debtors and the sale of houses surrendered by debtors who gave up and quit, and the agency went out of business in 1951.

In 1935, the Federal Housing Administration began to "insure" home mortgages. In case of default on an insured mortgage, the FHA stands ready to exchange its own marketable "debenture" for the mortgage, so that the creditor is secure against loss. To be insured, a mortgage must not exceed a stated percentage of the value of the house, as determined by conservative appraisal, and must provide for amortization of the principal through monthly installments

---

[20]U.S. Department of Agriculture, *Agricultural Statistics,* 1965, p. 508.

over a term of years. Home mortgages would not have been regarded as "bankable" before the Great Depression, but, with insurance, they are now very satisfactory bank assets. Commercial banks have held a sizeable share of the insured mortgages outstanding; their holdings totalled $7.7 billion in 1965 out of $38.5 billion outstanding.[21]

Since the war, FHA activities have been supplemented by the Veterans Administration, which also insures mortgages.[22] Besides, the Federal National Mortgage Association ("Fannie Mae") has bought mortgages from private credit institutions, so as to put them in funds for a fresh round of mortgage lending. FNMA operates on a large scale. In 1966 alone, it bought $2.7 billion of mortgages in the open market. It is sometimes accused of undermining Federal Reserve policies designed to curb inflation, and many observers have urged that FNMA activities be more closely coordinated with Federal Reserve operations.

---

[21] *Federal Reserve Bulletin,* April 1967, pp. 636, 637, excludes VA-insured mortgages.
[22] The VA also insures loans to veterans by banks for business purposes.

Part II

**Money,
Output,
and Prices**

Chapter 8

The Varieties of
Monetary Theory

The chief object of this book is to set forth those principles we must understand in order to formulate sensible economic stabilization policies. In Part I we examined the structure of the monetary and financial system. Now we are ready to examine the role of money and to explain how it affects economic activity. Chapters 8 through 11 study the various approaches economists have used to explain monetary phenomena. Chapters 12 through 14 provide an understanding of the statistical tools we use to measure monetary activity and economic performance. Taken together, the theoretical concepts and empirical guides form the economic framework with which we can evaluate and build effective stabilization policies.

Alternative approaches. Several different approaches to the study of money have been tried by economists. Three of these are:

1. The commodity approach
2. The transactions-velocity approach
3. The payments approach

Each of these ways of looking at money has some sense in it. The commodity approach and the transactions-velocity approach are not as useful as they once looked, but we still cannot afford to overlook them. The payments approach

143

in its several variants is essential for anybody who aims to understand business fluctuations.

The *commodity approach* starts by thinking of money as the "ghost of gold." It argues that the value of money is determined *through* the value of gold and that the value of gold is determined much like the value of any other commodity.

The *transactions-velocity approach* starts from the notion of a *stock* of money (or "means of payment") which "turns over" a measurable number of times as it circulates each year. The payments it makes are "transactions." The average number of times it turns over is its "velocity."

The *payments approach,* like the transactions-velocity approach, focuses attention on spending, but it looks at a range of reasons for spending, rather than the mechanistic connections between balances and spending that are emphasized by transactions velocity. The payments approach has several variants and we shall consider three:

> *A. The Interest-Investment Version,* which explores the connections between cash and interest rates, and between interest rates and investment. This is the version that is associated with the works of Wicksell and Keynes.
>
> *B. The Cash-Balances Version,* which explores the connection between people's demand for cash and their spending decisions. This is the version that is associated with the works of Pigou and Patinkin.
>
> *C. The Credit Version,* which explores the connections between lending and spending and regards the stock of money as a by-product of commercial-bank lending to business.

The commodity and transactions-velocity theories will be examined in this chapter. The payments approach in its several versions will occupy Chapters 9 through 12.

The commodity approach. This way of looking at money can be dealt with quite briefly. Two forms may be recognized—the "pure" and "revised."

In its "pure" form, the commodity theory tries to treat money as an ordinary commodity, viewing it as an aspect of gold. The value of gold is then explained as though it were set on a market in much the same way as the value of copper; this value is *transmitted* to the monetary unit.[1]

This view would be all right if we could suppose that the nonmonetary uses of gold completely overshadowed its monetary uses, but the facts are otherwise. Monetary stocks of gold have long been much larger than nonmonetary stocks, amounting to several years' gold production. If the monetary demand for gold collapsed, an ounce of gold would be much cheaper compared with other commodities; the dentists, jewelers, and industries that use gold would take decades to absorb the gold stock. The demand for gold is different from the

---

[1] For this point of view, see J. Lawrence Laughlin, *Principles of Money* (New York: Charles Scribner's Sons, 1903), chaps. i, viii, ix, and xi.

demand for other commodities *because* gold is linked with money. There is no use pretending that the nonmonetary demand for gold dominates the money situation.[2]

The "revised" form of the commodity theory does not insist that the demand for gold is just like the demand for any other commodity. It sticks to the point of view that money is essentially gold (or, if not redeemable, the "ghost" of gold). It regards the whole "superstructure" of paper money, bank credit, and so forth, as merely incidental. The market for gold still sets a value on gold, and it is this value that is transmitted to money. Commodities are thought of as having *gold prices* which are translated into money prices. The less gold there is in the dollar, the higher is the money price of a commodity that corresponds to a given gold price.[3]

In this less extreme form, the commodity theory helps explain some phases of economic history. As we said in the introduction, two units of account have sometimes existed side by side in a single country—one linked to gold and the other to local currency. If the gold unit was central in the thinking and accounting of business, this form of the commodity theory applied.

Facts *can be* as the revised commodity theory assumes, and sometimes they *have been,* but in the modern world the facts *are not* like that. People do not actually value goods and services in gold and translate their valuations into dollars. On the contrary, they value goods and services in dollars and translate these valuations into gold—*if,* indeed, they have any use for gold values, which they rarely do. That this is the way people reason may be seen from the history of the 1933–34 "devaluation" in the United States. When the price of gold was raised by government action from $20.67 to $35.00 per ounce, valuations in dollars should have gone up in proportion (by about 75 per cent) if the commodity theory were valid. But it never occurred to businessmen who fixed prices on a "cost-plus" basis to revise their cost figures. Prices fixed in contracts remained fixed, and doctors went on making their usual charge for office calls. Insofar as the devaluation raised prices, it did so by raising the dollar price of *foreign currencies* that were tied to gold and thus changing markets for goods that enter foreign trade.

Salvage from the commodity theory. The linkage of money to gold retains some importance because gold still enters the reserves of the monetary system. The production and private hoarding of gold (and, to a lesser extent, of silver) has to be watched, as do international movements of monetary metals.

---

[2] There may have been a time, in the dawn of history, when gold as a money took over a value from gold as a commodity. But strong evidence exists that gold has been "treasure" (that is, a form of wealth with an aura of glory about it) for thousands of years. Gold probably differed greatly from other commodities even before money existed.

[3] This view is essentially that of the late Professor George Warren, of Cornell (see G. F. Warren and F. A. Pearson, *Prices* [New York: John Wiley & Sons, Inc., 1933]), whose advice to President Roosevelt apparently had a strong influence on the "devaluation" of the dollar in 1933–34. Similar views seem to underlie much of the analysis by the late Gustav Cassel.

Several times in history, the production of gold has been so low as to check the expansion of the public's stock of cash needed to finance the growth of business. The long price declines of 1815–49 and 1865–96 are believed to have resulted from such gold shortages. Some analysts also think that a gold shortage explains the depression that several countries experienced during the 1920's and that most experienced during the 1930's.

A high level of gold production under a gold-based currency—or the introduction of silver into monetary reserves—can ease the monetary situation and permit expansion to replace deflation. It is no accident that big gold strikes (like those of 1849 in California and Australia and those of the 1890's in South Africa and the Yukon) have often heralded a change from periods of declining prices and sluggish business to periods of rising prices and active business.

The chief present importance of tying gold to money is that it fixes the income of gold producers. Mining gold (or silver) to sell to the government is one way to get an income, but such sales do not absorb any of the spending power of households or firms. The gold and silver are not paid for by increased taxes, but by printing gold or silver certificates. This makes gold production an inflationary force.

Looking at gold from the global standpoint, its chief importance is that it provides much of the income of South Africa, and northern Canada,—and a slice of the income of Russia and parts of the mountain states in this country. Gold is still basic, moreover, in international monetary relations, as we shall see in Chapter 18.

The transactions-velocity approach. When you buy things, you must pay for them. Money pays for things. The transactions-velocity approach starts out from these simple facts; it looks at money primarily as *means of payment.*

When we say that "money pays for things," we have to look out for a pitfall. As the introduction pointed out, a buyer of goods usually *goes in debt* to the seller, and when the buyer settles his debt, he usually pays by check—by putting his banker in debt to the seller. To be strictly accurate, we ought to say: Money can pay for things and sometimes does, but generally we pay for things with *debt*. The transactions-velocity approach has a trick for avoiding this difficulty. It labels a payment of the buyer's debt as "deferred payment" for the goods he bought. It then goes on as if all payments were alike—all "spot cash"—and calls them all "transactions."[4]

This way of looking at things has the advantage of connecting money directly with the flow of business. A few years ago, most American economists preferred the transactions-velocity approach to any other way of thinking about money. Since about 1930, difficulties have piled up. The notion of "velocity" (which we will look at shortly) has proved to hide more mysteries

---

[4] Transactions-velocity theorists often bring in the use of "book credit," however, as an influence on "velocity of circulation."

than it explains. While many able writers still use transactions-velocity analysis, most present-day monetary theorists prefer other approaches. But the transactions-velocity approach still makes a good starting point. While it does not take us as far as we could wish, it does make sense as far as it goes. The very weaknesses of this approach make it worth studying; they explain why we have developed other approaches.

The "circulation" of money and the notion of "velocity."   To *use* money in a transaction does *not use it up*. As soon as it has bought one piece of goods, a dollar of paper money or of bank deposits is ready to buy something else. Money "circulates" in a way that other things do not—a striking fact on which both professional economists and "cranks" alike base much of their monetary thinking.

To throw this aspect of money into clear relief, think of the nonmoney side of a "transaction"—the goods and services that money has bought. Services can never be exchanged a second time, while physical goods *can* be exchanged again, but very rarely are. *Two-way markets* do exist, to which the same pieces of goods return over and over again. The stock exchange and the real estate market are like this, and stocks and real estate "circulate" much like money. But most goods and services have *one-way markets* and do not circulate. The very purpose of buying goods would be lost if they were sold again in the same form in which they were bought. Buyers usually want the goods they buy *for use*—for household consumption or for processing in a factory. Even the retail merchant who does not aim to process goods combines them with services, so that, economically speaking, they cease to be the same goods. Most recent transactions-velocity analysis takes the one-way market as the standard case, and deals only incidentally with two-way markets.

Transactions-velocity analysis measures transactions in dollar value; it multiplies the unit price of each type of goods by the number of units. A given dollar volume may be financed by a large stock of money circulating slowly, or by a small stock of money circulating rapidly. This rate of circulation is what we mean by velocity. Some parts of the money supply circulate faster than others—dimes, for example, faster than $20 bills. If we could trace the movements of individual pieces of money (by putting a tag on each piece on January 1, asking each successive owner to put his name on the tag, and collecting all the tags on December 31), we would discover that a few pieces had stayed in the same hands all year, a few had changed hands only once, more had changed hands twice, and so on, up to a few which changed hands hundreds of times during the year. The notion of velocity in which we are interested amounts to an average rapidity of circulation that could be found by averaging the number of names on the tags.

We have to deal not only with payments in coin and paper money, however, but also with the much larger total of check payments, and there are no "pieces" of bank money to which we could possibly tie tags. Bank deposits circulate in the form of checks drawn fresh for each transaction, each check being a reincarnation of deposits embodied in a previous check.[5]

In this situation, the natural way to define velocity of circulation is as the ratio of dollar transactions to the stock of money—coin, paper money, and checking deposits.[6] Such a ratio is an implicit average of the number of times each dollar was used. Even this solution is not as simple as it sounds, because of the looseness of the term "transactions." There are at least six notions of velocity, corresponding to different definitions of total transactions:

(A) Some velocity calculations measure velocity by the ratio of "bank debits" to means of payment. A "debit" is the entry that the bank makes on your bank statement when it pays one of your checks. This is a very convenient form of measurement, but debits do not directly measure payments for goods and services. Debits in New York consist largely of purely financial transactions, and even at banks outside New York there is a large "fluff" of transactions that represent remittances between offices of the same firm, duplicate payments in connection with security and real estate dealings, checks cashed, loan repayments, and the like.[7] Debits, moreover, fail to cover currency transactions, except as these are represented by checks cashed.

(B) Some velocity calculations rest on estimates of total payments. These are built by adding together all the transactions that leave statistical tracks—including dealings in permanent physical assets and securities, speculative dealings in farm products and the like, as well as dealings linked with current production.[8]

(C) Seeking a coverage for "transactions" that is closer to the collection of things whose price level we hope to explain, some students prefer to limit their measurements to dealings linked to current output—including materials whose products are also coming on the market.

(D) Many economists prefer to measure transactions by the current-dollar value of Gross National Product. This is a series that is readily available back to 1929 (with somewhat shakier extensions as far back as 1869), and its "implicit deflator" offers the most usable index of the general price level.[9] On the other hand, this series includes substantial

---

[5] Usually the proceeds of one check cannot be traced into specific checks of later date. But if a person starts a bank account by the deposit of a single check, he is plainly using the same funds over again when he draws checks to pay his bills.

[6] Sometimes total "cash" (including time deposits as well as coin, paper money, and checking deposits) is taken as denominator of the velocity fraction. In the other direction, separate velocities for checking deposits and for coin and paper money are sometimes used in analysis. This plan implies separate measurement of the "transactions" that are settled in each form.

[7] For analysis of the relation of debits to transactions, see George Garvy, *Development of Bank Debits and Clearings and Their Use in Economic Analysis* (Washington, D.C.: Federal Reserve Board, 1952).

[8] For basis (B) or (C), data for 1936–42 may be found in the Federal Reserve tabulations on flows of funds and in Morris A. Copeland, *Study of Moneyflows in the United States* (New York: National Bureau of Economic Research, 1952), pp. 15, 174–75. These data describe financing though not gross asset turnover.

[9] Hence use of the "GNP deflator" in several of our charts.

noncash items—the rental value of owner-occupied homes, farm consumption of food, and the like—and excludes payments for materials and so forth.

(E) Some students prefer the less inclusive but more coherent index of National Income. But this has much the same drawbacks of under- and overinclusiveness as basis (*D*).

(F) For really long-period annual velocity estimates, before 1897, we have to depend on bank "clearings"—on the dollar value of checks that happen to come home to the bank on which they are drawn through its clearinghouse rather than over the counter or through a correspondent bank. Like bank debits, clearings in New York are dominated by financial operations. But clearings outside New York seem to give a reasonably good image of payments for dates through 1914, as outside debits do beginning with 1919.[10]

To interpret propositions about velocity and transactions, we must know which method of measurement is used. Older theoretical discussions run on basis (*B*), but with statistics on basis (*F*). More recent discussions[11] tend to run in terms of some variant of "income velocity," with concepts and statistics on basis (*D*) or (*E*).

The equation of exchange. Having defined velocity, we may now state the central core of the transactions-velocity approach. This is Irving Fisher's "equation of exchange":[12]

$$MV = PT$$

M is the stock of money, *V* its velocity of circulation, *P* is an index of prices, and *T* is an index of the *physical volume* of transactions.[13] As was noted above, we have a choice as to the dealings we call transactions. The price level represented by *P* in the equation must be interpreted as the price level of the goods and services that enter into the transactions we have chosen.

---

[10]Unfortunately, there is no way to check the clearings and debits series against each other, even though the clearings series has continued since 1919; for, as Garvy points out, the introduction of Federal Reserve clearing arrangements during World War I began to have a substantial impact on the proportion of checks cleared.

Garvy's study, moreover, indicates that the growth of clearings prior to World War I probably overstates the growth in total payments, and that the growth of debits since then has probably understated the growth in total payments.

[11]See in particular J. W. Angell, *Behavior of Money* (New York: McGraw-Hill Book Company, Inc., 1936) and *Investment and Business Cycles* (New York: McGraw-Hill Book Company, Inc., 1941), and E. M. Doblin, "The Ratio of Income to Money Supply: An International Survey" in *Review of Economics and Statistics,* August 1951, pp. 201ff.

[12]Irving Fisher, *Purchasing Power of Money* (New York: The Macmillan Company, 1911), pp. 26–27. If a separate velocity is set up for checking deposits, the equation runs $MV + M'V' = PT$, when *M* and *V* refer to coin and paper money outside banks, *M'* and *V'* to checking deposits. *Ibid.,* p. 53.

[13]Commonly such an index tries to measure the value of each year's volume of goods and services exchanged at the prices of a base year. This index and the price index have to be defined so that when they are multiplied together we have an accurate measure of the *dollar volume* (physical volume times current prices) of transactions.

This equation, we should stress, is a statement about *definitions* of M, V, P, and T, and like all such statements is necessarily true.[14] The equation merely says that the same dollar payments may be looked at from different points of view; it is not a finding about statistically determined facts. Its importance in relation to facts is chiefly that it enables us to locate some errors in what we think are facts. A statement of fact that contradicts the equation must contain an inconsistency of definition or an error of measurement, or both.

The equation of exchange is sometimes used as the basis for a monetary theory; it is not the same thing as the quantity theory of money, but is often used as a vehicle for expounding that doctrine. By making assumptions about V and T, economists have used it to relate M and P.

In order to turn the equation into a monetary theory, one must make these assumptions:

1. That changes in M will not induce inverse changes in V (for, if they did, they might leave MV unchanged or changed in the opposite direction);
2. That changes in M will not induce parallel changes in T;
3. That changes in P are not somehow brought about by nonmonetary forces in a way that will induce parallel changes in M or V or inverse changes in T; and
4. That changes in M are not overshadowed by changes in V or T as causes of changes in P.

To hold the quantity theory in the strictest sense one would have to go still further:

5. That V and T can be regarded as constants (perhaps with a simple trend in time); and
6. That P is incapable of influencing M, V, or T.

Careful quantity theorists have always qualified these propositions to allow for short-run aberrations. The classical statement of the quantity theory by Irving Fisher, for example, has a whole chapter[15] on "disturbance of the equation and of purchasing power during transition periods." Fisher argues that in "transition periods," when prices are rising or falling in response to monetary changes, forces outside the quantity theory are also at work. In particular, rising prices generate a demand for bank loans which will expand deposits—a case of prices affecting M. In addition, a depreciation of money in real purchasing power will incline holders to "get rid of it as fast as possible" and thereby increase

---

[14]If the facts yielded *independent and only approximately correct measures* of the four magnitudes separately, we should find the equation only approximately true of these measures. But for practical reasons cited above, an independent measure of velocity is out of the question. Velocity has to be both defined and measured so as to make the equation a truism.

[15]Fisher, *op. cit.*, Chapter IV.

V. T may also increase, since prices "have to be pushed up, so to speak, by increased purchases." Bank reserves limit the extent to which prices can expand *M*, and effects on *V* and on *T* are presented as though they are likely to wear off quickly, once prices have ceased to move in response to increased *M* and *V*. The same argument is paralleled for downswings of *M* and *P*.[16]

Thus the quantity theory is a long-run view. The proportional effect upon price levels of a difference in the stock of means of payment is expected to take hold only after the lapse of a "transition period," which may run into years.

The instability of velocity. The usefulness of the quantity theory in its transactions-velocity garb plainly turns on the stability of the "velocity of circulation." If *V* snaps back to a normal level after each disturbance, changes in *M* must exert strong pressure on *P* or *T*. If *V* shows a more complex reaction-pattern, we have to go much further to gauge the effect of monetary changes.

In the classical statement of the transactions-velocity analysis, the list of factors that affect *V* is framed to suggest a great deal of stability. Fisher[17] lists:

1. *Habits of the individual.*
   (a) As to thrift and hoarding.
   (b) As to book credit.
   (c) As to the use of checks.
2. *Systems of payments in the community.*
   (a) As to frequency of receipts and disbursements.
   (b) As to regularity of receipts and disbursements.
   (c) As to correspondence between times and amounts of receipts and disbursements.
3. *General causes.*
   (a) Density of population.
   (b) Rapidity of transportation.

These sound like things that will change only slowly and predictably. "Habits as to thrift" (item 1a) might wobble; but this possibility is not apt to distrub the reader's impression that the list implies stability. When we look at the facts, however, the notion of stability vanishes.

The record on velocity is represented by a set of curves (all more or less unsatisfactory) in Chart 8–1. Curve *V*–1 takes as the measure of velocity the ratio

---

[16]*Ibid.,* pp. 67ff. As a gauge of the change in professional attitudes, note: (*a*) the lack of explicit reference to unemployment in Fisher's account of the downswing; (*b*) his assertion (p. 62), in analyzing the "unhealthy increase in trade" on the upswing, that "the amount of trade is dependent, almost entirely, on other things than the quantity of currency, so that an increase of currency cannot, even temporarily, very greatly increase trade." This statement (quoted with the permission of the estate of the late Professor Fisher) implies that the upswing starts from prosperity rather than from a state of unemployment.

[17]Irving Fisher, *Purchasing Power of Money,* rev. ed. (New York: The Macmillan Company, 1926), p. 79. Quoted with the permission of the estate of the late Professor Fisher. A more recent version of the list (L. V. Chandler, *Economics of Money and Banking* [New York: Harper & Row, Publishers, 1948], p. 546) adds "the state of expectations," thus correcting the implication that changeable factors are unimportant.

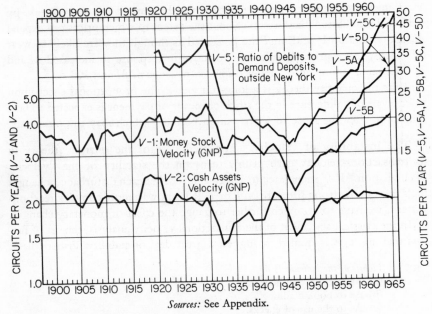

Sources: See Appendix.

Chart 8-1: Income and transactions velocity, 1897–1966.

of Gross National Product to the money stock. Curve V–2 shows the ratio of Gross National Product to total cash assets (money *plus* time deposits at commercial and mutual savings banks). Curves V–5, V–5A, V–5B, V–5C, and V–5D substitute bank debits for Gross National Product.

The curves that use Gross National Product (curves V–1 and V–2) are somewhat more stable than the curves that rely on commercial bank debits. The debits curve is clearly affected by the financial boom of the 1920's, despite the exclusion of New York debits. Velocity by every measure is far less stable than the transactions-velocity theorists were inclined to assume. From 1897 to 1930, the two income-velocity series (curves V–1 and V–2) seem to be nearly horizontal. Income-velocity fell sharply during the Great Depression and World War II, then rose again sharply. But the V-shaped curves from 1929 on do not restore the impression of stability given by pre-1929 data.

The changes in velocity since 1930 leave us with a choice of interpretations:

(1) The trend of velocity was roughly horizontal until 1929 or 1930, but something happened at that time to break the long-term trend;

(2) The trend of velocity has been downward throughout, but this trend was disguised by upward deviations during the inflation of 1917–20 and by the stock-market boom of the 1920's.[18]

---

[18]For an effort to explain this downward trend see Clark Warburton, "The Secular Trend in Monetary Velocity," *Quarterly Journal of Economics,* February 1949, especially pp. 86–90. This passage is reprinted in C. R. Whittlesey, ed., *Readings in Money and Banking* (New York: W. W. Norton & Co., Inc., 1952). For an explanation in terms of separate sector behavior, see the second edition of *Money, Debt, and Economic Activity,* pp. 163–65.

On either interpretation, the record is puzzling. The postwar increase of velocity lends some weight to the first hypothesis, but velocity has barely regained its pre-Depression levels. The first hypothesis, moreover, leaves the decline in velocity unexplained. The second interpretation runs counter to the classical list of factors explaining velocity, as these suggest a level or rising trend. Furthermore, it is hard to match with experiences of recent years. However we construe the trend, the velocity curve has fluctuated more widely and irregularly in recent years than before 1930.

Mechanical versus motivated models. The transactions-velocity approach may be described as a gamble on the existence of uniformities in aggregate monetary behavior that can be used to forecast events without themselves demanding much explanation. This mechanical approach seemed warranted by what was known about velocity down to 1930, but there is nothing built into the money system to keep velocity constant. If velocity were always jammed up against its technical maximum,[19] there might be no room for it to fluctuate. But velocity is actually far below this maximum.[20] Furthermore, it is decidedly unsteady. This is not to say that V is a useless concept. When we come to cash balances, we shall use it extensively as a measure of the demand for money. Our point is that V by itself does not offer a foundation for monetary theory. We cannot assume that V will be constant and go on to predict T or P from what we know about M. We must instead explain the fluctuations in V in order to construct a monetary theory, and engage in the sort of analysis that the transactions-velocity approach sought to avoid.

NOTES ON
ALTERNATIVE POINTS OF VIEW
AND SUPPLEMENTARY READINGS

For statements of the commodity theory, see:
G. F. Warren and F. A. Pearson, *Prices* (New York: John Wiley & Sons, Inc., 1933), chaps.-iv-v; and
G. Cassel, *Theory of Social Economy* (New York: Harcourt, Brace & World, Inc., 1932), chap. xi.
An international comparison of income velocities (extending the work of E. M. Doblin, referred to in footnote 11 above) was published by the International Mone-

---

[19]This maximum may be defined in terms of bank practices as follows: Suppose that every customer draws against funds deposited as soon as there has been time for their collection, but refrains from drawing on uncollected funds. Then holder-record deposits will be equal to the "bank float"—the amount of checks in the banks' check-collection machinery—and bank-record deposits (as entered on customers' statements) will be equal to the bank float plus the "mail float"—the amount of checks which drawers have subtracted on their checkbook stubs and recipients have not yet deposited.

[20]In terms of bank debits, checking deposits in downtown New York banks turn over ten times monthly, in other financial centers about five times monthly. Allowing for twenty business days a month and an average collection-time of $1\frac{1}{2}$ days (surely high), the technical maximum debits velocity would be at least fourteen per month.

tary Fund in *International Financial Statistics,* November 1951, under the title "Income Velocity of Money and the Rate of Interest."

For evidence on the behavior of different sectors, see the work of M. A. Copeland, referred to in footnote 8, and Raymond W. Goldsmith, *Study of Saving in the United States, 1897 to 1949* (Princeton: Princeton University Press, 1953). Also, Richard Seldon's treatment of the subject in *Studies in the Quantity Theory of Money,* Milton Friedman, ed. (Chicago: University of Chicago Press, 1956).

Recent studies on velocity appear in *Stabilization Policies,* a series of research studies prepared for the Commission on Money and Credit (Englewood Cliffs, N. J.: Prentice-Hall, Inc., 1963). In particular, see "The Relative Stability of Monetary Velocity and the Investment Multiplier in the United States, 1897–1958," by Milton Friedman and David Meiselman, pp. 165–268.

Chapter 9

The Stream
of Payments

Basic Notions

What do people spend? In Chapter 8, we looked at households and firms as spending their cash balances, and asked what determined how fast they spent them. This approach is somewhat artificial. The ordinary holder of cash is not in the position of the hero of the popular war song, who had "sixpence, jolly, jolly sixpence, to last him all his life." Cash is flowing in as well as out, and the volume of spending depends more directly on the rate of inflow than on the amount in hand, just as the working of an automobile's electrical system depends more on the generator than on the battery.

The payments approach presented in this chapter looks at people as spending *out of receipts* rather than out of balances. This approach was adopted in the 1920's by Foster and Catchings in the United States and by R. G. Hawtrey in England.[1] Present-day thinking along this line is largely derived from the work of the late J. M. Keynes, and this chapter is chiefly concerned with the

---

[1] See, for example, W. T. Foster and W. Catchings, *Business Without a Buyer* (Boston: Houghton Mifflin Company, 1927), and R. G. Hawtrey, *Currency and Credit,* 3rd ed. (London: Longmans, Green & Company, Ltd., 1928). Examples of similar thinking are readily found in writings of other countries and times. For example, Richard Cantillon (in 1755) analyzed the monetary effect of gold mining in payments terms; see the passage reprinted in A. E. Monroe, *Early Economic Thought* (Cambridge: Harvard University Press, 1924), especially pp. 264–66.

framework of Keynesian thinking. It also employs the Swedish distinction between "ex ante and ex post" magnitudes—between *expected* and *experienced* income, sales and so forth—to broaden the Keynesian approach.

The circuit of payments. If we are to think of the receipts of a household or firm as the main source of its outpayments we must know how far we can trace the payments from A to B to A. A's outpayments will be B's receipts, and thus the source of B's outpayments, which constitute receipts for A. We must be able to sketch a "wheel of payments" (or in the language of Foster and Catchings, a *circuit flow* of money).

A convenient place to break into this circuit is the consuming household. (See Chart 9-1.) The household's receipts consist chiefly of "personal income" —wages and salaries, dividends and interest, profits withdrawn from unincorporated business, and so forth.[2] The household makes its outpayments from

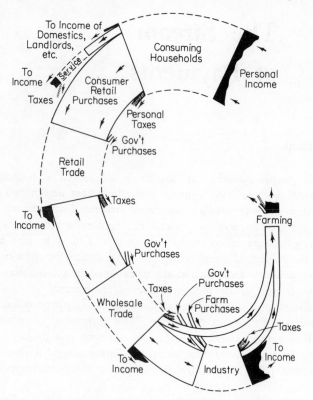

Chart 9-1: Destination of consumer expenditure.

---

[2] Since we are drawing a simplified sketch, we may leave out of account the household's receipts from borrowing, and selling securities or real estate. Complications that arise from such dealings will come into the discussion later.

its receipts, chiefly for the purchase of consumption goods and services and to the government for taxes. The bulk of these outpayments reappear as receipts for retail merchants.[3] The retailers, out of their receipts, pay wages, salaries, and other types of personal income, and some taxes. The bulk of their outpayments buy goods from wholesalers, and these purchases, in turn, constitute the bulk of wholesalers' receipts.[4] Wholesalers, again, make some personal income payments and pay their taxes, but the bulk of their outpayments are for the purpose of buying supplies. Here the stream of payments splits: part of the wholesalers' purchases are the products of industry;[5] part are farm products, acquired without substantial processing between the farm and the wholesale market. Industry makes personal income payments and pays taxes, and buys goods from the farms, while farmers make personal income payments, pay taxes, and buy goods from industry, thereby creating an eddy in the stream of payments.[6]

The image we get is of a stream of payments starting at the household and running to industry and farming—with more and more of the stream being diverted to households again as personal income payments, while another part is siphoned off as tax payments to the government. The stream is also reinforced by government purchases and by "eddies" of spending from stages more remote from the consumer. These injections of spending are not ordinarily large enough to make up for the income and tax diversions.[7]

If we ask about the sources of the personal income which consumers spend, we get a different view of the stream of payments (Chart 9–2). Part of personal income originates with government, part in farming, part in industry, part in wholesale and retail trade, and part in the service industries and rental housing. Part, as we have seen, returns directly to consumers as expenditures for personal services. As we go around the circle, we arrive at the image of a steam joined by many branches, and pouring out into the consumer's pocketbook.

Putting these two views together, and accounting for government as the receiver of taxes and as a maker of outlays, we finally arrive at Chart 9–3. This picture is much more complicated,[8] but it still makes sense to regard the diagram

---

[3] A small proportion of consumer outlay goes directly into the income stream as pay for domestic servants, and so forth. Part goes for services (for rental of houses, for haircuts, electric power), and the landlords and firms in the service industry pay out income and taxes. They also buy supplies from retail and wholesale trade—creating a stream of trade receipts that is omitted for simplicity in the diagram.

[4] The fact that some firms (such as the great chain groceries) combine retail and wholesale functions is neglected in this picture. So are the receipts of retail and wholesale trade from "industry."

[5] Internal payments within "industry" (for partly processed goods, mineral materials, machinery, and so forth) are not shown in this diagram.

[6] Actual farm purchases, of course, are distributed among all levels of trade.

[7] During World War II, of course, government expenditures grew to be about the same size as consumers' outlay.

[8] But it is much less complicated than would be necessary to register all payment flows in exchange for currently produced goods and services. Any attempt at full realism would have to increase the number of checking-stations within the general field labeled "industry"—

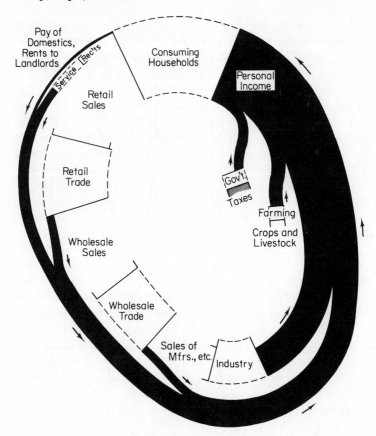

Chart 9-2: Sources of personal income.

as a great counterclockwise swirl of payments. At each checking-station (such as the household, wholesale trade, or farming) we have an inflow of receipts financing a flow of outpayments. From each checking-station we can trace most of the outpayments "downstream," and most of the receipts "upstream." Wherever we can trace a flow of money, we can also trace a flow of goods and services moving in the opposite direction. No piece of goods, however, goes clear around the circuit.

Adequacy in the flow of payments: "saving and investment." The flow of current output must be *approximately* self-financing. Each firm in the

recognizing construction, mining, various types of manufacture, and so forth. It would have to bring in payments for transportation, telephone, electric power, and so forth (payments that are made by every type of dealer in the economy). It would have to show many more "eddies" in the stream; and it would show transactions adding up to a larger multiple of income. Finally, it would have to allow for international transactions. But the general image would still be of the same type as that in the simplified diagrams.

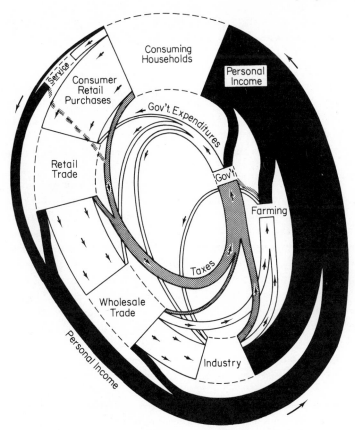

Chart 9-3: The circuit of payments.

system offers products for sale that are roughly equal in value to the firm's outlays for supplies, plus its personal income payments (including business profits distributed to owners), plus profits plowed back into the business (business saving), plus taxes paid by the firm.[9] The firm's "outlays for supplies" at one point of the circuit of payments constitute a market for the products of their suppliers. If we cancel out these transactions, the *net* product seeking sale must be roughly equal to the sum of personal income *plus* business saving and business taxes—or to personal income after personal taxes (so-called *disposable* income) *plus* business saving *plus* total taxes. This self-financing character

---

[9] Only "roughly," for any period, because of inventories. Supplies on hand at the beginning of a period contribute to output, while a part of new purchases and a part of current output go into stock. To get a strict equality, we have to put the value of the net increase in the firm's inventories on the left-hand side of the equation along with the value of product sold, or the value of any net decrease in inventories on the right-hand side along with the costs. But there is no use striving for precise equalities at this stage of analysis.

of economic activity is reflected in the diagrams by the rough equality of receipts and outpayments (shown by the width of the streams) at each of our checking-stations.

While disposable income plus business saving plus taxes *can* buy the current net output at satisfactory prices, they *need not* do so. It is conspicuous in economic life that consumers do not have to spend all of their incomes; they are free to save part, and almost always do.[10] Governments do not have to spend all their tax receipts, and business firms can cling to part of their net sales receipts. Every economic unit has the freedom to underspend its income—or to over-spend it.

For the moment, fix your eye on the consumer's freedom to save, and its consequences for the self-financing of markets. When consumers save part of their disposable income, they use some of their saving for direct consumer purchases of goods other than current consumables—notably for houses. These consumer purchases directly constitute a market for the output of industry. But much of consumer saving goes into token forms. Savers buy securities —government bonds, corporate stocks, and so forth. They put part of their saving into life insurance premiums, building up the cash values of their policies. In all but acute depression periods, they use part of their saving to build up their cash holdings, especially their savings deposits, but also holdings of money.

Money cranks love to argue that this token saving represents a "leak" in the monetary system and that this leakage is bound to bring the stream of payments to a halt. This will be true only *if:*

(a) No injection of funds elsewhere offsets consumer saving, *and*
(b) The net output of the system consists entirely of goods seeking sale to consumers.

Condition (*a*) sometimes holds, but a number of things may happen to keep it from being true. New money may be put into circulation to pay for the mining or importation of gold. Federal, state, and local governments may outspend their tax receipts. The country's exports may exceed its imports. Condition (*a*), then, is not *necessarily* true—and government policy could always make it false. But condition (*b*) is *never* true. Part of the output that is offered for sale is always bought by government. Except in serious depressions, much of that output consists of new plant and equipment that is bought by business to expand future production and of new houses for future use. These "capital expenditures" are called "investment" in the private language of economists.

---

[10] There are always some consuming households that outspend their income by running up debt or using up accumulated assets. But "negative saving" is usually far outweighed by the positive saving of other households.

Department of Commerce estimates (*Survey of Current Business,* July 1960) covering 1929–59 show negative personal net saving only in the acute depression years 1932 and 1933. If we could separate the saving of unincorporated business from those of households, it would probably turn out that household saving was always positive.

The fact that consumers save does not necessarily prevent production from generating markets adequate to keep itself going. To the extent that consumer income is used to pay taxes or is saved, it fails to provide a market for total current output. But government spending[11] and private investment outlays provide markets additional to those made by consumption. Markets will be self-balancing if *government expenditure plus investment equals the sum of taxes plus saving.*[12]

This proposition is the core of Keynesian income analysis. It plays the same role in the payments approach that the equation of exchange plays in transactions-velocity analysis. Like the equation of exchange, it is basically a truism, but is often used as the basis for elaborate theories. To see that this is so, let us restate it algebraically. We designate income paid out by Y and the value of total production by Z. We designate consumer spending by C, saving by S, taxes by T, business investment by I, and government spending by G.

Using these symbols we can write:

$$Y = C + S + T$$
$$Z = C + I + G$$

The first of these equations says that the income people receive must, in turn, be spent on consumers' goods, taxed away, or saved. The second of these equations says that the total of current output must be sold to consumers, to business (to provide for future production), or to the government.

If the income that is paid out is to finance the output that created it, Y must be equal to Z. But this tells us that

$$Y - Z = 0 = (S + T) - (I + G), \text{ or}$$
$$S + T = I + G$$

The sum of investment and the government's deficit (the excess of expenditure over taxes) is often called an "offset" to saving, but the investment that offsets consumer saving need not be financed directly by consumer saving. Business may pay for investment with funds drawn from idle business cash,

---

[11]Payments that the government makes to buy currently produced goods and services (services of officials, military supplies, highway construction, and so forth) must definitely be included here. Payments that are not connected to the purchase of current output (such as unemployment compensation, veteran's benefits, interest on the national debt, and tax refunds—what statisticians call "transfer payments") may be treated either as government expenditures or as negative taxes. Either way, however, the conclusions of the text hold.

[12]House construction is regarded for this purpose as a "business capital expenditure." If investment is measured gross, we must regard depreciation allowances as part of "gross saving." If investment is measured net of depreciation, only net business saving need enter our accounts of national saving. (We could even deal with investment net of all "inside financing" and treat business as having no saving.) On any basis used consistently, the conclusions of the text will hold: taxes plus saving must be balanced—on an *ex ante* basis—by government expenditure plus investment.

or funds borrowed from banks.[13] If the government has a budgetary surplus, it may pay off part of the national debt, and the proceeds may be used by ex-bondholders to finance business investment. What matters is not the linkage between specific parts of the saving flow and specific items of investment, but the overall matching between the amount of "offset" and the amount of saving.

The saving-investment relationship must be true for every level of income, because of the way in which we define our terms. In the first of our equations we have really defined S as the difference between Y and $C + T$. In the second of our equations we have defined I as the difference between Z and $C + G$. In effect, the first equation says that saving is income not spent, while the second says that investment is output not sold to consumers or to government. The second equation includes with investment the goods that were produced for consumers which consumers failed to buy. These are regarded as a form of investment because they are left in inventory when the year is over.[14]

In our discussion of the payments stream we said that Y and Z are equal, which is also the way in which our national income accounts treat them. If these totals are equal, these totals less consumption must also be equal. Saving plus taxes must be equal to investment plus government spending.

When we are examining a stable "equilibrium" level of income, the saving-investment equality takes on a deeper meaning. In order for a level of income to be self-perpetuating, *planned* saving plus taxes must be equal to *planned* investment plus government spending. To prove this proposition, suppose that consumer spending falls below what business had expected. This will not affect current production, for what is sold or left unsold has already been produced. Businesses will merely be left with a stock of unsold consumers' goods, and this stock of surplus goods will be reflected in higher inventories (in an increase of

---

[13]It used to be argued that consumers indirectly financed business by "putting savings in the bank." In recent years students of money have viewed this as a rather uninteresting half-truth. From the standpoint of any particular bank, lending power rises if it receives deposits that might have been in some other bank. At the same time, however, the lending power of the other bank fails. The fact that individual bankers see that their lending power depends on deposits is, therefore, inconclusive. If consumers' efforts to save in the form of bank deposits reflect a reduced willingness to buy newly issued corporate stock, banks as a whole gain no lending power. All that happens is that deposits that might have belonged to the corporations trying to float stock are now held by the savers who have refused to buy stock. Such a change does not give the banks any added ability to finance business.

Looking at the banking system as a whole, "putting savings in the bank" can enhance lending power only if it increases cash reserves or reduces reserve requirements. If savers pile up deposits by handing in coin and paper money or shift deposits into classes of banks with low reserve requirements (such as mutual savings banks) from banks with high reserve requirements, they increase the banking system's total lending power. But all these effects depend on what saving does to the *composition* of the outstanding mass of cash—not, in the first instance, on the *amount* of savings that people are trying to "put in the bank."

[14]If, of course, consumers buy more goods than business produced during the year, net investment in inventory will be negative; merchants will have to take goods off the shelf in order to satisfy consumer demand.

total investment). The shortfall in consumption will appear in both equations: as an increase of saving on the one hand, and an increase of investment on the other. Yet such a shortfall in sales will affect future production. Producers will cut back output in order to run down stocks. This will mean that Z next year must be smaller than what it has been, and that Y will also decline by the same amount.

In order that income may be stable from one period to the next, it is not enough that actual saving plus taxes equals actual investment plus government spending. What is needed to stabilize income is an equality of the *intended* magnitudes. Consumer and government spending must be as high as business-men expected if investment is to turn out as planned. This, in turn, requires that *planned* or *ex ante* saving plus taxes must match *planned* or *ex ante* business investment plus government spending.

It is in the *planned* or *ex ante* form that the investment-saving relationship has real significance, and it is in this sense that we will use it in later sections of this chapter, where we shall have more to say about planned and realized magnitudes.

Some Keynesian Building Blocks

The "propensity to consume."   This is what has been said so far: House-holds spend for consumption out of the personal incomes they receive, but usually do not spend *all* that they receive on consumption. This is rather vague; can we do better?

The line of monetary thinking that follows John Maynard Keynes offers as an answer the so-called consumption function. Given the community's habits and tastes and the distribution of income among different households, Keynes-ians argue that each possible level of income will yield a particular level of consumption. In Chart 9–4, consumption expenditure is measured vertically and income horizontally. The diagonal OD traces the locus of points at which spending would equal income. But, as already noted, consumer spending is usu-ally somewhat less than income. If income is OY_1, for example, so that a level of spending equal to income would be $Y_1D_1 = OY_1$, we would expect to find actual spending at Y_1C_1. The difference C_1D_1 represents saving. Similarly, if national income is OY_f, spending is Y_fC_f and saving is C_fD_f.

In the private language of Keynesian monetary theorists,

1. Curve C_1C_f traces out the "consumption function."
2. At any point, such as C_1 (corresponding to income OY_1):
   a. The *slope* of C_1C_f measures the "marginal propensity to consume," which is always supposed to be a fraction less than one.
   b. The *ratio* of C_1Y_1 to OY_1 (or of C_1Y_1 to Y_1D_1) measures the "average propensity to consume."

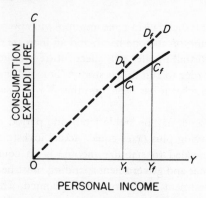

PERSONAL INCOME

Chart 9-4: Keynesian hypothesis on relation of consumption to income.

Because the "marginal propensity to consume" is supposed to be less than one, an increase of total income will result in both more consumption and more saving. In Chart 9–4, for example, $Y_f C_f$ exceeds $Y_1 C_1$, and $C_f D_f$ also exceeds $C_1 D_1$.

Much empirical work has been done on the shape of the consumption function. There have been dozens of statistical studies that attempt to pin it down.[15] These studies are agreed on one basic point. While many followers of Keynes were originally inclined to draw the consumption function curling over and flattening out as income levels rise, most of the statistical studies suggest that the function is linear. In the Keynesians' terminology, the statistics suggest that the marginal propensity to consume is about the same at all levels of income. The studies disagree on the average propensity to consume. Some long-period studies, and Milton Friedman's work with "permanent" income, suggest that the average propensity is also a constant. This would mean that the consumption function passes through the origin, instead of cutting the vertical axis, as would the function in Chart 9–4 were it extended to the left. Other studies, especially of short-run data, show that the average propensity declines as income rises. A higher *percentage* of income may be saved when income itself is high than when income is low. Most Keynesians would seem to favor this second conception of the consumption function, but the essential Keynesian argument is not at issue in this dispute. All that is required is that the consumption function slope upward, but less steeply than the diagonal OD in Chart 9–4.

Investment and "underemployment equilibrium." Production and employment can only be sustained if aggregate spending provides an adequate

---

[15]A summary of early efforts will be found in Robert Ferber's *A Study of the Aggregate Consumption Function* (New York: National Bureau of Economic Research, 1953). More recent efforts are described by Milton Friedman in *A Theory of the Consumption Function* (Princeton: National Bureau of Economic Research, 1957).

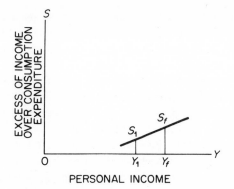

Chart 9-5: Implied relation of saving to national income.

market for output. This conclusion means that consumer saving must be balanced by spending of the other sorts which constitute investment.[16]

This finding—that in equilibrium saving and investment must match—enables us to read Chart 9-4 either forward or backward. If national income is Y_1, the diagram says, consumption spending will be Y_1C_1 and saving will be C_1D_1. But because saving must be matched by investment, income can be OY_1 *only if* investment is also C_1D_1.

For convenience, we may translate Chart 9-4 into another diagram (Chart 9-5). This shows the saving, instead of the consumption, that corresponds to each level of income. Y_1S_1 in Chart 9-5 is the same length as C_1D_1 on Chart 9-4, and Y_fS_f is the same length as C_fD_f. If we are told how much investment *will* be—and how much saving *must* be—we need only find the point on the S curve of Chart 9-5 that is the right height, and read off the equilibrium level of income by dropping a perpendicular to the OY-axis.

This line of argument leads directly to the Keynesian idea of an "underemployment equilibrium." Suppose that OY_f is the level of national income that will be reached if labor is fully employed,[17] while OY_1 is a level of income so

---

[16]Assume for the moment that government spending balances taxes; the effects of an unbalanced government budget will be brought in presently.

[17]Trying to define "full employment" seems to raise many people's blood pressure. Our definition for purposes of this book is aimed to be less exciting than many. We mean by "full employment" a situation where:

1. People who have jobs are reasonably content with their working hours and pace of work, and would not on the whole prefer to do more work at current rates of pay in order to increase their earnings.
2. People who are out of work can count on getting jobs which will use their skills, with pay and working conditions in line with those now current on such jobs, within the few days or weeks required to get in touch with possible employers and to change their residence or get extra training when required.

Just how many jobs and how much unemployment this definition permits will depend on the

low that it means an underemployment of labor. If investment is only Y_1S_1, equilibrium is possible at income OY_1 but not possible at the full-employment income level of OY_f. Only if investment can be Y_fS_f can we have equilibrium at full employment.

So far, we have not allowed for the possibility of a surplus or deficit in the government budget, yet government can be brought in without even redrawing the diagrams. "Income" in Chart 9–4 would ordinarily be interpreted as that part of personal income which is "disposable" after households pay their income taxes, social security contributions, and so forth.[18] But if we choose we can let Y measure "income" before taxes, and can consider the margin between the C curve and the diagonal OD to include taxes as well as saving. The S curve of Chart 9–5 must then be read as including saving plus taxes, and its shape must depend on the tax structure as well as on the public's attitudes toward saving. Most tax structures imply higher total tax payments as well as higher saving at higher income levels. If tax rates and definitions of taxable income remain unchanged, we can draw a single rising curve to show the sum of saving and taxes. When we do so, what must balance saving plus taxes is the *sum* of investment plus government spending. If investment alone is too small to provide full employment, government spending can be used to make up the difference. Alternatively, we can cut taxes to lower our saving schedule in Chart 9–5 until saving plus taxes just matches the existing levels of investment plus government spending.

The multiplier. Suppose that the level of investment changes. The equilibrium level of national income must also change in the same direction. But the change of income will include a change in consumption, because consumption depends on income. The differences in investment and in consumption (which add up to the difference in income) must, therefore, add to more than the initial difference in investment. The ratio of this added income to the added investment is called by Keynesian economists the *investment multiplier*.

In Chart 9–6, the consumption function is again represented by C_1C_2. Investment is set at $OI_1 = Y_1G_1$. The sum of consumption plus investment at income level OY_1 is represented by extending Y_1C_1 upward, by a distance equal to Y_1G_1, so that $Y_1D_1 = Y_1G_1 + Y_1C_1$. More generally, so long as investment is OI_1, the sum of investment and consumption is shown by curve E_1D_1, parallel to C_1C_2. Intersection D_1, the equilibrium point, shows that investment and the

---

characteristics of the labor force and of the labor market that determine the "normal" lag in placing a worker with a new employer. In the light of postwar experience, it seems reasonable to identify full employment with a situation where unemployment (as defined and measured by the Census) is about 3 to 4 per cent of the labor force.

[18]Certain taxes (such as sales taxes, cigarette stamps, and so forth) are commonly counted as part of consumption expenditure; the funds with which consumers will pay them are not subtracted out in obtaining "disposable income." But if we want to reinterpret Charts 9–4 and 9–5 to include government expenditure along with investment, we must treat this part of "expenditure" explicitly as taxes.

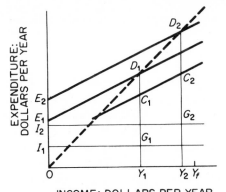

Chart 9-6.

consumption corresponding to income OY_1 just add up to equal income, since D_1Y_1 equals OY_1.

If investment is OI_2 instead of OI_1, the curve showing the sum of investment and consumption must be drawn higher—in position E_2D_2. ($E_1E_2 = I_1I_2$.) D_2 is now the equilibrium point, and OY_2 equilibrium income. The ratio of the income difference Y_1Y_2 to the investment difference I_1I_2 is the investment multiplier. The steeper the C curve (the higher the marginal propensity to consume), the greater will be the income difference Y_1Y_2, and the larger will be the multiplier.

The relationship between the marginal propensity to consume and the multiplier may be more convincingly developed by means of simple algebra. We write the change of income as the change in consumption plus the change in investment:

$$\Delta Y = \Delta C + \Delta I.$$

We then write the change in consumption as the change in income times the marginal propensity to consume:

$$\Delta C = mpc(\Delta Y).$$

This gives us:

$$\Delta Y = mpc(\Delta Y) + \Delta I,$$

or:

$$\Delta Y(1 - mpc) = \Delta I.$$

From this expression we obtain:

$$\Delta Y/\Delta I = 1/(1 - mpc).$$

The expression $\Delta Y/\Delta I$—the ratio of added income to added investment—represents the multiplier.

The larger the marginal propensity to consume, the larger the multiplier. If, for example, $mpc = 0.5$, the multiplier is $1/(1 - 0.5)$ or $1/0.5$, or 2.0. If $mpc = 0.9$, the multiplier is $1/(1 - 0.9)$, or $1/0.1$, or 10.

Multiplier formulae can also be constructed to show the effects of changes in taxes or government spending, in import spending or export receipts, on the level of national income. We shall use some of these formulae in Parts III and IV of this book.

The analysis just sketched shows a difference between one equilibrium position and another. But it does not tell *by what path* the economy will shift from one equilibrium to the other.[19] A dynamic "process analysis" can be framed only if we go on to add assumptions about the way people respond to change. One such assumption (linked with the name of Sir Dennis Robertson) is that consumer spending in each period is adjusted to the income level of the preced-

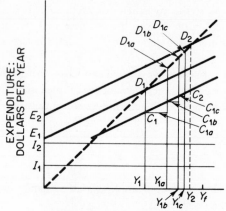

Chart 9-7.

---

[19]In fact, the analysis does not even show that if an original equilibrium is disrupted the resulting changes will in fact tend to a new equilibrium. The economy might oscillate indefinitely—even with widening swings. We shall show such a case in Chapter 10. It takes additional assumptions to tell what will happen in a Keynesian model of the economy when such a disturbance happens. The assumptions sketched in the text, patterned after J. R. Hicks, *A Contribution to the Theory of the Trade Cycle* (Oxford: Clarendon Press, 1950), p. 8, are far from being the only possible set.

ing period.[20] The results are sketched diagrammatically in Chart 9–7. Again, we start at equilibrium with national income OY_1, investment $OI_1 = C_1D_1$, and consumption Y_1C_1. Now we let investment rise to OI_2, and hold it at that level for several successive periods. In the first period after the change (Period A), consumption is still at Y_1C_1. This is because it is related to the original income level. Income is increased by exactly the amount of extra investment $I_1I_2 = Y_1Y_{1a}$, then, and is carried up to $OY_{1a} = Y_{1a}D_{1a}$.[21] In the next period (Period B), consumption will rise from $Y_1C_1 = Y_{1a}C_{1a}$ to a level corresponding to income OY_{1a}, that is, to $Y_{1b}C_{1b}$. With investment holding constant at $OI_2 = C_{1a}D_{1a}$, this gain in consumption will constitute a gain in income of $Y_{1a}Y_{1b}—C_{1a}C_{1b}$. Income for Period B will be OY_{1b}. Consumption will then adjust by rising to $Y_{1c}C_{1c}$ and so on. Beginning with Period B, each period raises income by a constant fraction of the last previous increase, moving income by decreasing steps toward a new equilibrium level OY_2.[22]

Multiplier analysis can thus be transformed into a sort of analytical subassembly and used extensively as an element in business cycle theories.[23] But this is as far as the analysis need be pushed for present purposes.

A complete Keynesian theory must go on to indicate what determines investment. This is the task that Keynes assigns to the interest rate and money, and the rest of Keynes' analysis will await our next chapter. We shall look at the several ways in which cash can affect income and payments. At this point we pause to examine the record on saving and income.

The record on saving. Just as the transactions-velocity approach can most easily be used if velocity is constant, so the Keynesian payments approach

---

[20]See D. H. Robertson, "Saving and Hoarding," *Economic Journal,* September 1933. The length of the "period" is left ambiguous; think of it as being in the neighborhood of three to six months. In more realistic analyses, economists tend to think of a delayed response of consumption to income, in terms of a "distributed lag." The consumption of a given calendar quarter will partly depend on that quarter's income, partly on income in the preceding quarter, partly on income in a few earlier quarters.

[21]Note, by the way, that saving and investment are equal at the end of Period A. As income is OY_{1a} and consumption is still at $Y_{1a}C_{1a}$ (equal to Y_1C_1), saving is now at $C_{1a}D_{1a}$, as is investment. This itself tells us that our system is not yet in equilibrium. Consumers had intended to save C_1D_1, but actually saved somewhat more. *Ex ante* saving and *ex post* saving are not yet equal; neither are *ex ante* saving and *ex ante* investment.

[22]In the diagram, each period closes half the gap, as the illustrative figures assign half the extra income to consumption. In general, the fraction of the last increase by which income rises is given by the marginal propensity to consume. Thus algebraically, successive increases in income in this model will run: $K = I_2 - I_1$; BK; B^2K; B^3K; and so forth, where B is the "marginal propensity to consume." These successive increases yield a "convergent series" with a sum that approaches as a limit $K/(1 - B)$.

[23]This is the procedure of J. R. Hicks' *Trade Cycle,* already cited. The other main ingredients in his theory are a function generating "induced investment" (tracing the effect of activity on investment in plant and inventories), and a ceiling and floor that limit fluctuations. In principle, this sort of analysis should be developed in terms of influences on anticipations. For simplicity, most analysts stick to mechanical assumptions like the Robertsonian consumption pattern used for illustration in the text.

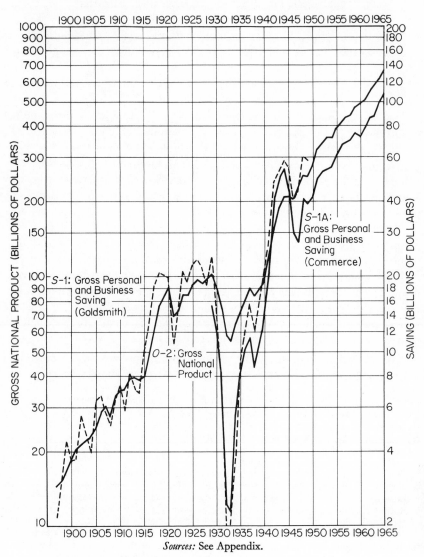

Sources: See Appendix.

Chart 9-8: Saving and income, 1897–1965.

is most useful if there is a stable relationship of saving to income. How far does the record justify such an assumption?

The longest estimate of annual saving with good credentials is presented as curve *S*–1 in Chart 9–8. To bring the record up to date, we have added Commerce Department estimates (curve *S*–1*A*) from 1929 to date. The saving series used are *gross;* they include depreciation allowances and the like, as well

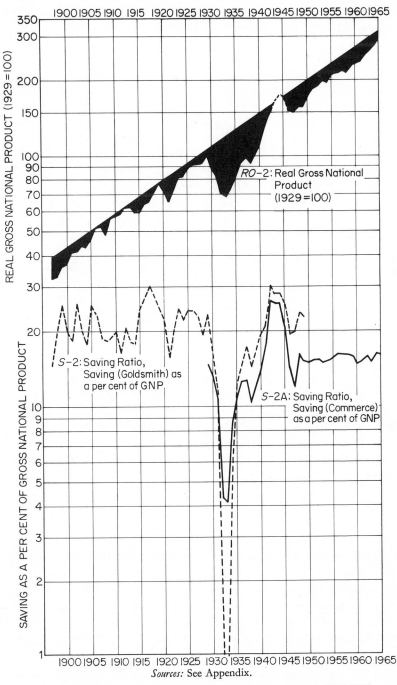

Chart 9-9: **The saving-income ratio and income fluctuations, 1897–1965.**

as the net saving of individuals and business. The chart compares the saving statistics with estimates of Gross National Product (curve O–2).

A glance will show the strong family resemblance between the curves of gross saving and that of Gross National Product. The curves are closely intertwined throughout the seven decades covered, indicating that gross saving is roughly one-fifth of GNP. The great upsurge of World War I, the slumps of 1920–22, 1930–33, and 1938–39, the new upsurge of World War II, and the postwar prosperity appear in the saving and GNP series, though saving fluctuates more sharply.

The Keynesian consumption-function hypothesis would require that saving remain a constant fraction of Gross National Product, or that it decline compared to GNP when GNP is falling and rise compared to GNP when GNP is rising.[24] To check the record against these predictions, we have plotted saving as a fraction of GNP in Chart 9–9, and have compared the saving-income ratio (curves S–2 and S–2A) to an index of GNP in 1929 prices (curve RO–2).

Like the stable-velocity theory of money, the Keynesian saving hypothesis seems to work best for the larger swings in aggregate activity. The saving-income ratio rises sharply during World War I and falls off sharply in the postwar depression of 1921–22. It declines precipitously in the early 1930's and falls off again in the 1938–39 recession. The ratio rises into World War II and declines sharply after the war, along with GNP.

The saving-income ratio moved erratically during the business fluctuations prior to 1914. It fell during some prewar recessions, but also declined or was low in some years of prosperity. In the 1950's and 1960's, by contrast, the ratio was unusually stable, and when it varied it generally moved in the "right" direction. Because it has had such an erratic history, however, we should not put too much confidence in its continued stability.

On balance, the record would seem to say, income alone does not determine saving. What people save would appear to depend on many things in addition to the level of income itself.

Anticipations and Surprises

The dynamic view of the flow of payments. The first part of this chapter dealt with the flow of payments along Keynesian lines. The Keynesian tradition, however, limits its applicability by dwelling too much on "equilibrium." The forces that it analyzes are bound to set up fluctuations and are not even certain to lead to the establishment of an equilibrium. We shall, therefore, ask how the flow of payments works when the economic system is out of equilibrium.

---

[24]It should be a constant fraction of GNP if the consumption function passes through the origin; it should vary more sharply than GNP if the consumption function is as drawn in Chart 9–4.

The clue to a dynamic analysis of payments lies in a very simple idea which we owe to the Swedish economists—that of looking at all transactions both *ex post* and *ex ante*. In the *ex post* view, we look back at each transaction as part of *experience*. In the *ex ante* view, we look ahead at the transaction from the standpoint of those who *expect* to take part in it. The difference between expectation and outcome—a difference which does not exist in equilibrium—must be taken into account in predicting what will happen next.[25]

The cash account. The rules of accounting require "balance" in the accounts we draw up for firms, households, and government. The items we enter on the left-hand side (assets, for example) must add up to the same total as those we enter on the right-hand side (liabilities, for example). This balance is brought about by including a "residual" item on one side of the account that is just large enough to make the total on its side balance the other side.

This rule of balance applies in particular to the cash accounts of spending units.[26] On the left-hand side of the cash account for any firm or household we enter:

> cash held at the outset;
> *plus* receipts from sales of goods and services;
> *plus* receipts from dividends and other remittances of profits from other economic units;
> *plus* receipts from financing (borrowing or sales of securities).

This sum equals initial cash plus total cash receipts.

On the right-hand side of the account we enter:

> payments for purchases of goods and services;
> *plus* payments of dividends, and so forth;
> *plus* payments for financing (lending, repayment of borrowings, purchase of securities).

This total is bound to fall short of the left-hand total by just the amount of cash held at the end of the period. Final cash constitutes the residual item which we enter on the right-hand side to make the account balance.

If we group firms or households together, the same rule of balance must

---

[25]An equilibrium outcome from the working of economic forces is perhaps best defined as an outcome *which, if expected, will happen*. The cruder conception of an equilibrium outcome as one which, if it happens, will go on happening until the determining circumstances change, is approximately the same idea.

[26]For purposes of analysis, it is simplest to regard short-term debts arising from sales of goods and services as constituting receipts from the sale of goods for the sellers, and as outlays for the buyers. "Accounts payable" (or receivable) are thus treated as a form of cash. This procedure is necessary because most sales are initially settled by setting up such debts. Borrowing on a promissory note, however, is regarded as "financing." This way of using terms is arbitrary but convenient. It also corresponds roughly to the usage of the Federal Reserve study of "flow of funds."

apply to the combined cash account—obtained by taking the sum of like items for all the members of the group. The reason is simply the mathematical rule about "equals added to equals." This section rests chiefly on such combined accounts.

Balancing cash accounts *ex post* and *ex ante*. The principle of balance in the cash account applies both *ex ante* and *ex post*. For any firm or household, the cash account for (say) July must balance as drawn up in anticipation on June 30, and as drawn up in retrospect on August 1, and if we add up the corresponding items in the cash accounts of all firms and households, we must also get a balance *ex ante* or *ex post*.

As the *ex post* accounts deal with actual events, items that relate to transactions between spending units must appear identically in the accounts of both units. The amount a retailer paid his wholesaler for a case of canned peaches, for example, must be the same on the books of both retailer and wholesaler. The amount the retailer borrowed at the bank must be the same on his books as on the banker's books. This standard of consistency does not apply to the *ex ante* accounts. The retailer may plan to pay a lower price for the case of canned peaches than the wholesaler plans to charge. The wholesaler, in fact, may not plan to sell them, although the retailer expects to buy them. The only item in the *ex ante* accounts for which we can guarantee consistency is the initial cash position—the one *ex post* item in the *ex ante* accounts, because it is already determined when the estimates are drawn up.

We have already come across one instance of a discrepancy between *ex ante* magnitudes. In periods of disequilibrium, *ex ante* saving-plus-taxes need not match *ex ante* investment-plus-government-expenditure.[27] As J. M. Keynes pointed out in his *Treatise on Money*,[28] decisions to save are taken primarily by consuming households, decisions to invest by business firms. As they are made by different people under the sway of different motives, the two sets of decisions cannot be expected to match with perfect smoothness. Matching is finally brought about by a Procrustean process that makes people do otherwise than they had intended.

Rough fulfillment of expectations for short periods. If we look about a month ahead, the general course of economic events is almost sure to be roughly anticipated by the managers of the firms and households that make up the economic system. Each firm or household plans to pay out approximately

---

[27]Note that neither saving nor investment appears as such in the cash accounts. Household income is roughly the amount received from sales of currently produced goods and services (consisting chiefly of wages, salaries, and profits withdrawn from business). To define saving, we add the excess of business profit over amounts withdrawn, and subtract household outlays for current consumables. Investment consists of any household outlays for goods not classified as current consumables, plus additions to inventory, plant, and equipment by businesses. There is a noncash element in both profits and additions to business inventory, plant, and equipment.

[28]New York: Harcourt, Brace & World, Inc., 1930; especially Vol. I, p. 175.

as much as it receives. If we are dealing with so short a period that there is no room for actual disbursements to diverge far from plans, about enough will be paid out to fulfill expectations as to receipts.

Some slack occurs in this calculation. Although total receipts may be as expected, individual firms and households may find the outcome very different from what they expected—some having more, some less. In any case, the equality of planned total expenditure and actual total receipts is only approximate. Even within a week or a month, plans for disbursements will not be followed precisely. The difference between complete fulfillment and "rough fulfillment" of expectations may substantially affect operations in subsequent periods. This line of inquiry will be followed up shortly. First, we must trace the consequences of rough fulfillment of expectations, for some of these consequences are rather striking.

1. The general *level of physical activity* (production and sales) during a "month" will roughly match expectations held by business at the start of the month. If businessmen are convinced that they are in a depression, and plan business outlays accordingly, the depression they imagine will occur. The same thing is true of optimistic expectations.

2. Any substantial *rise or fall in the physical volume of activity* during a "month" can also be traced to a general expectation of such a rise or fall in the minds of the business community. Small expansions or contractions may happen as a result of unanticipated events. But if the month is one of significant economic upswing or downswing, the swing must have been built into business plans at the beginning of the month.[29]

3. (A qualification.) Sales to consumers often differ substantially from expectations; and such surprises can considerably alter production schedules and investment within a few months.

4. Any marked *rise or fall* in the *prices* at which currently produced nonfarm output is sold will ordinarily have been built into business plans at the beginning of the month in which it occurred.[30]

5. Further, a high or low *level of profits* during the month will reflect an expectation of high or low profits at the beginning of the month— slanted up or down by market surprises.

---

[29]It is hard to believe that the rate of production, employment, and so forth, over the economic system as a whole can diverge by more than 1 per cent or even $1/_2$ of 1 per cent from *expectations* held a month earlier, except in case of war or major natural catastrophe—possibly, one should add, in case of unexpected major labor disputes. Yet a divergence of more than 1 per cent from the previous month's seasonally adjusted *actual* rate occurs quite frequently. This is because business is executing plans previously existing. Turning points in business seem often to be set off by an unexpected tapering-off of an upswing or downswing of sales.

[30]Prices of *previously existing* goods (real estate, securities, used automobiles and machinery, or crops in storage such as wheat and cotton) sometimes jump unexpectedly. A generally anticipated change in these prices, in fact, involves a paradox. If in December people agree that in January wheat will sell 50 per cent above its November 30 price, then wheat will actually be about 50 per cent above that price in December itself.

Surprises arising from inconsistencies in expectations. Next we must go behind the "rough correspondence" of outcome and expectations, and ask why any divergence is possible. The answer is that expectations are often *inconsistent*—either with each other or with external realities. A new firm, for instance, may expect to sell some goods next month which nobody is planning to buy. A firm may be planning to fill an order which its customer is planning to cancel. In such cases, one or both of the parties to the prospective transaction will find things turning out contrary to plan. Surprises are also in prospect if the grand total of final cash balances that spending units expect to hold diverges from the amount of cash that is actually going to exist.

One can map out the sources of surprises in some detail, but the process is so laborious that only a few results can find space here.[31] We will concentrate on surprises as to business receipts from sales of current output to nonbusiness buyers.

We must stress at the outset that each firm's receipts depend on the payments by other firms—directly as other firms are its customers, and indirectly as other firms pay out income to consumers. Each firm's receipts hardly respond to the effect of its own payments on consumer income. Firms that are overly optimistic about receipts and that budget their payments on the basis of their estimates of receipts are laying up unpleasant surprises for themselves but pleasant surprises for other firms.[32]

If any general departure of actual from planned income payments by business to nonbusiness groups occurs, business receipts will tend to diverge from expectations in the same direction.

If the plans of businessmen for interfirm dealings do not match, surprises will also result—not only on interfirm markets but also on the markets where business firms sell to nonbusiness groups. The income payments of firms which expect to sell to other firms are necessarily based on their own sales estimates, not on the unknown estimates of their customers. If the prospective sellers expect lower interfirm dealings than do prospective buyers, total business payments to nonbusiness groups will be inadequate to fulfill expectations.

Surprises may also result from monetary forces.[33] If business plans to enlarge its cash balances, but the monetary system does not produce an increase of total cash or a reduction in the cash balances of nonbusiness holders, business receipts from sales will fall short of expectations. If business plans to hold constant or

---

[31]For more details, and an algebraic statement of the underlying reasoning, see the note at the end of this chapter.

[32]There is an exception to this rule. If the overoptimistic firms revise their plans in the course of the period under study and dump inventories—selling more than expected at a lower price than expected—they may generate unpleasant surprises for others without having pleasant surprises themselves.

[33]Besides the factors discussed in this paragraph, the financing of business by households and by banks also comes in question; such financing is passed over here for simplification, but see the algebraic note to this chapter.

to reduce cash balances while total cash increases or the cash of nonbusiness holders falls, business receipts will exceed expectations and there will be pleasant surprises. This is interesting in relation to the government's tax and expenditure policy, for if the government has a deficit, it must either deplete its cash holdings, print new money, or induce the banks to "create credit" for the government's benefit.

Revision of estimates in the light of surprises. The plans businessmen carry into a month are bound to be revised in the light of experience. If experience during a month diverges from first expectations, estimates and plans for later months will be revised in the same direction.[34] If business entered July expecting an upswing of sales for both July and August, pleasant surprises during July will reinforce the expectation of an upswing during August. Unpleasant surprises will weaken this expectation, or cause it to be replaced by expectations of a downswing. We will always find some firms undergoing pleasant surprises and revising further estimates in an optimistic direction, at the same time that other firms are undergoing unpleasant surprises and making pessimistic revisions.

Not all of the revision of estimates is based on market experience. Political news, for instance, affects business estimates. The views of professional forecasters and engineers who look further into the future may also lead business to revise estimates, even though recent experience follows expectations. Each firm has some idea of how others are doing. If its own good or bad luck seems exceptional in relation to the fortunes of others, it may not expect good or bad luck to continue.

When looking at estimates of the future, one should know not only *in which direction* opinion expects affairs to go, but also *how closely different people agree* and *how confident* they are of their estimates. If recent events have been very different from expectations, people are very likely to hold different opinions of the future, and especially likely to feel uncertainty. This may increase the demand for cash assets—for reasons we shall examine shortly—and could produce the sort of situation in which unpleasant surprises are apt to occur in the next month.

The effect of experience on estimates may vary greatly with circumstances, and especially with people's notions of what is "normal." Shortly after a war,

---

[34]But if we think in terms of receipts from sales to nonbusiness groups, an exception must be made on account of inventory policy (cf. note 32). With aggregate receipts from sales just as expected, some firms will find their particular markets weaker than expected and might reap larger-than-expected receipts by selling off inventories at prices lower than they had expected to charge. If they do so, they will be unpleasantly disappointed as to markets but not as to receipts. Their sales, however, will drain receipts away from other firms, giving the other firms unpleasant surprises both as to receipts and as to markets.

In the other direction, if some firms decide to hold larger inventories than they had planned (in the hope of sales at better prices later on), they may have pleasant surprises as to markets but smaller receipts than expected. By driving away customers, however, they will create pleasant surprises for other sellers.

for instance, there may be a widespread conviction that prices are abnormally high. In this case, a drop in prices is apt to lead to a downward revision of price expectations for some time ahead. A rise, on the other hand, is not likely to affect estimates of prices more than a few weeks ahead. In such circumstances, *either* a rise or a fall of prices is likely to generate differences of opinion about future developments, thus increasing the proportion of dealers who take "bear" positions.

A depression may create a conviction that prices are subnormal. If there have not been major price declines in recent weeks, it may be easier to set up expectations that a rise is near than expectations that there will be a further fall. If the optimists have had hopes of recovery blasted several times (as happened in 1930, 1931, and 1932), faith in "normality" may fade. This sort of experience is probably one reason why recovery from long depressions is so difficult.

Revision of plans in light of new estimates. How businesses operate in any month depends primarily on the plans with which they entered the month. These, in turn, go back to previous estimates. The outcome will determine further estimates, which will lead to further plans. It is by following this chain of argument that "dynamic" monetary theory must proceed.

In an uncertain world, estimates and plans for the immediate future are always more concrete than for later dates. When entering July, business may have a *provisional plan* (based upon provisional estimates) for August, as well as a fairly detailed plan for July. When its provisional estimates are revised, its provisional plans have to be readjusted. But many elements in its plans for the next few months are already pretty well settled by past decisions. A firm that is a "going concern" has contracts, goods in process, stocks of perishable supplies, and commitments to employ labor, leaving little freedom to adjust production in the next few weeks or months. Output for the near future already exists in partly finished form; most costs are already "sunk," and can only be recovered by incurring the extra costs that are needed to ready the output for sale. Firms have somewhat more freedom in scheduling purchases of materials and labor than in scheduling output, as most of the materials and labor are used in the production of goods that are not yet near completion. But even input of perishable goods and of services (especially labor) can rarely be changed quickly and drastically without gross inefficiency.

Firms have much more freedom to make sharp quick changes in investment plans. To be sure, the rate of *completion* of investment goods is always rather rigidly fixed for some weeks or months ahead, for the same reasons that limit the short-term flexibility of other types of finished products. Houses that will be ready for occupancy next month are already near completion. Although revised sales estimates may be much more pessimistic about the sales price or rental value of such houses, it is worthwhile incurring the last 10 per cent of costs to recover most of the 90 per cent of costs that have already been "sunk" in the house. Even if revised sales estimates are much more optimistic, not much can be done at reasonable cost to bring extra houses to completion within the next couple of months. Similarly, machines to be installed next month are already well toward completion.

The volume of investment, though, is not so much a matter of *completion* of construction as of *work done* during the period under study. The work done may be altered somewhat, even within a few weeks, both by changing the pace of construction on projects already started, and by altering the rate at which new projects are launched. Finally, there is a great deal of scope for adjustments in inventory investment. Firms that have salable products on hand or in production may try to hasten their sale by price cuts, or may mark up prices to hold back goods for later sale. Similarly, supplies already bought may either be held in storage or put into processes leading to sale or further fabrication. Decisions to change the rate of future output show up in the important component of inventories called "goods in process." If output is to be expanded, it is first necessary to "fill the pipelines"—to increase the production of materials and parts used in the finished product. Until the bulge in production reaches final markets, the extra output appears in the "goods in process" part of the inventory account rather than in salable output. This bulge in inventories will be matched by an increase in personal income. If output is shrinking, the decline will first appear as a fall in inventories of goods in process (disinvestment), and personal income will decline relative to the flow of final output.

The *sensitivity* of investment plans to changes in sales estimates varies widely from one firm to another and from one time to another—particularly for investment in durable plant and equipment. We can always find some firms whose operations strain their facilities, while others are operating at a rate that leaves plenty of unused capacity. The latter are apt to be *insensitive;* they will plan little investment whether or not they expect an improvement of business. The former—those who are straining capacity—are likely to be *sensitive*. If their sales estimates grow more optimistic, their investment plans are likely to expand; if estimates grow more pessimistic, their plans are apt to contract.

These differences in sensitivity make the distribution of surprises very important. To forecast investment we must know which industries are experiencing pleasant surprises and which industries are having unpleasant surprises.[35] Differences in sensitivity also imply that the responsiveness of investment will depend upon business conditions. In times of high prosperity when most business is active and a great deal of investment in plant and equipment is planned or in progress, investment is apt to be highly sensitive to bad news. In times

---

[35]The accidental distribution of especially pleasant surprises among firms of greater and less sensitivity may explain a good deal of the wobble which is commonly observed from month to month in such series as construction contracts awarded.

of acute depression when most businesses have excess capacity, investment may be highly insensitive to good news or to bad.

Unintended investment and the equalization of saving with investment. Investment in inventories may be *unintended*.[36] If business is trying to reduce output, sales are likely to fall below estimates, for the process of cutting down output is apt to produce unpleasant surprises for the majority of firms. In such circumstances, businesses are likely to seek an increase of their cash holdings.[37] At the same time, the process of cutting down output is apt to involve a net credit contraction through repayment of loans, and consumers are apt to be scared into trying to build up their cash assets.[38] If consumers are not willing to spend as much as it takes to fulfill business sales expectations, sellers of goods must cut their prices more than planned, or accept an unintended growth of physical inventories of salable goods. At the same time, business will be cutting inventories of goods in process. This is a by-product of its cuts in production. Yet inventories of goods in process *plus* salable goods will shrink less than intended, and total investment will be greater than originally planned.

This unintended investment is one side of the process by which investment and saving are brought to *ex post* equality when there is an excess of *ex ante* saving. Two other processes are involved as well. One is an unintended reduction of saving that occurs when some households and businesses find their incomes less than they expected. The other is an increased government offset to saving that will occur on account of the decline in national income that results from the other adjustment processes; a decline in national income cuts into government revenue and usually increases certain government outlays.

If there is an excess of planned investment over *ex ante* saving, the process works in reverse. Any effort of business to expand production and inventories will raise consumers' incomes and will tend to make business sales exceed expectations. There will be an unintended reduction of inventories of salable goods that will reduce total investment below what was planned. There will also be unintended increases in saving and reductions in government's offset to saving.

---

[36]By "unintended" is meant here an act which is carried out reluctantly and in opposition to the plans for the current period that existed a few days earlier. Obviously, investment in inventories can rarely be involuntary in the extreme sense of running against an *unconditional* refusal of the firm to invest. A firm that is piling up inventory could ordinarily pile up less by making larger price cuts. Unintended inventory investment may be interpreted to mean acceptance of more inventory than had been planned *in preference to the greater evil* of making greater price cuts than had been planned.

[37]Ordinarily, a firm which is reducing its output does not aim to reduce its "net working capital"—that is, the sum of its cash, debts receivable, and inventories *minus* its short-term debts payable. If it plans to reduce the inventory component, it is presumably planning either a growth of cash or debt retirement, or both.

[38]Unemployment, however, may be forcing some consuming households to reduce their cash balances; and the effects of unemployment on the government budget may be leading the government to reduce its cash holdings or to increase the total cash supply by borrowing at the banks.

An Algebraic Treatment of the Stream of Payments

Expected and realized flows of payments. This note will illustrate the relationships between expected and actual receipts described in the text, and provide a foundation for the results sketched there. The procedure used represents an improved version of that developed in two articles by Hart in 1937–1938,[39] which, in turn, was developed from Swedish ideas.

A mimeographed paper on the saving-investment problem by Professor Erik Lindahl (1934) suggested much of the analytical structure, especially the useful device of subtracting an *ex post* from an *ex ante* equation. Professor Lindahl's *Money and Credit* (London: George Allen and Unwin, 1939), pp. 74–136, contains an elaborate development of his ideas.[40] Our divergence from his exposition results partly from our efforts at simplification, partly from the fact that we try to steer clear of *income account* concepts, on the ground that income for a period is not on an *ex post* basis even at the end of the period, since later experience may lead to a revaluation of assets which alters income accounts retrospectively. The *cash account* in which we deal can be finally closed the moment that the period studied comes to an end, so that the *ex post* basis is more definite.

Generalized cash account. A general system for handling these relations is embodied in the "generalized cash account" (Table 9-1). Each item in the cash account is assigned a letter, so that the cash account becomes an equation which holds as between two sets of algebraic symbols. Following the rule that "equals added to equals are equal," we can combine accounts by adding corresponding terms over the accounts of all the dealers in a group. These groups are taken to be five for present purposes: households; enterprises other than banks; banks; the outside world; and the state (central and local government).

The resulting equations are very simple in structure, since the only relationships here are additive. We merely carry out additions, subtractions, and transpositions from one side of an equation to the other; there is not a single division or a multiplication in the whole operation.[41]

---

[39]"Failure and Fulfillment of Expectations in Business Fluctuations," *Review of Economic Statistics*, May 1937, pp. 71–72; "Consumption Markets," *American Economic Review*, supplement, March 1938, pp. 122–25.

[40]A postwar version of Lindahl's system, applied to inflation and generalized to take account of the state and of foreign trade, is presented in Bent Hansen, *Study in the Theory of Inflation* (New York: Holt, Rinehart & Winston, Inc., 1951).

[41]This simplicity results from the modesty of our objectives. We are always content to stop with measuring one variable or the sum of a set of variables as the algebraic sum of a long list of other variables. An analysis which aimed to arrive at unique solutions in terms of specific magnitudes would have to posit a large number of other relationships among the variables in addition to this set of cash-account equations; and some of these other relationships would be much more complex algebraically.

TABLE 9-1

GENERALIZED CASH ACCOUNT

$*m(0)$	:	Cash held at the beginning of the period—always known from the outset;
$+_r g$	:	Receipts from sales of *goods* and services;
$+_r d$	:	Receipts from *dividends* and other items (including interest and withdrawals from unincorporated businesses) paid as profits;
$+_r t$	:	Receipts of *taxes* (for a government);
$+_r f$	:	Receipts from *financing* (borrowing or sale of securities);
$+n$	:	Creation of *new* money (printing by a government; net expansion of credit by a bank);
$=$		
$+_p g$	:	Payments for purchases of *goods* and services;
$+_p d$	:	Payments of *dividends* and other profit payments;
$+_p f$	:	Payments for *financing* (lending or purchase of securities);
$+_p t$	:	Payments of *taxes;*
$+m(1)$	:	Cash held at the end of the period.

MEANING OF SYMBOLS IN TABLES 9-1 TO 9-4

m	:	Dollars of cash (coin + paper money + bank deposits + accounts receivable less accounts payable), held at date (0) or (1).
g	:	Dollars paid for *goods* and services.
d	:	Dollars paid for *dividends* or other profit distributions.
t	:	Dollars paid in *taxes.*
f	:	Dollars paid in *financing.*
n	:	Dollars of *new* money created.

M, G, D, T, F, or N: A *combined* total of the corresponding items for *all* economic units in the group indicated by the small letter to the right of the M, G, D, T, F, or N. These letters denote:

h	:	*households* (including farmers), treated as consumers and as suppliers of labor and farm products;
e	:	*enterprises* (corporations and unincorporated nonfarm businesses, excluding banks);
b	:	*banks;*
w	:	the *world* outside the country under study;
s	:	the *state* (central and local governments).

An asterisk (*) to the left of the M, G, D, F, T, or N indicates an *ex post* measurement of actual sums experienced.

Absence of an asterisk indicates an *ex ante* measurement. A small $_p$ to the left of the G, D, F, or T indicates an estimate by the *payer;* a small $_r$, by the prospective *recipient*. M's are estimated by the holder; N's, by the money-creators.

Payment terms $(G, D, F,$ or $T)$ have two subscripts at the right: the first shows who is to receive the payment; the second, who is making the payment, by class of dealer.

Business account *ex ante*. The first application of our generalized account is to draw up a combined *ex ante* account for all business enterprises other than banks. The result appears in Table 9-2. The *ex post* account (not reproduced) would look exactly the same, except that the estimator subscripts would vanish and asterisks would appear on all terms to show their *ex post* character; thus, the term $_r G_{eh}$ would become $*G_{eh}$.

TABLE 9-2

COMBINED *EX ANTE* CASH ACCOUNT FOR ALL BUSINESS ENTERPRISES
(EXCLUDING BANKS) FOR THE PERIOD FROM t_0 UNTIL t_1

$*M_e(0)$	: Cash held by businesses at the outset;
$+_rG_{eh}$	: Prospective business receipts from sales of goods and services to households, as estimated at t_0 by prospective sellers;
$+_rG_{ew}$	: Prospective business receipts from export sales to the outside world (sellers' t_0 estimates);
$+_rG_{ee}$	: Prospective business receipts from sales of goods and services to another business (sellers' t_0 estimates);
$+_rG_{es}$	: Prospective business receipts from sales to government (sellers' t_0 estimates);
$+_rF_{eb}$	: Prospective business receipts from borrowing at banks (borrowers' t_0 estimates);
$+_rF_{eh}$	: Prospective business receipts from financing by consuming households (borrowers' t_0 estimates);
$=$	
$_pG_{he}$	: Prospective business payments to households for goods and services (chiefly labor services and farm products) as estimated at t_0 by prospective buyers;
$+_pG_{we}$	: Prospective import purchases (buyers' t_0 estimates);
$+_pG_{ee}$	: Prospective interbusiness purchases (buyers' t_0 estimates);
$+_pD_{he}$	: Prospective payments of dividends, and the like, to households (payers' t_0 estimates);
$+_pT_{se}$	: Prospective tax payments by business (taxpayers' t_0 estimates);
$+_pF_{be}$	: Prospective repayments of business loans, and the like, at banks (t_0 estimates of debtors);
$+_pF_{he}$	: Prospective repayments of loans, and the like, at households (t_0 estimates of debtors);
$+M_e(1)$	: Prospective business cash holdings at t_1 (t_0 estimates of prospective holders).

We may concentrate on the terms showing business receipts from non-business customers: the G terms on the receipts side, excluding $_rG_{ee}$. To make these terms stand out, the equation may be rearranged by transposing the other terms on the receipts side to the other side of the equation and changing the order of terms. The result is:

$_rG_{eh} + _rG_{ew} + _rG_{es}$	: Prospective receipts from sales to nonbusiness customers;
$=$	
$_pD_{he} + _pG_{he}$	: Prospective income payments by business;
$+_pG_{ee} - _rG_{ee}$	: The discrepancy between buyers' and sellers' estimates of interfirm dealings;
$+_pT_{se}$	: Prospective tax payments;
$+_qG_{we}$	: Prospective import purchases;
$+_pF_{be} - _rF_{eb} + _pF_{he} - _rF_{eh}$	: Prospective net repayment of financing;
$+M_e(1) - *M_e(0)$	: Prospective net growth of business cash holdings.

TABLE 9-3

COMBINED *EX POST* RECEIPTS OF BUSINESS FROM NONBUSINESS, DERIVED FROM NONBUSINESS ACCOUNTS

Account	Households	Rest of World	State	Banks	Combination
Business receipts	$*G_{eh}$ =	$*G_{ew}$ =	$*G_{es}$ =	0† =	$*G_{eh} + *G_{ew} + *G_{es}$ =
Taxes	$-*T_{sh}$	0†	$*T_{se} + *T_{sh} + *T_{sb}$	$-*T_{sb}$	$*T_{se}$
Income payments, etc.	$\begin{cases} +*G_{he} + *G_{hs} + *G_{hb} \\ +*D_{he} + *D_{hs} + *D_{hb} \end{cases}$	$+*G_{we}$ 0†	$-*G_{hs}$ $-*D_{hs}$	$-*G_{hb}$ $-*D_{hb}$	$+*G_{he} + *G_{we}$ $+*D_{he}$
Financing not touching business directly	$\begin{cases} +*F_{hb} + *F_{hs} \\ -*F_{bh} - *F_{sh} \end{cases}$	$+*F_{wb}$ $-*F_{bw}$	$+*F_{sh} + *F_{sb}$ $-*F_{hs} - *F_{bs}$	$\left.\begin{array}{l} +*F_{bh} - *F_{hb} \\ +*F_{bw} - *F_{wb} \\ +*F_{bs} - *F_{sb} \end{array}\right\}$	0
Financing touching business	$+*F_{he} - *F_{eh}$	0†	0†	$+*F_{be} - *F_{eb}$	$+*F_{he} + *F_{be}$ $-*F_{eh} - *F_{eb}$
Initial cash	$+*M_h(0)$	$+*M_w(0)$	$+*M_s(0)$	0	$+*M_h(0) + *M_w(0) + *M_s(0)$
Final cash	$-*M_h(1)$	$-*M_w(1)$	$-*M_s(1)$	0	$-*M_h(1) - *M_w(1) - *M_s(1)$
Money creation	0†	0†	$+*N_s$	$+*N_b$	$+*N_s + *N_b$

†Assumed zero for simplification. Other zeros are genuine. The zero in the *Combination* column must come from the addition by definition; the zeros in the *Banks* column arise from the logic of the credit-creation equation: see the text.

Derivation of actual business receipts from nonbusiness accounts.
The actual (*ex post*) receipts of business from nonbusiness buyers can be obtained
from the business accounts or from the accounts for nonbusiness dealers. The
second procedure is adopted in Table 9-3.

Each column of the table represents the application of the generalized cash
account to one of the major nonbusiness groups. The outlay items that constitute business receipts are put on one side of the equations. On the other side
are the receipts of the group in question, together with the other outlay items
(with minus signs because they are transposed to the receipts side). The fourth
column is the only one that calls for special explanation. Banks do not figure
significantly as customers of business. But their dealings with other sectors
have to be brought in to unsnarl the national accounts. This column is drawn
up as a credit-creation equation; it says that the amount of credit created equals
the sum of credits extended and expenses, taxes, and dividends paid *less* loan
repayments received (taken inclusive of interest). In combining the equations,
many of the terms that are positive for one class of nonbusiness dealers appear
with minus signs in the columns of other dealers. These terms, therefore, cancel.

The *Combination* column seems at first sight to say that in business "it is more
blessed to give than to receive," for it asserts that actual business receipts will
be larger as business:

Pays more taxes;
Pays more to employees and suppliers;
Pays more dividends;
Increases its loan repayments relative to its borrowings; and as non-
business holders have large initial cash balances.

The apparent paradox is a fraud. The proper interpretation of the result is that
each firm gains if *others* make large outpayments. If, of course, paying out more
will bring in more, the results are neutral, for business as a whole, to a first
approximation. The *composition* of outpayments will naturally affect the profit
situation.

Shortfall or overshot of business receipts as against estimates. It is
very illuminating to compare *actual* business receipts from sales to nonbusiness
groups (as derived in Table 9-3) with *prospective* receipts (as derived in Table 9-2).
This comparison may be made in the form of an algebraic subtraction of actual
from prospective receipts. The difference, if positive, represents a shortfall
of receipts as against estimates—an *unpleasant surprise* for business. The difference,
if negative, is an overshot—a *pleasant surprise*.

These subtractions lead to the equation shown in Table 9-4. This is most
readily interpreted by taking the numbered terms, singly and in appropriate
groups, and asking what it means if a term (or group of terms) is positive while
all others are zero:

(1) Receipts will tend to fall short of estimates to the extent that business cuts back its planned income payments to consuming households.

(2) Receipts will tend to fall short of estimates to the extent that business pays less taxes than planned. But note that the assumption that all other terms are zero implies that $*N_s$ and various terms involving government financing are all zero—that government will cut back spending because tax receipts are reduced. If government spending is unaffected, $*N_s$ will offset a cutback of taxes, government cash holdings will fall off, government will borrow at banks (creating a positive $*N_b$), or government will draw funds away from individuals by borrowing.

(3) Receipts will tend to fall short of estimates to the extent that import purchase plans are cut back. (Here note the proviso that the cash of the "rest of the world" is not changed, which implies that exports will drop to match the drop in imports.)

(4) Receipts will tend to fall short of estimates to the extent that business cuts back planned repayments or increases borrowings as against plans, giving consumers less spendable funds. (Note again, the effects of the proviso that other terms are constant: zero values for $*N_b$ and for the change in consumers' cash are involved.)

(5) Receipts will tend to fall short of estimates to the extent that inter-

TABLE 9-4

COMBINED EXCESS OF *EX ANTE* OVER *EX POST* RECEIPTS OF
BUSINESS FROM NONBUSINESS

$_rG_{eh} + {}_rG_{ew} + {}_rG_{es}$ $-*G_{eh} - *G_{ew} - *G_{es}$	} : Excess of anticipated over actual sales receipts of business from nonbusiness
=	
$_pD_{he} + {}_pG_{he}$ $-*D_{he} - *G_{he}$	} : Excess of planned over actual income payments by business to consuming households; (1)
$+_pT_{se} - *T_{se}$	} : Excess of planned over actual business tax payments; (2)
$+_pG_{we} - *G_{we}$	} : Excess of planned over actual import purchases; (3)
$+_pF_{he} + {}_qF_{be} - {}_rF_{eh} - {}_rF_{eb}$ $-*F_{he} - *F_{be} + *F_{he} + *F_{eb}$	} : Excess of planned over actual *net* repayment of outstanding loans by business to households and banks; (4)
$+_qG_{ee} - {}_rG_{ee}$	} : Discrepancy between buyers' and sellers' estimates of interfirm dealings; (5)
$+M_e(1) - *M_e(0)$	} : Planned increase of business cash holdings; (6)
$-*N_b - *N_s$	} : Actual decrease in stock of cash; (7)
$+ *M_h(1) + *M_w(1) + *M_s(1)$ $- *M_h(0) - *M_w(0) - *M_s(0)$	} : Actual increase in the portion of cash held by nonbusiness groups. (8)

Items numbered (1), (2), and (3) represent *cutbacks* as against plans in *current-account* payments to nonbusiness groups;

Item (4) represents a *cutback* in planned *financial* payments to nonbusiness groups;

Item (5) represents *inconsistencies* in plans as among business;

The sum of items (6), (7), and (8) represents *inconsistency* in businesses' plans for their cash balances in relation to the actual monetary situation—in relation to the creation of cash by the government and banks, and the demand for cash balances on the part of consumers, government, and foreigners.

business purchasers estimate transactions higher than interbusiness sellers.

(6) Receipts will tend to fall short of estimates to the extent that business plans to increase its cash. (Here, the proviso means that there is no growth of the cash stock, and that nonbusiness groups are not willing to let their portion of cash run down.)

(7) Receipts will tend to fall short of estimates to the extent that the total stock of cash is reduced.

(8) Receipts will tend to fall short of estimates to the extent that nonbusiness groups insist on increasing their cash holdings.

Or, using *groups* of these terms:

(1, 2, 3) Receipts will tend to fall short of estimates to the extent that business cuts back its current-account outpayments to nonbusiness groups.

(6, 7, 8) Receipts will tend to fall short of estimates to the extent that business plans for building up cash are inconsistent with the actual building up of the cash supply by credit creation and the willingness of nonbusiness groups to change their holdings.

Evidential value of the findings. We must not claim too much for these findings. They do not tell us what actually will result from a decision affecting any of these terms; such a decision will ordinarily have by-product effects on others. A tax cut affecting term (2), for example, will also affect terms (4), (7), and (8), as noted above. The most that we definitely know from an analysis running in terms of accounting truisms is that *statements inconsistent with the truisms must be false*. But this is actually a good deal of knowledge: it condemns many statements we might otherwise find plausible about business fluctuations.

NOTES ON
ALTERNATIVE POINTS OF VIEW
AND SUPPLEMENTARY READINGS

The fountainhead for the Keynesian version of the payments approach is, of course, J. M. Keynes, *General Theory of Employment, Interest, and Money* (New York: Harcourt, Brace & World, Inc., 1936), Book III.

Simplified versions of Keynes are legion, but most authoritative is perhaps A. P. Lerner, "Mr. Keynes' 'General Theory of Employment, Interest, and Money' " in *International Labour Review,* October 1936). Other excellent presentations are Alvin H. Hansen's *A Guide to Keynes* (New York: McGraw-Hill Book Company, Inc., 1953), and Dudley Dillard's *The Economics of John Maynard Keynes* (Englewood Cliffs, N. J.: Prentice-Hall, Inc., 1948).

Our analysis has not made very much use of the multiplier. For a more extensive treatment, see G. N. Halm, *Monetary Theory,* 2nd ed. (New York: McGraw-Hill Book

Company, Inc., 1946), pp. 399–416, and R. M. Goodwin, "The Multiplier," in S. E. Harris, ed., *The New Economics* (New York: Alfred A. Knopf, Inc., 1947), pp. 482–99. The first edition of this book did without the concept. But it is quite plain from the use of multiplier analysis in such work as J. R. Hicks' *Trade Cycle* (Oxford: Clarendon Press, 1950) that acquaintance with it will be essential to any reader who wants to get far with current monetary literature.

The final part of this chapter reflects the view of E. Lindahl, *Studies in the Theory of Money and Capital* (London: George Allen and Unwin, 1939), Part I. Our emphasis on the self-fulfilling character of *widely held* business expectations, an idea conspicuous in Keynes' *Treatise on Money,* is further developed in K. E. Boulding, *Reconstruction of Economics* (New York: John Wiley & Sons, Inc., 1951).

Chapter 10

Money and the Stream of Payments: The Interest-Investment Approach

The classical view. The main line of monetary thinking—from David Hume and Adam Smith in the eighteenth century to Irving Fisher in the twentieth—paid little attention to the connections between interest and money, nor did it assign the rate of interest much influence on spending. The interest rate was pictured as the price paid for the economic service performed by the saver. Interest was thought to equilibrate the supply of current saving with the demand for saving to finance investment. Money was thought to affect spending directly, since velocity was assumed to be independent of the money supply, and so spending was expected to respond proportionately to changes in money.

The main relation between interest and money stressed by this line of theorists was the adjustment of the interest rate in the face of the price-level changes caused by money. A creditor who had lent $100 in return for $105 one year later was not really being paid for his "abstinence" or "waiting" if prices rose 10 per cent during the year. To give him a "real" return of 5 per cent, he would have to obtain $115.50 in exchange for his $100. Insofar as people sensed a movement of prices, inflation would bring about an increase in contract interest rates, while deflation would bring about a fall in rates. Such a movement of contract rates of interest can be observed historically, but the movement is disconcertingly small. Bondholders who acquired securities during an inflation uniformly realized a negative "real" rate of interest.

189

Natural versus market rates.   Monetary developments actually do affect interest. The banking system can alter the interest charges on loan contracts while bank loans free the financing of investment from the decisions of savers because investment can be financed by the creation of money. Economists have consequently tried to work out theories that make room for monetary influences upon the rate of interest.

One such theory distinguished between *natural* and *market* rates. The rate that would equilibrate saving and investment was the natural rate; the rate set by banks was the market rate. If the market rate were below the natural rate—because the natural rate had risen with an expansion of investment opportunities, or because the market rate had fallen as bankers sought more assets—borrowing would increase and investment spending would expand. This would push up production and prices. By the same reasoning, a market rate above the natural rate would lead to a contraction of spending and a fall in output and prices. This view led to the business-cycle theories that are linked with the name of the Swedish pioneer, Knut Wicksell, and encouraged the belief that the economy could be stabilized by a sophisticated monetary policy. The banking system would merely detect the tendencies of the natural rate and adapt the market rate to these tendencies.

The Keynesian view: liquidity preference.   The Keynesian analysis of income and output also connects interest rates to the money supply and relates the interest rate to the level of spending. This theory of interest is centered in the notion that a small cash supply leads to a high rate of interest, and a large cash supply to a low rate of interest, with the additional proviso that expanding the cash supply cannot lower interest rates beyond a certain point.

The rate of interest, in Keynesian thought, represents the terms on which a holder of cash—can lend it out.[1] To the extent that he actually holds cash, he has rejected the lending option. He must have done so because the advantages of having cash on hand and the risk of lending it out outweigh the advantages of a later repayment with interest.[2] The risk at issue here is not the risk of default, but of a capital loss that the lender might suffer if he had to transfer the loan to another holder prior to its final maturity. The lower the rate of interest that the lender can get, the smaller the reward for taking this risk and for giving up the advantages of holding onto cash.

---

[1] In talking of "the" rate of interest, Keynesians imply that the whole wide range of rates on different kinds of loans can somehow be reduced to a common footing. The supposition is that "the" rate refers to a long-term loan on which the creditor is sure the debtor will literally fulfill his contract (such as a loan to the government), and that differentials reflect "risk premiums" on loans where there is some recognized hazard of default on principal or interest.

[2] Keynesian analysis assumes that "cash" yields no interest. In actual fact, some interest was paid on checking deposits in the United States prior to 1933. Even now, some holders of checking deposits may get "implicit interest" if their bankers would increase service charges were their balances reduced. In such cases, it is the *interest difference* to which Keynesian analysis must refer.

The advantages of holding cash will be examined closely in the next chapter. The point here is that the holder of cash can enjoy those advantages more fully if he puts a larger proportion of his wealth into cash. If the interest rate is low, so that he gives up little by holding cash, he may hold more cash and fewer earning assets than if the interest rate were high.[3] Given his total wealth, we can draw a curve that measures how much he will hold in cash at each interest rate. With interest measured vertically and cash horizontally, such a curve would slope downward to the right. Next, we can add together the cash balances of all households and firms for each interest rate. This will give us a curve such as that in Chart 10-1. The Keynesians call it the "liquidity-preference schedule."

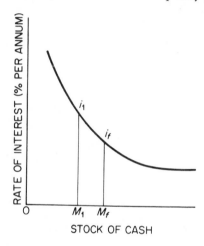

Chart 10-1: Keynesian liquidity-preference schedule.

This diagram can be read in either of two directions. Given the quantity of cash, the curve tells us how much the interest rate must be. If cash is OM_1, the rate of interest must be M_1i_1. If the central bank increases the stock of cash from OM_1 to OM_f, the rate of interest must fall to M_fi_f. This proposition corresponds to what we know about the way in which central banks operate. When the central bank wants to enlarge the money supply, it may go into the open market and buy government securities, bidding up the prices of bonds and thereby lowering the market rates of interest. In its open-market operations, the central bank is really persuading people to accept cash in place of bonds, and so must reduce the interest reward that is available on bonds. The diagram can also be read from the interest rate to the money stock. It tells us how much

---

[3] Students of economic theory will see an exception. The person whose affairs we are analyzing may get most of his income as interest, and he may be so impoverished by low interest rates that he has to give up the luxury of holding a lot of cash, even though it costs him less to hold it. This is the same principle on which people will work for lower wages when hungry—an example of the "income effect."

cash must be extant for a certain rate of interest to prevail. If we want the interest rate at $M_1 i_1$, we must see that OM_1 of cash is outstanding.

The way we have drawn the liquidity-preference curve implies (in line with Keynesian tradition) that there is a floor to the rate of interest—that at some minimum interest rate, "liquidity preference becomes absolute."[4] Keynesians insist that such a floor must exist for at least two reasons: (1) Lenders have in mind some standard of "normal" interest rates and refuse to buy bonds when rates are far below "normal" because they fear that rates will return to "normal" and impose capital losses on bondholders. (2) The cost at which lenders can administer their portfolios is somewhat above zero, and they will not lend unless that can cover the costs of asset management. This notion of a floor to the rate of interest plays an important part in Keynes' concept of underemployment equilibrium, and we shall say more about it later.

The rate of interest and the level of investment. Having outlined the Keynesian approach to interest rates, we are now able to set out the Keynesian theory of investment.

The Keynesian theory of investment is based on the proposition that businesses planning on expansion must compare the return they can obtain on money put into the business with the return the money would earn if used to buy bonds or other securities. If the rate of return on funds put into the business (the "marginal efficiency of capital," in Keynesian language) exceeds the rate of return available on the securities (the market rate of interest just discussed), business will use its funds to enlarge plant or inventory. But if the marginal efficiency of capital is below the rate of interest, business would be wiser to buy outside securities.[5]

The marginal efficiency of capital can be calculated if we know the cost of the machinery or inventory the firm plans to buy and the income this machinery or inventory will earn for the firm in the future. If we let C stand for the cost of the machinery, and let R_1, R_2, R_3, $\ldots$, R_n stand for the annual receipts that the machinery will yield in each year from 1 through n, we can calculate the marginal efficiency of capital, r, using a standard discount formula:

$$C = \frac{R_1}{(1+r)} + \frac{R_2}{(1+r)^2} + \frac{R_3}{(1+r^3)} + \cdots + \frac{R_n}{(1+r)^n}.$$

Keynesians would argue that r will decline with an increase in the level of investment per month or per year. This proposition follows directly from

---

[4] This means that as somebody gives our cash-holder more wealth, he will insist on taking the whole of the addition in cash.

[5] The same point can be put in terms of a decision to borrow money. If the costs of borrowing (the market rate of interest) are smaller than what the firm can earn with borrowed money (the marginal efficiency of capital), the firm should borrow the money. But if the cost of borrowing exceeds the marginal efficiency of capital, the firm would be foolish to borrow money. Keynes, incidentally, pointed out that this concept of marginal efficiency is identical with what Irving Fisher called "the rate of return over cost."

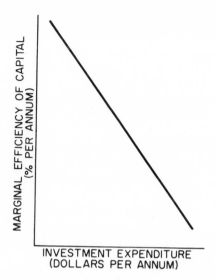

Chart 10-2: The marginal efficiency of capital.

the law of diminishing returns. The more machines we produce per year, the higher the cost of production of machines; but the higher C, the lower r. The more machines we produce, moreover, the smaller the output from one more machine; but the smaller this additional output and the smaller R, the smaller the marginal efficiency of capital, r.

For these and other reasons, we may draw a schedule that shows the marginal efficiency of capital falling as the level of investment per period is increased. Chart 10-2 shows such a schedule, whose use will let us predict the level of investment once we know the rate of interest, for investment will be expanded in each period until the marginal efficiency of capital is equal to the rate of interest. Once we know investment, we know the level of income and output. We have completed the Keynesian connection that runs from the stock of cash to the level of income and output.

A modified Keynesian system.   One major flaw in the Keynesian analysis as explained above is that it ignores a second link between the stock of money and the level of total output. The argument as we have described it runs from the money stock to interest and investment, and goes on from investment to the level of output. But it does not lay bare the connection that runs in the opposite direction—the influence of output and income on the demand for money. The higher the national income, the more cash will be demanded at a given interest rate. If income is rising but the stock of cash is fixed, the rate of interest will also rise and choke off the growth of income.

One way to deal with this connection is to show what the interest rate would be at each level of income and cash—to draw a separate liquidity preference

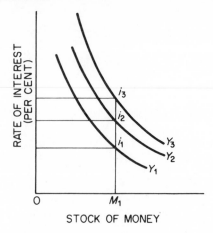

STOCK OF MONEY

Chart 10-3: Income, interest, and the money stock in a modified Keynesian analysis.

curve for each separate level of national income. A set of liquidity preference curves is shown in Chart 10-3. Suppose that income is at Y_1 and that the money stock is at OM_1. This would mean an interest rate of $M_1 i_1$ and a level of investment that could be determined from Chart 10-2. If that level of investment, working through the "multiplier," gives an income level of just Y_1, the Keynesian system with which we are working is in equilibrium. If, however, that level of investment gives us a higher income level, for example Y_3, our simple Keynesian system will not be in equilibrium. Income level Y_3 gives us a new liquidity preference curve, resulting in a higher interest rate. A higher interest rate, in turn, means a lower level of investment, and a reduction of investment means a lower level of income. To locate an equilibrium position, we must jump from diagram to diagram until we find an income level consistent with the interest rate that produces that level of income.

A second way to handle this problem is one favored by Alvin Hansen, a leading American expositor of Keynesian economics. Hansen would divide the demand for money into two parts—a transactions demand (M_1) that depends on the level of income, and a speculative demand (M_2) that depends on the interest rate. The speculative demand (M_2) can be described by a diagram we have already drawn; merely change the label on Chart 10-1, replacing the "stock of money" with the "speculative demand for money." The transactions demand can be described by Chart 10-4, which shows the transactions demand rising with the national income.[6]

---

[6] One cannot actually segregate transactions—demand balances from speculative—demand balances. The distinction is entirely artificial, but is convenient for purposes of exposition. Note, moreover, that these two motives for holding money do not come near to exhausting the list. We shall say more on this subject in the next chapter. For the present, we shall subsume other motives under Hansen's "transactions demand."

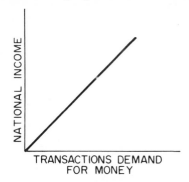

Chart 10-4: The transactions demand for money in a modified Keynesian system.

Because M_1 and M_2 must add up to the total stock of money, we can always describe the latter as the total money stock *minus* M_1. This is what we do in Chart 10-5. In the lower right-hand quadrant of that diagram, we replot Chart 10-4, but flip it over and turn it upside down. This converts it into a schedule that shows the transaction demand as a subtraction from total cash. If the total money stock is OA and the income level to start is OB, the transactions demand for cash turns out to be CA and the speculative demand for cash must be OC. But if M_2 is OC, the interest rate must be CD. With the interest rate at CD, we know from the investment-demand curve in the top left-hand quadrant (which is turned around to run from right to left) that the level of investment must be OE. As the final step, we invoke the saving function (Chart 9-5), turned on its side in the lower left-hand quadrant of Chart 10-5. If investment is OE, saving must be OE. But if saving is OE, income must be OB.

As we have drawn the diagram, we end with the same income level at which we began. If this had not happened, we would have had to start again, choose another income level and go around the diagram in the same counterclockwise fashion. After several tries, we would find that income level which is precisely consistent with the curves in the chart. The last step would be to inscribe a rectangle within the diagram, which is tantamount to solving the simple Keynesian system the chart portrays. If one of the curves in the chart were to change its position, we would have fit a new rectangle within the curves and would solve the changed system for income, investment, and interest, just as we have done with the system in Chart 10-5.

We can use Chart 10-5 to show the role of money an dmonetary policy in Keynesian analysis. Suppose that income level OB is below that which corresponds to full employment. If we increase the stock of money to OA', we lower the interest rate to CD', raise investment to OE', and lever up income to OB'. A monetary expansion can increase income and employment in a Keynesian system. Similarly, a contraction of the money stock will raise the rate of interest, lower investment spending, and cut down income and employment. However,

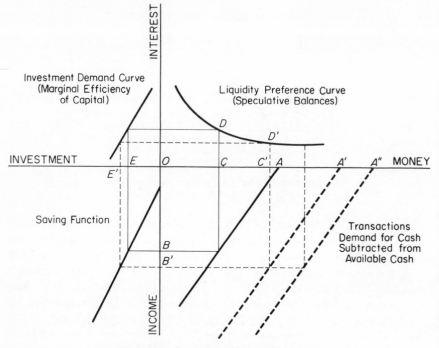

Chart 10-5: A modified Keynesian system.

an increase of the money stock beyond OA' would not lead to a further increase in income and employment, because the liquidity-preference curve in the top right-hand quadrant becomes horizontal for cash balances larger than OA'. Here, then, is the significance of the so-called "liquidity trap." If liquidity preference becomes "absolute" at an interest-rate level higher than the one that would give full employment, monetary policy is powerless to combat unemployment. A further increase in the money stock cannot lower the interest rate and is not able to raise investment and income.

The four-part diagram we have just presented can also be used to show the system's path to equilibrium. In Chart 10-6 we have redrawn the four curves of Chart 10-5 and started our Keynesian system at the same initial position. The money stock is again OA, the interest rate is at CD, investment at OE, and income is again OB. Now suppose that a lag occurs in the adjustment of the system to a change in the money stock. When the supply of money is increased to OA_1, the level of income does not immediately change. In consequence, the whole increase of money goes into speculative balances (which, therefore, increase from OC to OC_1), driving down the interest rate to C_1D_1. This increases investment to OE_1 and raises the level of income to OB_1. When income is OB_1, transactions balances are A_1C_2. The stock of speculative balances falls to OC_2 and the interest rate rises to C_2D_2. This lowers investment to OE_2 and cuts

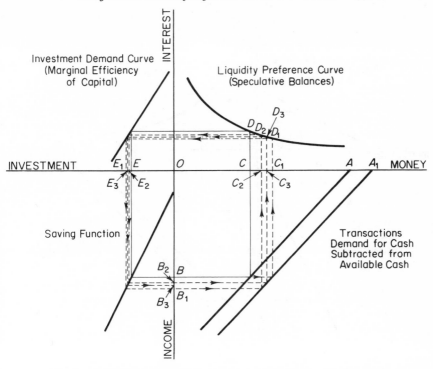

Chart 10-6: Converging flustuations in a modified Keynesian system.

back income to OB_2. When income is OB_2, speculative balances are OC_3, and the interest rate is C_3D_3. Investment must become OE_3, and income must rise to OB_3. We could go around the diagram several times more, but we need not, as a pattern is already emerging. At the first stage, income jumped from OB to OB_1. At the second stage, income fell from OB_1 to OB_2. And at the third stage, income rose from OB_2 to OB_3. Note now that OB_2 is higher than OB, while OB_3 is lower than OB_1. Each decline of income is smaller than the increase that preceded it, and each increase of income is smaller than the preceding decline. The oscillations that the system produces grow gradually smaller as the interest rate, investment, and income seek out the equilibrium implied by the money stock OA_1.

The fluctuations in income that occur during adjustment may not "damp out" as in Chart 10-6. They may instead grow larger at each step in the process, so that our Keynesian system will not tend toward equilibrium when it is disturbed. Chart 10-7 illustrates this possibility. It is identical to Chart 10-6 in every respect but one—its investment demand curve is much more elastic, so that changes in the interest rate will cause very large changes in investment.[7]

---

[7] The same result could be achieved by changing one of the other schedules—making the liquidity-preference curve steeper, or reducing the marginal propensity to save (increasing the multiplier) to make for larger income changes as investment changes.

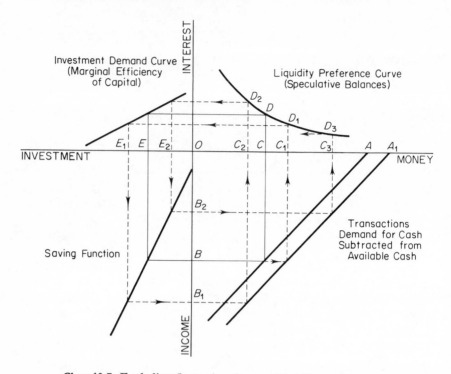

Chart 10-7: Exploding fluctuations in a modified Keynesian system.

Note what happens when this system is disturbed. As in Chart 10-6, income at first rises to OB_1 when we change the money stock from OA to OA_1, and raises the interest rate to C_2D_2. C_2D_2 is larger than CD, so OE_2 must be smaller than OE. Income at the next stage must be OB_2, very much smaller than OB, and the interest rate must fall all the way to C_3D_3. In this diagram, each increase of income must be larger than the previous decline, while each decline in income must be larger than the previous rise. The Keynesian system in Chart 10-7 can never seek out equilibrium. It will continue to oscillate once it is disturbed.[8]

Other criticisms of the Keynesian approach.   The model we have just discussed was meant to correct one flaw in Keynes' system—his neglect of the "causal arrow" that runs from income to the demand for cash. There are a number of other weaknesses in the Keynesian approach.

We have already seen that saving and consumption are not neatly related to income. The Keynesian consumption function is as stable as most simple economic relationships, but it is not sufficiently stable to be used without qualification. This is even more true of the marginal efficiency of capital.

---

[8] Note, however, that the system will not oscillate in ever-larger swings. This is because the interest rate cannot fall further than C_3D_3, so that income cannot rise above the level that matches this interest rate.

The term itself may lead the unwary to expect stability in the schedule. It sounds like some sort of technical characteristic of productive equipment (like the thermal efficiency of a locomotive) that depends on engineering and can only change by invention and the gradual installation of improved equipment. Actually, the marginal efficiency is a very subjective variable, as Keynes took pains to observe, that represents the *expectations* of business as to the returns from investment. If businessmen come to expect higher prices for their output, they will expect larger receipts to result from installing a piece of equipment. In terms of the symbols used before, they will anticipate a larger series $R_1 \ldots R_n$. If the cost of the equipment is stable, they will impute a higher marginal efficiency to proposed investment in new equipment.[9] Keynes himself suggested that fluctuations in production and employment are mainly the result of fluctuations in marginal efficiency.

In the development of Keynesian ideas, the theory of investment has changed in two ways: (1) increasing skepticism has developed about the influence of interest rates on investment; (2) more emphasis has been placed on business volume as a determinant of investment.

Faith in interest-rate reductions as a stimulus to investment was badly shaken by the experience of the 1930's. After 1932, interest rates in the United States were very low by accustomed standards, yet unemployment hung on and investment was much lower than in the 1920's. Economists interviewed businessmen about the influence of interest rates on their investment calculations, and came back with answers that did not jibe with theory. Interest rates were found to play a role in decisions about buildings, public utilities, and transportation equipment, but not in decisions about manufacturing equipment or inventory investment.[10]

---

[9] If the greater optimism about future prices is so general that businessmen scramble for the equipment and bid up its price, it may come to have the same marginal efficiency as before. Even so, the current dollar volume of investment that corresponds to a given level of marginal efficiency will have been increased by the amount of the price increase on the equipment. Either way, a greater optimism about future product prices will shift the investment demand schedule to the right.

[10] Postwar studies have come to much the same conclusion. See, for example, H. F. Lydall, "The Impact of the Credit Squeeze on Small and Medium-sized Manufacturing Firms," *Economic Journal*, September 1957. These surveys have been severely criticized, as by William H. White, "Interest Inelasticity of Investment Demand," *American Economic Review*, September 1956. A thorough review of this issue is found in James R. Schlesinger, "Monetary Policy and Its Critics," *Journal of Political Economy*, December 1960.

Note, however, that the construction-utilities-transport exception is a very large gap in the generalization that interest rates do not affect investment, for these lines almost always account for well over half of investment. The importance of interest calculations in such long-term investment decisions can readily be seen in housing. If you are going to buy a house on monthly payments, you have to ask whether the monthly amount of interest and principal (plus taxes, insurance, and so forth) that you must pay to retire the mortgage is more or less than rent. Obviously, the answer depends on the interest rate and the period of repayment. But if the period of repayment is constant (for example, at fifteen years), interest at 5 per cent accounts for just about half of the early payments and a change of $1/2$ per cent in the rate of interest appreciably changes the monthly payments.

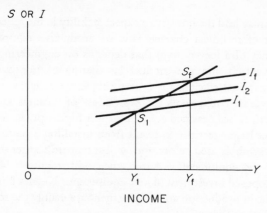

INCOME

Chart 10-8: Investment and income as affected by income and interest.

The effect of business activity on investment fits easily into the Keynesian system and has been adopted by most Keynesian economists. It presumably arises through pressure on productive facilities. We have come across it in our discussion of anticipations. When a business is operating near capacity, it can reduce operating costs by putting in new machinery, enlarging buildings, and so forth. The marginal efficiency of capital shifts to the right as operations' expand. Taking income as a rough measure of "activity," we may set up a diagram to illustrate the argument. In Chart 10-8, the S curve that shows how saving relates to income is carried over from Chart 9-5. Investment is represented by a series of curves that also run from southwest to northeast, showing higher investment at higher income levels.[11] Each curve is drawn for a given interest rate, the highest curve representing the lowest interest rate. If we start with the rate of interest that corresponds to investment curve I_1, income must be OY_1 and saving (and investment) Y_1S_1. To raise income and employment, we must lower the interest rate. To reach income OY_f, we must lower the rate of interest to that level that corresponds to curve I_f. This will raise saving (and investment) to Y_fS_f, thereby raising income to the desired level.

If income had no effect on investment, the investment curves in Chart 10-8 would be horizontal, and a larger interest rate reduction would be needed to secure a given increase of income and employment. If interest rates had no effect on investment, there would be just one investment curve in Chart 10-8,

---

[11]This is an *approximation* to the idea that investment depends on activity, a notion often given a slightly more elaborate formulation. It is argued that the *level* of investment depends upon the *rate of increase* of income (or output). The level of investment yields an addition to the total stock of productive equipment, but it is this total stock of capital goods that should be aligned with the level of output. This more sophisticated argument is neatly set out by Paul A. Samuelson, "Interactions Between the Multiplier Analysis and the Principle of Acceleration," reprinted in *Readings in Business Cycle Theory* (Homewood, Ill.: Richard D. Irwin, Inc., 1951).

and no amount of interest rate manipulation could increase the level of income and employment.[12]

Another main line of criticism of Keynesian analysis is that it puts too many things in each of its baskets. It works with sweeping "aggregates" instead of looking closely at the components of income and output. At a few points, Keynesians allow for the fact that the same aggregate may have different effects according to the way it is divided among households or firms. But "disaggregation" should be carried out more often, especially when considering consumption and investment. We have seen how important it can be for the study of investment. The distribution of surprises among firms and industries can profoundly affect the overall level of investment spending.

A third main criticsm of Keynesian analysis is that the more extreme Keynesians pay too little attention to motives for holding cash and, therefore, attach too little importance to the stock of cash. These economists argue that the money supply can only affect spending by way of the interest rate. They brush aside much of traditional monetary theory, deprecating the other effects of cash on consumption and investment. In our opinion (and in the opinion of some other "moderate" Keynesians), this reaction has gone too far. When we allow for the effects of uncertainty, we find that consumption and investment are apt to be directly influenced by the stock of cash.

The direct influence of the demand for cash is considered in Chapter 11. We begin with a more complete examination of the motives for holding cash than is usually offered by Keynesian theorists. Using that list, we trace out the impact of the demand for cash on spending-unit behavior.

NOTES ON

ALTERNATIVE POINTS OF VIEW

AND SUPPLEMENTARY READINGS

The readings listed at the end of Chapter 9 contain much material on Keynesian interest and investment theory. A useful modified model of Keynesian equilibrium is set out by J. R. Hicks, "Mr. Keynes and the 'Classics': A Suggested Interpretation," *Econometrica,* April 1937.

---

[12]By drawing only one saving curve by the same token, we imply that saving is unaffected by interest. Actually, some economists would hold that at a given level of income the rate of interest does affect saving. But most economists seem to be ready to agree that, within the range of interest rates that usually prevail on United States government long-term securities, the effect of interest rates on saving may not be large enough to pull the S curves for different interest rates far apart on the diagram.

Chapter 11

Money and the Stream of Payments: The Cash-Balances Approach

Motives for Holding Cash

Introduction. While Keynes himself made an enormous contribution to our understanding of the demand for cash,[1] most simple Keynesian models, like the one in Chapter 10, do not give sufficient attention to people's motives for holding money. This is why Keynesian models attach too little importance to money and monetary policy. In order that we may fully appreciate the influence of money, we must look much more closely at the demand for money.

Who holds the cash? To survey the motives for holding cash, we must have some idea of the way in which cash is distributed. Is the typical holder of cash a wage-earner? An old lady on an annuity? A big corporation? We know from bank statistics (Table 11-1) that the lion's share of demand deposits is held in very large accounts. Financial and nonfinancial corporations held 45.3 per cent of adjusted demand deposits at the beginning of 1961, the former had average balances of $27,333, the latter average balances of $20,600. A vast number of individuals have checking accounts, but most of these cash balances

---

[1] The argument of this chapter, indeed, rests largely on the work of Keynes, *General Theory of Employment, Interest, and Money* (New York: Harcourt, Brace & World, Inc., 1936) and J. R. Hicks, "Suggestion for Simplifying the Theory of Money," *Economica*, February 1935; and *Value and Capital* (Oxford: Clarendon Press, 1939). But it will go a good way beyond their position, especially in handling uncertainty.

TABLE 11-1

DEMAND DEPOSITS, BY OWNERSHIP JANUARY 25, 1961*

		Per Cent of Total Accounts	
Type of Owner	Average Size of Account (in dollars)	By Number of Accounts	By Amount on Deposit
All owners**	$1,866	100.0	100.0
Nonfinancial business:			
Corporate	20,600	3.4	37.8
Noncorporate	3,395	6.4	11.9
Financial business:			
Corporate	27,333	0.4	7.5
Noncorporate	9,000	0.3	1.7
Farm operators	1,464	4.8	3.7
Individuals (personal)	701	79.2	29.7
Nonprofit organizations	1,767	5.1	4.8
All other owners†	31,000	0.2	2.8

Source: Federal Reserve Bulletin, April 1961.

* Detail may not add to total because of rounding.
**Excludes government and interbank deposits.
† Trust departments of banks and foreign owners.

are relatively small and they account for only 29.7 per cent of total demand deposits.

Even now a large number of families do not have checking accounts. Only

TABLE 11-2

CONSUMERS' HOLDINGS OF LIQUID AND INVESTMENT ASSETS, DECEMBER 31, 1962

	Percentage of Spending Units Holding			
Size of Spending Units- 1962 Income (dollars)	Some Liquid Assets*	Checking Accounts	Savings Accounts	Some Investment Assets
All income classes	79	59	59	31
Under $3,000	56	34	36	15
$3,000–$4,999	74	52	52	20
$5,000–$7,499	86	63	62	30
$7,500–$9,999	96	79	78	41
$10,000–$14,999	96	87	83	56
$15,000–$24,999	100	96	87	73
$25,000–$49,999	99	95	87	93
$50,000–$99,999	100	97	60	96
$100,000 and over	99	99	42	99

Source: Dorothy S. Projector and Gertrude S. Weiss, *Survey of Financial Characteristics of Consumers,* p. 114. Published by the Board of Governors of the Federal Reserve System, 1966.

*Includes checking accounts, savings accounts, United States government savings bonds, and shares in savings and loan associations. Excludes currency.

a third of spending units with incomes below $3,000 were reported as having checking accounts in 1962 (Table 11–2), units the proportion of spending and holding checking accounts generally increased as the size of their portfolios increased (Table 11–3). These data on personal balances and the large average size of corporate accounts suggest that we should regard the checking-deposit component of total cash assets as mainly administered by business firms and persons of large affairs.

Apparently, time deposits are held mainly by households, although foreign holdings of dollars are sometimes placed on time deposit at commercial banks. Once again, however, savings accounts are not uniformly distributed among consuming units. Only half of the households with incomes below $5,000 were reported as having savings accounts in 1962 (Table 11–2), and better than half of the households that had time deposits had accounts smaller than $500 (Table 11–3). Considerable concentration occurs even in the holdings of this component of total cash, though probably less than with respect to checking accounts. We should assume that time deposits are held mainly by individuals, but that these individuals are largely drawn from the middle and upper income groups.

Evidence on holdings of paper currency is fragmentary. Incomplete surveys of business cash suggest that most of the currency belongs to households, but the fact that more than a quarter of the currency outstanding is in denominations

TABLE 11-3

THE SIZE OF CONSUMERS' PORTFOLIOS OF LIQUID AND INVESTMENT
ASSETS, DECEMBER 31, 1962†

	Per Cent of Spending Units with			
Size of Portfolio (dollars)	*Some Liquid Assets**	*Checking Accounts*	*Savings Accounts*	*Some Investment Assets*
Zero	21	41	41	69
$1–$499	99	70	56	4
$500–$1,999	98	74	72	27
$2,000–$4,999	98	69	86	48
$5,000–$9,999	98	74	89	67
$10,000–$24,999	98	81	86	75
$25,000–$49,999	100	89	81	93
$50,000–$99,999	100	92	88	99
$100,000–$499,999	100	100	72	100
$500,000 and over	100	100	74	100

Source: Dorothy S. Projector and Gertrude S. Weiss, *Survey of Financial Characteristics of Consumers,* p. 114. Published by the Board of Governors of the Federal Reserve System, 1966.

*Includes checking accounts, savings accounts, United States government savings bonds, and shares in savings and loan associations. Excludes currency.

†This is merely a rearrangement of the data in Table 11-2 by size of portfolio rather than by income group.

of $50 or over—denominations that are not too common in the average person's wallet—does suggest that currency is also concentrated. The concentration must be less than with bank deposits, but is still important enough to warrant our attention.

Putting the evidence together is not easy. As checking deposits are more than half of the total cash supply, we can be sure that business and wealthy individuals hold a large slice of that total. Our theories about motives for holding cash can, therefore, assume businesslike behavior in cash management, along with a connection between cash holdings and the markets in stocks and bonds. Our theories about the consumers' transactions demand for cash are apt to be less relevant to an explanation of total cash holdings, yet theories that connect cash management to consumers' saving patterns must be taken seriously in view of the rather wide distribution of total time deposits.

A list of motives for holding cash. At first glance, households and firms would seem to have little reason to hold a cash balance day after day. Cash cannot be eaten, worn, slept in, or used to keep off the weather. Since it is valued only because it can be used to buy other things, why should cash be kept unspent?

One might reply that when one person spends cash, somebody else gets it; *using* cash does not *use it up*. The total amount of cash in existence is determined by the forces studied in Part I. It arises from bank loans to private parties, from government deficits, importation and mining of gold, and so forth. The sum of individual holdings is simply the total of cash that is brought into existence by these transactions. But this explanation does not get us far—it would only be adequate if everyone always passed cash on at the earliest possible moment, and each dollar was owned by its present holder only because he had not yet had time to spend it. In the language of Chapter 8, this would imply a velocity up to the mechanical maximum, which can only happen in hyperinflation.[2]

Economists use a more or less standardized list of motives for holding cash. These motives can be classified as follows:

1. *Transactions Motive.* Holding enough cash to carry the holder past some foreseen trough in his holdings—to absorb the excess of cash outlays over cash receipts until the arrival of a foreseen substantial receipt.
2. *Margin-of-Safety* (or *Precautionary*) *Motive.* Holding enough cash to cushion the ill effects of an unexpected outlay or of a failure of receipts, and to safeguard financial respectability.

---

[2] A friend who was a child in Germany during the great inflation of 1923 recollects that as soon as the father of the family got his pay, the money was parceled out among the six children–to be spent right away, because prices would be so much higher later in the day. If everybody happened to bring home nothing but toothbrushes, barter could be set up with neighbors. This is a sample of the processes by which velocity is maximized in "hyperinflation" —raising prices much faster than the stock of money grows.

3. *Investment Motive.* Holding cash as the embodiment of wealth because the holder cannot see his way clear to put his wealth into any other form.

4. *Speculative Motive.* Holding cash because the holder is waiting for something he wants to buy to come down in price.

We cannot divide the cash balance of a given holder into definite parts representing each of these motives. The same cash balance may "double in brass." If, for example, a holder has accumulated cash for speculative purposes, he also has a margin of safety, so that his needs under the second motive are swallowed up in those under the fourth. Besides, the different motives shade into one another. In analyzing them, it is less important to keep them distinct than to keep track of the common element that binds them all together—*the adaptation of business dealings to uncertainty.*

The transactions motive. The transactions motive is a matter of avoiding the inconveniences, expenses, and annoyances that occur when we run out of cash. Every household or firm has lean periods "when everything goes out and nothing comes in." When we have cash on hand or cash coming in, and can foresee such a lean period coming, we make sure that we will enter that lean period with enough cash to see us through.

The working of the transactions motive depends on the factors listed by Fisher in his discussion of velocity. People who are paid weekly need less cash for transactions purposes than people with the same yearly income who are paid monthly. People who run up a bill at the grocer's and settle the bill on payday need less cash (as of two days after payday, for example) than those who buy exclusively at cash-and-carry stores. People who are able to borrow, and do not mind doing so, need less cash than those who feel that borrowing is a sin.

The size of an individual's transactions needs depends on how far that person looks ahead, and which future receipts and expenditures he assumes to be beyond his control.[3] It also depends on whether he has any reason for holding a minimum transactions balance. A cash-holder may be subject to bank service charges if his balance dips below a certain level; then he has a transactions motive to keep his balance equal to this minimum *plus* any excess of outlays over receipts that he anticipates.

The particular assets that can serve transactions needs depend on the nature

---

[3] If you depend on a fixed monthly salary of $100, and expect to spend $80 next month and $120 the following month, your minimum need just before next payday is zero, so far as these two months are concerned. If you expect to spend $120 next month and $80 the following month, your need just before payday is $20. If, however, in the third month you expect to spend $200, extending your "horizon" to three months raises your need to $120.

If some spending is optional, you may be able to cut your initial need by planning to spend less. In view of the greater freedom of action you enjoy for more remote dates (having "more time to turn around") and in view of uncertainty about future conditions, it is not worth extending your horizon for definite cash calculations very far into the future. But it is imprudent not to look at least two or three months ahead.

of those needs. If a man is about to take a trip during which he will deal entirely with strangers, he will need coin and paper money. If he is about to make a number of payments to people by mail, he will need a bank balance subject to check. But if he plans an elaborate vacation next summer and has plenty of time beforehand to change his banking arrangements, a savings account can fill his needs just as well as a checking account or a roll of bills. For fairly remote requirements, noncash assets serve in lieu of cash.[4]

The margin-of-safety motive and the principle of linkage of risks. Future transactions are *uncertain*. Few of us could make a precise estimate of all our receipts and disbursements. Reliable advance estimates can be made for selected items, but the uncertain items are more numerous and usually more important.

As cash is not ordinarily an income-yielding asset, it might seem that income prospects would be maximized by cutting cash holdings to a minimum. But a margin of safety in cash holdings is not a luxury, paid for by accepting reduced income prospects. A margin of safety makes income prospects better rather than worse. The reason for this is called the *Principle of Linkage of Risks*.

An old proverb says, "Misfortunes never come singly." Our affairs are often arranged so that if one thing goes wrong, many others will go wrong in consequence. A motorist on a long trip may make a close estimate of his cash requirements and take just enough currency with him to pay for gasoline and meals. If he is unlucky enough to be arrested for speeding, misfortunes pile up at a great rate. He not only has to pay the fine, but also suffers a night in jail, the ignominy and expense of having to wire his friends for funds, and perhaps substantial loss by not arriving in time to attend to his business. A similar chain of misfortunes would be set off if his car were to be crippled and need emergency repairs.

The same kind of thing can happen in business. Suppose that a small firm has made large sales on credit to a customer who goes bankrupt. This means that certain cash receipts will not come in when expected, if at all. If the firm has figured its cash position closely, the customer's bankruptcy creates a need to push sales harder than intended, to dun other customers into paying up more quickly, get more credit from suppliers, borrow more at the bank, and so forth. The loss will start a chain of consequences that work the wrong way. Price cuts to push sales may induce customers to postpone purchases in the hope of further price cuts. Pressure on customers to pay more promptly may lose good will and interfere with sales; it may start gossip that will hurt our firm's credit rating. Suppliers are likely to wonder whether our firm is still a good credit risk;

---

[4] Whether we say that a United States Savings Bond serves a transactions requirement for a future month of heavy outlays or regard the cashing of such a bond as a future item of cash receipts is a purely arbitrary decision. Whichever language we use, the holder needs less currency and bank deposits for transactions purposes than if the bond disappeared from his list of assets.

to apply for increased credit may be just the way to persuade them that they should be reducing their advances. A loan application at the bank that arises from the firm's loss will not necessarily be rejected, but the applicant for a "distress loan" must expect the banker to probe into his affairs with embarrassing closeness. If gossip begins to spread that our firm has asked for a bank loan and been refused, the firm's credit rating with suppliers will suffer and its other troubles will be compounded. A loss of receipts threatens to strip the firm of its working capital, might force it to liquidate some of its physical assets at a forced sale, and could even drive it into bankruptcy. The "going-concern value" of the assets of a competently managed firm exceeds their "breakup value" at forced sale; if the firm has to sell some of its assets to meet a shortage of cash, this excess of going-concern value evaporates.

These chain reactions can be avoided by allowing a margin of safety in the cash position. Had our motorist carried enough extra cash to pay his fine, his troubles would never have compounded. Had our firm held enough cash to take its loss in stride, its earning power would not have been impaired. *A stronger cash position weakens the linkage of risks,* so that one misfortune will not bring another in its wake.

In more pleasant directions, a stronger cash position also guarantees the ability to seize opportunities. Our motorist might have found for sale the puppy his daughter wanted for her birthday. With extra cash, he could have taken it along. Our firm might have been offered a large batch of materials at a very good price—a chance to lower its costs for several months ahead. Without extra cash, it could not buy ahead except by cutting down its purchases of other materials or of the labor needed to use the materials, so that the bargain offer would not be useful.[5] Here again, a strong cash position is not a luxury bought at the expense of reduced income prospects, but is itself a way to improve income prospects.

The margin-of-safety motive can be served by "near-moneys," although these are not useable for making payments. If our motorist carried savings bonds with him, he could get cash at any bank in case of need, but could hold onto his bonds if no emergency developed. Our firm could use marketable securities for the same purpose. These assets must not be essential to the holder's operations, and must promise to yield almost as much on quick sale as they would if the holder took plenty of time to market them. Our motorist, for example, could get cash for his tires or for the watch on his wrist. But if he sold the tires, he would have to stop his trip, and if he sold the watch he would get much less than it would cost him to replace it. To provide a margin of safety, noncash assets must be "liquid."

---

[5] Where the need for cash arises from a stroke of good luck rather than bad, however, the prospects of getting a bank loan are brighter. Borrowing power at the bank is a more useful substitute for cash when seizing opportunities than when trying to cover losses.

The margin-of-safety motive and financial respectability. Some households or businesses may not feel the need for a margin of safety in response to the uncertainty of their forecasts. But nearly everyone is subject to social pressure to allow such a margin for the sake of financial respectability.

A strong credit rating is one of the most important intangible assets a firm or household can have. To be known as one who sails too close to the wind is bad for credit. Our firm or household may never actually get into trouble by carrying a low cash balance, but those who know that its cash is low are apt to suspect rash management.

As has been remarked, the surest way to get a bank loan is to show that you do not need it. Borrowers who always allow a margin of safety can count on getting loans at low interest. Borrowers who keep their cash balances low are usually looked on with skepticism by the low-interest lenders, particularly commercial banks. They will be shunted over to lenders who make heavier charges, or loaded with inconvenient and humiliating collateral requirements. In terms of interest costs, it may pay the borrower to forego present profitable uses of funds in order to get low-interest loans later on.

Many firms and households in a country like the United States probably manage their affairs by rule of thumb rather than by precise calculations of probable gain and loss. The tradition of financial conservatism, built up partly by the example of successful firms and households and partly by the "educational" campaigns of banks, gives a prominent place to the principle of a safety margin in cash holdings. During the 1920's, many firms adopted a financial policy that allowed them to avoid bank borrowing in all circumstances. The sad experience of the firms that did not do so (and of individuals who had borrowed to buy securities) during the contraction of bank loans which started in 1929 caused even more vigorous efforts by business to gain emancipation from a dependence on banks. Those who sought emancipation during the interwar period may have acted on their own analysis of the needed margin of safety or on revised rules of thumb that were coming to be accepted as financial respectability. In either case, the "margin-of-safety motive" was at work.

Prolonged prosperity since World War II may have somewhat weakened the margin-of-safety motive. Businesses and individuals have shown an increased willingness to borrow, and appear to be carrying smaller cash balances in relation to transactions requirements, for velocity has increased sharply in the 1950's. But margin-of-safety considerations still affect cash-management decisions and could reappear strongly in the event of a sharp business downturn.

Credit rationing and the demand for cash assets. Our discussion of the margin-of-safety motive and the linkage of risks brings out a fact hinted at in a previous chapter.[6] The demand for cash assets or, more broadly, for liquidity, is sharply affected by *credit rationing*.[7]

The linkage of risks would not exist, and there would be no margin-of-safety motive, if everyone could borrow all he honestly believed he could repay at a market rate of interest. Anyone threatened with business losses because of a shortage of cash could get out of trouble by using his borrowing power.

But the loan market cannot be like that. Lenders cannot be sure of the honesty, good judgment, or business prospects of would-be borrowers. An exhaustive investigation of a borrower's credit standing is too expensive. Lenders take refuge in rules of thumb that relate borrowing power to the supply of collateral, or to the borrower's ratio of current assets to current liabilities, or of net worth to debt, or both.

This rationing of would-be borrowers affects their affairs in several ways.

1. Some borrowers (probably the majority by number, but not usually the largest firms or the richest households) would like to borrow more at the interest rates they now pay, but credit rationing prevents them from borrowing all they want.
2. Most borrowers are conscious of limits to their lines of credit, and have to scale down their operations to correspond to those limits.[8]
3. Most borrowers have to allow for the danger that their lines of credit may shrink, and make their margins of safety large enough to cover this possibility.
4. To reduce this danger, or to expand their lines of credit, most borrowers have incentives to show financial prudence.

These effects of credit rationing explain why an increase of liquidity for a firm or household weakens the linkage of risks and increases the range of expenditures that can safely be undertaken. The direct effect of money on expenditures as distinct from indirect effects (other than through changes in interest rates) hinges on this relationship between liquidity and the linkage of risks.

The investment motive.　Some holders of money choose to hold it simply because they see no income-yielding alternative.

---

[6] See Chap. 3.

[7] In a broader view, what is at issue is *capital rationing*. On capital rationing as an influence on business planning and upon the working of interest, see A. G. Hart, *Anticipations, Uncertainty, and Dynamic Planning* (Chicago: University of Chicago Press, 1940; reprint, New York: Augustus Kelley, 1951), pp. 39–50, 67–74.

[8] Lines of credit are frequently neglected in the study of monetary phenomena. When discussing the "creation of deposits," we should suppose that as loans and deposits are expanding, an expansion of unused lines of credit also occurs. Easy money increases the public's liquidity directly, by setting up a flow of payments from actual borrowers to their suppliers, and also indirectly, by increasing unused lines of credit which potential borrowers treat as money substitutes. The same direct and indirect influences are at work in reverse when a contraction of credit occurs.

There is a deep-seated tradition in our middle-class society of "keeping capital intact." Some people are spendthrifts who cannot hang on to cash or property of any kind, but most—including the majority of those who save or inherit substantial sums—feel that to "dissipate capital" is a sin, and will avoid doing so if they can.

Most wealth belongs to people who probably know of various ways to invest it for income. But a good many who own a little capital and struggle to keep it intact do not see any practical way to keep it except in cash. They may hold paper money, but are more apt to have savings bonds or a savings account at a bank.

People like this will succeed in saving when they are in full health and jobs are easy to get. They may have to use up their savings when they are caught by ill health or unemployment, when they have young people to educate, or when they reach retirement. On balance, this group of savers-in-cash are likely to gain ground in times of high employment. Very likely they accounted for a good part of the growth in currency, time deposits, and United States Savings bonds during World War II.

In the early postwar years, many people who had been steady savers used their wartime savings to finance new cars, furniture, and appliances, to move to California, or to travel in Europe. But net liquid savings continued to rise.

The speculative motive. A large proportion of the total money stock is held by households and firms actively interested in owning noncash assets —stock-exchange securities, real estate, inventories, and productive equipment. Some of the cash requirements related to dealings in these assets are straightforward transactions requirements. A man who has decided to buy a house, for instance, has to build up cash for his down payment. But the greater part of cash holdings that relate to these asset dealings must be viewed as *speculative* —linked with purchases that will only be made after the price has dropped or news comes in that makes the asset in question more attractive.

In some instances the cash-holder's interest in the asset market is *purely* speculative; he is waiting for a chance to buy an asset in order to sell it on the same market later, at a higher price.[9] More often, the cash-holder wants the asset for use—to contribute direct services, as does a house; to contribute to production, as does a machine; to yield cash income, as does a bond or a dividend-paying stock. Even when the buyer wants assets for use, he cannot entirely avoid speculation. A holder who expects to use an asset himself may also be on the lookout for a favorable chance to sell it. Anyone who wants to own assets has to make guesses about the best time to buy. If he can postpone his purchase, he will not knowingly buy something whose price will soon fall sharply.

---

[9] This implies a two-way market; cf. Chapter 8.

When someone deliberately sells a noncash asset or foregoes its purchase because he thinks its price is likely to fall, he is described in speculative lingo as a "bear." A bear hopes to gain by holding cash until the price decline has occurred. If he operates on a two-way market, he is able not only to postpone purchases, but also to sell his present holdings and increase his cash.[10] If facilities exist, as on stock and organized commodity exchanges, he may go even further and sell short, collecting cash now or later in exchange for a promise to deliver noncash assets at an agreed future date. The bear who sells short is gambling on "covering" his contract by buying the asset cheap before he has to deliver.

Very often, one who is a "bear" on asset A is a "bull" on another asset B. He thinks he can gain by selling asset A and holding cash, but he thinks he can gain even more by selling asset A and investing the proceeds in asset B. If a bear holds cash, he must be bearish not only on asset A but also bearish (or, at least, not bullish) on all of the other assets in which he is interested.

This list of other assets need not include all the assets in the economic system. Most holders of cash are not prepared to commit themselves to a limitless range of assets, but rather operate within a restricted list. If a stock-market speculator takes a bear position and holds cash, we can infer that he forecasts a general fall in stock prices. But it does not follow that he is forecasting a fall in other prices—in real estate, foreign currencies, or commodities. He may simply be refusing to bet on any forecast of those other prices. If the list of assets that a person will consider becomes very short, the speculative motive for holding cash merges with the investment motive already discussed.[11]

This limitation of interests to a restricted field applies especially to managers of "other people's money." The administrator of a trust fund, for example, is commonly limited to bonds and mortgages. If he cannot find desirable investment opportunities of this sort, he will let cash accumulate in the trust account as its present portfolio of bonds matures. He may be *almost* sure of price increases in stocks, real estate, or commodities, but he cannot—or will not—move onto these markets with the money entrusted to him. Corporation managers may also pile up cash because they lack appropriate ways to spend it. A corporation is ordinarily organized to carry on a stated line of business. An oil company will deal in oil lands, refining and distributing facilities, or the securities of other oil companies it might want to control. If it is not prepared to buy such assets at a given moment, the company may pile up cash far beyond transactions and precautionary requirements. The officers of the company may feel certain that

---

[10]Note that this description of bearishness coincides with our description of the Keynesian liquidity-preference curve. That curve has a "floor" because potential bondholders are persuaded that interest rates are "subnormal"—that interest rates are going to rise in the very near future.

[11]In many discussions, the investment motive is not handled separately. There is nothing logically wrong with treating it as a limiting case of the speculative motive, but treating the two separately makes the situations we are discussing easier to recognize.

houses, wheat, or railway shares are going to rise in price, but may not feel free to put the company's cash into such assets.

Uncertainty in the speculative motive. You cannot be a bear unless someone else is a bull. If everyone agrees that a certain railroad share will soon be worth only 80 per cent of what it sold for yesterday, today's quotation must quickly fall to 80 per cent of yesterday's. If at today's price someone is bearish, someone else must hold a *different opinion.* The bear cannot place his bet on a price decline unless somebody else is sufficiently optimistic to place a bet against that price decline.[12]

Even with such a difference of opinion, the bears may not hold cash *if* the bulls finance their purchases by borrowing from the bears. In the late 1920's, billions of dollars' worth of "brokers' loans for the account of others" were outstanding through New York banks. A part of this lending was virtually self-financing because the bears lent out some of the money they had received from sales of stock. But the bulls cannot usually draw directly on the bears' cash balances for lack of suitable financial machinery.[13] If the bears are not themselves bullish on other assets, a sharpening of the difference of opinion means an increased total demand for cash.

Just as different people forecast asset prices differently, a single individual is likely to make forecasts that are not entirely clear-cut. Uncertainty may be described as a difference of opinion *within* a person's mind. A person's judgment on a particular price may take a compound form: (1) that the price is more likely to rise than to fall over the next few months; but (2) that a fall is possible

---

[12]This argument relates to future prices of durable assets like securities and storable commodities. Everybody may agree that strawberries will cost less next year without lowering this year's price.

[13]Banking might be thought to constitute such machinery, but it actually does not. Bankers cannot transfer customers' balances to other customers without consent. The mere fact that some customers are accumulating funds does not increase the banks' lending power, for a shift in the ownership of deposits leaves total reserves and reserve requirements unaltered. If, of course, increased bearishness increased the proportion of *time deposits* (with lower reserve requirements), there would be an automatic increase of lending power; in general, however, the bear has no incentives to make such a shift. He ordinarily expects to use his funds so soon that he would get no interest on his time deposits.

Development of a difference of opinion about future asset prices is likely to bring an increased flow of loan applications from bulls or their brokers. If the banks have unused lending power, the supply of cash is likely to expand. If banks are "loaned up," however, loan applications can only be filled by denying loans to others, unless the central bank makes more reserves available.

In general, our monetary institutions have evolved in such a way that the shift of cash from bulls to bears, *plus* the increased money supply generated by bank lending to bulls, will fall short of the increased cash holdings desired by the bears. Limits upon borrowing against stock-exchange collateral or real estate also reduce the moneyness of these assets. Intensified disagreement about security prices is thus a deflationary factor. Speculative assets are apt to be better money substitutes at high than at low prices, so that a stock-market or real-estate boom will be inflationary on balance, until the price rise has nearly ceased and bearishness increases rapidly.

over the next few months; *and* (3) that the price is quite likely to go lower before it rises. The speculator's best policy is quite different under such a compound guess than it would be if he knew that the price would rise steadily on a stated timetable, for several months ahead.

Speculators rarely put all their eggs in one basket. Now and then, "plungers" stake everything on a bullish or bearish forecast about a particular price, but most speculators mix bullish and bearish behavior. They *differentiate* their portfolios of property held so as to include different kinds and different degrees of risk.[14] As uncertainty grows, speculators will seek to add cash to their portfolios. The speculative and margin-of-safety motives converge at this point, for a risky speculative position intensifies the linkage of risks. A bull speculator who has stretched his cash position to the limit and has bought stock "on margin" is vulnerable to a chain of calamities. If the price of his stock falls, his broker may call upon him to put up more cash, and the bull must either disrupt his other operations or sell his stocks at just the moment when he is more than ever convinced that the stock is bound to go up.

The speculative demand for cash is probably intensified by the interplay of taxes and "selective credit controls." The tax rates on capital gains from securities held more than six months are much lower than the rates that apply to the ordinary income of upper-bracket taxpayers. These taxpayers are, thereby, attracted to speculative operations, but the Federal Reserve sets minimum cash margins on the purchase of stock-exchange securities. These margin requirements have recently ranged from 50 per cent to 100 per cent of the securities' purchase price. Because of these requirements, it now takes much more cash to swing a speculative operation than it did in the 1920's.

Near-moneys in the demand for cash.   The concept of cash used thus far includes money and time deposits, and matches the usage generally followed in accounting. But *cash* might have been defined more narrowly to omit deposits not subject to check, or more widely to include short-term government securities and savings and loan shares.

Had a narrower concept of cash been adopted, we would have had to talk differently about several topics, but the substance of the argument would have been the same. The importance of time deposits as a substitute for checking deposits would have needed recognition regardless of definitions. Nor can we ignore the monetary importance of life insurance cash values, savings and loan association shares, and Treasury securities merely because these and similar claims are not included in our notion of cash.

Whether a claim can actually be used for payment is only important in relation to the transactions motive. If cash is wanted for margin-of-safety or

---

[14]The speculator's problem in differentiating his portfolio is much the same as that which a banker faces in deciding how to balance his portfolio of assets, except that the range of assets from which the banker has to choose consists almost entirely of debts receivable.

speculative reasons, direct use in payment does not come in question. An asset can be a substitute for cash if it is *liquid* (if it has moneyness), and is a *non-operating asset*.

Liquid, you will recall, means the holder is confident that he can get a stated price for the asset on short notice. Because price certainty and the speed with which it can be realized are both matters of degree, moneyness itself is a matter of degree.[15] With cash, moneyness is complete,[16] but all debts receivable have some degree of moneyness that shades off as the date of repayment recedes and as the debtor's credit standing becomes more doubtful. Debts payable have *negative moneyness,* varying with the date of maturity and the probability of being able to renew.

An asset is nonoperating if the owner can part with it without upsetting his affairs. Many highly liquid assets, such as inventories and debts receivable from customers, are operating assets because an effort to cash in on them would cut into a firm's ability to sell its products.

Another way of ranking assets as money substitutes is to ask whether the owner will consider selling them. Assets of varying moneyness may be priced so low that the holder would prefer to keep them either for use or for speculation. In some instances, holders set up taboos around certain assets. Many holders of life insurance refuse to borrow on their policies and plan their affairs so that they can avoid doing so. In other instances, as with bonds, owners may consider selling at high prices, but will refuse to sell them at a discount unless, of course, they come to expect a default on interest or principal.

Room exists for debate as to the degree to which assets are regarded as money substitutes. Most observers think that short-term government securities are prized chiefly as money substitutes, but that life insurance cash values, though a contractual claim that is very liquid, are held chiefly by policyholders who refuse to draw on them.

An effective money substitute can only be defined in the light of the way people feel and behave. We may be sure that the list of substitutes is quite long, and that the makeup of the list varies continually.

Cash Balances and Spending Decisions

Introduction. Our discussion of the reasons for holding cash lends some support to the Keynesian hypothesis connecting cash to interest rates. The speculative motive for holding a cash balance is related to actual and prospective asset prices and to asset yields. Our discussion supports also the view that the demand for cash can directly affect outlays for goods and services. To be caught

---

[15]Cf. the discussion of liquidity in banking.

[16]This statement might be made a definition of "cash." But it seems more sensible to define cash in accounting terms and to make this statement as an *approximately correct description* of cash so defined.

short of cash can be so dangerous that households and firms may regulate their spending on goods and services in order to maintain an adequate cash balance. Spending units with excess cash may use that cash to buy goods and services, not merely to buy stocks and bonds. These possibilities are at the core of the cash-balances approach to monetary theory.

Early versions of the cash-balances approach. The cash-balances approach has a certain similarity to transactions-velocity analysis. Like the transactions-velocity approach, it has a long history and has been widely used, especially in England.[17] In addition, it was also adopted as a way of expounding the quantity theory of money.

But a fundamental difference exists between the two analyses. The central question in transactions-velocity analysis was *how rapidly money is spent.* The central question in cash-balances analysis is why the holders of cash *haven't spent it yet.*[18] It is not a mechanical analysis, but a study of volition.

This aspect of cash-balances analysis and its connection to the quantity theory are neatly illustrated by Alfred Marshall's version of the cash-balances doctrine.[19] Marshall suggested that the people of a country would want to "keep by them" money that was equivalent to a certain stock of real goods and services. The *aggregate* purchasing power of the country's money stock would then be equivalent to this mass of goods. The purchasing power of a unit of money would be the pro rata share of each piece of money in the mass of goods. The more pieces of money, the smaller the purchasing power of each piece—the higher, that is, the prices of the goods and services involved.

The cash-balances approach was long identified with English economists at Cambridge, and presented in terms of a "Cambridge equation" that differs sharply from the "Fisher equation" of Chapter 10. In an article, published in 1917, on which most discussions of the equation rest,[20] Professor Pigou chose to stand his price-level concept on its head, letting P represent the price of money in terms of goods. Turning the formula right side up, to make the price level

---

[17]Among twentieth-century British economists, Alfred Marshall, A. C. Pigou, D. H. Robertson, and J. M. Keynes (in the earlier stages of his monetary thinking) took this approach. On the Continent, similar analysis was developed by Leon Walras, founder of the "Mathematical School," who based his monetary doctrines on the concept of an "encaisse désirée," or the amount of cash that people wish to hold.

[18]In an effort to focus attention on this point, R. G. Hawtrey coined the term "the unspent margin" to describe the public's total holdings of coin, paper money, and checking deposits. (See his *Currency and Credit,* 3rd ed. [London: Longmans, Green & Company, Ltd., 1928], p. 47.)

[19]A. Marshall, *Money, Credit and Commerce* (London: Macmillan & Co., Ltd., 1923), pp. 44–45. The evolution of Marshall's views from older work, running back into the eighteenth century, is hinted in a footnote, *ibid.,* p. 47.

[20]A. C. Pigou, "Value of Money"; reprinted in American Economic Association, *Readings in Monetary Theory* (New York: McGraw-Hill Book Company, Inc., 1951), pp. 161–83. The equation is presented on p. 165, but in a slightly different form.

that of goods in terms of money, his equation becomes:

$$kRp = M$$

Here, as in the Fisher equation, M may be taken to represent the stock of money, and p is an index of prices not very different from Fisher's P.[21] The other terms have no precise equivalent in Fisher's formulation.

R is defined as "the total resources, expressed in terms of wheat, that are enjoyed by the community," and k as "the proportion of these resources that it chooses to keep in the form of titles to legal tender."[22] Then kR measures the demand for money as the equivalent of a quantum of commodities.

If we think of kR as the batch of goods to which people want to hold a monetary equivalent, the price-level index p takes on a somewhat different meaning than Fisher's P. When an individual price changes, the effect on the index depends on the weight that the index gives to the commodity in question. A commodity may have a very different weight in an index of transactions from that which it has in an index of the wealth-equivalent of money. Compare, for example, bread and antique furniture. Bread is overwhelmingly more important in the flow of transactions, but antique furniture may be more important in an index of the wealth-equivalent of money. This is because it is bought mainly by prosperous people who carry more cash in relation to their payments than does the average bread consumer. To buy antiques, you have to watch for the things you want, and have the cash on hand to snap them up. It would not be at all surprising if antiques motivated more cash-holding than bread.

But this difference in the Fisher and Cambridge price indexes[23] should not be overrated. Well-constructed indexes of P and p would run reasonably parallel, as many of the most important commodities would have similar weights in both indexes, and the prices of commodities with a heavier weight in p than P would probably not rise or fall more than those that are important in index P.

Waiving the difference in price-level concepts, we can rewrite the Cambridge equation in the form $\dfrac{M}{P} = kR$ and the Fisher equation in the form $\dfrac{M}{P} = \dfrac{T}{V}$ and infer that $kR = \dfrac{T}{V}$. If $\dfrac{T}{R}$ were constant, kV would also be constant, while any change in V would imply an inversely proportionate change in k.

---

[21]We use a small p rather than a capital P, to stress the fact that this term is the reciprocal of what Pigou called P, and (as will appear later) slightly different from Fisher's P.

[22]*Readings in Monetary Theory,* p. 165. "Resources" is an ambiguous term which might refer either to stocks (wealth) or to flows (income). Most of the references to resources in Pigou's article seem to imply the wealth interpretation, but some imply income.

[23]Worked out by J. M. Keynes in his *Treatise on Money* (New York: Harcourt, Brace & World, Inc., 1930).

We can regard k as the reciprocal of V,[24] and can translate any monetary statement framed in terms of the Cambridge equation into the terms of the Fisher equation.

But the equations are not fully equivalent. The cash-balances argument can do several things that the transactions-velocity approach cannot: (1) It can deal with the way that *uncertainty* affects economic behavior. (2) This tie-up makes it much more applicable to "transition periods." (3) It looks at money as a form of property and can clear up the relations of money and "near-moneys." Above all: "It brings us at once into relation with volition—an ultimate cause of demand—instead of with something that seems at first sight accidental and arbitrary."[25]

Criticisms of the Cambridge equation. The Cambridge equation is often a target for captious criticisms. One recent writer objects that the equation implies that cash is held "exclusively. . . for expenditure on consumption goods."[26] It is hard to reconcile this with the frequent references to business motives by Pigou and the other Cambridge writers. The idea that cash represents command over goods and services is just as applicable to firms as to households. Inactive balances held because the owners *may* find it desirable to finance future purchases from assets can also be looked at in his way.

The Cambridge equation does not do full justice to the ideas it aims to represent. First, representing the demand for money by a quantum of goods (kR) is clumsy. We do not represent the demand for apples by a quantum of cash, but by a schedule relating the number of apples demanded to various factors affecting that demand.

Second, the Cambridge equation does not provide an explicit place for the several demand-determining factors. The equation was originally meant to suggest that people want to hold cash balances equal to a fraction of their income plus a fraction of their wealth.[27] Unless income and wealth are separately listed in the equation, it looks as though cash is linked exclusively to income. The liquidity-preference doctrine suggests that interest rates may help to determine

---

[24] In his discussion of the translation from one equation to the other (p. 173 of the article cited above), Pigou points out that the constancy of T/R holds for "given conditions of production and trade." In a recession from a prosperity into a depression, the real volume of production (T) would shrink greatly relative to real wealth. If, therefore, we take R to refer to wealth, V and k would not move inversely. Suppose that V starts at 10 *per annum* and that V and T each fell by 20 per cent and that wealth merely stopped growing. If T/R were 1.0 at the outset, then k would be 0.1. Then we get $T/R = 0.8 = kV$ and we find that while V has fallen 20 per cent, k remains constant at 0.1.

[25] J. R. Hicks, "A Suggestion for Simplifying the Theory of Money," in *Readings in Monetary Theory*, p. 174.

[26] E. S. Shaw, *Money, Income and Monetary Policy* (Homewood, Illinois: Richard D. Irwin, Inc., 1950), p. 348.

[27] Cf. A. Marshall, *Money, Credit and Commerce* (London: Macmillan & Co., Ltd., 1923), pp. 44–45.

the demand for cash. A better way to express the cash-balances concept would be to write:

$$M = f(Y, W, i, X)$$

when M stands for the stock of cash, Y for national income, W for national wealth, i for interest, and X for such other determinants as the *distribution* of income and wealth, price expectations, and the degree of uncertainty about business forecasts.[28] This equation explicitly mentions three of the variables that are probably important in the determination of the demand for cash. The level of income is closely linked to the transactions motive, while income, wealth, and interest rates affect the investment and speculative motives. Our uncertainty about prices, incomes, and outlays is subsumed under the blanket variable X, which stands for many of the influences affecting the margin-of-safety motive for holding cash balances.

The real-balances effect. Some recent writers have used a variant of this demand equation as the basis for a "refutation" of Keynesian postulates on money, interest, and income.[29] These economists write the demand for "real" money balances in terms of "real" income, "real" wealth, and other variables:

$$M_r = \frac{M}{P} = g(Y_r, W_r, i, X).$$

They then point out that a doubling of prices and of the nominal money stock (M) will satisfy this demand equation at unchanged levels of "real" income, "real" wealth, and interest rates.

This conclusion is unexceptionable, but is made to support a series of propositions that are open to dispute. First, it is used to argue that prices and the money stock are uniquely related—that a doubling of the nominal money stock will *cause* prices to double, leaving "real" income and wealth as they were before. This is a rigorous restatement of the familiar quantity theory of money.

The real-balances theorists also use their demand equation in an assault on the Keynesian notion of underemployment equilibrium. Suppose that

---

[28]Cf. the monetary equations developed by Lawrence Klein in *Economic Fluctuations in the United States, 1921–41* (New York: John Wiley & Sons, Inc., 1951), pp. 95–101.

[29]See, especially, Don Patinkin, *Money, Interest, and Prices,* 2nd ed. (New York: Harper & Row, Publishers, 1965). The argument developed at length by Patinkin was stated earlier by Professor Pigou and sometimes referred to as the "Pigou effect." For Pigou's own formulation see his "Economic Progress in a Stable Environment," reprinted in *Readings in Monetary Theory* (New York: McGraw-Hill Book Company, Inc., 1951). Pigou's original argument had a long-run flavor; Patinkin's version does not appear to draw a distinction between short- and long-run phenomena.

investment falls off, so that income and employment decline as in a Keynesian model. Such a decline of employment must touch off a fall in wages which, in turn, will be reflected in lower costs and prices. A fall in prices is formally equivalent to an increase in the nominal stock of money; a decrease of P in the equation given above has the same effect on M_r as an increase of M. If the stock of "real" money is increased by falling prices, the public will be inclined to spend some of their money balances; at the initial level of "real" income, let alone the reduced level caused by the drop in investment, the demand for "real" money balances will be smaller than the enlarged available supply. This increase of spending by consumers and business must raise output and employment. It will continue until output and employment are back to initial levels.

The real-balances analysis may be easily illustrated by an adaptation of Chart 9–5. Suppose, as in Chart 11–1, that "real" investment is initially at I_o, so that "real" income is at OY_f. Consider, next, the consequences of a fall in investment to the level I_1. If the saving schedule, S_o, were to stay put, the level of income would fall to OY_1. This would cause a fall in wages and prices, and would thereby raise the "real" stock of money. That increase would raise consumption (lower saving) for each level of "real" income. In effect, the saving schedule would drop from S_o to S_1. This would restore income to OY_f, so that full employment would once again prevail. If the real-balances effect does not at once bring income back to full-employment levels, wages and prices will continue to fall. This will shift the saving schedule downward some more and, in the end, bring income back to OY_f.

The same result could be achieved by an increase in the nominal stock of money with wages and prices constant. Yet real-balances theorists prefer to stress wage and price changes rather than money-stock changes. They seek to show that the economy is self-equilibrating—that a decline of investment (or of another component of spending) will be offset by price-induced spending changes that the drop in investment itself sets off.

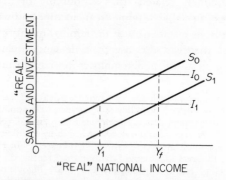

Chart 11-1: The real balances effect and full employment equilibrium.

The real-balances argument is extremely elegant. But it has decisive drawbacks as a guide to policy. It is based on very restrictive assumptions and attempts to apply it may have disequilibrating by-products.[30]

One assumption often made in discussions of the real-balances effect is that there is no "money illusion"—the supposition that holders of money are only concerned with its real value. While this may be true of most people in the long run, there are significant exceptions. Some spending units have fixed money obligations or deal in assets that have fixed money prices. These units must partly gear their money holdings to their nominal debts or nominal assets. The phrase "money illusion" evokes disapproval, but those who display it may not always be irrational.

Another assumption crucial to the argument is the supposition that price changes affect debtors in the same way as creditors. Although this is given an innocuous label—the "neglect of distribution effects"—the assumption is hardly innocuous. We have already argued that debtors and creditors may be differently affected by price-induced changes in the real value of debt.[31]

Still another assumption in the real-balances approach is that wages and prices are perfectly flexible. If prices do not fall when output drops, the "real" stock of money will not increase and there will be no growth of consumer and business demand to take up the slack in output and employment. This assumption of flexibility does not square with the facts. Wages and prices will rise when there is excess demand, but do not as easily fall when there is unemployment.

The assumptions we have listed are connected to the assertion that the economy is self-equilibrating. They relate to the effect and likelihood of falling wages and prices when a drop in output and employment occurs. One may also object to the real-balances analysis of the effects of an increase in the nominal money stock. Real-balances theorists often neglect to indicate how additional money comes into being, yet the way in which money is created can itself affect the demand for money. If the central bank purchases government bonds, it is apt to change the public's asset preferences. By bidding up the price of bonds (lowering interest rates), the central bank will enhance the speculative motive

---

[30]This list of objections is far from exhaustive. There are many more complex objections to the real-balances approach, especially to the version Patinkin has produced. See, for example, G. C. Archibald and R. G. Lipsey, "Money and Value Theory: A Critique of Lange and Patinkin," *Review of Economic Studies,* XXVI, no. 1 (October 1958).

[31]See Chapter 6. There is a further point to be made in this connection. A fall in commodity prices is tantamount to an increase in the "real" stock of bonds outstanding. Quite apart from its impact on the net worth of creditors and debtors, such an increase can affect economic activity by way of its impact on interest rates. A fall in prices causes an equi-proportional increase in "real" cash balances and "real" bonds outstanding. It need not cause an equi-proportional increase in the demand for cash and the demand for bonds. As the real wealth of asset-holders increases on account of the fall in prices, the demand for bonds may grow faster than the demand for cash, or the demand for cash more rapidly than the demand for bonds. We do not know which one has the higher wealth-elasticity of demand.

for holding cash.[32] If money is put into circulation by a government deficit that is incurred to pay a veterans' bonus, the transaction in itself does very little to increase the demand for money. The veterans who receive it will be apt to spend it promptly. Those from whom they buy, getting money for goods from inventory, are likely to spend the money to replenish inventory. The whole sequence of events set up by increasing the stock of money will depend on the way that money is created.

The decisive objection to most real-balances reasoning is that it neglects the role of expectations. A fall in wages and prices caused by a drop in output can easily generate pessimistic business forecasts and can cause consumers and businesses to cut back their outlays. This increase of "bearishness" might easily swamp the equilibrating influence of the real-balances effect.

All of this is not to criticize a demand-for-money equation that relates desired "real" money balances to income, wealth, and interest rates, but merely to say that such an equation falls far short of being a complete theory of money. No one can quarrel with the proposition that a doubling of nominal money and of the price level would satisfy the demand equation at unchanged levels of income and wealth.[33] But this comes close to being a truism and is very different from the assertion that a doubling of money balances will *cause* prices to double.

Some evidence exists to support the contention that the level of real balances has an effect on spending, but we would be imprudent to rely upon this one effect as our main route out of depressions. The evidence suggests that the demand for money is a better restraint upon inflation than a cushion against recessions. People with excess money are not likely to increase their spending in a deliberate effort to dispose of cash balances. Rather, an excess of money allows them to neglect their cash positions when making major spending decisions. Cash balances have sometimes *increased* hugely, as in the 1930's, without causing an increase of spending or upward pressure on wages and prices, but cash balances cannot be allowed to *decrease* indefinitely in relation to income or outlays. There must come a point at which we are short of cash, whether because the money stock is shrinking or because prices and output are growing. When this happens, holders of money may try to build up cash assets; they may even cut back spending in order to restore an adequate margin of safety. Anyone who does not consciously conserve his cash will soon find it "slipping through his fingers." He need not keep his eyes glued to his cash requirements or holdings, but if he does not cast frequent glances at his cash position, he will eventually become "illiquid." He may get good value for the money he spends, but will nevertheless

---

[32]In some analyses, this possibility is ruled out by an ingenious but unrealistic extension of the assumptions that there are no distribution effects and no money illusion. Businesses are said to borrow more as soon as prices begin to rise, so as to hold constant the "real" interest payments and indebtedness of the business sector. Business, however, is hardly apt to borrow money simply to satisfy an economist's yearning for symmetry in monetary analysis.

[33]Even this proposition, however, relies on the unrealistic assumptions concerning distribution effects that we have already criticized.

find himself surrounded by possessions that he cannot use effectively for want of a cash balance.

Evidence on the demand for cash. The cash-balances approach to monetary theory argues that the holders of cash can mold the nominal supply of cash to match the real demand—variations in aggregate spending will alter the price level so as to translate a given stock of nominal cash balances into the desired stock of "real" balances. To what extent has this actually happened? The record on "real" cash holdings is presented graphically in Chart 11–2, which shows the scale of the public's demand for cash in periods of steady prosperity, traces

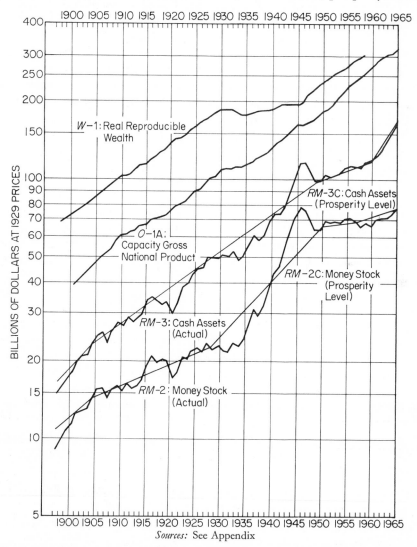

Sources: See Appendix

Chart 11-2: Wealth, output, cash assets, and the money stock, at 1929 prices, 1897–1965.

a trend between such periods, and locates deviations from that trend associated with depressions and inflations. The cash stocks are deflated for price changes using the Gross National Product deflator—the most comprehensive price index available.[34]

"Real" cash for each year from 1897 to 1965 is shown by the jagged curve RM-3 in the middle of the diagram. We also give an estimate of "real" money stocks (curve RM-2), as money is the largest component of total cash assets. Curves RM-3C and RM-2C gauge the trend of the public's demand for cash and its demand for money. These curves are derived by looking more closely at behavior in periods of approximate economic stability—periods when people could look back on at least a year of high-level production (over 90 per cent of potential) and when prices were not changing faster than 5 per cent per annum. From 1889 to 1965, we had six such periods lasting longer than one year: 1889–92, 1903–5, 1926–29, 1949–50, 1955–57, and 1963–65.[35] Curves RM-2C and RM-3C are constructed by taking the average of money or cash holdings in these periods as "prosperity-level" points and connecting these prosperity-level points to produce a continuous curve.

To provide a perspective for gauging the growth of "real" cash, Chart 11–2 offers two reference curves—curve W–1 for reproducible wealth and curve O–1A for productive capacity. All of the curves are drawn on a semilogarithmic scale, so that equal rates of growth are shown by equal slopes on the graph.

The prosperity-level curve for "real" cash (or any other reasonable trend line for cash) rises at roughly the same rate as reproducible wealth and productive capacity, at least up to 1930. The wealth curve levelled out during the depression and war, but has since resumed its increase at a rapid rate. Cash assets grew rather slowly during the 1950's but increased rapidly in the early 1960's. Note that the money stock proper, curves RM-2 and RM-2C, grew more rapidly than wealth, capacity, and total cash assets during much of the period under study, but slowly in the latest decades.

Consider the deviations of the "real" cash curve from its estimated prosperity level. Until 1916, these deviations were relatively small—rarely over 10 per cent in either direction. The trough of "real" cash in 1917–20 reflects the war-induced inflation and the reduced intensity of the margin-of-safety and speculative motives that are likely to occur when people realize prices are rising sharply. This is the nearest thing to a recent observation of the demand for cash on a purely transactions basis. The sharp rise in the "real" value of cash assets in the early 1930's also testifies to a change in the mixture of motives, reflecting an acute bearishness after 1929 that intensified the speculative and margin-of-safety

---

[34]While the resulting unit for measuring money stocks is called a "1929" dollar, it could be thought of as the quantum of commodities visualized in the Cambridge equation. For year-to-year comparisons, undeflated current-dollar figures for cash are more appropriate, especially if prices are separately graphed.

[35]Several single years in the period under study also satisfy our test of "approximate economic stability."

motives. The sudden drop in "real" cash assets after 1932 probably indicates an ebb in transactions requirements on account of depression. Note that the "real" money stock, as contrasted with total cash assets, dropped at the very outset of the 1930's. This may be because money, narrowly defined, is the preferred medium for satisfying a transactions requirement.

In 1941–42, we seem to have had the beginnings of another inflationary slump in the "real" value of cash—a slump like that in 1917–20. Price control prevented an alignment of "real" demand and supply, while rationing caused a piling up of liquid assets. Although people had more cash than they needed, the inflation that could have matched supply with demand was temporarily repressed. After the end of direct controls, the growth of nominal money and cash assets was outpaced by a rise in prices; an inflation finally brought the "real" cash stock into line with previous trends. This adjustment was rapid but far from instantaneous. The demand for goods and services, especially for investment goods, remained high relative to income for some time. Excess demand continued to push up prices until the excess of liquidity had largely evaporated. In the 1950's, the growth of "real" cash was very sharply curtailed by rising prices and the policies of the Federal Reserve. The cash-balances approach would argue that the public accepts this constraint. Otherwise, it would say, prices could not have risen throughout the 1950's. Cash-balances analysis might attribute this slower growth of "real" cash assets to a new reduction of the margin-of-safety and speculative motives that are associated with rising prices and a long period of relative prosperity. The high levels of employment and output that prevailed in the 1950's may have greatly reduced business fears of a major slump and diminished the margin-of-safety demand for "real" cash assets.

"Real" cash balances grew swiftly in the 1960's because increases in interest-rate ceilings on savings and time deposits permitted financial institutions to offer high returns on corporate and individual deposits. The rate of growth of "real cash assets" was much higher in the 1960's than the growth of "real" money, narrowly defined. This suggests a greater willingness on the part of cash-holders to accept close substitutes for money—to let time deposits do some of the work for which we used to rely on money.

Velocity as a measure of the demand for cash assets. We suggested earlier that the reciprocal of velocity can be used as a rough index of the demand for cash. At the very least, it is an index of the demand for cash balances relative to level of income. In order that we may look at velocity from this standpoint, we reproduce our basic velocity series in Chart 11–3. The curve V–1, one may remember, is the ratio of Gross National Product to the money stock. The curve V–2 is the ratio of GNP to the money stock *plus* time deposits. We add to these basic series three other velocity measures. The curve V–3 compares GNP with a more inclusive measure of cash assets. It adds United States Treasury bills to money *plus* time deposits. The curve V–4 compares GNP with a

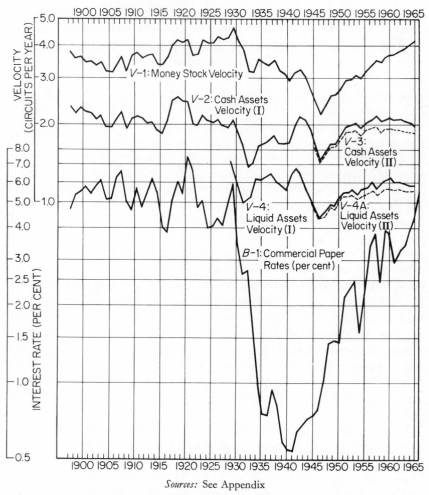

Sources: See Appendix

Chart 11-3: Income velocity and interest rates, 1897–1965.

measure of liquid assets we have used before—the sum of money *plus* time deposits, savings and loan shares, and United States Savings bonds. Curve *V*–4*A*, finally, adds Treasury bills to the measure of liquid assets used in *V*–4.

The fluctuations in velocity already discussed make more sense when interpreted in the light of cash-balances analysis.[36] The drop in velocity after 1929—a drop that may now be regarded as an increase in the demand for cash relative to income—may be interpreted as reflecting the increase of precautionary and speculative demands already discussed in connection with Chart 11–1. The postwar increase of velocity may now be regarded as the result of an inflation-induced decrease in the strength of these same motives.

---

[36]See Chapter 8.

The velocity curves which relate to cash and liquid assets behave somewhat differently than money-stock velocity. For one thing, they returned to pre-Depression levels at the end of the 1930's, with curve V–3 topping its 1929 peak as early as 1942. This suggests a dropping off of the investment and speculative motives near the end of the long depression. Balances held to satisfy investment and speculative motives are more apt to take the form of time deposits than are balances held to satisfy a transactions motive. As investment opportunities started to reappear with recovery from the depression, asset-holders again began to switch from cash and liquid assets to stocks and bonds. Cash-assets velocity and liquid-assets velocity rose by more than money-stock velocity in the late 1920's and early 1940's.

These velocity curves were somewhat more stable than money-stock velocity from the mid-fifties to the mid-sixties. This is consistent with our earlier suggestion that rising prices and sustained prosperity greatly reduce the margin-of-safety motive for holding cash, and may also reflect a shift to money substitutes as a result of the rise in interest rates that curve B–1 describes. Moreover, the higher interest offered by financial institutions on savings and time deposits in the 1960's undoubtedly has persuaded some holders of money to accept time deposits and other near-moneys in place of their checking deposits.

A danger exists in using the rate of interest as the chief way to interpret the demand for cash, because there are so many imperfections in capital markets. Households and firms may not dare to shift from money toward other earning assets, or may not be able to shift their funds as they desire. The causal vectors *from* interest *to* the demand for cash are not altogether clear. Vectors running in the opposite direction may be very much stronger. The cash position of households and firms may strongly influence interest-rate levels. If the economy is saturated with cash, interest rates will tend to sag as the holders of cash seek earning assets. If cash is definitely short, interest rates will rise. Those who are pinched by the cash shortage will not go on holding bonds at very low yields; they will sell to raise needed cash until bond prices fall so far that they cannot afford the sacrifice of further sales at prices far below those expected to rule presently. Firms pinched by the cash shortage will be willing to float their own bonds, even at rather high coupon rates or discounts below face value. As our modified Keynesian model suggested, the money market tends to tap speculative balances by pushing bond prices down (interest rates up) until those who were bears before have become bulls and are willing to buy bonds and release needed cash.[37] The interest rate may not be a powerful in-

---

[37]These propositions may help to explain why short-term rates are so much more volatile than long-term rates of interest. Households and firms with a temporary excess of cash are apt to lodge their surplus holdings in short-term government or business securities rather than in longer-term bonds or stock. When cash is temporarily plentiful, short-term rates are likely to be low relative to long; this has happened in both of the recessions of the 1950's. If, however, households and firms are caught short of cash, they are more apt to sell short-term securities (or to refrain from buying new ones as the old mature) than to sell long-term bonds on which they can suffer a larger capital loss with each percentage-point fall in market yields. When cash is scarce, short-term rates rise rapidly and are not unlikely to leap over long rates, as in the booms of the 1950's.

fluence on business decisions, but it remains an excellent thermometer, useful for measuring the demand for cash.

NOTES ON

ALTERNATIVE POINTS OF VIEW

AND SUPPLEMENTARY READINGS

The classical statements of the cash-balances point of view will be found in:
A. Marshall, *Money, Credit and Commerce* (London: Macmillan & Co., Ltd., 1923), Chapter 4.
A. C. Pigou, "Value and Money," *Quarterly Journal of Economics,* 1917–1918, pp. 38–65.
J. M. Keynes, *Tract on Monetary Reform* (New York: Harcourt, Brace & World, Inc., 1924), pp. 81–95; *Treatise on Money* (New York: Harcourt, Brace & World, Inc., 1930), chap. XIV.
For a tracing of similar points of view in French and Austrian economics, see A. W. Marget, *Theory of Prices* (Englewood Cliffs, N.J.: Prentice-Hall, Inc., 1938), Vol. I, index references under names of Menger and Walras; and "Leon Walras and the 'Cash-Balance Approach' to the Problem of the Value of Money," *Journal of Political Economy,* 1931.
Perhaps the most useful statement of this approach is J. R. Hicks, "A Suggestion for Simplifying the Theory of Money," *Economica,* February, 1935.
The "real-balances effect" and its implications for monetary theory has had intensive discussion. The most useful papers are probably:
A. C. Pigou, "The Classical Stationary State," *Economic Journal,* 1943, pp. 343–51.
Don Patinkin, *Money, Interest, and Prices,* 2nd ed. (New York: Harper & Row, Publishers, 1965), and his "Price Flexibility and Full Employment," *American Economic Review,* September 1948, pp. 543–64.
L. A. Metzler, "Wealth, Saving and the Rate of Interest," *Journal of Political Economy,* April 1951.
Milton Friedman has applied his notion of "permanent income" to the task of explaining income-velocity changes in a cash-balances framework. He finds that velocity calculations using "permanent income" produce much more stable estimates of velocity than those we have used. For an outline of his argument, see his "The Demand for Money: Some Theoretical and Empirical Results," *Journal of Political Economy,* August 1959, pp. 327–51.

A NOTE ON

THE MARGIN-OF-SAFETY MOTIVE

IN RELATION TO INVENTORIES AND INSURANCE

In order to put monetary theory in its proper relation to general economic theory, we should stress that the margin-of-safety motive discussed in the text applies to other things besides cash holdings. The same logic, for example, is at work in inventory decisions and insurance. The margin-of-safety motive for holding cash is really only a special case of a very general principle, that of meeting uncertainty by preserving freedom to change a course of action as fuller information comes in.

The holding of inventories resembles the holding of cash in many ways. Inventories of materials, of semifinished goods awaiting further processing, and of salable products are held partly because of transactions needs—because the inflow and outflow of goods are irregular and cannot be made to synchronize perfectly.[1] An important margin-of-safety element also exists. If inventories of materials are cut too close, delay in an expected delivery or acceleration of output (or the discovery of defects in materials on hand) will throw operations out of stride. Workers may stand idle and other materials may deteriorate. If inventories of salable goods are cut too close, a delay in output means that orders cannot be filled and that sales will be lost to competitors. As with an inadequate cash balance, an inadequate inventory intensifies the *linkage of risks,* so that any one misfortune will generate others, and may prevent the seizure of favorable opportunities as these arise.

Insurance is the clearest case of allowing a margin of safety to cover uncertainty. There would be inventories in the absence of uncertainty, but there would be no insurance, for uncertainty makes it *mutually* advantageous for the insurance company and the policy-holder to do business with each other. If a house were sure to burn, the company could not afford to insure it; if it were absolutely fireproof, the owner would not pay premiums. Insurance, then, is a good place to study the role of the uncertainty we have seen affecting cash.

A key fact about insurance is that premiums always exceed actuarial value.[2] A fire insurance company has to cover losses of two types, losses from fires that its policy-holders could not avoid, and fraudulent losses that go undetected, as policy-holders sometimes destroy insured property or pad legitimate claims. Besides meeting both types of losses and covering the cost of limiting fraudulent losses, the company has to cover its office and selling expenses and also make a profit.

Why do people pay billions of dollars for insurance when the odds are against them in this way? Partly because they do not know the odds, and partly, perhaps, because they hope insurance will ward off danger. Many people feel that to lack protection is to tempt providence. We make a joke of this superstition, telling people who go without raincoats that they will bring on the rain, but most people's attitude contains an undercurrent of seriousness. More objectively, insurance companies try to combat the very hazards they insure against. Taking insurance may be a way to get valuable safety advice, although this is often handed out impartially to the insured and the uninsured alike. Yet the willing-

---

[1] The well-known influence of seasonal fluctuations on inventory is one example of the forces creating such transactions needs.

[2] This term means the "objective probability" of a loss—or the percentage of the sums at risk the company's experience shows that it will have to pay on the class of risk in question.

ness to insure probably comes largely from the factors used in the text to explain the margin-of-safety motive—financial respectability and *linkage of risks*. Those who do not insure against certain hazards are considered rash by the community. Where the risk is physical injury to another person, as in automobile insurance and employers' liability, insurance is often compulsory.[3] Conventional standards of prudence do not apply to all the varieties of insurance on the market; prospective parents are not thought rash if they fail to insure against having twins. But people who overlook life insurance, fire insurance, automobile liability insurance, and so forth, endanger their credit rating, and will pay a price in higher interest and an intensification of the risks of illiquidity.

The respectability argument for insurance brings to light a neglected factor affecting the margin-of-safety motive for holding cash—the importance of standards of prudence in handling *other people's money*. A salaried business manager who is thinking about fire insurance is almost forced to take it out, whether or not he thinks the risk is worth the premium. If the firm has a fire, he will be thought prudent if he has taken out insurance, but may find his whole career blighted if he has not. There may be no serious fire loss during the term of the policy, but he will rarely be praised or promoted for saving needless insurance premiums. In the theory of money, the same force makes it prudent to hold too much cash rather than too little. A manager who gets his firm into trouble by keeping too little cash is punished, while one who enhances the firm's earning power by cutting down cash may not be praised, even though his luck may hold and his firm may escape injury.

The linkage-of-risks factor is also brought out very clearly by life insurance. Suppose that a man has a son who proposes to take the long and expensive training required to become a doctor. Think what will happen to the son's training if after he has started medical school his father dies and leaves a widow and younger children without life insurance. The loss of the father's earning power will lead to a second loss: the son will have to abandon his professional training. This linkage of risks must be foreseen when the son starts his premedical work. Unless the family can see to it that the son may continue his studies, whatever happens, it may not be worth making sacrifices to finance his medical training. A life insurance premium will divorce the risk of the father's death from the risk that the son cannot finish his training—a fact which raises the value of life insurance.

---

[3] With automobile insurance, social policy is influenced by the suspicion that some people who fail to insure, having no property the courts could seize for the benefit of the injured party, are expecting to take refuge in bankruptcy, if they run over somebody. People who do not choose to insure are sometimes excused if they can prove that they have enough property to make good such a claim.

Chapter 12

Lending and
the Stream
of Payments

Monetary theory and monetary policy. The major varieties of monetary theory examined thus far dictate very similar monetary policies. They all attach great importance to the stock of money (or cash) as a determinant of output, employment, and price levels, and consequently direct the central bank's attention to the size of the money supply. The interest-investment analysis *and* the cash-balances analysis suggest an expansion of the money stock to increase output and employment, and a shrinkage of the money stock to curb inflation caused by excess demand.

A third approach to the analysis of spending looks upon the money stock somewhat differently, and offers different advice to the central bank. It is more concerned with the flow of credit—with lending by banks and other institutions —than with the stock of cash that may be created by commercial-bank lending. It looks upon the money stock merely as a by-product of lending to business and government, and upon the demand for money merely as an imprecise limit to the pyramid of credit and debt that can be erected upon a given monetary base.

This is a very recent approach to monetary analysis. It is still taking shape in the technical literature, so a rigorous presentation comparable to those possible for the other approaches is as yet difficult. But because it comes close to being the theory of money that guides United States monetary policy, something should be said about it here. The Federal Reserve would appear to be more interested in the control of lending than in control over the stock of money or cash.

The credit-flows approach. The credit-flows approach to monetary phenomena can best be set out if we consider a simple economy consisting of several persons (or sectors), each earning an income from production.[1] If each person or sector were to spend all of his income, the total demand for goods and services would just match total output; the economy would be working at full capacity. If, however, one person were to save a part of his income, while others continued to spend all of theirs, aggregate demand would fall short of aggregate output and, in subsequent periods, output and employment would probably drop. In order to maintain capacity production, someone must spend more than his income to offset saving by another person. The credit-flows doctrine is concerned with the financing of this deficit spending. It asks how such deficits are financed, and tries to spell out the implications of a change in the volume of financing or in the terms on which it is offered.

Such deficit spending might be financed by the persons who are saving; savers might be willing to lend their savings to the persons seeking to spend more than they earn. This sort of financing does occur in our economy, and on a very large scale. Individuals who buy United States Savings Bonds are placing funds at the disposal of the federal government to finance its deficit spending. Similarly, those savers who buy newly issued corporate stock or corporate bonds are placing funds at the disposal of business which can finance deficit spending. But direct transfers of cash from savers are not the only way of financing the deficits in which we are interested. These may be financed by the creation of new money—by bank lending, a major function of the banking system and the one most heavily stressed by credit-flows analysis. The credit-flows approach looks upon the creation of cash as a by-product of the lending process. It does not entirely neglect the previously mentioned routes by which an expansion of the money stock may stimulate spending by reducing the rate of interest or increasing real balances, but argues that the most important effect of cash creation is that it facilitates spending by deficit households and firms. It says that this spending is the primary and dominant consequence of deposit creation, and accounts for most of the inflationary impact of an increase in the money stock when resources are fully employed.

An economy which segregated savers from deficit sectors and forbade direct transfers of cash would constantly have to enlarge its money stock. This would be its only way of financing the deficits required to offset saving. When cash can be transferred, full employment can be sustained with less deposit creation, and may even be feasible without an addition to the money stock. Savers may not be willing to transfer all their savings directly to deficit spending units, but may place their remaining savings with nonbank credit institutions that

---

[1] The example that follows is an elaboration of one we set out in Chapter 6, where we described the process of liquid-assets creation.

can transfer it to these units. In the process, these institutions will create their own debts to savers—time deposits, savings and loan shares, and insurance policies. The credit-flows approach looks upon these debts in much the same way as it looks upon money, regarding them as by-products of the lending process. They are, of course, different from the deposits created by commercial banks. First, they are created in a process preliminary to the financing of deficits, while the demand deposits of commercial banks are created in the act of financing these deficits. Second, they are money substitutes, not means of payment, a fact which will grow in importance at a later stage of analysis.

Credit flows and business fluctuations. The supply of finance does not adapt itself to the demand. The supply of finance is distinct from the demand by deficit sectors, and even different from the volume of saving. A shortage of finance can curb deficit spending, while a glut of finance can stimulate it. The lending process may cause the total of deficit spending to differ from the planned volume of current saving, and thereby influence the level of output and prices.

The supply of finance can be divided into three parts: (1) the part of current or past saving which is directly furnished by savers; (2) the part of current or past saving which is furnished through credit institutions; (3) the volume of lending by commercial banks that is matched by the creation of new demand deposits. This flow of loanable funds may differ greatly from the volume of saving in a given month or year. It may fall short of planned saving if savers decide to build up cash balances, rather than lend their savings to business or place them at the disposal of the nonbank credit institutions. It may exceed planned saving, even in the absence of deposit creation, for the savers themselves may decide to run down their cash balances—to lend out more money than they have saved during the month or year in question. When we allow for bank lending, there is even less likelihood that saving will precisely match the flow of loanable funds.

If lending exceeds saving, output and prices are likely to rise; if lending falls short of saving, output and prices may fall. This can be demonstrated by relating the notion of deficit spending used in this chapter to the saving-investment relationship developed in Chapter 9. The deficits we are discussing are roughly equivalent to *ex ante* investment *plus* government spending.[2] This sum must equal *ex ante* saving *plus* taxes if income, output, and employment are to be stable from one period to the next. If the total of finance that is forth-

---

[2] The correspondence is only approximate. The deficits we have in mind are really differences between total outlays and receipts in each sector. The business deficit would be business investment *less* the total of business saving and business cash balances that was directly used to finance business investment; the government deficit would be government spending *less* the total of taxes and government cash balances that was used to finance government expenditure. There could also be a household deficit if households spent more on consumables and investment goods than they could finance out of total income and a reduction of household cash balances.

coming sufficiently stimulates business investment, or encourages households to spend beyond income, *ex ante* business and household investment can exceed *ex ante* saving, so that total output and, perhaps, prices will be raised during the period. If there is a shortage of finance, investment may drop below *ex ante* saving *plus* taxes, depressing output, employment, and prices.

Some evidence on credit flows. The data in Chart 12-1 are designed to evaluate this credit-flows hypothesis in the light of American experience during the past half century. The top curve (curve *RO*–2) is Gross National Product in 1929 prices—the curve used before to represent business fluctuations. As usual, we have drawn a peak-to-peak trend line astride this curve. The middle curve in the chart (curve *W*–2) is an estimate of end-year nonfarm inventories—of the value at 1929 prices of raw materials, semifinished goods, and marketable output held by producers, processors, and sellers. The bottom curves (curves *RM*–11 and *RM*–11*A*) describe the end-year total of bank loans outstanding,[3] other than for real-estate or securities purchases. This curve has also been corrected for price changes; it is deflated by the same price index that was used on curve *W*–2. The bank-loan series has two parts: its first segment (curve *RM*–11) includes loans to consumers; its second segment (curve *RM*–11*A*) does not. As the two curves are not far apart when they overlap, we may assume that consumer loans were small in the early twentieth century.

We have chosen to use inventories as the link between bank loans and Gross National Product because inventory investment has had a strategic place in the business cycle, and because the traditional rules of prudent banking singled out the financing of business inventories as a proper use for bank credit.[4] Few components of Gross National Product have been as volatile during business fluctuations, and few are as likely to move in consonance with commercial-bank lending.[5]

This connection between inventories and total output is confirmed by a comparison of curves *W*–2 and *RO*–2. They move in very close sympathy. Every decline of Gross National Product is matched by a drop in inventories or by a marked reduction in their rate of growth. Every retardation in the

---

[3] Changes in the real value of loans outstanding are only an approximation to new net lending, because the real value of loans outstanding can be considerably affected by price-level changes.

[4] See pp. 36–37.

[5] The connection between Gross National Product and inventories is not as simple as might be assumed. First, the inventory series is concerned with total stocks; a decline in inventory investment that depresses Gross National Product need not depress total inventories. Such a reduction in net inventory investment will merely slow the growth of total inventories, unless that net investment is actually negative. Second, inventories may move counter to production close to the turning points of total production. This is because unsold goods and raw materials can accumulate when demand and production decline, while an increase of production may cause a reduction in inventories of raw materials, and an increase of final demand can cause a reduction in inventories of final output. We have already discussed this "unintended" inventory investment in our survey of the payments stream. See, especially, p. 180.

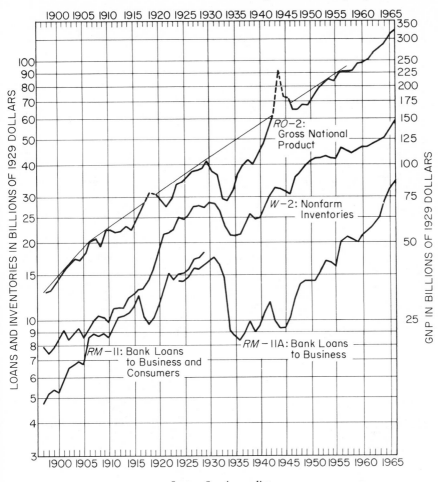

Chart 12-1: Bank loans, total business inventories, and gross national product, at 1929 prices, 1896–1966.

growth of Gross National Product is also reflected in the inventory curve, either by an actual drop or by a decline in the rate of growth of stocks. Every acceleration in the growth of total production is also reflected in the inventory curve, although less clearly than the recessions or retardations. There are one or two wobbles in the inventory series that have no counterpart in the output curve—inventories fell in 1901, but there was no drop in GNP. These slight discrepancies do not mar the striking correspondence between the two curves in Chart 12-1. The figures do not tell us which changes were cause and which effect, but do suggest a connection worth study.

Consider next the relationship of the inventory curve to the two series that describe bank loans outstanding. This connection is not as close as the one we have just examined, but inventories and bank loans are related. The inventory reductions of 1904 and 1909 are clearly reflected in the bank-loan curve. There is an independent reduction of bank loans during World War I, a disturbance that can be explained within the credit-flows framework. This drop in bank loans reflects the growth of business profits and a consequent increase in industry's capacity to finance its inventories without resort to the banks—indeed, to repay loans that were arranged before the beginning of the war. After the war, the link between inventories and bank credit is again visible. The sharp growth of inventories after 1925 is markedly reflected in the bank-loan curve, and the sharp drop of inventories after 1929 is matched by a drastic drop in bank loans outstanding. The two curves separate in World War II, for the same reasons as in World War I, but they again move in harmony after the war, and fluctuate together throughout the 1950's and mid-1960's.

This connection between bank loans and inventories may be used to explain the relationship of cash assets to total output. What is more important, it may help to explain the loosening of that relationship in the 1950's.

Until the end of World War I, bank loans and bank deposits moved together. The bank-loan series in Chart 12-2 (curves M-11 and M-11A) travel parallel to the bank-deposit curve (curve L-4). Commercial-bank deposits, as we have seen, are the major part of total cash assets. During the 1920's, deposits continued to increase, while bank loans to business were rather stable, the consequence of increased bank lending for securities purchases and construction. The business-loan series, during this period, matches production as closely as cash assets. Business loans grew a bit more slowly than inventories or total production (Chart 12-1), but real cash assets rose more rapidly than did Gross National Product (Chart 11-2). During the 1930's, the loan and deposit curves moved parallel again, although they were much further apart than they had been before World War I. They both declined sharply in the early 1930's, then moved along similar routes into World War II. The greater distance between them was the result of commercial-bank purchases of United States government debt. The government borrowed heavily in the 1930's, and on an even larger scale during World War II.

It is in the postwar period that the credit flows approach does best by contrast with its rivals. During the 1950's, real cash assets grew quite slowly and the real money stock actually declined. In the early 1960's real cash assets grew more swiftly than the real money stock (Chart 11–2). Production, by contrast, continued to grow. The total of bank loans grew apace with inventories, and inventories in their turn grew with Gross National Product. The difference in rates of growth between the money stock and output may be explained by the divergence between the paths of bank loans and bank deposits. Bank lending to business grew in comparison with deposits, following a path more closely consonant with production than the money stock or total cash assets.

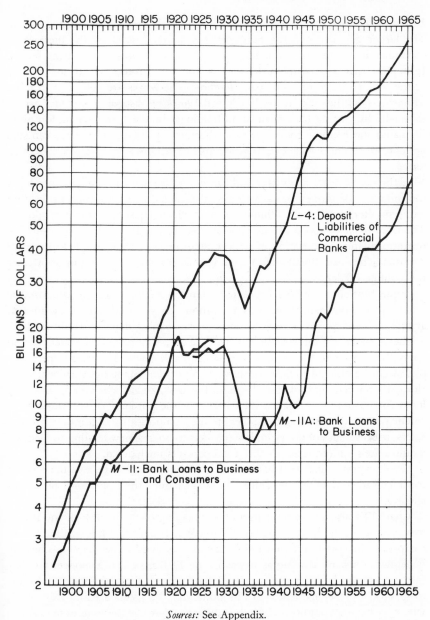

Chart 12-2: Bank loans and bank deposits, at current prices, 1896–1966.

Credit-flows analysis and monetary policy. Charts 12–1 and 12–2 describe two phenomena that have received much attention in recent years. Note, first, the increased distance between curves *L*–4 and *M*–11*A* in Chart

12-2 and the fact that the loan series has recently risen faster than deposits. The larger gap between the two curves is partly caused by the increase of consumer loans and by bank holdings of United States government bonds. It implies that a growth in deposits is not now prerequisite to an increase in the volume of commercial-bank lending. The banks are able to lend more to business, as they did in the 1950's and 1960's by disposing of other assets, especially by cutting back their bond holdings. In effect, this separation gives the banks more elbow room to finance business spending. The banks can step up loans to business whenever they are able to sell off other assets on agreeable terms.

If the credit-flows analysis is right in emphasizing loans and playing down the influence of money or cash stocks, the banks' ability to increase lending without altering deposits diminishes the effectiveness of monetary policy. The traditional weapons of our Federal Reserve—rediscounting, open-market operations, and the variation of reserve requirements—are designed to control deposits. They can directly affect lending only insofar as lending must increase the volume of deposits.

Some economists who have called attention to this problem propose the reform of reserve requirements as a solution. They would replace the present system, which applies a reserve ratio to the banks' deposit liabilities, with a scheme based on the structure of bank assets. The proposed system would apply these ratios to the various commercial-bank assets. The banks, for example, might be obliged to hold a reserve of 5 per cent against government securities, 10 per cent against their loans to business, and 20 per cent against their loans to consumers or against their loans for the purchase of securities. Such a scheme could discourage changes in the composition of commercial-bank assets, because sales of government securities to finance new lending to business would raise required reserves with total deposits unchanged.

Other experts admit that bank lending is important, but believe the existing methods can cope with asset shifts. We will examine their position later in this chapter.

Chart 12-1 also shows a separation, a spreading of the bank-loan and inventory curves during most of the post-World War II period. Although the spread narrows somewhat in the mid-1960's, it indicates that business is not as heavily dependent on bank lending as it was in the 1920's, so that a monetary policy that only controls the banks may not come near to limiting industry's access to finance. Further evidence on this point may be gleaned from Table 12-1, where we have set out flow-of-funds statistics to describe the sources of business cash. These data derive from money-flows data collected by the Federal Reserve System, and start where income statements usually end. The first lines show what businesses have left after paying wages, rents, interest, dividends, and taxes. The sum of the first two lines gives the total of finance that was supplied

TABLE 12-1

SOURCES AND USES OF FUNDS, NONFINANCIAL BUSINESS, 1961–65

(dollar amounts in billions, rounded to nearest $0.1 billion)*

	Total, 1961–65	
Sources and Uses of Funds	*Corporate*	*Noncorporate*b
Sources of funds:		
1. Gross saving from business operations		
1a. Undistributed profits after taxes	$74.1	‡
1b. Capital consumption allowances	153.3	$68.6
2. Funds raised from outside business		
2a. From owners	4.2	−9.5
2b. By sales of corporate bonds and of mortgages	37.2	22.8
2c. By sales of U.S. government bonds	2.7	——
2d. By net borrowing from banks**	17.8	10.2
2e. By other borrowing	4.1	6.4
2f. By trade indebtedness	28.4	4.6a
3. Total from all sources	$321.8	$103.1
Uses of funds:		
4. Used in business operations		
4a. Gross investment in plant, etc., and in inventory	$209.4	$99.6
4b. Loans to customers†	80.2	——
5. Added to deposits and currency	−4.4	3.4
6. Used to buy other financial assets	26.8	——
7. Total funds used	$320.8	$103.0
8. Funds not accounted for and rounding error	$1.0	$0.1

Source: Federal Reserve Bulletin, January 1967.

*Detail may not add to total because of rounding.
**Other than mortgage loans.
†Trade credit extended, consumer credit extended, and finance paper.
‡All profits are treated as though paid out to owners; profits ploughed back are listed as funds raised from owners.
aNet of change in trade receivables, hence not comparable with corporate entry.
bIncludes farm sector.

by production and commerce. The remaining lines tell how businesses raised the rest of the money used to build new plants, accumulate inventories, finance customers, and increase cash balances. Out of a total of $321.8 billion collected by corporations in a five-year period, $227.4 billion came from profits and depreciation allowances, and two-thirds of the remainder were raised by sales of new stocks and new bonds. Only $17.8 billion of the total—a little more than 5 per cent—was raised by borrowing from commercial banks. Unincorporated business relied more heavily on the banks, but even this sector borrowed less than a quarter of what it needed for investment and lending.

One may argue that these flow-of-funds statistics understate the contribution of commercial banks. The banks may have supplied additional finance by purchasing new business securities. But the more comprehensive data in Table 12-2 do not lend much support to this line of criticism. During the same five-year period covered by Table 12-1, the banks acquired slightly more than a third of the debt issued by other sectors. Moreover, their acquisitions were less than those of other credit institutions.[6]

The data represented by Tables 12-1 and 12-2 have led some economists to express severe doubts as to the effectiveness of monetary policy. They point out that a large part of investment is financed with the savings of the investor himself; much of business investment is financed with after-tax profits that have

TABLE 12-2

SOURCES AND CONSIGNMENT OF CREDIT INSTRUMENTS BY SECTOR, 1961–65
(dollar amounts in billions, rounded to nearest $0.1 billion)*

	Total, 1961–65		
Issuing or Purchasing Sector	*Issued*	*Purchased*	*Net Borrowing*
Consumers and nonprofit organizations	$119.2	$1.5	$117.7
Farmers and noncorporate nonfinancial business	39.3	—	39.3
Corporate nonfinancial business	63.3	6.3	57.0
Government	59.2	37.0	22.2
Financial system	31.3	277.5	−246.2
Banking system**	—	119.6	—
Savings and insurance institutions	—	132.6	—
Other financial institutions	—	25.3	—
Rest of world	15.1	3.5	11.6
Total	$327.4	$325.8	—
Not accounted for and rounding error	—	−$1.6	+$1.6

Source: Federal Reserve Bulletin, January 1967.

*Credit instruments as defined for this purpose include federal obligations other than savings bonds, state and local government debt, corporate stocks and bonds, mortgages, consumer credit, securities loans, other bank loans, and miscellaneous loans. Trade credit is not included, nor are the debts of financial institutions, such as savings and loan shares or life insurance policies.

**Includes monetary authorities and commercial banks. Commercial banks account for $103 billion of this total.

---

[6] These gross purchases by households do not include acquisitions of fixed money obligations—of time deposits at mutual savings banks, of savings and loan shares, and of life insurance policies and pension equity. It is not proper to regard the household sector as a net deficit sector in the sense given to that term in this chapter. While households were net borrowers, on the definitions used by Table 12-2, they acquired the debts of credit institutions not shown by this table. In effect, this table is meant to describe borrowing by the final users of credit and the initial destination of the debt instruments issued by borrowers. As a fair approximation to the ultimate position, we could add the purchases of savings institutions to the acquisitions of the household sector. This would indicate that these purchases were financed by households who acquired the money substitutes issued by credit institutions.

not been distributed as dividends. It is also said that the nonbank credit institutions are not subject to Federal Reserve control.

While the Federal Reserve System has no direct contact with these institutions comparable to its contact with commercial banks, many economists argue that it has an indirect influence on the asset choices of nonbank institutions. By altering the level and direction of interest rates, the Federal Reserve may affect their activities by discouraging the sales of government securities with which these institutions sometimes finance their purchases of business debt, and, more directly, by scaring them away from large purchases of newly issued business bonds.

The reasoning that underlies this proposition is much like that outlined in the discussion of commercial banks.[7] When the Federal Reserve sells government bonds, it depresses bond prices, raising interest rates. At the same time, it alters expectations as to the future of interest rates. The impact of such sales on the asset choices of credit institutions depends partly on the change in interest-rate levels, but even more heavily upon the change in expectations induced by a movement of interest rates.

A lower level of bond prices (higher interest rates) is held to discourage sales of government bonds by the credit institutions that seek to buy new business debt. Holders who sell their bonds below par and below what they paid for them have to register a realized capital loss. If they hold onto their bonds until prices recover, they will not realize a capital loss, and may actually score a gain *relative to present prices*. Many holders of bonds are reluctant to realize such losses, for capital losses put a stamp of finality upon mistakes in portfolio policy.

A downward movement of bond prices may also discourage large sales of bonds. Falling bond prices signal bearishness in the bond market, and threaten even lower levels and larger capital losses if institutional holders sell more government bonds. An important possibility exists that falling bond prices will discourage institutional purchases of new corporate securities. A decline of bond prices, however small, may generate uncertainty about ultimate yields and prices, and cause investors to shy away from new issues until they can confidently predict the level at which prices will settle.[8]

---

[7] See pp. 100–101.

[8] How effective such a decline in prices will actually be must depend upon the *elasticity of expectations*—the ratio of expected future price changes to current price changes, in which both changes are expressed as percentages. If that elasticity is high for moderate declines in price (if a fall in bond prices brings a drastic downward revision in people's expectations of future bond prices), a moderate decline in bond prices induced by open-market sales can induce a large decline in market quotations. During this decline, institutional investors are very likely to abstain from new purchases. If the elasticity of expectations is low, a small drop in prices induced by open-market sales may not cause a prolonged suspension of new business borrowing, for the institutional investors will not be deterred from purchases. The initial fall in bond prices will not be followed by large private sales, so that the rate of interest will be quickly stabilized and the flow of borrowing will be resumed.

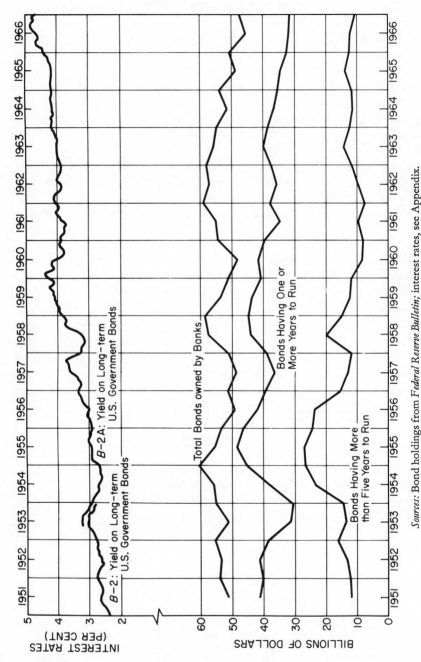

Sources: Bond holdings from *Federal Reserve Bulletin;* interest rates, see Appendix.

Chart 12-3: United States government securities owned by commercial banks, 1951–1966.

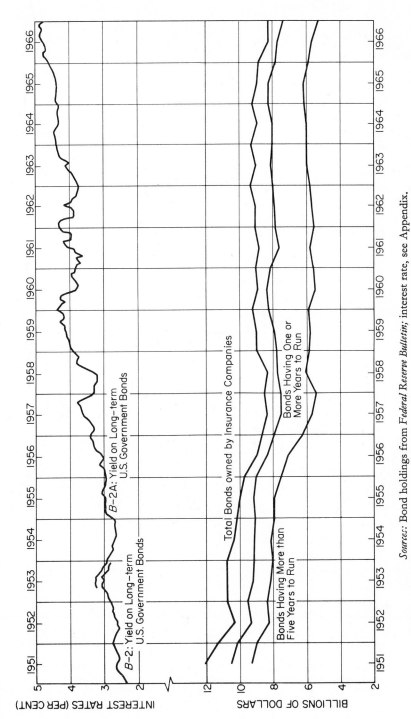

Source: Bond holdings from *Federal Reserve Bulletin;* interest rate, see Appendix.

Chart 12-4: United States government securities owned by insurance companies, 1951-1966.

243

The same set of arguments can be applied to defend monetary policy against the charge that it can be undermined by banks. If commercial banks are reluctant to take losses on their sales of government securities, they may hesitate to sell their bonds when bond prices are falling and interest rates are in flux. If they are reluctant to take capital losses, they cannot step up lending without increasing deposits, so those weapons of the Federal Reserve that effectively limit deposit-creation may be adequate to control the level of bank lending to business.

Evidence on the locking-in effect.   Data on interest rates and commercial bank holdings of government securities are set out in Chart 12-3.[9] These data do not give the "locking-in" effect as much statistical support as one might hope. During the fifteen years covered by the chart, there were three declines in commercial-bank bond holdings. In the first (1955 to mid-1957) and second (1959), the declines were concentrated at the long end of the banks' bond portfolios and each occurred in a period of increasing interest rates. The third decline (1963 to mid-1966) was less pronounced and not as heavily concentrated in bonds with a maturity of five or more years. Through the fifteen-year period, the banks disposed of bonds when the demand for loans was rising, and enlarged their bond portfolios when the demand for loans was sluggish.

A similar pattern can be found in the holdings of insurance companies. The curves in Chart 12-4 describe a steady decrease in the companies' holdings, a decrease that was especially rapid during the 1955–57 boom. Once again, they assign the bulk of the decrease to the long end of company portfolios.

These statistics are not decisive, for they do not really show that the banks and insurance companies suffered losses on account of their sales. As time passes, long-term bonds gradually approach maturity, so a bank or insurance company that has neither bought nor sold bonds would display a shrinking portfolio and an increasing concentration of short-term bonds. The decline of long-term holdings shown by banks and insurance companies may not indicate outright sales at low bond prices, but merely a refusal to buy new bonds as the old ones moved out of the long-term category. The actual reduction of bond holdings could have occurred as issues matured—not by way of sales, but as encashments. The banks and insurance companies need not have realized capital losses on the shrinkage of their bond portfolios.

This explanation raises a problem more damaging to the locking-in hypothesis than the data in Charts 12-3 and 12-4. It suggests that credit institutions may be able to avoid capital losses because their portfolios of government debt include a very wide range of maturities. The credit institutions may be able

---

[9] This chart and the one that follows use ordinary arithmetical scales instead of the semilogarithmic scales we have employed in most of our diagrams. This is because we are interested here in the addition of several magnitudes—of long-term, medium-term, and short-term bonds held by the commercial banks. Additive relationships do not emerge clearly on semilogarithmic paper.

to sustain their lending to business merely by refraining from new bond purchases—by letting the bonds that they hold come to maturity and turn into cash.

Interest rates and loanable funds. Another objection can be made to the argument that interest rates can control lending. The same increase of interest rates that is supposed to "lock in" lenders may provide those same lenders with additional money to lend. An increase of interest rates may persuade the holders of money to cut back their money balances in exchange for money substitutes—for example, time deposits, Treasury bills, and finance-company paper. These money substitutes bear handsome interest rates when the demand for finance is high or rising. By issuing them, credit institutions can obtain extra cash and increase lending without selling government bonds.

The credit-flows approach assigns several functions to the rate of interest. Most important, it regards the rate of interest as a measure of conditions in the markets for finance. The interest rate may not be the most important item in a loan contract, but changes in interest rates on new loan contracts are indicative of changes in other contract terms. The interest rate is a barometer that gives us a clue to the availability of credit. Second, the interest rate is regarded as an instrument that can be used to affect lenders' preferences. By altering interest rates through open-market operations, the Federal Reserve may be able to affect the supply of finance. Finally, the interest rate is a measure of the demand for money balances, just as in Keynesian thinking and in the cash-balances approach. The terms on which holders of money are willing to part with it help to determine the supply of finance in the credit-flows analysis.

NOTES ON
ALTERNATIVE POINTS OF VIEW
AND SUPPLEMENTARY READINGS

This chapter draws heavily on the works of John G. Gurley and Edward S. Shaw, especially on their articles, "Financial Aspects of Economic Development," *American Economic Review,* September 1955, and "Financial Intermediaries and the Savings-Investment Process," *Journal of Finance,* May 1956. For a criticism of their approach, especially of their innovations in terminology, see J. M. Culbertson, "Intermediaries and Monetary Theory," *American Economic Review,* March 1958. Our presentation of the credit-flows approach also draws on the works of Sir Dennis Robertson, especially on *Essays in Monetary Theory* (London: P. S. King, 1940).

The alleged impact of interest rates on lenders' preferences is sometimes called the "Roosa doctrine" in honor of one of its leading expositors. See R. V. Roosa, "Interest Rates and the Central Bank," in *Money, Trade, and Economic Growth, Essays in Honor of John Henry Williams* (New York: The Macmillan Company, 1951). This argument has been widely criticized in the journals. See, for example, Warren L. Smith, "On the Effectiveness of Monetary Policy," *American Economic Review,* September 1956, and John H. Kareken, "Lenders' Preferences, Credit Rationing, and the Effectiveness of Monetary Policy," *Review of Economics and Statistics,* August 1957.

Chapter 13

How Price
Levels Change

Excess Demand and Price Changes

Inflation and deflation. In the older economic literature, the terms *inflation* and *deflation* referred to parallel movements of prices and the money stock. But, like so much else in monetary theory, these terms have been redefined by the shift of emphasis away from price levels and the quantity theory. Here are definitions more in accord with present-day professional usage.

    1. *Inflation:* an upward movement of price levels.
    2. *Deflation:* a downward movement of production and employment, and of those prices that are flexible.[1]

This lack of symmetry in the definitions implies that many prices can be raised much more readily than they can be lowered. This is one cause of the asymmetry. Because money prices do not fall when there is a decline of demand, such a reduction of demand is reflected in sales volume and, eventually, in output.

    Our discussion of business fluctuations has dealt extensively with the role of money in deflations; now we turn to the connection between money and

---

[1] Note that the concept of deflation comes very close to matching the business-cycle concept of downswing, but an upswing may be noninflationary.

inflation. Beginning with the effect of excess spending power[2] on price levels, we bring in the influence of cash balances and liquidity, and then take a closer look at the mechanics of price determination in order to put the monetary influences in a proper perspective.

Inflation from the payments standpoint: excess spending power from current income. The best starting point for an analysis of inflation is the payments approach of Chapter 9. If people try to spend more than the value of forthcoming output at current prices, there is every likelihood that prices will rise.

Most serious inflations in industrial economies have occurred during or just after wartime. War mobilization pulls workers out of their previous jobs. It puts them in uniform or sets them to work producing munitions. This shifting of producers does not reduce civilian demand for goods and services; the people set to work for the government by mobilization are likely to have larger money incomes.[3] But instead of producing goods that will soak up spending power on the civilian market, they are producing things that never come to market.

If the starting position is one of unemployment, as in the United States when rearmament started in 1940, there may be a phase of "guns plus butter" —civilian output may expand fast enough to match increased spending power without a price rise. Workers who were unemployed replace those diverted to war work. As mobilization proceeds, the growth of civilian output is stopped or reversed, while money income keeps on growing. Unless civilians are shaken out of their normal spending patterns, inflation sets in, as it did in the United States early in 1941.[4] If consumers go on spending a normal share of this income, while business continues investment to expand plant and inventory in line with expanding consumption, and if government spending keeps on growing as it does in wartime, there is more spending than the available output of civilian goods and services can absorb at unchanged prices.[5]

---

[2] This term needs emphasis. We speak of *spending power* rather than purchasing power, because of the threat of price increases. If your wages go up, your power to *spend* increases. But your power to *purchase* will not increase if the rise of your wages is outpaced by the rise of prices on the goods you aim to buy. You may easily find yourself spending more to purchase less.

[3] Many of the uniformed fighting forces have their money incomes reduced, but most of the added civilian government workers and nearly all of the munitions workers have increased money incomes.

[4] This date illustrates the fact that inflation may set in before the initial unemployment is entirely absorbed. This beginning of inflation is interpreted in terms of bottlenecks—barriers to the expansion of output that cannot be forced at once, though there is still labor available.

[5] The inflation after the Korean outbreak of June 1950 was a peculiar case. Anticipations of inflation led to a powerful "cost-push" and an active speculative demand for goods. But military spending did not rise rapidly—it was actually outpaced by revenue, so that the government had a large surplus of cash income over cash outgo early in 1951. Then, something very like a business-cycle downswing in the civilian sector—a reaction from speculative buying—offset the growing deficit later in 1951.

War inflation can be prevented or stopped, but only by an appropriate pattern of anti-inflationary policies. Tax increases can reduce the amount of disposable income, and thus drain off excess spending power. Controls to allocate scarce equipment and materials among businessmen and a rationing of goods to consumers can limit total opportunities to spend, especially if these direct controls are supported by price control. Positive incentives to save, such as Payroll Savings Plans and drives to sell war bonds, can be offered. But if these policies are lacking or weak, inflation breaks through.

Postwar inflations represent slightly different sets of forces. Just after a war, government spending is still swollen, and a good part of the labor force is still employed in activities that do not put goods on the civilian markets. The after-effects of war leave business with abnormally strong incentives to invest; wartime restrictions leave a backlog of accumulated needs for houses, machinery, factories, stores, and inventories. At the same time, war controls are apt to weaken. This weakening of controls is especially acute in defeated countries (such as Germany after World War I), where the government may even be unable to collect normal taxes.

Nothing exists in the arithmetical logic of the payments approach to keep an excess-spending-power inflation from breaking out at any time when employment is fairly high. If consumers chose to spend all their after-tax income and governments to spend all their tax revenue, *any* net investment by business in excess of business saving would overbalance the market and give us intended spending in excess of what supplies can absorb without inflation. But, in fact, consumers always save something in prosperity, governments often spend less than their tax revenues, and business does not often push investment beyond what intended business saving, consumer saving, and government surpluses can offset. In peacetime, our economic system has not been very vulnerable to inflation, but it may prove more vulnerable in the future.

Cash balances and liquidity in the inflation process. The payments-approach account of inflation is only an approximation. We can improve it by bringing in some of the cash-balances thinking of Chapter 10.

War tends to increase the public's stock of cash assets and of noncash assets that are near-moneys. Modern governments that spend beyond tax revenues, because of war, borrow at banks, causing the creation of deposits. Even the bonds sold to the nonbank public become liquid assets. To make the pressure stronger, banks are encouraged to finance war industries. This expansion of liquid assets may or may not be regarded as the primary cause of war inflation. At least, it explains why the inflation is not brought to an end by forced curtailment of private spending because of an inadequate cash supply.

Cash-balances elements count still more heavily when we come to postwar inflations. At the end of a war, both households and firms are likely to come out with liquid assets that are very large in relation to transaction needs. This was conspicuously the case in the United States after World War II. This high liquidity reinforces the backlog of demand for civilian goods that were scarce during the war, especially durable goods, such as houses and machinery. With so much liquid wealth on hand, households and firms are well along toward their savings goals and can afford to ease up on saving. They can budget expenditures close to incomes, and can let saving give way, rather than other expenditures, when some outlay runs higher than planned. Corporations can afford to pay out bigger dividends. At the same time, households and firms have an incentive to bring their asset holdings back toward balance by turning some of their liquid assets into operating assets (houses or business plant and inventory) that will bring in income. Thus the liquidity position inherited from the war encourages low saving and high investment. This tendency is accentuated if, as in 1946–47, efforts to preserve "cheap money" for the Treasury enhance the banks' ability to lend to business.

Our comparative immunity to peacetime inflations can also be interpreted in cash-balance terms, with the emphasis on the *demand* for cash balances. Under peacetime conditions, a rise of prices may tend to enhance bearishness.[6] The bears' desire to swap other assets for cash limits the price increase directly and tightens the monetary situation. If the bears refuse to disgorge the cash they get by selling assets, the cash supply of the rest of the community tends to run down, an effect which is plainly anti-inflationary. Unless the government has to spend much more than it can raise by taxes, the cash supply is not likely to increase at a rate that will facilitate a large rise in prices. Here we have a testimonial to the usefulness of deep-seated views about the normality of certain prices for durable assets, and the usefulness of skepticism of market prices above normal.

Hyperinflation. Under some circumstances, the demand for cash may cease to be a drag on rising prices. If prices are rising rapidly enough to make large inroads on the purchasing power of cash balances, the demand for cash may be sharply reduced and decisions about cash balances can accelerate the increase of prices. In such a situation, called *hyperinflation,* the value of the currency unit almost disappears. Prices rise to thousands or millions of times their initial level as people search for assets other than cash to satisfy their precautionary and speculative demands, and economize to the limit on transactions requirements. The unit of account is itself deserted, and the only way out is to abolish the existing currency and set up a new one. Hyperinflation has often occurred in countries that have been badly defeated in war. The leading cases are the German mark and Russian ruble after World War I. The Confederate dollar had a similar fate in the last months of the Civil War, as did the Chinese and Hungarian currencies after World War II.

Repressed inflation. We have already alluded to ways of stopping an

---

[6] For a time, however, it may reduce the dispersion of opinions about future asset values, thus reducing the demand for cash and making the boom cumulative up to the point where differences of opinion again become acute.

inflation without a full correction of the underlying imbalances, through controls of prices and wages. Unless the imbalance is slight, such a repression of inflation also requires rationing and allocation rules to keep goods flowing at controlled prices to the people who have claims to them, and diligent policing to check the growth of black markets outside the regular channels of trade with prices above ceilings.

Such a situation is called *repressed inflation*. How much stress *it has to stand* depends upon the size of the *inflationary gap*—the excess of demand over supply at existing prices.[7] How much stress it *can stand* depends upon the administrative strength of its price and supply controls, and upon the co-operativeness of the population.

Even a successful repression of inflation has its drawbacks. Work incentives are weakened because people have such large liquid assets relative to current earnings, or to the cost of living at controlled prices. Any areas that are left uncontrolled, such as amusements, tend to get more than their share of manpower. Price-controlled producers concentrate on the most profitable items and offer consumers a poorly balanced assortment. If the administrators yield to the temptation to issue just a few more ration coupons than are justified by the supply of goods, consumers must spend endless hours standing in line. If inventories are held low to make rationed allotments as generous as possible, the usual interruptions of supply through bad weather or strikes throw whole chains of production out of gear.[8]

To get out of a repressed inflation, we may choose among three methods. One, adopted by the United States in 1946, is to drop controls and let prices rise. A second, pursued by Belgium after World War II, is to correct the current budget situation and block the liquid assets left over from previous deficits. The third is merely to wait for a change in the economic climate. This last may be a very good policy if reason exists to expect a lucky turn in foreign trade or a decline of business investment after certain urgent projects are completed. But if liquidity is very high, the wait may be long and painful.

Costs and Prices

The inflation spiral. Inflation is often described as a spiral, with price increases leading to wage increases, and wage increases leading to another round of price increases. In order to see how such a spiral occurs, to understand its

---

[7] Another way to interpret the gap is as an estimate of the flow of saving (over and above that normal to the income situation in view) which must be made to avert inflation. In this sense, of course, the gap can be estimated not only for repressed but for open inflation. For open inflation, the estimate is essentially *ex ante;* the rise of prices precludes testing what would have happened at constant prices. See Milton Friedman, "The Inflationary Gap," *American Economic Review*, September 1942.

[8] For example, see J. R. Hicks' interpretation of the British production crisis in early 1947 ("The Empty Economy," *Lloyds Bank Review*, September 1947). It seems to be a large-scale model of what we called, in Chapter 11, the "Principle of Linkage of Risks."

pacing, and to forecast its limits, we must take a closer look at the way prices are set, and especially examine the role of cost in price determination.

Some markets still exist on which sellers decide what quanity they are going to sell, and let an impersonal market decide the price.[9] But most transactions are on markets where someone consciously *decides* what the price shall be.

1. Sometimes one party to a transaction decides the price. Sellers of standardized commodities, for instance, ordinarily set a price and sell what they can at that price. After a while they may change the price if sales are much better or worse than expected. The standard rates of pay set up by employers with large staffs doing standardized work are another example of unilateral price making.
2. Sometimes prices are separately set for each transaction by close bargaining between buyer and seller. This happens when contracts are let for the construction of a building, or when orders are placed for machinery built to the buyer's specifications.
3. Sometimes prices are set for a whole series of transactions by negotiations between buyer and seller. A wage agreement reached by collective bargaining sets a price for the man-hours of labor that are to be bought by the employer, as does a contract between an employer and an individual specialized worker. Similar contract prices are set for power, the use of hired trucks, auto parts, and many other things. These contracts often set the price, but let the buyer set the quantity.
4. Sometimes, finally, government intervenes to set prices or to establish a ceiling or floor for prices reached by private decisions.

All these ways of setting prices can be influenced by demand conditions. Prices will be different if there is unemployment and deflationary pressure than if employment is good and there is inflationary pressure. But pricing decisions cannot be described simply as reactions to the monetary situation. Pricing has a momentum of its own, so the same monetary situation may yield different results if pricing is carried on differently.

We will describe the major nonmonetary influences that give pricing its independent momentum, and show how the reasoning of earlier chapters must be adjusted to allow for these influences. Many of the questions we will discuss are still at the forefront of professional discussion and research. Our account will, of necessity, be incomplete, but it would be a greater error to ignore these questions than to make errors in their analysis.

Costs in commodity pricing.   Sellers of commodities who are in a position to decide about prices[10] commonly think in *cost-plus* terms. *Cost,* for this

---

[9] A typical example of this sort of pricing was the practice of shipping livestock on consignment to an agent at the market. The shipper would receive whatever his agent could get, less shipping costs and his agent's commission. Occasionally, the shipper would get a bill for expenses exceeding the value of his shipments instead of a check.

[10]These are sellers who have the power to alter their rate of sales by varying production, or by varying purchases of merchandise, and who do not deal on markets that are so impersonal as to deprive sellers of buyers if their prices are above the market.

Farmers are unable to decide about prices on both counts; the most they can do is to hold

purpose, means operating costs that are directly linked with the commodity sold. The *plus* is a margin to cover overhead costs and profits.[11]

Two broad types of *cost* situation may confront sellers in this position.

1. Sometimes the chief operating cost is the wage bill, based on fixed wage rates, or a combination of such wage costs with outlay for materials that sell at rigid prices. This situation points to a fairly stable level of direct operating costs per unit of output, common in the manufacture of metal products and other highly finished goods.
2. Sometimes the chief direct operating costs are for materials that have flexible prices. This situation is common in merchandising, and in food processing, where farm products are the main materials and the processing itself is not very expensive.

Cost pattern (*1*) is likely to lead to rather rigid prices, or to prices that move by discrete steps. Changes in operating costs that look temporary are often absorbed by the producer, not passed on to his buyers by way of higher prices. Changes that look permanent enter quickly into pricing formulae, especially if they affect all of the firms in an industry. A firm that has to work its staff overtime at time-and-a-half wage rates in order to catch up after a mechancial breakdown will not raise its prices to recover the increase of costs. But when that firm signs a new contract with its unionized workers, it will refigure its costs and raise its prices if the new contract greatly raises its normal level of wage costs.

Cost pattern (*2*) is apt to lead to fairly flexible prices, although the *markup,* or spread between costs and prices, may be very rigid. Changes in input prices are quickly passed through to customers by changes in selling prices.[12]

So much for the cost side of cost-plus pricing. What about the "plus"? Is it calculated so as to offset cost changes?

---

goods off the market if they think prices are too low, and even here they have little freedom. Most sellers of manufactured goods (including most processed farm products) have some such freedom.

For an illuminating discussion of the theory of markets, stressing the distinction between "price takers" and "price makers," see T. Scitovsky, *Welfare and Competition* (Chicago: Richard D. Irwin, Inc., 1951), pp. 12–26.

[11]This view on pricing is not in contradiction to the marginalist view set forth in most textbooks on price theory. The two points of view can be made to match pretty well *when allowance is made for anticipations and uncertainty.* For monetary analysis, the cost-plus approach (with the marginalism between the lines, as it is in much business thinking) gives a simplification that does not involve a serious loss of analytic accuracy.

[12]A lag may occur in this process of transmitting cost changes because accounting systems often attach a cost change to specific physical assets that may not be used in production for some time. This lag would be shortened if businesses calculated prices on the basis of replacement cost. This would raise the prices of goods already on sale as soon as raw materials costs began to rise. The chief reasons for sticking to acquisition cost seem to be business routine and effects on competitors' behavior. To change prices on goods that already have price tags on them is bothersome, expensive, and upsetting to cost-accounting systems. It also may upset tacit agreements among competitors to apply standard markups, and a period of cut-throat competition may result.

The items that the *plus* is intended to cover—overhead and profit—do not vary directly with output. Some are sums that remain the same for low and high levels of output; managerial salaries and bond interest are of this type. Some are joint costs relating to several kinds of output and can only be allocated arbitrarily. The cost of heating a factory in which many products are manufactured is an example of a joint cost. How much is charged to each *unit of output* will depend partly on the number of dollars that must be covered during a given month, and partly on the number of units of product over which the charge can be spread.[13]

Pricing policies may be based on a high breakeven point, designed so that the unit charge for overhead and profit, multiplied by the amount of output, will yield a loss unless output is large. They may be based on a low breakeven point, in which case profits are huge if a great deal can be sold at the price set. The breakeven point used in price policy will reflect a compromise between *expected* sales volume and *normal* sales volume. A firm that expects abnormally large sales may be satisfied with a lower markup on unit operating costs than it would seek when smaller sales are in prospect. It is less likely to commit itself to a low margin (a high breakeven point) than it would be if it expected these very large sales to continue as the normal condition.

While what we have said has referred to the prices sellers *would like to charge,* it often happens that they feel forced to charge less.[14] Sometimes they try prices figured on a cost-plus basis and find that these will not work. If sales are so slow that the breakeven point cannot be reached, it is often better to take a loss by selling a great deal at unexpectedly low prices than by selling unexpectedly little at the intended price. Unpleasant surprises as to sales volume thereby lead to price cuts.[15] Department stores, for instance, ordinarily price new goods on a cost-plus basis; after the goods have been in stock a while, the unsold remainder goes on sale at a reduction. Thus, averaged, realized markups may fall short of initial markups. Sellers can often predict that cost-plus prices figured by normal formulae will prove too high, so it may be better to offer a frankly unprofitable price from the beginning and sell a moderate amount than to charge a price that ought to be profitable and sell too little to approach the breakeven point.

The *plus* element in cost-plus pricing is not immovable, but neither is it so supple that we can expect cost changes to leave price levels unaffected. We must ordinarily expect changes in operating costs to be passed on by pricing policy.

---

[13]The margin *per unit* is also affected by standards of fairness. Management may balk at cutting its gross profit per unit below a certain minimum, and may feel that it would be unfair (or costly to good will in the long run) to push gross profit per unit above a certain maximum, whatever short-run profit calculations may say.

[14]Here is where marginal considerations begin to creep in between the lines; cf. footnote 11 above.

[15]Price increases in response to unexpectedly good sales are apparently much less common.

Wage determination.　The most important part of costs is the level of wages. If wage rates per man-hour in any industry rise faster than output per man-hour, the result is the kind of cost increase that results in higher price. If a depression lowers wage rates, or if improved productive methods sharply increase output per man-hour in an industry, the result is the kind of cost decrease that comes through in prices. In practice, wage increases often come along with improvements in production; the net effect of these joint changes may or may not raise costs.

Wage determination is complicated, and much dispute occurs among the experts as to how it works. But a few well-settled facts can be sorted out, and these are the ones we shall emphasize here.

Most wage rates are set by the conscious action of people we can identify, not by impersonal forces. Workers do not offer their services unconditionally and they do not auction them off to the highest bidder. In some parts of the labor market, wages are fixed by bargaining between single workers and employers, and both sides are strongly influenced by notions of fairness. In other parts of the market, employers have established scales that apply to all workers they hire. A third part uses wage scales fixed by collective bargaining between employers and labor unions.

Although many employers can fix the wages they pay, either by posting schedules or by individual bargaining, they cannot fix them casually. If an employer sets wages too low, his workers may leave to find better jobs. Even in times of general unemployment, when workers may not easily change jobs, an employer who tries to pay too little may find himself losing his working force. As retirement, illness, and death pull workers out of his shop, an employer who pays too little will have trouble hiring replacements.

Those individual employers who fix wage scales are often obliged to change them. In depressions before 1940 (more intense than we have experienced since World War II), some employers found they must cut wages as the only way to get a necessary cut in costs and meet competition on the selling market. These wage cuts and the related price cuts are best seen as the *joint effects* of an acute depression. In prosperity, employers raise wages to keep in line with competing employers and thereby prevent a loss of workers. These wage increases appear as *causes* of price increases, but these wage and price increases are also likely to be the joint effects of increasing demand.

The joint relationship of wages and prices to the level of aggregate demand deserves special emphasis. Rising prices are often blamed on wage increases, which may be their *proximate* causes, for they can raise costs and jack up prices. But the wage increases may themselves result from the pressure of demand on labor markets. The wage level serves to transmit inflationary pressures, and especially to raise administered prices when there is excess demand.[16]

---

[16]Sometimes it transmits demand pressures to the wrong industries. An increase of demand may raise wage rates that enter into the prices of goods which are not in excess demand. But even such a wage increase as this serves to reallocate resources. By raising the prices of goods that are not scarce, wage increases may reduce the sales of those goods, releasing labor and raw materials for use where they are scarce.

Wage rates may exert an independent influence on price levels. Wage rates set by collective bargaining are affected by the same influences that determine nonunion wages, but are somewhat more rigid, and are even inclined to rise in the absence of a demand pull. During a business downswing, unionization and collective bargaining strengthen the obstacles to wage cuts. While a labor contract is in force, employers have little freedom to reduce wages. During an upswing, unionization and collective bargaining probably weaken the obstacles to wage increases, except insofar as wages are rather rigid during the life of a contract. The threat of a strike when the contract ends makes it worth an employer's while to go further and faster than he otherwise would. In industries that are strongly unionized, an employer is more apt to accept union demands because he knows that his competitors will be confronted with the same demands, and he will be able to raise his prices without suffering a significant drop in sales.

Collective bargaining by strong unions makes it likely that money wage rates will go on rising whatever the state of demand, unless, of course, there is severe unemployment. Moderate unemployment may actually increase the bargaining power of a strong union—a matter of politics rather than of economics. The outcome of a strike depends heavily upon the state of public opinion and on the several ways that government can intervene. Unemployment makes the public more sympathetic to the unions as underdogs, and raises the responsiveness of government to union pressure. As the labor market is now organized, it may take a large increase of unemployment to keep wage rates from rising faster than output per man-hour and to keep wages from pushing up the price level.[17]

Seemingly labor unions might lose interest in getting wage increases that push up prices, calculating that the loss of real wages through subsequent price increases would cancel much of the wage increase. But this consideration is much too weak to guarantee that wage increases will be held within the limits of price stability. Many workers are convinced that employers can give large wage increases without increasing prices; organized workers decline to take the responsibility when employers raise prices. Besides, the effect of wage increases on the cost of living cannot be blamed on any one union. Unless each union can be sure that scaling down its wage demands will cause all other unions to scale theirs down in proportion, every union's members will gain by increasing their own money earnings as much as possible. Most organized workers share with the rest of us what we have called the "money illusion." They feel that a dollar is a dollar, and do not ordinarily worry that the purchasing power of the dollar may leak away through price increases caused by their own wage demands.

Government price fixing.   Another nonmonetary influence on price levels is price fixing by government action. The government affects several sets of prices.

---

[17]This likelihood is reinforced by the interplay of wages and farm prices discussed in the section that follows on "Government price fixing."

1. Prices of large concerns that are influenced by "moral suasion";
2. Public utility and transportation rates that are set by regulatory agencies;
3. Wage rates that are supported by minimum-wage legislation;
4. Retail prices that are supported by resale-price-maintenance legislation;
5. Farm prices that are propped up by our farm-price-support program.

1. "Moral suasion" on the pricing policies of large firms is one more factor conducive to price rigidity. The hold that government has over these pricing policies lies partly in the fact that the decisions of big business have widespread economic effects, so that the managers of large firms feel a sense of public responsibility, and quietly consult government officials about many policy decisions. Business responsibility for the public welfare is reinforced by the antitrust laws. A big firm that moves out of line with apparent public policy, especially by announcing a dramatic price increase, is likely to lose good will with the public and with government officials. But the attempted use of explicit "guidelines" for prices and wages in the 1960's has shown the debility of suasion.

2. Transportation and utility rates are controlled by the fixing of maxima by federal and state governments. Rates are usually cut, when the regulatory commissions are convinced that existing rates yield more than a fair profit.[18] Rates are raised on an application from the companies, but only if the commission is satisfied that existing rates yield less than a fair profit.

This system of rate regulation has often brought about rate increases in depressions, because profits fall with declines in rail traffic, power consumption, and so forth. Rate decreases may sometimes be ordered in times of good business, just when prices in general are on the rise. It takes so long to get rate changes approved by the commissions that their timing is uneven. The effect of regulation on the trend of rates is debatable, but it is fair to say that transportation and utility rates make up a very rigid and rather large component of business costs, pointing toward a rigidity of commodity prices.

3. The most direct government influence on wage rates is the setting of legal minima. This influence is reinforced by the rule that firms selling commodities to the federal government must conform to specified labor standards. Government has indirect ways of influencing wages that are even more effective. First, government employs a large proportion of the nation's clerical workers and certain administrative and professional workers, and its pay schedules affect what private employers will give these workers. Government almost never cuts its rates of pay, and sometimes gives increases—a pattern tending toward the short-run stabilization of salaries and an upward trend over long periods. Second, government has a strong influence on the outcome of labor disputes.

---

[18]If some classes of rates are cut because they are held to be out of line with others, and thus unfair to customers, other classes of rates are raised unless the profit standard calls for lowering the general rate level.

How this influence is used depends on predilections of the administration in Washington and in major state capitals. In recent years, government has rarely taken the employer's side when a wage cut is at issue, and has frequently taken the union's side when an increase is at issue. This is another reason for our finding that the wage level may have an upward trend almost irrespective of monetary conditions. Third, standards of unemployment compensation, assistance to workers changing jobs, and relief will affect wage rates.

4. During the interwar period, federal, state, and local governments made laws that encouraged rigidity in merchandising markups and, on the whole, a widening of these markups. Manufacturers were allowed to fix retail prices for their products and to cease supplying dealers who undercut these prices. Anti-chain-store laws and similar measures were adopted to discourage merchandising methods that could narrow wholesale and retail margins. Though somewhat weakened by recent court decisions, these laws increase the power of manufacturers and dealers to resist price decreases, and enable some price makers to push their prices up even in the face of deflationary pressures.

5. The most important single government influence on prices is its program to support farm prices. The measures it has adopted to bolster farm prices have varied from time to time. It has discouraged the planting or harvesting of crops that are likely to have low prices.[19] It has stood ready to buy farm products at stated prices, or to make loans upon them at high valuations and permit the farmer to surrender his crop rather than repay the loan by selling the crop. These programs have saddled the government with large holdings of farm commodities and have driven it to find ways of disposing of the surplus without depressing prices—by selling them abroad at reduced prices, by giving them away under food stamp plans, by selling human food for livestock feed, and so on.[20]

Farm price policy and wages interact upon one another. Pressures upon government to raise farm prices are increased when wage rates rise, while an increase of farm prices pushes up the food component of the cost of living, touching off a drive for higher wage rates. In times of deflation, a drop in farm prices or in wages will ease the pressure on government to *raise* the other, but will rarely produce an effective reduction.

Tax costs. The government also influences prices by way of taxes, for many taxes operate as costs that go into prices. From this standpoint taxes may be classified into three broad groups:

---

[19]Spokesmen for organized farmers have pointed out that this program merely does for agriculture what industry does for itself—restricts sales for the sake of price maintenance. We are not concerned here with the soundness of public policies that compensate farmers through public restrictions on farm output. Our point is that government intervention to support or raise farm prices, particularly when compounded with the forces that raise wages, makes the price level an active rather than a passive part of the monetary situation.

[20]"Soft-currency sales" of food to underdeveloped countries under Public Law 480 during the early 1960's largely absorbed "surplus stocks" of wheat and some other commodities; but output restrictions continued.

1. *Operating costs*—taxes set up so that the total tax bill varies in proportion to output or to input.
2. *Overhead costs*—taxes that remain the same irrespective of output or profits.
3. *Shares in profits*—taxes that vary with net profits, and which are not properly "costs."

This grouping is not absolutely clear-cut, but will serve our purposes.

1. Among operating-cost taxes, the most important are retail sales taxes, excise taxes, import duties, and the payroll taxes that finance social security. Changes in these taxes are among the permanent changes in operating costs that are immediately passed on to customers in higher prices. If the prices that go into costs are flexible, these taxes may be shifted backward by way of a reduction in wages and in the prices of materials. Even with cost rigidity, this outcome is likely in the long run, but in the short run, changes in these taxes are a distinct nonmonetary influence on the prices of finished goods.[21]

2. Overhead-cost taxes act on prices through the *plus* in cost-plus pricing; examples are property taxes and annual license fees for dealers in certain commodities. Changes in these taxes ordinarily affect the *plus* to which the taxpayer feels entitled. They may or may not affect what he is actually able to get. If the tax is evenly levied on everyone in a line of business, as is a license fee for running a bar, it is very likely to be shifted. If not, it is apt to fall upon net profits or else to be capitalized in the value of some asset which is taxed, as may happen in real-estate valuation.

3. Taxes on shares in profits are not ordinarily shifted—they do not enter directly into prices.[22] The chief taxes in question are the corporation income tax and the individual income tax, insofar as individual taxpayers are in business for themselves. In general, such a tax does not alter profit incentives very much,[23] or affect bargaining power in price negotiations, but there are exceptions.

---

[21]Note that a *subsidy* applied per unit of a commodity is just the opposite of an operating-cost tax—a tax with a minus sign. Adoption of such subsidies will lower finished-goods prices if shifted forward, will raise input prices and wage rates if shifted backward, and in either case will narrow the spread between input prices and wage rates, on the one hand, and prices of finished goods, on the other.

[22]Here we take a "traditionalist" stand, rejecting arguments by some distinguished economists (notably Richard Musgrave) to the effect that corporate profits taxes are shifted. These arguments seem to us to neglect important parts of the evidence—notably the reduced share in national income of the richest group of individuals. This redistribution is hard to explain on the assumption that this tax is shifted.

[23]If all such taxes were at flat rates and applied to the *average* income of the taxpayer over a long period, the rate of tax would not make much difference in business decisions. If one decision would make a company's income *before* tax $10,000,000, and an alternative decision would make it $9,000,000, the relative merits of the two decisions would be identical for a 10 per cent tax or a 50 per cent tax. The main loose end in this proposition is *leisure;* a 50 per cent tax might make it worthwhile to earn less (or more) than a 10 per cent tax. In practice, however, taxes are progressive rather than flat-rate, and the averaging of income for tax purposes is so imperfect that taxpayers with fluctuating incomes pay much heavier taxes than taxpayers with steady incomes of the same average size.

Some firms are free to charge higher prices, and would if they could keep a good share of the resulting profits. But raising prices to increase profits may call down public wrath and lead to an antitrust prosecution, advertise the level of profits to potential competitors, or lead workers to make much more burdensome wage demands. Higher income taxes may reduce such threats and encourage higher prices, for the public may be mollified if a large slice of the extra profits are taxed away.

The operating-cost taxes (sales, excise, and so forth) are most likely to influence the price level. To increase these taxes is to raise prices. Such a tax increase will also increase the government surplus if government expenditures are constant, and increasing the surplus reduces the probability of agreeable surprises for sellers, while increasing the likelihood of unpleasant surprises. At the same time, higher prices will increase transactions requirements for cash. The finding that an increase of these taxes will raise price levels does not contradict our earlier finding that such an increase in government revenues is deflationary. These tax increases lead us into a situation in which prices are higher but inflationary pressures are weaker than they would have been at lower prices.

The role of anticipations.   On the markets where businessmen regard prices as found and not made—markets for securities and speculative commodities, in particular—expectations are crucial. Today's price is primarily a reflection of what dealers think prices will be later, and only very incidentally a regulator of today's commodity flow to consumption. If people think these prices abnormally high, the market is especially liable to a sharp slump; if people think them abnormally low, prices may rise abruptly.

Where prices are more definitely administered, price expectations play less of a role, but expectations of a change in cost may be very important. A forecast of higher wage costs may take hold in product prices almost as strongly and promptly as an unexpected actual increase in wage rates.

The Interaction of Cost and Demand Elements

The inflation spiral once again.   We began our discussion of costs and inflation with a reference to the notion of a spiraling inflation. We are now in a position to explain such a spiral of prices and costs.

Why don't inflationary pressures send prices sky high at once? A superficial analysis would suggest that this could happen. If there is an excess of spending power that leads to a rise in prices, someone necessarily gains. The income generated by a flow of goods is equal to the value of these goods at current prices. When prices go up, income is increased. This extra income means added spending power, which, if exercised, means more income, another round of spending, and so forth ad infinitum.

That this process does not send prices skyrocketing is partly because excess spending power is not fully exercised. Part of the bulge in income is siphoned off by taxes, part is diverted into savings. The people who gain income directly from a demand-induced price increase are profit receivers—farmers, shopkeepers, and nonfinancial corporations. These are the groups that have a high propensity to save out of additional income. If the underlying cause of inflation is a government deficit, *income will rise until the additional saving is large enough to offset the deficit.*[24]

Our study of the pricing process also helps in understanding why the increase of prices is gradual and limited. Many prices and most wage rates are rather rigid in the short run. This rigidity converts some of the excess demand into delivery delays and shortages rather than into higher prices. It keeps excess spending power out of the hands of the wage-earners who have the smallest propensity to save.

Once the administered prices are drawn into the inflationary process, the spiral takes on a new aspect. If wages start to rise because of the pressure of demand or because they are tied to prices by so-called escalator clauses, a new dual pressure forces up the price structure. Some of the extra spending power finds its way into wage-earners' wallets, bolstering the pressure of demand, and costs begin to rise and push up the otherwise rigid prices.

A wage-price spiral of this kind can easily outlive the excess spending that started it. An increase of wages that inflates prices will set up a new demand for higher wages. Another round of wage increases may be inevitable if many union contracts include escalator clauses, but this new round of wage increases gives another push to prices, sending them on up the spiral.

Fortunately, this sort of spiral need not continue indefinitely. It may encounter monetary barriers, for rising prices will reduce real cash balances, increasing buyers' resistance to further price increases and thereby stiffening management's resistance to the granting of new wage increases. Escalator clauses rarely raise wages by enough to offset past price increases; each wage increase that is meant to recompense workers for past price increases will be smaller than the one that preceded it and will exert less pressure on the cost and price structure. Finally, the growth of productivity will diminish the impact of rising wages on the level of costs and, through costs, on prices. The spiral may gradually slow down and, in the absence of new bouts of excess spending, come to an end. But it will have lasted longer and pushed prices higher than if the cost-price elements had not been drawn in.

Our analysis of cost changes illustrates another point—an inflation can begin

---

[24]This helps to explain a paradox often noted during World War II: In an inflation whose causes are readily measured, it is easier to make an accurate forecast of saving than of most other economic magnitudes. Saving has to rise to match the government deficit; how much of a rise in money income and in prices must occur before this increase of saving has been attained will vary with circumstances.

without an appearance of excess demand. The steady upward drift of wages and of federal programs in aid of the farmer can touch off a spiral of prices much like the one just considered. These autonomous forces can work back upon the state of demand. If nonmonetary forces are driving prices up, many people will come to expect an increase in their money incomes and may step up their spending in a way that will accelerate the increase of prices. An increase of costs may touch off inventory investment, which will show up in bank loans, creating cash to support the inflation. In the short run, at least, the monetary situation and the level of aggregate demand may be profoundly affected by nonmonetary pressures.

At the same time, these autonomous forces may be inhibited by the monetary situation. A growth of business activity calls for a growth in the money stock; a stoppage in the growth of cash has always been linked with a business recession. If the stock of cash is held constant in the face of rising prices, a deflation of production and employment may occur. Whether a shortage of cash will also stem the rise in prices depends on the sensitivity of price makers to business conditions. If unions push up wages in the face of rising unemployment, a restriction of the cash supply may only be able to stabilize prices at disastrously high levels of unemployment. The price rigidities and drift of wages considered in this chapter may greatly reduce the efficiency of monetary policy as a weapon to combat increasing prices.

NOTES ON

ALTERNATIVE POINTS OF VIEW

AND SUPPLEMENTARY READINGS

On the nature and process of inflation see:

Bent Hansen, *A Study in the Theory of Inflation* (New York: Holt, Rinehart & Winston, Inc., 1951).

A. G. Hart, *Defense Without Inflation* (New York: 20th Century Fund, 1951).

Charles L. Schultze, *Recent Inflation in the United States,* a Study Paper for the Joint Economic Committee of Congress (Washington, D.C.: U. S. Government Printing Office, 1959).

The debate over "cost push" has involved some of the best minds in economics. For a sampling of viewpoints, see *The Relationship of Prices to Economic Stability and Growth,* a Compendium of Papers for the Joint Economic Committee of Congress (Washington, D.C.: U. S. Government Printing Office, 1958). The papers by Abba P. Lerner, Martin J. Bailey, Milton Friedman, and J. Fred Weston are especially interesting.

A comprehensive review of inflation theories is found in Martin Bronfenbrenner and Franklyn D. Holzmans article, "Survey of Inflation Theory," *American Economic Review,* September 1963, pp. 591–661.

A NOTE ON

THE MEASUREMENT

OF PRICE LEVELS

Economists have long used index numbers to measure price-level changes, but the kind of index number used has changed because of changes in our ways of looking at the processes of price determination.

The classical division of price theory into a theory of price-level change and a theory of relative prices explains the way in which index-number theory has grown up. A natural counterpart of the quantity theory of money is the view that there are pervasive general price movements affecting all prices *in the same direction and in the same proportion.* All prices do not change in this way, but the quantity theory regarded the scatter of price changes as a reflection of supply-and-demand changes working on relative prices. Suppose that the "general price level" drops 33⅓ per cent, that steel prices are unchanged, and that wheat prices drop 66⅔ per cent. The quantity theorist would say that *if* the monetary situation had held the "general price level" constant, steel prices would have risen by 50 per cent and wheat prices would have fallen by 50 per cent.

The quantity theory of money assigned to index numbers the task of measuring the "objective mean variation of prices"—the supposed common element in all price changes. It implied that the problem of measuring price-level changes was logically much the same as the problem of measuring physical magnitudes—the "acceleration of gravity," for example. However carefully done, apparently identical experiments in physics will yield somewhat different observations. The correct answer is estimated by taking the results of careful and well-equipped experimenters, correcting them for the "personal equation" of the observers, and averaging these corrected figures. The more observations of good quality, the better the estimate. By this reasoning, only prices that represent well-ascertained open-market quotations on commodities of clear-cut specifications (such as the prices of grains, fibers, and metals) could be included in a price index, and as many such prices as possible should be included. The change in each price should be expressed by taking the price for the date under study as a percentage of the price for a "base date," and the resulting percentages should be averaged. This average of the percentages would then be regarded as the desired "objective mean variation." To illustrate, an index representing wholesale prices in 1932 as compared with 1929 would be computed as follows:

		Average Prices		
Commodity	*Unit*	*1929*	*1932*	*1932 % of 1929*
Wheat, no. 2 hard, Kansas City	Bushel	$1.180	0.494	41.86
Wool, Ohio, medium grades, Boston	Pound	.467	.196	41.97
Butter, creamery, extra, N. Y.	Pound	.449	.210	46.77
Shoes, men's, black calf, lace, oxford	Pair	3.467	3.092	89.18
Coal, bituminous, mine run	Ton	3.953	3.638	92.03
Oak, plain, white, no. 1, mill	1,000 ft.	57.623	41.635	72.25
Ammonia, anhydrous, N. Y.	Pound	.140	.155	110.71
Paper, wrapping, manila, no. 1, jute, N. Y.	100 lbs.	9.125	9.125	100.00
Average of prices in 1932[1]				74.71

[1] A further corollary of applying the "theory of error" used in physical and astronomical

Because wholesale price quotations were the most reliable that economists could get, indexes of wholesale prices were believed to measure the "general price level."

Economists today are usually interested in measuring the effects of price changes on *specific groups of people*. The also want to know the extent to which price changes "inflate" changes in national income, the receipts of farmers, or other money flows that correspond to physical-volume changes. To handle these problems, we need another kind of price index—one that measures changes in the money value of "baskets of goods and services" of constant physical composition. Each such "basket" is meant to represent the sort of thing that a specific group of persons or firms buys or the sort of thing that it sells. Examples of these "market-basket" index numbers are the "index of consumers' prices" (alias the "cost-of-living" index), the indexes of prices paid by farmers and prices received by farmers, and the U.S. Bureau of Labor Statistics wholesale price index.[2] To compute these index numbers, we calculate the cost of a "market basket" of goods for each date and reduce it to a percentage of the cost of that "basket" at a "base" date. When such an index is at 150 (or 200), we may say that the "basket" it represents is half again as expensive (or twice as expensive) as it was in the base year.

---

estimates is to average these prices by use of a "geometric mean"—to take the average of the logarithms of the "price relatives" for individual commodities as the logarithm of the index number. This was recommended by such nineteenth-century economists as W. S. Jevons. In this example, it would give an index of 69.63 instead of 74.71.

[2] Note that the wholesale price index is a mixed basket of goods, including those manufacturers buy and sell, things farmers buy and sell, and so forth. As a result, we cannot say whether a rise in that index is good or bad for anyone in particular.

Chapter 14

Key Facts
on Fluctuations

Everyone knows that business has ups and downs. Some years are remembered as times of prosperity, others as years of "hard times" and heavy unemployment. Some years have seen prices soaring; others have seen prices decline.

Controlling business fluctuations is the foremost problem of economic policy in the United States. Our way of life is on trial before the world. We cannot afford mass unemployment, either economically or politically. Neither can we afford stagnation: Sufficient evidence is found in the social costs—especially in the accumulation of Negro unemployment resulting from the retarded growth of the United States economy from 1956 to 1964.

In order that we may fulfill our international obligations without impairing living standards at home, we must provide for a steady increase in aggregate output. As we provide for growth and attempt to combat employment we must also be careful not to slip into inflation. Successful stabilization policies will balance these goals so that the economy prospers and supports the democratic political institutions which safeguard our liberties and freedom.

Unemployment and Loss of Potential Output

Selection of facts. We cannot talk about the ups and downs of business in a vacuum. Facts are essential, although a *complete* description of fluctuations is out of the question. Economists have given many hundreds of man-years to collecting data on fluctuations and hundreds more to analyzing them. They have already filled a rather large library of published books and papers, not to mention a huge mass of worksheets, at the National Bureau of Economic Research, the United States Department of Commerce, and other centers of research. Despite this research, the data are still seriously incomplete.

The only course is to focus attention on a few key statistics, each of which summarizes a lot of information—broad-gauged measures of national income, physical production, employment, and major groups of prices. These summary figures carry most of the information about fluctuations that a citizen or statesman needs in order to understand the nature of employment-price policy.

The study of these data is only a part of our task. We cannot hope to arrive at an adequate basis for policy judgments (or for personal business decisions) just by poring over charts and tables. The notion that the facts will tell their own story and shape themselves into patterns which explain everything is a reincarnation of numerology. It is on an intellectual par with astrology, the forecasting of history from measurements of the Great Pyramid, and the invention of systems to break the bank at Monte Carlo. Statistical measurements are useful only in conjunction with sensible theories. After we have looked at the statistics we shall have to theorize about them—to construct hypotheses that are consistent with the data.

Even in conjunction with sound theorizing, statistics will not work miracles. We would like our facts to "prove" a set of theories on which we can build sound policy proposals, but facts cannot really prove theories.[1] They can merely help us to *reject* hypotheses that do not square with experience and to conserve the remaining hypotheses in order that they may face further facts. Hypotheses that survive a number of such ordeals by fact, and that tie in logically with other surviving hypotheses, may begin to serve us as a guide to policy.

Living a while with the facts will give us a "feel" of the problem that is essential. We get an impression of what is large and what is small, and learn that certain families of hypotheses always come a cropper, while others go over the factual hurdles much more easily.

Nonfarm employment and output. We begin our survey of the data with two broad statistical categories—nonfarm output and employment. This is because most workers are employed in "industry and commerce," in manufacturing, mining, construction, trade, transportation, and the whole

---

[1] This limit to the value of evidence is not a peculiarity of economics, but part of the general logic of "scientific" thinking in all fields. Sometimes a crucial experiment is said to "prove" some general principle. But this is to use the term "proof" rather loosely and casually. What is meant is that the experiment—in conjunction with related experiments and with a structure of theories that we use to interpret experiments—squares with the general principle, and that this whole complex of knowledge makes the principle "highly probable." This sort of finding is rather different from a formal proof as generally understood.

range of service trades like amusements, medicine, and beauty parlors. Most of these workers are employees, although several million are self-employed. We will leave to one side employment in government and farming, since neither of these sectors throws workers into unemployment when the markets for goods weaken. The waves of unemployment that we want to study represent mainly failures to get a job in industry or commerce.

The employment statistics for industry and commerce are presented in Chart 14-1. Commercial and industrial employment since 1889 is represented by National Bureau and Department of Commerce estimates (curves *E*–4, *E*–5) since 1914, and by Professor Frickey's index of manufacturing employment (curve *E*–3) for 1889–1914. All these curves display a rapid upward drift, which is a reflection of the nation's economic growth.

The underlying growth in available manpower is best traced by drawing lines to connect successive peak years, when practically everyone wanting a job was at work. The years 1892 and 1906 are examples, and are used to place a trend over curve *E*–3. Similarly, 1920, 1929, 1942, 1953, and 1965 are used

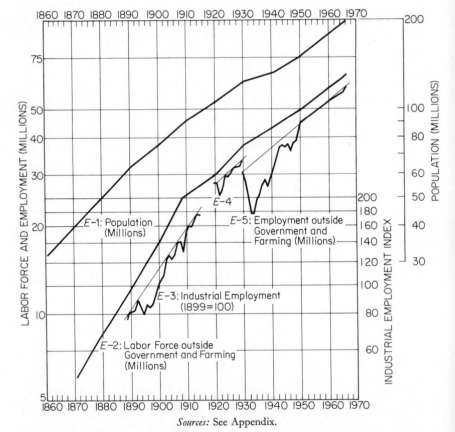

Sources: See Appendix.

Chart 14-1: Population, the labor force, and employment, 1860–1966.

to set the growth line for curves *E*–4 and *E*–5. When the curve of actual employment drops below the growth line, part of the labor force is idle. The amount of unemployment may be roughly gauged using the percentage by which the two curves separate.[2] The number of unemployed that would be found by a Census inquiry might be somewhat higher or lower. Unemployment brings the wives and children of jobless workers onto the labor market, so that several members of the family may be reported as unemployed.[3] Note that most of the successive peaks fall on very smooth curves. This testifies that a projection of the number of workers available can be made with reasonable accuracy by extending the curve drawn through recent peak levels of employment. For confirmation of this hypothesis we need only look at the decennial labor-force estimates made by the Bureau of the Census. These estimates of the labor force outside farming and government trace a curve (curve *E*–2) that closely parallels our peak-to-peak projections.

Looking more closely, you will see that curve *E*–3 rises faster than curves *E*–4 and *E*–5—at about $3\frac{1}{2}$ per cent a year as against about $2\frac{1}{2}$ per cent. This break in the rate of growth of the labor force results from the sharp cut in immigration at the time of World War I. Immigration was interrupted late in 1914, and stringent immigration laws went into force early in the 1920's. The same break in trend may be seen in curve *E*–2, the Census series, and less dramatically in curve *E*–1, the decennial Census estimates of total population. Curve *E*–2 outgrows curve *E*–1 most of the way across the diagram because the ratio of farmers to total workers has declined. The number of farm workers stopped growing about 1910, leaving the whole growth in the number of workers to reinforce "industry and commerce" (except as they were absorbed into the growing work of government). Note that population picks up again after 1940, yet the labor force does not, because the babies who swelled our population in the 1940's and 1950's were barely beginning to enter the labor force as the 1950's ended. There is, indeed, a slight retardation in the growth of the labor force after 1950, reflecting the low birth rates of the 1930's.

Curve *E*–5 shows clearly the mass unemployment of the 1930's. Industrial and commercial employment was below 90 per cent of potential all the way from 1931 through 1940.[4] From 1932 through 1936, and again in 1938, employment was below 80 per cent of potential and for 1932 and 1933, the two worst years of the Great Depression, was about 70 per cent.

Looking across the diagram, the depression of the 1930's is plainly the worst in the record, but far from the only one. Employment dropped below 90 per

---

[2] Since the graph is "semilogarithmic," the actual curve will always be the same vertical distance below the growth curve if the same percentages of the potential labor force are employed.

[3] The typical Census standard of unemployment is that a person is "out of work, able to work, and looking for a job." The fact that some of the unemployed would cease to look for a job if *somebody else* in the family found one is not registered.

[4] If we were using figures for periods shorter than a year, we should find employment dropping below 90 per cent of potential before the end of 1930 and below 80 per cent before the end of 1931.

cent of potential in the post-World War I slump of 1921 (curve *E*-4), and again in the 1908 slump (curve *E*-3). In the 1890's there was a dragging depression, with industrial and commercial employment steadily below 90 per cent of potential from 1894 through 1899.

We do not have dependable yearly statistics of employment further back than 1889, but a good clue to employment history may be found in *output*. Curve *O*-3 in Chart 14-2 traces Kendrick's gross nonfarm product index; curve

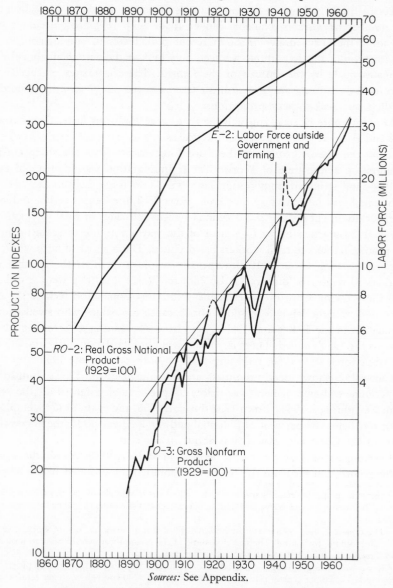

Sources: See Appendix.

Chart 14-2: The labor force and nonfarm output, 1860-1966.

RO–2 traces real Gross National Product in 1929 dollars (including farming and government) from 1897 to 1966. Growth lines are drawn through the peaks on the same principle as for the employment curves. These output curves show much the same characteristics as the industrial-and-commercial employment curves. This should not be surprising since, by and large, they reflect the product of that employment. The output curves show more "amplitude"—dropping below potential by a somewhat larger percentage, and showing somewhat larger year-to-year percentage changes. In addition, they have more rapid growth trends, reflecting the rise in output per worker.

Following the output curve back of 1890, we find two years of serious depression in the 1880's and another major depression (with output below 90 per cent of potential for four years, 1874–78) in the 1870's.

With this evidence before us, plainly mass unemployment is not just something that happened once, in the 1930's. Our economic system has known few long stretches of smooth operation—if "smooth operation" means 90 per cent of full-employment industrial output. Since 1870, there have been only five "smooth" peacetime periods exceeding three years in succession:

1870–73
1879–83
1885–92
1923–29
1946–66

Of the eighty-eight peacetime years (counting the Spanish War period, 1914, 1940, the Korean War, and the Vietnam War as "peace"), these smooth stretches cover only forty-seven years. The nearest things to sustained prosperities were 1879–92, 1899–1913, and 1946–66. But these periods were punctuated by the rather serious recessions of 1884–85, 1904, 1908, besides perceptible recessions in 1900, 1911, 1949, 1954, 1957, and 1960. The fact that we have recently experienced one of the longest spells of prosperity in the record must not blind us to the long-standing tendency of our economy to undergo spells of unemployment.

We could easily supplement the production series of Chart 14-2 with a host of related data—the indexes of manufacturing production compiled by Persons, Fabricant, and the Federal Reserve System, the estimates of finished-goods production by Shaw, and so forth.[5] These sources would occasionally conflict with curves RO–2 and O–3. The Day-Persons index of manufacturing output would show a slowing down of growth; its peak-to-peak trend line would gradually bend downward in the nineteenth century. Some of the alternative statistics would put World War I output below the growth line, and some would time fluctuations differently in the nineteenth century. By and large, however, these other series would confirm the patterns displayed by Chart 14-2. They

---

[5] See Chart 26 of the 2nd edition of this book. Some of these series are used in later parts of this chapter.

would have very similar growth rates to curves RO–2 and O–3 and similar estimates of lost output in the major and minor depressions.

"Cycles" in perspective. The employment and production statistics we have just examined exhibit the familiar "peaks and valleys" "of "business cycles." But peaks and valleys are not the best geological metaphor. The curves look more like the profile of a gradually sloping plain that has been eroded away in parts, like the Great Plains of our West.

The evidence strongly suggests that when production is high, it comes up against a rather clear-cut ceiling—but a ceiling which itself rises through time. Chart 14-2 indicates that this ceiling may be the limit of available manpower. Its rise reflects the growth of the working force plus the growth of productivity that comes with improvements of productive technique, the education of workers, and so forth. There is no "floor" that corresponds to this ceiling. Industrial-commercial output can drop to very low percentages of potential. It seems to have dropped below 60 per cent at the bottom of the Great Depression of the 1930's.

The record as a whole suggests something seriously wrong with the economic machine. Time after time, the machine slowed down just as it reached capacity levels. On the other hand, the enormously improved record since World War II suggests that at least part of the defects in the machine must have been cured.

Fluctuations in Prices and Components of Output

Price patterns. This second section of the chapter deals chiefly with prices of different types of output. For background, we shall pause briefly to look at historical price patterns.

The notion of price levels is by no means simple and some of the problems were discussed in the supplementary note to Chapter 13. However we have chosen to define "the price level," it has oscillated violently. To interpret these gyrations has always been one of the chief tasks of the economist. The history of the price level in the United States since 1860 is traced by the price curves P–1 and P–2 in Charts 14-3 and 14-4. P–1 is the official index of wholesale prices and can be used to tell the story for earlier years. It shows a rough similarity to P–2 for the years after 1896, although its swings are wider. P–2 represents the price level of total output—the figure by which we divide current-dollar estimates of Gross National Product to reduce them to 1929 dollars. These price curves show well-marked peaks for each of our three major wars (1865, 1920, and 1948) and if traced back further, would show another (1814) for the War of 1812. They also describe the gradual inflation that has afflicted us since World War II.

In Charts 14-3 and 14-4 we also present two families of components of each price index. Wholesale prices of all commodities (P–1) are compared with

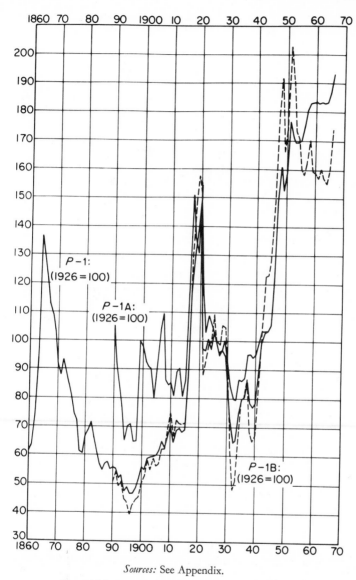

Sources: See Appendix.

Chart 14-3 : Wholesale price patterns, 1860–1966.

two of their main components—metals and metal products (curve *P–1A*) and farm products (curve *P–1B*) in Chart 14-3. The deflator of GNP (curve *P–2*) is compared in Chart 14-4 with its main components—price indexes for consumer durable goods (curve *P–2A*), consumer nondurable goods (curve *P–2B*), consumer services (curve *P–2C*), construction (curve *P–2D*), and producer durable goods (curve *P–2E*).

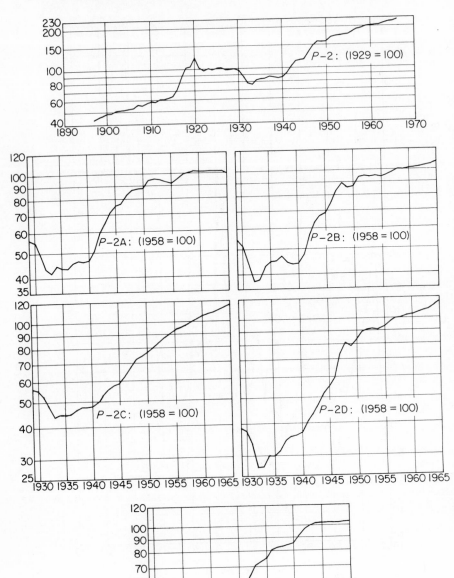

Sources: See Appendix.

Chart 14-4: GNP deflator, 1897–1966, and components, 1929–1965.

First observe that all of these curves take part in every major swing in prices, although they reflect these swings in differing degree. The drop early in the 1890's, the strong upsurge around 1900, the World War I inflation and postwar recession, the depression of 1929–33, the partial rebound thereafter, and the rise during and since World War II are characteristics of all the price curves.

A second central fact is that prices are high or rising when output is high, not when it is low. When we compare Charts 14-2, 14-3, and 14-4 we see that the downswings of prices come when output is either falling or already depressed. The upswings of prices come when output is high or rising rapidly relative to capacity.

This proposition that prices move *parallel* with output rather than inversely also holds for the major sectors of industrial output that will be studied below. In agriculture, however, prices frequently move inversely to output, which is testimony to the fact that farm output is insensitive to markets, but sensitive to the weather.

Examining the variations of pattern shown by the major price groups would be interesting, but space permits just a few comments. Of the groups shown, metals and metal products (curve *P–1A*) seem to have had less flexible prices between the wars than before World War I. This fact probably registers the growing importance of conscious price making and of price understandings among competitors. The relative sluggishness of the consumer-services curve (*P–2C*) through the 1940's and early 1950's testifies to the stabilizing influence of rent control and utility regulations. The effects of price control can be seen also in the producer-durables curve (*P–2E*) for 1942–45. The sharp relative rise in construction costs (curve *P–2D*) since 1939 probably explains part of the large shift of resources into construction activity.

One is tempted to read into long-term price history some sort of tendency for prices to work back to a "long-run normal" level after wartime increases. Taking 1913 as 100, the record of wholesale prices works out as follows:[6]

War	*Prewar*	*Peak*	*Immediate Postwar Trough*	*Deepest Trough Before Next Major War*
War of 1812	152 (1812)	221 (1814)	148 (1816)	86 (1849)
Civil War	87 (1860)	189 (1865)	119 (1871)	67 (1896)
World War I	98 (1914)	221 (1920)	139 (1922)	93 (1932)
World War II	110 (1939)	236 (1948)	222 (1949)	———

These figures suggest that this temptation should be resisted. War and postwar price booms admittedly become top-heavy and lead into price declines.

---

[6] BLS index for all commodities transferred from 1926 = 100 to 1913 = 100. From *Historical Statistics,* pp. 233–34, and *Federal Reserve Bulletin,* December 1951, p. 1563.

But in only one case (the War of 1812) did the speculative reaction quickly carry prices back to prewar levels. The long price declines which took place between wars were ground out by long and grueling depressions—particularly those of the 1870's, 1890's, and 1930's. There is nothing built into the system that can induce a depression of just the right size and duration,[7] and if we succeed with the policy of full employment to which the nation is committed by the Employment Act of 1946, we cannot expect prices to sag so far. Over the decades, price-making policies and technical advances in production may give us a gradual decline of price levels, but this is not necessary nor likely, in view of the price-making processes that will be analyzed later.

The farm sector. The record of agricultural fluctuations is spread out in Chart 14-5. Farm production is represented by curve O–11 (Gross Farm Product 1889–1953) and by the series representing gross farm output in 1939 dollars (curve O–12). Since the peak years of farm production represent years of good weather, rather than of good markets, we have drawn the trend lines through averages of five-year periods (1886–70, 1875–79, 1882–86, 1895–99, 1902–6, 1911–15, 1946–50).

As may be seen by comparison with the curve O–1, the growth of farm output has slowed down greatly relative to total output. The farm sector's contribution to the Gross National Product (curve O–12) shows an uptrend of only $\frac{1}{2}$ of 1 per cent per year. The gradual rise of farm productivity since 1910 has been used to release manpower (curve E–5) as well as to boost output.

The fluctuations of farm output (the curves O–11 and O–12) are very different in timing from those of industrial output (curves RO–2 and O–3 in Chart 14-2). The sharpest decline of output below trend, it is true, comes in the 1930's, but it primarily reflects the drought rather than the depression. The depression of the 1870's has no counterpart in the farm-output curve, and the industrial slump of 1884–85 coincides with peak farm output. In the 1890's, the peak years of farm output (1895–98) again come in an industrial slump. The farm and nonfarm output curves resemble each other in 1907–8 and 1921–23, but this is probably accidental. The unresponsiveness of farming is linked with the smoothness of the farm employment curve (E–6); this series shows few traces of industrial fluctuations.

Although farm prices show a pattern of year-to-year changes that strongly resembles the industrial-production curve, it would be as easy to make out

---

[7] In gold-standard days (see Chapter 18), there was such an outside pressure. Given world conditions as they were at the time, the United States could not have maintained the gold standard without a serious depression in the 1890's, and could not have resumed gold payments at the pre-Civil War gold price in 1879 had there not been a serious depression in the 1870's. The prices of 1872 or 1893 would have led to unbearably heavy gold exports in 1879 or 1899. Whether the gold standard could have been maintained without heavy price deflation in the 1930's is open to argument. In view of our very large share of the world's gold reserves and of global production and trade the gold standard might have survived a successful anti-deflation policy. At least, the prospects of the gold standard would have been no worse than under the policies actually adopted!

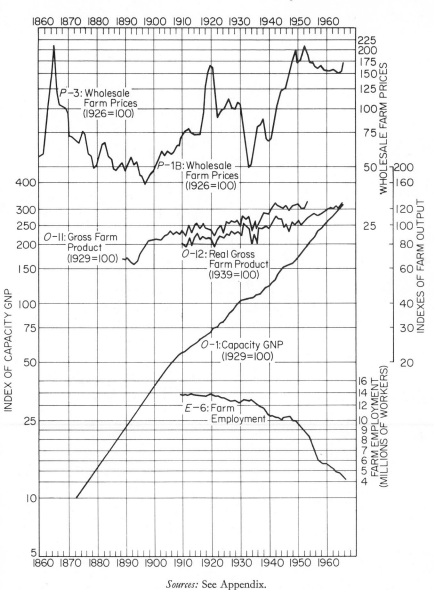

Sources: See Appendix.

Chart 14-5: Farm prices, employment, and output, 1860–1966.

a case for inverse movement as for parallel movement between farm prices and farm production.

Construction. Building construction is also peculiar, but in a very different way from agriculture. Like manufacturing and commerce, construction responds to markets, and slumps far below capacity when markets are inade-

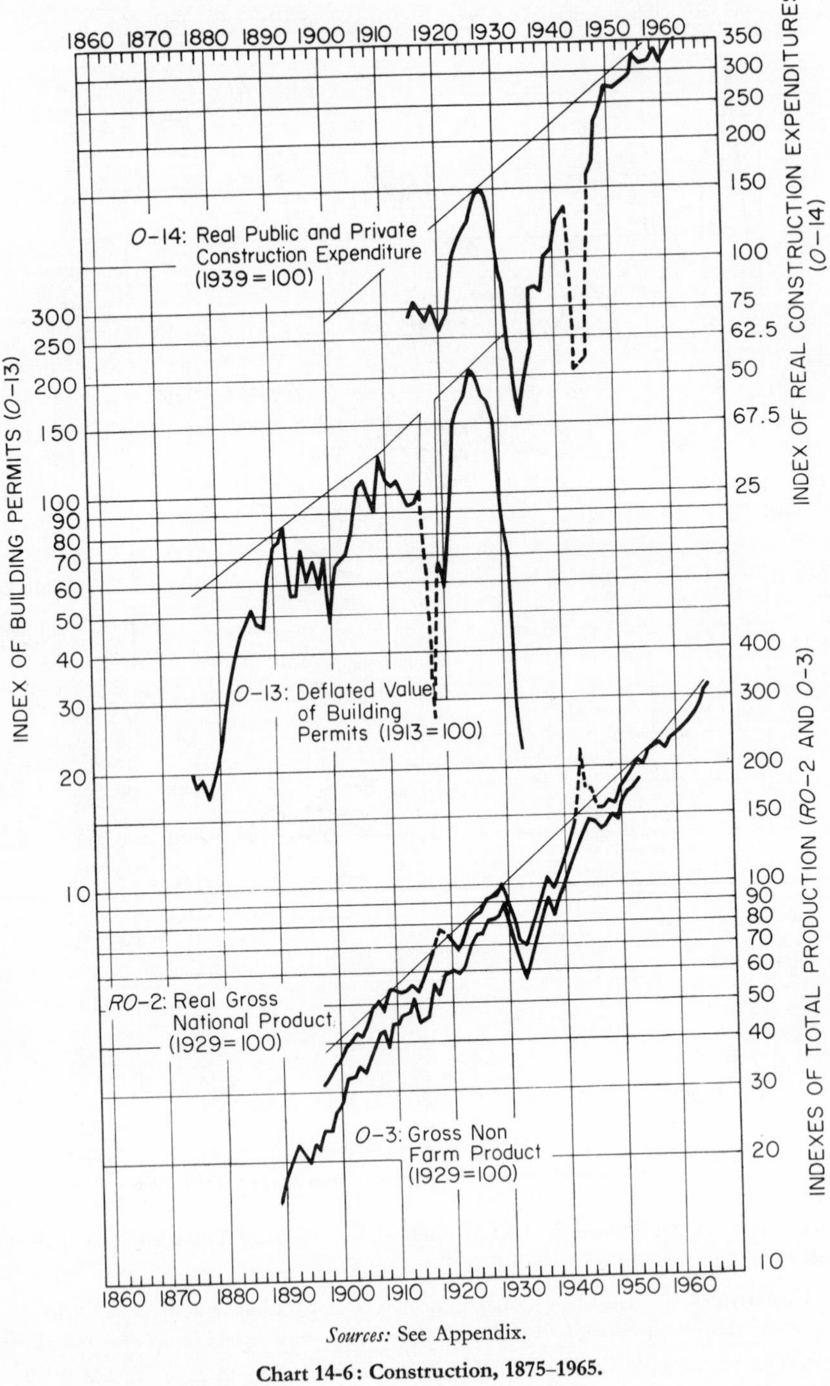

Sources: See Appendix.

Chart 14-6: Construction, 1875–1965.

quate to provide employment for all of its workers at prices that will cover building costs. Peak construction years are always years of good business in general, and construction is almost never booming (as farm output often is) when industrial production is in a slump. Yet construction activity shows peculiarities in timing, and a prodigious amplitude to its fluctuations; the interrelations of its peaks differ from those of industry.

The available long-term series on physical construction activity are spread out in Chart 14-6. From 1915 to date (curve O–14) we have Department of Commerce estimates of the value of construction put in place in 1939 dollars; for 1875–1933 (curve O–13), we have Newman's index of the value of contracts awarded in 1913 dollars. For reference, curves RO–2 and O–3, measuring total industrial and commercial activity, are carried forward from Chart 14-2.

The first fact to strike the eye is that construction varies by an enormously wider percentage range than production in general. Two of the great troughs (1917–18 and 1942–45) represent the interruption of construction by war. The trough of the 1930's, the deepest of all, represents the impact of depression, with construction falling to as low as 30 per cent of its preceding (1927) peak.

Lines drawn through the peak years of the construction curves suggest slower growth for construction than for industry, perhaps because so much building is linked with population growth. But the sense in which these peak-to-peak lines represent potential full-employment activity is different from what it is for industry. First, construction is so high at its peaks only because its slumps leave a catching-up problem; if employment and construction were more steady, construction peaks would presumably be lower. Second, the smooth growth of capacity suggested by linking the peaks is not so meaningful for construction. Because construction peaks lie many years apart, there is time for skilled workers to retire or to drift off into other occupations[8] and for contracting organizations to fall apart between peaks. Training of new workers is probably concentrated in a few years close to the peaks.

The great peaks of construction come at times of high industrial prosperity (the early 1890's, 1920's, early 1950's, and early 1960's). The great industrial depressions (the 1870's, 1890's, and 1930's) have counterparts in the construction curves, with interesting similarities in the timing of recovery. But construction shows much independence in timing. Its upturn of 1920 and its downturn of 1927 ran counter to the direction of swing in industry. The industrial upswing of 1915–17 had no counterpart in construction. These differences of timing are strategic in the history of the interwar period.

Services. A large part of economic activity yields *services* rather than material goods as its products. Some of these services are adjuncts to the material goods that come from manufacturers or farmers, like the services of merchan-

---

[8] Labor-force estimates by Paul Douglas, included in the corresponding chart of the first edition of this book, show a noticeable attrition of construction workers between 1915 and 1920. In the 1930's, the disappearance of construction workers may have been large.

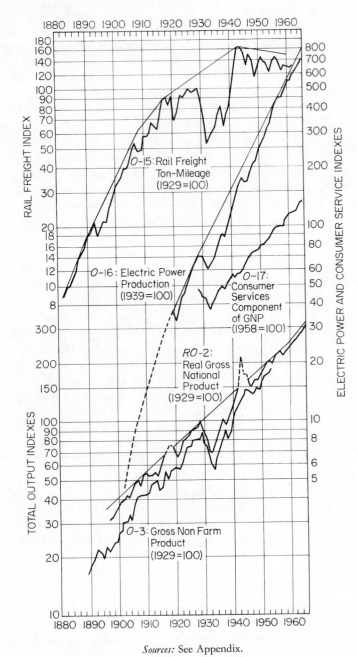

Sources: See Appendix.

Chart 14-7: Production of services, 1882–1965.

dising and freight transportation. Some are "pure" services, like electric power,[9] medical care, haircuts, amusements, passenger transport, and the use of house-room.[10] Government activity is often classified as a service activity, although we do not treat it as such here.

We have no satisfactory overall measurements of service activity. We do have some data for segments of the service field, which are spread out in Chart 14-7.

Curve O–15 measures railway freight traffic, in ton-miles. In the prewar period, rail freight outpaced industrial production in growth; but since World War I, freight has lagged behind. This change in relative trend is mainly the result of competition from trucking. Rail freight rose so fast during World War II because the truckers were handicapped by the gasoline shortage. The pattern of peaks and troughs for freight is much like that for industrial output, but with considerably greater amplitude. Judging by World War II experience, the growth of freight-handling potential continued after traffic began to ebb away.

Curve O–16 measures electric power (kilowatt-hours) production. It has an extremely rapid uptrend, with departures from capacity levels about as wide as those of industrial activity.

Curve O–17 records the consumer-services component of real Gross National Product. This series is heavily weighted with the rental value of housing, which is rather fully occupied at all times. As a result, curve O–17 sticks rather close to its uptrend. It barely shows the Great Depression, and rises smoothly (perhaps suspiciously so) through the war and postwar period.

On the whole, changes in service production do not by themselves account for any large fraction of changes in overall activity. The investment needs of the service industries (of railways, power, telephone, housing, and the like) are very heavy however, so a slackening in the growth of demand for services may undermine investment in durable goods.

Mining. Mineral production is covered by a long sweep of statistics, some of which appear at the top of Chart 14-8. The current authoritative index is that of the Federal Reserve Board (curve O–19), which takes us back to 1919. Overlapping curve O–16 and going back to 1899, we have the index of the National Bureau of Economic Research (curve O–18). There are no comprehensive indexes that go still further back, but bituminous coal, the main component of prewar mineral production, can be traced back before the Civil War, and is shown here (as curve O–20) for 1865–1929.

---

[9] Conventionally, the line between "services" and "goods" is drawn between electricity and cooking gas. But for some purposes gas is thrown in with electricity, which it strongly resembles economically.

[10] We pay rent for *room-years*—which are related to houses much as passenger-miles are related to railways. Both rent and the price of railway tickets constitute payment for services.

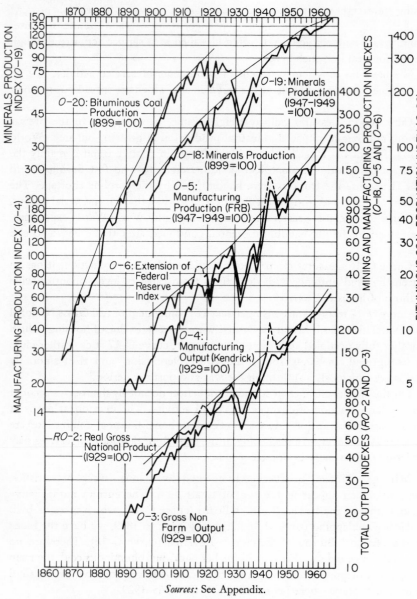

Sources: See Appendix.

Chart 14-8: Mining and manufacturing production, 1860–1966.

Mineral production in the nineteenth century outgrew industrial output, as measured by curve *O–3*, but for the interwar and postwar periods grows somewhat more slowly than aggregate output, as measured by curve *RO–2*. It shows almost exactly the same time shape as industrial output, except that

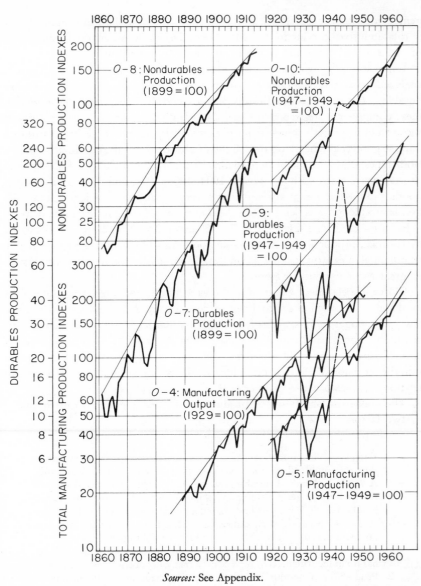

Sources: See Appendix.

Chart 14-9: Manufacturing production, durable and nondurable goods, 1860–1966.

its swings are somewhat wider. Its peaks come in the same years with those of general production, and trace out a fairly smooth growth curve.

Manufactures—durable and nondurable. Manufacturing is the most important sector of the industrial economy. The family resemblance between the manufacturing curves (*O–4, O–5,* and *O–6*) spread out in Chart 14-8, and the general industrial curves (RO–2 and O–3) reflects the large share of manufacturing in total industrial production. The two sets of series show a marked coincidence of peaks and troughs and rather similar long-term growth rates.

For reasons that will soon grow clear, manufacturing activity is ordinarily analyzed separately for durable goods (primarily metal products) and nondurable goods (manufactured foods, textiles, and the like). Curves representing these components are traced in Chart 14-9. Both types of manufactured goods show smooth growth trends from peak to peak, but our capacity to produce durable goods has tended to grow slightly faster than that for nondurable goods. Both types show the major depressions of the 1870's, 1890's, and 1930's, and shorter depressions with troughs in 1904, 1908, 1921, and 1924. But durable-goods production jumps up and down very much more violently. Durable-goods production was below 60 per cent of potential in a great number of years —in 1876–78, 1894, 1921, 1921, 1931–35, and 1938–39. In each of these years, by contrast, production of nondurable goods was less than half that far below its potential. Year-to-year changes in durable goods are commonly several times as great as in nondurable goods.

Closer inspection of Chart 14-9 shows a number of interesting differences in shape as between the two lines of production. Nondurable goods make fewer and longer swings, and sometimes fail to participate in the smaller slumps of durable-goods production. The nondurable curves lack the double peak of 1890–92, barely show the durable-goods recessions of 1900 and 1914, and skip the recession of 1927. There is little evidence of any significant lead-and-lag relationship between the two series.[11]

The greater instability of the production of durable goods is caused chiefly by two factors:

1. Purchases of durable goods are commonly postponable. Because they are durable, these goods yield services over a long stretch of time. A would-be buyer of durables can generally make those he already has serve a little longer if a slump in his income (or in his optimism) makes him hesitate to buy as he had planned. If business activity falls off, the user of such goods often can use a smaller flow of services, and can postpone adding to his stock of durables. In a slump, for example, the owner of a fleet of taxicabs is called on for fewer cab-miles and so has no immediate need to replace cabs that wear out.
2. Production of nondurable goods is partly made up of manufactured food and other products relying on materials that come from the farm; this influence is a stabilizing one.

---

[11]The quarterly curves presented in the first edition of this book show a slight tendency for the nondurable curves to register downturns earlier than the curves for durables. But when we allow for the fact that durable goods (being made largely to buyers' specifications *after* they are committed to buy) have decision dates several months ahead of purchase, there seems to be no systematic difference of timing here that will bear weight in interpreting the record.

The evidence presented in Chart 14-9 casts an interesting sidelight on the hypothesis of a steady growth in productive potential around which much of this chapter is organized. Like minerals, power, and railway transport, both sectors of manufacturing have production peaks that lie on a fairly smooth growth curve. This suggests that a fairly specific pool of resources is available for each purpose and matches fairly well with the known specialization of productive facilities and skilled workers, and with the regional concentration of groups of industries.

Past and future instability in construction and durables. Of all the components of output examined above, construction and the manufacture of durable goods—which includes machinery, ships, and so forth—showed the greatest instability, with minerals close behind. If national policy were to smooth out aggregate actual production close to its potential line, it would either have to smooth out these curves or to induce *offsetting fluctuations* in the production of nondurable goods and the various service industries so that they would absorb manpower from construction, durables, and minerals.

On the record, we must not hope for very large short-run transfers of labor across these occupational boundaries. The fact that separate smooth potential curves can be traced for durables and for minerals testifies that these branches of work hold their labor force even in the long run. This is supported by the direct evidence of labor-force studies. Construction is capable of changing its share of the labor force somewhat more readily—but not very much within a year or two. We may, of course, hope to reduce the tendency of nondurables to swing *parallel* with durables. If we could avoid these parallel changes, we could somewhat reduce fluctuations in durables by removing those fluctuations of demand for durables that arise from the effect on consumer incomes of unemployment in the nondurable and service trades. It would be particularly desirable to offset fluctuations against each other *within* the durable goods and construction fields. We cannot stabilize each part of the durables sector separately, but may be able to offset a fall in one such sector with a rise in another.

We are bound to have some fluctuations in the future if only because we have had them in the past.[12] The size and composition of our existing stock of houses, factories, passenger automobiles, trucks, railway equipment, industrial machinery, and so forth, reflect past fluctuations in production and almost require future fluctuations. Both the Great Depression of the 1930's and the war years were lean times in the building of apartment houses and single-family

---

[12]By this we mean: (1) that we cannot avoid having fluctuations in certain items so long as individual business firms can accept or reject opportunities to buy equipment, buildings, and so forth, according to their own business judgment; and (2) that if we could avoid fluctuations in these items by influencing business (and supposing the *means* of influencing business to be entirely unobjectionable in itself), it would in many cases be bad social policy to do so. A temporary postwar bulge in the building of houses and automobiles, for instance, was manifestly desirable despite the problems it might create when subsequent cutbacks came.

houses. This meant a backlog of replacement demand in the postwar period. Similarly, World War II left us with a large stock of fairly good ocean freighters. It made no sense to build more in the postwar years, except to keep the ship-building industry alive as a military reserve. By the 1960's, these ships became so seriously worn and obsolete that we accepted a decline in the *operation* of American ships in lieu of a rapid upswing in their *construction*. When we have a stock of durable items of uneven age and fairly even service life, it is an arith-metical impossibility to stabilize simultaneously the *stock* and the *rate of inflow* of newly produced goods into stock, for the *rate of outflow* is bound to be irregular.

But while there are large groups of goods (such as ships and passenger automobiles) with fairly uniform service lives, there are others (such as houses) whose service life and quality can be improved by repairs and alterations. As a long-run matter, we can expect those fluctuations in demand that result from the peculiar age-grouping of the existing stock to grow milder *if* we can avoid major slumps for a couple of decades. Service life varies among groups of goods, even though there are groups *within which* service life is fairly standard-ized.

We may outlive this problem of recurrent fluctuations in the demand for durables that echo past fluctuations in output. But it is bound to be serious in the first ten or twenty years after a set of sharp fluctuations such as those of the Great Depression and World War II. If we cannot absorb periodic cut-backs in the various lines of durable production and construction without a serious general slump in activity, the new fluctuations will build a fresh set of future problems into our productive outfit. The main problem of stabiliza-tion policy is to offset the declines in each line of durables production with a rapid increase in the demand for other types of durable goods.

NOTES ON
ALTERNATIVE POINTS OF VIEW
AND SUPPLEMENTARY READINGS

For a general account of theories of the business cycle, the standard reference is G. Haberler, *Prosperity and Depression*, 4th ed. (Cambridge: Harvard University Press, 1958). The student may be interested to verify the astounding fact that many theories describe the boom as growing out of a full-employment "equilibrium" rather than out of a depression—probably a by-product of the tradition that an adequate theory must be capable of explaining how a cycle could arise in a previously stable economic system.

At the textbook level, firsthand thinking is embodied in A. H. Hansen, *Business Cycles and National Income,* expanded ed. (New York: W. W. Norton & Company, Inc., 1964), and R. A. Gordon, *Business Fluctuations,* 2nd ed. (New York: Harper & Row, Publishers, 1961).

At the level of monographs and treatises, the most useful are probably:

J. A. Schumpeter, *Business Cycles* (New York: McGraw-Hill Book Company, Inc., 1939), 2 vols.

E. R. Frickey, *Economic Fluctuations in the United States* (Cambridge: Harvard University Press, 1942).

A. F. Burns and W. C. Mitchell, *Measuring Business Cycles* (New York: National Bureau of Economic Research, 1946).

J. R. Hicks, *A Contribution to the Theory of the Trade Cycle* (Oxford: Clarendon Press, 1950).

A number of authoritative articles by various economists are reprinted by the American Economic Association in *Readings in Business Cycle Theory* (New York: The McGraw-Hill Book Company, Inc., 1944).

Chapter 15

Money in
Business Fluctuations

Questions of fact. Now that we have looked at the patterns of fluctuations in output and prices, we must turn back to money. Is money influential in these fluctuations?

It helps to confront the facts with a checklist of questions. We shall ask these about the data:

1. At downturns and in downswings, how does cash behave? Is the public short of cash and is the stock of cash shrinking?
2. In recoveries, is growth in the cash stock helpful?
3. Over upswings and downswings, are the swings in output and prices of the same general magnitude as the swings in the stock of cash?
4. Is a steady growth in cash needed for steady prosperity? Or does such steady growth generate inflation?

Annual data. For a quick overall view, we may compare the annual figures of nonfarm output with annual figures for the cash supply in Chart 15-1. You will see at a glance that such a comparison gives an affirmative answer to our first three questions for the prewar and interwar period. (We shall examine the postwar period presently.) Down to 1941, every major slump in output is marked by a dent in the cash-supply curves. The sharpest downswings of output (the 1870's, 1890's, 1908, 1921, and 1930's.) have corresponding

286

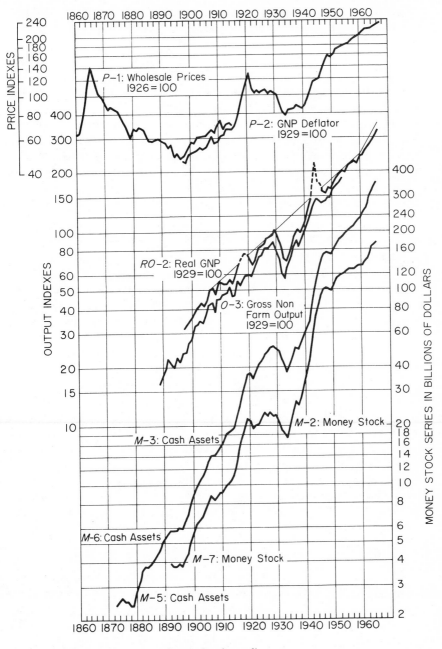

Chart 15-1: Output, prices, and the money supply, 1860–1966.

downswings in cash; milder downswings in the 1880's, 1904, 1914, 1924, 1927, and 1938 are marked by perceptible checks in the growth of cash.

Recoveries from the great depressions (1879–81, 1897–1902, 1933–36, and 1938–41) are marked by a very rapid growth of cash, while the milder recovery periods also show up in the rate of growth of cash. During and just after both world wars, there was a rapid growth of cash when output was already full. The price data show these as periods of inflation.

These figures are too rough to say much about the *direction* of causation. They could be used to argue that cash fluctuations cause business cycles, or that business activity alters the demand for cash and the banking system responds by changing the supply. We must go inside individual years and add certain supplementary evidence. This is done below in three separate stages—for the period 1899–1914; for the interwar period; and for the postwar period.[1]

Cash, output, prices, and interest, 1899–1914. The data for this period are spread out in Chart 15-2. Cash (curve M–10) is represented by the public's deposits at national banks (adjusted to eliminate duplication caused by items in the process of collection), at the call dates that came five times a year. Output is represented quarterly by a backward extension of the Federal Reserve index of manufacturing production (curve O–22).[2] Prices are represented by a bimonthly average of the Bureau of Labor Statistics index of wholesale prices (curve P–1C). The fine tracery of curve B–1A describes the course of interest rates, as represented by bimonthly averages of open-market rates on "prime commercial paper."

The evidence provided by this chart is subject to some dispute. The fluctuations in output can be detected in the cash curve, but the downturns do not show up very clearly. The decline in output in 1899–1900 is merely reflected in a leveling out of the cash curve, as is the recession of 1903–1904. There was an absolute decline of cash in the recession of 1907–1908, but it was much smaller than the large drop in output.

During the upswings in production, cash seems to have played a more active part. It increases at every upswing (1900, 1904, 1908, and 1912). The upswing of 1900 was slightly preceded by an upturn of the cash stock, as were the upturns of 1908 and 1911. In 1904, by contrast, cash lagged behind the erratic recovery of business.

The interest-rate curve in Chart 15-2 gives us some additional evidence on the role of money. Note that a sharp peak in rates occurred at the start of each business decline—at the end of 1899, at the end of 1903, and in the second

---

[1] The 1870's and 1880's were surveyed in earlier editions of this book. The evidence they provide is broadly consistent with that we shall develop from the periods surveyed here.

[2] This index, for 1899–1930, by Woodlief Thomas, was published in *Federal Reserve Bulletin*, January 1931, p. 46. A monthly interpolation of the index was worked out by L. P. Ayres and published in his *Turning Points in Business Cycles* (New York: The Macmillan Company 1939), p. 203 (used here by permission of the publisher). Monthly figures are reduced here to quarterly averages.

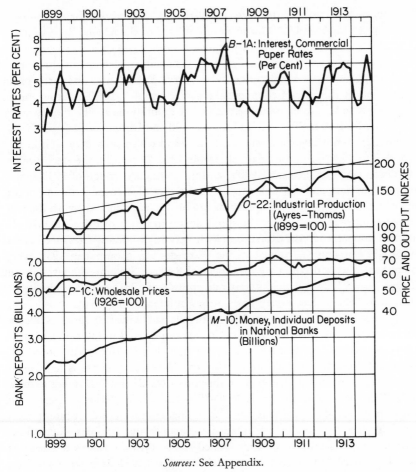

Sources: See Appendix.

Chart 15-2: Output, interest rates, money, and prices, 1899-1914.

half of 1907 when we suffered a sharp panic. These peaks in money rates would seem to indicate a shortage of cash at the onset of each business decline. Interest rates were slow to rise in each business recovery—in 1901, 1905, 1909, and 1912. This might indicate that the cash supply was ample until output was near to full recovery—that new cash shortages did not develop until output ran ahead of the money stock.

The price series in Chart 15-2 sheds some light on the links between money and prices. Note that the steady growth in bank deposits did not cause a continuing inflation. Prices rose slowly in most of the period. When they rose abruptly, as in 1899, 1902–1903, 1907, and 1909–1910, it was not just because the money stock was growing, but also because output was crowding its trend line. An increase in the money stock may help to boost prices, but this chart suggests that it is rarely a sufficient stimulus.

Cash, output, prices, and interest, 1919–41.   The record for the interwar years appears in Chart 15-3. Output is represented by the Federal Reserve index of industrial production, seasonally adjusted (curve *O*–21). Cash is represented by the stock of money (curve *M*–8). Prices are again represented by the Bureau of Labor Statistics wholesale price index (curve *P*–1*C*). And interest is again represented by the rate on commercial paper (curve *B*–1*A*). The output, price, and interest series are bimonthly averages of monthly data. The money stock data is for June 30 in 1919–21, and for June 30 and December 31 for 1922–41.

The larger movements of output, prices, and cash match very well in this period. The 1920 peak, the relatively stable 1923–29 plateau, the steep decline and deep trough of the early 1930's, and the secondary trough of 1938 appear in prices, output, and the cash supply. Interesting differences of timing occur, however, notably the strong upturn of production early in 1921, with the cash supply and prices still falling, the slight downward drift of prices in 1923–29, and the stoppage of cash expansion (with very high interest rates) well ahead of the 1929 downturn. Note, too, the sharp decline in output in 1931, when interest rates were driven up by the Federal Reserve System. The leveling out of cash before 1929 and the interest rate episode of 1931 are prize exhibits for those who believe that money has a strong influence on activity.

The milder fluctuations of the 1920's are reflected in the cash series as fluctuations in its rate of growth. Although in this respect and in the smoothness of the price curve, the period is something like that of 1899–1913, there is a significant difference in the interest pattern. The interest curve is less jagged than in earlier periods, and, except for the years 1921–22 and 1931, tends to move parallel to the output curve. In 1899–1914 and earlier periods, interest and output had moved inversely. In the 1920's, fluctuations of interest rates ("managed" by the Federal Reserve) tended to smooth out business fluctuations, whereas before World War I they tended to accentuate business fluctuations.

The apparent difference of timing at the trough of 1932–33 is partly spurious. There was no call date between December 1932 and June 1933, but in between there was a sharp trough in cash. During the "bank holiday" of March, almost all bank deposits were effectively out of action for a few days. After the first jump in 1933, prices rose very gradually for three years, with another jump in 1936–37 (though production was far below full-employment levels). In 1941, as full employment approached, another sharp price rise occurred, marking the beginning of a war inflation comparable to that of World War I. Much more interesting than these price rises is the stability of prices in 1938–40, though the money stock was expanding rapidly during those years.

Cash, output, prices, and interest, 1945–66.   The last in this series of exhibits is Chart 15-4, which carries the record from World War II to 1966. This chart continues the production curve used in Chart 15-3, and continues the wholesale price index, but puts curve *P*–1*C* on a 1947–49 base. It also uses commercial paper rates (curve *B*–1*A*), but adds another measure of interest

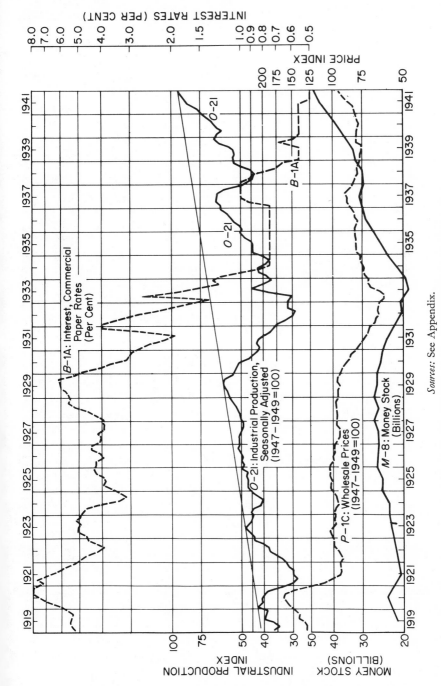

INTEREST RATES (PER CENT)

PRICE INDEX

B–1A: Interest, Commercial
Paper Rates
(Per Cent)

O–21

O–21

O–2I: Industrial Production,
Seasonally Adjusted
(1947–1949=100)

B–1A

P–1C: Wholesale Prices
(1947–1949=100)

M–8: Money Stock
(Billions)

INDUSTRIAL PRODUCTION
INDEX

MONEY STOCK
(BILLIONS)

Sources: See Appendix.

Chart 15-3: Output, interest rates, money, and prices, 1919–1941.

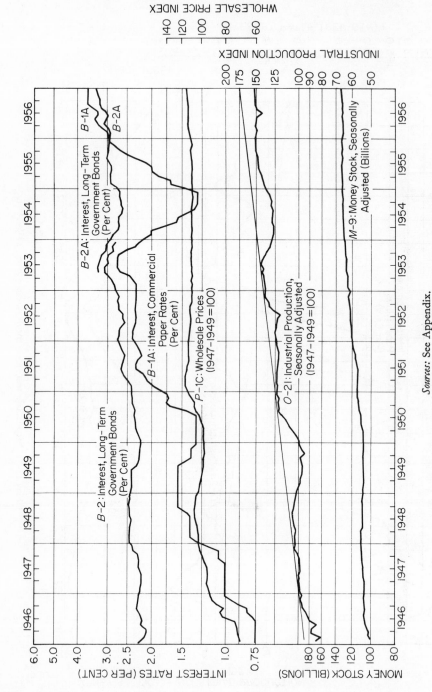

WHOLESALE PRICE INDEX

INDUSTRIAL PRODUCTION INDEX

B-1A

B-2A

B-2A: Interest, Long-Term
Government Bonds
(Per Cent)

B-1A: Interest, Commercial
Paper Rates
(Per Cent)

P-1C: Wholesale Prices
(1947–1949=100)

O-2I: Industrial Production,
Seasonally Adjusted
(1947–1949=100)

M-9: Money Stock, Seasonally
Adjusted (Billions)

B-2: Interest, Long-Term
Government Bonds
(Per Cent)

INTEREST RATES (PER CENT)

MONEY STOCK (BILLIONS)

Sources: See Appendix.

Chart 15-4: Output, interest rates, money, and prices, 1946-1966.

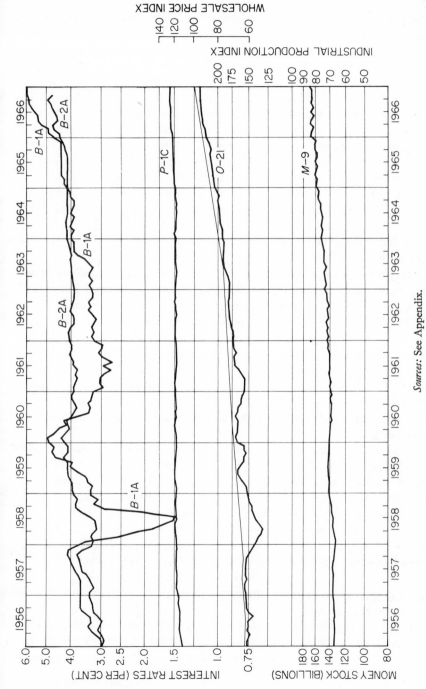

Source: See Appendix.

Chart 15-4: Output, interest rates, money, and prices, 1946–1966

293

rates—the yield on long-term government bonds (curves *B*-2 and *B*-2*A*). As a measure of the cash supply, it uses seasonally adjusted monthly estimates of the money stock (curve *M*-9). All of these curves are plotted monthly, except for Gross National Product which is quarterly.

In this postwar period, the output-cash relationship seems to be weakened, and some new propositions begin to emerge. Note the stability of the money stock throughout the twenty-year period described by Chart 15-4. The money supply has increased, but very gradually, and it has barely dropped during recessions. The recession of 1948–49 is marked by a very small dent in the money stock—a leveling out that began before production turned down and that lasted beyond the midpoint of the 1949–50 recovery. The recession of 1953–54 is not even marked by a pause in the cash curve, and during the subsequent recovery there was no sharp growth in the money supply. In the 1957 and 1960–61 recessions the money supply did shrink in absolute terms, but on both occasions it rose before the recovery periods were really underway.

The interest-rate curves in Chart 15-4 tell us something more about money. They suggest that there were large changes in the demand for cash during each one of the postwar recessions. Interest rates declined a bit in the recession of 1948–49, falling off after production had turned down and rising after recovery started. Again, in the recession of 1953–54, there was a sharp fall in short-term interest rates. In the subsequent recovery, interest rates rose greatly, and short rates topped long. This same pattern was repeated in the recession of 1957–58. Interest rates also fell during the 1960–61 recession and remained relatively stable until the end of 1965 when extreme tightness in the money markets raised both short-term and long-term rates to their highest levels since 1929.

These interest-rate changes suggest that money was important in the postwar period. They indicate that the demand for cash changed as the level of business output moved up and down. These changes in demand were not matched by changes in supply, and the public found itself more liquid as business reached its cyclical low, instead of being short of cash through the business decline. This experience contrasts favorably with prewar recessions, when the supply of cash moved parallel with changes in production. Any decline in the demand for cash that was caused by a business downturn was usually matched and sometimes swamped by a decline in the supply of money. The public was left less liquid as business activity fell, instead of being well supplied with cash and able to finance recovery.[3]

The postwar data in Chart 15-4 also help to answer our question about growth. Note that in the postwar period the money supply has grown more slowly than "capacity production." It has grown apace with actual production.

---

[3] We shall have more to say about this contrast between prewar and postwar experience. It is, perhaps, the most significant single accomplishment of the Federal Reserve System.

This suggests—though tentatively—that links exist between money and growth. It is possible that a faster growth in the stock of cash would have pushed the production curve closer to its trend line. On the other hand, our simple projection of the 1929–53 growth line may exaggerate the growth potential of recent years; the economy may not be running as far below capacity as this chart indicates. But note that what growth we have had in the money stock has not run parallel to the wholesale price curve. Prices rose sharply just after the war, again at the outbreak of war in Korea, and for a third time in the middle of the 1950's. The first of these increases may be regarded as a delayed reaction to wartime growth in the money stock. It would have come earlier if we had not used price controls during and just after the World War II. But the later increases in prices cannot be linked to money-stock changes.[4] Prices might not have risen as fast had the money stock been falling since World War II. Still, it is hard to connect the actual price changes with the actual growth in the money supply. The two curves in Chart 15-4 are rarely synchronized.

Conclusions. This review of the past half-century tells heavily in favor of money as an influential factor in fluctuations. Returning to the questions we posed at the beginning:

1. Most major downturns have come when the stock of cash began to shrink (or, at least, ceased to grow with rising productive capacity). Most major downswings have been accompanied by a decline in the stock of money—with interest rates high enough, early in the decline, to contradict the notion that the public was voluntarily retiring excess cash by paying off bank loans.
2. Most recoveries from depression have been accompanied by a growth in the stock of cash going far beyond the normal rate of growth, with a timing that suggests that cash was very influential.
3. In major disturbances (major depressions and inflations), the swings in the stock of cash have been of the same general size as swings in output and/or prices. Within the periods of stable prosperity, output fluctuations were of greater amplitude than fluctuations in the stock of cash.

---

[4] We may easily show that the inflation of the 1940's was not out of line with money-stock changes, but that the later rise in prices was larger than money-stock growth:

	1941	1948	1959
GNP deflator (average in year)	100	167	213
Money stock (average in year)	100	242	309
Capacity GNP	100	124	176
Money stock deflated by capacity GNP	100	195	175

Up to 1948, the growth in the money stock, adjusted for increases in capacity production, far exceeded the increase of prices. But by 1959, the growth of the money stock, adjusted for capacity production, had fallen far behind the increase of prices.

4. The periods of fairly steady prosperity (1899–1914, the 1920's, the 1950's, and early 1960's) have also been periods of steady growth in cash. But in the 1950's and 1960's, the stock of cash and actual output have both grown more slowly than capacity production. A steady growth of cash has not always caused inflation, but a rapid growth of cash when production was near to potential has often caused prices to rise rather sharply.

The fact that these hypotheses stand up under inspection is useful in the making of policy, but by themselves they do not tell us all we need to know. In recent years the problems of output and employment have also been given close study. Economists have constructed new short-run theories to explain output changes and have given them more attention in long-run theories of growth. As these problems have moved into the foreground, the price level has ceased to be the sole problem of monetary theory. In the late 1930's, it was pushed nearly out of sight and attention focused almost entirely on employment. Experience with inflation during and since World War II has brought the price-level problem back into prominence, but alongside the employment problem, not in place of it. Economists have been seeking to solve both problems—to provide for full employment and economic growth while maintaining a stable price level. This is the complex of problems that will concern us in Part IV.

NOTES ON

ALTERNATIVE POINTS OF VIEW

AND SUPPLEMENTARY READINGS

The most comprehensive study of the relation between money and economic activity was made by Milton Friedman and Anna J. Schwartz in *A Monetary History of the United States, 1867–1960* (Princeton: Princeton University Press, 1963). Their conclusions support the role of money as a major causal factor affecting the level of economic activity and the rate of economic growth. A good summary of their views is found in Milton Friedman and Anna J. Schwartz, "Money and Business Cycles," *The Review of Economics and Statistics,* February 1963, Supplement, pp. 32–64. Other economists' comments, which support or criticize their methodology and conclusions, are found in the Supplement on pp. 64–78.

Part III

International
Monetary
Relations

Chapter 16

How National Monetary Systems Mesh

Introduction. A book on money and monetary policy is no place for a thorough review of international economic relations; international trade and finance were among the first subjects to attract the attention of economists and have produced an enormous specialized literature. But international transactions link the separate national monetary systems into a network that does require attention if we are to understand the task and limits of domestic monetary policy.

International transactions serve to transmit business fluctuations from one country to another; they affect each country's output, employment, and price level. That is why major business fluctuations have coincided in the major countries—why so many countries experienced a serious depression in the 1930's and shared in some degree the American recessions since World War II. Conversely, national policies that affect output and price levels also affect a nation's transactions with the outside world and influence the national balance of payments. The debt instruments issued by the government, banks, or businesses of one country may be held by the government or citizens of another country, as near-moneys or as earning assets.

These and other links between national monetary systems suggest that we must briefly intrude upon the domain of the international economist, to survey the transactions that enter a nation's balance of payments and study the foreign-exchange market in which those transactions are ultimately centered. In the next chapter, we shall examine the notion of "payments equilibrium" and the many ways in which equilibrium may be attained, stressing those methods of adjustment that most directly involve monetary policies, but looking briefly at other techniques. In Chapter 18, we shall examine other aspects of international finance, looking most carefully at the structure of international monetary reserves, at the role of gold and of the United States dollar, and at such intergovernmental institutions as the International Monetary Fund.

Throughout Part III, we shall stress the need for intergovernmental co-operation—for the co-ordination of national policies to avoid a disruption of international payments such as that which occurred in the 1930's and seriously impeded recovery from the depression.

Two-money transactions. The distinguishing characteristic of an international transaction is that it ordinarily involves two moneys. A British textile mill that wishes to buy American raw cotton would like to pay for it in pounds sterling, but the American seller usually asks to be paid in dollars. Hence, sterling has somehow to be turned into dollars, and three prices must be used in the calculations: the price of cotton (delivered to England) in pounds sterling, the price of cotton (delivered to England) in United States dollars, and the price of the pound sterling in terms of the United States dollar.[1] These prices are not independent of each other—the sterling price of cotton must equal the dollar price of cotton *divided by* the dollar price of sterling. If cotton costs $120 per bale, its sterling price must be exactly £50 (fifty pounds), for one pound will buy just $2.40, and £50 will buy $120.

Two-money transactions are not confined to commodity dealings. Households have to cover tourist expenditures when travelling abroad and must deal in foreign-currency units. Gifts between households in different countries, such as remittances by Americans to their relatives in Europe, also involve a transformation of one currency into another. Governments deal extensively in foreign currencies, both as a matter of economic policy[2] and for the conduct of government activities—the support of embassies and troops abroad, the financing of development in low-income countries, and so on. There are also two-money dealings for financial purposes. Banks and individuals buy foreign securities or take speculative positions in foreign currencies themselves, buying when they expect the price of a currency to rise (appreciate) in terms of another currency, and selling when they expect the price of a currency to fall (depreciate) in terms of another currency.

---

[1] We shall often talk of the "price of the pound" here in Part III, for we will use the pound sterling as typical of foreign-currency units. When we do so, we mean the *number of dollars one must give up to buy one pound.* That price, of course, could be recalculated to give us the number of shillings one can buy for a dollar. As there are twenty shillings in a pound, and the pound costs about $2.40, one dollar would purchase slightly more than eight shillings. Throughout this discussion, however, we shall stick to the first version—the number of dollars required to buy one pound.

[2] See the section entitled "The foreign-exchange market," below.

The foreign-exchange market. The purchases and sales of foreign currency that are involved in two-money dealings take place on the so-called "foreign-exchange market." Like most markets, this one has two groups of participants: (1) the businesses, householders, and government agencies that have need of foreign currencies in the course of their day-to-day operations or come into possession of such currencies and wish to convert them into domestic money; (2) the dealers that supply final users with the currencies that they need and buy from the users the currencies that they acquire.

Transactions between users and dealers (retail transactions) normally take place at prices set by the dealers. Dealers *post* these prices hour by hour according to the state of the market.[3] The dealers will sell you bank notes if you want them, but do most of their business in *sight bills*. The sight bill is very much like the bank draft used in domestic commerce. It is an order issued by one bank to another, directing the second bank to pay a sum of money to the person presenting the bill. An American businessman owing £1,000 can buy from his New York bank a draft drawn on the British bank at which his own bank has its sterling account. That draft will order the British bank to pay the businessman (or his creditor) £1,000, and to debit the account of the New York bank. By this means, the businessman will obtain and pay over £1,000 merely by writing a check on his own account for the dollar equivalent of £1,000 (plus the commission charged by his own bank). The £1,000 come from an inventory held by his New York bank for just such purposes. The draft involved in this transaction is called a sight bill because it must be honored when presented. The foreign-exchange dealers also offer *bills of exchange* payable at some future time— in thirty, sixty, or ninety days, or even longer intervals. These time bills allow businessmen to protect themselves against changes in the price of a foreign currency.[4]

Transactions between dealers (wholesale transactions) occur when a dealer

---

[3] The dealer's commission may be included in the rate he posts, but more often is stated separately from the posted rate.

[4] These time bills are sometimes called *bank bills* or *bank paper*. They will be sent to the market on which they are drawn and presented to the prospective payors for verification that they are valid. When they have been accepted by the payor, they become *acceptances* drawn on the market in which the payor resides, and can be discounted like any other piece of commercial paper. In earlier decades, these deferred bills were issued by merchants, not by specialists in foreign exchange, and were called *trade paper*. When a buyer of commodities wanted credit for a few weeks, he could endorse the bill that was sent to him by his supplier, thereby indicating his intention to pay for the goods in a few weeks or months. His supplier might then discount the bill with a specialist in commercial paper. Trade paper such as this was more easily discounted if countersigned by a banker. It was then known as two-name paper. Much of the world's trade was financed by this sort of commercial paper in the nineteenth century. The London discount houses specialized in the purchase of commercial paper that was created in the course of international commerce. They came to know the credit standing of every major merchant dealing in internationally traded commodities. The banks also participated, serving as endorsers of trade paper. They stood ready to open "acceptance credits"—promises to endorse a stated volume of trade paper for a given merchant or firm. During the 1950's, the use of trade paper revived, and a thriving business in acceptances is again conducted by the British banking system. Acceptances are extremely popular in the financing of certain commodity shipments, notably the annual Australian wool crop.

feels the need to replenish his inventory of a particular currency or to cut down on an inventory he has accumulated by purchases from the public.[5] They are arranged by telephone calls from dealer to dealer, just like transactions in United States government securities. They are executed by means of cabled orders, directing a bank in a foreign financial center to transfer a bank balance from the account of one dealer to the account of another. These cabled messages accomplish vast transfers in a matter of minutes, and explain why the exchange rates at which dealers operate are called *cable rates or telegraphic transfer* (TT) *rates* in the jargon of the market.

This hour-by-hour process of wholesale trading determines foreign-exchange rates. A dealer who seeks to acquire pounds sterling calls around to others to get the best price. As the balance between orders and offers shifts in this very active market, the price of each currency moves up and down.

The way a dealer manages his balances of pounds sterling, francs, marks, or lire can best be analyzed using the list of motives for holding money developed in Chapter 11. The dealer's main motive for holding a currency is, of course, a transactions motive. He needs a balance of pounds sterling in order to satisfy his customers' requirements, and the size of his sterling balance will be heavily influenced by the volume of business his customers do with Britain. But a prudent dealer will hold more sterling than would be justified by a best estimate of anticipated customer purchases; he will hold a balance large enough to give him a margin of safety. If a dealer receives an order for sterling large enough to deplete his balance, he must enter the open market to buy sterling at the cable rate. Having just sold sterling at a posted price that corresponded to the prevailing cable rate, he may take a loss when replenishing his balance if, in the process, he drives up the cable rate.[6] Finally, every dealer is apt to display a well-developed "speculative" motive. If he expects the price of sterling to rise in the very near future, he will build up his balance in London. If he expects the price of francs to fall within a few weeks, he will reduce his balance in Paris.

This matter of speculation deserves additional space because it can profoundly affect the system of exchange rates and can exert great pressure on the balance of payments. The method of speculation we have just described—the

---

[5] They also occur when a dealer gets an order from a customer that is too big to handle out of his working inventory. Large businesses often hold working balances of their own if they are continuously involved in foreign transactions. Insurance companies, oil companies, and the like hold their own working balances and so stand midway between the users and the dealers in their connection with the foreign-exchange market. They do not buy foreign currency at posted rates, but work through the dealers to get the best rate possible in the open market where the dealers operate.

[6] He could, of course, avoid an outright loss by channeling the order received from his customer directly into the wholesale market and charging his customer whatever it cost to round up the pounds needed by the customer. But even this procedure involves a kind of loss, for the dealer may earn less as a pure broker than he would as the supplier of the sterling ordered by the customer.

purchase of a currency expected to appreciate and sale of a currency expected to depreciate—is not the only method that dealers can employ. A dealer anticipating a decline in the dollar price of the franc can arrange to profit from that decline by selling francs on the *forward* (futures) market. By issuing time bills rather than sight bills, he can commit himself to supply francs at a stated time some weeks away. If the price of the franc has fallen by the time the bills fall due, the dealer can round up the francs he needs to make good his promise and can earn a profit in the bargain.[7]

Arbitrage and speculation. The speculator's hallmark is his willingness to make commitments based on forecasts, knowing that an error in his forecasts can involve him in a loss. Hence, *forward* dealings in foreign exchange are speculative if the sellers cannot be sure of supplying what they have promised without taking a loss in the process. Speculative dealings have been common in the last two decades; British experience since World War II has been marked by many episodes. But the bulk of forward-exchange transactions are not really speculative. A dealer who has made a forward commitment usually *covers* that commitment by adding to his inventory of the currency he is pledged to deliver. The profit in these dealings comes mainly from commissions, but also arises from arbitrage. If the price of the pound sterling for forward delivery is higher than its price for spot delivery, a dealer can often make a profit by swapping spot for forward pounds. He can buy sterling at the cable rate and sell it for delivery thirty days hence. This sort of arbitrage across time helps to keep the spot and forward prices from straying very far apart. Dealers will buy pounds spot to sell them forward until the difference between spot and forward prices is no larger than the interest cost of holding pounds instead of dollars. If interest rates in London are two percentage points lower than those in New York, a dealer who holds sterling for one month sacrifices 2/12 of 1 per cent in interest. If the premium on forward sterling is larger than this fraction of the spot rate, dealers will be induced to sell sterling forward and buy it spot; they will gain more on the swap than they will lose in interest. Arbitrage transactions will increase the supply of forward sterling and the demand for spot sterling, tending to narrow the premium on forward pounds until it is no larger than 2/12 of 1 per cent.

Dealers engage in another sort of arbitrage—moving across currencies rather than time. Suppose that a pound costs $2.40 in New York and a Canadian dollar, $0.92. If, at the same time, the pound costs $2.59 in Canadian funds, an alert dealer can make a profit by sending funds in a circle. He can buy £1,000 in Toronto for just $2,590 in Canadian funds. He can then sell the £1,000 in New York acquiring $2,400 in American funds. But $2,400 in American funds will purchase

---

[7] By the same token, a dealer who has issued time bills in a currency that gives signs of appreciating can cover what amounts to a speculative position by acquiring a larger inventory of the currency in question. In the jargon of futures markets, this is known as *hedging*.

roughly $2,609 in Canadian funds, leaving the dealer with a gross profit of $19 Canadian dollars. This illustration overstates the margin at which crossrate arbitrage actually occurs. Arbitrage begins as soon as the margin can cover the costs.

Arbitrage can also be carried on in combinations of foreign currencies, foreign securities, commodities, and so on. If the Amsterdam price of Chrysler stock (translated into dollars through the price of the Dutch guilder) is above the New York price, a profit can be made by selling Chrysler for guilders, selling the guilders in New York, and buying Chrysler in New York. Obviously, few of us are qualified to be arbitrageurs. One needs an unquestioned credit standing in many countries, a nose for a bargain, the power of quick decision, and the ability to juggle rapid-fire telephone conversations (often in different languages) without becoming confused.

These specialists are as useful as they are rare, for they spare the businessman interested in a single transaction the trouble of scanning all the international markets. The ordinary businessman can rest assured that arbitrageurs have exhausted every chance to make a profit by the roundabout ways of paying for foreign purchases.

The balance of payments and the foreign-exchange market.   Because most international transactions involve an exchange of currencies, the foreign-exchange market serves as a mirror of a nation's foreign transactions. This is why the market interests us. Under certain circumstances,[8] it can also play an active part in adjustment processes that have great importance, but under the arrangements currently governing most major currencies, the market's main function is to signal changes in the nation's foreign commerce and foreign investment.

Balance-of-payments accounts also give us a second picture of national transactions with the outside world. These accounts are nothing more than an adaptation of the cash-transactions equation used in Part II. They explain changes in the cash-holdings of the nation, using "cash" to mean the nation's holdings of foreign currency *less* foreign holdings of the nation's own currency. They summarize the nation's transactions with the outside world and the impact of those transactions on the national cash position.

The foreign transactions of the United States may be classified into two broad groups: (1) *current-account transactions,* which alter the total of goods and services available for consumption by Americans; and (2) *capital-account transactions,* which are dealings in financial instruments or real property. Transactions on both current and capital accounts will be reflected by a change in the *cash account.* Those that would increase our cash-holdings (in the absence of other transactions) are listed in the current or capital account with a plus sign; those that would decrease our cash-holdings are listed in one of these accounts with a

_____
[8] See pp. 321–25.

minus sign. In the cash account itself, increases in American holdings of foreign currency are listed with a minus sign, as required by the conventions of double-entry bookkeeping; increases in foreign holdings of American currency are listed with a plus sign.

Merchandise exports and imports are the largest items on current account, but are not the only ones involving current consumption. Americans travelling abroad, who pay for meals, hotel rooms, and plane fare, are doing much the same thing as Americans at home who consume imported goods; they are using the services of foreign factors of production. At the same time, their transactions tend to reduce our cash-holdings, so that their purchases from foreigners are listed with a minus sign in the current account. Similarly, foreigners who lease cargo space in American ships or pay interest on money borrowed from Americans are making claims upon American factors of production, just like foreigners who buy American exports. These transactions are also listed on current account, but with a plus sign, as they tend to increase American cash balances.

American purchases of foreign securities and repurchases of our own debt instruments are listed with a minus sign on the capital account. They increase our stock of assets (or decrease our liabilities), but tend to reduce our holdings of foreign currency or to increase foreign holdings of United States dollars.

Some transactions do not fit neatly into the current or capital accounts. When, for example, Americans send money to their relatives abroad, or when our government gives a grant to a foreign government, our cash balances tend to decline. Yet we do not receive consumable goods in return for our outlays, nor do we obtain a negotiable instrument that signifies foreign indebtedness to the United States. Hence these *unilateral transfers* are not strictly current transactions, but neither do they belong on the capital account. Here and in most other presentations, they are forced into the current account (as offsets to the flow of goods and services).

In order that we may become fully familiar with the conventions of balance-of-payments accounting and perceive the connections between the balance of payments and the foreign-exchange market, let us work through a set of illustrative transactions and enter them in a hypothetical balance-of-payments tabulation for the United States.

> 1. Foreigners buy $1,000 worth of United States merchandise. They pay for it by purchasing a dollar sight bill from a British bank and endorsing that bill over to the American manufacturer.

This transaction involves an entry on the current account; merchandise exports (Item *A* in Table 16–1) is credited with $1,000. It also involves an entry on the cash account; foreign-owned balances at American banks (Item *H*) are reduced by $1,000 as soon as the sight bill used in the transaction has travelled from the bank where the American manufacturer deposited it to the bank where the British exchange dealer has his dollar account. Note that this transaction has increased the total of cash assets owned by Americans. The total deposit liabilities of American banks have not been changed by the transaction, but dollar deposits have been transferred from the account of the British bank to the account of the American manufacturer.

> 2. An American buys $500 worth of British goods. He pays for them by borrowing the sterling equivalent of $500 from a British bank.

This transaction also involves an entry on the current account; merchandise imports (Item *B*) is debited by $500. The financing, however, does not affect United States cash holdings. Instead, there is a $500 increase of United States borrowing (Item *F*). The justification for assigning a plus sign to this borrowing and a minus sign to the purchase becomes clear when we break this transaction into two separate steps. The American buyer begins by borrowing the sterling equivalent of $500 from a British bank and adds the money to his balance in London. The borrowing increases American cash and is therefore recorded with a plus sign in the capital account. The American buyer then spends his balance on the goods he is importing. This transaction reduces American balances by $500, and offsets the increase caused by the borrowing that preceded it. Note that this transaction does not change the total of cash assets held by Americans, but that it does decrease the liquidity of the American public, insofar as an increase of indebtedness is an offset to liquidity.

> 3. An American tourist pays a $50 hotel bill with a traveler's check bought from an American bank before his journey. The hotelkeeper deposits the check in his own bank, which sends the check to the American bank that issued it.

This transaction leads to a minus sign next to tourist spending (Item *C*) on the current account. After the financing is complete, it leads to a plus sign on the cash account—an increase in foreign holdings of American dollars (Item *H*). This transaction, by the way, also reduces American liquidity. It does not change the total of dollars in existence, but transfers dollars from an American to a foreign bank.

> 4. The United States government lends $300 to a foreign government for use by that government in its development program. The foreign government spends $200 on American goods and uses the other $100 to buy German goods.

Like the second transaction above, involving a bank loan, this complex sequence can best be recorded if it is divided into two parts. First, our government transfers $300 to the dollar bank account of a foreign government. As this trans-

TABLE 16-1

HYPOTHETICAL BALANCE OF PAYMENTS FOR THE UNITED STATES

Item and Text Example Number	Credit (+)	Debit (−)
Current account		
A. Merchandise exports (1)	1,000	
(4)	200	
(5)	250	
B. Merchandise imports (2)		500
Balance of trade	950	
C. Tourist expenditure (3)		50
Balance on current account	900	—
Capital account		
D. United States government loan (4)		300
E. United States direct investment (5)		750
F. United States borrowing abroad (2)	500	
Balance on capital account	—	550
Net current and capital balance	350	—
G. Increases (−) in U. S. balances abroad (5)	750	250
Net Increase (−)	500	
H. Increases (+) in foreign dollar balances (1)		1,000
(3)	50	
(4)	300	200
Net Increase (+)	—	850
Net increase (−) in U. S. cash (G + H)	—	350

action increases foreign cash and reduces the net cash position of the United States, it is recorded in the capital account (Item *D*) with a minus sign, and under foreign balances (Item *H*) in the cash account with a plus sign. Next, the foreign government spends $200 on American goods. This creates a $200 credit next to exports (Item *A*), and a $200 debit next to foreign balances (Item *H*). The final stage in this transaction does not affect our balance of payments, as it merely involves a transfer from one foreign balance to another.

5. An American company builds a plant abroad, spending $500 for the purchase of land and the erection of a building, and $250 on machinery which it buys in the United States. It pays for the land with sterling bought from an American bank, and for the machinery with a check drawn on its ordinary bank account.

This final transaction can most easily be analyzed by asking what would have happened to our balance-of-payments statistics if the American company had bought a building abroad instead of erecting a new one and had commissioned its previous owner to buy equipment for the building. American assets abroad would have increased by $750, and the sterling balance of an American bank would have fallen by the same amount. Hence, direct investment (Item *E*) would have been debited in the amount of $750 and American balances (Item *G*) would have been credited with $750. The building's former owner, however, would now spend $250 on American equipment. Were he to buy $250 from an American exchange dealer, American balances abroad would rise by the foreign-currency equivalent of $250, as would the domestic bank account of the American company selling the equipment. American exports would also increase by $250. When these two steps were put together, American balances in foreign banks (Item *G*) would be lower by the equivalent of $500, and American exports (Item *A*) would be up by $250. These two credit items, combined, would exactly offset the $750 debit under direct investment. When the transaction described above is executed as originally supposed, the balance-of-payments table will record these same three changes. Note, that this transaction reduces domestic cash assets by $500; the firm building the factory has $750 less, but the firm selling it equipment has $250 more. This reduction of cash assets, moreover, has been accompanied by an equal shrinkage of total deposits. The deposit liabilities of American banks have fallen by $500, as have their balances held abroad. The change in American cash assets exactly matches the decrease in American banks' holdings of foreign currency.

We are now ready to summarize the five transactions listed in our hypothetical balance-of-payments table. We start by taking the difference between exports and imports—the so-called *balance of trade*—which stands at +$950 in our table. Next, we add in the service transactions (there is just one in this example), to calculate the *balance on current account*. This stands at +$900 in our example and represents the *net addition to domestic income that accrues from the nation's foreign transactions*. For this reason the balance on current account enters the national-income accounts. Receipts from sales to foreigners and investment income earned abroad are treated as income flows injected into the domestic income stream, analogously to business investment. Purchases from foreigners are treated as leakages from that same stream, analogously to domestic saving. Hence, the national-income equations we described in our study of the payments approach must now be amended to take account of foreign transactions. The national income (national product) must be defined as:

$$Y = C + I + G + X - M,$$

where Y is income (product); C, I, and G are consumer, investment, and government spending, respectively; X is spending by foreigners on domestic output; and M is the part of total domestic spending that leaks out of the income stream by way of imports and other income payments to the rest of the world. We can simplify this equation for the purposes of Part III by substituting one letter, H, for $C + I + G$, letting H (for home) be total domestic spending. In this case, $H - M$ stands for domestic spending on home-produced goods, while $X - M$ stands for the net contribution of foreign transactions to total spending on home goods. In our table, the $900 balance on current account corresponds to $X - M$; it is the excess of income received from commodity and service sales and from American property abroad, over income paid to foreigners for commodity and service purchases and on foreign property in this country.

Next, we look at the capital account, and strike a balance of asset transactions. In our example, that balance comes out at $-$550. This indicates that the dollar value of the assets Americans acquired abroad exceeded American borrowing and sales of domestic assets to foreigners.

Putting together the current and capital accounts, we get a net balance of $+$350. This final figure must be matched by an increase of United States cash holdings *less* any increase in foreign holdings of United States dollars. In the table, it appears as a reduction of foreign balances in the United States larger than the reduction of American balances abroad. American dealers in foreign exchange ran down their holdings by $500, but foreigners dealing in United States dollars cut back their inventories by $850. This increase of our net cash assets matches the increase in domestic liquidity. Although total bank deposits have fallen on account of transaction (5), balances owned by Americans have increased by more than total deposits have fallen. Some $850 of dollar deposits at American commercial banks have been transferred from foreign ownership to the accounts of American business.[9]

The pattern of payments displayed in our example illustrates one of many possibilities. In the table we have constructed, the United States ran a sufficient surplus on current account to finance its transfers and net asset purchases, and also to increase its cash-holdings. In effect, its current-account surplus served as a form of saving; it comprised an excess of income over outlay that could be used to acquire earning assets and to finance an increase of cash balances. One could construct examples that display a different pattern. The United States could run a deficit on current account and could finance that deficit, plus net asset acquisition, by reducing its total cash assets.

Official intervention in the foreign-exchange market. The five transactions that comprise our hypothetical balance of payments have all involved "retail" dealings in the foreign-exchange market; the net cash requirements of business and consumers have been met out of dealers' balances. As a result of retail transactions, however, the dealers' inventories have been depleted.

---

[9] There has, of course, been a $500 increase in short-term indebtedness to foreigners. If a dollar of this indebtedness decreases liquidity by as much as a dollar's increase in cash assets increases liquidity, we would have to conclude that Americans are less liquid than they were before.

We must now consider the monetary consequences of the dealers' efforts to reconstitute their balances.

Suppose, for purposes of illustration, that each dealer seeks to bring his balance back to what it was at the start of the period that witnessed our five transactions. On this assumption, American dealers will try to buy the foreign-currency equivalent of $500, while foreign dealers will seek to acquire $850 of United States dollars. The first thing to note about this situation is that the Americans' demand for $500 worth of foreign currency will help to satisfy the foreigners' demand for additional American money. The Americans' demand for foreign bank balances is also an offer to supply $500 of American bank balances at the existing rate of exchange between dollars and foreign currency. By the same token, the foreigners' demand for dollars is also an offer to supply the foreign-currency equivalent of $850 in United States currency. American dealers can thereby acquire the foreign-currency equivalent of $500, and foreign dealers can acquire a $500 balance at American banks, without putting any pressure on the prevailing exchange rates.

At this point, however, the foreign-exchange market has still to deal with a foreign demand for $350 in American bank balances (the difference between the $850 that foreigners seek and the $500 that Americans offer at the existing exchange rate). This *excess demand* for dollars (an *excess supply* of foreign currency) remains to influence the foreign-currency price of the United States dollar.

If foreign-exchange rates were free to fluctuate in the market, any such an excess demand for American currency would drive up the price of the dollar in terms of foreign currencies. Such an increase in the price of the dollar (a depreciation of foreign currencies in terms of the dollar) will normally call forth an increased demand for foreign currencies and will reduce the demand for American dollars.[10] To anticipate our discussion of balance-of-payments adjustment under flexible exchange rates, the depreciation of foreign currencies will reduce the dollar cost of foreign merchandise and raise the foreign-currency price of American merchandise.[11] As a result, businessmen and consumers in the United States will increase their purchases from other countries, while foreign businessmen and consumers will reduce their purchases from the United States.[12] In the expecta-

---

[10]This proposition requires qualification because the foreign-exchange market may be unstable and because speculative influences can upset an otherwise stable market. These points are discussed in Chapter 17.

[11]If the pound sterling costs $2.40, a British car selling for £700, will cost exactly $1,680 in the United States (before allowing for tariffs and transport costs). A depreciation of the pound sterling to $2.00 will reduce the dollar cost of the car to just $1,400. By the same token, an American drill press costing $2,400 will cost £1,000 in Britain when the pound sells for $2.40, but will rise in price to £1,400 when the pound falls to $2.00.

[12]Note, however, that Americans will not necessarily increase their purchases of foreign currency. If the American demand for foreign goods is inelastic, total dollar outlays for foreign goods will decline when foreign goods get cheaper, and may fall by enough to reduce American purchases of foreign currency, although Americans will acquire more units of foreign currency per dollar spent. By the same token, an inelastic foreign demand for American goods can mean a larger foreign-currency outlay for American goods despite the increase in the foreign-currency cost of American merchandise. These are the possibilities we had in mind when we referred to unstable markets in footnote 10.

tion of an increased demand emanating from Americans, dealers in foreign currency are likely to build up their balances. They will offer additional dollars to foreign dealers, helping to fill the $350 excess demand for dollars that set off the change in exchange rates. At the same time, foreign dealers in American money are likely to cut back their balances in anticipation of a smaller demand by the public, and will forego purchasing some of the $350 that they initially sought to buy. Eventually, the market will establish an exchange rate at which the foreign dealers can buy the dollars they still want.

Some exchange rates have been free to fluctuate as we have assumed. For many years, the United States dollar price of the Canadian dollar was allowed to respond to changes in supply and demand, and moved up and down, hour by hour. But most exchange rates are not allowed to fluctuate as widely as would be required to equate supply and demand. The rules that were formulated after World War II, when the International Monetary Fund was established, fix the price of each major currency in terms of gold, and thereby fix a *par value* for each currency in terms of every other currency that has a gold price. The United States dollar is valued at 0.888671 of a gram of fine gold, which corresponds to the familiar $35.00 per troy ounce of gold. The pound sterling is valued at 2.13281 grams of fine gold, equivalent to nearly 292 shillings per troy ounce of gold. As a result, the pound exchanges for 2.13281/0.888671 dollars, or for $2.40 per pound.

In practice, few governments actually trade currency for gold, or gold for currency, to maintain the gold values of their currencies. The United States is almost unique in this respect. Instead, governments intervene in the foreign-exchange markets to maintain the exchange-rate parities implied by the gold valuations.[13] They do not seek to preserve perfect stability, but are committed by the Articles of Agreement of the International Monetary Fund to keep the exchange rates within 1 per cent of those that are implied by the gold valuations.[14] The British government, through the Bank of England, stands ready to buy sterling with foreign currency whenever its price falls close to $2.38, and to sell sterling for foreign currency whenever its price rises near to $2.42.[15]

The British government and most others hold a cash reserve of gold and foreign currency with which they conduct these operations; this reserve may be

---

[13]This amounts to maintaining the gold valuations, because a currency that has a constant price in terms of United States dollars has a constant price in terms of gold.

[14]This 1 per cent margin around parity is reminiscent of the margin that existed under the gold standard which prevailed before World War I and in the 1920's. Under that gold standard, an American wanting pounds sterling could buy them in the open market or could buy gold in New York, ship it to London, and sell it to the British authorities in exchange for sterling. If the dollar price of sterling rose far enough above the par value implied by the gold price of sterling and the gold price of the dollar, it was cheaper to send gold to London than to buy sterling directly for dollars. As a consequence, the dollar price of sterling could never rise above this so-called *gold export point*. There was a similar lower limit to the price of sterling (the gold import point), for a price lower than this limit would bring British gold to New York to buy dollars more cheaply than they could be purchased on the open market.

[15]Actually, the British government enters the market well before prices reach these limits. It has sold sterling (bought foreign currency) at prices much below $2.42.

regarded as a supplement to the inventory held by the private dealers in foreign exchange. An increase in the demand for foreign currency which dealers are unable or unwilling to meet is at first reflected in an increase of the prices at which foreign currencies are traded against the home currency. As the government is committed to prevent this depreciation of its own currency, it will move into the market and sell foreign currency from its own reserve, mopping up the excess supply of its own currency that is the counterpart of any excess demand for foreign money.

Under this system of fixed exchange rates, changes in official reserves take the place of changes in exchange rates. They measure the extent of official intervention in the foreign-exchange market and, therefore, the gap between private supply and private demand. To show such changes in the cash account, one must separate the change in official holdings of gold, foreign currencies, and other cash assets from the changes in private cash holdings; one must rearrange the cash account of Table 16–1. In our previous example, all foreign-exchange dealers sought to reconstitute their own inventories of foreign currency. This would bring the Bank of England into the market as a net seller of $350 (a net buyer of nearly £146). Once all balances have been transferred to their new owners, the cash account will look like this:

	+	–
Increase (–) in *private* United States balances abroad	0	0
Increase (+) in *private* foreign dollar balances	0	0
Increase (+) in *official* foreign dollar balances	0	350

The last line in this group shows the decline in British reserves resulting from official intervention to stabilize the dollar price of the pound sterling. It is known as the *balance on official settlements,* and is widely regarded as the best summary measure of disequilibrium in the foreign-exchange market. The $350 reduction in official dollar holdings indicates a balance-of-payments surplus for the United States (a reduction of foreign reserves and, therefore, of United States reserve liabilities); it likewise indicates a balance-of-payments deficit for the United Kingdom.

Changes in official reserves have an important effect on the banking system and the money supply. When the Bank of England undertakes to provide $350 from its own reserves, it will place an order, in London or abroad, for the sterling equivalent of $350 (for £146, to the nearest pound, at $2.40 per pound), and will feed the $350 into the foreign-exchange market as payment for the sterling it has ordered. The Bank of England keeps a dollar balance at the Federal Reserve Bank of New York. When it has sold dollars to British dealers, it must write a check on that account. The British exchange dealers will deposit the check in an American commercial bank, and the bank will send it on to the Federal Reserve. The commercial bank will end up with $350 in its balance at the Federal Reserve. Central bank intervention has done what none of our five transactions could do unaided: it has increased the total of commercial-bank reserves, enlarging the credit base in the United States. At the same time, it has cut back the British credit base. To pay for their newly acquired dollars, the British dealers must pay nearly £146 to the Bank of England—the sterling equivalent of the $350 they have on deposit at an American bank. This £146 payment to the Bank of England reduces the credit base in Great Britain.[16]

Thus, retail transactions in foreign exchange can cause important changes in liquidity; they involve a redistribution of existing bank deposits and, sometimes, a change in total deposits. But wholesale dealings have a much more powerful monetary impact. They can alter the credit base, permitting an expansion of deposits in the country whose currency is in excess demand, and forcing a contraction of deposits in the country whose currency is in excess supply. These powerful monetary counterparts of official intervention in the foreign-exchange market can, of course, be offset by open-market operations or by a change in reserve requirements. But if the central bank lets them stand, they may help to eliminate the basic economic conditions that caused them to happen. Monetary changes are one way of altering a nation's balance of payments—of changing its demand for foreign currency relative to the foreign demand for its own currency.

The United States' balance of payments. Balance-of-payments tables for the United States are organized to show the current, capital, and cash accounts and to identify the balance on official settlements. Data for 1965 and 1966 are given in Table 16–2. Note that there was a very large current-account surplus in each of those two years, but also a very large capital outflow. In consequence, the cash account showed a decline in the net cash assets of the United States. More importantly, there was a *deficit* in the balance on official settlements over the two years taken together. In 1965, United States' reserve assets (gold, foreign currencies, and automatic drawing rights at the International Monetary Fund) fell by $1.2 billion while reserve liabilities (the dollar balances of foreign governments and central banks) rose by $82 million. The deficit was $1.3 billion. Our own and foreign governments had to intervene in the foreign-exchange market to prevent a fall in the foreign-currency price of the dollar. In 1966, there was a further fall in United States reserve assets but a larger fall in reserve liabilities, resulting in a $225 million surplus.

---

[16]This description would not be much modified if the Bank of England started out with gold, rather than dollars at the Federal Reserve. Starting with gold, the Bank of England would buy dollars from the Federal Reserve, which acts as the agent for the United States Treasury for gold transactions. This would supply the Bank of England with the dollars to continue its transaction just as we described it in the text. The gold movements listed in Table 16-2 (and discussed at length in Chapter 18) arise mainly in this way. Governments that need dollars for foreign-exchange-market operations buy those dollars with the gold they hold as a cash reserve. Governments holding more dollars than they need trade those dollars in for gold at the Federal Reserve.

TABLE 16-2

THE UNITED STATES BALANCE OF PAYMENTS, 1965–66

(millions of dollars, rounded to nearest $1.0 million)

Item	1965		1966	
	Credit	*Debit*	*Credit*	*Debit*
Goods and services:				
Merchandise exports*	26,244		29,168	
Merchandise imports		21,472		25,510
Transportation and travel	3,770	5,112	4,162	5,571
Military expenditures	844	2,921	847	3,694
Miscellaneous services	2,401	969	2,617	1,088
Income on investments	5,888	1,729	6,245	2,047
Balance on goods and services	6,944		5,102	
Unilateral transfers:				
United States government grants (net)		2,166		2,278
Private gifts (net)		658		647
Balance on current account	4,120		2,177	
Capital account:				
United States government loans and claims (net)		1,575		1,531
Direct private investment (net)		3,418		3,543
Other United States private investment (net)		325		670
Foreign investment in United States (net)	178		1,710	
Balance on capital account		5,140		4,034
Errors and omissions		415		302
Balance on current and capital account		1,435		2,159
Cash account**				
Increase (+) of *private* foreign dollar balances	131		2,384	
Increase (+) of *official* foreign dollar balances	82			793
Increase (−) of United States reserve assets†	1,222		568	
Balance on official settlements	1,304			225
Balance on cash account	1,435		2,159	

Source: United States Department of Commerce, *Survey of Current Business.*

* Merchandise exports exclude about $1.9 billion in shipments of military hardware financed by grant assistance. Corresponding grant assistance is excluded from government grants.

**This cash account does not appear in the Commerce Department tabulations. It is constructed by separating the change in foreign short-term claims on the United States from the total of foreign investment given in the official tabulation and adding the change in United States reserve assets. Changes in United States' private holdings of foreign currencies, which figured prominently in our hypothetical balance of payments, have been small in recent years and are included in "Other United States private investment," rather than in our cash account.

† Includes United States' gold stock, holdings of convertible currencies, and IMF gold-tranche position.

NOTES ON

SUPPLEMENTARY READINGS AND

ALTERNATIVE POINTS OF VIEW

The standard treatise on the balance of payments is James E. Meade, *The Balance of Payments,* Volume I of *The Theory of International Economic Policy* (London: Oxford

University Press, 1951). The operations and structure of the foreign-exchange market are described clearly by Alan R. Holmes and Francis H. Schott, *The New York Foreign Exchange Market* (New York: Federal Reserve Bank of New York, 1965). The balance-of-payments accounts of the United States are surveyed in *The Balance of Payments Statistics of the United States: A Review and Appraisal* (Washington, D.C.: U.S. Government Printing Office, 1965); note, in particular, chap. ix, which discusses the several ways of measuring surpluses and deficits (and which endorses the official-settlements concept used in this book).

Chapter 17

The Processes of Balance-of-Payments Adjustment

Equilibrium in the Foreign-Exchange Market

Supply and demand curves for foreign exchange. The description of the foreign-exchange market in Chapter 16 suggests that the workings of this market can be described by supply and demand curves similar to those used to analyze markets for goods and services and for other assets. The demand for foreign exchange will depend upon the price of foreign currency, along with prices at home and abroad, domestic and foreign interest rates, and the level of real income. These variables are determinants of the demand for foreign goods and services and for foreign assets. They are, therefore, determinants of the demand for foreign exchange. The higher the price of foreign currency in terms of home currency, the more expensive are foreign goods relative to home goods and the smaller the demand for foreign exchange; the higher are home prices relative to foreign prices, the greater the demand for foreign goods and for foreign exchange; the higher are foreign interest rates relative to home interest rates, the greater the demand for foreign securities and foreign exchange; and the higher the domestic national income, the greater the demand for all goods and services, the demand for foreign goods and services, and the demand for foreign exchange.

This list of variables is not complete. Trade and payments controls, including tariffs, influence the demand for foreign exchange. So, too, do expectations of

316

potential buyers concerning future prices and exchange rates, because these affect the timing of foreign-exchange purchases.[1]

The demand for foreign exchange can be graphed in the usual way—as a curve connecting the quantities demanded with the prevailing exchange rates. Such a graph is presented in Chart 17-1, where the number of foreign-currency units (pounds) is measured along the horizontal axis, and the price of the foreign-currency unit (dollars per pound) is measured along the vertical axis. The demand curve in Chart 17-1 slopes downward (from left to right) to indicate that the quantity demanded increases as the pound depreciates—that Americans will buy more pounds sterling as British goods and services grow cheaper in relation to competitive home products.

The curve in Chart 17-1 does not neglect the many other variables that affect the demand for foreign exchange. It treats those variables as determining the position of the curve. An increase of income in the United States would be reflected in a rightward shift of the demand curve for pounds.

At one point in Chapter 16 we noticed that a demand for foreign currency will always correspond to an offer of domestic money. This proposition may be used to translate Chart 17-1 into a supply curve of American dollars. If the price of the pound is \$2.40 and Americans seek to purchase £1,000 at that price, the supply of dollars must be \$2,400; the offer to purchase £1,000 is an offer to sell \$2,400. If we multiply the price of the pound, given on the vertical axis of Chart 17-1, by the number of foreign-currency units demanded at that price, we derive the corresponding offer of dollars. Thus, the supply of dollars at the exchange rate OF is equal to the product $OF \times OD$, or to the area of the rectangle $ODEF$. The supply of dollars at the exchange rate OC is equal to the product $OC \times OA$, or to the area of the rectangle $OABC$. Note one important point: As the price of the pound rises (as the pound appreciates) from zero to OF, the supply of dollars increases steadily; the relevant rectangles grow in size until they form the perfect square $ODEF$. As the price of the pound rises beyond OF, the supply of dollars decreases steadily, falling to zero when the price of the pound reaches the level OK. In Marshallian terms, the demand curve for pounds is inelastic ($\epsilon < 1$) at prices lower than OF, has unit elasticity ($\epsilon = 1$) at the price OF, and is elastic ($\epsilon > 1$) at prices higher than OF.[2] These characteristics of the demand curve will prove helpful very shortly.

---

[1] Dealers' expectations are especially important in this respect. This discussion will treat the dealers' net demand (as reflected in inventory changes) as a part of the market demand. In effect, the analysis will compress retail and wholesale dealings, regarding them as a combined private demand for foreign-currency units. If a gap appears between the amount of currency demanded at a particular exchange rate and the amount that is forthcoming at that same exchange rate, the gap must be filled by official purchases of domestic or foreign currency if the exchange rate is to be kept stable.

[2] The elasticity of a demand curve is defined as the percentage change in quantity caused by a small percentage change in price. Algebraically, it is $-(dQ/Q)/(dP/P)$, where dQ is the change in quantity and Q the quantity being sold at the current price, dP is the change in price and P the current price. If we were concerned exclusively with commodity trade, we could

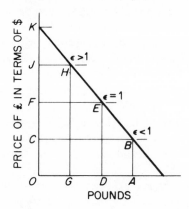

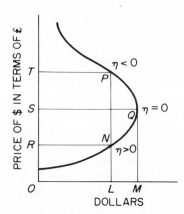

Chart 17-1: The demand for pounds.   **Chart 17-2: The supply of dollars.**

The supply of dollars we have been discussing is described by Chart 17-2. There, the vertical axis measures the price of the dollar in terms of the pound; this is the *reciprocal* of the price in Chart 17-1 (the price of the pound in dollars turned upside down). There, moreover, a *distance* along the horizontal axis corresponds to an *area* in Chart 17-1. Thus, the distance OL in Chart 17-2 corresponds to the area $OGHJ$ in Chart 17-1; both measure the number of dollars that will be offered by Americans when the price of the pound stands at OJ, so that the price of the dollar stands at OR. Similarly, the distance OM corresponds to the area $ODEF$; both measure the number of dollars that will be offered when the price of the pound is OF and, therefore, the price of the dollar is OS.

---

show that the elasticity of demand for foreign exchange is identical to the elasticity of the demand for imported merchandise. The demand for foreign exchange, C_d^f, can be written as $P^h Q/R$, where P^h is the home price of the imported commodity, Q is the quantity purchased per period, and R is the price of foreign currency in terms of home currency. Those who know the calculus will see that:

$$\frac{dC_d^f}{dR} = \frac{1}{R}\left[\frac{dP^h}{dR} \cdot Q + \frac{dQ}{dP^h} \cdot \frac{dP^h}{dR} \cdot P^h\right] - \frac{P^h Q}{R^2}$$

Multiplying both sides by R, and replacing $\dfrac{dP^h}{dR}$ by its equivalent, $\dfrac{P^h}{R}$, we obtain:

$$\frac{dC_d^f}{dR} \cdot R = \frac{P^h Q}{R}\left(1 + \frac{dQ}{dP^h} \cdot \frac{P^h}{Q}\right) - \frac{P^h Q}{R}$$

Dividing both sides by $\dfrac{P^h Q}{R}$ and replacing it with its equivalent, C_d^f, we emerge with:

$$\frac{dC_d^f}{dR} \cdot \frac{R}{C_d^f} = \frac{dQ}{dP^h} \cdot \frac{P^h}{Q}$$

But the left-hand expression in this equation, when prefixed by a minus sign, is the elasticity of demand for foreign exchange, while the right-hand expression, prefixed by a minus sign, is the elasticity of demand for an imported commodity.

The reader who finds this bewildering need not be alarmed. He can skip the next footnote too, if he is willing to accept some assertions in the text as matters of faith.

When the price of the dollar is higher than OS (when the price of the pound is lower than OF), the supply curve in Chart 17-2 begins to bend back upon itself; the supply of dollars begins to shrink when the pound cheapens and the dollar becomes expensive. This is another way of describing what we observed earlier. When the price of the pound falls below OF, the rectangles in Chart 17-1 grow smaller than $ODEF$. Thus, the number of dollars on offer when the price of the dollar is OT is the same as when that price is OR; the rectangles $OGHJ$ and $OABC$ are exactly the same size and both correspond to the distance OM in Chart 17-2.

The elasticity of the supply curve in Chart 17-2 (denoted by the symbol η) is related to that of the demand curve in Chart 17-1. When the demand curve for foreign exchange is elastic, the supply curve has an elasticity ranging between one and zero; when the demand curve has unit elasticity, the supply curve has zero elasticity; and when the demand curve becomes inelastic, the elasticity of the supply curve becomes negative.[3]

---

[3] The relationship between elasticities can be established algebraically. The supply of home currency, C_s^h must equal RC_d^f (the demand for foreign currency *times* the price of foreign currency). The elasticity of supply of home currency can be defined as:

$$\eta = \frac{dC_s^h}{dR'} \cdot \frac{R'}{C_s^h}$$

where R' is the price of home currency in terms of foreign currency ($R' = 1/R$). We can rewrite this expression as:

$$\eta = \frac{d(RC_d^f)}{dR} \cdot \frac{dR}{dR'} \cdot \frac{R'^2}{C_d^f}$$

But by the basic rules of the calculus:

$$\frac{d(RC_d^f)}{dR} = C_d^f + \frac{dC_d^f}{dR} \cdot R, \text{ and } \frac{dR}{dR'} = -\frac{1}{R'^2}$$

Therefore:

$$\eta = \left[C_d^f + \frac{dC_d^f}{dR} \cdot R \right]\left(\frac{-1}{C_d^f} \right) = \left[-\frac{dC_d^f}{dR} \cdot \frac{R}{C_d^f} - 1 \right]$$

But $-\dfrac{dC_d^f}{dR} \cdot \dfrac{R}{C_d^f} = \varepsilon$, the elasticity of demand for foreign currency, so that $\eta = \varepsilon - 1$. We can use this same method to relate the elasticity of supply of foreign currency and the elasticity of foreign demand for home currency. The supply of foreign currency is $C_s^f = C_d^h/R$, so that:

$$\frac{dC_s^f}{dR} = \left[\frac{dC_d^h}{dR} - \frac{C_h^d}{R} \right]\frac{1}{R} = \left[\frac{dC_d^h}{dR'} \cdot \frac{dR'}{dR} - \frac{C_h^d}{R} \right]\frac{1}{R}$$

$$= \left[\frac{dC_d^h}{dR'}\left(\frac{-1}{R^2} \right) - \frac{C_d^h}{R} \right]\frac{1}{R} = \left[-\frac{dC_d^h}{dR'} \cdot \frac{R'}{C_d^h} - 1 \right]\frac{C_d^h}{R} \cdot \frac{1}{R}$$

But $-\dfrac{dC_h^d}{dR'} \cdot \dfrac{R'}{C_h^d}$ is ε', the elasticity of demand for home currency, and C_d^h/R is C_s^f, so that:

$$\frac{dC_s^f}{dR} \cdot \frac{R}{C_s^f} = \varepsilon' - 1 = \eta', \text{ the elasticity of supply of foreign currency.}$$

We will use this formula in just a moment.

Defining equilibrium.   The conversion of a demand for foreign currency into a supply of home currency is something more than a geometrical *tour de force*. It is prerequisite to the analysis of the foreign-exchange market. Just as the demand curve for foreign currency can be remade into a supply curve of domestic currency, so a foreign demand curve for domestic currency can be remade into a supply curve of foreign currency. The foreign demand curve for American dollars can be translated into a supply curve of pounds sterling and, in Chart 17-3, is set against a demand curve for pounds like the one plotted in Chart 17-1.

Neglect, for a moment, the demand curve $D'D'$, and fix your attention upon the point E at which the demand curve DD intersects the supply curve SS. At this point (and at the point U), the demand for pounds is exactly equal to the supply forthcoming from purchases of dollars. An exchange rate established at OR could be perpetuated for as long as the demand and supply curves stood still. There would be no excess supply of pounds to depress the price of pounds or to require official intervention. But a price that can perpetuate itself from period to period is what economists usually call an "equilibrium" price. Hence, an exchange rate that matches supply with demand may be regarded as an "equilibrium" exchange rate.[4] By the same token, the international transactions that correspond to OA sterling payments at the exchange rate OR may be regarded as signifying equilibrium in the British balance of payments.

This notion of equilibrium in the balance of payments implies a definition of disequilibrium that corresponds quite closely to common usage. If there is an excess demand for sterling or an excess supply, so that the exchange rate changes or requires official support in the foreign-exchange market, the balance of payments may be said to exhibit a kind of disequilibrium.[5] To illustrate, suppose

---

[4] Some authorities would not be satisfied with this definition. They would require that an equilibrium exchange rate clear the market for foreign exchange at full-employment levels of national income (and under certain other restrictions). But this is to burden the notion of equilibrium with policy considerations. If we wish to denote an exchange rate which clears the market at full employment or without exchange restrictions, we should use some such term as the *full-employment equilibrium exchange rate* or the *free-trade equilibrium exchange rate*.

We should note that our definition of an equilibrium exchange rate has several pitfalls. First, any shift in the supply or demand curve owing, for example, to a change in tastes, can be offset by a change in levels of income. There will be a different equilibrium exchange rate for every combination of the variables listed in the domestic and foreign demand equations.

Second, a given exchange rate may always be maintained by variations in trade and payments controls to offset changes in demand or supply. Part of any disequilibrium can always be suppressed by restricting the demand for imports or forcing potential importers and investors to obtain a license before they buy foreign exchange. In what follows, we shall assume that trade and payments controls are not changed, save where explicitly indicated. Specialists will say that this assumption does not solve the problem; it merely translates the problem into the task of defining an *unchanged* system of trade and payments controls—a difficult task at best. But it will serve the purposes of an introductory survey.

[5] Such a disequilibrium cannot always be measured *ex post*, by looking at official transactions in foreign exchange or at the movements of the foreign-exchange rates. A balance-of-payments disequilibrium will set up price and income movements that will shift the demand and supply schedules and will obscure part of the disequilibrium. We shall say more about these shifts later in this chapter.

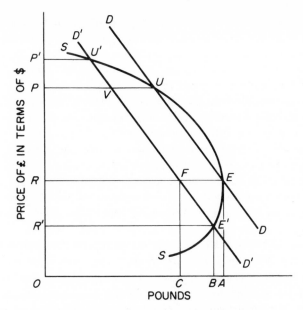

Chart 17-3: Equilibrium in the foreign market.

that the demand schedule shifts to $D'D'$. At the old exchange rate, OR, there is now an excess supply of sterling, equal to the distance EF (or AC). To preserve the exchange rate OR, the Bank of England must buy EF pounds and feed $EACF$ dollars into the market from its official reserves.

A currency whose price is too high, causing a deficit like the one described in the diagram, is sometimes said to be *overvalued*. One that is priced too low, causing a surplus, is said to be *undervalued*. A deficit or disequilibrium in Great Britain's balance of payments could go on for some time without causing much concern, but there is a limit to British reserves and to the dollars Britain can borrow from other governments and international institutions. Eventually, the British must act, to alter the positions of the curves and restore equilibrium at the exchange rate OR, or to let the exchange rate leave OR and achieve a new equilibrium at OR'.[6] In later sections of this chapter we shall examine the several ways in which public policy can shift the curves so as to prevent a loss of reserves and to maintain the existing exchange rate. In the balance of this section, we shall study the use of changes in exchange rates as a method for combatting balance-of-payments disequilibria.

Flexible exchange rates and payments equilibrium. The Bank of England could deal with the disequilibrium implied by the gap EF by with-

---

[6] There is a third possibility—to ration the available supply of foreign currency by means of exchange control. This is what Great Britain and other countries did during and after World War II. In recent years, however, most major countries have been moving away from exchange control toward the use of the market mechanism as the way to combat payments crises.

drawing from the market and permitting supply and demand to establish a new equilibrium. Were the Bank to cease buying pounds at the exchange rate OR, there would be downward pressure on the price of sterling, and the price of the pound would fall to OR'. At that price, a new equilibrium would be established; demand and supply are each equal to OB pounds per unit of time.

Many economists advocate this approach to balance-of-payments problems, regarding it as a way to avoid direct controls and the painful income changes that may be required to shift the demand and supply curves. There are, however, objections to exchange-rate adjustment by free-market forces.

First, the market for foreign exchange may be unstable. Suppose that the initial equilibrium had been at OP rather than OR. With a leftward shift in the demand for pounds, there will be an excess supply of pounds in the market— of UV pounds per unit of time. The nearest equilibrium is at the price OP'— at a higher price of sterling—but the market will not find it. In a competitive market, excess supply will drive down the price and there will be a drastic fall in the price of sterling, from OP to OR'. The market will impose heavy costs on the British consumer by raising the home prices of imported goods.

This is the possibility to which we alluded in Chapter 16. It can arise whenever the sum of demand and supply elasticities for foreign currency is negative. At point U in Chart 17-3, the supply curve is flatter than the demand curve and negatively sloped; the supply elasticity is negative and larger in absolute value than the demand elasticity. The sum of the elasticities is negative and the market for foreign exchange is unstable.[7]

Next, one must alow for the influence of speculation, which may operate to drive the exchange rate in the wrong direction or to push it in the right direction, but past the new equilibrium level. Suppose, once more, that the price of the pound is OR in Chart 17-3 and that there is a drop in the demand for sterling. As the price of the pound begins to fall toward OR', holders of sterling may begin to unload their balances, so that the price of sterling may be driven below OR'.[8] Speculation of this kind could induce larger shifts in the

---

[7] Using the derivation in footnote 3, above, this condition may be translated into another statement—one that is often employed in international-trade theory. If the foreign-exchange market is to be stable:

$$\varepsilon + \eta' > 0$$

But η' is equal to $\epsilon' - 1$, where ε' is the foreigners' elasticity of demand for foreign exchange. Hence, the above condition may be rewritten as:

$$\varepsilon + \varepsilon' - 1 > 0 \qquad \text{or} \qquad \varepsilon + \varepsilon' > 1$$

This says that the sum of the two demand elasticities (the elasticity of American demand for pounds and the elasticity of British demand for dollars) must sum to more than unity if depreciation is to improve the balance of payments. This condition, often called the Marshall-Lerner-Robinson condition, after the three economists who derived it independently, is a sufficient condition for successful depreciation or devaluation.

[8] Such a speculative assault upon sterling may be shown in the diagram by a further temporary shift in the demand curve for pounds—a movement to the left of $D'D'$.

allocation of resources than those that are required by changes in economic conditions, because they could cause wider fluctuations in exchange rates than those that are warranted by basic supply and demand changes. If, of course, speculators buy sterling as its price falls (in the expectation of a later price increase) and sell it as its price rises (in the expectation of a later price decline), they will narrow exchange-rate fluctuations. Speculation can be equilibrating. Experience with the Canadian exchange rate in the 1950's is heartening. Although free to fluctuate widely, the price of the Canadian dollar moved within a rather narrow range. Yet a steady inflow of capital from the United States kept the Canadian dollar at a premium in relation to the United States dollar; there were no large disturbances to produce significant fluctuations in its price and thereby to induce large-scale speculation. Hence, we do not know how speculators would have behaved in the event of major changes in supply or demand.

Theorizing on this point is not much more helpful. Some economists have maintained that speculation must be equilibrating, as speculators operating any other way would soon vanish. They argue that speculation can be disequilibrating only if speculators buy a currency when its price is high and sell that currency when its price is low, in which case they will suffer losses and will eventually go broke. Unfortunately, the problem is a bit more complex than this argument implies. Speculation can be disequilibrating (in that it widens exchange-rate fluctuations) if speculators sell foreign currency as its price *falls* and buy foreign currency as its price *rises*. This is not the same as buying high and selling low. Dealers can buy on the upswing, but when price is still low, and sell on the downswing, but when price is still high relative to the price at which they bought. Speculators who operate to widen exchange-rate fluctuations need not go broke; they can make a profit (though not the largest profit).[9]

The adjustable peg. There is another method of exchange-rate adjustment that can be used to correct balance-of-payments disequilibria. Instead of withdrawing from the foreign-exchange market and allowing the forces of supply and demand to produce an equilibrium price, a government might try to estimate that equilibrium price and to reset its support price accordingly. If, as in Chart 17-3, the British government finds itself forced to buy pounds in support of the price *OR,* it can establish a new price for pounds in the neigh-

---

[9] This paragraph derives from a series of theoretical examples offered by William J. Baumol ("Speculation, Profitability and Stability," *Review of Economics and Statistics,* August 1957). In these examples, Baumol confronts the speculators with price movements generated by ordinary, nonspeculative transactions and asks how the activities of speculators will affect those price movements. His examples have been criticized on two grounds. First, his speculators may never realize their profits (they will, instead, continue to accumulate foreign exchange), and the price of foreign exchange will go on rising. Second, his "nonspeculators" base theis own transactions on the trend in the exchange rate, not just the current rate, and are, to that extent, making speculative judgments. For a more thorough discussion of Baumol's exampler (and a counterexample in which speculation is equilibrating regardless of timing), see Lester G. Telser, "A Theory of Speculation Relating Profitability and Stability," *Review of Economics and Statistics,* August 1959.

borhood of *OR'*, instead of permitting the private dealers to seek out that new price by competitive trading. Periodic changes in support price are more common than flexible exchange rates. They are the method of exchange-rate adjustment envisaged by the Articles of Agreement of the International Monetary Fund. Governments are supposed to obtain IMF approval for changes in exchange rates larger than 10 per cent of "par",[10] but the Agreement prefers periodic adjustments in par values to a continuous adjustment by way of private dealings; it prefers *devaluation* to *depreciation*.[11]

Occasional adjustments in support prices might meet one of the two difficulties posed by flexible exchange rates. If the price of the pound were at *OP* in Chart 17-3, and there were an decrease in the demand for sterling that called for a new equilibrium price at *OP'*, governments could make an adjustment in exchange rates that could not be brought about by private dealings. Private dealers would bid down the price of sterling, instead of raising it to *OP'*. Governments, by contrast, could set the price at *OP'* and thereby achieve a new equilibrium with the smallest change in rates. To fix the support price at *OP'*, however, governments would have to know much more about market conditions than is usually known by governments or dealers. It would have to have data on demand and supply elasticities, as well as a forecast of dealers' behavior. In practice, then, governments are not likely to strike the right price. They are apt to overshoot the mark, as some say Britain did in its 1949 devaluation, or to fall short of the right price, so that a second devaluation is needed later on.

Periodic adjustments, moreover, invite a form of speculation that is always disequilibrating. Traders who anticipate a devaluation are apt to sell the currency whose price is expected to fall. This will put additional pressure on the price of that currency and on reserves, and may force a devaluation that might otherwise be resisted. This sort of speculation is quite likely because the speculator is offered an irresistible proposition—a "heads I win, tails you lose" gamble on the exchange rate. If he guesses right on government policy (if the support price is lowered), he makes a large windfall profit by selling the currency in question and buying it back at a lower price. If he is wrong in forecasting policy (if the support price is not lowered), he has only to reconstitute his holdings of the currency after the devaluation scare is over. The only costs of speculation are the commissions that a speculator must pay to sell a currency and buy it back if he is proved wrong.

---

[10]In some cases, especially in 1949, the IMF had no choice but to accept large exchange-rate changes. Otherwise, the governments involved would have gone ahead in defiance of the Fund. More recently, the IMF would seem to have exerted considerable influence on exchange-rate policy. It has begun to modify its position on flexible exchange rates, mainly by allowing several underdeveloped countries to adopt fluctuating rates in lieu of multiple-rate systems and other discriminatory devices.

[11]The uncompromising position adopted in the Articles of Agreement doubtless reflects the governments' dissatisfaction with the flexible exchange-rate systems that were tried in the 1930's. During the decade 1929–39, but especially after 1931, a number of governments adopted flexible exchange rates. The result (to be described in Chapter 18) was unsatisfactory.

The postwar history of sterling lends support to this criticism of the adjustable peg. In each of Britain's postwar payments crises, there has been heavy speculation against sterling. In 1949, Britain ran a deficit in her balance of payments, partly because of the United States' recession. She might have survived her difficulties without devaluation if her foreign-exchange holdings had not been eroded by speculation, as well as by her payments deficit. Holders of sterling sold it in the foreign-exchange market, and Britain's debtors held off paying what they owed, hoping that they could buy the sterling they needed at a much lower price in terms of other currencies. This bear speculation greatly increased the outflow of reserves and forced devaluation.[12] In 1951 and 1955, similar speculative outbursts aggravated Britain's balance-of-payments deficits and enlarged her reserve losses, bringing Britain closer to devaluation than she would otherwise have been. The British government had to impose stringent monetary policies, costly in income and employment, in order to preserve the exchange rate. In 1956 (during the Suez crisis), and in the summer of 1957, there was renewed speculative pressure against the pound, even though Britain's balance of payments was in good condition. During the 1960's, moreover, the British payments deficit worsened and the pound faced three severe speculative attacks. In late 1964, the uncertainty created by domestic economic difficulties was compounded by the election of a new Labour government. In 1966, wage increases, a seamen's strike, and the Rhodesian crisis brought speculative activity to another peak. Britain's balance of payments position deteriorated sharply in 1967. Aggravated by several factors—the closing of the Suez canal after the Arab-Israeli war, the American and West German economic slowdowns, and a nationwide dock workers walkout—the trade gap in October was the worst in more than three years. Massive speculative pressures finally forced Britain to devalue the pound again in November 1967.

Income, Expenditure, and the Balance of Payments

Income changes and payments adjustment.   While there are important obstacles to changing exchange rates as a way to secure equilibrium in the balance of payments, this approach to the problem of payments adjustment has gained much popularity in recent years. The alternative methods of payments adjustment are still more difficult to use. Controls on foreign trade and the rationing of scarce foreign exchange tend to provoke retaliation by other countries and badly distort trade patterns. In addition, they are very difficult to admin-

---

[12]We are not arguing that the devaluation was wrong or unnecessary. Price changes in Britain, compared with those in the outside world, may have required a devaluation of the pound sterling. But the decision was made in haste, under speculative pressure, and the price of sterling was reduced somewhat more than might have been necessary to correct the payments position.

ister. A government cannot effectively conserve foreign exchange by regulating some transactions and not others; a prohibited transaction can often be disguised so as to slip into an approved category.[13] At the same time, monetary and fiscal policies, while capable of restoring equilibrium in the balance of payments, may do so at the cost of unemployment and a reduction in real income.

To reveal the connection between monetary policies and the balance of payments, we must go back to the basic equation that defines national income. In Chapter 16, we presented a revised income equation that defined the gross national product as a sum of consumer, business, and government spending $(C + I + G)$ and of export receipts *less* import outlays $(X - M)$. We suggested that total domestic spending, $C + I + G$, could be denoted by a single letter, H, so that income might be redefined as total domestic spending on home products $(H - M)$ plus foreign spending on home products (X).

Let us now divide total domestic spending into two parts: H^a and H^d, using H^a to denote the autonomous part of total domestic spending—the part that does not depend on national income[14]—and H^d to denote the part that does depend on the national income. Let us also suppose that H^d is a linear function of national income:

$$H^d = cY$$

The coefficient c in this equation is similar to the Keynesian "marginal propensity to consume." It is the ratio of additional spending to additional income, just as the "marginal propensity to consume" is the ratio of additional consumer spending to additional consumer income. By the same token, the complement of c (that is, $1 - c$) is analogous to the Keynesian "marginal propensity to save." It is the fraction of extra income that is not spent, and will be denoted by s in our analysis.[15]

We may also divide M into two parts: M^a which is independent of income, and M^d which depends on income. Induced import spending, M^d, may be written as a linear function of income:

$$M^d = mY$$

---

[13]Controls over foreign investment, for example, can often be evaded by falsifying documents pertaining to commodity trade. If import spending is not closely controlled, an importer can obtain funds for the purpose of foreign investment by reporting his purchases abroad at a higher price than he will actually have to pay.

[14]This term H^a is the total of business investment (I), government spending (G), and that level of consumer spending which would occur at zero income (from the origin of a consumption-function diagram to the intersection of the consumption function with the vertical axis).

[15]Note, however, that if investment is dependent on the level of income, s will be smaller than the "marginal propensity to save." Our s represents "net domestic leakage"—saving resulting from an increase of income less the offsets to saving that are also the result of an increase of income.

The coefficient m in this equation is known as the "marginal propensity to import."

We could go on to divide X into two parts—that which is independent of income and that which depends on national income by way of its connection to income abroad and, therefore, to foreigners' import spending. Here, however, we shall treat X as though it were entirely autonomous. We shall neglect the foreign repercussions of an income change.[16]

We can now replace H and M in the income equation with the separate components of H and M, and can then replace H^d and M^d with their equivalents, cY and mY:

$$Y = H^a - M^a + X + H^d - M^d = H^a - M^a + X + cY - mY$$

Next, we can rewrite the income equation in terms of small changes (Δ's), can regroup terms, and can solve the equation for changes in income:

$$\Delta Y = \Delta H^a - \Delta M^a + \Delta X + c\Delta Y - m\Delta Y$$

$$\Delta Y(1 - c + m) = \Delta H^a - \Delta M^a + \Delta X$$

$$\Delta Y = \frac{\Delta H^a - \Delta M^a + \Delta X}{1 - c + m}$$

This final equation is similar to the multiplier equation developed in Part II. The multiplier here, however, is $\dfrac{1}{1 - c + m}$, which is smaller than the corresponding multiplier for a closed economy, $\dfrac{1}{1 - c}$. This is because there are two leakages from the income stream of an open economy. First, we have the net domestic leakage, $1 - c$ or s, which is roughly equivalent to saving in a closed economy. Second, we have an import leakage, m, which has no counterpart in a closed economy. In what follows, we shall write the foreign trade multiplier in terms of these leakages, replacing $1 - c$ with the net domestic leakage denoted by s.

We may write another equation to describe the impact of the disturbances ΔH^a, ΔM^a, and ΔX on the current-account balance of payments. First, define a change in the current-account balance as:

$$\Delta B = \Delta X - \Delta M$$

But ΔM is divisible into $\Delta M^a + m\Delta Y$, and $m\Delta Y$ is equivalent to $\dfrac{m}{s + m}$ $(\Delta H^a - \Delta M^a + \Delta X)$. Hence, the balance-of-payments equation turns into:

---

[16]These, however, are considered in an algebraic note at the end of this chapter.

$$\Delta B = \Delta X - \Delta M^a - \frac{m}{s+m}(\Delta H^a - \Delta M^a + \Delta X)$$

$$\Delta B = \Delta X\left(1 - \frac{m}{s+m}\right) - \Delta M^a\left(1 - \frac{m}{s+m}\right) - \frac{m}{s+m}\Delta H^a$$

$$= \frac{s}{s+m}(\Delta X - \Delta M^a) - \frac{m}{s+m}\Delta H^a$$

Now we can calculate the changes in income and in the current-account balance that are caused by a change in total spending, ΔH^a, a diversion of spending from home goods to imports, ΔM^a, and a change in exports, ΔX. For a change in home spending, for example, we set ΔM^a and ΔX equal to zero, and ask what the change in income will be per dollar of extra home spending. This change is $\frac{1}{s+m}$ dollars per dollar of extra home spending, and the corresponding change in the current account is $\frac{-m}{s+m}$. These solutions are reproduced in the first row of Table 17-1, under columns (2) and (3). Column (2) tells us how income will change per dollar of disturbance; column (3) tells us how the current account will change per dollar of the same disturbance. The remaining lines in Table 17-1 give comparable data for other disturbances.

Table 17-1 contains much interesting information. Note, for instance, that the decrease of income that is caused by an increase of imports helps to offset the impact of that import increase on the current-account balance. Were income unaffected by an increase of imports, the current-account balance would deteriorate by ΔM^a. As income is reduced, however, there is a secondary fall in the level of imports, so that the final deterioration in the current account is only $\frac{-s}{m+s}$ of the initial import increase. In short, the induced income change has an equilibrating effect on the current account and, in consequence, on the overall balance of payments. An increase of exports has an analogous effect. It stimulates income and imports, reducing the favorable balance which extra exports create.

If there were no net domestic leakage (if s were zero), the expressions in column (3) would be radically different. An increase of domestic spending would worsen the current-account balance by an amount exactly equal to the increase of home spending. This is because an injection of spending would induce successive rounds of spending and raise the national income until the import leakage out of income had risen to offset fully the initial injection of domestic spending. The process would be perfectly analogous to that which we described in Part II. In the case of extra import spending, ΔM^a, or an export boom, ΔX, there would be another startling change in the current-account entry. In each instance, ΔB would go to zero, bringing the current-account balance back into equilibrium. An autonomous increase of imports would

TABLE 17-1

EXPENDITURE DISTURBANCES, THE NATIONAL INCOME, AND THE CURRENT-ACCOUNT BALANCE*

(changes in dollars per dollar of disturbance)

Nature of Disturbance	Effect on		Change in Domestic Spending Needed to Offset Effect on Current-Account Balance	Effect of (4) on National Income	Change in Domestic Spending Needed to Offset Effect on National Income	Effect of (6) on Current-Account Balance
	National Income	Current-Account Balance				
(1)	(2)	(3)	(4)	(5)	(6)	(7)
Increase of autonomous domestic expenditure (ΔH^a)	$\dfrac{1}{m+s}$	$\dfrac{-m}{m+s}$	-1	$\dfrac{-1}{m+s}$	-1	$\dfrac{m}{m+s}$
Increase of autonomous import expenditure (ΔM^a)	$\dfrac{-1}{m+s}$	$\dfrac{-s}{m+s}$	$\dfrac{-s}{m}$	$\dfrac{-s}{m(m+s)}$	1	$\dfrac{-m}{m+s}$
Increase of export receipts (ΔX)	$\dfrac{1}{m+s}$	$\dfrac{s}{m+s}$	$\dfrac{s}{m}$	$\dfrac{s}{m(m+s)}$	-1	$\dfrac{m}{m+s}$

*Neglecting foreign repercussions (treating export changes as autonomous). For the corresponding expressions when foreign repercussions are taken into account, see the algebraic note at the end of this chapter. Effects of disturbances are measured in terms of the marginal propensity to save, s, and the marginal propensity to import, m; for definitions, see text.

cut back income until it had generated an induced decline of imports just large enough to offset the extra autonomous import spending. An autonomous increase in exports would raise the national income and generate extra import spending just large enough to offset the increase of exports. In the absence of domestic leakages, expenditure disturbances on the balance of payments would be self-correcting, but the restoration of payments equilibrium would be at the expense of income and employment or, in the case of an export increase, would be inflationary.

Further effects of disequilibrium. In practice, of course, domestic leakages occur, so balance-of-payments disturbances like those we have considered are not self-correcting. The income changes brought about by autonomous shifts in home spending, exports, or imports leave a continuing disequilibrium in the current account and, as a consequence, in the overall balance of payments. But these same shifts in spending and the balance-of-payments disequilibria to which they give rise. They affect the stock of money, interest rates, and the availability of credit, and do so in ways that help to restore equilibrium in the balance of payments and foreign-exchange market.

A good starting point for the analysis of these phenomena is the fact, already mentioned, that stabilization of the exchange rate requires official intervention in the foreign-exchange market. When central banks intervene in that market, bank reserves must change, forcing a contraction of the money stock in the country with a payments deficit and allowing an increase in the country with a payments surplus.[17] Whether by way of the interest-investment nexus, the real-balance effect, or credit flows, this change in money stocks will alter the level of spending in each country. There will be a secondary decrease of domestic spending (ΔH^a) in the country with a payments deficit and a secondary increase of domestic spending in the country with a payments surplus. These secondary changes will act to restore equilibrium on the balance of payments.

Suppose that there is a deficit in the balance of payments and that bank reserves shrink because the government is buying its own currency in the foreign-exchange market to support the exchange rate. The money stock will probably decline, raising interest rates, reducing real balances, and limiting the banks' ability to lend. This means a fall in domestic spending (a negative ΔH^a) that will operate to improve the current account and to reduce the balance-of-payments deficit; a decrease of domestic spending will improve the balance of payments by $\dfrac{m}{s + m}$ dollars per dollar of decrease in domestic spending.

These monetary counterparts of disequilibrium in the foreign-exchange market will continue to operate for as long as there is need of official interven-

---

[17]This assumes that the central bank does not operate to neutralize the bank-reserve effect of a change in foreign exchange or gold holdings. It also assumes that the banking systems of both countries are fully loaded up at the start.

tion. They will exert a smaller additional impact in each successive period, for the money-stock changes will grow smaller as the payments deficit is closed. They operate, however, in a cumulative fashion and will go on working until the deficit vanishes. The money stock of the deficit country will continue to shrink until governments withdraw from the foreign-exchange market; the money stock of the surplus country will continue to grow.

Columns (4) and (5) of Table 17-1 can be used to analyze this monetary counterpart of payments disequilibrium. The first entry in column (4) shows that a balance-of-payments deficit resulting from an increase of domestic spending must give rise to a matching decrease in domestic spending if payments equilibrium is to be restored. This can be accomplished by money-stock changes. Column (5) shows that the requisite decrease of spending will just offset the income effect of the initial increase in domestic spending. In the jargon of international economics, the monetary counterparts of a deficit resulting from changes in domestic spending will restore *internal balance* as they re-establish *external balance*.

Money-stock changes can also offset the payments impact of an increase in imports or exports. In these cases, however, those changes will intensify the conflict between internal and external balance. The changes in domestic spending needed to offset an import increase will reduce the national income while they work to erase the payments deficit. Column (5) of Table 17-1 indicates that the necessary change in domestic spending will reduce income by $\dfrac{s}{m\,(m+s)}$ dollars per dollar increase in imports. This implies a combined reduction of $\dfrac{m+s}{m\,(m+s)}$ or—dollars per dollar of import increase—a larger reduction than that which was caused by the initial increase in imports.

Built in monetary changes may occur too slowly to satisfy a government having payments problems. In this case, the government may use the weapons of monetary policy to reinforce the built-in monetary changes. If, for example, a deficit appears on the balance of payments, the central bank can raise interest rates and sell securities in the open market to produce a more rapid reduction in the money stock. Notice, however, these same monetary weapons can also be used to interfere with the restoration of payments equilibrium. A conflict in policy aims between the preservation of external and internal balance may often be resolved in favor of the latter, for most governments are committed to the preservation of full employment. In this case, the central bank may try to raise domestic spending so as to combat the income effects of an increase in imports. This is what happened in the United States during the recession of 1960–61. At that time, there was a gaping deficit in the balance of payments and a tendency for bank reserves to fall on account of the resulting gold outflow. The Federal Reserve decided to combat the recession instead of working to combat the deficit. It bought securities in the open market so as to prevent a decline in bank reserves.

Such a policy may worsen the payments deficit that caused the decline of income. The increase of domestic spending needed to offset the income effect of an increase in import spending will worsen the current account by $\dfrac{m}{m + s}$ dollars per dollar of increase in imports (see column [7] of Table 17-1). The combined deterioration in the current-account balance will amount to one full dollar per dollar of import spending, the sum of the entries in columns (3) and (7).

A conflict such as this is a frequent cause of devaluation. A country that seeks to maintain internal balance while combatting a payments deficit is obliged to act against its deficit in the foreign-exchange market, or to impose direct controls in order to stem its foreign-exchange losses.[18]

We have now described two important processes that operate to alter the current-account balance when that balance is disturbed by changes in demand for exports or imports: the income effects of the initial disturbance; and the impact of the money-stock changes set up by the disturbance (and the resulting surplus or deficit in the overall balance of payments). This description of adjustment under fixed exchange rates has to be expanded in two directions. First, we must ask how changes in internal prices can foster adjustment. Second, we must look at the capital account, as the locus of possible disturbances and as the locus of possible adjustments.

Price effects and payments adjustment. If a country is near full employment, an increase of aggregate spending, whatever its cause, is apt to generate an increase in wage rates and prices. A decrease of spending is apt to have the opposite effect, although wages and prices do not fall easily or quickly, and this opposite effect may be less significant. These two price effects can combine to rectify a surplus or deficit in a country's balance of payments.

Suppose that a country experiences an increase in world demand for its exports. Its current-account balance will show a surplus (or a smaller deficit). Total spending on its output will rise, and the increase of spending will be reinforced by the money-stock changes already discussed. If it was close to full employment before the increase in its exports, wage rates and prices will start to rise, and this will have the same effect as an appreciation of its currency in the foreign-exchange market. At any constant exchange rate, its own goods

---

[18]A country that starts out with unemployment and external balance may also have need of devaluation in order to *maintain* external balance as it acts to eradicate unemployment. An increase of home spending to create jobs is bound to produce a payments deficit, unless separate action is taken to combat that payments deficit. Note, further, that a country can turn this process on end. It can restrict imports (by tariffs, quotas, exchange controls, or devaluation) so as to raise its national income. A reduction of imports will raise the national income by $1/(m + s)$ dollars per dollar of import reduction. But this sort of policy amounts to "exporting" unemployment—to shifting the burden of unemployment from one country to its trading partners. It is sometimes called a "beggar-my-neighbor" policy and is a shortsighted way to maintain full employment. We shall have more to say about this sort of policy in the next section of this chapter and in Chapter 18.

will become more expensive relative to foreign goods, causing a reduction in the foreign demand for its exports and an increase in its own demand for imports. These changes in exports and imports will tend to restore equilibrium in the balance of payments.[19]

Price effects may not be powerful or suitable in the very short run. Wages and prices will not fall fast or far in the deficit countries because they are fairly rigid, even in the face of substantial unemployment. Wages and prices will not rise rapidly in the surplus countries as monetary and fiscal policies will be used to combat inflation. Over the longer run, however, internal price changes may have an important part to play—and may operate without absolute reductions in the money wage rate. In most industrial countries, wage rates tend to rise year after year. But this increase in wages need not cause an increase in prices if it is matched by an increase in productivity, and this also rises, year after year. If, then, there is need for a change in relative price levels—an increase in some countries' prices relative to those of other countries—the change can sometimes be accomplished by reducing the rate of increase of money wages, not cutting the wage level absolutely. If wages rise more slowly in one group of countries and the rate of growth of productivity is not affected, labor costs and prices will fall in those countries, or will rise more slowly than in other countries. Price levels can be realigned gradually, altering trade flows and the balance of payments.

Disturbance and adjustment on capital account. Capital flows can be important causes of international disequilibria and can be affected by public policies so as to restore an equilibrium. We have already mentioned one type of disturbance on capital account—speculative movements out of weak currencies in anticipation of devaluation. We have also mentioned one type of adjustment on capital account—movements of cash balances by arbitrageurs who seek to maximize interest earnings (after allowing for the cost of forward-exchange cover). We have now to mention some other disturbances and to explore the policy problems associated with attempts to alter the capital account.

There are several types of capital flow—direct investments in foreign plants, purchases of foreign securities (stocks and bonds), bank lending to finance foreign trade, interest arbitrage, and outright speculation (which may involve transactions in long-term securities or in money-market paper and bank deposits). Each type derives from different motivations. Direct investment, for example, results from a comparison of profit prospects in different countries and, increasingly, from a comparison of profits on exports to a foreign market with profits on production in that foreign market. Profit prospects, in turn, involve comparisons of prospective wage rates, labor productivity, the costs of other inputs, and national tax rates. Decisions to buy foreign securities

---

[19]The criterion for an improvement in the balance of payments through changes in domestic prices is the same as the criterion governing a change in exchange rates—the Marshall-Lerner-Robinson condition derived in footnote 7.

involve a comparison of current and prospective yields. Decisions to issue securities in a foreign market involve a comparison of interest rates and of underwriting costs (which vary widely from country to country because capital markets vary in size and efficiency). Interest arbitrage depends on a similar comparison of interest rates and on the cost of covering in the forward foreign-exchange market.[20]

Persistent differences in profitability between one country and another can generate large amounts of direct investment. In the late 1950's and early 1960's, industrial profit rates were higher in Europe than in the United States, and European markets were growing very fast. American industry responded to this situation with massive investments in European plants. During that same period, moreover, interest rates were higher in Europe, so that foreign governments, municipalities, and corporations issued new securities in the New York market. The very large capital outflow from the United States, direct and portfolio, was a major cause of the United States balance-of-payments deficit. The capital outflow, together with United States foreign aid, was larger than the current-account surplus.

There are, of course, three ways to deal with a large capital outflow. First, one could try to cut back the outflow itself. Second, one could try to attract foreign capital as a continuing offset to the outflow. Third, one could try to create a current-account surplus large enough to pay for the capital outflow. One's choice among these options will depend on several considerations. Consider the position of the United States. As a large, high-income country, it generates a very large volume of saving, and some part of that saving should perhaps flow to other countries, including the other high-income countries which generate less saving compared to their investment needs. On this view, the United States should not restrict foreign investment, but should instead enlarge its current-account surpluses. Some say, moreover, that United States investment in Europe represents an important form of financial intermediation: American savers, personal and corporate, have a taste for risk-bearing equity investments; European savers put a higher premium on safe, liquid investments. Hence, American saving flows to Europe through direct investment in manufacturing, while European saving flows to the United States through the cash account, the acquisition of money-market assets, and time deposits at American banks.[21] On this view, the United States should not restrict its capital outflow but should instead attract foreign investment in the United States—the further

---

[20]See pp. 303–304.

[21]Some who take this view go a step further. They argue that the whole United States deficit of recent years, measured by the growth of foreign official dollar holdings and the reduction of the United States gold stock, is a by-product of financial intermediation. Central banks who acquire gold and dollars are investing in liquid assets, just like individuals and corporations. For more on this view, see Charles P. Kindleberger, "Balance-of-Payments Deficits and the International Market for Liquidity," *Essays in International Finance*, No. 46 (Princeton: Princeton University Press, 1965).

accumulation of dollar bonds, money-market paper, and bank deposits—as an offset to United States direct investment in Europe and elsewhere. In brief, the right response to any disequilibrium, whether on current or capital accounts, depends on judgments as to the desirable allocation of new saving and the real resources transferred by current-account balances.

Suppose, however, that one decides to restrict an outflow of capital or to encourage an offsetting capital inflow. One could use direct controls, but these tend to break down over time (or to require a growing network of supporting regulations as investors find ways to avoid existing restrictions). One could use the tax system to reduce net profits or net yields on foreign assets. The United States has done this sort of thing. In 1962, it tightened the tax treatment of income earned on direct investments. In 1964, it imposed an interest-equalization tax to reduce the yield on foreign securities held by United States citizens: the tax is levied on the purchase price, reducing the net yield to the investor (or raising the net cost to the borrower). Finally, one could use monetary policy.

An increase in home interest rates, relative to foreign rates, will operate to cut back every form of foreign investment. Direct investment will be affected because it will be more expensive to raise the required funds. Portfolio investment, long term and short term, will be affected because domestic assets will be more attractive relative to foreign assets. But this use of monetary policy to influence the capital account raises two problems. First, there may be an offsetting change in forward foreign-exchange rates. Second, an increase of interest rates has internal costs—lower real output, higher unemployment, and slower economic growth—that cannot always be offset by changes in other economic policies.

The risk of countervailing changes in the forward foreign-exchange rate can be explained quite easily. Early in Part III, we said that an increase in one country's interest rates will cause *arbitrageurs* to buy that country's currency on the spot market and, at that same time, to sell the country's currency on the forward market. The spot purchase is required in order to acquire money-market assets. The forward sale is required in order to protect the arbitrageur against a devaluation of the currency in which he is investing. Hence, an increase in one country's interest rate will increase the spot demand for its currency and will increase the forward supply. The spot price of the currency will rise, the forward price will fall, and the forward discount (spot price *less* forward price) will grow, discouraging continued arbitrage. In order to sustain the capital inflow caused by covered arbitrage, the central bank may have to push the interest rate higher and higher, or may have to intervene in the forward foreign-exchange market, buying its own currency with foreign currency at a constant forward discount (smaller than the difference between its own interest rate and the interest rates in foreign countries). Some central banks have adopted this policy; others are reluctant to do so because they do not want to assume an ever-growing obligation to deliver foreign currency when forward contracts mature.[22]

Some of the domestic costs of high interest rates can be offset by resort to the other instruments of economic policy. A decrease of tax rates to stimulate domestic consumption, domestic investment, or both, will help to sustain output and employment. An increase of government spending will have similar effects. In general terms, fiscal policies can be assigned to stabilize aggregate demand when monetary policy has been assigned to alter the capital account and stabilize the balance of payments. There is an *optimum policy mix* for each combination of internal and external aims.[23] Notice, however, that one cannot be indifferent to the several ways of using fiscal policy for internal balance. A decrease of personal tax rates that increases household spending on consumer goods does not offset the growth-depressing effects of high interest rates; a decrease in corporate taxes that increases investment would be a better choice. Note, too, that major changes in fiscal policy are time consuming. It took two years for Congress to approve the tax reductions of 1962 and 1964.

The International Spread of Business Fluctuations

Income effects and the transmission of business fluctuations.   Because income changes in one country affect its demand for imports, and one country's imports are another's exports, income changes in one country affect income levels abroad. An increase of income in one country (a positive ΔH^a) increases that country's imports by $\left(\dfrac{m}{m+s}\Delta H^a\right)$. This increase of imports is an increase of exports by some other country and augments the national income of that other country by a multiple of the increase in its exports.[24]

The monetary counterparts of an autonomous increase in income and of the resulting payments deficit also act to increase income abroad. A deficit in one country's balance of payments is a surplus for some other country and

---

[22]Notice, however, that a successful combination of interest-rate policy and forward-exchange policy will bring foreign currency into the central bank (there will be excess demand for the country's own currency on the spot market). This increase in foreign-currency reserves is ample backing for the central bank's forward commitments.

[23]For more on the *optimum policy mix,* including the dynamic properties of a system in which monetary policy for external balance is run by the central bank and fiscal policy for internal balance is run by the treasury, see Robert A. Mundell, "Monetary and Fiscal Policy for Internal and External Stability," *International Monetary Fund Staff Papers,* March 1962, pp. 70–79.

[24]As a first approximation to that increase of income, we may multiply the first country's additional imports by the income multiplier for an increase in exports given in column (2) of Table 17-1. We multiply $\{[m/(m+s)]\Delta H^a\}$ by $1/(m'+s')$, where m' and s' are the import and domestic leakages of the second country. This gives us $m\,\Delta H^a/(m+s)(m'+s')$. More accurate formulae, allowing for further repercussions, are set out in the algebraic note at the end of this chapter.

is apt to increase bank reserves in that other country, stimulating spending and lending, and producing a secondary income effect in the other country. This mechanism for the spread of fluctuations from country to country is not so rigid as to make output and prices move uniformly. While the 1929 peak in the United States represented virtual full employment, the next high point (1936–37) was a "submerged peak" with considerable unemployment. In Great Britain, however, the 1937 peak came about as close to full employment as that of 1929.[25] But there is a striking similarity in the prewar business annals of the United States, England, France, Germany, and Austria. They all show a peak in 1872–73, a depression in 1874–77, another peak in 1881–82, and a depression in 1884–85; peaks in 1889–90, 1899–1900, and 1906–07, a depression in 1908, and a peak in 1912–13.[26] The interwar period displays a similar coincidence of turning points, although not as close as in the prewar annals.

This record suggests that we need to look for four sorts of forces that affect the timing of fluctuations in different countries.

1. International factors that work parallel in different countries *without* going through the nextwork of world trade: wars and threats of war, changes in productive methods, shifts in labor relations, and so forth.
2. Local factors that bring diversity in the timing of fluctuations: booms in real estate and securities, local financial panics, technical developments in localized industries, crop variations, and elections.
3. International developments which benefit one country at the expense of another: devaluations, tariff changes, and other protectionist devices; the effects of depression on the prices that industrial countries pay for raw materials.
4. International developments by which one nation's booms or slumps cause *parallel* movements in other countries.

Items (3) and (4) are the immediate concern of international monetary policy, but (1) and (2) may greatly influence the overall outcome.

The United States as a source of fluctuations. There has been a tendency to picture the United States as the villain of international monetary history, a way of thinking especially fashionable among Europeans since World War II. Economists in Europe have been somewhat complacent about their ability to maintain full employment given external stability. They are still skeptical about

---

[25]Sir William Beveridge, in *Full Employment in a Free Society* (New York: W. W. Norton & Company, Inc., 1945), p. 111, shows that 1.25 million were unemployed in Great Britain in 1929, and 1.56 million in 1937. The percentage of workers unemployed (*ibid.,* p. 47) was 10.4 per cent in 1929 and 10.8 per cent in 1937. In the United States, according to B.L.S. estimates, 1929 unemployment was under 3 per cent; 1937 unemployment was about 13 per cent.

[26]Willard L. Thorp, *Business Annals* (New York: National Bureau of Economic Research, 1926), pp. 78–84.

the ability of the United States. Their concern was reinforced by our 1949 recession and the inflation of 1950–51.[27]

The very mild American recession of 1948–49 was associated with a stiff loss of exports for foreign countries. Measured by quarterly estimates of gross national product in current dollars, the recession amounted to a mere 4 per cent drop from peak to trough. From October 1948 to June 1949, however, United States imports of goods and services dropped by 10 per cent in dollar value, and our imports from some European countries fell by as much as a third. Not all of this drop was caused directly by the recession in current consumption of imported goods. The direct effects of the recession gave credence to (accurate) rumors that European currencies would be devalued, and these rumors gave American importers an incentive to sell off their inventories and replenish them later.

The post-Korean inflation of 1950–51 gave foreigners another reason for concern. American attempts to build up inventories pushed raw-material prices sky-high, and the resulting rise in the dollar value of United States imports, combined with the after-effects of the 1949 devaluations, brought a sharp improvement in Europe's international position. Britain was so much better off at the end of 1950 that American aid was ended. But during 1951–52, Britain and the outer sterling area felt a backlash from the boom. Raw-material prices dropped sharply, pushing Britain and the sterling area into deep difficulties.

Assuming that major American fluctuations are a thing of the past would not be prudent. Some of the factors which made us unstable in the prewar and interwar periods are still at work, and we have not yet confronted a rigorous test of our ability and willingness to combat a massive swing in aggregate demand. Nor can we neglect the likelihood that fluctuations will arise elsewhere in the world. International disturbances are still reciprocal. In fact, the balance between Europe and the United States may have shifted in the 1950's. We have had recessions, but so have the countries of Europe, and their 1958 recession reduced United States exports by more than our own recession reduced United States imports.[28] The global recession of 1957–58 adversely affected the United States balance of payments, not the European balance of payments.

Policies to combat the spread of fluctuations. A nation that confronts the prospect of depression, because of a recession or stagnation abroad and a reduction of its exports, can select one of four policies. First, it can accept

---

[27]What may be more important, the less-developed countries doubt that the industrial countries, as a group, can grow steadily enough to provide expanding markets for raw materials and tropical foodstuffs—the principal exports of the less-developed countries—and postwar experience has given them ample reason for concern. Their export prices and proceeds have been very sensitive to mild fluctuations in levels and growth rates of aggregate demand in the industrial world. Their exports dropped sharply during the 1957–58 recessions in Europe and the United States and another smaller drop occurred in 1966–67 when the industrial economies grew rather slowly.

[28]Our total imports were strongly bolstered by the flood of automobile imports; the public shopped abroad for compact cars when Detroit was slow to produce them.

a reduction of its own income as the way to maintain external balance. Second, it can retreat behind trade controls, to bolster domestic spending as a substitute for exports and reduce imports so as to conserve foreign-exchange reserves. Third, it can devalue its currency to augment its exports and reduce its imports. Finally, it can allow the burden to fall on its balance of payments; it can bolster domestic spending but not cut its imports, thereby sustaining an outflow of foreign-exchange reserves.

The first of these policies is virtually impracticable under conditions prevailing today. Most major countries, whether developed or underdeveloped, are committed to preserve high levels of national income and to combat unemployment by every available method. They cannot put the maintenance of payments equilibrium ahead of their commitment to domestic prosperity.[29]

Many countries chose the second or third options during the Great Depression of the 1930's. Each nation sought to battle the Depression on its own. One after another, they resorted to exchange controls, import restrictions, or devaluation.

Exchange control began to be important with the "Stand-still Agreement" of 1931,[30] which authorized the German authorities to prevent the use of foreign exchange earned by Germans for the repayment of foreign debts (except for the gradual retirement of debts under the agreement itself). Transfer of German funds owned by non-Germans was also restricted. The agreement aimed to make German holdings of foreign currencies, including export proceeds, freely available to pay for German imports. These controls were tightened by the Nazi government and were extended to countries under Nazi influence. "Second-class citizens" who wanted to emigrate were allowed to convert a mere fraction of their property into foreign funds, and had to hand over most of the remainder to pay for the privilege. Limitations on the use of funds to buy certain imports were used ruthlessly to influence foreign governments.[31]

During World War II, the United States and other allied countries were forced to use similar controls. Funds belonging to Axis nationals were frozen so that they could not be used to buy supplies for the Nazi war machine. The

---

[29]We should at once add that these objectives may not be in conflict. If, for example, a payments deficit is caused by excessive domestic spending—if the nation is "living beyond its means"—deflationary policies that restore external balance are not inconsistent with the full-employment pledge. We have already seen that a domestic boom and the consequent balance-of-payments deficit can both be combatted by a reduction of domestic spending. This was the lesson offered by the formulae on the first line of Table 17-1.

[30]At about the same time, exchange control was adopted in the raw-material countries of Latin America and in some countries of Eastern Europe.

[31]A further development under the Nazis was the bilateral "exchange clearing." Countries such as Yugoslavia, whose exports to Germany exceeded imports from Germany, were required to put the proceeds of sales to Germany into special clearing accounts under German control. A stated percentage of the balance in this clearing account had to be spent on German goods. In effect, the poor countries that were forced into these clearings found themselves obliged to lend to Germany. When German export deliveries fell behind schedule, these countries piled up clearing balances that could not be used to buy goods elsewhere.

funds of some friendly countries were frozen too. Great Britain ran up debts to India and Egypt for raw materials and for the maintenance of troops stationed in those countries. By agreement, the proceeds of British military spending went into *blocked sterling*. Latin American suppliers of food and raw materials accepted some payments in this same form. These blocked sterling balances, amounting to £3 billion or nearly $14 billion, were a great barrier to the relaxation of exchange control after the war. If these funds had been released suddenly, the great bulk would have been converted into dollars, more than absorbing the proceeds of the United States' loan to Britain in 1946, and greatly increasing the pressure on scarce American export goods. When the British did relax their exchange controls in the summer of 1947, a massive run on sterling forced the reimposition of exchange restrictions after merely six weeks of limited convertibility. Finally, Britain and other European countries restricted their own residents' access to foreign funds and required that exporters surrender their foreign-currency earnings.

During the 1950's, the European governments worked with patience and imagination to dismantle these exchange controls and to restore full convertibility. At the beginning of the 1950's they established a European Payments Union to facilitate the movement of funds within Europe. Later, they liberalized their import restrictions on American goods and made the terms of settlement within EPU more closely comparable to those that would prevail under complete convertibility. At the end of 1958, they gave outsiders virtual freedom to deal in European currencies, and some of them removed the remaining restrictions on purchases and sales by their own citizens.

The experience of the 1930's and of the early postwar years has made most governments wary of exchange control and of devaluation. Too often, they were used aggressively, and even when employed defensively, they tended to worsen the position of some other country and to provoke retaliation.

Riding out periods of disequilibrium.   Bound by commitments to full employment, to liberal trade policies, and to stable exchange rates, governments today must adopt the fourth option—to ride out foreign business fluctuations as balance-of-payments disequilibria. There have been tentative efforts to organize an international policy toward business fluctuations, but these have not borne fruit. A closer coordination of monetary and fiscal policies is emerging within the European Common Market. But attempts at close coordination between Western Europe and the United States have not yet succeeded. There has been much discussion of national policies in the Organization for Economic Cooperation and Development (OECD), but there have been no substantial changes in national attitudes. Still less can we expect global efforts, embracing the low-income countries of Asia, Africa, and Latin America. For the present, seemingly, the best that we can do is to improve the arrangements enabling each country to ride out balance-of-payments disturbances. Governments must be assured of access to adequate foreign-exchange reserves. This is the problem of world liquidity that will occupy our attention in the final chapter of Part III.

NOTES ON
ALTERNATIVE POINTS OF VIEW
AND SUPPLEMENTARY READING

The processes of adjustment discussed in this chapter are described in more detail by James E. Meade, *The Balance of Payments,* Volume I of *The Theory of International Economic Policy* (London: Oxford University Press, 1951). The notion of an equilibrium exchange rate (and a somewhat different definition of equilibrium than the one we have used) is discussed by Ragnar Nurkse, *Conditions of International Monetary Equilibrium* (reprinted in *Readings in the Theory of International Trade* [New York: McGraw-Hill Book Company, Inc., 1949]).

The case for flexible exchange rates is set out by Milton Friedman, *Essays in Positive Economics* (Chicago: University of Chicago Press, 1953), pp. 157–203. See, too, Egon Sohmen, *Flexible Exchange Rates: Theory and Controversy* (Chicago: University of Chicago Press, 1961); Sohmen has much to say on speculation and on the forward foreign-exchange market. On Canada's experience with flexible exchange rates and speculation, see Paul Wonnacott, *The Canadian Dollar, 1958–1962* (Toronto: University of Toronto Press, 1965). The use of fiscal and monetary policies for internal and external balance is analyzed by Robert A. Mundell, "Monetary and Fiscal Policy for Internal and External Stability," *International Monetary Fund Staff Papers,* March 1962.

On the observed historical connection between business cycles in different countries, see W. L. Thorp, *Business Annals* (New York: National Bureau of Economic Research, 1926). On the cyclical behavior of U.S. exports, see Ilse Mintz, *Cyclical Fluctuations in the Exports of the United States Since 1879* (New York: National Bureau of Economic Research, 1967). Experience with exchange control in the 1930's and postwar years is described in several of the works listed at the end of the next chapter. The impact of the 1950–51 inflation on Britain and the sterling area is described by P. B. Kenen, *British Monetary Policy and the Balance of Payments, 1951–57* (Cambridge: Harvard University Press, 1960), chaps. i and iii. Recent balance of payments developments are summarized in the *Annual Report* of the International Monetary Fund.

For more on the need for policy co-ordination, see Richard N. Cooper, *The Economics of Interdependence* (New York: McGraw-Hill Book Company, 1968).

AN ALGEBRAIC NOTE ON
THE FOREIGN-TRADE MULTIPLIER
WITH FOREIGN REPERCUSSIONS

The multiplier formulae used in the text of Chapter 17 neglected the "feedback" of spending that occurs when the income of one country changes, changing the exports and incomes of other countries. A change in expenditure by one country alters its imports, other countries' exports, and hence the income levels of other countries. A part of the change in other countries' incomes is then fed back into the income stream of the first country by way of an increase in the other countries' imports.

In order to appraise the impact of these feedbacks upon the argument of

Chapter 17, we shall now develop foreign-trade multipliers that take explicit account of the feedback effects. We shall look at two countries (I and II) to see how expenditure changes in the first country affect spending in the second and to examine the impact of expenditure changes in both countries on the balance of payments.

We begin with income equations just like those in the text, using the subscripts 1 and 2 to identify parameters and variables pertaining to the first and second countries:

$$\Delta Y_1 = \Delta H_1^a - \Delta M_1^a + \Delta X_1 + (1 - s_1 - m_1)\Delta Y_1 \tag{1}$$

$$\Delta Y_2 = \Delta H_2^a - \Delta M_2^a + \Delta X_2 + (1 - s_2 - m_2)\Delta Y_2 \tag{2}$$

If we regard country II as the conglomerate of outside countries that have dealings with the first, the marginal propensity to import of country II (m_2 in equation 2) must be regarded as relating to imports from country I alone. Goods that travel from one part of the conglomerate to another wash out in the process of aggregation.

Next, we can write equations translating the exports of each country into the imports of its trading partner:

$$\Delta X_1 = \Delta M_2 = \Delta M_2^a + m_2 \Delta Y_2 \tag{3}$$

$$\Delta X_2 = \Delta M_1 = \Delta M_1^a + m_1 \Delta Y_1 \tag{4}$$

Equations (3) and (4) can be used to replace the export variables in the income equations; in place of equations (1) and (2), we have:

$$\Delta Y_1 = \Delta H_1^a - \Delta M_1^a + \Delta M_2^a + m_2 \Delta Y_2 + (1 - s_1 - m_1)\Delta Y_1 \tag{1a}$$

$$\Delta Y_2 = \Delta H_2^a - \Delta M_2^a + \Delta M_1^a + m_1 \Delta Y_1 + (1 - s_2 - m_2)\Delta Y_2 \tag{2a}$$

Now we group terms in equation (2a) to give us an expression for ΔY_2 that resembles the multiplier formula used in the text:

$$\Delta Y_2 = \frac{1}{s_2 + m_2}[\Delta H_2^a - \Delta M_2^a + \Delta M_1^a + m_1 \Delta Y_1] \tag{2b}$$

This expression can be used to replace ΔY_2 in the income equation for the first country. Substituting in equation (1a) and regrouping terms, we come out with another expression for the change of income in the first country:

$$\Delta Y_1 = \Delta H_1^a + \left(\frac{m_2}{s_2 + m_2}\right)\Delta H_2^a + \left(\frac{m_2}{s_2 + m_2} - 1\right)\Delta M_1^a$$

$$- \left(\frac{m_2}{s_2 + m_2} - 1\right)\Delta M_2^a + \left(1 - s_1 - m_1 + \frac{m_1 m_2}{s_2 + m_2}\right)\Delta Y_1 \tag{1b}$$

A further rearrangement of this equation brings us to the formula that we seek:

$$\Delta Y_1 = \frac{(s_2 + m_2)\Delta H_1^a + m_2\Delta H_2^a - s_2(M_1^a - \Delta M_2^a)}{s_1 m_2 + s_2 m_1 + s_1 s_2} \qquad (1c)$$

Were we now to substitute this expression for ΔY_1 in equation (2b) and work through the required rearrangement, we would produce a symmetrical expression for the change in income in the second country:

$$\Delta Y_2 = \frac{(s_1 + m_1)\Delta H_2^a + m_1\Delta H_1^a - s_1(\Delta M_2^a - \Delta M_1^a)}{s_1 m_2 + s_2 m_1 + s_1 s_2} \qquad (2c)$$

The current-account-balance equation for this set of income equations will be written from the standpoint of country I:

$$\Delta B_1 = \Delta X_1 - \Delta M_1 = \Delta M_2^a - \Delta M_1^a + m_2\Delta Y_2 - m_1\Delta Y_1 \qquad (5)$$

Substituting the expression in equation (1c) for ΔY_1 and the expression in equation (2c) for ΔY_2, we obtain the following statement after regrouping terms:

$$\Delta B_1 = \frac{s_1 s_2}{s_1 m_2 + s_2 m_1 + s_1 s_2}\left[\Delta M_2^a - \Delta M_1^a + \Delta H_2^a\left(\frac{m_2}{s_2}\right) - \Delta H_1^a\left(\frac{m_1}{s_1}\right)\right] \qquad (5a)$$

Using equations (1c), (2c), and (5a), we may now determine the income and balance-of-payments effects of any one of four "autonomous" changes, ΔH_1^a, ΔH_2^a, ΔM_2^a, and ΔM_1^a, and can tabulate those effects as we did with the "autonomous" changes considered in the text. The results are set out in columns (2), (3), and (4) of Table A in this note. They are expressed as dollar changes per dollar of variation in the "autonomous" variable. The denominator, D, stands for the expression $s_1 m_2 + s_2 m_1 + s_1 s_2$, which appears in each of the income equations and in the balance-of-payments equation.

The table displays a pattern very similar to that evinced by Table 17-1 in the text. An increase in domestic spending in either country raises income at home and abroad. An increase in import spending by either country (more accurately, a diversion of expenditure from home products to imported goods) decreases income at home but raises income abroad. An increase in domestic spending causes a deterioration in the current-account balance and balance of payments of the country where domestic spending increases. A diversion of home spending to imports also causes a deterioration in the balance of payments.

Like Table 17-1 in the text, Table A assigns a strategic role to the marginal propensity to save. Note that all the entries in column (4) would be zero if one or the other marginal propensity to save were equal to zero.

TABLE A

BALANCE-OF-PAYMENTS DISTURBANCES AND THE NATIONAL INCOME, ALLOWING FOR FOREIGN REPERCUSSIONS*
(changes in dollars per dollar of disturbance)

Nature of Disturbance (1)	Effect on Income in		Change in Current Account of Country I (4)	Change in Spending (5)	Change in Domestic Spending by Country I needed to Correct the Current-Account Balance	
	Country I (2)	Country II (3)			Effect on Income in	
					Country I (6)	Country II (7)
Increase in domestic spending by country I (ΔH_1^a)	$\dfrac{s_2+m_2}{D}$	$\dfrac{m_1}{D}$	$\dfrac{-m_1 s_2}{D}$	-1	$\dfrac{-(s_2+m_2)}{D}$	$\dfrac{-m_1}{D}$
Increase in domestic spending by country II (ΔH_2^a)	$\dfrac{m_2}{D}$	$\dfrac{s_1+m_1}{D}$	$\dfrac{m_2 s_1}{D}$	$\dfrac{m_2 s_1}{m_1 s_2}$	$\dfrac{m_2 s_1}{m_1 s_2}\cdot\dfrac{(s_2+m_2)}{D}$	$\dfrac{\left(\frac{s\,m_2}{s_2}\right)}{D}$
Increase in import spending by country I (ΔM_1^a)	$\dfrac{-s_2}{D}$	$\dfrac{s_1}{D}$	$\dfrac{-s_1 s_2}{D}$	$\dfrac{-s_1}{m_1}$	$-\dfrac{s_1}{m_1}\cdot\dfrac{(s_2+m_2)}{D}$	$\dfrac{-s_1}{D}$
Increase in import spending by country II (ΔM_2^b)	$\dfrac{s_2}{D}$	$\dfrac{-s_1}{D}$	$\dfrac{s_1 s_2}{D}$	$\dfrac{s_1}{m_1}$	$\dfrac{s_1}{m_1}\cdot\dfrac{(s_2+m_2)}{D}$	$\dfrac{s_1}{D}$

*The denominator, D, used in this table stands for the denominator of the multiplier formula: that is, $s_1 m_2 + s_2 m_1 + s_1 s_2$.

The table gives evidence to support our contention that a boom or depression in one country spreads to others via foreign trade. An increase of H^a in either country raises income in the other country; a decrease of H^a in either country lowers income in the other country.

The last three columns of Table A reproduce one of the exercises mentioned in the text. Column (5) indicates the change in domestic spending that must be accomplished to offset the balance-of-payments impact of the disturbance listed in the corresponding row of column (1). To calculate the entries in column (5), we derive an auxiliary equation from equation (5a), showing the balance-of-payments impact of a change in domestic spending:

$$\Delta B_1' = \frac{-m_1 s_2 \Delta H^{a'}}{s_1 m_2 + s_2 m_1 + s_1 s_2} \tag{6}$$

We then require that:

$$\Delta B_1 + \Delta B_1' = 0 \tag{7}$$

Substituting the arguments of equations (5a) and (6) for ΔB_1 and $\Delta B_1'$ in equation (7), we can match $\Delta H^{a'}$ against each disturbance to learn how large that term must be in order to offset the balance-of-payments impact of each disturbance. Thus, the first entry in column (5) tells us what should be intuitively obvious—that the impact of an increase in home spending can be offset by a subsequent reduction of equal size. The second entry in column (5) tells that the impact of an increase of home spending by country II can be offset by an expansion of home spending in country I. The third and fourth entries are symmetrical, telling us that spending must be reduced to offset a shift to imports by country I, and must be increased to offset a shift to imports by country II.

Columns (6) and (7) of the table tell us what will happen to income on account of the changes in home spending listed in column (5). Thus, the first entries in columns (6) and (7) indicate that the needed change in spending will exactly offset the changes in National Income produced by the initial disturbance (the changes listed in columns [2] and [3]). The next entries in columns (6) and (7) tell us that the spending changes in country I needed to restore equilibrium on the balance of payments are apt to magnify the income changes produced by the initial increase of home spending in country II. This suggests that balance-of-payments problems caused by domestic-spending changes are best dealt with by the country experiencing the autonomous spending changes, not by its trading partners. The third lines in columns (6) and (7) reproduce the conclusions listed in the text when we dealt with expenditure shifts. The changes in home spending needed to correct the balance of payments tend to compound the domestic deflation caused by an autonomous increase of imports.

Chapter 18

International
Financial
Arrangements

The Search for Liquidity Before World War II

The gold tradition. For decades, economists, bankers, and statesmen considered that there was but one asset that a nation ought to hold as an international cash reserve. Gold was long regarded as *the* international money, and the gold standard as a system of simple rules that could guarantee economic health.

As an interpretation of history, this view is an oversimplification. Silver, rather than gold, was the chief monetary metal through most of human history. The older moneys have names (*pound, mark*) which refer to weights of silver. The oldest names for coins (*shilling, crown, dollar*) apply traditionally to silver coins, while many of the most venerable gold coins (*guinea, sovereign*) date only from the eighteenth century—and, please note, are English. The gold tradition owes much to Great Britain's dominance in international finance during the eighteenth and nineteenth centuries. London was the unchallenged financial capital of the world, and Britain was on a gold standard, in law, if not in fact. The gold standard came to be regarded as the proper arrangement for economically advanced countries; other monetary systems were considered as makeshift arrangements suitable only for colonial or backward areas.

The world did not come near to a universal gold standard until 1879, when the United States resumed the redemption of its paper money after the Civil

War. A mere thirty-five years later, World War I broke up the gold standard. There was a brief resumption, starting in 1925, but it was shattered by the crisis of 1931.

The gold standard did not provide a foolproof system of rules for economic policy. During its heyday, the world experienced the great depression of the 1890's—a downward drag on prices that was quite plausibly interpreted as the result of insufficient growth in the world's gold stock, relative to the growth of population and production. There was a rather serious creeping inflation in 1899–1913, and financial crises occurred in 1883, 1893, 1904, and 1907. The attempted restoration of 1925–31 witnessed chronic unemployment in Great Britain and Germany, the American stock-market boom and crash of the 1920's, and the recession that began in 1929, producing mass unemployment in every major country by 1931, when the gold standard collapsed.[1]

Yet the gold tradition still has vitality. Since World War II, governments have sought to build new financial arrangements. In many important respects, these amount to a modified gold standard, although gold metal itself may play a smaller role in their functioning. The gold tradition, moreover, still sets the tone for conservative thinking on monetary questions. Hence, the world's previous experience with gold and the gold standard deserves our close attention. At the very least, we may hope to understand the errors made in earlier periods, so as to avoid their repetition and financial catastrophes such as those they brought on.

Working of the gold standard. A gold standard has been defined as an arrangement whereby the value of a monetary unit and the value of a defined weight of gold are kept at equality.[2] Governments have maintained this equality by offering to buy and sell gold at stated prices. When two or more countries have made such offers, they can be said to have established an *international gold standard*. Under this sort of arrangement, a balance-of-payments disequilibrium is ordinarily covered by gold movements.[3]

Gold-standard arrangements sometimes broke down because one country ran out of gold, or because its government expected to do so and acted as though

---

[1] One can argue that the gold standard helped to stabilize international *politics*. See K. Polanyi, *The Great Transformation* (New York: Holt, Rinehart & Winston, Inc.), chap. i, where it is argued that the gold standard made a decisive contribution to the long period of peace before 1914. Polanyi's contention is that several threats of war were staved off because "international high finance" persuaded governments that they could not afford measures that would break down the standard.

[2] D. H. Robertson, *Money*, 4th ed. (London: Nisbet & Co., Ltd.), p. 64. Robertson points out that this definition is framed "with a certain low cunning." It avoids the vexed question of whether money gets its value from gold or gold gets its value from money. It is also framed to cover gold prices fixed by law and gold prices fixed by discretionary administrative decisions.

[3] Note that present-day arrangements satisfy both of these requirements, albeit indirectly. Few governments deal directly in gold, but most of them stabilize their currencies in terms of the dollar which is, in turn, directly connected to gold. Today, moreover, a balance-of-payments deficit is not necessarily covered by movements of gold, but it is covered by movements of currencies that are tied to gold.

it already had. During the thirty-five years after 1879, however, all the major industrial countries were on a gold standard which was thought to insure them against running out of gold. A gold standard was supposed to provide an automatic adjustment mechanism that would reverse any gold flow. That mechanism was similar to the one described in Chapter 17, but was supposed to work by price effects rather than by variations in real income. When gold left a country, that country's stock of cash assets was reduced, directly and indirectly. The gold loss transferred cash to outsiders through the flow of trade; it also reduced bank reserves, inducing a domestic credit contraction that reduced cash assets further. This shrinkage of the cash stock was expected to deflate prices and wages in the country losing gold, while a corresponding growth of the cash stock was expected to inflate foreign prices and wages. The result, according to gold-standard doctrine, was a shift in relative costs of production that would expand the deficit country's exports and reduce its imports. This would shift its balance of payments so as to stop the gold flow. In addition, the decline in the deficit country's exchange rate to its gold export point, together with an increase of interest rates as bank reserves were pinched, would make it profitable for bankers in all countries to keep short-term loan funds in the country losing gold, and this could help to keep the gold loss from going to extremes so long as bankers had confidence in the deficit country's currency.

Unfortunately, this "classical" explanation of the adjustment process proves too much. First, it requires that the country losing gold permit and reinforce the shrinkage of cash assets implied by the gold loss. Actually, few countries obeyed these "rules of the game."[4] Second, correction via price-wage deflation in the country losing gold and price-wage inflation in the country gaining gold would have taken a good deal of time. On the record, by contrast, periods of gold export rarely exceeded a few months, except for countries that were large gold producers. In the view of present-day analysts, the process of adjustment must have occurred by way of the direct income effects described in Chapter 17; not by way of monetary movements ascribed to a payments deficit and a gold outflow.[5] Adjustments occurred mainly through changes in real incomes and employment, rather than through changes in wages and prices. Prices were not sufficiently flexible in the industrial countries to permit a speedy adjustment and also to maintain full employment—except, of course, when world prices

---

[4] On the "rules of the game," see Ragnar Nurkse's discussion in *International Currency Experience* (Geneva: League of Nations, 1944); also Arthur Bloomfield, *Monetary Policy Under the International Gold Standard, 1880–1914* (New York: Federal Reserve Bank of New York, 1959).

[5] In the pivotal case of Great Britain, another equilibrating monetary influence was at work. An increase of interest rates and a tightening of credit in London could cause a worldwide shortage of short-term credit, especially of funds used to finance international commodity trade. Such a tightening of credit could force dealers in raw materials to cut back inventories and thereby to lower the prices Britain had to pay for her principal imports. On this point, see Peter B. Kenen, *British Monetary Policy and the Balance of Payments, 1951–57* (Cambridge: Harvard University Press, 1960), chap. ii.

were drifting upward so that countries gaining gold could make most of the adjustment through price increases, while countries losing gold could participate by inflating more slowly.

Gold in 1919–31: Gold-exchange standards. Between the two World Wars, gold had a stormy history. In the early 1920's, the monetary authorities of every major country were anxious to re-establish an international gold standard. After Great Britain had renewed gold payments (at the prewar parity) in 1925, and France had done so (at a lowered parity) in 1926, there was jubilation among central bankers. The restoration seemed to be well under way. But disillusion came in 1931, and by 1936, the gold-standard arrangements were in ruins again.

In the efforts at re-establishment, early in the 1920's, two problems loomed large: (1) A number of countries were impoverished by World War I. To build up adequate gold reserves by running current-account payments surpluses or by borrowing abroad seemed beyond their means. (2) If gold reserves were to bear their traditional relation to domestic bank notes and deposits, there would not be enough gold to go around, unless the United States parted with a large share of its huge gold reserve. The experts feared that there might be an international scramble for gold, resulting in tight money and worldwide deflationary pressures. This concern was justified, as we shall soon see.

The remedy adopted was a systematic effort to *economize* gold. First, gold was concentrated in the hands of central banks, instead of circulating as coin or serving as a commercial-bank reserve.[6] Second, many countries adopted a *gold-exchange standard;* they used sterling balances in London or dollar balances in New York as reserves for their central banks.[7] As these balances could be invested in safe, income-yielding assets (short-term Treasury securities, or acceptances), the poorer countries profited by this device; the interest they earned on their reserve balances could be used to offset interest owed on foreign debt.

Breakdown of interwar gold arrangements. The gold-exchange standard was not a sure safeguard against a scramble for gold. If countries with balances in London or New York started to bring them home in gold, they could denude the center countries of their own gold reserves and bring about a financial crisis. French monetary policy went far to realize this possibility. When the franc was stabilized late in 1926, the Bank of France held a mixed reserve of gold and foreign exchange. In 1928, the Bank was required by law to hold every increase of reserves in gold and to cease building up its foreign-exchange holdings.

---

[6] The United States, which had more gold than it needed, was less economical. There was some circulation of gold coin (especially in California, where the habit of carrying gold survived from gold-rush days). Moreover, the Treasury continued to issue gold certificates—a special type of paper money amounting to a warehouse certificate for gold coin. These gold certificates in circulation constituted a hidden reserve for the Federal Reserve. By hanging onto these bills when they came in from circulation and issuing Federal Reserve notes to replace them, the Reserve banks could build up their reserve ratios.

[7] India was on the gold-exchange standard before World War I, and similar arrangements had existed elsewhere. Never before, however, had the system been so widely used.

Because the franc was undervalued and French reserves mounted rapidly in the late 1920's, other European countries experienced a serious gold drain.[8] Finally, in the summer of 1931, France and other countries converted their sterling balances into gold, fearing a suspension of gold payments by Great Britain, and accomplishing precisely what they had feared. Britain left the gold standard and allowed the pound to fluctuate in relation to the dollar and other currencies.

The crisis of 1931 split the countries of the world into two main monetary groups, although a few splinter countries went their separate ways. One group consisted of countries that had maintained gold-exchange standards based on sterling and had strong ties with Great Britain. These countries continued to use sterling balances as reserves and, with some exceptions, to stabilize their own exchange rates in relation to the pound; they became the sterling area.[9] Another group—the United States and European "gold-bloc" countries (France, the Netherlands, Belgium, and Switzerland)—tried to continue the gold standard with gold reserves held at home. The splinters included the fascist countries and Japan, Balkan countries which Germany could dominate, and countries which had been outside the dominant arrangements of the 1920's, notably Russia and China.

The prestige of gold, as well as the prestige of sterling, was shaken by Britain's decision to leave the gold standard in 1931. In fact, gold suffered more than sterling. Great Britain and most of the sterling area enjoyed a business upturn in 1932, while the countries that adhered to gold, including the United States, continued to lose ground until 1933. The last countries to maintain pre-Depression gold parities, the European gold bloc, sustained serious unemployment for several years after 1932, while Britain was recovering.

The prestige of the gold-standard *rules* also sagged. At one time or another in the 1930's, every major country was led into damaging policies by adherence to those rules. Each country was forced to raise interest rates and contract bank credit in the midst of a depression, manifestly worsening the depression. Almost every country found the going easier once it had dropped gold or raised its official gold price.

Causes of the breakdown.   One cause of the breakdown in the 1930's

---

[8] French reserves stood at $0.7 billion from 1919 through 1926. They climbed steadily to $1.3 billion at the end of 1928, and to $2.1 billion at the end of 1930. The gold reserves of *all* central banks and governments outside the United States and France declined from $5.1 billion at the end of 1928 to $4.6 billion at the end of 1930, despite a rise of $0.9 billion in world stocks. The United States absorbed $0.5 billion; France, $0.8 billion. See Federal Reserve Board, *Banking and Monetary Statistics* (Washington, D.C.: U.S. Government Printing Office, 1943), pp. 544–45.

[9] These countries included the British dominions (except Canada), Portugal, and the Scandinavian countries. A number of Latin American countries attached their currencies to sterling after steering an independent course for a while, but broke away again after World War II.

The British monetary authorities came into the position of a "super-central bank" and, during World War II, managed to align the exchange controls of the sterling countries. On the formation of the sterling area, see Brian Tew, "Sterling as an International Currency," *Economic Record,* June 1948.

was the scarcity of gold mentioned above—the fact that paper money and bank deposits were much larger relative to gold stocks than they had been before World War I. This scarcity of gold might have been cured by an increase in the price of gold, so that an ounce of gold would correspond to more dollars, pounds, francs, and so on. But this alternative was never considered seriously in the United States and was rejected by Great Britain; governments preferred to economize gold and to adopt the shaky gold-exchange standard.

Another cause was the *maldistribution of gold*. The United States and, at a crucial stage, France had such large shares of the world's gold that the residue was inadequate for other countries. In 1913, the United States had held less than a quarter of the world's gold reserve; by 1923, we held about 45 per cent. By 1928, when most other countries were back on gold, we still held about 37 per cent, and in 1933, after the collapse, about 35 per cent. Under these circumstances, many people were convinced that most other countries could not capture and retain sufficient gold to make the standard workable.

The disproportionate share held by the United States was blamed by many analysts on "America's refusal to accept her creditor position."[10] Prior to World War I, we were paying interest and repaying principal on the foreign capital invested in American railways and other enterprises. We had to have an export surplus. During World War I, however, Europeans sold off their American securities and borrowed from the United States to finance the war effort. With the balance of property income and debt repayment reversed, we should have developed an import surplus, but continued to have an export surplus. We were not prepared to adapt ourselves by making it easier for imports to come in; on the contrary, we raised tariffs in 1922 and 1930. We were prepared to buy more foreign securities, but not on a sufficient scale to close the gap, and not as a steady practice; gold imports were called in as the balancing item.

Although there is much truth in this analysis, it is one-sided. Foreign countries could have cut down their imports from us had they really set much store by gold. Our gold imports represented the foreigner's implicit preference for goods over gold. This preference, if strong enough, can make a gold standard unworkable, for it leads to a paring down of gold reserves, so that a short run of bad luck can then exhaust them.[11]

---

[10]The drift toward France, in the period 1927–32, was interpreted in terms of undervaluation of the franc when the new rate of exchange was set in 1926. The renewed drift toward the United States, beginning in 1934, was also linked with undervaluation—this time, of the dollar.

[11]It is for this reason that underdeveloped countries and colonies rarely maintain sound currencies on their own. Most underdeveloped countries spend every windfall instead of building up international reserves. American economic history before 1776 is full of complaints about the lack of hard money in the Colonies—a lack reflecting the simple fact that anyone who happened to get some hard money could always think of something useful he would rather have. Every business felt itself starved for capital; liquidity was a luxury; and when anyone got into trouble through lack of liquidity, he would be defended by his neighbors and by the colonial legislature. The same phenomenon may be traced in the attitude of the "backwoods" toward the "tidewater" soon after the Revolution and in the "wildcat banking" of the nineteenth-century frontier.

American devaluation, 1933–34.   After Great Britain went off the gold standard, the American deflation, already in process, grew much worse. The slump did not reach bottom until the banking crisis of early 1933. One feature of this crisis was the hoarding of gold and gold certificates.

An early act of the Roosevelt administration was to pry gold out of hoarding. The Emergency Banking Act of 1933 (passed on March 9) empowered the President to "regulate or prohibit" transactions in gold and foreign exchange and the hoarding of gold. An executive order of April 5 required gold holders, including commercial banks, to exchange their gold or gold certificates for other cash at a Federal Reserve bank. It also required licenses for gold exports. On April 18, the government began to refuse applications for export licenses, and an executive order of April 20 put an absolute embargo on gold exports. The value of the dollar in terms of gold-bloc currencies began to fall immediately, and for several months thereafter exchange rates were determined by the market. The dollar dropped to about 85 per cent of parity in May, then to 70 per cent in July.

Meanwhile the President's powers were enlarged by fresh legislation. The Thomas Amendment to the Agricultural Adjustment Act of 1933 authorized the President to fix the weight of the gold dollar, but not to reduce it by more than half. A Congressional resolution held that debt contracts calling for payment in gold dollars should be treated as calling simply for dollars.

Beginning in September 1933, the government began again to quote an official gold price. But the new prices were fixed "on a twenty-four-hour basis." Starting at $29.62 an ounce, compared with $20.67 before the gold embargo, they fluctuated for several weeks, moving with foreign-exchange rates. The fluctuations were designed to give American gold-mining concerns as good a price as they could have obtained by export in the absence of the embargo. Beginning October 25, however, the price was deliberately raised above the foreign price of gold. From this point on, all changes were increases, and foreign gold was bought, along with domestic gold. The official price was set at $31.36 on October 25 and was raised by twenty-one successive jumps to $34.01 on December 1. It was finally fixed at $35.00 an ounce on February 1, 1934. This price amounted to a 41 per cent reduction in the gold content of the dollar. It was not described as permanent, but no further changes have yet been made.

This gold policy was apparently based on the theory (implied by the language of the Thomas Amendment) that raising the price of gold would produce a proportionate increase in commodity prices.[12] We have already paid our respects to the commodity theory of money, and will have something more to say about price raising as a technique for recovery in Part IV.[13] Broadly speaking, however, the policy failed as a method of raising American prices. Except for

---

[12]See G. F. Warren and F. A. Pearson, *Prices* (New York: John Wiley & Sons, Inc., 1933). The views of Professor Warren were apparently very influential in shaping gold policy.

[13]See Chapter 20.

a few commodities with important world markets, like wheat and cotton, most price increases in the period must be ascribed to the cost-boosting operations of the National Recovery Administration, the crop restrictions of the Agricultural Adjustment Administration, and the effects of a rising national income.

If the gold policy had any effect, it was, paradoxically, to loosen most of the connections between gold and ordinary business—the very connections which had fostered the belief that gold was directly connected with prices. The anti-hoarding regulations deprived firms, households, and commercial banks of their gold holdings. The Gold Reserve Act of 1934 went further, prohibiting direct gold ownership by Federal Reserve banks. The anti-gold-clause resolution of June 1933 (backed by subsequent court decisions) rooted out whatever hold gold might have had on business accounting.

Most important of all, our devaluation upset the remaining gold-standard countries. Reducing the dollar to 59 per cent of its old parity left it badly undervalued in relation to the French, Belgian, Dutch, and Swiss currencies. Despite the rise in United States national income, which might have been expected to enlarge imports relative to exports, our exports outgrew our imports from 1933 to 1934. Furthermore, the American devaluation, coming after the depreciation of the pound, increased the likelihood that the gold-bloc countries would devalue their own currencies. Gold began to flow to the United States, out of the countries that had tried to keep their old gold prices. By the end of 1936, the last pre-Depression gold price had been surrendered.

The tripartite agreement, 1936–39. With the United States gold price settled, other currencies gradually aligned themselves with the dollar. From early 1934, the British Exchange Equalization Account kept the pound-dollar rate in the neighborhood of $5.00, and most of the sterling area was carried along. Canada, whose dollar had fallen relative to ours in 1931–32, came back to a dollar-for-dollar exchange rate.

When the gold-bloc countries gave up the struggle to maintain their overvalued currencies, they also aligned themselves with the dollar. The belga had been worth 14 cents before our devaluation and was above 23 cents during 1934. When Belgium devalued in April 1935 (the first of the gold-bloc countries to do so), the belga dropped slightly below 17 cents.

The French devaluation in October 1936 was the occasion for a formal agreement among Britain, France, and the United States. This tripartite agreement did not fix definite parities for the three currencies, but pledged the three countries to consult on future exchange-rate moves, to avoid competitive depreciation, and to use their stabilization funds for smoothing the day-to-day course of the exchange rates. Other countries, notably the Netherlands, Belgium, Switzerland, and Brazil, adhered to the agreement. It proved elastic enough to handle further devaluations of the French franc, when France could not hold down its price level, and to absorb speculation against the pound between the events at Munich (September 1938) and the outbreak of war (September 1939). Gold continued to flow into the United States after 1936, but the drain on other countries' gold reserves was arrested. This could occur because of a sharp rise in the dollar value of gold production, especially in Canada and South Africa.

The Search for Liquidity After World War II

Wartime planning for recovery.   The advent of World War II shattered hopes for a consolidation of the financial structure that was emerging under the tripartite agreement. Britain imposed new and comprehensive exchange controls in order to prevent the enemy from using sterling assets to purchase war materials and to conserve scarce foreign exchange for the purchase of munitions and essential foodstuffs. Even with these drastic restrictions, Britain came close to exhausting her own foreign-exchange holdings and had to sell most of her long-term assets abroad. Had the United States not begun the Lend-Lease program in 1941, Britain might have been starved into capitulation for want of dollars to buy food.

Soon after the United States entered the war, British and American experts began planning for postwar reconstruction. They were anxious to improve upon the piecemeal methods used after World War I, especially to avoid the creation of a war-debts problem like the one which bedeviled financial diplomacy in the 1920's, and to produce arrangements capable of generating an adequate volume of foreign-exchange reserves.

The British, under the leadership of Lord Keynes, came forward with the most ambitious proposal. While they were not ready to discard gold as a means of settlement, they proposed the creation of a new means of settlement to be used concurrently with gold. The Keynes plan would have established a *clearing union* to finance international transactions—to serve the double function of a clearing house and a central bank. If Britain acquired francs through her operations in the foreign-exchange market, she could ask France to redeem them through the clearing union. France could repurchase the francs with a check drawn on the clearing union, instead of paying with gold or dollars, and could run up a debt at the clearing union (technically, an overdraft), within agreed limits. The clearing union would have created an international means of settlement by way of its lending to deficit countries, and every government would have been committed to accept the clearing union's IOU's, just as they now accept gold or dollars (and may soon start to accept a new form of claim on the international Monetary Fund).

The Keynes plan proposed a dramatic break with tradition. By creating an international central bank, it would have given more elasticity to the supply of reserves, just as the creation of our own Federal Reserve System gave elasticity to the supply of American currency. The United States, however, was not prepared to accept anything this radical. It had doubts about the feasibility of the British proposal, and more important, it feared that the Keynes plan would give other countries a blank check to draw on the United States. If other countries could borrow from the clearing union, they could run payments deficits with the United States during the years immediately following World War II, at a time when we anticipated serious shortages of goods in this country.

The American government *was* willing to assist in the work of postwar recovery. As early as 1945, it agreed to lend Britain $3,750 million, to be repaid over ninety-nine years. We also agreed to the establishment of an International Bank for Reconstruction and Development. This bank issues its own bonds in major financial centers and lends the money raised by those bonds to governments engaged in reconstruction or economic development.[14] At the time, however, we were not prepared to give the outside world the large claim upon our resources that was implied by the Keynes plan. Instead, the United States proposed an arrangement that would serve to mobilize convertible currencies and make them available to countries having balance-of-payments problems. We were willing to pool reserves, rather than give an international agency the power to create additional reserves. The American proposal was accepted after protracted negotiation, and an International Monetary Fund was established by the Bretton Woods Agreement of 1944.

The International Monetary Fund. The International Monetary Fund is set up as an autonomous organization, although affiliated with the United Nations. Its members are national governments (thirty-five at the outset, 109 in 1968) which ratified the Agreement drafted at Bretton Woods and subscribed the gold and national currencies required to launch the Fund. They include almost all non-Communist countries except Switzerland. Each member is assigned a quota upon joining the Fund; this quota determines its subscription to the Fund's capital, its drawing rights, and its voting power. One-fourth of each country's subscription is payable in gold or United States dollars, the remainder in the member's own currency. As of August 1968, quotas totalled $21.2 billion, of which $5.2 billion had been subscribed by the United States.[15]

The Fund is controlled by a Board of Governors, representing all the member countries. It is managed by a group of twelve Executive Directors, elected by the Governors, who exercise the voting power conferred on member govern-

---

[14]The bank also lends money to private business, but only if the loan is guaranteed by the government of the country in which the business is located.

[15]IMF quotas were increased in 1959 and in 1965, raising total Fund resources from $9.2 billion and $14.0 billion respectively. The United States subscription was $2.8 billion before the 1959 increase and $4.1 billion before the 1965 increase. In 1963, ten major industrial nations agreed to make an additional $6 billion available to the Fund on a conditional stand-by basis. The United States pledged $2 billion to this supplementary fund. The agreement is known as the General Arrangements to Borrow.

ments by their quotas. The United States quota gives this country enough votes to choose one Director.

The first task of the Fund was to set up a system of exchange-rate parities expressed in terms of gold or the United States dollar. By December 1946, parities for thirty-two countries and various dependencies had been announced. By 1968 par values had been established for the vast majority of Fund members.[16] Members, we said earlier, are supposed to hold the prices of their currencies within 1 per cent of parity.

Under the Agreement, however, room exists for an orderly adjustment of parities—for depreciation or appreciation that will not trigger competitive responses by other countries. Every country retains the right to vary its parity between 90 per cent and 110 per cent of the initial parity. Consultation with the Fund is required in these cases, but the Fund's consent is not required. For changes outside these limits, the Fund's consent is needed, but the Agreement binds the Fund to accept changes "necessary to correct a fundamental disequilibrium."[17]

The Fund has been unable to keep all its members in line. France had adopted an agreed parity, but went over to a no-par system in 1948, without Fund approval. In 1949, the Fund "considered and concurred in proposals" for a drastic devaluation of the pound sterling and twelve other currencies. But the concrete proposal to drop the pound from $4.03 to $2.80 seems to have been formulated by London and Washington, then presented to the Fund in a form that left no room for modification. Recently, the Fund has had greater influence upon exchange-rate policy. This is probably connected to the revival of its currency transactions after 1955, a revival described below.

The Fund is a pool supplementing each member's own reserves. In case of need, a member country may "purchase" foreign currencies from the Fund in exchange for its own currency. A member's drawing rights, however, are circumscribed: No member is ordinarily allowed to draw more than one-quarter of its quota subscription in any twelve-month period, and no member is entitled to go on drawing after Fund holdings of its own currency have risen to 200 per cent of its quota. More important, drawing rights are not automatic. The Fund may refuse drawing rights to any government that is not trying its best to combat its balance-of-payments problem. A country that is losing reserves on account of an outflow of capital may even be asked to stem the outflow by exchange control.[18] A country that is losing reserves on account of inflation is

---

[16]Many of the remaining cases are countries which have but recently joined the Fund.

[17]The Agreement, however, does not define a "fundamental disequilibrium"; if a country is able to balance its international accounts, but accepts unemployment to do so (as did Britain in the 1920's), is that country suffering from "fundamental disequilibrium"?

[18]This is the one instance in which the Bretton Woods Agreement explicitly sanctions the use of exchange control. The Fund's resources were meant for use in times of temporary current-account disequilibrium, not to finance deficits owing to large-scale capital flight.

expected to combat the inflation by monetary and fiscal policies.[19] Countries that wish to draw the currency equivalent of their gold subscriptions receive "the overwhelming benefit of any doubt that may arise in connection with a request for a drawing." Countries that wish to draw currency equivalent to the second quarter of their quotas can "confidently expect a favorable response to their applications, provided they are making reasonable efforts to solve their problems." But the criteria for larger drawings are very strict, including "well-balanced and adequate programs to restore balance, to establish or maintain the enduring stability of the currency at a realistic rate of exchange, and to prepare the conditions for repayment of the drawing."[20]

In recent years, the Fund has made a number of exceptions to its limit on annual drawings. It has also negotiated "stand-by" arrangements with several countries, similar to agreements made by commercial banks with their major borrowers.[21] The Fund commits itself to honor a member country's application to purchase stated amounts of foreign currency. The Fund made its largest stand-by agreement with Great Britain in November 1967, helping to turn back a speculative onslaught against sterling after the Labour government devalued the pound.

The Bretton Woods Agreement runs in terms of rights to "purchase" foreign currencies; the word "loan" is taboo in Fund discussions. But each purchase is the subject of an agreement between the member and the Fund, including provisions for "repurchase" of the member's currency. Thus, the Fund treats members who want to purchase currencies as though they were borrowers, and even refers to their "credit-worthiness."[22]

To prevent Fund transactions from becoming one-way flows, the Agreement obligates members to repurchase their currencies from the Fund when they are able to do so (and regardless of ability, after a fixed term of years). A member country whose reserves rise above its quota must use a slice of those reserves to repurchase its currency from the Fund, if the Fund already holds a balance in that currency exceeding three-quarters of the country's quota.

The Fund is designed to forestall economic warfare. To this end, the Bretton Woods Agreement commits members to abstain from a number of objec-

---

[19]Some critics of the Fund complain that it has gone too far in its insistence on anti-inflationary policies. A country suffering from a payments deficit on current account can always improve its position by cutting back domestic spending (see Chapter 17). Whether it should do so, however, is another matter. A country may have to accept substantial unemployment or, at the very least, a reduction in its rate of economic growth, before restoring current-account equilibrium. In defense of Fund policies, it may be said that the Fund has often permitted a devaluation where alternative anti-inflationary policies threatened unemployment or a drastic reduction in the rate of growth. This has been especially true of its attitude toward the less-developed countries.

[20]International Monetary Fund, *International Reserves and Liquidity*, pp. 80–81. This passage paraphrases a resolution adopted by the Fund in 1952.

[21]See p. 57.

[22]International Monetary Fund, *Annual Report for 1952*, pp. 42, 87.

tionable monetary practices, including the rationing of foreign exchange, discriminatory currency arrangements, and multiple-exchange arrangements. Other international agreements (especially the General Agreement on Tariffs and Trade) aim to stop the use of import quotas. But the ban on exchange control and discrimination was not immediate or unconditional. Exceptions were made to limit capital transfers, to provide for the transitional use of controls after World War II, and to handle "scarce currencies."

The "scarce-currency" clause was expected to be the most important exception. It was designed to protect other countries from a postwar depression in the United States. Should the Fund be in danger of running out of one currency (read "the American dollar"), it must ration its supply of that currency among other countries. Once a currency is declared to be "scarce," moreover, other governments may restrict its use as they see fit. They may discriminate against the exports of a "scarce-currency" country. The dollar was in short supply after World War II (but for a reason different from the one that was anticipated), yet was never designated as a "scarce currency." The IMF hoarded its supply of dollars, instead of using them liberally to assist countries in deficit with the United States. As a result, the dollar was never "scarce" within the meaning of the Bretton Woods Agreement.

The postwar dollar shortage.   In its first two years of operation, the International Monetary Fund came to the assistance of several countries suffering from shortages of foreign exchange. During 1947–49, it sold $725 million to member countries. But the Fund could not begin to cope with the foreign-exchange problems of the European countries and of other areas devastated by World War II. Despite their strict exchange controls and import restrictions, these countries sustained large deficits, especially with the United States. These deficits were mainly the result of war damage; imports ran at record levels and exports were depressed because of the damage done to farms and factories, shortages of industrials materials, and labor scarcities. They were aggravated by excess liquidity in most European countries; currency holdings were abnormally large, and the pressure of excess demand caused prices to rise rapidly or, where price controls and rationing were used, produced black markets in a wide variety of consumers' goods.

At the end of the War, the United States made a large "lump-sum contribution" to recovery—its subscriptions to the IMF and the International Bank for Reconstruction and Development, and its $3,750 million loan to Britain. It also increased the lending authority of the Export-Import Bank, a government agency that makes foreign loans. The United States financed *relief* programs in war-stricken areas, through the United Nations Relief and Rehabilitation Administration (UNRRA) and through the Allied military governments administering ex-enemy territories. But Washington was not prepared to continue outright grants-in-aid for *reconstruction*. As a result, the European countries were nearly stripped of their remaining reserves in 1946 and 1947. Britain's brief experiment with convertibility worsened the situation, diverting some of the proceeds of the 1946 American loan to Britain's creditors outside of Europe. The unusually severe winter of 1947 also played havoc with recovery plans and Europe's balance-of-payments position, by greatly increasing fuel consumption.

The United States came gradually to realize that recovery would take longer and would be harder than had been anticipated, and that large Communist parties in France and Italy might capitalize on mass discontent at the forthcoming elections. In March 1947, President Truman asked Congress for $400 million in aid to Greece and Turkey. In June 1947, General George Marshall, then Secretary of State, proposed a massive program of assistance for recovery, and in April 1948, a four-year European Recovery Program was approved by Congress.

The American recession of 1948–49 produced a new crisis in Europe's financial position. The sharp drop in United States imports put new pressure on sterling and other European currencies, and this pressure was compounded by rumors that sterling would soon be devalued. At the beginning of 1949, Britain's gold and dollar reserves stood at $1,912 million; by September 18, they had fallen to $1,340 million—a drop of some 30 per cent. Britain was finally forced to devalue the pound from $4.03 to $2.80, and a dozen countries followed suit, including France and several members of the sterling area.

It is hard to appraise the results of this devaluation, as a different stimulus to sterling-area exports arose just nine months later. The outbreak of the Korean War set off a wave of scare buying in the United States; government and business bid frantically for imported raw materials, seeking to forestall critical shortages should the war engulf our major suppliers. The ensuing increase in raw-materials prices was injurious to Britain, which imports raw-materials—but beneficial to other sterling countries, so the two together were not hurt by the price increase. In early 1951, however, as prices were leveling out, the outer sterling countries began to increase their imports. The income effects of the previous boom had worked themselves through to import demand and were augmented by a relaxation of import controls; the outer sterling countries were trying to spend the windfall incomes that Britain hoped to use to cope with higher import prices. To make matters worse, Britain was subjected to heavy inflationary pressures as she began to participate in Western rearmament. The munitions industries bid resources away from export production. The position reached crisis proportions late in 1951, when raw-materials prices began to drop, cutting into the income of the outer sterling countries. This time, however, Britain did not resort to devaluation. She tightened her import controls and revived domestic monetary policy as a means of reducing expenditure, thereby to cut imports and release goods for export.

Having weathered the crisis of 1951, Britain and other countries in Western Europe steered a very steady course toward recovery and the liberalization of international trade. Even as the 1951 crisis threatened to undo the progress already made, the governments of Europe were setting up a European Payments Union. This arrangement was similar to Keynes' clearing union. At the end of every month, each European country reported its net credit or debit position vis-à-vis other European countries. These were offset against each other insofar as possible, and net balances were settled, partly in dollars and partly in credit. During the period when dollar reserves were very scarce, EPU credits served as partial substitutes for those reserves.

The return to convertibility. As the 1950's wore on, the European countries rebuilt their reserves from the 1951 low, liberalized their trade and payments controls, and took steps to make their currencies more nearly convertible. In March 1954, the London gold market was reopened for the first time in more than a decade. At about the same time, the rules governing EPU settlements were hardened; a larger fraction of net indebtedness had to be settled in dollars, reducing a debtor country's access to EPU credits. This meant that European countries had less incentive to import from Europe instead of the United States—less incentive to discriminate against dollar goods. A deficit with other European countries was nearly as costly of dollar reserves as a deficit with the United States.

The United States recession of 1953–54 caused some trouble for the outer sterling countries, but it did not impair the stablity of sterling. Britain's position remained fairly strong. New difficulties did crop up in 1955–56, because of an investment boom, but these were successfully met by monetary and fiscal policies and by assistance from the International Monetary Fund. The IMF came alive in 1956, after seven years of inactivity. In the fiscal year ending April 1957, its currency sales totalled $1.1 billion, twice as large as the cumulative total for the preceding seven years. In December 1956, the Fund sold $561 million to Britain and put the rest of Britain's quota on a stand-by basis, helping London to ward off a bout of speculation occasioned by the fighting in the Middle East and the closing of the Suez Canal. Soon thereafter, the Fund helped France to protect the franc; rumors of impending devaluation and of an appreciation of the German mark, coupled to continuing domestic inflation, had run down French reserves.

At the end of 1958, the franc was devalued. At the same time, however, it was made convertible for nonresidents, along with all the other major currencies of Europe. Henceforth, all foreigners holding Europe's currencies could convert them into dollars. Some countries went further, lifting all restrictions on their own residents, and other countries followed in the 1960's. The European Payments Union was brought to an end, for there was no further reason to conserve dollar earnings, and a new European Monetary Agreement came into force. This new Agreement established a "little IMF" to assist European governments facing payments deficits. It also guaranteed the dollar value of bank balances owed by European central banks to one another.

From 1958 through the mid-1960's, Europe enjoyed a large payments surplus—the mirror image of the U.S. payments deficit mentioned in Chapter 17. The Common Market countries gained reserves steadily, and two of them, Germany and the Netherlands, were moved to revalue their currencies in March 1961, but Britain continued to have problems. It was forced to borrow from foreign central banks and to draw large amounts from the IMF: $1.5 billion in August 1961 and $1.0 billion in November 1964. Britain's fundamental disequilibrium finally forced her to devalue the pound in November, 1967 moving from $2.80 to $2.40.

The current situation, then, is very different from the days of dollar shortage. Europe (apart from Britain) has a payments surplus; we have a deficit. The first large United States deficit occurred in 1958, with a marked weakening of the trade accounts. Exports leveled out, while imports rose suddenly. Thereafter, the trade balance grew back into surplus, but the very large increase in foreign investment discussed in Chapter 17 shifted the problem to capital account. There was steady growth in direct investment and a large increase in bank lending to foreigners, as the United States' commercial banks began to expand their international operations. In the mid-1960's, foreign investment leveled out, owing partly to the use of informal controls (formalized in 1968) and the interest-equalization tax, but the payments deficit continued, as military spending on the Vietnam war placed a direct burden on the balance of payments and, by fostering inflation in the United States, damaged the trade accounts.

Looking over a full decade of American deficits, some experts conclude that United States policies have been defective, or that some basic adverse change has affected the competitive position of the United States. Other experts stress the shifting nature of the United States deficit—from merchandise account in 1958–59, to capital account in 1960–64, to government and trade accounts in 1965–68—and argue that we have had a long run of bad luck. The truth would seem to lie between these two extremes. One fundamental change has occurred in our competitive position: The European economies have recovered from World War II and are able to challenge the United States in world markets. That same recovery, moreover, has attracted American capital to Europe. In different terms, the United States payments problem is not an indictment of current United States policies but measures the success of past United States policies in aid of European recovery. At the same time, one must give considerable weight to the several independent, "autonomous" disturbances that have afflicted the balance of payments—the sudden and striking "internationalization" of American business and banking, the growing American market for foreign products, the large costs of the Vietnam war.

Whatever the diagnosis, one thing is clear. The United States cannot run deficits much longer. It cannot accumulate short-term liabilities and lose gold indefinitely. This challenge poses an immediate problem for American policy and a long-run problem for the international monetary system.

The new gold-exchange standard. The return to convertibility in 1958 was made possible by an enormous increase in the international reserves of the

European countries—an increase that continued into the 1960's. A portion of this increase came from newly mined gold, but much more of it came by way of United States deficits—an increase in the liabilities of the United States and reductions in its gold stock. The statistics in Table 18–1 show a $33.6 billion increase in the reserve assets of other countries from 1948 through 1966. Of this total, $30.7 billion came by way of deficits in the United States balance of payments. These deficits started in the early 1950's and grew quite large in and after 1958.[23] Of the $30.7 which came from United States deficits, $11.1 billion was taken in gold. The rest, $19.6 billion, was left on deposit with American banks or invested in money-market paper. The increase in world liquidity, then, has been the result of the construction of a new gold-exchange standard.

This new standard, however, is not elastic. It cannot create additional reserve assets without also undermining the reserve position of the United States. Table 18–2 shows to what extent this has already happened. In 1950, total United Stated assets exceeded total liabilities by a threefold margin; by 1966

TABLE 18-1

THE INCREASE OF INTERNATIONAL LIQUIDITY, 1948–1966*

(billions of United States dollars; rounded to nearest $0.1 billion)

Source of increase	Amount End 1948 to End 1966
World gold production and reported Soviet sales of gold	$17.9
Increase in United States short-term liabilities	19.6
United States gold losses	11.1
Equals gross increase of reserves	48.6
Less increase in holdings by international institutions	15.0
Equals increase in holdings by other countries **	33.6

Sources: International Monetary Fund, *International Financial Statistics.*

* Excluding Soviet-bloc countries, but including Soviet sales of gold to noncommunist countries.

**This total overstates the increase in world liquidity because it neglects the change in Britain's position as a reserve-providing center. During the period covered by this table, Britain's liabilities to foreigners declined by $2.3 billion and her own gold and dollar holdings remained constant. This means that the gold, dollar, and sterling holdings of countries other than the United States increased by $31.3 billion (by $33.6 less $2.3).

---

[23]The fact that the United States ran deficits over this whole period does not contradict our earlier assertion that the world suffered from a dollar shortage in the early postwar years. It would have run a large deficit with the United States had we not been willing to provide substantial grants-in-aid and long-term loans.

our assets were only two times our liabilities. In 1950, our gold and reserve assets were more than two-and-a-half times greater than our short-term obligations to all foreigners and nearly eight times greater than our liabilities to foreign official institutions. By 1966, reserves were less than *half* our total short-term liabilities, and were also smaller than our obligations to foreign official institutions. Since 1966 the situation has grown worse.

The United States still holds a large quantity of gold, and the decision, in march 1968, to terminate gold sales in London, letting the price rise for private buyers, will help to conserve American gold. Nevertheless, the decline in the United States gold stock and the erosion of the nation's reserve position have caused grave concern among international bankers as well as academic and government economists. The weakened cash position of the United States invites potential speculation against the dollar—speculation that could develop into a major attack on the gold exchange standard. Pessimists indeed say it is

TABLE 18-2

INTERNATIONAL FINANCIAL POSITION OF THE UNITED STATES: 1950 AND 1966

	1950	*1966*
Assets:		
1. Gold and other reserve assets.*	24.3	14.9
2. Deposits and short-term claims on foreigners:		
Privately owned	1.5	10.6
Government owned**	0.3	2.8
3. Long-term claims on foreigners:		
Private direct investments†	11.8	54.6
Privately owned stocks and bonds	4.3	14.9
Other privately owned claims on foreigners	1.4	6.1
Government claims on foreigners‡	10.8	21.2
4. Total assets	54.4	125.1
Liabilities:		
5. Short-term obligations to foreigners:ᵃ		
To foreign central banks and governmentsᵇ	3.6	17.9
To other foreignersᵇ	6.0	15.5
6. Long-term obligations to foreigners:		
Foreign direct investments in the United States	3.4	9.1
Other foreign claims on the United States	4.6	17.9
7. Total liabilities	17.6	60.4

Source: United States Department of Commerce, *Survey of Current Business,* September 1967, p. 40.

* Other reserve assets are convertible currencies held by the Treasury and Federal Reserve *plus* the United States' gold-tranche position in the IMF.

**Includes United States government holdings of foreign currency whose use is subject to foreign consent.

† Book valuation: understates current market value.

‡ Includes claims payable in inconvertible foreign currencies.

ᵃ Includes United States government bonds and notes.

ᵇ Figures for 1950 are approximate; the recorded total of short-term liabilities, \$9.6 billion, cannot be accurately divided between foreign holders.

underway. In 1964 and 1965, the Bank of France used its dollar holdings to buy nearly $1.3 billion of gold from the United States. Thereafter, it declined to accumulate dollars; the whole French payments surplus was taken in gold, just as it was in 1928–31. French policy helped to destroy the first gold-exchange standard. It could destroy the new one, if imitated by the other central banks.

Here, then, is the long-term problem to which we referred above. The United States must prevent a further erosion of its reserve position; it must eliminate its balance-of-payments deficit. Doing so, however, it will slow down the growth of world reserves, for new gold production is not very large (and much of that production goes into private hoards or industrial processes). How, then, can governments, acting together, provide for future growth in world reserves? What lies beyond the gold-exchange standard?

Proposals to Increase World Liquidity

A catalogue of proposed reforms. This problem has provoked new interest in proposals for international monetary reform. Economists and others interested in these matters have revived several old schemes and have proposed a series of new arrangements to cope with the need for additional reserves and with the problems posed by a gold-exchange standard. Governments have also done work on the problem, and, in 1967, came to a new agreement which most experts hailed as a major step forward. We cannot analyze all of these suggestions and plans, but will look briefly at three of the proposals for radical reform and at a few of the more modest suggestions, including the official plan.

The commodity-reserve-currency proposal. The most radical reform that has been suggested is one that would remove gold from monetary arrangements. It was originally designed for use in a single country, but has also been offered as a basis for international monetary arrangements.[24] It gains additional

---

[24]The plan was originally put forward by Benjamin Graham in *Storage and Stability* (New York: McGraw-Hill Book Company, Inc., 1937). It was taken up by Professor Frank Graham (no relation), of Princeton University, in several articles in the *American Economic Review*. A revised version, calling for an international rather than merely a United States commodity standard, was published in Benjamin Graham, *World Commodities and World Currency* (New York: McGraw-Hill Book Company, Inc., 1944). For recent views of the commodity-reserve-currency proposal, see E. M. Harman, *Commodity-Reserve Currency* (New York: Columbia University Press, 1959) and Albert G. Hart, "Monetary Reform to Further Economic Development," *Political Science Quarterly,* September 1964, pp. 360–74.

12 bushels of wheat,	16.3 pounds of tobacco,
12$^1/_2$ bushels of corn,	6.3 barrels of petroleum,
87 pounds of cotton,	7,480 pounds of coal,
25 pounds of wool,	204 pounds of wood-pulp,
24 pounds of rubber,	506 pounds of pig-iron,
34 pounds of coffee,	35 pounds of copper,
9$^1/_4$ pounds of tea,	4 pounds of tin.
300 pounds of sugar,	

current appeal because it would help to solve one of the principal problems facing the less-developed countries. These nations are exporters of raw materials and are exposed to special hazards in international trade because the prices of raw materials tend to fluctuate widely. The commodity-reserve-currency scheme (also known as the Graham Plan) is designed to stabilize the level of raw-materials prices and would thereby assist the less-developed countries in maintaining payments equilibrium.

The heart of the scheme is a standing government offer to buy and sell several commodities. There would be no attempt to fix the prices of individual commodities. The government or international agency would offer to buy *a bundle of warehouse certificates,* each certificate in the bundle giving control over a stated quantity of one commodity.[25] There would be a stated buying price for the bundle, but this offer would not keep individual prices from varying. If wheat could be bought more cheaply, the price of some other commodity on the list would have to be higher. Fixing the price of the composite would keep all of the prices from rising or falling *at once,* but some could rise provided others fell.[26] Graham proposed that the agency responsible for managing the standard should not merely announce its buying and selling offers and wait for people to accept them, but should actively seek chances to buy and sell on the stated terms. The agency would watch commodity markets hour by hour. Whenever it observed a combination of prices which enabled it to buy a hundred-dollar unit for as little as $95.00, it should immediately place buying orders on all the commodity markets involved and continue to buy until the price of the unit climbed above $95.00. Whenever it saw a chance to sell a hundred-dollar unit for as much as $105.00 it should immediately sell on all the markets, and continue selling until the price sagged below $105.00.[27]

To make good on its selling offers, the agency would have to own a suffi-

---

This list is aimed to represent these fifteen commodities on a basis which straddles their relative values in world production and world exports in 1937. If the scheme were started with prices well above 1937, Graham would propose reducing the quantities; if a price level 200 per cent of 1937 were accepted, for example, the quantities would be scaled down by half.

[25]For example, in *World Commodities and World Currency* (p. 45), Benjamin Graham suggests that a $100 unit of commodities might include:

[26]The scheme thereby avoids the rock which wrecked gold-silver bimetallism: namely, the difficulty of fixing more than one price when trends in production costs diverge. The fact that silver production was cheapened relative to gold production was a great source of monetary strain from 1879 to 1896.

The famous economist Alfred Marshall proposed to avoid this same strain by a method with much the same logic as the Graham Plan. Marshall's plan (which he called "symmetallism" in contrast with "bimetallism") was to fix the price for a *pair* of metal ingots—a small one of gold mated with a large one of silver, both of fixed weight. The price of silver could then fall on condition that the price of gold rose.

[27]The proposal for a spread between buying price and selling price would keep every trifling price fluctuation from bringing the reserve agency into the market. But a spread smaller than that used here might suffice.

cient reserve of commodities, just as a gold-standard government has to own a sufficient reserve of gold and claims on foreign currencies. But if it were endowed with some of the existing national stockpiles of surplus farm products and strategic minerals, it might be able to start work at once, without waiting for an opportunity to buy a reserve on the open market.

The chief claim for the plan is that it would exert a direct stabilizing influence on the price level. If the commodities involved were sufficiently important, their prices could scarcely be stable when commodity prices in general were rising or falling strongly. If, then, the commodity-reserve agency were successful in stabilizing the price of the composite, its influence would reach out *through* the commodities in the composite to stabilize commodity prices on a wider front. Consider the prices of meat and dairy products. These commodities are not on the sample list of commodities, and could not be,[28] but the list does include grains, and grain is the most important cost item for livestock and dairy production. In consequence, stabilizing the composite would set limits to the fluctuation of grain prices and somewhat wider limits to the fluctuation of livestock prices. Look at this same argument in a different way. If meat prices tend to fall because of a slump in demand, grain prices will fall too; livestock raisers will demand less grain. This reduced demand for grain will push down the price of the composite to the $95.00 buying price, and official purchases will drain off grain along with the other commodities in the composite, keeping grain prices from falling as far as they otherwise would. Less grain will be fed to animals, the flow of animals will be restricted, and meat prices will fall less than they otherwise would. This sort of stabilization effect is too indirect to dominate each and every market. But if there is a slump in the demand for *most* finished goods, most of the raw materials which make up the composite will have a reduced private demand, and the effect of official buying will be felt on most markets.

We have just looked at the *price* effects of the scheme. There would also be *income* effects. When the composite was pressing against its $95.00 price floor and the reserve agency was buying, the incomes of producers would be maintained just as if private parties were buying. But the funds used for the purchases would not come out of the stream of private expenditure;[29] the reserve agency

---

[28]To be suitable for inclusion in a commodity reserve, a commodity must be: (1) compact and durable enough for storage; (2) well enough standardized and graded to make price quotations definite; and perhaps (3) free enough from monopoly control so that manipulation of its price will not put pressure on the composite. (Point 3 is debatable; some critics challenged Graham's inclusion of tin on this ground.)

[29]The agency could print paper money (analogous to gold certificates) against the goods it bought; this paper money (or checks written by the agency) would go into banking channels, building up the public's deposits at commercial banks, the reserves of the commercial banks, and the claims of the central bank on the commodity-reserve agency. Thus, there would be no taxes to finance these purchases; they would be self-financing in just the same sense that gold purchases are self-financing. When the agency sold commodities, it would be obliged to retire commodity certificates; but the proceeds of sales would provide checkbook funds to pay for the certificates retired.

would be adding to the income stream. This increased income would combat the recession in output and income that lay behind the decline in prices. If, by contrast, the composite rose to its $105.00 price ceiling, sales by the reserve agency would withdraw funds from the income stream.

Like a gold-reserve system, a commodity-reserve system could become disorganized. Reserves might pile up until the warehouses burst, or might run out in a period of continuous inflationary pressure. If the upward pressure on prices were strong enough, the commodity-reserve currency would have to be devalued—the physical quantities of goods backing the $100 unit would have to be reduced.

The international variant of the commodity-reserve-currency scheme might offer an alternative to the gold standard or gold-exchange standard if countries could be persuaded to accept a basic monetary reconstruction. It could also operate side-by-side with the present gold-exchange standard. The $100 commodity-reserve-currency unit could be given a fixed price in terms of gold, so that countries might exchange the new currency for gold bullion, and vice versa. This combined arrangement would look to the commodity-reserve scheme to provide needed additions to reserves, while preserving the "money-ness" of present gold stocks. Under either system—a pure commodity-reserve arrangement or a new "bimetallism"—the International Monetary Fund (perhaps through a subsidiary) would make the buying and selling offers for warehouse certificates and would own the commodity reserves.[30]

Such an international arrangement would provide the reserves needed to maintain the volume of world trade in periods of international economic contraction. A recession in the industrial countries that tended to reduce raw-materials prices would bring the IMF or its subsidiary into commodity markets to support the price level by commodity purchases. The agency would not only help to stem the price decline, but would also provide the raw-materials producers with the funds they need to sustain their imports from industrial countries. In case of an inflationary disturbance in international trade, the plan would have a slight damping effect; sales of commodity bundles out of the central stock would absorb income, these same sales would also curtail the number of commodity units to which central banks had equivalent claims at the IMF, and it would exert anti-inflationary pressure by a squeeze on monetary reserves. The point of impact of this pressure would be the reserves of the countries whose nationals were purchasing raw materials. The cyclical characteristics of the plan, accordingly, are rather satisfactory. On the other hand, one may not want the trend of monetary reserves to depend on the course of raw-material markets.

---

[30]Countries depending on a single export product (Venezuela's oil, Malaya's tin, Cuba's sugar) might want further protection through buffer-stock plans for particular commodities. Graham regarded these plans as compatible with the basic scheme so long as they did not go further than to stop price declines at some such floor as 80 per cent of the average price of the preceding five years.

What is now the "farm surplus problem" might transform itself into the secular-inflation-of-reserves problem.

Increasing the price of gold.   The present gold-exchange standard might also be replaced by a pure gold standard if new gold production could be increased sufficiently to provide the additional reserves nations will require in the years ahead. An increase in the dollar price of gold might have this effect.[31] First, it would enlarge the dollar value of present gold production. Second, it would stimulate new gold production by raising the price of gold relative to mining costs. Third, it would increase the dollar value of existing gold stocks, providing a large, once-over increase in the dollar value of present reserves.

During the past few years, this solution to the problem of world liquidity has gained a number of advocates,[32] and rumors of a change in the dollar price of gold have circulated every time an exchange-rate crisis has seemed imminent. The United States, however, has been an adamant opponent of any increase in the gold price. Part of its opposition has been based on tradition and national pride. An increase in the price of gold is tantamount to a devaluation of the dollar and a partial repudiation of dollar liabilities. There are, however, better reasons for opposing an increase in the price of gold.

An increase in the gold price would bring windfall profits to countries that produce gold. The major beneficiaries would be South Africa, the Soviet Union, and Canada. For political and strategic reasons, if no other, the United States is not anxious to augment the purchasing power of South African and Soviet gold production.

An increase would bring windfall profits to the countries that happen to hold gold and would penalize the countries that now hold reserves in New York or London. The major European countries, especially France, Switzerland, and the Benelux, would be the major beneficiaries, for they hold most of their official reserves in the form of gold. The less-developed countries would lose out, for many of them hold dollar or sterling balances rather than gold. An increase in the price of gold would enlarge reserves, but would make for an even more lopsided reserve distribution than now prevails.

An increase in the price of gold would not be a substitute for the present gold-exchange standard unless that increase were sufficiently large to align the dollar value of the world's gold stock with present global reserve needs, and also to align the dollar value of new gold production with the steady increment in global reserve needs. This is because an increase in the price of gold might undermine the international moneyness of the dollar and of sterling. Were such an increase to occur, few countries might be willing to hold dollars, save for irreducible working balances, because the increase could be taken to forecast

---

[31]For maximum effectiveness such a change in the dollar price of gold should be accompanied by a simultaneous change in the gold content of other currencies.

[32]See, for example, Jacques Rueff and Fred Hirsch, *The Role and the Rule of Gold: An Argument,* Essays in International Finance, No. 47 (Princeton: Princeton University Press ,1965).

a series of later changes in the gold price that would also benefit the holders of gold and penalize the holders of dollars. Governments might want to hold all of their reserves in the form of gold. Notice, moreover, that a gold price set to align present reserves with present requirements might not align incremental gold supplies with incremental requirements. Stock equilibrium may not coincide with flow equilibrium.

Proposals for transforming the IMF. Many critics of the present gold-exchange standard have proposed that it give way to an international currency, partly based on gold, to be administered by the International Monetary Fund. They would go back to an arrangement very much like Keynes' clearing union.

The best-known proposal of this kind is the one advanced by Robert Triffin.[33] It would require every country to hold a fraction of its total reserves on deposit at the International Monetary Fund, and would empower the Fund to "create" deposits by making loans to countries short of reserves. In addition, the Fund would be empowered to engage in open-market operations and to purchase dollar balances from countries that now own them in exchange for newly created IMF deposits.

Triffin's proposal has two objectives. First, it is designed to replace existing national balances of gold and foreign exchange with a new international currency—deposits at the International Monetary Fund. The minimum deposit requirements and the Fund's open-market operations would gradually gather existing gold holdings and dollar balances into the IMF.[34] This transfer of national balances to international ownership, when complete, would protect reserve currency countries against the sort of crisis that has assailed them in the past, when foreign governments and other holders sought to convert their balances into gold or to switch their holdings from one reserve center to another. The Fund would not be likely to transfer its balances from New York or London, and national governments would no longer have the opportunity to do so, as they would be obliged to hold their reserves as deposit balances with the IMF. The centralization of national reserves at the IMF would accomplish the same purpose that was served by the creation of the Federal Reserve System. Because our commercial banks hold their reserve funds as deposits at the Reserve banks, we are no longer in danger of the domestic panics that used to occur when commercial banks switched their reserve deposits from one financial center to another.

Second, the Triffin proposal would provide an "elastic" international cur-

---

[33]This proposal is outlined in his *Gold and the Dollar Crisis* (New Haven: Yale University Press, 1960).

[34]Thus, the Fund would start with assets comprising gold and foreign exchange. Gradually, it could convert its foreign-exchange holdings into gold, and after a few years of operations, it would also acquire the short-term IOU's of countries borrowing from the Fund. In the end, the Fund's assets would be similar to those of other central banks; gold and government debt (except that the debt would be a special kind created in connection with national borrowing from the IMF).

rency. Lending by the IMF would generate additional reserve balances that could be used as a means of international settlement. At the same time, Triffin seeks to meet the major objection that was leveled against Keynes' plan for a clearing union. He would set narrow boundaries to IMF lending and would thereby limit the rate of increase of total reserves. In addition, he would perpetuate the Fund's present policy of refusing aid to governments that do not make adequate efforts at restoring payments equilibrium.[35]

Triffin suggests that reserve balances at the Fund be convertible into gold, and that countries might continue to hold large amounts of gold. But these would seem to be transitional arrangements. In the end, the Triffin plan points toward a monetary system very much like that which prevails in the United States. The IMF would hold most of the gold stock, and national governments, much like commercial banks, would settle net indebtedness to one another by transfers of balances at the IMF.

Triffin's proposal is the most comprehensive of the schemes outlined in recent years. It comes closest to establishing an international central bank. But governments are not prepared to go so far or fast. Their own plan, described below, matches certain features of the Triffin plan, but grants much less power to the IMF.

More modest reforms. Subsequent to Triffin's own proposal, several other plans were put in circulation. Some of these sought greater powers for the IMF, some sought to strengthen the reserve position of the United States, the center country of the gold-exchange standard.

The first general increase in IMF quotas occurred in 1959, giving the Fund additional resources and giving its members additional drawing rights. Thereafter, many experts argued for a further increase of quotas as the right way to strengthen the monetary system. Some went a step further, suggesting that the IMF be given the authority to borrow convertible currencies, thereby to supplement its own resources.[36] Two more steps were taken along these lines. Quotas were increased again in 1965, and ten major countries agreed that they would lend their currencies to the IMF if it required additional resources to meet a major threat against the monetary system.[37] But larger quotas and the

---

[35]Note that the Triffin proposal has one expansionist feature that Keynes' plan lacked. Triffin would give the Fund power to take the initiative in the creation of new reserves: The Fund would be entitled to engage in open-market operations.

[36]See E. M. Bernstein, *International Effects of U.S. Economic Policy: A Study Paper Prepared for the Joint Economic Committee of Congress* (Washington, D.C.: U.S. Government Printing Office, 1960), pp. 84–86. See, too, Peter B. Kenen, "International Liquidity: The Next Steps," *American Economic Association, Papers and Proceedings of the Seventy-Fifth Annual Meeting,* 1963, pp. 130–38.

[37]See pp. 355–58 above. Supplementing these new multilateral arrangements, a number of countries have set up bilateral credit arrangements. Participating central banks have agreed to "swap" currencies should either party to the arrangement encounter balance-of-payments problems. The United States has made a number of "swap" agreements with European central banks and has drawn on those credit facilities several times. Britain, too, has made

concomitant increase in countries' drawing rights are not a perfect substitute for larger reserves. Access to drawing rights is not automatic, and currencies drawn must be repaid within a fixed number of years. These steps, then, did not quell the demand for fundamental reforms of the system.

A second set of plans for partial reform envisaged the creation of a "collective reserve unit" (CRU) outside the IMF. The CRU would have been backed by national currencies, would have been issued in fixed amounts to a limited number of countries, and would have circulated among that group of countries in a predetermined relationship to gold. A deficit country belonging to the group could settle its deficits in gold and CRU, and each country belonging to this inner group would have agreed to hold its own reserves according to a formula —so much in gold, so much in CRU. This proposal went a step further than those which proposed an expansion of the Fund. It involved the creation of *new* reserve assets to supplement gold and the dollar. At the same time, it had two deficiencies: First, CRU would be used and held in a fixed relationship to gold, so that the supply of CRU could not be increased unless the supply of gold was increasing too. Second, the CRU proposal excluded the less-developed countries, who felt that they should have some share of the new reserves created by any international agreement.

Another set of proposals sought to strengthen confidence in the United States dollar—to forestall conversions into gold like those that France made after 1964. Many experts argued that the United States should offer a gold-value guarantee on dollars held by foreign central banks. If foreign central banks were assured of reinbursement (in dollars) in case of any increase in the dollar price of gold, they would not hesitate to hold their reserves in dollars; they would not convert their dollars into gold.[38]

This proposal has much merit, and might stave off crises. It might even allow an expansion of dollar liabilities through continued United States deficits, imparting elasticity to total reserve supplies. But it has not found favor in Washington or foreign capitals. Some foreign governments might like a guarantee on the dollars they hold, but do not want to hold additional dollars and do not want to give the United States leeway to finance additional deficits. Although Britain has recently given a dollar-guarantee to countries which agree to hold reserves in sterling, the United States is not likely to do so.

Progress toward reform. Early in the 1960's, ten major governments

---

extensive use of "swaps," and has incurred large short-term debts this way. She has also borrowed under the so-called Basle agreements set up in 1961 and renewed several times thereafter on an informal, *ad hoc* basis. Most recently central banks have agreed to give Britain additional medium-term credit to pay off sterling balances held by other countries.

[38]Some people have suggested that such a guarantee be extended to private holders of dollars, not just central banks and governments. But any such extension would be difficult. It is hard to draw a dividing line between foreign-dollar holdings (cash assets) and foreign investments in the United States. Foreign holdings of Treasury bills might qualify as dollar holdings and obtain a guarantee, but what about foreign holdings of long-term government bonds, corporate securities, and real property?

(those that had subscribed to the General Arrangements to Borrow) began official consultations on proposals for reform. For some years, they denied the need for major reform. Eventually, however, they conceded that additional reserves might be required and that those reserves would have to be furnished by new arrangements—not by gold production or by United States deficits. At one point, it looked as though they might endorse the CRU and would limit the creation of new reserves to a handful of advanced, industrial countries. In 1966, however, they endorsed the universal distribution of reserves, and in 1967, submitted a formal plan that was adopted by the Governors of the IMF. As this is written, the new plan, which cast a series of amendments to the Bretton Woods agreement, is being ratified by IMF members. The new proposal, even when ratified, will still be a "contingency plan" that will not come into effect unless a vast majority of IMF members (those holding 85 per cent of the total votes) agree that new reserve ought to be created. If and when it comes into being, however, it will mark a major step from the gold-exchange standard—a step toward the collective management of international liquidity.

Under the new plan, every member of the International Monetary Fund will receive a new set of Special Drawing Rights (SDR's). The members of the Fund will vote on the amounts to be created in successive five-year periods, and each member will receive a share of the total equal to that country's share in present Fund quotas. These Special Drawing Rights will be quite different from ordinary drawing rights in the IMF. Ordinary drawing rights are used to buy currencies from the Fund; the new SDR's can be used to buy currencies from other countries. If the United States has a payments deficit, it may use its SDR to buy marks from Germany or francs from France.[39] The drawing rights transferred to Germany or France will be added to their own SDR's; they become a part of regular reserves, to be used when Germany or France run into deficit. The current proposal, then, comes near to the Triffin and Keynes plans in one important respect; it creates a new reserve asset on the books of the IMF, one that can be transferred from country to country at the initiative of those that have deficits.[40]

The use of Special Drawing Rights has three limits. First, no country can be asked to accept unlimited amounts. Each country may refuse to accept SDR's if its current holdings are three times as large as its own cumulative allocation of new drawing rights. If, for example, the United States is credited with $200 million per annum in the first five-year period, its total holdings will reach $1,000 million after five years, and it need not then accept more than $2,000 million in transfers from other countries. Second, no country can use *all* its

---

[39]Alternatively, it may buy back dollars held by the German or French central banks.

[40]In one respect, the current plan goes further than the Triffin plan. Triffin allowed for the conversion of IMF deposits into gold; the new plan has no such option. Note, too, that the new plan is different from the CRU proposal; the new asset may be held and transferred independently of gold.

SDR's for any length of time. Provisional rules call for the "reconstitution" of a country's holdings if, over five years, its actual holdings have averaged less than 30 per cent of its cumulative allocation. In practical terms, a country may use some of its SDR's all of the time and all its SDR's some of the time, but may not use all its SDR's all of the time. Finally, member countries are expected to use their SDR's to finance balance-of-payments, not just to alter the composition of their own reserves; no country can use SDR's to buy dollars from the United States, then to use the dollars for the purchase of gold, seeking to substitute gold for SDR's.

No one can tell how this plan will work out. If very small amounts of SDR's are created, the plan will not supplant the gold-exchange standard. If, instead, large amounts of SDR's are brought into being within the first decade or so, the plan will be a major innovation in international monetary relations. The new plan is not as flexible as the Triffin plan, which would tie the creation of new reserves to the incidence of payments deficits and would grant the IMF additional discretion by permitting it to conduct of open-market operations. But it is much more flexible than some of the other plans that have been proposed in recent years, and it is, above all else, the first concerted attempt to manage the supply of world reserves.

NOTES ON
ALTERNATIVE POINTS OF VIEW
AND SUPPLEMENTARY READINGS

On international financial history during the interwar period, see R. Nurkse, *International Currency Experience* (Geneva: League of Nations, 1944), and W. A. Brown, Jr., *The International Gold Standard Reinterpreted,* 2 vols. (New York; National Bureau of Economic Research, 1940).

On the preliminary British and American plans for postwar financial arrangements, see J. H. Williams, *Postwar Monetary Plans and Other Essays* (New York: Alfred A. Knopf, 1945), Part I, and Jacob Viner, "Two Plans for International Monetary Stabilization," *Yale Review,* Autumn 1943. The postwar negotiations that set up the present IMF are described by R. N. Gardner, *Sterling-Dollar Diplomacy* (London: Oxford University Press, 1956).

Postwar financial developments in Europe and the European Payments Union are detailed by Robert Triffin in *Europe and the Money Muddle* (New Haven: Yale University Press, 1957). The adequacy of present international reserves is discussed in *International Reserves and Liquidity* (Washington, D.C.: International Monetary Fund, 1958), and in Robert Triffin, *Gold and the Dollar Crisis* (New Haven: Yale University Press, 1960), Part I. Triffin's own proposal is contained in Part II of the same volume. For a theoretical treatment of the gold-exchange standard and a discussion of its instability, see P. B. Kenen, "International Liquidity and the Balance of Payments of a Reserve-Currency Country," *Quarterly Journal of Economics,* November 1960. For recent views of the commodity-reserve-currency proposal, see E. M. Harmon, *Commodity-Reserve Currency* (New York: Columbia University Press, 1959), and Albert

G. Hart, "Monetary Reform to Further Economic Development," *Political Science Quarterly,* September 1964.

A summary of recent proposals for reform of the international monetary system is contained in Fritz Machlup and Burton Malkiel, eds., *Plans for Reform of the International Monetary System* (Princeton: Princeton University Press, 1962). For comments on these plans and additional proposals, see Joint Economic Committee, *Guidelines for International Monetary Reform* (Washington, D.C.: U.S. Government Printing Office, 1966).

Part IV

**Stabilization
Policy**

Chapter 19

The Framework for
Stabilization Policy

A General Interpretation of Fluctuations

The future of fluctuations. Should we decide that business fluctuations are part of our environment, like the weather, or like the deep commitment of our society to continue with scientific discovery and invention even though we risk destruction? Or should we think of fluctuations as an evil to be combatted?

Some sort of answer to these questions can be found in our discussion of fluctuations and monetary theory. We stand with those who think fluctuations are to be combatted, but believe that the sources of fluctuations are very deep-rooted in our way of life, and that *fluctuations in components of economic activity* are not only unavoidable but desirable. The policy question is how to make fluctuations in one component offset fluctuations in another.

In this section, we will spell out some of the implications of this proposition, and seek to dispel misunderstandings that arise in discussions of fluctuations.

"Incentives" versus "markets." The interpretation of the record offered in earlier chapters rests largely on the relation of "markets" to production. When markets are inadequate, output and employment usually shrink. When production is inadequate, prices begin to rise. This interpretation may seem to be in conflict with the widely held view that prosperity depends on adequate incentives for business, but the apparent conflict is a fraud. Conflict appears

377

to arise because politicians and journalists often talk as though the provision of certain other incentives (low tax rates, the elimination of "government competition with business," and of various types of government regulation) would make worry about markets unnecessary, and because those concerned with other incentives tend to *oppose* concern with markets.[1] It is quite proper to worry that emphasis on markets may overshadow other incentive problems, but actually the benefits of other incentives are largely lost if markets are too weak.

Obviously, the market idea is an incentive idea. The strongest incentive for any firm to increase its output and employment is to have more orders from customers. The emphasis on sales and sales promotion in American business is evidence for this interpretation. The effects of strengthening markets may show up in increased prices rather than increased output. But the facts that the sales organization of every business is always hungry for orders, and that the producing and purchasing organizations take pride in seeing that orders are filled, speak strongly for the view that markets are a powerful production incentive. If this incentive falls below a certain level, moreover, other incentives fail. What affects the decision to install a new plant? Increased freedom from regulation, tax allowances, and the restoration of a climate that will strengthen the businessman's pride in his work will all be unavailing if markets are so weak that the businessman cannot sell the output of the plant he already has.

Incentives other than markets cannot safely be neglected. In the production of consumers' goods and of goods to be sold to government, output is pulled along by suction from the buyer's end of the pipeline.[2] When it comes to investment, the initiative is clearly with business. Investment is always aimed at the production of future output, so that adequate markets are an essential ingredient of investment incentives. But confidence in future markets is not mechanically determined by the present state of markets. While influences on current markets via consumer spending power and government purchases may be very favorable to investment, a lack of other incentives may hold investment down.

It is not the business of this book, which is primarily concerned with money and banking, to explore the problem of incentives. We must, rather, emphasize markets because the problem of markets lies almost entirely in the jurisdiction of the student of money—the payments approach in its several versions is the best that the economist has to offer on this side. We will discuss some of the

---

[1] To the extent that businessmen are persuaded that measures to stabilize markets are bad medicine, unfortunately, these measures do have adverse psychological effects on investment decisions. If the "market" considerations were really of secondary importance, it might be worth soft-pedaling them to avoid this effect. But all the evidence shows that they are of primary importance. To keep them out of sight would be to yield to blackmail. The proper solution for the propaganda-created conflict is to convince businessmen (by argument and by favorable experience) that the conflict is a fraud.

[2] Even here we must not overlook the role of advertising in stimulating consumer demand. The businessman is not passive, but enjoys considerable initiative.

effects of *levels* of taxation, but the differential effect of different *types* of taxation has to be left to books on public finance. This leaves much of the strict incentive effect of business taxes in the background, for an incentive structure favoring large production and investment is not achieved simply by allowing large after-tax profits. Fat profits may even get in the way of activity.[3] The incentives that count are those *at the margin;* policy should design an incentive system that makes it more profitable to produce more instead of less, rather than to make any particular level of production profitable.

Taxation is not the only issue we shall leave to one side. Patterns of labor relations, steps that can be taken to give businessmen a greater responsibility in the formulation of stabilization policies—all these are major problems in relation to incentives which we can mention only incidentally.

The price issue. The problem of price stability is closely related to the problem just discussed. Many discussions of markets take for granted that prices will not rise unless markets are stimulated beyond the level needed to reach full employment. This is a risky assumption, as may be seen from the analysis of price making in Chapter 13. Prices can rise before we reach full employment, partly because business and labor enjoy some influence over key prices, but also because businessmen may not make the decisions to expand output and employment when markets expand. They may fail to satisfy an increase of demand, causing a round of price increases and involuntary saving.

This line of thought also leads into questions we cannot handle within the field of money and banking. The problem leads over into *price economics* (the domain of economic theory in the narrow sense), and into the politics and sociology of the organizations that make prices—business firms, trade unions, trade associations, interest-groups, government offices, and legislatures. We will say something about their influence in the chapters that follow, but our account will be frankly inadequate—and could not be otherwise without using most of economic analysis and borrowing heavily from the other social sciences.

Alleged advantages of depressions. Some people think depressions are a good thing. Like most economists, we take the opposite view. Depressions have some useful by-products, but too few to pay for the damage they do.

A venerable doctrine in Christian morality holds that we should be grateful for the "trials" of this life because they are good for our characters, so some people welcome depressions as an opportunity for us to show our fortitude. Most of us feel that our lives would have been poorer if some of the hardships had been left out. But the world in our lifetime is likely to offer adequate exercise

---

[3] If comfortable profits can be made too easily, there may be no spur for initiative. Perhaps the best incentive combination for production and investment is one where the existing situation is unprofitable but where profits can be restored by expanding output and modernizing plant. Yet ample profits have one favorable effect on investment which policy must take into account. They permit large business saving, which in turn, increases business borrowing power. Thus, ample profits mitigate the handicaps to investment imposed by capital rationing.

for our moral fiber. Trials can be overdone. People capable of fine things may be strained past the breaking point; the wake of business fluctuations is full of moral wreckage.

Depressions help to weed out inefficient firms and promote an overhaul of methods and leadership in surviving firms, while the hothouse climate of inflation can keep inefficiency alive. But the frost of depression does not single out weeds. Many promising enterprises are also killed by that frost because they happen to be at a tender stage. Inefficient firms may even survive a depression if they happen to have adequate financial backing.

Others claim that depression stimulates invention, for necessity is its proverbial mother, and hard times galvanize people into finding new and effective ways to do things. But there are offsetting losses. Depression diverts planning efforts into improvising stopgaps to protect the firm against the slump. Business plans for further development go into the wastebasket, or have to be set aside until they are out of date, and the benefits of forward-looking engineering and production management are frittered away.

Depressions help to break down monopolistic combinations and price rigidities, but they also build up the fears that drive businessmen and workers into defensive price-making combinations. A climate is created in which such combinations can command political support—even from people who will suffer from higher prices—on the grounds that the groups involved are entitled to set up defenses against future depressions.

Depressions may enhance industrial discipline and efficiency, for the fear of unemployment may stimulate a worker to work hard and to stay on good terms with the foreman. But the fear that jobs may be scarce is also the motive behind collective labor actions we call *slowdown* and *featherbedding*.

Perhaps the most important by-product of depression is its power to correct the inflationary drift. Barring a revolution in price-making patterns, prices will probably drift upward in most prosperous periods. In addition, intermittent national emergencies occur and give wages and prices an upward jerk. If there are no intervening periods when prices get reduced substantially, we can expect secular inflation at a fairly rapid rate. But we should be reluctant to accept major depressions as the method for stabilizing prices. A depression like that of the 1930's is too much to pay for a price-level correction. We must hope that mild recessions can exert a sufficient downward pressure on prices, or we will have to seek other ways of controlling inflation.

The obverse of this connection between prices and depressions may be even more important. If we shrink from ever taking the risk of a mild depression, we are bound to have a secular inflation. Anti-recession measures are likely to include easy money, tax concessions, the expansion of public works, financial favors to farmers, and, if political log-rolling plays a part, wage-rate increases.[4]

---

[4] Note that this list of measures is not our recommendation, but a forecast of what politics will generate if an effort is made to forestall recessions by taking countermeasures when they threaten.

If these measures are sometimes adopted to combat recession threats that prove illusory, they will generate an inflationary combination of cost-push and demand-pull. Refusal to tolerate any risk of unemployment will thus accentuate the risk of inflation.

Note, finally, that depressions in individual industries can yield society most of the gains we have been discussing, and that the effectiveness of individual-industry depressions is not enhanced by having all industries depressed at the same time. On the contrary, the toning-up effect of a depression in any one industry is at its best if other industries are prosperous. The workers, managers, buildings, and so forth, released by the collapse of an inefficient firm, can find uses in other industries. Such a collapse in a general depression may leave these productive resources with no place to go.

Self-generation of fluctuations.   Another way of looking at the "silver lining" of depressions is the suggestion that we have to suffer through them as the price of the ensuing prosperity, with an implication that an attempt to tinker with depression may somehow keep the ensuing prosperity from happening.

At its crudest, this argument is an inversion of the old fallacy: *post hoc ergo propter hoc.* Depressions come before prosperities and must, therefore, cause them. We should not be too impressed with this sequence. If a depression is followed by a second depression rather than by prosperity, our recording apparatus simply says, "Long depression, isn't it?"—and long depressions have happened. All we may infer from the alternation of depressions and prosperities is that both do happen and that they cannot both happen at once.

A more sophisticated version of this argument holds that depressions correct the deficiencies of past prosperities. In prosperity, it is said, something happens to create an imbalance that makes the continuation of prosperity impossible, and the downswing eliminates this imbalance. This view has some merit; on the whole, however, we probably get upswings *in spite of* depressions rather than *because of them,* except insofar as depression shifts public policy.

Clearly, some kinds of imbalances that occur in prosperity can be corrected in depression. We sometimes get "overbuilt" during a boom. If in an ensuing depression construction is low, we may gradually develop a nationwide housing shortage (owing to population growth, fire losses, and so forth), which will make it easier for us to be prosperous some time in the future. If building costs rise during an expansion of construction and keep on rising after building starts to shrink, the construction industry may "price itself out of the market," and a reduction in building costs suggests itself as the natural remedy.[5] A depression is

---

[5] In such a situation, a temporary slump in private construction may become unavoidable; if building costs are falling at all rapidly, builders may refuse to put up new structures that will compete with structures built later at lower costs. Unless it is possible to increase public construction and simultaneously cut building costs (two processes likely to get in each other's way), a slump in *total* construction may become unavoidable. But it should be possible to get revival as soon as costs have hit bottom.

a way to reduce building costs, but a general depression does not reduce building costs *relative* to other prices, for the prices that enter into building costs are among the most rigid. A general depression cuts other prices, including the rental values of existing buildings, more rapidly than building costs, so that the imbalance becomes worse instead of better. If the depression can be confined to building, prospects are better; it is the spread of the depression from building to general business that does the mischief. The policy implication is plainly that a mild stimulation of other industries is probably needed to give us the benefit of corrective price declines in industries that are overpriced.

A similar argument applies when a downswing is set off by business decisions to reduce excessive inventories. The natural and healthy reaction of a firm burdened by excessive inventories is to hold a clearance sale and slow down purchases. But if everyone does this at once, we get a general recession. Each firm's effort to unload inventories reduces the general level of income and interferes with the sales of other firms. The fall of activity and sales reduces the *denominator* of the inventory-sales fraction, by which businesses judge the adequacy of inventories. Thus the process may fail to improve the excessive inventory ratio that set off the slump, and may even make it worse.

We run into similar problems if the initial imbalance is an unsound financial position of debtors. Pressure on debtors to pay off their debts does reduce outstanding debts, but it also cuts down the volume of business, reducing the debtors' incomes on which their credit standing depends. In 1930, in 1931, and in 1932—after one, two, and three years' effort, respectively, to cure the unsound credit situation of 1929—the credit situation was more unsound than ever. Financial conditions for prosperity were undermined, not built up, by the use of depression as a corrective.

A depression will aggravate imbalances if it is confidence to sustain prosperity that is lacking. Depression teaches people not to trust the promises of debtors, the purchase commitments of customers, the safety of banks, or the competence of governments to safeguard their welfare. It is likely to engender hasty experiments in economic policy that are more certain to scare investors than to produce desired results. If a depression lasts too long and cuts too deep, it may even weaken the foundation of mutual trust among citizens and prevent cooperation to get the nation's work done. The real possibility of such a paralysis through crises of confidence is illustrated by the difficulty of getting the French economy under way again after World War II. France's difficulties were partly the result of the Nazi occupation, of weak current policies, and of memories of the inflation in the 1920's, but also in good part the result of the rifts that opened during the dragging depression of the 1930's. Even the mild, chronic "stagnation" of the United States economy in 1956–65 seems to have weakened mutual trust through its differential effect on minority groups.

The notion of a general depression as a healthy corrective for economic ills should be rated as dangerous nonsense. We may find ourselves forced to accept an occasional depression because public policy has erred, because it has not been able to find a well-timed offset for a slump in some important sector. But we should not take comfort in the delusion that by meekly going through the wringer of depression we are fostering recovery. Recovery will come only with the advent of some expansive force strong enough to offset the imbalance that set off the recession *and* the handicaps to recovery that depression itself creates.

Room for policy. The data in Part II and in the following chapters show that different spells of prosperity have been built on different combinations of spending—consumers' spending, debt-financed government spending, and business spending for plant and inventory. They also indicate that the composition of spending within each category has varied extensively, and that *within* a stretch of prosperous years, the foundations of prosperity may shift a good deal.

Any long-continued prosperity must probably rest on such a shifting foundation. We must expect, even welcome, fluctuations in construction, agricultural exports, and automobiles; and, for reasons we cannot explore here, will probably experience serious fluctuations in business inventories. If we succeed in avoiding major depressions, it will be because we are lucky enough or skillful enough to have some of these elements take a turn for the better just when—or just after—others take a turn for the worse.

Waiting very long for the spontaneous appearance of these offsets would be rash, even though the risk in waiting is somewhat smaller now that we have a monetary framework that will not compound a recession by monetary deflation. But for reasonable security against major slumps, we still need measures to temper the instability of the components of investment, and to make it less likely that several will decline at once.

Coping with inflationary tendencies is equally difficult. In the past, the economy seemed immune to peacetime inflations. The economics of inflation appeared to be a branch of war economics, useful on special occasions. But the nearest approach to peace we are apt to see will probably include frequent international crises, so that inflation will be a recurrent problem. In addition, we have developed institutional arrangements that may make inflation the normal prospect.

Policy Priorities and Related Matters

Employment vs. prices. The primary business of monetary policy—or more broadly, of monetary-fiscal policy[6]—is economic stabilization. By this we mean controlling tendencies toward inflation and toward mass unemployment. But should one of these stabilization objectives take priority? And are they compatible with other social objectives?

---

[6] Including monetary aspects of taxation, public expenditures, and so on.

A strong tradition exists in economics that would divert monetary-fiscal policy toward price-level stabilization. This would call for measures to expand the stock of cash (and perhaps also to reduce the demand for cash assets) in case prices begin to fall, and for contractionist measures in case prices begin to rise. The price-stabilization tradition was born before economists worried much about unemployment, but its present-day supporters,[7] though cognizant of unemployment problems, still come out with the traditional answer.

The argument for giving price-level stability unconditional priority may be summarized as follows: (1) Unemployment is ordinarily accompanied by falling prices; in this case, nothing is lost by letting prices guide monetary-fiscal policy, since falling prices will call for much the same counteraction as an assault upon unemployment. (2) If the rules of policy and actual experience can convince businessmen that they may look forward to stable prices, an initial fall of prices will encourage inventory accumulation and equipment-buying in the expectation of a return to the previous price level, rather than encourage business buyers to await further price declines. (3) Admitting that the contractionist measures needed to stop a price rise may sometimes create avoidable unemployment, the sponsors of a price-level-stabilization standard argue that monetary-fiscal policy should not be held liable for unemployment of this sort. In such a case, they maintain, those who have power to decide what prices shall be are probably raising their prices in the face of unemployment.[8] If these people (trade unionists, business leaders, farm organizations, and so forth) were put on notice that such behavior would force monetary policy to generate unemployment, the responsibility would be theirs.[9]

At the other end of the spectrum of professional opinion is the view that monetary-fiscal policy should be guided solely by the level of employment. An increase of unemployment, whether or not accompanied by a price decline, would warrant action to expand the money supply or to increase people's disposable income by fiscal policy. Although prices may advance when unemployment is serious, this school of thought would recommend continuing anti-recession measures and the use of other lines of policy (price control?) to cure the price inflation.

The arguments against a pure price-level-stabilization standard seem to us over-whelming, although they are political arguments rather than "pure economics": (1) Is it realistic to suppose that we can prsuade trade-union, business, and farm groups to forego price increases by threatenineg to generate unemployment if they misbehave? We may be able to appeal to these groups in the name of

---

[7] Notably W. J. Fellner, of Yale, and several University of Chicago economists—Milton Friedman, the late Henry C. Simons, and L. W. Mints.

[8] See Chapter 13. Note, however, that a price-level risem ight spring from a crop failure that raises food prices. A price-level-stabilization standard for policy ought strictly to be set up with some sort of correction factor for crop fluctuations.

[9] For this point of view, see W. J. Fellner, *Monetary Policies and Full Employment* (Berkeley: University of California Press, 1946), pp. xii and 229–30.

the public interest. We may be able to move them by warning of the misfortunes that will fall upon them—notably, the unfavorable publicity that will undermine the political support on which they rely. But the leaders of these groups and their key constituents are personally secure against any moderate growth of unemployment, so we cannot threaten them with misfortunes that will actually fall upon quite different people who may become unemployed. (2) Any successful national program of economic stabilization requires general understanding and acceptance by the public. A program aimed at employment objectives (with or without price objectives grafted on) has the sort of legitimate appeal around which public consensus can be built. Price-level stabilization alone may never catch the public's imagination to the same degree.[10]

The common-sense solution, it would seem, is to set up employment *and* price goals as objectives. A real risk exists that the two objectives may come into conflict, as price-making forces have an upward bias, and what we should do in case of conflict is a difficult question. By setting up a dual objective, we say that stabilization policy has suffered a defeat if employment *or* the price level gets out of hand.

Supplementary objectives. Stabilization policy has other goals to consider.[11] Of these, human freedom is paramount. It is all too easy to mouth empty formulae about freedom in relation to economic policy—or, at the other extreme, to pretend that such talk is mere sentimentality or a verbal smoke screen to defend the *status quo*. Yet there is plenty of substance in the view that freedom should be the overriding goal of society. If you look inside the employment-price issues themselves, this is what you find: The individual's independence and an equality of opportunity—not mere creature comforts—are the real stakes.[12]

Less important than freedom, but not to be ignored, is the goal of efficiency—getting enough output from our input on each job; securing an efficient allocation of manpower and other resources among jobs; and improving productivity by invention and education. Conflicts can arise between efficiency and employment. Some devices for maintaining employment (especially featherbedding) impair efficiency. But in the large, the objective of employment and the goal

---

[10]For a well-reasoned argument to the contrary, see G. L. Bach, "Monetary-Fiscal Policy, Debt Policy, and the Price Level," *American Economic Review,* Papers and Proceedings, May 1947, pp. 228–42. It must be said also that widespread opposition to cuts in federal tax rates in 1961–66 seems to have rested largely on anti-inflation sentiment.

[11]Among the lesser goals, one that has a special claim upon monetary policy is the vested interest of small business in bank-loan financing. Small firms, unable to float securities on the open market, depend much more on bank loans than do large firms. Any development that weakens the lending power of banks thereby imposes a differential handicap on small business. Monetary policy must take this consideration into account, but cannot give it unconditional priority over steps to further employment-price objectives.

[12]Equality of opportunity does *not* mean merely an equal chance in a lottery; it implies designing the economic "game" so that success depends more on skill and diligence than on good luck.

of efficiency are thoroughly consistent. Output per man hour, on the whole, rises when unemployment shrinks and falls when unemployment grows. Unemployment is itself a glaring waste of resources, socially speaking, and we can often more easily afford other types of inefficiency than unemployment. Unemployment also means inefficiency in the distribution of goods, because it reduces the incomes of the unemployed.

Freedom and planning. Some people[13] seem to think that economic planning necessarily involves a sacrifice of freedom and of efficiency, but we disagree. Co-operation among individuals and among organized groups is needed to keep freedom and efficiency alive, and this co-operation is likely to break down if we relapse into an alternation between disastrous slumps and inflations. To avoid slumps and inflations, we need some sort of planning. The question, then, is not "Plan or no plan?" but "What kind of plan?" And on this more sensible question, the standards of freedom and efficiency offer good guidance. We may pose the problem as a contrast between two extreme notions of planning: at one extreme, installing a "boss" or "czar"; at the other, "framework planning." The first gives an official broad discretion and the authority to issue orders to individual firms or households. The second sets up a framework of rules so designed that people can do what they like provided they do not break the rules, and ultimately find that the rules bring their actions into harmony.[14]

The boss system is antithetical to freedom. People show a healthy reluctance to have bosses tell them which employers to work for, where to live, where to trade, what to buy, and what to sell for what price. The other extreme— framework planning—has a much more pleasing aspect. Unfortunately, it is utopian.

The vice of the boss system is its affinity to political corruption. The official whose range of discretion premits him to grant or withhold large gains (profits, wage increases, or tax abatements) is under a triple temptation—to benefit

---

[13]Notably F. A. Hayek (*Road to Serfdom* [Chicago: University of Chicago Press, 1944]). Hayek is ready to concede that there must be monetary policy and budget policy. But his main points are that uncritical enthusiasm for planning makes for a facile acceptance of measures designed to further private rather than public interests, and that essential freedoms may be breached by reaching out for the handiest way to administer a plan. In arguing these perfectly valid points, Hayek somehow conveys an impression that having a plan to guide the economic system is inherently vicious. (This impression is especially strong among those who know Hayek's book only by its title.)

[14]A homely parable can easily be found in traffic control. One remedy for traffic congestion at a busy corner is to introduce a czar in the form of a policeman with a whistle. He looks at each car (taking note, if he wishes, of the driver's signals), and tells the driver whether to stop, continue, or go right or left. Another remedy is to introduce framework planning in the form of a "cloverleaf interesection." By overpassing one road and building the necessary connecting links, everyone can be restricted to a choice of going straight ahead or turning right, but can still take any road he wants away from the corner without getting in anyone else's way. By the time the policeman with the whistle has forced you to go straight ahead two or three times when you wanted to turn, you will appreciate the beauties of framework planning (that is, assuming the proper signs have been posted to tell you how to proceed!).

those with whom he comes in contact, out of sheer amiability; to win approval and votes for a political party or a faction (or merely for his office); or to pave the way for a promotion or even to line his pocket with bribes. The process of swapping favors between government agencies and private interests (whether they are corporations, or trade unions, or less sharply organized interest-groups) is corrupting to the favored people and to the structure of social control, as well as to the officials involved.

The pure framework system suffers from the vice of inflexibility. In a changing society, an unchanging set of rules grows less and less relevant to the set of problems with which the community must deal.[15] Unless the framework can be kept in perfect adjustment, we find ourselves tempering its application by "rules of reason," and bossism creeps in the back door by the process of interpretation.

The most promising compromise is what we may call *framework-incentive planning*. Our planning intelligence should go into the mapping of a set of rules for economic affairs that can serve for long periods with only gradual change. The discretionary elements in policy should then be focused upon the management of impersonal and impartial measures that can be carried out with full publicity. Discretionary policy should not consist in the promulgation of directives to particular firms or households, but in the application of measures that will influence private decisions by changing the incentives that underlie those decisions—largely by affecting markets.

Where money fits in. When you start to look for evenhanded measures that can influence the economy through incentives, you inevitably light upon monetary and fiscal policies. These include bank-reserve requirements, open-market operations in government securities (whether by the Federal Reserve or the Treasury), international monetary policy, tax rates and the rules of accounting set up in connection with taxes, and government spending.

Most other stabilization measures can be classified either as parts of the framework or as discretionary measures that call for the issue of directives to private parties and that do not fit into a framework-incentive-planning program. In the first group (parts of the framework) are the legal rules governing property, contract, collective bargaining, and so forth, and those taboos that aim at keeping people from injuring each other. The taboos include anti-monopoly rules, health and safety regulations, and many other familiar controls.[16] Among the stabilization proposals that involve directives are a number of nonmonetary control suggestions—proposals for the direct control of private investment, for peace-time price and wage control, for the manipulation of collective bargaining to

---

[15]In the previous metaphor, cloverleaf intersections will cease to make our traffic self-regulating if we start traveling in helicopters rather than autos.

[16]For an inventory (and a convincing showing that even the "anti-planners" have come to take familiar controls for granted), see J. M. Clark, *Social Control of Business*, 2nd ed. (New York: McGraw-Hill Book Company, Inc., 1939), Parts I and II.

produce shifts in wages and profits, for controls over the use of foreign exchange, and for the direction of labor into urgent jobs. On the boundary between the two groups lie the less impersonal monetary-fiscal measures, such as selective control of bank loans and security holdings, installment credit regulations, margin requirements for speculation, and public works. These tend to require the issue of directives from government to private parties, but are rather promising areas for using discretionary authority because they involve general rules that remove the temptation for abuses.

The forecasting problem: how to tell when to do what. You could easily use this book as a work of reference, to find out what measures might be adopted to nip an inventory boom, to stimulate investment in durable goods, to offset a reduced demand for cash balances resulting from a more direct routing of payments, or to forestall an imminent slump in consumer spending on semidurable and perishable goods. A catalogue of remedies, however, is not enough. To say what should be done in the event of a particular threat to economic stability is rather like telling a farmer what to plant when there will not not be enough rain in August. That is very useful advice *if* we can also tell him how much rain will fall. The farmer cannot guide his planting by evidence that is not available to him at the time he has to put in his crops.

Economic policy is like farming in that we have to decide what to do before we do it, and what we do will often make a difference long after it has been done. Economic policy must depend heavily on economic forecasting— *differential* forecasting of the swing in future affairs that will occur if we take a certain step, and *absolute* forecasting of future affairs if we do not take that step.

The first thing to note about economic forecasting is that it is inaccurate. Whatever happens, someone will always appear to say that he predicted it, and he can often prove that he did. But if you look back into his record, you will always find that the person who was right this time was often wrong before, and you can sometimes show that he got the right answer for the wrong reasons. Someone is always right, moreover, because the guessers are shooting in such a variety of directions that all of the possible guesses are always being made.[17] But most forecasts err somewhat, and major errors of forecasting are hard to avoid.

The fact that forecasting is inaccurate does not mean that economists have no sound advice to offer. It would be nice to know just what will happen, both with and without the policy measures we advise. But if we face the fact that the future is uncertain, we can often give good advice about preparing for uncertainty, which affects some parts of our forecast much more than others. A good deal of stability exists in some basic behavior patterns; this is the foundation for framework planning. Forecasting then, can give sensible approximations.

---

[17]The monopolistic competition theorists have a name for this class of phenomenon; they call it "differentiation of the product."

The uncertainty of forecasts creates two policy issues:

(1) Automatic *versus* discretionary policy.
(2) Forestalling *versus* remedial action.

Policies can be designed that will be automatic, and will go into action when trouble develops *before* we have time to size up the situation, make fresh policy decisions, and put them to work. If a complete set of automatic stabilizers adequate to meet all contingencies could be devised, we would be freed of most of our forecasting difficulties. Unfortunately, the automatic stabilizers cannot do the whole job. They have to be supplemented by discretionary policy measures calling for fresh legislation from time to time, administrative action within rules laid down by legislation, or a combination of the two.[18]

Discretionary policies can be either preventive or remedial. Given good enough forecasting, the best alternative would be to forestall trouble. If forecasting is too unreliable, however, efforts to forestall an inflation give us an avoidable depression (or vice versa). When in 1957 the Federal Reserve acted upon forecasts that inflation would continue, it took action that may have worsened the 1957–58 recession. Fears of recession seem to have given policy an inflationary slant in 1967. Our uncertainty about the future forces us to rely heavily on policies for arresting or reversing undesirable trends before they go dangerously far.

Nonmonetary Stabilization Policies

The plan of Part IV. The balance of this book will survey monetary and fiscal policies for economic stability—the use of reserve requirements, open-market operations, discount policy, debt management, taxes, and public expenditure to prevent inflations and recessions. In effect, it will examine the work of the Federal Reserve System and some of the responsibilities of the Treasury, the Bureau of the Budget, the Federal Home Loan Agency, the Federal Deposit Insurance Corporation, and the Federal Housing Administration.

Chapters 20 and 21 will review business fluctuations since World War I and tell the story of stabilization policy against that background. Chapter 22 will look more closely at fiscal policy and appraise the contribution of automatic stabilizers and the role of tax-rate changes and government spending. Chapter 23 will look more closely at monetary management since the "Accord" of 1951 that freed the Federal Reserve System from its obligation to support

---

[18]The difference between automatic and discretionary policy is parallel to the difference between having automatic sprinklers in the ceiling and having an old-fashioned fire extinguisher in a wall bracket. The sprinklers will go into action as soon as a fire raises the temperature, even though nobody is in the room. The fire extinguisher needs an operator and does not go into action automatically, but it can do some jobs that the sprinklers cannot.

government bond prices. It will devote special attention to the measurement of Federal Reserve responses to changing economic conditions and to the examination of key monetary-link variables as transmitters of Federal Reserve policy. Part IV concludes with proposals to improve the monetary system.

As none of these chapters gives explicit attention to the place of nonmonetary measures, we shall look at these policies in this section. We shall pay special attention to wage-price policies, then turn to proposals for the manipulation of private investment to maintain a steady rate of economic growth and to aid in the solution of certain special problems.

Price policies in economic stabilization. The price problem in economic stabilization has two parts—the problem of avoiding a rise in the price level, and the problem of varying *relative* prices so as to keep pockets of unemployment from developing.

The problem of price levels is connected to the problem of employment. Measures that will call forth a larger *physical volume* of output (and, hence, raise employment) may also push up prices, while measures to discourage a rising level of prices through tighter credit, higher taxes, and so forth, may easily lead into a slump in employment.[19]

Some economists feel that the only way out of this dilemma is to make prices fully flexible. Such a policy, if *completely successful,* could automatically maintain full employment and leave us with just one worry—the price level. But a *partial success* is all we can expect, and this could do more harm than good. People who talk increased price flexibility seem to mean making trade unions accept wage reductions.[20] But the unions that are most open to pressure are those that could do little for economic stabilization by making their wages flexible, while those whose acceptance of flexibility might help most toward stabilization are in a sufficiently secure position to keep making wage gains. A flexibility in construction costs, including construction wages, might greatly steady the physical volume of construction, but the unions involved are able to oppose wage concessions.[21] A flexibility in grocery clerks' wages, defended by a relatively weak union, may be attainable, but would have little effect on output or employment. Insofar as the drive for flexibility means "union-busting" (and this often seems to be its political meaning), it may merely widen the disagreements between business and trade unions. The co-operation we

---

[19]A jingle by Kenneth Boulding neatly sums up the policy dilemma of stabilization:
Divergent policies we seek
For markets strong and markets weak,
But hoping to avoid this crisis:
Too weak for jobs, too strong for prices.

[20]We have heard also vigorous criticism of rigidity in business pricing practices. See, for example, Charles L. Schultze, *Recent Inflation in the United States: A Study Paper for the Joint Economic Committee of Congress* (Washington, D.C.: U.S. Government Printing Office, 1959).

[21]Building workers might prove willing to accept lower hourly wage rates in a mild slump in exchange for steadier employment under "annual-wage" arrangements; this chance of developing flexibility in construction costs is one promising reserve for future slumps.

need in our attempt to achieve stabilization is not likely to thrive on a diet of threats.

Our main concern as to flexibility should probably focus on the longer-run flexibility needed for an effective development of new industries. If the firms that control new products and new processes are not bold enough in cutting product prices to expand their markets and in bidding up wages to staff their expansion, the gains of technical progress may be frittered away.

Whether or not the government aims for price flexibility, it is increasingly entangled in pricing decisions. The government is deeply involved in the pricing of farm products, and is often drawn into wage disputes. Unless we discontinue wage negotiations on a national scale, a condition hard to imagine, there is no way for the government to escape a share of responsibility. Government officials are frequently called in to arbitrate labor disputes, and cannot refuse without precipitating major strikes. Wherever there is leeway in the terms of settlement, or the possibility of shortening a strike, public opinion has a strong influence on the outcome, and government policy has a strong influence on public opinion. Government, in short, must have a wage policy—avowed or unavowed, consistent or inconsistent, constructive or destructive, but still policy.

In the early post-World War years, strong labor-union support existed for the use of wage policy to stabilize employment via the distribution of income. There was then widespread fear of a major slump, originating from inadequate consumer spending. A wage-raising campaign, it was argued, would transfer income from profits to wages, raising consumer spending to a larger proportion of the national product and dissipating the threat of a slump. Unfortunately, the large wage increases that were actually made passed through to consumers in higher prices, and the chief effect of the wage campaign was to boost the wage level and the price level further above interwar levels. The price increases also boosted the value of goods in inventory, as those goods could be sold in competition with goods produced at higher costs. Inventory profits thus fattened total profit figures on the books of business, and produced the statistical basis for further rounds of wage increases.

In our judgment, this scheme should be written off the books as unsound, at least until we have better ways of gauging correct wages and better methods for regulating prices. Business might conceivably make prosperity impossible by insisting on an excessive spread between direct costs and prices, and unions might make prosperity impossible by insisting on wage schedules too high relative to productivity.[22] But the only relevant measures that have been proposed in this field are depression-forestalling wage increases. These might reduce investment demand more than they increased consumer demand. Even if they did not discourage investment, they might prove self-defeating and

---

[22] See J. M. Clark's "separate concurring statement" in United Nations, *National and International Measures for Full Employment* (Lake Success: United Nations, 1949), pp. 100–104.

inflationary. Employers will try to pass on their cost increases in higher prices unless a slump actually sets in. Price control could prevent a transmission of wage increases by way of higher prices, but combined with price control, a wage-boosting scheme would be regarded as confiscatory by businessmen. Certain that profits would be snatched away for the benefit of employees, businessmen would not risk capital in new equipment and buildings, and a stagnation of investment is almost certain to set in. Even without price control, the adoption of such a wage policy would be a very ominous change of climate from the business standpoint.

The wage problem may actually be of an opposite kind to that we have been discussing. During the postwar years, wage increases have been at least as rapid as we should like—if not, indeed, too rapid. This is not to say that labor should be blamed for inflation since World War II, or that wages have led prices upward. It is to assert that postwar wage increases have helped to fasten the price level into its new notch after every bout of inflation. The problem of wage policy is to facilitate wage increases in appropriate cases, but still to hold down the general average of wage rates so as to keep the price level from climbing higher. The requirements of stabilization policy do not give us a comprehensive guide to labor policy, but they do give a basis for criticizing some of the popular wage standards. Two such standards that command a great deal of public sympathy, but make an unhealthy combination, need special comment.

1. In many wage disputes, labor appeals to a standard called "in-lining." A wage increase is claimed for certain workers on the ground that they are underpaid compared with other workers (in the same industry or another) whose skills and working conditions are similar. This standard is somewhat slippery in application, as there are always a variety of other workers with whom a comparison may be made. The parties to the dispute can often make plausible cases for wage figures quite far apart, but a close look will commonly narrow the range of doubt. A general rule of economic policy supports in-lining. If different groups of workers are really interchangeable, they should be paid the same wage in all uses, and should be used up to that point at which their marginal contribution is equal in each use.[23]

2. In other cases, labor appeals to a profit standard. Workers claim a wage increase if their employers' profits are high, particularly if the gain in profits arises from increased efficiency. A combination of standards (1) and (2) can be an inflationary mixture. Whenever one group of workers has its wage boosted because its employers have large profits, it becomes better paid than some other group whose employers have smaller profits. An increase for one group under standard (2) always creates a case under standard (1) for some other group. Similarly, increases under standard (1) normally boost costs for the employers whose wage rates rise; and the competitors of these employers thereby gain an

---

[23]In application, the common-sense rule is to slant the decision toward the upper edge of the range of doubt if the occupation in question needs recruits, and toward the lower edge if it is overstaffed.

advantage that will boost their profits. Increases under standard (1) also create a case for increases under standard (2); the two combined may generate a spiral.[24]

From the standpoint of stabilization policy, we can easily see that the villain of the piece is standard (2), although there are cases where standard (2) makes good sense. If profits rise because of an increase in efficiency, and *that increase comes because the workers involved are making special efforts which other workers do not match,* there is a clear claim for higher wages—and the higher wages are not inflationary. But if the gain in profits and in efficiency comes from the application of science to production, the case is very different. The resulting gain in productivity creates a claim to a general increase in the *wage level.* There ought to be a gradual rise in wages for *all* workers (not just for those in the industry where the improvement centers), accompanied by an upward drift of prices in industries with stagnant technology and a downward drift of prices in advancing industries.

The question of price policy is still more ticklish than that of wage policy, and works back into the wage question. During World War II, price-control was fairly successful in all the English-speaking countries; one is tempted to argue that price control in peacetime as well, should be used to control inflation below full employment. Unfortunately, the remedy is not as good as it sounds. Even when price control was buttressed by wartime patriotism, it was a struggle to keep evasion within bounds. Black-market dealing sprang up, and hidden price changes were made by shifting quality labels. Our experience with price control in the postwar transition (1945–46) and during the post-Korean inflation (1950–52) was discouraging. Production was distorted by profitable ceilings on some trivia and unprofitable ceilings on some essentials. The political drawbacks of price control also loomed large. Price control is inherently control by directive, rather than by impersonal rules—particularly if the control is more elaborate than a mere price freeze, and if the quality of goods has to be watched. It is exposed to all the perils of bossism if it is kept simple, and quickly piles up a mountain of red tape if accompanied by restrictions on the administrators.

The problem of price policy is compounded by its relation to farm policy. During the 1930's and the war period, farmers grew used to having their prices fixed by government officials working under the watchful eye of farm-minded Congressmen. They also came to evince great sensitivity to wage increases, seeking compensation whenever wages rose sharply. Trade unions resent any

---

[24]Note that an increase of profits owing to a rise in final demand in an isolated sector of the economy can start such a spiral and spread across the economy. Inflation, then, can begin without a general excess of demand, and without an initial autonomous push from wage rates or other costs. This analysis, incidentally, provides a plausible interpretation of the American inflation in the late 1950's. While there was idle capacity in some sectors, there was excess demand in others. This pressure raised profits in some industries and began a spiral of the type just described.

policy resembling wage control, unless it is accompanied by price control, and price control is taboo with businessmen and very unpopular with the farmers. In short, government price-wage policy is subject to claims from three powerful groups—claims that are far from consistent with one another, and still less consistent with the needs of less organized groups that want uninterrupted production and reasonable prices.

Under these conditions, the natural impulse of the politician is to yield a little to each organized group. Furthermore, the pressures leave him one path of escape. Farmers may want to see lower wages, but will gladly accept higher farm prices instead. Trade-unionists would like food cheaper, but can be consoled with higher wages. Businessmen would like lower costs, but are cheerful as long as they can add what they regard as a suitable profit to the costs originating in wages and farm prices. The politician is perpetually tempted to please one group by raising its selling prices, and then to compensate others by doing the same for them. The result is "log-rolling inflation."

This process seems unsound, both morally and practically. It implies a perpetual deception of wage-earners—by promising higher wages, then snatching back part of the increase by lowering the purchasing power of the wage-earner's dollar. Even if wage-earners were simple enough to be taken in by this trick, its fairness would certainly be questionable.

Stopping log-rolling inflation, however, will be difficult, even if we resolve to do so. We have reached a point in our political development where price relations, notably the relation of wages to farm prices, depend heavily on political compromises. Such compromises will sometimes break down and have to be renegotiated, and a successful renegotiation is likely to involve a "retreat to a higher price line." There are ways to get price reductions that will cancel the upward effect of these increases. One is a tremendous acceleration of technical progress, to permit an unprecedentedly rapid drop of finished goods prices compared with wages and farm prices. Another is to cut prices and wages through a major depression. The first is highly desirable, but somewhat unlikely. The second is moderately likely, but most undesirable. All in all, price rises will probably outweigh price declines during the coming decades.

Direct controls of investment and the public economy. Our discussion of fluctuations should have shown clearly that unsteadiness in private investment is of key importance in fluctuations and in the process of economic growth.[25] Investment is a large component of total spending and also is the means by which we provide for future increases in the national product. Monetary and fiscal policies can *influence* investment, but they may not be able to *stabilize* aggregate investment at a high level—to conjure up fluctuations in one component of investment to offset fluctuations in some others. Nor can monetary-

---

[25]We include in "investment" residential and other construction, the manufacture of producers' durable equipment, inventory accumulation, and the goods-and-services balance in foreign trade.

fiscal policy guide the *distribution* of aggregate investment by industry or by region. Yet we may have to guide its distribution so as to redevelop the chronically depressed areas that account for a large part of our unemployment. We need to look at the possibility of stabilizing investment and affecting its allocation through direct controls, an examination best made sector by sector.

Federal, state, and local governments are bound to have policies toward housing. These policies seek to provide a decent minimum for low-income groups, and, by means of land-use rules, to keep filth, noise, smoke, and general squalor from invading people's living-places. In the postwar years, a strong government effort has also been made to facilitate home purchases. It began with aid to veterans and spread into a general program in aid of mortgage financing. With a record rate of family formation and with residential construction far in arrears because of the depression and World War II, house building gained tremendous momentum after the war, and despite some fluctuations, has on the whole remained high ever since.

The government has also provided a good deal of multiple-unit housing and has subsidized private low-rent housing.[26] The scale and timing of these projects can obviously be affected by government policy. It would indeed be possible to design government policy so as to provide those responsible for economic stabilization with complete control over one component of residential construction.

The construction of private upper-bracket housing, like the higher-priced suburban developments, is much less amenable to direct control. So is the private construction of factories, office buildings, stores, theatres, garages, and so on. These fields of construction are directed by upper-income-bracket individuals and by business firms, and no special reason exists to count on stability, nor any effective way to achieve it. In times of acute pressure, as after a war, limitations on the flow of building materials and the manipulation of building permits can restrict construction and build up a backlog of projects. So long as such a backlog of demand presses against the system of controls, private building as a whole can be kept below some ceiling. If one project is dropped, an alternative can be called up from the queue. But once the backlog runs out, there is no way of controlling the volume of private construction. Government cannot force people to build more homes or to erect factories that will stand idle. Private construction can be kept below a ceiling, and thereby spread out at a stable level, but it cannot be sustained in the face of a decline in the demand for new buildings.

Note, however, that government may be able to affect the regional distribution of heavy construction, especially of factory construction. A manufacturer

---

[26]This is a sample of what Sir William Beveridge called "joint" public and private enterprise. See *Full Employment in a Free Society* (New York: W. W. Norton & Company, Inc., 1945), p. 133. We also have an increasing amount of construction by life insurance companies and savings banks (on the whole, medium-rental rather than low-rent projects), which is more open to public influence than is most private construction.

will not build a factory unless he anticipates an adequate demand for the products that factory will supply. Once he has decided to build, however, his choice of site may be influenced by government policies—especially by tax treatment. Some locations may be better than others because they are closer to raw materials or to the final market, but the appeal of inferior locations can be substantially enhanced by public policy. There have been experiments of this kind in recent years. A number of states and municipalities have offered tax concessions— ranging from outright tax holidays to favorable depreciation rules—in order to attract industry. The federal government has made some more modest concessions to bring industry into areas of substantial unemployment.

The construction of public utilities (power plants and transmission lines, railways, pipelines, telephones, and so forth) is on a somewhat different footing. These enterprises are not strictly private; for the most part, they fall into the *joint* field, and a few, notably in electric power, are fully socialized. Furthermore, a small number of large firms are of key importance, enabling government to influence the timing, scale, and regional allocation of investment by moral suasion, or even by striking negotiated bargains with individual firms. If necessary, government can extend the area of public ownership in the utilities field. As we are dealing here with regulated monopolies that use a fairly well-stabilized technology, the margin in efficiency between private and public operation is often fairly narrow, and by no means always in favor of private enterprise. An expansion of public enterprise in the utilities field might make the timing of investment more readily controllable.

Producers' outlays on durable equipment—machinery, trucks, store fixtures, lighting equipment, and so forth—are another volatile component of total investment. Critics of free enterprise consequently argue that we do not make full use of the resources that have the most to contribute to economic growth by producing such equipment, in contrast to the Communist economies, where these resources are in continuous use. But government controls over this component of investment would be very difficult to administer in our environment. Because durable equipment is so heterogeneous, controls over production or sales would have to be drawn in fine detail, and would spawn a vast bureaucracy. Such controls could not be free of bossism and might waste resources by pushing the wrong lines of production or by adapting equipment poorly to production needs. (All the Communist countries of Eastern Europe have been struggling with such sources of inefficiency in recent years.) Equally important, production or sales control could not sustain producers' outlays for durable equipment. Like controls over construction, they could only spread out a backlog of demand, were such a backlog already in existence. It is also hard to justify government controls over producers' purchases, except on stabilization grounds. This makes government intervention difficult, as business still distrusts stabilization policy—especially where that policy runs counter to the businessman's own version of his best interest. Stabilization policies may sometimes obtain acceptance masked by some other public purpose. But that is impossible in this case. Monetary and fiscal policies would seem to be government's best way of stabilizing producers' outlays on durable equipment. By fostering an adequate market for the producers' final output and by evening out the flow of financing, they can sustain his interest in plant expansion.

Inventory investment is a very tempting field for the inventors of direct-control gadgets. Success here could help enormously in economic stabilization, although the discussion in Part II has suggested that monetary and fiscal policies are not very effective in this area. Yet the practical problems of devising an effective control mechanism (let alone one that is also free of bossism) seem to be nearly hopeless. During World War II, the War Production Board experimented with a sort of inventory control. Firms were not supposed to show an unreasonable increase of inventory. But to avoid a host of separate investigations and hearings, the Board set its definition of "reasonable" so high that the rule was not really restrictive. In principle, of course, we could use a tax on *changes* in inventory, or one with variable rates on the *total* of inventory held, to penalize producers that change inventories sharply. Such an arrangement, however, might shatter on the difficulty of obtaining reliable data on inventories at sufficiently frequent intervals to be useful in stabilization.

NOTES ON

ALTERNATIVE POINTS OF VIEW

AND SUPPLEMENTARY READINGS

On the role of money in a system of "framework-incentive planning," see H. C. Simons, *Economic Policy for a Free Society* (Chicago: University of Chicago Press, 1948), pp. 40–77, 160–83.

For an influential view on the relationship among various policy goals, see W. H. Beveridge, *Full Employment in a Free Society* (New York: W. W. Norton & Company, Inc., 1945), pp. 18–39 and 242–58. Sir William's views on nonmonetary policy in relation to employment and prices (*ibid.,* pp. 124–31, 170–75, and 194–207) are also of interest as an antidote to the view that public spending policies to combat unemployment are all-sufficient.

A broad-gauged view of the stabilization problem is J. M. Clark's *Guideposts in Time of Change* (New York: Harper & Row, Publishers, 1951). A brief account of the problem, with special attention to the dispersion of professional opinion, is given in a subcommittee report to the American Economic Association (by Emile DesPres, Milton Friedman, A. G. Hart, Paul Samuelson, and D. H. Wallace), "The Problem of Economic Instability," in *American Economic Review,* September 1950. See also the recommendations for domestic stabilization policy in the report on *National and International Measures for Full Employment* (Lake Success: United Nations, 1949), pp. 73–87.

Extensive discussion of the wage-price issue will be found in D. H. Wallace's 1953 report for the 20th Century Fund (focused on the effects of economic mobilization), and in David McCord Wright, ed., *The Impact of the Union* (New York: Harcourt, Brace & World, Inc., 1951). See also J. R. Hicks, "The Instability of Wages," *Three Banks Review,* September 1956, and his "Economic Foundations of Wages Policy," *Economic Journal,* September 1955. On measures to stimulate economic growth, see *Employment, Growth and Price Levels: Staff Report to the Joint Economic Committee of Congress* (Washington, D.C.: U.S. Government Printing Office, 1959), chap. viii, and the Committee's *Hearings* on the same subject in 1959.

The conflicts among stabilization policy goals are examined in *Money and Credit,* the report of the Commission on Money and Credit (Englewood Cliffs, N.J.: Prentice-Hall, Inc., 1961), chap. i.

Chapter 20

The Economic Annals: 1919—1951

Why review the annals? This chapter is a brief review of business fluctuations and stabilization policy in the United States from the end of World War I up to the Treasury-Federal Reserve Accord in 1951. The next chapter tells the story of the first fifteen years of post-Accord economic activity. The two chapters interpret events in the light of the monetary theory of Part II. There are several reasons for such a review.

1. Having a clear notion of what an economist means when he calls up a date to illustrate a type of situation is useful. Years have personalities whose acquaintance you must make in order to follow an argument about recent economic events, just as you need some acquaintance with the personalities of John Kennedy and Lyndon Johnson to keep track of a political argument.

2. The review gives you a chance to see whether the sort of monetary theory that we offer can be used to interpret reality. This opportunity is limited, as there is room here for only a very brief and incomplete sketch. It would be best to assume that the details we mention are selected in a way that will make our theories look respectable, but you can perhaps decide whether the facts have to be strained to fit, or whether the theory is reasonably realistic.

3. The history of stabilization policy tells us something of policy-forming habits the United States has developed and gives our later discussion of monetary and fiscal policy a relevance it could not otherwise have.

399

The post-Armistice boom, 1919–20.   For a few weeks after the Armistice of November, 1918, employment and production were sharply disturbed. Munitions production was cut off in full swing, although the wartime shipbuilding program was extended for several months. There were some delays in planning peacetime operations and finding markets for civilian goods. For three or four months, some prices declined.

By the spring of 1919, business was on the upgrade. Industrial production shot up, construction contracts mounted, and department-store sales expanded. War workers and demobilized servicemen quickly found jobs. In the last months of 1919 and the first months of 1920, we had full employment.

This postwar upswing had a strongly inflationary flavor. Consumer-goods prices rose steadily until the middle of 1920, and the HCL (high cost of living) was a household word. Most groups of prices reached peaks more than double 1913 levels; in June 1920, food and clothing were even a third above early 1919 levels. Business buyers had trouble getting supplies and found they had to place each new order at a higher price than the last. With prices rising and deliveries delayed by railroad labor difficulties, buyers tried to buy ahead and build up inventories rather than to wait and buy later at higher prices. This led to a pyramiding of orders—buyers asked suppliers for more than they meant to take, in the hope of getting a fraction of what was ordered. Statistics of department-store stocks, the only major inventory series clearly visible at the time, show a sharp rise late in 1919 and early in 1920.

On the financial side, the United States Treasury apparently ran a heavy cash deficit in the first half of 1919, a small deficit in the second half, and a surplus of receipts over expenditures early in 1920. Banks started to expand loans early in 1919, and continued until late in 1920. The public's cash assets (coin and paper money outside banks plus bank deposits) rose from $34.6 billion in mid-1919 to $39.6 billion in mid-1920, or by 14 per cent in a year. But the terms of lending were stiffened late in 1919, by Federal Reserve action; all of the Reserve Banks raised their rediscount rates. Interest rates were high and rising from then until late in 1920.

The boom evidently rested on a combination of factors. The Federal cash deficit and Federal Reserve easy-money policy to aid war financing had created inflationary pressures that continued for nearly a year after the Armistice, although the policies of both agencies were working *against* inflation by early 1920. European countries were buying heavily here throughout 1919 and 1920, paying largely with the proceeds of loans from our government, which thereby continued to exert inflationary influence after they had ceased to figure as government outlays. This foreign buying was reflected in an export surplus: commodity exports exceeded $200 million in almost every month down to the middle of 1920, and totaled $4 billion for 1919. (This amount compares with a national income of under $70 billion.) Construction grew rapidly, as did automobile sales. Inventory expansion absorbed a considerable share of output.

More broadly, the boom was supported by backlogs of demand at home and abroad, similar to those that made for inflation after World War II; by an inflationary financial situation (the expansion of bank loans replacing a Treasury deficit as the source of fresh cash for the public); and by a general sense of psychological release from war tension.

The slump of 1920–21.   The boom broke during 1920. It was brought to an end by: (1) the top-heavy speculative situation in commodities—with inventories as large as they were only because business expected rising prices; (2) a sagging of exports relative to imports; and (3) monetary deflation.

The top-heaviness of the boom was itself enough to guarantee some sort of setback. Firms had felt justified in buying ahead of requirements, because they expected that they would have to pay more if they waited. Yet prices eventually advanced to a level that was felt to be abnormally high. People were willing to buy and hold goods at prices they thought excessive only because they believed that they could count on finding other people who would be foolish enough to take over the overpriced goods at still higher prices. But, when a representative owner of goods counts on finding a "sucker" to give him his profit, collapse becomes inevitable; the holders will eventually realize that they themselves are the worst suckers of all. When they arrive at this moment of truth, they will try to unload and will break prices.[1]

At the time, a favorite explanation of the break was a "buyers' strike" on the part of consumers. Economists have been inclined to belittle this explanation, alleging that consumers would not take this initiative. In the light of our experience in 1951, however, 1920 should perhaps be re-examined. There is excellent evidence that consumer resistance to high prices helped to break the inflation that began with the Korean War.

The monetary stringency of 1920 resulted from deliberate actions by the Federal Reserve System. During World War I, it had permitted and even fostered a great credit expansion to facilitate war spending. This expansion rested on: a lowering of commercial-bank reserve requirements when the Federal Reserve Act went into force; the gold imports of 1915–17 with which the Allied countries paid for some of their war purchases; and an expansion of Reserve bank credit (Reserve holdings of rediscounts, acceptances, and government securities) that was undertaken to keep Treasury securities at good prices. The Federal Reserve did not support bond prices by open-market purchases, as it did in World War II, but it stood ready to buy private debt and thus indirectly to facilitate purchases of government securities by commercial banks and the public.

---

[1] This sort of top-heaviness characterizes a genuine boom, as distinct from the prosperity on which a boom is superimposed. The famous Florida land boom of the early 1920's, the stock market boom of the late 1920's, and various suburban real estate booms have been like this. Boom psychology does not usually affect all classes of assets at once. Thus, in 1919–20 there was a boom in commodities and farm real estate, but stock dealers did not share in the excitement, and the stock market began to fall late in 1919.

It set preferential rediscount rates on so-called "war paper"—IOU's written by banks and individuals to raise the cash they needed for purchases of government bonds. By the end of the war, member-bank rediscounts, including "war paper," exceeded total commercial-bank reserve balances, so that owned reserves were below zero and the banks were operating entirely with *borrowed* reserves.[2]

Once the Treasury's debt operations seemed to be under control, the Federal Reserve set about raising interest rates. All of the Federal Reserve Banks raised rediscount rates at least twice between October 1919 and June 1920. Starting at 4 per cent or $4\frac{1}{2}$ per cent in October 1919, the rates at all the Federal Reserve Banks had risen to 6 per cent by February 1920, and, at four of the more important banks, went on to 7 per cent in June. No reductions were made until the spring of 1921. The commercial banks responded by raising the rates charged on loans to customers. These reached a peak of about 7 per cent in the winter of 1920–21. Rates on open-market commercial paper had ranged from $5\frac{1}{8}$ to $5\frac{3}{8}$ per cent during most of 1919, and rose to $8\frac{1}{8}$ per cent for July-November 1920. Yields on every type of bond rose on about the same timetable (that is, prices fell). Most bonds were already selling below par value in 1919, and went down still further in 1920. United States government bonds (*Liberty bonds*) had averaged 92 per cent of par in 1919, and were down to 82.6 per cent in August 1920.

The Federal Reserve Banks did not appreciably change their holdings of government securities during this high-interest period. The System had not yet recognized the power of open-market operations and did not begin to use them as a monetary weapon until 1922 or 1923. In early 1922, the individual Reserve Banks purchased government securities to maintain their income in the face of declining rediscounts. As the System came to understand the monetary impact of these purchases, it began to coordinate the separate transactions of the individual Reserve Banks. Federal Reserve holdings of acceptances dropped by several hundred million dollars during 1920. This intensified the shortage of reserves, and the commercial banks virtually stopped loan expansion in the middle of 1920. During the autumn, they actually began a rapid contraction of loans outstanding.

A case for monetary deflation as *the cause* of the *downturn* is difficult to make. Loans continued to expand slightly for several months past the middle of 1920, presumably because the banks were making loans to firms in distress. High interest rates and the associated decline in bond prices presumably reduced the availability of bonds and of unused line of credit as money substitutes, and

---

[2] In June 1917 (when the use of reserve balances as sole legal reserves became effective), member banks had $1.05 billion of reserve balances and $0.20 billion of rediscounts. Owned reserves were, therefore, $0.85 billion. But they had to get new reserve funds to meet a drain of paper money into circulation; the currency figure rose from $3.78 billion in June 1917 to $4.95 billion in December 1918, and to $5.41 billion in October 1920. In addition, the growth of the public's deposits built up reserve requirements. The need for larger reserves forced a growth of rediscounts to a peak of $2.81 billion (October 1920); at this stage, reserve balances were $1.82 billion, so that owned reserves were *minus* $0.99 billion.

thereby tended to increase the demand for cash assets. Although the business downturn happened too soon to be the result of this monetary contraction, the credit contraction was fairly sharp once it started. The loans of member banks fell continuously from a high of $19.9 billion in November 1920 to a low of $17.1 billion in March 1922—a drop of about 15 per cent. The public's stock of cash assets apparently dropped about 5 per cent, mainly between November 1920 and June 1921.[3] This deflation doubtless contributed to the speed and depth of the *downswing* once that downswing got started.

The timing of the 1920 downturn is fascinating. The National Bureau of Economic Research has set its "reference date" for the downturn at the very beginning of 1920. In retrospect, however, one can see signs that the boom was breaking up even before the start of the year. The net export balance reached its peak in the spring of 1919. Thereafter, imports increased as the export capacity of other countries began to revive, and our exports sagged after the spring of 1920. Residential building contracts showed a clear downturn in the middle of 1919, and nonresidential construction contracts slipped at the turn of the year. Securities prices (stocks as well as bonds) began to subside late in 1919. In production, nondurable manufactures reached their high point at the start of 1920, sagged off very slightly during the spring, and began to fall rapidly in June. Durable manufactures were almost as active in the third quarter of 1920 as in the first, and the slump in durables was not clearly visible until late autumn. Department store sales reached a peak in May 1920, and held near peak levels through the summer.

As the Federal Reserve Board said in its *Annual Report for 1920:*[4] "It was not until the spring of 1920 that it became generally recognized that reaction had set in, and that the country was passing through the most acute stage of transition from wartime delirium to the more normal conditions of peace." What gave the slump public recognition was the clear-cut break in prices in the spring of 1920.[5] Wholesale prices of various groups of commodities reached their peaks

---

[3] After this date, the effect of a gold inflow on cash assets roughly offset those of the loan contraction.

[4] P. 1. This report went to press in February 1921.

[5] A Federal Reserve Board comment on prices in the report just cited (p. 8) makes fascinating reading in the aftermath of World War II:

> The equilibrium of prices could have been maintained only through an increased or at least sustained buying power, as well as disposition to buy on the part of the public, which was not existent. Consequently, it became evident after the first quarter of the year that the buying or consumptive power was not sufficient in volume to absorb the greater quantities of goods which were being steadily produced and offered to the public. The practical question accordingly arose whether reductions in prices would not be necessary in order to move the current output of manufactured goods. In some lines an effort was made to solve the problem through a voluntary restriction of production, but it soon became evident that such measures were inadequate, and accordingly substantial reductions in prices of some articles which had reached a high level were announced by producers.

in April or May of 1920, and then broke decisively. Retail prices turned down sharply in June. This meant a clean reversal of the speculative inventory situation. Instead of building up inventories, business was trying to cut them down. This inventory break was probably decisive in setting off the spectacularly rapid downswing.

By December 1920, the downswing had carried nondurable manufacturing down to two-thirds of its peak level of early 1920, but nondurable production began to increase early in 1921. Durable manufactures, by contrast, started to decline later, and kept on declining until, in the summer of 1921, they fell to less than half the highest levels reached in 1920. Wholesale prices also fell drastically to a 1921 trough not much over half the 1920 peak level, although a third above prewar prices. And consumers' prices continued to fall into 1922, reaching a trough about one-fifth below the 1920 peak, although more than 50 per cent above prewar levels.

Recovery to full employment, 1921–23. The National Bureau reference date for the beginning of the upswing after the slump comes in the late summer of 1921, but as with the preceding downswing, there was a wide scatter in the dates at which the major elements of activity began to move. The sequence in physical activity was roughly the same as in the downswing. Construction paced the rise, with residential construction improving from the first month of 1921, and other construction beginning to gain two months later. Nondurable manufactures began to rise at about the same time as construction, while durable manufactures did not turn up until late in the summer—about the time of the reference date. Mining had been last to fall, holding up until the end of 1920, and was also last to recover. The upswing might have started earlier— at the very end of 1921—but was interrupted by the coal strike of 1922; there were no strong gains in mineral output until late in 1922.

The strain on the banks and, through the banks, on business, eased steadily in 1921–22. Gold began to come in from abroad late in 1920, and during 1921, there was a rise of more than $700 million in the gold stock. At the same time, money in circulation dropped—by over $900 million during 1921—benefiting the reserve position of the banks. Using the reserve funds from these two sources, member banks were able to pay off most of their rediscounts. By the end of 1921, rediscounts were down to $1.14 billion, leaving member banks with $0.61 billion of owned reserves out of $1.75 billion in total reserve balances. By the middle of 1922, rediscounts were down to $0.46 billion, reserve balances were up to $1.82 billion, bringing owned reserves to $1.36 billion. In the spring of 1921, furthermore, the Federal Reserve banks belatedly began lowering rediscount and acceptance rates; the rediscount rates came down to 4 per cent and $4\frac{1}{2}$ per cent by the summer of 1922. In response, open-market money rates in New York began to drop gradually early in 1921. This drop grew faster later in the year, and was paralleled by a drop in the rates charged on customers' loans. Bond yields showed similar changes. Interest rates in 1922 were well below their 1919 levels, and, in many sectors, below prewar prosperity levels. The shrinkage of bank loans continued until early 1922, but after the middle of 1921, apparently, the banks did not put much pressure on customers to repay.

The upturn in physical production took place before prices ended their decline. Only one important price series was rising before production started up —the rent series, which had the unique record of rising throughout the decline of business.[6] Farm prices began to rise in the summer of 1921, just about the reference date of the upturn. But wholesale prices of industrial commodities did not begin a sustained rise until March 1922, while consumers' prices kept on declining until the summer of 1922.

Once the upswing in output was underway, it took hold vigorously. Industrial production rose from two-thirds of potential in mid-1921 to about 95 per cent of potential in fifteen months—a gain of nearly 2 per cent per month. Virtually all lines of activity were close to full-employment levels by the end of 1922, despite the setback of the coal strike. There was also a fairly sharp upswing of commodity prices, and the stock market rose by a good 60 per cent from its low point in August 1921 to the March 1923 peaks. At the time, these price developments caused some worry; in perspective, they look like healthy correctives to the price distortions of the 1920–21 recession.

Several factors apparently fostered this recovery. Most important was the strong demand for housing and other buildings, evidenced by the buoyancy of rents. Although construction had been high before the war, it had fallen behind in 1917–18, and a backlog of demand had piled up. There was also a backlog of demand for producers' durable equipment—machinery, trucks, and so forth. Another powerful factor was the automobile. It had been "sold" to the American public by this time, but its production had been checked by the war.

At the time, much stress was placed upon "confidence" as a stimulus to recovery. Whatever Europeans thought, most Americans believed that we had won a victory in World War I (we then called it *the* World War), and that our way of life had proved itself and was gaining well-deserved imitation. The success of the Federal Reserve in steering us through the 1920 crash without a suspension of cash payments and wholesale bankruptcies gave ground for belief in the soundness of our monetary and business arrangements. The election of November 1920 was a triumph for political conservatives who doubtless benefited from the fact that they had been in opposition rather than in office when prices fell and unemployment climbed. The new administration's slogan of "back to normalcy" suited the times. It is hard to tell how heavily we should weight these factors in a balanced explanation of the upswing. But at the very least, there were no barriers on the side of confidence which could have kept

---

[6] Rents had risen much less than most prices during the war, largely owing to the rent controls of state governments which were relaxed in 1920–21.

other favorable factors from working. And as the profitability of construction depends largely on returns in the distant future, confidence must be regarded as part of the basis for the rise in construction that paced the recovery.

The "new era": 1923–29. With 1923, the country entered on a stretch of fairly continuous high employment, often called at the time the "new era" or (with pleasing alliteration) a "plateau of permanent prosperity." Analysts of business cycles recognize three distinct peaks in this period, in 1923, 1926, and 1929, and two troughs, in 1924 and 1927. But in the seven-year stretch, industrial production was above 90 per cent of potential during sixty-two of the eighty-four months, and never got below 80 per cent. The 1924 and 1927 recessions were too brief and shallow to be spoken of in the same breath with the 1920–22 depression, let alone that of the 1930's.

From the Armistice until 1923, developments in the United States had much in common with developments in Europe. The post-Armistice boom of 1919–20 and the 1920–22 depression were international affairs, although the timetable differed somewhat from country to country. When the next upswing brought a disastrous inflation to a number of European countries, observers in this country became alarmed at *our* 1923 price flurry.[7] To be safe, the Federal Reserve put on the brakes by tightening up slightly on credit. Acceptance buying rates were raised in stages, beginning with September 1922. And early in 1923, the three Federal Reserve Banks (including New York) that had a 4 per cent rediscount rate were leveled up to the $4\frac{1}{2}$ per cent rate of the other nine. Federal Reserve holdings of government securities were reduced, and in October 1923, member bank borrowings were up to $0.87 billion and owned reserves down to $0.97 billion. The interest rates charged by banks stiffened in response, as did bond yields. The pressure was much less severe than that of 1920–21, and did not last so long; but it continued until the middle of 1924, when a decline of both prices and business activity was clearly visible. The downturn from 1923 to 1924 is consequently attributed by many authorities to Federal Reserve pressure.

This downturn was well marked in the production of durable and nondurable manufactures and minerals, but many people scarcely noticed the recession. It did not show up in construction; on the contrary, construction reached new highs in the first half of 1924. Despite price declines, it barely appeared in the curve of dollar sales at department stores. Recovery took hold quickly and strongly; industrial output remained below 90 per cent of potential for only

---

[7] It is a little hard, with hindsight, to share these fears of 1923. The Continental inflations were in countries whose governments were spending heavily and could not or would not raise enough revenue to cover the bulk of expenditures, and where confidence was badly shaken. In Great Britain, which had more or less paralleled our 1919–22 experience, the recovery did not come back to a full-employment level, let alone generate inflation, and signs of chronic unemployment were visible in 1923. In view of the "hand-to-mouth buying" practices adopted by much of American business after 1920, we were not in great danger of another top-heavy inventory boom.

nine months. The 1924 recession, in the end, was not much more than a ripple on the economic stream. That it was short and mild may have been the result of an easy money policy that was largely motivated by the Federal Reserve's desire to cooperate in the re-establishment of gold standards abroad. Interest rates were kept low to avoid attracting gold from Europe to New York.[8]

The years 1925 and 1926 brought solid prosperity. Industrial production grew in line with the normal growth of potential, and held steadily above 90 per cent of potential. Farm prices rose rather sharply in 1925, but rents ended their long rise, and crested at the beginning of 1925. Other prices were reasonably steady.

With the edge taken off the housing shortage, a slight fall occurred in residential construction in 1926. But total construction reached its postwar peak in 1926, thanks to a further rise in other forms of construction. Durable manufactures and minerals flagged somewhat in 1927, with durables dropping briefly below 80 per cent of potential in the autumn of 1927.[9] Industrial production as a whole (both branches of manufacturing plus mineral production) was below 90 per cent of potential for less than a year, and by a narrow margin. By the latter part of 1928, durables and nondurables came back close to full-employment levels and stayed there through most of 1929. Construction, however, fell off from 1927 to 1928 and again, more sharply, from 1928 to 1929.

Toward the end of the 1920's, policy attention was focused on the stock market. From a low point late in 1923, stock prices climbed almost uninterruptedly until late in 1929. The increase of prices exceeded 1 per cent a month and brought them to a peak more than triple their 1923 level. The Federal Reserve, however, had maintained an easy money policy from the middle of 1924 to the middle of 1928. Discount rates sometimes ran as high as $4\frac{1}{2}$ per cent, but most member banks were not heavily in debt, while setbacks in the growth of bank loans and of the public's cash assets were rare and mild. Discount rates were actually reduced early in 1927 with an eye to European monetary conditions.[10] But this 1927 episode hardly deserves the criticism it has so often received; it was hardly the decisive factor in building the stock-market boom to a top-heavy stage. The small decrease in discount rates in 1927 was not needed to give stock prices their upward momentum, although a sharp increase in discount rates might have discouraged borrowing for stock-market speculation had such an increase been made as early as 1927.

In any event, the stock market did reach a top-heavy stage, and by 1929 was visibly supported only by the "find-a-worse-sucker" psychology. It was

---

[8] See E. A. Goldenweiser, *American Monetary Policy* (New York: McGraw-Hill Book Company, Inc., 1951), pp. 141–42.

[9] This slump was widely attributed to the shutdown of the Ford plant at the time when Model T was dropped and Model A was introduced, but the effect seems too large relative to the alleged cause.

[10] See Goldenweiser, *American Monetary Policy,* pp. 145–46.

ripe for a crash. The Federal Reserve, meanwhile, had taken alarm.[11] In early 1928, it had raised rediscount and acceptance rates to their highest levels since 1921. The rediscount rate was 6 per cent at the Federal Reserve Bank of New York, and 5 per cent at other Federal Reserve Banks. Government securities and acceptances at the Reserve Banks were worked down from about $0.9 billion in 1928 to about $0.2 billion in the summer of 1929. Member banks were thrown into debt, and in July 1929, had rediscounts of $1.1 billion. Owned reserves were just about half as large as the $2.3 billion in total reserve balances. The interest rates charged by banks, especially on the stock-exchange call loans that the Federal Reserve was trying to curtail, were higher than they had been for years.

The 1929 crash will be examined presently. First, let us turn back to seek the basis of the "new-era" prosperity. That prosperity was supported by a combination much like the one that launched prosperity in the revival of 1922–23: (1) the backlog of construction demand; (2) the automobile and its accessories, including highway construction; and (3) "confidence." We must also allow for two additional props: (4) the growth of demand for consumers' durables, financed as were automobiles by consumer credit; and (5) an export surplus that was financed by American purchases of foreign securities to the tune of $1 billion a year, and by gold imports when our purchases flagged. All of these factors combined to generate a large volume of investment.

Looking back, it is hard to understand America's complacency about the "permanence" of our "plateau." We had worked through the construction backlog, and we had ample warnings in the successive downturns of construction components, and especially in the decline of total construction during 1928. The terms on which we were making foreign loans implied that foreign borrowing power might run out. German municipalities were among our most important borrowers; their prewar debts had been wiped out by the inflation of the early 1920's, and they were diligently borrowing up to their debt limits and in total disregard of Germany's capacity to service overseas debt. The Latin American countries were also heavy borrowers, and their capacity to incur debt was also limited. For much of the new era, American agriculture was in trouble, and there were recurrent warnings that the market for automobiles could become saturated.

Stabilization policy has much to answer for in the 1920's. It probably could not have prevented a weakening of the props to prosperity, but it should have anticipated this inevitable weakening and made efforts to offset the decline of construction, the drop in foreign borrowing, and other changes that could end prosperity. As things turned out, it had nothing in reserve.

Crisis and recession: 1929–31. The National Bureau's reference date for the 1929 downturn comes late in the spring. Nondurable manufactures

---

[11]The White House and Treasury continued to issue cheerful pronouncements, often timed to offset pessimistic Federal Reserve utterances.

started to decline at that time, durable manufactures at midyear. Construction, as noted above, was already on the downgrade in 1928, and in the aggregate, declined again in 1929. Commodity prices were declining mildly throughout 1929, except for food prices, which increased for several months in the middle of the year. The stock exchange crash of September—the great dramatic event of 1929—came when business volume and commodity prices were already on the downgrade. But the psychological change brought about by the crash presumably speeded up the drop in output in the autumn.

The year 1930 was one of worsening depression. At its start, industrial output was already below 90 per cent of potential; by the year's end, it was only about 65 per cent. Stock prices rebounded early in the year, but turned down again in April. All classes of commodity prices fell rapidly, and unemployment became a matter of grave public concern. Discontent over the downswing had much to do with the Democratic victory in the 1930 Congressional elections, which left us with a Republican President and Senate but a Democratic House of Representatives.

Early in 1931, business looked better. For several months the production of durable and nondurable manufactures rose slightly, as did the output of minerals. There was a pause in the decline of farm prices. Many analysts felt that the country was ripe for recovery, and it was at this time that President Hoover made his much-ridiculed but rather reasonable guess that "prosperity is just around the corner." These hopes of recovery were soon to be dashed. The downswing was renewed as 1931 wore on.

In 1928–29, the Federal Reserve had imposed a tight-money policy, with interest rates high and commercial banks heavily in debt. Whereas through most of the "new era" there had been a fairly smooth growth in bank assets and in the public's cash assets, the public's cash holdings fell during the first half of 1929. Business loans grew a little as funds were supplied from the reduction of investments and some new bank capital. But, on the whole, there was still monetary stringency.

Late in 1929, after the market crash, the Federal Reserve turned to an easy-money policy. Rediscount rates were lowered several times; the New York Federal Reserve Bank, for instance, cut its rate from 6 per cent to 5 per cent on November 1, 1929, to $4\frac{1}{2}$ per cent on November 15, to 4 per cent on February 7, 1930, to $3\frac{1}{2}$ per cent on March 14, to 3 per cent on May 2, to $2\frac{1}{2}$ per cent on June 20, to 2 per cent on December 24, and, finally, to $1\frac{1}{2}$ per cent on May 8, 1931. The Federal Reserve Banks also expanded their holdings of government securities and acceptances, and lowered member-bank borrowings to about $200 million in the spring of 1930. But despite this easing of the reserve position, commercial banks continued to contract credit. Their loan rates fell much less than rediscount rates, the published averages dropping from just over 6 per cent late in 1929 to about $4\frac{1}{2}$ per cent early in 1931. This decline in average rates may have been caused by the refusal of credit to high-rate borrowers, not by a reduction in the rates charged to particular customers. The loans of all commercial banks combined dropped from $36.0 billion at the end of 1929 to $32.0 billion at the end of 1930, and to $29.2 billion in June 1931. The public's cash assets dropped from 54.5 billion at the end of 1929 to $53.2 billion at the end of 1930, and to $52.5 billion in the middle of 1931.[12]

Apart from easing the position of banks, government policy consisted mainly of efforts at maintaining confidence. After the stock-market crash, as before, there were frequent official testimonials to the soundness of the American economic system. The President urged businessmen not to cut wages, and to hold up the volume of construction.[13] A special effort was made, moreover, to stabilize farm prices. A Federal Farm Board was set up in 1929 and armed with a revolving fund of $0.5 billion to finance agricultural co-operatives, including specially created "stabilization co-operatives," that were trying to hold farm products off the market. But the slump was so severe that prices went down despite this withdrawal of goods from the market. The Treasury's policy was conservative. Throughout the "new era," there had been an excess of Treasury cash income over cash outgo. This surplus was continued through the middle of 1930. Thereafter, an increase in outlays and the effects of depression on tax revenues combined to produce a deficit.[14]

Prolonged panic: 1931–33. The signs of recovery that appeared early in 1931 were washed away by new financial catastrophes originating in Europe. The United States may have been ripe for recovery, but the rest of the world was going from bad to worse. Great Britain and Germany, as well as several other countries, had suffered from chronic unemployment during the 1920's. But long exposure to chronic depression did not immunize them to a further

---

[12]The fall in the public's cash assets was thus only $2.0 billion from the end of 1929 to the middle of 1931, against a $6.8 billion fall in commercial-bank loans. The discrepancy is accounted for by: (1) a growth of $2.2 billion in commercial-bank investments; (2) a growth of $1.0 billion in mutual-savings-bank earning assets; (3) heavy write-offs of loans deemed uncollectible—especially at closed banks.

[13]Several branches of public-utility construction, particularly the building of railroad facilities, actually reached their interwar peaks in 1930.

[14]Quarterly (cash basis) figures are given as follows by H. H. Villard in *Deficit Spending and the National Income* (New York: Farrar, Straus & Company, 1941), p. 285:

Date	Expenditure	Receipts	Excess of Expenditure
1929:			
July–Sept.	$ 782	$980	$−199
Oct.–Dec.	802	939	−137
1930:			
Jan.–Mar.	820	924	−104
Apr.–June	893	989	− 96
July–Sept.	1,056	843	213
Oct.–Dec.	1,068	831	237
1931:			
Jan.–Mar.	1,048	705	343
Apr.–June	1,162	652	510

decline. Confidence abroad had never fully recovered after World War I and was shaken again in 1931. The loss of American markets as this country's depression deepened and as imports encountered the massive tariff wall we had enacted in 1930,[15] along with a stoppage of our foreign lending, increased unemployment in Europe and led to a sharp financial crisis.

This financial crisis began to take shape in Austria in the late spring of 1931. The Kredit-Anstalt, the chief bank of Vienna, fell into difficulties. This led many people to doubt the solvency of German banks that had loans in Austria. In the summer of 1931, the "Stand-still Agreement" stopped transfers of funds out of Germany. But the crisis then spread to London, as British banks had lent money to Germans. Foreigners (including Americans) with funds on deposit in London tried to repatriate them before the British ceased to pay at par.

Just at this time, and probably as a reflection of the European crisis, American finance took a turn for the worse. Although our economy was seriously depressed by this time, confidence had not been badly shaken. The surest sign of panic—a conversion of bank deposits into paper money—had barely appeared. Down to the very end of 1930, currency in circulation was lower each month than in the same month a year before. There was a wave of bank failures at the very end of 1930, but it did not apparently scare the public very much, and in the first months of 1931 currency in circulation was about $4.3 or $4.4 billion—up only $0.1 billion from 1930. That confidence was still strong is also shown by the fact that the prices of municipal and corporate bonds were at record highs in May 1931. But in June 1931, we had another serious wave of bank failures; the currency circulation started to climb rapidly, and bond prices began to sag.

Britain, we said earlier, went off the gold standard in September 1931, and thereby shifted the international pressure to New York. Foreigners began to say that the dollar would be next to go, and in October 1931, large sums were transferred abroad (especially by foreign central banks), cutting our gold reserves by over $400 million. The remaining $4.0 billion was just $0.3 billion short of the highest pre-1931 figure on record. Yet our bankers and financiers were badly shaken.

The Federal Reserve reversed its policy of easy money in what was either a slavish adherence to the traditional rules of the gold standard or an unwarranted panic at our small gold loss. The New York Federal Reserve Bank jumped its rediscount rate from $1\frac{1}{2}$ to $2\frac{1}{2}$ per cent on October 9, and to $3\frac{1}{2}$ per cent on October 16. Acceptance rates also were raised. The Reserve Banks bought some securities, but not enough to offset the effects of gold losses and of the public's withdrawal of currency from the banks; rediscounts shot up from about $250 million to $1,025 million between early September and the end of 1931, bringing the owned reserves of member banks down from $2.1 to $1.3 billion.

---

[15]This was the Hawley-Smoot Tariff of 1930, the highest in our history, once called the "Holy Smoke Tariff" by a student with more insight than accuracy.

The commercial banks tightened up on credit. In the last three months of 1931 and the first six of 1932, bank loans were shrinking by more than $0.5 billion per month. From the middle of 1931 to the middle of 1932, the public's cash assets fell from $52.4 to $45.0 billion. Bond prices sagged, and the prices of corporate stocks fell by a third from March 1931 to September, and by 58 per cent of their September level through June 1932. Loans secured by stocks "froze" in bankers' hands, as did business loans.[16] Hundreds of banks closed in each month of late 1931, blocking large masses of deposits.[17]

This stretch of history is unedifying. Our financial leaders, including the Federal Reserve authorities, yielded to panic, and official explanations do not make matters look any better. In their 1931 report, the Federal Reserve Board remarked drily that "after the middle of September, in view of the outflow of gold from the country and of currency into hoarding, the Federal Reserve Banks increased their rates on discounts and acceptances."[18] The Treasury called for drastic cuts in government spending, and for tax increases to yield $1.1 billion per year. Congress granted these requests—and compounded the damage by levying $650 million of the new taxes as excise and stamp taxes on commodities and services.[19]

Although it contributed to deflation through central-bank policy and taxation early in 1932, the government did start trying to combat the depression—or at least to mitigate its effects. Congress passed legislation that established the Reconstruction Finance Corporation and that freed the hands of the Federal Reserve (the Glass-Steagall Act).

The RFC and the shift in banking policy were an effort to stem the panic on what commentators at the time called the "trickle-down" system. The RFC was empowered to lend to distressed banks and to railways, in order to keep trouble from spreading from these weak spots. The abrogation of artificial collateral rules that had tied up gold[20] put the Federal Reserve in a position to

---

[16]Metaphors are tricky. In physics, pressure liquefies solids; in banking, pressure freezes what is liquid.

[17]Perhaps $1 billion of the $7.5 billion shrinkage in the cash assets of the nonbank public during the twelve months ending June 1932 was the result of the blocking up of deposits in suspended banks. About $1.6 billion was on deposit in banks that suspended, but part of this amount was released by the reopening of the banks or the sale of their assets to surviving banks.

[18]*Annual Report for 1931*, p. 6. This report was drafted with the aid of a good deal of hindsight, bearing the date of June 6, 1932. Comments made in the 1932 *Annual Report* (pp. 16–19) imply regret at having kept the member banks short of owned reserves, but offer retrospective excuses based on restrictive rules applying to the Federal Reserve banks themselves.

For strong evidence that the Federal Reserve authorities were disastrously slow to size up the damage their deflationary policy was doing, see H. H. Villard, "The Federal Reserve System's Monetary Policy in 1931 and 1932," *Journal of Political Economy*, December 1937. For a qualified defense of the Federal Reserve's action (based chiefly on policy pressure exerted by the Bank of France), see Goldenweiser, *American Monetary Policy*, pp. 158–61.

[19]The tax increases were requested to preserve the "unimpaired credit of the Federal Government." See Secretary of the Treasury, *Annual Report for 1932*, p. 256.

[20]See above, pp. 406–408. The Federal Reserve was previously required to post "collateral" for Federal Reserve notes—up to 60 per cent in acceptances or rediscounts, and not

ease the plight of bankers. In both cases, the major immediate beneficiaries were the big businesses; ordinary mortals were expected to benefit indirectly, through the unfreezing of credit. In the summer of 1932, however, $500 million of federal funds were made available for unemployment relief—distributed by the RFC as loans (later canceled) to the states.

The Federal Reserve Bank of New York cut its rediscount rate from $3\frac{1}{2}$ to 3 per cent on the very day (February 26, 1932) that Congress changed the gold rules by passing the Glass-Steagall Act.[21] A further cut to $2\frac{1}{2}$ per cent was made in June, when the Chicago Bank also cut to $2\frac{1}{2}$ per cent. All the other Federal Reserve Banks, however, held their rates at $3\frac{1}{2}$ per cent throughout 1932 and early 1933.[22] Acceptance rates were cut in several stages, and reached 1 per cent (for sixty- to ninety-day bills) in June. During March, the Federal Reserve began to build up its holdings of government securities, but the increase did not become rapid until April. The RFC, meanwhile, had started operations at the end of January, and by June had loaned $420 million to banks and $139 million to railways. Bank failures slowed down in the spring, some coin and paper money returned from hoarding, and by May, bank rediscounts had fallen below $500 million. Interest rates dropped somewhat and bond prices recovered a little. But stock prices kept on sagging, and the liquidation of bank loans did not stop.

In the middle of 1932, business volume began to revive after its long decline. Mining began to expand in June, nondurable manufacturing in July, and durable manufacturing in August. At the middle of the year, wage-and-salary payments began to grow, despite a continued cutting of wage rates, and department-store sales improved a little. A new spurt of bank failures broke out in June and early July but was stopped, at the cost of seriously crippling the rescue operations of the RFC.[23] Commodity prices recovered slightly and the average of stock prices rose by 72 per cent from June to September.

Before long, however, a fresh decline set in. Commodity prices were on the

---

less than 40 per cent in gold, but to use enough gold to make up any deficiency of rediscounts and acceptances. With the huge rise in the note circulation during 1931–32, the requirement tied up most of the Reserve's gold, even though rediscounts were so heavy that commercial banks were deflating credit at a great rate. Open-market purchases of government bonds to give the banks more owned reserves would have reduced rediscounts and would thereby force the substitution of gold for rediscounts as collateral. The slowness of the Federal Reserve authorities to start such open-market purchases is doubtless explained by the artificial gold stringency. On the other hand, this explanation offers no justification whatever for the System's failure to increase its holdings of acceptances, or for the two-month lag in taking advantage of the new law to start open-market purchases.

[21] The official enactment date is February 27—the date of President Hoover's signature.

[22] Two of the Reserve banks (Richmond and Dallas) had raised to 4 per cent instead of $3\frac{1}{2}$ per cent in October 1931, and came back into line at $3\frac{1}{2}$ per cent in January 1932.

[23] The most conspicuous bank in trouble at this time was the Central Republic Bank of Chicago, and the head of the RFC (General Dawes) was an officer of that bank, on leave. Given its responsibilities and policies, the RFC had no alternative but to grant the Central Republic the loan that averted its failure. Yet there was a great outcry that General Dawes in his official capacity was rescuing General Dawes in his personal capacity; and thereafter, the RFC's lending policy was more timid.

downgrade again in September, nondurable manufacturing turned down in November, and durable manufacturing in December. The Democratic victory in the November election was a shock to conservatives, and a renewed loss of confidence may explain the fresh wave of hoarding and bank failures that began in December. Certainly the political hiatus between the election of President Roosevelt in November and his inauguration in March explains the helplessness of government to stem the panic. In the early weeks of 1933, currency in circulation rose from $5.7 to $7.5 billion, and rediscounts at the Federal Reserve Banks went up from $0.3 to $1.4 billion. Persistent runs threatened to carry down sound banks as well as weak ones; in several states, governors took the responsibility of declaring "bank holidays." Five states had closed all of their banks at the end of February, and seventeen others followed in the first three days of March. One of the first acts of the new administration was to make the bank holiday nationwide.

As the new President and Congress took office, the country was almost paralyzed. Industrial production was down to about 40 per cent of potential, having been below 50 per cent for a solid year. Unemployment exceeded 15 million, and many of the employed were on short hours. Construction was almost at a standstill. Stock prices, although above the 1932 low, were about one-fifth of 1929 levels. Farm prices were below 40 per cent of 1929, and commodity prices, other than those of farm and food products, were below 80 per cent of their 1929 levels. Hourly factory wages were also below 80 per cent of 1929.

Partial recovery under the "first New Deal": 1933–35. Beginning in March 1933, there was a rapid upturn, Most of the banks were reopened, with a tacit government guarantee of their safety that was soon made explicit by the establishment of the Federal Deposit Insurance Corporation. Bank loans and investments expanded, creating fresh deposits. The home-loan and farm-loan agencies described in Part I were set to work, and the RFC stepped up its activity.

The new administration and Congress set about fashioning a recovery program (the "first New Deal") that rested mainly on two agencies—the National Recovery Administration and the Agricultural Adjustment Administration. The NRA operated chiefly through *codes* that it established for various industries. These aimed to spread employment by reducing work hours, to stop "chiselers" from price-cutting forms of competition, and to raise prices and wages. They were reached by agreement among the firms in each industry and were subject to approval by NRA. Many of them were actually designed to raise profits and to tighten up price-raising and price-maintaining arrangements.[24] Pending the adoption of the industrial codes, business was made to obey a "blanket code"

---

[24]It is no mere coincidence that this experiment with "self-government in industry" as the core of economic policy came at the time when Fascist Italy and Nazi Germany were moving toward economic control through a "corporate state"—that is, a structure of comprehensive business cartels, subject to government supervision and regulation.

that raised wages, shortened hours, guaranteed labor's right to bargain collectively, and checked "chiseling" on prices. The "triple A" aimed to raise farm prices, mainly by restricting acreage for major crops.

Manufacturing output jumped in the spring of 1933, and until 1935, seesawed between the mid-1933 level and a few points lower. Employment held its gains thanks to work-spreading. Prices jumped and then continued to rise more smoothly, while cash expansion was about in line with the price rise. This brisk rise in output, followed by stagnation, can be traced to the inventory boom that NRA produced. Merchants had cut down their inventories during the slump, and needed more stock to handle even a partial revival of sales. In addition, NRA guaranteed against a further cut in prices while threatening a sharp rise of money costs. For a few months there were very strong incentives to expand inventories, but the resulting spurt in output was bound to be reversed.[25]

The new administration came in pledged to economy. Government salaries were cut, and despite generous grants to state and local governments for the finance of relief programs, the combined net income-increasing expenditures of government were lower through most of 1933 than they had been in 1932.[26] The government had started a public works program, but it took more than a year for these public works to begin operating on a sufficient scale to offset reductions in state and local construction.

The administration declined to work for international recovery. At the London Conference in the summer of 1933, it refused to commit this country to a definite program of international co-operation, and late in 1933, it devalued the dollar.

The first New Deal, then, was basically a program of price boosting and monetary expansion. In the end, this combination did not work. Activity revived a bit, but only to a less acute depression level. Thanks to fuller employment at shorter hours and more generous relief, actual suffering from the depression was much mitigated. But the level of activity was not high enough to revive private investment; most firms still had excess capacity. From the monetary standpoint, the price-boosting campaign largely nullified monetary expansion. The gain in cash balances was roughly offset because firm and households needed more cash to do the same volume of business at higher prices.

Upswing: 1935–37. In 1935 conditions changed, and a definite upswing finally set in as private investment revived. The system of codes had been swept away, to everyone's relief, by an adverse court decision. There was a rise of public works expenditures, new work relief programs, and so forth, but they were roughly offset by the increase of tax yields at higher-income levels, and the

---

[25]Despite this spurt, there was a net decline in physical inventory for 1933 as a whole.

[26]See H. H. Villard, *Deficit Spending and the National Income* (New York: Farrar, Strauss & Company, 1941), p. 323. "Net income-increasing expenditures" means roughly the excess of cash outgo over cash income. Villard's monthly series (1929–39) covers state and local governments as well as the federal government.

income-increasing expenditure on which some people based their hopes for recovery was lower through most of 1935 than in 1934. It was mainly a growth of business investment that sparked recovery, as capital outlays for private investment ran above $6 billion in 1935, as against less than $3 billion in 1934.

The upswing continued into 1936, backed by a heavy government deficit and the continued growth in the cash supply. In the summer of 1936, more than a billion dollars of cash was distributed as a bonus to veterans. While output was still well below capacity, some people began to feel prosperous. There was a great deal more building, and all the investment accounts showed a gain.

Early in 1937, for the first time since 1929, some observers were actually worried about inflation. In retrospect, 1936 and 1937 appear as seriously depressed years. But at the time, people were acclimated to depression, so businessmen, politicians, and economists were able to persuade themselves that a reasonable prosperity had been regained. Industrial production was back to 1929 levels, and stock prices were above 80 per cent of the 1928 average by late 1936, and still rising. Stock prices, indeed, were about as high relative to 1928 levels as were commodity prices. Meanwhile, commodity prices had started to rise fairly rapidly, including some prices that are normally "sticky." This increase could be traced to a sharp rise of wages, which in turn testified to the success of the great new industrial unions, notably the steel workers. The unions' organizing drive threatened users of commodities with interruptions of supply through strikes and with higher labor costs, therefore helping to touch off a very rapid increase of business inventories in 1936–37.

This turn of events produced a turn in policy. Every since 1933, the federal government had been trying to stimulate business, albeit wrong-headedly at times. In 1936–37, government policies began to resist a further increase of spending. Relief expenditures were cut down, and the pressure for public works was relaxed.[27] Commercial-bank reserve requirements were raised, and excess reserves were cut down from a peak of $3 billion at the beginning of 1936 to about $0.8 billion in the middle of 1937. Banks reduced their holdings of securities, while the growth of loans was slowed down early in 1937 and reversed at mid-year. For the first time since 1933, the public's cash assets declined slightly.

The 1937–38 recession.   Policy in 1937 sought to taper off the expansion. Instead, it helped to bring on a sharp recession. This recession was dramatized

---

[27] The actual history of outlays for public construction (according to the *Survey of Current Business*) is as follows (in billions of current dollars):

Year	1929	1930	1931	1932	1933	1934	1935	1936	1937	1938	1939
Federal	$0.16	0.21	0.27	0.33	0.35	0.43	0.47	0.51	0.54	0.47	0.54
State and local	2.33	2.65	2.39	1.53	1.03	1.19	1.12	1.54	1.61	1.62	2.13
Total	$2.49	2.86	2.66	1.86	1.38	1.62	1.59	2.05	2.15	2.09	2.67

by another stock-market collapse. Stock prices at first sagged a bit from their peak in March, then recovered nearly to the previous peak. In August however, they began an uninterrupted slide, reaching about 57 per cent of the March peak at the end of the year. In March 1938, there was another drop that carried stock prices down to 49 per cent of the 1937 peak.

As in 1929, production sagged before the dramatic stock-market break. Department-store sales and nondurables output reached their peaks in May and sagged during the summer. In September, durable manufacturing suddenly dropped, the decline in nondurables grew more rapid, and there was a rapid fall in employment and payrolls all over the economy. Consumers cut down their spending, and food prices fell sharply during the autumn. For a while, department stores and others practically stopped placing new orders, and the business outlook became very dark. By early 1938, payrolls were down to two-thirds of mid-1937 levels; durable manufacturing, to just about half; and nondurable, to about three-fourths. The need for an expansive public policy was as clear as it had been in the depths of the depression.

In April 1938, therefore, the Federal Reserve lowered reserve requirements by enough to add about $1 billion to excess reserves. Meanwhile, a gold inflow had added about $0.4 billion. This stopped the shrinkage of bank assets and permitted an expansion of bank lending (with a renewed creation of deposits) beginning in the summer of 1938. Work relief was expanded again, from early 1938 on, so that the government's net income-increasing expenditures were up to about $300 million monthly in the second half of the year.

Business activity responded to these policies. Nondurable manufacturing and department-store sales began to show substantial monthly gains, beginning in June, and durable manufacturing followed a month or two later. Factory employment, payrolls, and personal income payments all showed a marked upturn in the summer. By the end of 1938, things were definitely on the mend, although activity was still below early-1937 levels.

Continued recovery and the war boom: 1939–41.   By the time that recovery was well under way, Hitler's diplomatic victory at Munich (September 1938) made a European war overwhelmingly likely. The economic recovery of 1939–41 consequently displayed elements of a war boom from the start, but contracyclical domestic policies also helped. During 1939, the government continued to push expansion with large net income-increasing expenditures. The expansion of the cash supply went on at about the 1933–36 rate. By the end of 1939, manufacturing output was back to the peak levels of 1937, and, after a brief setback early in 1940, it pushed on toward full-employment levels. Unemployment was below four million at the end of 1941.[28]

---

[28]An unemployment level comparable to 1923 and 1929 would have been about two million rather than four million. But since war preparations centered on manufacturing, this part of output reached full-employment levels earlier than general employment.

In 1940, prices hardly budged from the levels reached after the 1937 recession. But wage rates began to rise late in the year; by the beginning of 1941, food prices were on the upgrade; and in the late spring, the whole price level was in motion. From February to December 1941, the cost of living rose by just under 1 per cent per month. This movement was fostered by American rearmament and by the spending of European governments, reinforced by Lend-Lease, from early 1941. Gold imports expanded bank reserves, and the combined spending of the governments (plus a growth in bank loans) expanded the cash supply. There was no cash shortage to damp the expansion or the price inflation.

War prosperity, 1942–45: repressed inflation.   After the Pearl Harbor attack brought us actively into the war in December 1941, stabilization policy was overhauled. The public and the government were concerned about inflation, and price control was introduced to check it. "Selective price control," on a more or less informal basis, had already been at work in 1941—chiefly on metal products. In April 1942, however, the Office of Price Administration issued "General Max"—an order requiring each seller of goods to charge no more than the prices which he had charged during March 1942. Most foods were at first exempted from control by a provision in the enabling act that barred food price ceilings which would hold farm prices below 110 per cent of parity.[29] Hence clothing prices, rents, and the wholesale prices of nonfarm commodities leveled off at once, but food prices kept on rising into 1943.

The system of controls represented a general *stabilization compromise* among the major interest-groups in the economy. The trade unions accepted a no-strike agreement and a "wage freeze" (subject to exceptions) in exchange for a "price freeze" on rents and clothing (and on most foods from 1943 onward). Business accepted price control, allocations, and an excess profits tax with effective rates at about 80 per cent in exchange for the labor concessions. Farm groups eventually accepted controls over food prices in exchange for favorable farm prices; where necessary, subsidies on food were used to close the gap. Food rationing served to secure a reasonably fair sharing of supplies, which were ample by prewar standards but too low to match high wartime levels of personal income.

Monetary policy was mainly passive during the war. The Federal Reserve subordinated other objectives to the support of government bonds prices. It pegged the whole structure of interest rates on Treasury obligations and stood ready to buy securities at the pegged rates. Its purchases, of course, expanded bank reserves. There were limits on consumer credit, but these were largely ineffective, as the goods normally bought on credit were in short supply. Fiscal policy was moderately restrictive. Congress voted unprecedentedly high tax

---

[29]"Parity" (a concept developed and applied to farm legislation during the 1930's) is a ratio between an index number of prices received by farmers and an index number of prices paid by farmers, computed for the base period 1910–14. From values far below parity in the 1930's, the ratio rose until it crossed the parity line in 1941; through the war and early postwar period, it ranged from 115 to 120 per cent of parity.

rates, made easier to bear and to collect by arrangements to withhold taxes on wages and salaries at the source of income. Exemptions were pushed down until most income-receivers were taxable. There were also heavy increases in excise duties, but the tax increases fell far short of mounting war expenditure. Government debt and the public's cash assets kept on climbing.

With the Treasury cash deficit reaching more than $50 billion a year at the peak of the war effort in 1943 and 1944, there was a large *inflationary gap*. Consumers earned record incomes by producing war goods as well as civilian goods, but they could buy only the civilian goods, and taxes did not whittle personal income down sufficiently to match consumer spending with the value of civilian goods at existing prices.[30] To balance the account, an abnormally high proportion of income had to be saved. This saving was fostered by positive inducements—payroll savings plans for war bond purchases and bond drives. It was also achieved by the reduction of normal negative saving (spending by workers temporarily unemployed, college expenses, the retirement of the elderly, foreign travel for the prosperous, and long vacations). Finally, it was achieved by the sheer absence of chances to buy the goods that were wanted—because those goods were rationed, because they were not in the shops, or because shopping was too difficult.[31]

During most of the war we had full employment. In fact, several million extra people joined the labor force—chiefly the young wives of servicemen and others who wanted to participate in the war effort. Unemployment was kept down to a few hundred thousand. This unexpected windfall of labor power enabled the United States to mobilize more than 12 million men and women for the armed forces, to supply them and to furnish large supplies for our Allies, and yet to avoid any serious setback in domestic consumption.[32] Total output was beyond any previous estimates of capacity. On the other hand, the sellers' market permitted a markdown of quality; goods that would have ordinarily proved unsalable found ready buyers. Accordingly, the measurement of physical output

---

[30]Cf. the discussion of the inflation process above, Chapter 13.

[31]The fact that saving could be induced in this way reflected the public's general expectation that goods would be available later at prices they were used to. This expectation played a large part in the success of price control in the face of an inflationary gap much larger than economists and OPA officials thought was safe. On this point, see George Katona, *War Without Inflation* (New York: Columbia University Press, 1942), and *Price Control and Business* (Bloomington, Indiana: Principia Press, 1945).

Perhaps the best brief analysis of the war economy from this standpoint is J. K. Galbraith, "The Disequilibrium System," *American Economic Review,* June 1947, pp. 287–302.

[32]Economists kept predicting that the growth of war production and the armed forces would cause a decline in production of nondurable goods for civilian use—besides the decline in durables that resulted from putting automobile plants, electrical supply factories, and so forth, into war work. But the physical volume of consumption (except for durables) seems to have kept on growing until 1945. This growth helps to explain the unexpectedly thorough success of wartime price control. People were called upon to save money, but were allowed to consume more, too. If they had been called upon to save still more and consume less, their resistance might have broken down the controls.

during the war is difficult, and the size of the peacetime productive capacity that the war experience demonstrated is open to argument.[33]

Demobilization and postwar inflation: 1945–47. During the war, the demobilization process was expected to involve serious transitional unemployment. This forecast was based on three arguments: (1) Such a spell of transitional unemployment had happened in the winter of 1918–19, although the shock was much smaller than was expected after V-J Day. (2) Early in 1945, the government was buying nearly half of a $200 billion national product, and was expected to cut its buying in half immediately after victory; how could business take such a shrinkage of markets in its stride?[34] (3) Millions of men would be discharged from the armed forces within a few months after victory, and more millions would be laid off from war plants—how could they be put into peacetime employment without delay for retooling, and so forth? Anxiety was so great that some government officials were reported to contemplate holding sevicemen in uniform for a time to keep from overloading the labor market. A White House denial of any such intention was required before the air was cleared.

These same fears prompted Congress to enact a pledge that government would work to maintain maximum employment and production in the postwar period. The Employment Act of 1946, containing this promise, established the Council of Economic Advisers to assist the President in the formulation of stabilization policy, and called upon the President to submit an annual Economic Report in which he would describe economic prospects and propose action to combat fluctuations. The Employment Act did not promise *full* employment, but went much further than had any previous declaration by the federal government.

The actual outcome was very different from the expectation. Although the armed forces were not greatly reduced before V-J Day, cutbacks in war production had already reduced manufacturing employment to approximate peacetime levels. Layoffs at the termination of war contracts were only about 2 million—a fraction of what had been expected. Manufacturers, moreover, were confident that they would soon need workers, and apparently hesitated to part with employees for fear that they could not rehire them when needed. The excess profits tax greatly reduced the cost of holding on to workers.[35]

---

[33]One cynical economist says that what the war demonstrated was "our capacity to produce unparalleled quantities of junk." Anybody who watched the distintegration of cardboard toys and wooden bread-boxes that the statistics rated as equivalent to prewar metal products, or who noticed how often wartime shoes had to go to the cobbler's, can sense the way in which figures exaggerated our productive achievements.

[34]For a while there was hope of a tapering-off period after the European war terminated. But stiff Nazi resistance delayed V-E Day until within a few months of V-J Day.

[35]If an employer found that he had no use for the workers retained and took a loss on their wages, he would reduce his profits subject to excess profits tax by the amount of the wages—or else acquire an "unused excess-profits-tax credit" which would entitle him to a tax refund. In effect, the tax left government to absorb more than 80 per cent of any loss incurred. On the other hand, failure to hold together an adequate work force could cripple operations after the war, and the loss this would entail was likely to come out of the corporation's own money. Thus, the calculation on keeping workers came out "heads we win, tails we don't lose."

The Census figure for actual unemployment never rose above 3 million during the demobilization period of 1945–46.

Output did fall quite sharply for a while, as plants were rearranged and pipelines filled with goods for civilian production. But nondurable manuactures were expanding by the end of 1945, and durables by March 1946. Actually, outside of manufacturing and mining, activity was scarcely checked at all.

Although the employment and output situations were better than expected, prices and distribution behaved badly. Food rationing was dropped in the autumn of 1945, on the strength of a temporary gain in food supplies achieved by draining the military pipelines. The excess profits tax was repealed, effective at the end of 1945, breaking up the stabilization compromise. If business could "cut a melon," organized labor, released from its no-strike pledge, did not intend to be left out. And if organized labor could have wages increased, organized farmers intended to obtain corresponding price increases. Price control soon ran into difficulties. Patriotic incentives to comply with inconvenient regulations quickly weakened, and manufacturers concentrated on lines where price control allowed them the best profits, badly distorting supplies. Broadcloth shirts, priced for $3.00, and costing 20 cents to launder, were out of stock at the haberdasher's; consumers had the privilege of buying $8.00 sport shirts that cost 50 cents to dry-clean. Builders could get some sorts of hardware, but nails were very scarce; and so it went.

Businessmen, moreover, had no intention of accepting cost increases from higher wages and farm prices without boosting their prices. Moderate advocates of price control felt that employers would have to be allowed to pass cost increases through to their customers in order to avoid a complete breakdown of controls.[36] But OPA officials felt that once the price level was allowed to get in motion, the game of control was up. In the end, apparently both were right: effective price control was probably impossible in the climate of the moment.

The legal powers of the OPA were timed to expire June 30, 1946. In the shadow of the oncoming Congressional election, Congress was not inclined to extend controls for long and waited until the last minute. It finally approved an extension in late June, but this was vetoed by President Truman as inadequate. There was then a hiatus of several weeks before another renewal act was passed and signed. It was plain that the resuscitated OPA would not live long. Farmers, gambling on a termination of controls, held off selling their livestock in hopes of better prices. The resulting meat shortage made the termination of key food-price controls a political necessity just before the election, and thereby justified the farmers' price gamble.

During the summer hiatus, and again on termination of price controls, there was a sharp rise of prices. This was largely an alignment of quoted prices with the "black-market prices" that had gained importance in the spring (and even

---

[36]For an example of this line of reasoning, see M. G. deChazeau, A. G. Hart, *et al.*, *Jobs and Markets* (New York: Committee for Economic Development Research Study, McGraw-Hill Book Company, Inc., 1946), chap. iv.

more during the attempted revival of price control in the early fall). Late in the year, merchants and some manufacturers actually made determined efforts to roll back certin key prices, and it looked as though prices might be reaching their peak. But price increases picked up momentum again in 1947. The wage increases of early 1946 were followed by a smaller "second round" in early 1947. The catastrophic winter in Europe, plus delayed damage from the wartime disorganization of European society, led to a very heavy export surplus throughout 1947–financed partly by American loans, partly by gold shipments. In addition, the United States was hit by bad crop weather and a serious corn crop failure that left farmers with too little feed to maintain an adequate flow of meat to market over the next crop year. This paved the way for a sharp rise of food prices and a third round of wage increases.

Beginning in 1948 there was finally a small but definite recession that may have marked the terminus of the World War II inflation. Yet it may have been merely a breathing spell, as there were some indications that the inflationary forces were not yet exhausted; the renewed inflation after June 1950 did not merely reflect post-Korean events.

In the postwar part of the inflation (1946–48), monetary policy played an important but undignified part. The wartime accumulation of unspent income had been allowed to take highly liquid forms—cash and short-term or redeemable securities rather than securities that could not readily be cashed. This helped to feed the inflation, as it led consumers to spend an abnormally high proportion of their disposable income in 1946–47. Similarly, the wartime accumulation enabled many business firms to embark on plant expansion without serious financial limitations.

The inflationary effect of the wartime accumulation was reinforced by postwar credit expansion. Many consumers and firms wanted credit to support their spending, and got it readily. The Federal Reserve's open-market powers were still being used to hold down the yields (and hold up the prices) of Treasury securities, not to restrict bank reserves. Consequently, any bank that ran short of reserves could get more by passing some of its holdings of government securities over to the Federal Reserve. Each bank that did so brought about the creation of new reserve funds for the banking system as a whole, as did nonbank credit institutions that sold bonds to the Federal Reserve to get funds for an expansion of their mortgage loans. Many banks were, therefore, able to expand lending without actually taking action to replenish their reserves. This monetary pressure helps to explain how we experienced inflation in the face of a sizable Treasury surplus of cash income over cash outgo.

As in 1919, the Federal Reserve gradually moved back into a position where it could exert restraint. In mid-1947 it allowed an increase of rates on short-term Treasury securities; and at the end of 1947, the "support level" for prices of government securities was marked down. For all that, the Federal Reserve maintained a ready market for government securities, and permitted an easy bank-reserve position. When a recession finally came, it could not be attributed to monetary restraint, but to a reversal of business inventory policy—coupled with a slackening of construction and of business investment in producers' durable goods.

Recession and recovery: 1948–50.   The recession that began late in 1948 was basically an inventory adjustment. As consumer demand slackened from its record postwar level, business found its stocks of goods rising too rapidly, and set about reducing them. During the third quarter of 1948, nonfarm business inventories rose at a seasonally adjusted annual rate of $4.1 billion (at 1954 prices). Thereafter, inventories fell; in the second quarter of 1949, they were declining at an annual rate of $4.6 billion, and in the next two quarters fell at an annual rate of $3.1 billion. There was also a decline in the rate at which business was installing new equipment. Gross business spending on producers' durables fell from $22.8 billion in 1948 to a seasonally adjusted annual rate of $18.5 billion in the final quarter of 1949.

The inventory cuts and reduced outlays for plant and equipment quickly affected production. Nondurables production reached a peak in June 1948, and declined gradually through April 1949, for a total drop of 7 per cent from peak to trough. Durables production turned down later, but fell much more sharply. It reached a peak in July, turned down in October, and did not level out until the summer of 1949. It fell by a full 18 per cent from peak to trough. Unemployment rose sharply during 1949—from 4.0 per cent in the final quarter of 1948 to 7.1 per cent a year later.

Monetary policy during the recession was a compound of contradictions. Because the Federal Reserve System was committed to peg the prices of government securities, it actually *sold* government bonds early in the recession, thereby reducing bank reserves. It did so because the recession had reduced the demand for credit, lowering interest rates and raising bond prices. Fortunately, the System was able to gain Treasury concurrence in a modification of its support commitment. On June 28, 1949, the Federal Reserve announced that it would henceforth seek the "maintenance of orderly conditions" in the bond market. This meant that it would continued to *support* bond prices, but would not act to prevent a *rise* in those prices. The System could cease its sales of government securities. In the meantime, it had reduced commercial-bank reserve requirements in several steps to offset the impact of its open-market sales. At central reserve city banks, for example, reserve requirements dropped from 26 per cent to 22 per cent. The Federal Reserve also eased the margin requirements that govern borrowing for the purchase of stock-market securities, and liberalized its restrictions on consumer installment credit. The latter were allowed to lapse at mid-year, when the legislation that had authorized them finally expired.

Fiscal policy during the recession was not much more helpful than monetary policy. At the beginning of 1949, President Truman actually called for tax increases, believing that there was still a danger of inflation. He did not rescind his request until the middle of 1949, but even then did not recommend tax reductions to combat the recession. Yet there was a tax cut during the recession —one that had been enacted a year earlier by the Republican Congress over Mr. Truman's veto. In this instance, Congress and the President were each rescued by the other's error. It was probably wrong to have voted a tax cut in 1948, but very helpful to have had one effective in 1949. In any case, tax receipts declined during the recession, partly because of the cut in rates, but also because taxable income was falling. The federal government ran a cash deficit in the second quarter of 1949, and smaller ones in each of the next two quarters.[37] The government also ran a deficit on income-and-product account in every quarter of 1949.[38]

Recovery from the recession began in the middle of 1949. Nondurables production, we said before, reached its trough in the spring, and rose steadily thereafter. It passed its prerecession peak in January 1950. Durables production turned around in October 1949 (twelve months after it started to decline), and reached its prerecession level in April 1950. Unemployment was back to its prerecession level in the second quarter of 1950. The recovery was supported by an increase in residential construction that may have been connected to the easing of mortgage restrictions early in 1949. There was actually a boom in home building early in 1950, that may have been helped by the operations of the Federal National Mortgage Administration ("Fannie Mae") which put money into the mortgage market during the recession and recovery. The recovery was also supported by an increase in consumer spending, made possible by the stability of disposable income and the payment of a large dividend on veterans' life insurance policies in early 1950. Thanks to the drop in taxes and to increased federal transfer payments, personal income after taxes fell but briefly and slightly during the recession. It dropped by about 1 per cent from the final quarter of 1948 to the first quarter of 1949, but increased in the succeeding quarters. Thus the economy was definitely on the upgrade (though not every body recognized the fact) when war broke out in Korea in June 1950.

Mobilization and inflation: 1950–51.   With recollections of World War II still very fresh, people reacted to the Korean crisis much as though the country were entering a new global war. Memories of shortages impelled consumers to buy goods while they were still available—there was even an hysterical run

---

[37]Data on the government's cash budget are seasonally adjusted estimates from the Staff Report of the Joint Economic Committee, *Employment, Growth, and Price Levels* (Washington, D.C.: U.S. Government Printing Office, 1960), pp. 309–10. Many of the other data in this chapter also come from that report.

[38]The income-and-product account data record the government's spending on goods and services; the cash budget records its total receipts and outlays. Neither set of figures is quite the same as the conventional budget—which is the one politicians usually have in mind when they argue over government spending, surpluses, and deficits. For a comparison of the three sets of figures, see *Economic Report of the President* (Washington, D.C.: U.S. Government Printing Office, 1960), p. 218.

on sugar supplies in the summer of 1950. With goods disappearing from the shelves, merchants ordered heavily. Government compounded the pressure on resources by placing huge orders for armaments and by encouraging the construction of defense plants.

This great increase of buying is reflected in the statistics. Consumer spending soared from an annual rate of $214.2 billion in the second quarter of 1950 to an annual rate of $225.6 billion in the third quarter of that year. Spending on durable goods accounted for $7.5 billion of this increase, for a 25 per cent expansion. Nonfarm inventory investment mounted to an astonishing annual rate of $14.5 billion in the fourth quarter of 1950, and continued at an annual rate of $11.5 billion during the first half of 1951. (All of the above figures are in 1954 prices.) There was a sharp increase in manufacturers' unfilled orders for durable goods. These stood at $21.7 billion at the end of June 1950, reached $36.6 billion at the end of the year, and stood at $64.1 billion twelve months later.

The brief war boom completed recovery from the 1949 recession. It brought unemployment down to 3.3 per cent in 1951 and boosted durables production by 13 per cent from June 1950 to April 1951. But the boom was most prominently reflected in price movements. The government's index of wholesale prices rose 16 per cent from mid-1950 to its peak in February or March of 1951. This pressure on prices was the result partly of increases in the current consumption of raw materials, but mainly of speculative buying. Prices rose because buyers thought they would rise and were buying far ahead of requirements.

The government moved to fight inflation with a variety of weapons. It reimposed price and wage controls in January 1951, and revived selective credit controls—restrictions on installment buying and mortgage terms. It also used the more orthodox monetary and fiscal policies.

Between the first and second halves of 1950, Defence Department orders of military hardware rose from $1.9 billion to $8.7 billion, and in the first half of 1951, soared to $17.4 billion. Yet the government succeeded in maintaining a cash surplus of $3.1 billion in the second half of 1950 and of $3.6 billion in the first half of 1951. This was possible partly because actual Defense Department outlays lagged behind orders,[39] but also because tax collections reached record levels in the first quarter of 1951. Congress voted large tax increases in the autumn of 1950, including increases in personal and normal corporate taxes, and an excess profits tax. A survey of postwar fiscal policy prepared for the Joint Economic Committee of Congress comments as follows upon this period:

---

[39]The stimulus to business that is provided by an increase in Defense Department buying probably occurs sometime after orders are placed, for it takes time to start production. But stimulus probably precedes the actual government spending on military hardware, as payments are not made until delivery. Thus, the data on orders (strictly speaking, data on "obligations") are probably indicators of what will happen, while actual outlays, as recorded in the budget, probably tell us what has already happened.

In retrospect, the period of Korean hostilities, mid-1950 to mid-1953, may be regarded as the high-water mark of postwar fiscal policy. The very large and sharp increase in defense demands, coming on top of a rapid recovery in total demand, represented a major disturbance originating in the Government sector. Compensatory fiscal action was both prompt and more nearly adequate than at any other time in the postwar era.

The speculative boom of 1950 and early 1951 was supported by a large increase in bank lending. The business loans of commercial banks rose by $6.8 billion, or by about 40 per cent, between June 1950 and March 1951. The cash assets of the public (adjusted time and demand deposits, and currency in circulation) rose by $6.9 billion, or by 4 per cent, in the second half of 1950. In early 1951, a sharp drop in cash assets helped to brake the increase of commodity prices; cash assets fell by $4.4 billion in three months. Yet this decline was really a by-product of fiscal policy—of the record tax collections early in 1951—rather than a reflection of restrictive monetary measures. The Federal Reserve Board raised reserve requirements by two points and increased the rediscount rate from $1\frac{1}{2}$ per cent to $1\frac{3}{4}$ per cent. Yet banks had adequate access to extra reserves because the Reserve Banks were still committed to support bond prices. By selling government securities, the commercial banks were able to obtain the reserves they wanted for credit expansion.

NOTES ON

ALTERNATIVE POINTS OF VIEW

AND SUPPLEMENTARY READINGS

For a general view of economic fluctuations in the United States and other countries in the interwar period, see J. A. Schumpeter, *Business Cycles,* 2 vols. (New York: McGraw-Hill Book Company, Inc., 1939), chaps. xiv and xv (pp. 692ff.). A brief and lively account of the interwar annals of the United States is given in J. A. Schumpeter and A. Smithies, "The American Economy in the Inter-War Period," *American Economic Review,* Papers and Proceedings, May 1946, pp. 1–27. R. A. Gordon's *Economic Fluctuations* (New York: Harper & Row, Publishers, 1952) offers two solid chapters (pp. 360–445) which deal with the annals since 1919.

On the wartime system of price controls and rationing, see J. K. Galbraith, "The Disequilibrium System," *American Economic Review,* June 1947.

For a sprightly account of the stock-market crash of 1929, see J. K. Galbraith, *The Great Crash* (Boston: Houghton Mifflin Company, 1955). On the deflation after 1929, see Lionel Robbins, *The Great Depression* (New York: The Macmillan Company, 1935), and H. H. Villard, "The Federal Reserve System's Monetary Policy in 1931 and 1932," *Journal of Political Economy,* December 1937.

Federal Reserve policy is reviewed by authors who have been close to it in K. R. Bopp, "Three Decades of Federal Reserve Policy," in Federal Reserve Board, *Federal Reserve Policy* (Washington, D.C.: Postwar Economic Studies, 1947), and E. A. Goldenweiser, *American Monetary Policy* (New York: McGraw-Hill Book Company, Inc., 1951). A listing of "principal policy actions of the Federal Reserve System," 1919–51, with explanations, was submitted by the Board to a Congressional committee and was published by the Joint Committee on the Economic Report, in *Monetary Policy and the Management of the Public Debt* (Washington, D.C.: U.S. Government Printing Office, 1952), pp. 216–33. A fascinating mathematical analysis of interwar American development is offered by J. Tinbergen, *Business Cycles in the United States of America, 1919–32* (Geneva: League of Nations, 1939). This study has been followed up at the Cowles Commission by Lawrence Klein, *Economic Fluctuations in the United States, 1921–1941* (New York: John Wiley & Sons, Inc., 1950). These mathematical studies seem to be inconclusive; but they are very suggestive of possibilities for an interpretation of the annals which would put less stress both on policy and on shifts in the public's attitude than ours has done.

Chapter 21

The Economic Annals:
1951—1968

The revival of monetary policy: 1951–52. During the inflation of 1950–51 and the corresponding credit expansion, the Federal Reserve System grew more and more restive under Treasury dominance. Its commitment to keep interest rates low rendered the System impotent to control bank lending or the volume of deposits. In 1947 and after, it had gained some room to maneuver by letting short-term rates rise. It could offset some of its purchases of long-term Treasury securities by selling Treasury bills and certificates, but it could not actually compress bank reserves, as the banks could always sell more long-term bonds to gain reserves.

Gradually, the Federal Reserve won support of its campaign to regain the initiative in monetary matters. In January 1950, a Congressional committee under the chairmanship of Senator Paul Douglas had said that "an appropriate, flexible, and vigourous monetary policy, employed in coordination with fiscal and other policies, should be one of the principal methods used to achieve the purposes of the Employment Act."[1] In August of 1950, the smoldering conflict between the Federal Reserve and the Treasury burst into the open. The Federal Reserve had just raised its rediscount rate when the Treasury announced a new offer of medium-term securities at $1\frac{1}{4}$ per cent—a rate in line with the market

---

[1] Subcommittee on Monetary, Credit, and Fiscal Policies of the Joint Committee on the Economic Report, *Report on Monetary, Credit, and Fiscal Policies* (Washington, D.C.: U.S. Government Printing Office, 1950), p. 1.

before the rediscount-rate change, but far too low with the rediscount rate at 1¾ per cent. In effect, the Treasury challenged the Federal Reserve to let a government security issue flounder in the open market. The Federal Reserve Banks rescued the Treasury, but not without displaying a reluctance and irritation that finally carried the issue to the White House. Finally, the Treasury and Federal Reserve reached an "Accord." The precise terms of that March 1951 agreement have not been made public, but its effects were immediately obvious. The Treasury pitched its next long-term issue at 2¾ per cent, rather than at the 2½ per cent yield that had prevailed ever since World War II. The Federal Reserve, for its part, made a subtle change in the standing instructions it had issued for the conduct of open-market operations. Previously, the System was to operate for the "maintenance of orderly conditions." Now, it would operate to "prevent disorderly conditions." This apparently meant that the System would intervene to prevent wide price fluctuations, especially on the eve of major Treasury operations, but that it would no longer keep long-term rates at or below 2½ per cent. In the future, therefore, sales of Treasury securities by the banks or nonbank public would no longer cause an increase of commercial-bank reserves, as the Federal Reserve Banks would not have to intervene in support of bond prices and interest rates.

In the months immediately following this "Accord," the Federal Reserve acted very cautiously, buying government securities in the open market to ease the transition from pegged interest rates. Free reserves remained positive through 1951 and the first half of 1952.[2]

Credit expansion nevertheless halted in 1951. The total loans of commercial banks were stable from March 1951 to mid-1952, and cash assets hardly changed. The demand for credit tapered off with an end to panic buying in the spring of 1951. The price level actually receded as the demand for raw materials was sharply curtailed, although the prices of metals and machinery did not fall very much as the pressure of defense spending continued to support them, and the government's index of retail prices (the cost of living index) kept on rising right through 1951.

Production was rather stable after its initial upsurge. Durables output fell

---

[2] Free reserves, the reader will recall, are the difference between excess reserves and member-bank borrowing from the Federal Reserve System. Free reserves are a useful index of the pressure on commercial banks, as a decrease of free reserves means a decline of excess reserves, an increase of rediscounting, or both. This, in turn, means a decrease in the supply of reserves relative to the demand, or, in the case of increased rediscounting, pressure on the banks to repay debts to the Federal Reserve banks.

While Chapter 5 used "owned reserves" as a measure of reserve pressure, this chapter will use free reserves, because free reserves seem to be more closely watched by the Federal Reserve itself. The level of free reserves has become the accepted measure of credit-creating power in the postwar period. Note, however, that a reduction in free reserves does not necessarily imply or foreshadow a decline in commercial-bank lending. Whether such a decline occurs will depend upon the banks' willingness to remain in debt to the Federal Reserve (and the Reserve banks' willingness to countenance sustained indebtedness), and upon their willingness to dispose of other assets in order to make new loans.

back slightly in the summer of 1951, and rose again in 1952. Nondurables output declined from the January 1951 peak, but it also rose early in 1952. Unemployment was low. The eighteen months ending December 1952 were characterized by prosperity and remarkable stability—a prosperity and stability that owed much to government stabilization policies.

Defense procurement ran at high levels in 1952, with new Defense Department obligations totalling $33.2 billion, as compared with $30.5 billion in 1951. But the government ran a surprisingly small cash deficit in the second half of 1951 and in 1952, despite the fact that defense outlays were catching up with orders. For its part, the Federal Reserve System began to operate vigorously on bank reserves. It bought government securities in the second half of 1952, but its purchases were insufficient to match commercial-bank reserve needs. As a result, member-bank borrowing rose rapidly in the middle of 1952—from about $580 million in June 1952 to about $1,075 million in July. Free reserves turned negative in September as commercial bank indebtedness came to exceed excess reserves by some $400 million. They fell to *minus* $875 million in November and December, and stood at *minus* $650 million in the first quarter of 1953.

Retrenchment and recession: 1953–54. The restrictive monetary and fiscal policies of late 1952 were justified by the course of production and prices. By December 1952, durables production was 14 per cent higher than it had been in the first half of the year; unfilled orders for durable goods stood at $73.2 billion, compared with $64.1 billion at the end of 1951. Unemployment was at a low 2.8 per cent in the final quarter of 1952, and federal spending on goods and services was running at an annual rate of $66 billion and was heavily concentrated on durable goods. Wholesale prices had levelled out after their long decline, and the index of retail prices was rising at a faster clip.

The beginning of 1953 saw a sharp reversal in the prospects for government spending. A new administration took office with the promise to cut back spending. There was a reduction in new procurement even before the end of the Korean war. New obligations for military hardware fell by 40 per cent from 1952 to the first half of 1953 and were cut to just $1.2 billion per quarter after the Korean armistice in late July.

The new administration's financial policies also put the economy under deflationary pressure. The Secretary of the Treasury, George Humphrey, had promised a lengthening of the national debt, and to that end issued $1.2 billion of new thirty-year government bonds paying $3\frac{1}{4}$ per cent interest in May 1953. This new bond issue came onto the market as interest rates were rising rapidly. The key Treasury bill rate stood at 2.8 per cent in April, compared with an average of 1.77 per cent in 1952; the yield on long-term government bonds stood at about 2.97 per cent, compared to an average of 2.68 per cent in 1952. The Federal Reserve had raised its rediscount rate from $1\frac{3}{4}$ per cent to 2 per cent in January 1953. The cash assets of the public had been shrinking, partly because of the seasonal bulge in Treasury tax receipts. The new thirty-year bond issue brought long-term rates above 3 per cent. It was in great demand at first, but went to a discount within a few weeks, as bondholders grew bearish on prices and cut back their holdings. It was widely thought that Secretary Humphrey would countenance still higher yields in his efforts to lengthen the federal debt.

The reduction of federal spending and the sharp rise in interest rates early in 1953 help to explain the recession which developed during the summer. Durable production fell rapidly after July, declining by some 16 per cent to March 1954. Nondurables output also peaked in July, and fell by 6 per cent through December. Unemployment rose from a low of 2.7 per cent in the first three quarters of 1953 to a peak of 5.9 per cent in the final quarter of 1954.

As usual, the recession produced a sharp reversal in inventories. Having increased at an annual rate of $3.6 billion in the first half of 1953, nonfarm business inventories dropped at an annual rate of $4.3 billion in the final quarter of 1953, and at an annual rate of $3.0 billion in the first half of 1954 (estimates in 1954 prices). The inventory run-off, however, does not appear to have been an important *cause* of the 1953 recession. In 1949, remember, the turnaround in inventories had set off the decline in production; in 1953, by contrast, that turnaround had followed the decline in production. The decline itself was triggered by the reduction of federal spending[3] and by cuts in business spending on plant and equipment. The latter did not show up in our National Income statistics until the final quarter of 1953 (when spending on producers' durables dropped by 13 per cent from their average level in the first nine months of the year). But it was presaged by a decline in new orders for durable goods, which fell sharply in the third quarter of 1953.[4]

Fortunately, the Federal Reserve moved vigorously to combat the 1953 recession. Even before the downturn was fully apparent, the Reserve banks had eased the pressure on bank reserves. During the bond-market crisis of May and June, the System had bought $900 million of government securities. In July, it reduced reserve requirements on demand deposits—by 2 percentage points at central reserve city banks, and by 1 percentage point at other commercial banks. During the second half of 1953, it bought another $1.7 billion of government securities, pursuing its policy of "active ease." In the first half of 1954, the rediscount rate was lowered in two steps—from 2 per cent to $1\frac{3}{4}$ per cent, and from $1\frac{3}{4}$ per cent to $1\frac{1}{2}$ per cent. Reserve requirements were cut back again, but this time on time deposits as well as on demand deposits.

The reserves of member banks quickly reflected these anti-recession measures. Free reserves turned positive in June 1953, and climbed to an average

---

[3] While federal payments for goods and services did not actually decline until the first quarter of 1954, new orders for defense hardware had dropped before production fell off.

[4] This decline, incidentally, may be partly attributed to government policies—to the sharp decline in new government orders for military hardware and to the efforts by the previous administration to speed up spending in defense plants during the Korean crisis. The latter probably caused business to anticipate its requirements by a year or so, so as to benefit from special tax concessions.

of $600 million in the first half of 1954. Interest rates fell sharply as the recession wore on. The Treasury bill rate dropped from 2.23 per cent in June 1953, to 0.65 per cent in June 1954, and averaged only 0.93 per cent in the second half of 1954. The yield on long-term Treasury bonds also dropped and averaged 2.52 per cent in the second half of 1954. The earning assets of commercial banks grew substantially, with loans climbing by $5.2 billion from mid-1953 to the end of 1954, and investments, mainly government securities, rising by $13.2 billion in the same eighteen-month period. The cash assets of the public matched this increase; they rose from $192.6 billion in June 1953, to $210.2 billion at the end of 1954, or by 9 per cent.

Monetary policy, it should be said, had to carry much of the load. The new administration had promised to balance the federal budget, as well as to cut spending, so it hesitated to cut taxes, even as spending fell. In May 1953, President Eisenhower had asked Congress to extend the excess profits tax and to postpone scheduled reductions in normal corporate rates. As a consequence, these tax cuts did not come into force until the recession was well under way, although a cut in personal taxes did go into force as originally scheduled. Note that, once again, a tax reduction came into force during the recession, having been voted before the recession began. Had some taxes not been already scheduled for reduction or abrogation, there might not have been any tax cut during the recession.[5]

The decline in taxable income brought about a reduction in tax receipts long before the tax cuts went into force. The federal government had run a $1.4 billion cash deficit in the first quarter of 1953. Despite cuts in spending thereafter, its deficit grew to $2.6 billion in the second quarter of 1953, and continued at $2.0 billion in the second half of the year. The deficit on income-and-product account was still larger. It run at an annual rate of $11.8 billion in the final quarter of 1953, and at $10.6 billion in the first quarter of 1954.[6]

Once again, disposable income was stable during the recession, the decline in taxes and the increase of transfer payments having partially offset a reduction in wages and other earned-income payments. As a result, consumer spending was also stable. It did decline between the final quarter of 1953 and the first

---

[5] Our emphasis on this point should not be taken to imply that the tax cuts were less effective than they would have been if they had been voted as anti-recession policies. We merely wish to stress the fact that discretionary fiscal measures have actually been rather rare in the postwar period—that the right things were sometimes done to combat recessions, but that they were often done for the wrong reasons.

[6] As between the first and fourth quarters of 1953, government spending rose by an annual equivalent of $1.4 billion, while receipts declined by the annual equivalent of $5.3 billion. The deficit consequently grew by an annual equivalent of $6.7 billion. As between the fourth quarter of 1953 and the first quarter of 1954, government spending declined by an annual equivalent of $4.3 billion, but receipts declined by the annual equivalent of $3.0 billion. As a result, the deficit shrank by about $1.3 billion. The $3.0 billion reduction of tax revenue, by the way, was mainly caused by a decline in corporate tax accruals, owing to the reduction in tax rates, not by a decline in actual receipts.

quarter of 1954, but by less than 2 per cent. And it rose very rapidly afterward, topping prerecession levels in the third quarter of 1954.

Construction was also firm during the recession. In fact, it rose sharply during 1954—by a full 13 per cent between the first and fourth quarters. This boom in building was partly because of a relaxation of mortgage terms and an increase in the ceiling on interest charges for veterans' mortgages and for mortgages insured by the FHA.[7]

Despite the support from construction and consumer spending, the recession of 1953–54 dragged on for a long time. Durables output hit bottom in March 1954, but did not begin to rise until autumn; nondurables rose earlier, but at a crawl, and unemployment was still at 5.4 per cent in the final quarter of 1954. The Federal Reserve, therefore, prolonged its policy of "active ease" through 1954 and into the early months of 1955.

Economic advance: 1955–56. Then, recovery gathered strength. The demand for durables—by business and consumers—grew rapidly in the early months of 1955, and the Gross National Product rose from an annual rate of $366.1 billion in the second half of 1954 to an annual rate of $389.5 billion in the second quarter of 1955. There were remarkable increases in every component of private spending, but an especially sharp upturn in consumer durables and in residential construction. Sales of consumer durables rose by some 18 per cent between the second half of 1954 and the second quarter of 1955. The automobile industry enjoyed a record year as its new models sprouted their first fins. (More important, of course, was the availability of automatic transmissions on standard models for the first time.)

Behind this increase of final demand, there loomed an even more powerful force to promise expanding activity in the months ahead. Heavy industry began to lay plans for an expansion of capacity, and orders for durable equipment began to rise. By the end of 1955, the durables' sector of manufacturing was working hard, and unfilled orders from consumers and producers were a full 20 per cent higher than at the end of 1954. The Federal Reserve index of durables production passed its prerecession peak in July, and was well above that level at the year's end.

The upsurge of business in 1955 was quickly reflected in the demand for credit. Consumer indebtedness (installment loans) grew by $2.5 billion in the first

---

[7] It would seem paradoxical that an increase in rates could stimulate mortgage financing in this way. One must remember, however, that the major deterrent to construction in a period of high interest rates may not be the reluctance of borrowers to pay high rates, but the reluctance of lenders to take on mortgages when open-market rates are much higher than the rates charged on mortgages. The interest ceiling on veterans' mortgages (and a similar rigidity in FHA rates) causes money to slip away from the mortgage market in periods of tight money. The increase of rates on veterans' mortgages during the 1953–54 recession, coupled to a sharp reduction in other interest rates, brought money back to the mortgage market and gave a needed boost to residential construction.

half of 1955, and by another $2.9 billion in the second half. The business loans of commercial banks rose by $2.0 billion in the first half of the year, and by another $3.6 billion during the second half. Finally, the boom began to push up prices. Wholesale prices began to rise in the middle of 1955, while retail prices and wage rates quickened their advance.

The Federal Reserve System, however, was slow to change its posture. It did not abandon "active ease" until January 1955, and did not begin to "lean against the wind" until April. Then it raised the rediscount rate from $1\frac{1}{2}$ per cent to $1\frac{3}{4}$ per cent, and began to compress bank reserves. Free reserves turned negative at the end of July, as rediscounts mounted relative to excess reserves. In August and September, the Reserve banks again raised their rediscount rates, and brought them to $2\frac{1}{2}$ per cent in November. Yet the cash stock went on growing throughout the year—from $205.3 billion in March 1955, to a seasonal peak of $216.6 billion at the year's end.

The System did not begin an intensive attack on the boom until the early months of 1956. In January, it sold $1.4 billion of government securities, partly to offset a seasonal increase in bank reserves, and in March and April raised the rediscount rate to $2\frac{3}{4}$ per cent. During the balance of the year, it held down the total of bank reserves, despite an increase in reserve needs, and in August 1956, raised the rediscount rate to a full 3 per cent. It continued its offensive in 1957, selling another $1.8 billion of government securities during the first half of the year, and forcing the rediscounts of commercial banks up to $1.0 billion in June 1957.

This increased pressure on the banks, and on the supply of credit, was markedly reflected in the level of interest rates. During 1955, the Treasury bill rate had risen from 1.17 per cent to 2.56 per cent. By the end of 1956, it stood at 3.23 per cent. The yield on long-term government bonds went from 2.57 per cent to 2.97 per cent during 1955, broke through 3 per cent in July 1956, and stood at 3.58 per cent in June 1957. Other interest rose in similar fashion. Rates on large business loans (short-term loans larger than $200 thousand) rose from an average of 3.50 per cent in 1955 to 3.97 per cent in June 1956, to 4.23 per cent in June 1957, and to 4.62 per cent at the end of 1957.

Federal Reserve policy was supported by a more restrictive fiscal situation. The government had run a small cash deficit in 1955, but attained a large cash surplus in 1956, and a smaller one in the first half of 1957. The income-and-product accounts displayed a government surplus in 1955 as well as in 1956; in 1955, it was $3.8 billion; in 1956, $5.1 billion. This surplus was mainly accomplished by way of an increase in receipts which was the result of the increase in taxable income. Tax policy was also working to stimulate business spending on plant and equipment. The Internal Revenue Code had been revised in 1954 to permit more generous depreciation allowances. The great growth of investment in 1955 and 1956 cannot be attributed solely to these tax revisions, but the new tax code was nonetheless a stimulant.

Business activity levelled out in 1956, possibly because of monetary stringency, but also, perhaps, because the investment boom had run its normal course. Durables output ran below its peak level during most of 1956, while nondurables were on a similar plateau. Unfilled orders for durable goods were higher at the end of 1956 than at the end of 1955, but new orders had levelled out, and eased off slightly in the first half of 1957. The Gross National Product (in 1954 prices) remained in the neighborhood of $400 billion, the level it had reached late in 1955. Unemployment was slightly lower than in 1955, but not nearly as low as it was in the year preceding the 1953 recession.

Prices, however, continued to rise in 1956. By the end of the year, wholesale prices (other than those of foodstuffs) had advanced by 6 per cent over their 1955 levels. They were paced by the prices of metals and metal goods, which were up by 12 per cent. Wholesale prices tended toward stability early in 1957, but the index of retail prices went on rising. Retail prices had advanced by 3 per cent in 1956, and rose by another 3 per cent in 1957. Wage rates were also up from their 1955 levels, and were still rising in 1957. By 1957, in short, everything had been brought to a plateau—except the price level.

Recession and recovery: 1957–59. Deeply committed to the quest for price stability, the Federal Reserve System "overstayed" the boom of 1955–57, as it may have overstayed the recession of 1953–54, by prolonging "active ease" into the recovery. As we have already said, the major production indexes were nearly stable in 1956 and early 1957. But after August 1957, durables output turned down sharply and declined by 33 per cent during the next eight months. Nondurables dropped more gradually and reached a low earlier, but fell by 8 per cent in late 1957 and early 1958.

Advance indications of a decline appeared somewhat earlier. Durables production actually peaked in February 1957, and there was a slight drop in new orders for durables during the first half of 1957, as well as in the level of unfilled orders. Yet the Federal Reserve banks actually raised the rediscount rate as late as August, lifting it from 3 per cent to $3\frac{1}{2}$ per cent. The System, moreover, kept free reserves negative until the end of the year, and seemed very reluctant to relax credit long after the recession had started. In November, it described itself as "fostering sustainable growth"; in December, as "cushioning adjustments and mitigating recessionary tendencies"; and, finally, in March 1958, as providing "monetary ease." By March, we should note, the recession had been underway for seven months! The System, however, was doing more than it was saying. In November 1957, most of the Reserve Banks had lowered their rediscount rates to 3 per cent, where they had been before the dubious August increase, and the fourth quarter 1958 rate of growth in adjusted owned reserves was the highest since 1954. In January 1958, rediscount rates came down again, and free reserves became positive as the volume of rediscounts fell. In February, and again in April, the System reduced reserve requirements. And in March and April, the rediscount rate was cut again—to a low of $1\frac{3}{4}$ per cent. Interest rates fell sharply during the recession. The Treasury bill rate had been at 3.59 per cent in October 1957; by March of the next year, it stood at 1.35 per cent; and by June 1958, fell to a low of 0.88 per cent. The decrease in long-term yields was, as usual, somewhat milder, but it was sufficient to produce widespread speculation in government bonds.[8] Mortgage financing grew much easier as money came back to the mortgage market, while rates on short-term business loans dipped below 4.0 per cent for a short while.

Commercial-bank loans were remarkably stable during the recession, and the banks greatly increased their investments; their holdings of government securities rose by some $12 billion from September 1957 to November 1958. As a result, the public's cash assets rose sharply, from $220.9 billion in September 1957, to $229.5 billion in June 1958, and to $237.0 billion in November 1958.

The banks' purchases of government bonds were of great assistance to the Treasury, for the federal government ran a huge deficit during the depression. There was a cash deficit in every quarter of 1958, and a still larger deficit in the first half of 1959. As a result, the Treasury borrowed heavily, and its marketable debt rose by $15.9 billion during 1958 and 1959.

No tax cut was made during this recession, although many observers urged one. The government deficit was wholly the result of a decline in tax receipts and of increased spending. Congress increased federal grants to the states for unemployment compensation and enacted an expanded housing program. These programs helped to sustain disposable income and, therefore, personal consumption.

By the usual measures, this recession was very deep. Durables output fell by a third in eight months. Unemployment rose from 4.2 per cent in the summer of 1957 to 7.5 per cent in April 1958. But the recovery from this recession was also sharp. Durables production had regained prerecession levels by March 1959 and was well above its previous peak at the start of the steel strike in July. Nondurables output, moreover, passed its previous peak in July of 1958, and was 11 per cent above that peak one year later. The recovery came about without a renewed increase in prices. Prices had leveled out during the recession and were virtually stable during 1959. The retail index rose somewhat, but mainly because of an increase in the prices of services.

As the recovery got underway, the Federal Reserve tried to improve on its timing. It began to tighten up on bank reserves even as production was starting to rise. The growth of effective owned reserves fell sharply from the first

---

[8] As the text implies, long-term rates rarely drop as sharply as short-term rates. In this instance, however, there were special circumstances at work to keep long-term yields up and to reduce short-term rates very sharply. The Treasury was selling long-term bonds during the recession, while the Federal Reserve was buying short-term securities in the course of its open-market operations. We shall have more to say on these points in the next chapter.

The speculation in government bonds, incidentally, came to a sudden end during the summer. At that time, the Federal Reserve System was forced to intervene decisively to prevent an old-fashioned bond-market crisis.

to the second quarter of 1958 and became negative in the third. The Federal Reserve raised the rediscount rate in September of 1958, and three times more during the next nine months. By September 1959, the rate stood at 4 per cent —its highest level since 1930. Free reserves turned negative again in December 1958, and ran at *minus* $400 million in the early months of 1959. There were sharp increases in market rates and a new tightness in the mortgage market. Treasury bills were priced to yield a full 4.57 per cent at the end of 1959, and long-term governments averaged 4.27 per cent. The banks were charging an average of 5.24 per cent on large short-term business loans, and nearly 6 per cent on their smaller loans. The cash assets of the public were nearly stable in 1959 and the first half of 1960.

Recession and recovery once again: 1960–62. Several signs indicated that the economy had entered a recession early in 1960. Inventory accumulation —the bellwether of postwar recessions—steadily declined from a positive annual rate of $11.4 billion in the first quarter to a negative annual rate of $3.0 billion in the last quarter. GNP rose slightly to an annual rate of $505 billion in the second quarter and then leveled off to $503 billion during the last half of the year. Corporate profits declined steadily, mortgage financing dropped $1.5 billion below 1959 levels, and unemployment rose to reach 6.8 per cent by the end of the year.

During 1960, bank credit rose by $8.4 billion, moderately more than in 1959. Loans rose by only $5.8 billion, against an increase of $11.9 billion in the preceding year. The slower pace of bank lending, despite the larger volume of funds available, was caused by the lessened total demand for credit by all major sectors of the economy. Banks, therefore, were able to add about $2.4 billion to their holdings of United States government securities, thus reversing the heavy liquidation that had taken place in 1959.

The Federal Reserve moved to reduce monetary restraint early in the year. By April Federal Reserve open-market operations had the effect of easing the reserve position of the banks, and net, positive free reserves existed through December. The System waited until June, however, to lower the discount rate from 4 per cent to $3\frac{1}{2}$ per cent. In September the rate was again cut to 3 per cent. Some observers have felt that the discount rate should have been lowered earlier than June and that the System should have purchased governments more extensively in the spring. Toward the end of the year the Federal Reserve did take additional steps to promote monetary ease. In two successive moves in September and December, reserve requirements against demand deposits for central reserve city banks were reduced from 18 per cent to $16\frac{1}{2}$ per cent and the central reserve city category was eliminated. Most important, from the point of view of providing reserves, all vault cash at commercial banks was made available for meeting reserve requirements. As a partial offset, requirements for country banks were raised from 11 per cent to 12 per cent.

The nation had become acutely aware of its balance of payments difficulties during 1960. During the 1950's the nation had been running balance of payments deficits, but they averaged only $1 billion a year and did not place pressure on our gold stock since foreign nations put much of their newly earned dollar reserves in deposits with American banks. From 1958 onward, the deficits increased sharply and averaged $3.7 billion annually. Moreover, they had begun to draw down the nation's gold reserves. The gold stock had declined by over $2 billion from 1949 to 1957; during the next three years it dropped $5 billion. Not only had our balance of trade narrowed, but nations had become well stocked with dollar reserves and chose to convert substantial portions of their export earnings to gold. The continued deterioration in the balance-of-payments and gold-reserve position would affect domestic economic policy decisions throughout the sixties.

As 1961 began, business activity had been contracting for eight months. The decline proved to be the mildest of any postwar recession. Following the pattern of other business downswings, the largest single element in the 1960-61 decline was a shift in inventory investment from a $5 billion annual rate of accumulation in the second quarter of 1960 to a $4 billion liquidation in the first quarter of 1961. In contrast, final demand—GNP less changes in inventories —continued to inch upward throughout 1960 and barely declined at all in early 1961.

By the end of the first quarter of 1961, signs appeared to indicate that the recession had been reversed. All major components of domestic demand contributed to the growth of GNP, and total production rose to a record rate of $542 billion by the fourth quarter, $41 billion above the level at the beginning of the year. The industrial production index regained its previous peak in July 1961 and climbed 13 per cent between February and December 1961. Prices remained relatively stable; consumer prices increased only 1.1 per cent and the wholesale industrial price index even declined slightly. Unemployment remained a serious problem as it never dipped below 6.7 per cent during the year.

The Federal Reserve maintained a basic policy of ease throughout 1961. Net free reserves averaged $500 million during the year, and total liquid assets held by the public increased sharply. Commercial-bank time deposits grew by a record $11 billion, savings and loan shares rose by $9 billion, and the money supply increased by $5.6 billion.

Again the balance of payments performance was unsatisfactory, even though there was improvement over 1960. The balance on goods and services improved to $5.5 billion, and the total deficit (liquidity basis) declined to $2.4 billion. Gold sales abroad also declined but were still $0.9 billion in 1961. Part of the improvement was caused by the dropping of the "bills only" policy early in the year. The Federal Reserve resumed open-market operations in all sectors of the government bond market. The System purchased long-term governments —particularly in the three- to six-year range—to keep interest rates low to encourage economic expansion at home. At the same time it sold Treasury bills to raise short-term rates and discourage the outflow of dollars and gold.

In 1962 the economy continued its advance, although not so rapidly as had been predicted when the year began. GNP rose to $560 billion, an increase of $40 billion over 1961. The quarter-to-quarter increases in GNP were not as great as the advances made during the last half of 1961. In particular, inventory accumulation dipped sharply in the middle of the year. Some of the business slowdown could be attributed to depressed confidence which followed a presidential price roll-back in the steel industry in the spring which perhaps triggered the major decline registered in the stock market. To help restore business confidence, Congress liberalized depreciation guidelines and approved a 7 per cent tax credit for business investment.

Monetary policy continued toward ease during the year. In July, the Federal Reserve reduced stock-market margin requirements to 50 per cent, and in October reserve requirements on time deposits were reduced from 5 per cent to 4 per cent, releasing an additional $780 million in reserves. Net free reserves moved between $350 and $450 million during the year. Bank loans and investments rose by $18 billion, the largest increase since World War II, and were composed primarily of real estate and consumer loans. Short-term interest rates were maintained at 1961 levels (they fluctuated between 2.72 to 2.87), while long-term rates fell on balance from 4.1 to 3.8 per cent.[9]

On the first of the year, the Federal Reserve raised Regulation Q ceilings on the interest rates offered by commercial banks on savings and time deposits. Commercial banks responded to the higher ceilings and offered large-denomination negotiable certificates of deposit to institutional depositors. Time and savings deposits increased by a record $16 billion and provided the banks with additional loanable funds which were subject to low reserve requirements.

Despite the policy of ease, aggregate demand did not rise sufficiently to bring unemployment below 5.5 per cent during 1962. Prices however, were under little upward pressure. The wholesale industrial price index did not rise in 1961, and the consumer price index rose by only 1 per cent. Part of the price stability can be credited to the government's policy of providing wage-price guidelines to business and labor. Despite the criticisms of labor and management, 1962 wage and price increases were kept within the 3.2 per cent guidelines.

Increased international cooperation contributed to a slight improvement in the nation's balance of payments. In February 1962, the Federal Reserve resumed open-market operations in foreign exchange, which helped to stabilize the international money markets. It also initiated swap agreements with several nations to minimize exchange-rate fluctuations. The year's deficit was 2.2 billion and gold sales totaled $.9 billion.

Expansion and growth: 1963–65.   As 1963 opened, the recovery had lasted

---

[9] Open-market policy in the early 1960's was known as Operation Twist. See Chapter 23.

twenty-two months but the chronic problems of high unemployment and balance of payments difficulties persisted. During the year GNP rose to $590.5 billion, and the industrial production index rose six points. A residential construction boom and an unusually strong demand for autos contributed to the advance. Prices continued to remain stable. The consumer price index rose by 1 per cent during the year, while the wholesale industrial price index experienced a 1 per cent decline. Unemployment remained a serious problem and averaged 5.7 per cent over the year.

Monetary policy became slightly more firm than in 1962 although it was still heavily weighted toward ease. Net free reserves averaged $300 million during 1963 compared to $400 million in the previous year. The discount rate was raised ½ of 1 per cent in July, in a move designed more to stem the outflow of dollars than to initiate a period of monetary restraint. Short-term rates moved upward sharply in late summer and stabilized at higher levels at the end of the year. The Treasury bill rate in December 1963 was 3.52 compared to 2.87 in 1962; long-term government yields had also increased from 3.87 to 4.14. Stock-market prices rose 16 per cent in 1962 and in November the Federal Reserve raised margin requirements to 70 per cent.

Despite the tightened money conditions, bank credit increased 8 per cent in 1963, almost equal to the rise in 1962. Demand deposits rose $3.5 billion and time deposits rose $14 billion. Aided by a further rise in Regulation Q interest ceilings in July 1963, the large increase in time deposits helped cushion the reserve position of banks. During the year banks continued to shift their portfolios out of United States governments into mortgages and tax-exempt issues of state and local governments.

Balance of payments difficulties continued to plague the nation's leaders. The deficit rose to an annual rate of $5 billion in the second quarter of 1963. To stem the outflow of funds, the President proposed an interest equalization tax on foreign securities in July. Although it was not enacted until a year later, the proposal requested that the tax be made retroactive to July 1963. Uncertainty over the final tax rate had the effect of dramatically halting capital outflows into the foreign bond market throughout 1963. As a result the payments deficit for the year was held to $2.7 billion. Gold outflows also showed a sharp improvement and fell to $460 million—the smallest gold loss since 1958. An increase in gold sales from the Soviet Union helped the United States position.

Concern over high unemployment continued into 1964, and many economists cited an inadequate level of aggregate demand as the primary culprit. After more than a year of discussion and political maneuvering, Congress enacted an across-the-board tax cut in March 1964 which immediately reduced personal withholding rates from 18 per cent to 14 per cent and pumped $10 billion into the economy. As a result of the increased purchasing power and spending, GNP rose to $631 billion, an increase of nearly 7 percent over 1963. By year-end unemployment had declined to 5.2 per cent, the lowest rate since the 1955-57 boom. Economic growth did not put much upward pressure on prices although the CPI and wholesale WPI began to rise as the economy moved closer to full capacity productivity. The CPI rose 1.4 per cent, while industrial wholesale prices increased 0.5 per cent.

Monetary policy moved further away from ease in 1964. Interest rates on short-term market instruments rose slightly but, on the whole, paralleled movements in 1963. Banks found themselves moving toward tighter positions as net free reserves declined to an average of about $100 million. In late November the Federal Reserve raised the discount rate from $3\frac{1}{2}$ to 4 per cent to prevent an excessive outflow of funds following the Bank of England's lending rate increase from 5 to 7 per cent. The Board of Governors indicated, however, that this action did not imply any restriction on domestic credit availability and continued to follow an expansionary policy by supplying sufficient reserves to banks to permit a record 8 per cent growth in bank credit. The balance of payments again proved troublesome in 1964. The total deficit was $2.8 billion, and the flow of dollars into foreign bonds resumed after the interest equalization tax was enacted in August. On the brighter side, the monetary gold holdings of the United States declined by only $125 billion as other sources of supply including large Russian sales and increased new production helped satisfy the international demand for gold.

1965 marked the fifth consecutive year of the nation's longest peacetime expansion. From the first quarter of 1961 to the fourth quarter of 1965, GNP had risen by $142 billion for an average growth of $5\frac{1}{2}$ per cent per year. Unemployment had fallen from 6.9 per cent in 1961 to 4.1 per cent by the end of 1965. By itself, 1965 was a banner year. GNP rose to $681 billion, an increase of $7\frac{1}{2}$ per cent over 1964. Corporate profits increased $13\frac{1}{4}$ billion (before taxes and after an adjustment for inventories) to $73 billion—which, in absolute *and* relative terms, was the largest and sharpest rise since 1959.

Commercial-bank credit increased by record amounts. Business loans rose by $11 billion in 1965 compared to $6 billion in 1964. Time deposits rose by a record amount of $20 billion in contrast to $15 billion in 1964. Bank-reserve positions continued to tighten during the year. Net free reserves averaged minus $150 million and became negative for the first time since 1959. The short-term Treasury bill rate reached 4.37 in December—the highest rate since January 1960 and the long-term government rate rose to 4.43 at the end of the year. Prices reflected the tightened credit conditions: the consumer index rose nearly 2 per cent and the wholesale industrial index rose by more than 1 per cent. As interest rates edged upward, monetary authorities shifted to a position of restraint: on December 6 the Federal Reserve raised the discount rate from 4 to $4\frac{1}{2}$ per cent and increased the maximum interest ceiling on time deposits having a maturity of thirty days or more to $5\frac{1}{2}$ per cent.

1965 was also marked by new efforts to reduce the outflow of dollars and gold.

The President instituted a "voluntary restraint" program to encourage United States businessmen to restrict their overseas investments and loans to no more than a 5 per cent increase over their 1964 commitments. In September Congress extended the interest equalization tax for nineteen months and broadened it to cover the purchase of short-term foreign bonds. Congress also eliminated the required 25 per cent gold cover against the reserve deposits of member banks with the Federal Reserve Banks. The action released some $5 billion in gold to meet international claims on the dollar.

As a result of these measures, the balance of payments showed distinct but not sufficient improvement. The total deficit in 1965 was $1.3 billion but the gold outflow increased to $1.7 billion. A major factor contributing to the gold losses was the French governments sudden unwillingness to use dollars as a domestic reserve. Another serious problem was the decline in the balance of trade from $8.5 billion in 1964 to $6.9 billion in 1965. Imports had increased sharply in 1965 and were $3.6 billion more than in the previous year.

Prosperity and payments problems: 1966–68. During 1966 the forward moving economy showed signs of inflationary pressures. Although GNP increased $60 billion to reach $743 billion in 1966, real GNP increased only $27 billion. The consumer price index rose more than 3 per cent over the year, and the wholesale industrial price index also moved upward by more than two points—the largest increase since the expansion began.

From early 1966 onward the heavy business demand for credit placed upward pressure on interest rates. The long-term government rates rose also and reached 4.80 per cent in August before sliding off to 4.65 per cent in December. Treasury bill yields reached 5.36 per cent in October—the highest levels in forty years. Net free reserves had turned negative in late 1965 and fluctuated around minus $350 million during most of 1966.

Labor market conditions became tighter in 1966, and the unemployment rate went below 4 per cent during most months of the year. Wages rose more than in any year of the expansion, and settlements in many major industries resulted in 5 per cent annual increases. The 1962 wage-price guidelines were by-passed so many times that the President revoked them in his 1967 *Economic Report.*

A major cause of the inflationary pressures came from increased defense expenditures associated with the Vietnam War. The national defense budget rose $10 billion in 1966 and totaled $60 billion at year-end. In addition, corporate investment expenditures reached $61 billion, a $16\frac{1}{2}$ per cent increase over 1965. In October Congress suspended the 7 per cent investment tax credit to dampen the inflationary impact of business spending.

The Federal Reserve took strong steps to curb the inflationary pressures in the absence of major fiscal restraints. In July 1966 the System raised time-deposit reserve requirements against the initial $5 million of deposits from 4 per cent to 5 per cent. In September the rate was raised again to 6 per cent.

Interest rate ceilings on small-denomination short-term certificates of deposit were lowered from $5\frac{1}{2}$ per cent to 4 per cent, and ceilings on other time deposits were maintained despite the general rise in interest rates. CD's swiftly lost their competitive position, and banks lost $3 billion in time deposits from August to November 1966. Congressional legislation in September coordinated the interest ceiling regulations on commercial-bank time deposits, mutual savings bank deposits, and savings and loan shares.

The tight-money policy began to take hold by the end of the year. Bank credit expanded by only $18 billion, a decline of $10 billion from the 1965 peak. By December interest rates had fallen from their late summer highs, and net negative reserves declined to $150 million as compared to the negative $450 million average during the first three-fourths of the year. A "mini-recession" in new orders, durable-goods production, and stock prices appeared in late 1966 and early 1967.

Despite the tightened credit conditions at home, the balance-of-payments position did not improve noticeably. The deficit remained at $1.4 billion, although the gold outflow declined to $0.5 billion. The President's voluntary restraint program was extended in an effort to diminish the flow of investment funds abroad.

Credit conditions continued to ease in 1967. In March the Federal Reserve initiated a two-step reduction in reserve requirements on passbook savings deposits and on the first $5 million of time deposits. This action released $85 million of reserves to the banking system. In April the System reduced the discount rate from $4\frac{1}{2}$ per cent to 4 per cent. Short-term interest rates continued to decline during the first half of 1967, but long-term rates reversed their downward trend as early as February and by the middle of the year had approached their 1966 highs. The high long-term rates reflected a variety of pressures including a record amount of securities issued by state and local governments and nonfinancial corporations in the first half of the year. Short-term rates rose in mid-summer and remained at high levels for the year. The money stock grew 6.5 per cent in 1967, nearly three times the increase of the previous year.

The 1967 first quarter GNP performance was disappointing since the economy remained at the same level as the final quarter in 1966. After Congress restored the 7 per cent investment tax credit in the spring and credit market conditions eased, GNP resumed its upward climb. By year end GNP rose to $785 billion but in real terms the increase was disappointing. In 1966 real GNP had risen 5.8 per cent; in 1967 the increase was but 2.6 per cent. Spurred by inflationary federal expenditures for the Vietnam War, the consumer price index rose nearly 3 per cent in 1967 while the wholesale price index rose 1.6 per cent. Repeated Presidential requests for a 10 per cent income tax surcharge to alleviate inflationary pressures in the economy were ignored by Congress despite the low 1967 unemployment rate of 3.8 per cent.

The nation's balance of payments position worsened considerably during the year. Private investment expenditures, tourism, and the Vietnam War contributed to a record $3.7 billion payments deficit and a $1.1 billion gold outflow. After the British devaluation, the Federal Reserve moved to tighten credit and strengthen the dollar by raising the discount rate to $4\frac{1}{2}$ per cent in November and increasing reserve requirements against demand deposits by 0.5 per cent in December.

In January 1968 the President asked for stronger measures to stem the dollar outflow by requesting tighter restrictions on overseas investment, a tax on tourism, and once again, an income tax surcharge. Congress did not respond and anticipating possible United States devaluation, speculators moved massively against the dollar in overseas gold markets. To counter these fears, the Federal Reserve raised the discount rate to 5 per cent in March and again to $5\frac{1}{2}$ percent in April while Congress removed the 25 per cent gold reserve requirement against Federal Reserve notes. Sustained speculation forced the London gold market to suspend operations in mid-March while the United States and six Western European nations agreed to supply no more gold to private buyers. A two-price system for gold was established: one, the official monetary price of $35 an ounce for transactions among governments and the other, a free market price, among private buyers.

A 10 percent income tax surcharge was finally approved by Congress in June. GNP rose $71 billion, or 9 percent in 1968 but much of this increase reflected higher prices. Consumer prices, for example, rose more than 4 percent —their largest advance in 17 years. The balance of trade had narrowed dramatically by year-end and it was clear that long-run economic stability depended upon the adoption of monetary and fiscal measures which would stem domestic inflationary pressures, reduce payments deficits, and restore overseas confidence in the American economy.

NOTES ON

ALTERNATIVE POINTS OF VIEW

AND SUPPLEMENTARY READINGS

An historical analysis of the criticisms of monetary policy since the thirties is made by James Schlesinger in "Monetary Policy and Its Critics," *Journal of Political Economy,* December 1960, pp. 601–16.

A well-written review of recent monetary developments is found in "Postwar United States Monetary Policy Appraised" by Henry C. Wallich and Stephen H. Axilrod, *United States Monetary Policy,* rev. ed., Neil H. Jacoby, ed. (New York: Frederick A. Praeger, Inc., 1964), pp. 116–54.

Yearly summaries of economic developments are contained in the annual reports of the Federal Reserve Bank of New York and in the Economic Report of the President prepared by the Council of Economic Advisers.

Chapter 22

An Appraisal of Fiscal Policy

The Budget and Stabilization Policy

Plan of the chapter. This chapter seeks to appraise the role of fiscal policy in economic stabilization—obviously rather a large job. The present chapter has a great deal of work to do. As this book has been chiefly concerned with money and monetary policy, it has not said enough about fiscal policy to let us begin straightaway with an evaluation of the record. We have to look first at the techniques of fiscal policy and to appraise the contributions it *can* make.

The first section of this chapter will examine some of the goals that could be adopted to guide fiscal policy. It starts with the traditional objective, an annually balanced budget, then looks at proposals for balancing budgets across cycles—for running deficits in recessions and surpluses in prosperity. The second section evaluates the contribution of the automatic fiscal stabilizers—the role of the changes in receipts and spending that come about *because of* business fluctuations. The final section looks at discretionary measures—the role of tax-rate changes and of special spending programs.

The annually balanced budget. Conservatives usually argue for an annually balanced budget (or for a budget surplus if there is government debt to retire). This was the official standard in most Western countries until quite recently, and still commands some support in both the Democratic and Re-

445

publican Parties.[1] Unlike so many rules of government, it has been observed more often than it has been broken.[2]

From the standpoint of stabilization policy, the annual–balance standard leaves much to be desired. It has not worked well as an economic stabilizer and can actually work as a destabilizer. The annually balanced budget calls for increased tax rates and cuts in government outlays whenever there is a slump —measures that are apt to intensify the slump.[3] It encourages tax cuts and increased spending whenever there is a boom—measures that are apt to intensify the boom. If we want to get effective stabilization, we must improve upon this rule.

Yet the annual-balance standard has had tremendous advantages that alternative plans may lack, though they are superior for stabilization purposes:

1. It gives a yardstick for measuring the urgency of public spending.
2. It directs attention to the *composition* (as distinct from the size) of revenue and spending.
3. It gives safeguards against inflation.

Let us examine these advantages one by one.

1. A yardstick for gauging the urgency of public spending is an absolute essential. There is never any lack of claimants for public money. Most localities have pet development projects that could absorb a large amount of resources. That hardy perennial, rivers and harbors development, could alone absorb many billions of dollars annually. Roads, public buildings, and recreation facilities have immense possibilities. Our military leaders, having "discovered billions" during World War II, have an unlimited appetite for spending money. No clear limits exist to expenditure on soil conservation, housing and rehabilitation of cities, purification of air and water, public health, and education. Some projects can be barred quite easily as doing more harm than good. But if we had the resources, we could expand government spending by tens of billions a year in directions that would give us real benefit. There are, in addition, millions of people with valid claims to government "transfer payments"

---

[1] We should say, however, that many advocates of a balanced budget have in mind the legislative (or conventional) budget, while economists more often talk of the cash budget which covers all of the government's receipts and outlays or of the budget as reflected in the national accounts, which treats many taxes as they *accrue* rather than as they are later paid.

[2] In the United States, the federal government ran only twenty-seven deficits in the 121 peacetime years from 1792 to 1930. From the Civil War through 1930, there were only two peacetime years (1894 and 1909) in which the deficit was as large as 10 per cent of expenditure.

[3] Before World War I, the adverse effect on domestic stability may have been mitigated by the character of the taxes involved—mainly general property taxes for local governments and import duties for the federal government. Local governments were not under pressure to raise tax rates or cut expenditures in a slump unless property-tax collections fell into arrears. Federal tariff increases had the effect of shifting the trade-account balance with foreign countries in a "favorable" direction—tending to revive employment here and to export unemployment to Europe.

—veterans, farmers, the aged, the unemployed, the handicapped, and the young in need of education.

We must set limits to government spending, based on what the community can afford. Spending must be cut back below its beneficial maximum. To judge whether the boundary is well chosen, we have to weigh one proposal against another. If better schools fall outside the boundary, we say in our saner moments, free entertainment on TV must also be "extramarginal." But there are always several margins to consider. If we expand one line of government spending, we can cut back other spending, *or* we can raise taxes, *or* increase the deficit. Most people find it easiest to visualize raising taxes, so that the burden of a specified tax increase may be our best way to measure the cost of an increase in spending.

2. People fall too easily into the habit of looking only at the total of revenue and expenditure (or merely at the size of the surplus or deficit), when they are not disciplined by the goal of an annually balanced budget. Yet the composition of revenue and of expenditure needs close analysis, along with the size—not only from the standpoint of value received and general fairness, but also from the standpoint of stabilization policy. A sales tax probably reduces consumer spending more per billion of revenue than an income tax. A budget balanced by means of increased sales taxation may have a more powerful anti-inflationary impact than one balanced by increased income taxation. On the expenditure side, a billion dollars spent on highways will probably absorb more resources than a billion dollars of government "transfer payments," since the recipients of transfer payments may save a part of the cash they receive from government. Similarly, road building may stimulate private investment, while factory construction by government would depress it. Policy analysis gains a good deal if we ask what can be done in the direction of stabilization within the framework of a balanced budget, even though other fiscal rules may prove better in the end.[4]

3. While inflation is possible with a balanced government budget (witness American experience in 1947 and 1950), an acute inflation is not likely. Advocates of old-fashioned soundness in public finance greatly stress this fact, while the more "modern" views on taxation sound rather different. But you must not overrate the divergence. Modern views hold that the basic justification for taxation is that it offsets the inflationary pressure produced by government expenditures.[5] The production of goods and services for government generates

---

[4] In Great Britain a good deal of stress is put on this side of fiscal policy. Cf. U. K. Hicks, *Public Finance* (Cambridge, England: Cambridge University Press, 1947), and the 1944 "White Paper," *Employment Policy,* American ed. (New York: The Macmillan Company, 1944), pp. 24–26.

[5] For a neat exposition of this point of view, see the "Functional Finance" chapter of A. P. Lerner's *Economics of Control* (New York: The Macmillan Company, 1944), especially pp. 307–8 and 316–21. In this view, public expenditure should be carried to a margin at which an extra dollar of public spending in each direction would be just equal in its effect on public welfare to a foregone dollar of private expenditure. But no one knows where this crucial margin lies.

income, just as does production for sale to private parties. Therefore, taxes must siphon off enough income to bring spending power into line with supplies available for private consumption.

Enough taxation, by this standard, is enough to avert inflation, but different taxes exert different effects on private spending. Hence, it may prove hard to reach a working agreement as to how much taxation is enough. Furthermore, if "enough" is admitted to be a matter of judgment, politicians will always be tempted to set their tax goals too low (taxes being unpopular), and thus to err on the inflationary side.[6] These difficulties may be sufficiently intense to justify an annual balancing of the budget—as a rule of thumb that will yield smaller errors in tax policy than alternative rules, and minimize the consequences of poor forecasting.

Budgets balanced but not annually. Some of those who reject the standard of annual balance would ignore entirely the notion of balance. But there are ways to preserve the advantage of balance and, at the same time, escape its drawbacks by deleting the word *annual* from the formula.

The first of these alternative formulae for balance is a scheme to balance the budget *over a business cycle*—running deficits in depression and surpluses in prosperity, and planning to have the surpluses match the deficits over a stretch of years. Schemes of this sort were widely discussed just before World War II, under the label of Swedish budgets. The name testified to Swedish pioneering in this area and to the actual adoption of such a scheme in Sweden—just in time to be shelved because of wartime difficulties.

Cyclical balancing of the budget would preserve many of the basic advantages of annual balancing. The symbols would still be there and business confidence would probably stand up better than if budget-balancing were abandoned. New lines of government expenditure would call for new taxes, and the public's willingness to accept new taxes would still serve as a test of the public's earnestness in demanding new government projects. The standard would call for an excess of Treasury cash income over cash outgo in prosperity, giving substantial safeguards against serious inflation.

Yet uncertainty always exists as to the shape of the next business cycle—whether it will be long or short, sharp or mild, and with or without a price rise on the upswing. Consequently, there is bound to be uncertainty about tax revenue and about those expenditure items that have a tendency to vary with the cycle.[7] To insure that balance actually occurs over the cycle as a whole would require certain guarantees. One such proposal has been to treat a fifth

---

[6] Another temptation, stressed by advocates of "economy in government," is to let expenditures grow whenever there is any reasonable hope that existing taxes are nearly adequate and new taxes need not be levied.

[7] Some programs tend to grow with business volume, notably the provision of facilities to ease "bottlenecks," such as new post offices and airports. Others rise as business volume shrinks, such as payments to the aged, to the unemployed, to veterans, and to farmers.

of each year's deficit as a mandatory debt-retirement expenditure in each of the ensuing five years.

Proposals of this sort commonly run in double harness with schemes to segregate the government's "operating budget" from its "capital budget," and to use the latter as an economic stabilizer. The capital budget would plan public works and so forth some time in advance, and the authorities in charge of public works would have legislative authorization to carry out a stated list of projects in the next year—always more than are urgent. If the economy is prosperous, many projects would be postponed. If the economy is depressed, the lag between authorization and construction would be shortened so that the list of projects authorized-but-not-in-progress would be worked *down*. This plan would cause actual *capital outlays* to outrun new authorizations in bad years but fall short of authorizations in good years.

Budgets balanced but not annually: "agreed-high-level" balance. The Swedish budget overcomes some of the objections to annual balance. In particular, it provides that if a deficit is produced by a slump, taxes need not be raised at once. But this standard still calls for higher taxes after a slump has gone on for some time. The longer the slump, the more likely a tax increase before complete recovery, which is apt to interfere with recovery.

A way around this difficulty that still preserves the virtues of budget-balancing was suggested by Beardsley Ruml[8] and promoted year after year by the Committee for Economic Development. "Its basic principle is to set tax rates to balance the budget and provide a surplus at agreed high levels of employment and national income and thereafter to leave them alone unless there is some major change in national policy or condition of national life."[9] This plan differs from the Swedish standard because it lacks machinery that will guarantee the averaging out of deficits and surpluses over a business cycle. If the cycle should actually contain a predominance of prosperous years, there would be a surplus over the cycle as a whole. If depression should dominate a cycle, there would be a deficit over that cycle.

This standard would still call for an increase in taxes if government expenditures were expanded, and for expenditure cuts if taxes were reduced. It would require that same comparison at the margin between taxes and expenditures on which budget-balancers rely to prevent government extravagance. At the same time, it would be freer from dependence on business forecasting than either of the other budget-balancing standards.

Budgets deliberately unbalanced? The proposals for cyclical balance and for "high-level balance" both take it for granted that business will go on

---

[8] See the pamphlet, *Fiscal and Monetary Policy*, by Beardsley Ruml and H. Chr. Sonne (Washington, D.C.: National Planning Association, 1944).

[9] Committee for Economic Development, Research and Policy Committee, *Taxes and the Budget* (New York: Committee for Economic Development, 1947), p. 22, quoted by permission.

having fairly sharp ups and downs. They aim at reducing or eliminating the tendency of government budgets to make fluctuations worse, but they are not aimed mainly at active countermeasures. Both would set a bottom to depressions higher than the one we would reach under annual balance. Either variant would reduce the government's receipts and increase its outlays during a depression, but both would make the budget a passive element in stabilization policy. The stimulus that fiscal policy could provide during recoveries would weaken as soon as partial recovery brought the budget back toward balance. To do very much better than this, we would require more active fiscal policies than are contemplated by either version of the proposal for cyclical balance. The government may have to take deliberate measures to prolong its budget deficit during recovery and to enlarge its budget surplus during prosperity. A formulation of policy guidelines put together as far back as 1949 by a group of sixteen economists meeting at Princeton seems still to be in advance of official and public opinion. The key passages in their report run as follows:

> ... In conditions of continued prosperity, a modified version of the balanced budget rule could be used as a guide: taxes should grow or shrink corresponding to desired changes in expenditures. Thus proposed increases in expenditures would be exposed to the traditional test of whether they are worth their cost in terms of taxes.
>
> However, if recent events and the outlook for the near future pointed, on balance, toward unemployment and deflation ... new government programs should still be considered on their merits, but the additional taxation that in prosperous times would accompany them should now be deferred. Taxes that are deferred in these circumstances should be put into effect as soon as that can be done without impeding recovery. There should be no delay in making the tax reductions warranted by any reductions in government expenditures. ...
>
> On the other hand, if the weight of the evidence appeared to be on the inflationary side, the opposite policy should be followed. Tax reductions that would normally be in order should be deferred; and tax increases should anticipate expected increases in expenditures.
>
> Where there is a definite expectation, justified by events, of serious recession or inflation, more strenuous fiscal action would be called for, and the policies described above should be supplemented by emergency fiscal action.[10]

This formulation would salvage most of the advantages of budget balancing without requiring actual balance over some fixed number of years. The budgetary tests would survive to check any tendencies toward extravagance, but stabilization policy would not be placed in a straitjacket by the need for exact balance during a particular business cycle.

The government may have to take more positive measures to enlarge its budget deficit during recovery or to enlarge its budget surplus during pros-

---

[10] Joint Committee on the Economic Report, *Monetary, Credit, and Fiscal Policies* (Washington, D.C.: U.S. Government Printing Office, 1949), pp. 437–38.

perity. On these occasions the fiscal target is no longer the annually or cyclically balanced budget but is instead a desired full-employment level of output.

In 1964 the government enacted a $10 billion tax reduction during an expansion period when expenditures were growing and the budget had been incurring annual deficits.[11] Unemployment was greater than 5 per cent and government economists were willing to incur larger budget deficits in the short run to stimulate aggregate demand, achieve a higher rate of economic growth, and promote a fuller use of economic resources. The budget target was known as the "full-employment surplus": a designated excess of government revenues over expenditures which would prevail at 4 per cent unemployment.[12] The tax cut was successful: in the first half of 1965 unemployment was under 5 per cent, and the federal budget was running a $1.2 billion surplus until the Vietnam War expenses began to climb. The 1964 tax reduction marked the first time that government was willing to cut taxes at the same time that federal expenditures were rising. Effective stabilization policy was not placed in a straitjacket by the need for budget balance over a designated period of time or during a particular business cycle.

The Automatic Stabilizers

As will appear when we try to sum up this chapter, there are a number of contradictions in public opinion and official positions toward fiscal policy for economic stabilization. *Discretionary* changes in fiscal policy are a highly controversial subject. But there is relatively complete acceptance of one branch of stabilizing fiscal policy—the use of the so-called *automatic stabilizers*.

The central idea of stabilizing fiscal policy has been to try to correct a drift toward unemployment by shifting the government's budget in the direction of a deficit, or to correct a drift toward inflation by shifting the budget in the direction of a surplus. Automatic stabilizers are devices which tend to produce such shifts toward deficit or surplus at appropriate times *in consequence of standing arrangements,* without requiring fresh policy decisions. A number of such devices are in use in the United States; and in our judgment the fact that the country's economy since World War II has come closer to running at full employment without inflation than ever before reflects above all the effectiveness of these devices.

An inventory of automatic stabilizers. Our discussion will commence by listing and analyzing the automatic stabilizers now in operation. Then we

---

[11]Federal expenditures rose from $111.4 billion in fiscal 1963 to $117.1 billion in fiscal 1964; the federal budget deficit was $1.2 billion in fiscal 1963 and $1.9 billion in fiscal 1964 (National Income Accounts).

[12]The full-employment surplus is defined in the *Economic Report of the President,* 1962, pp. 78–84.

will survey the possibility of setting up further stabilizers or strengthening those already at work. Finally, we will consider the limitations of the automatic-stabilizer devices.

The prime example of an automatic stabilizer is unemployment compensation. When a worker loses his job, his income from employment begins within a few days to be replaced in substantial part by compensation (if he is lucky enough to be in "insured employment," as not everybody is!). The money comes out of an "Unemployment Trust Fund," in which the employment offices of the various states "deposit" insurance contributions and from which they can "withdraw" to pay the unemployed. Scheduling payments to individual workers is automatic—it happens as a matter of office routine, with no need to formulate new legislation, persuade Congress to enact it, appoint chiefs for a new agency, hire a bureaucracy, or work out procedures to implement a new policy. Any time that unemployment grows, the number drawing compensation and the scale of the benefits paid will rise, and the Unemployment Trust Fund will tend to run down as withdrawals exceed deposits. Whether this is called an element in the government's "fiscal deficit" depends on the labels put on different operations; but clearly we are looking at a procedure for raising government outlays relative to receipts.[13]

Another very powerful stabilizer exists in the currently collected income tax on individuals. Most of the tax is collected by employers who withhold tax on wages and salaries on behalf of the Treasury.[14] If an earner loses his job, ceases to earn overtime pay, or misses his Christmas bonus because his company is less prosperous than last year, his "take-home pay" is reduced by only 80 per cent or 85 per cent of the cut in his "nominal" pay (which, however, is not nominal but very real as a cost for his employer). Thus the drop in disposable income in a recession is mitigated, in a way which automatically pushes the government toward deficit by reducing revenue. In the oppo-

---

[13]We may take this opportunity to point out that on the fringe of automatic-stabilizer arrangements there are often *destabilizers*. In the case of unemployment compensation, there are two. In the first place, many states work with "merit-rating" schemes which impose lower contributions on employers whose record shows that few of their employees become unemployed. A recession, of course, causes many employers to show less "merit," and thus has some tendency to increase contributions, partly (and with a lag) offsetting the rise of benefits. In the second place, if unemployment is severe and longlasting, an increasing proportion of those drawing benefits "exhaust" the number of weeks they can draw under the rules before they find new jobs. Benefits, therefore, have some tendency to fall instead of rising if a recession passes certain limits of severity. But it has been found in the more severe postwar recessions that the existence of "UEC" makes it relatively easy to back up automatic stabilizers through discretionary action. It is possible (as has been done on two postwar occasions) to get Congress to appropriate for an "extension" of compensation to long-term unemployed.

[14]In the 1967 fiscal year, for example, collections on the federal individual income tax were $69.3 billion, of which $50.5 billion was collected by withholding. Another $18.8 billion was collected in other ways (by quarterly payments of "estimated tax" and final payments), while $9.6 billion was refunded—largely because of "overwithholding" on taxpayers who did not claim full exemptions, were unemployed part of the time, and so forth.

site direction, if inflation pushes up pay scales, take-home pay is increased only by 80 per cent to 85 per cent of the difference, the remainder going to build up government revenue and push the budget toward surplus.

Another important automatic stabilizer is the corporation income tax, which since the Korean war has been at rates between 40 per cent and 50 per cent. This means that well toward half of any swing in "corporate profits before tax" takes effect in pushing the federal budget toward deficit on a downswing of business and toward surplus on an upswing or in an inflation. The stabilizing effect is enhanced by a feature of the tax which many economists would regard as illogical-though-convenient: corporate taxable income is significantly raised on an upswing and reduced on a downswing by "inventory profits." Since on a rising market, the *replacement cost* of goods sold is higher than the *acquisition cost* on which most accounting profits figures are based, this may mean that a company is taxed on the privilege of maintaining its inventory level. But the swing of taxable income relative to GNP, and hence the automatic-stabilizer effect of the tax, is clearly greater as inventory profits and losses enter the tax base. The fact that income after tax moves so much less than income before tax helps corporations avoid dividend cuts in a downswing and expand dividends on an upswing. The stabilizing effect of the tax must be seen as operating also through reducing fluctuations in the ability of corporations to finance investment in plant and equipment and in inventories out of "internal cash flows." If the flow of funds available to corporations for distributions-plus-investment fluctuated by the full range of profits before tax, there might be a powerful "feedback" to strengthen business fluctuations because of a stronger tendency to invest in times of high profits and prosperity.[15]

How far other taxes should be regarded as automatic stabilizers is more debatable. Most taxes have some tendency to bring in more revenue on an upswing and less in a recession. But in some cases (notably that of state and local taxes on real estate), the effects lag so far behind changes in activity that they have no real tendency to make the budget fluctuate countercyclically. Sales taxes, which are collected soon after the transactions on which they rest, doubtless contribute something to stabilizing fiscal policy through "automatic" swings. The same is true of "employment taxes" (social security contributions); though for many workers earnings run so far above the maximum limit to which these taxes apply that even wide fluctuations in income do not affect their contributions.

On the side of expenditures, we have already seen that unemployment

---

[15]Some analysts would argue that the stabilizing effect of the tax on dividend distributions is easily overrated because in any event "corporate saving" (the part of income which is neither set aside for the tax collector nor paid out in dividends) provides a cushion which enables companies to avoid cuts in dividends in a recession, and to reduce the tax swing might merely increase the swing in corporate saving. But since the rate of flow of corporate saving is a significant factor in "internal financing of investment," this argument does *not* show that to reduce the corporate tax would not weaken the system of automatic stabilizers.

compensation involves an automatic shift toward deficit in a recession. There is also some tendency for the number of people depending on public assistance to rise in a recession and fall in an upswing; but for a number of reasons, most likely the automatic-stabilizer effect of public assistance is weak.[16] One might also expect some stabilizing influence from the government's farm outlays, since movements of farm prices are powerfully influenced by consumer demand as income fluctuates. But the vagaries of weather and of politics, and the lags in policy adaptation, are strong enough to bar any very strong countercyclical tendency in federal farm programs.

The counterstabilizer of the debt limit.   Economists have long recognized a certain tendency for expenditures of state and local governments to go along with the curve of private activity rather than show a stabilizing tendency to bulge in recessions and contract on upswings. We have just seen that the countercyclical tendency which might be expected from public-assistance programs is very much attenuated by budget considerations. The fact that state and local revenues are somewhat cycle-sensitive (chiefly because they rest rather heavily on sales taxes, plus state income taxes) puts pressure on state and local governments to cut back current expenditures in a recession, but permits expansion on a business upswing. Furthermore, there is some tendency for *capital expenditures* of state and local governments to be cycle-sensitive. For one thing, many of these expenditures (such as provision of streets, schools, water supply, and drainage) are a response to geographical shifts of activity that depend on active private construction. For another, city governments and to some extent state governments operate under *debt limits* (often a prohibition on a debt that exceeds a certain ratio to the assessed value of real estate). A recession stops the growth of the debt limit, and thus calls for caution in capital expenditures. Fortunately for economic stabilization, these influences work largely on *decisions* to make capital outlays, and the actual outlays follow with a lag of months or years, so that recession-caused cutbacks ordinarily come after other forces have started a recovery. But this feedback of recession on state and local capital expenditures might give a second downward kick to a recession which lasted longer than those we have experienced since World War II.

Another destabilizing influence works through the *federal* debt limit, whose importance economists on the whole have underrated.[17] The authority of the Secretary of the Treasury to borrow funds on the credit of the United States

---

[16]Public assistance goes largely to families which lack an effective "bread-winner"; even in a moderate recession, not many families on relief have heads who normally support the family by their earnings. In addition, while in principle the various states set minimum standards and give each family on relief enough to meet the minimum (so that one would expect outlays to move proportionately with the number on the rolls), agencies operate largely with fixed budgets; so when there are more applicants, there is a tendency either to undercut the minimum (for example by being dilatory about providing for clothes and furniture) or else to be more restrictive in admissions. Finally, the effect of recession on relief rolls, such as it is, comes in with a substantial lag as the unemployed exhaust their compensation claims.

[17]An example is the lack of references to the topic in previous editions of this book.

rests legally on legislation in which the Congress sets a ceiling to the total amount of government securities that may be outstanding. Much of the time, the Treasury is working under a temporary authorization to exceed a "permanent limit" which is far below the actual volume of government securities outstanding. The need to get such a temporary authorization extended (or if possible to get the regular limit raised) forces the Treasury to go hat in hand to the Congress every year or so, except when there is a surplus so that the existing limit remains livable.

The "economy bloc" in Congress has hit upon the notion that federal outlays can be held in check by the combination of a strict debt limit and niggardliness in levying taxes. In principle, Congress is supposed to control expenditures through the appropriation process. But in fact the expenditures of a given year (especially for defense) are made largely out of unexpended funds from previous appropriations. When it comes even to new appropriations, Congress finds itself morally committed by "programs" previously adopted—largely by promises implicit in legislation the Congress itself has passed with considerable enthusiasm. The Budget Message of the President, which is supposed to guide appropriations, is primarily a forecast of what will happen in the next year if accepted programs are carried out, rather than an expression of will about the next year's operations. Furthermore, Congress never takes legislative action (as do the Parliaments of such countries as Canada and the United Kingdom) on the budget as a whole, but enacts a series of appropriation bills each focused on the program of some agency or cluster of agencies. The strategy of the "economy bloc" is then to put pressure on the executive branch to spend less than Congress has appropriated, by tailoring the combination of tax policy and debt-limit policy so as to make it impossible to spend as much as approved programs and appropriations call for. Allocation of funds among programs is then thrown back upon the executive branch—with prohibitions, however, on cuts in certain programs which are especially popular in Congress.[18] Incidentally, Congressional hearings on the debt limit are always used to force spokesmen from the executive branch to proclaim their allegiance to principles of conservative finance—thus setting limits to the power of these spokesmen to seek public support for "modern" fiscal policy by appeals to public opinion.

This sort of Congressional pressure must have a real tendency to shrink federal government outlays (both for public investment and for current opera-

---

[18]Since the "economy bloc" holds (not without reason) that there are chronic wastes in government which go on in good years and bad, we find that both tax increases and tax decreases are made the occasion for squeezes on expenditures. Thus, the tax cut of 1964 had a good deal of support from Congressmen who did not believe that reducing taxes would help restore full prosperity but *did* believe that a lower level of revenue with application of the debt limit would help hold a lower level of government outlays over the coming years. When in 1967 a tax increase was proposed to offset inflationary pressures from the Vietnam War, influential members of Congress made it plain that they would accept the tax increase only if it was coupled with drastic executive action to cut nondefense spending; though the logic of the "new economics" would suggest that tax increases and expenditure cuts were substitutes rather than complements.

tion) in a recession, while leaving them much more free to expand on a business upswing. There is no way to trace these influences through in specific numerical calculations. Yet, plainly, officials who must make decisions whether to let contracts, hire personnel, or commit the government to grants to state and local governments must be powerfully influenced. If they have authority to spend which carries forward into the next fiscal year, the *amount* they will carry forward will be smaller if they are confident that new funds will be easy to get next year. If they are spending this year at a rate which will use up all their money before the end of the fiscal year (as often happens), they will continue to expand or will cut back according to their prospects of getting White House support and Congressional acceptance for a "deficiency appropriation." Either directives from higher officials or the spontaneous action of lower-echelon officials trying to be "realistic" in the political context will have the effect of cramping federal expenditures in a recession and making them expand rather freely in an upswing.

Measurement of automatic stabilizers.   While the automatic-destabilizer influence upon expenditures of the debt limit does not lend itself to numerical measurement, one can gauge roughly the quantitative intensity of the automatic stabilizers represented by taxes and unemployment compensation. We may measure by the proportion of any swing in GNP which tends to be transformed into a swing in government deficit by the device in question. For the main items under *federal* operations we present rough figures in Table 22-1 which show what happened during the years 1954–63—a period when as it happened no major changes were made in tax rates. The table makes comparisons between high and low points of activity measured by the proportion of apparent potential GNP that got produced. To reduce random errors, we have taken averages for the peak or trough quarter together with the quarters just before and after it.

> *Unemployment compensation,* though never more than a fraction of 1 per cent of GNP, swings by an appreciable proportion of the change in GNP. We may place its contribution as an automatic stabilizer in the range from 6 per cent to 9 per cent of the swing in GNP.
>
> *Personal taxes* seem to contribute less than would be expected. Though the federal taxes covered by the table account for about 8 per cent of the level of potential gross product, they account for only about 5 per cent on the average of the swings. We must allow also for the presence of state and local personal taxes, and may assume that the data shown in the table underrate their effectiveness.[19] But with total personal taxes

---

[19]The apparent movement in the wrong direction in 1959–61 is made up of a small increase in the personal-tax proportion of GNP during the period when the economy was "moving sidewise" from early 1959 to early 1960, followed by a drop in the actual fall of GNP after early 1960. There was a general upward "drift" of personal taxes relative to GNP during the period 1954–63 as a whole, because personal exemptions were not revised upwards as increased productivity and somewhat higher prices raised income per capita. But if the personal-income-tax swing were as strong as suggested in earlier editions of this book, the effect should be more strongly visible in the table.

TABLE 22-1

PERCENTAGES OF POTENTIAL GNP REPRESENTED BY ACTUAL
GNP AND BY TAXES AND UNEMPLOYMENT COMPENSATION:
FEDERAL LEVELS AND INCREMENTS DURING PERIOD OF
TAX STABILITY 1954–63, BY QUARTER YEARS.
(1 per cent of apparent full-production level of GNP taken for three
quarter-years centered at peak or trough)

| *Variable* | *GNP* | Federal Tax Collections or Accruals | | | *Unemployment compensation* | *Total (with sign of UEC reversed)* |
		Personal	*Corporate*	*Indirect*		
Levels at peaks and troughs:						
Trough: 1954:2	94.68	7.56	4.48	2.54	0.53	14.05
Peak: 1955:4	98.70	7.97	5.03	2.64	0.30	15.34
Trough: 1958:2	89.86	7.46	3.46	2.33	0.80	12.45
Peak: 1959:2	93.42	7.65	4.35	2.41	0.47	13.94
Trough: 1961:1	90.10	7.85	3.59	2.35	0.73	13.06
Upswing stage 1963:3	94.08	8.16	3.97	2.44	0.43	14.14
Increments between above dates:						
1954–55	+4.02	+0.41	+0.55	+0.10	−0.23	1.29
1955–58	−8.84	−0.51	−1.57	−0.31	+0.50	−2.89
1958–59	+3.56	+0.19	+0.89	+0.08	−0.33	+1.49
1959–61	−3.32	+0.20*	−0.76	−0.06	+0.26	−0.88
1961–63	+3.98	+0.31	+0.38	+0.09	−0.30	+1.08
Sum without regard to sign	23.78	1.22	4.15	0.64	1.62	7.63
Increments as per cents of GNP-increment:						
1954–55	100.0	10.2	13.7	2.4	−5.7	32.1
1955–58	100.0	5.8	17.8	3.5	−5.7	32.7
1958–59	100.0	5.3	25.0	2.2	−9.3	41.7
1959–61	100 0	−6 0*	22.9	1.8	−7.8	26.5
1961–63	100.0	7.8	9.6**	2.3	−7.5	27.1
Mean without regard to sign	100.0	5.1	17.4	2.7	−6.8	32.1

Source: Calculations by AGH from U.S. Government finance tables in *National Income and Product Accounts of the United States.*
  *Anomalous movement.
 **Affected by changes in credit, etc.

recently about 11 per cent of GNP, we should probably place their contribution as automatic stabilizers somewhat lower—say at 8–11 per cent of any swing in GNP.

Corporate taxes, because of the great amplitude of taxable corporate income relative to GNP, show a contribution which is several times

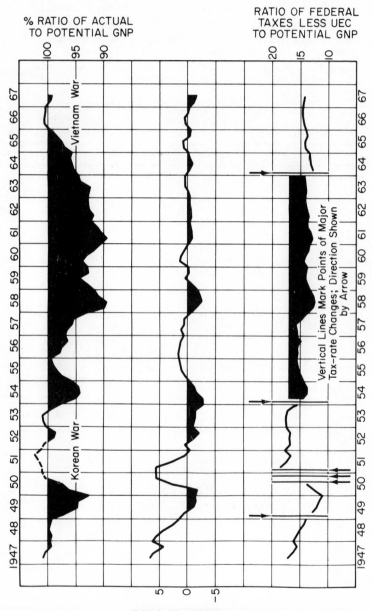

Chart 22-1: Federal surplus or deficit and major items of "automatic stabilizers" shown as ratios to potential GNP, quarterly, 1947–1967.

as great as one might expect from the fact that the federal levies covered in the table averaged less than 5 per cent of GNP. We may place their contribution in the range from 14 per cent to 20 per cent of any swing in GNP.

Other federal taxes seem to have moved more or less in proportion to GNP, and we may place their automatic-stabilizer contribution at 2 per cent to 3 per cent of any swing in GNP.

We should allow also for social security contributions (omitted from the table because changes in contributions were dominated by changes in the rates assessed against employers and employees, and were affected seriously also by a large expansion of coverage), and for various state and local taxes. If we add up the *minimum* estimates of contribution for the items covered by Table 22-1, we arrive at 31 per cent of any swing in GNP, so that it seems conservative (taking account of omitted items) to place the total automative-stabilizer effect at more than a third. The *maximum* estimates add up to 43 per cent for the items of the table, and something must be added for omitted items. Table 22-1 suggests 32.1 per cent; but if we regard as "abnormal" the items marked * and **, we conclude that the best estimate is 35 to 40 per cent.

An interesting comparison can be made by examining the effect of the automatic stabilizers on the surplus or deficit shown by the federal budget. This is done on a quarterly basis for 1947–67 in Chart 22-1. All figures are measured in per cents of "apparent potential gross product." The top curve shows the course of actual as against potential GNP, with shortfalls at the most seriously depressed points (in 1958 and 1961) of over 10 per cent. The middle curve shows the federal surplus or deficit as measured in the national accounts, which plainly shows a strong tendency to move in the same direction as GNP, and by an appreciable fraction of the movement in GNP. The third curve shows the course of revenue from federal taxes (not including social

---

Source: *National Income and Product Accounts of the United States: Statistical Tables* and continuation (data from 1963:1 onwards) in *Survey of Current Business,* July 1967.

"Potential GNP" is obtained in 1958 dollars by a logarithmic straight-line interpolation between values of real GNP for 1947, the four quarters ending June 1953, and 1966. (The slight excess of actual over "potential" in 1966 results from a minor discrepancy between the official annual figures and quarterly figures for 1966; that for 1950–51 is assumed to represent "overemployment" during the Korean war.

Potential GNP in current dollars (not included here because it does not enter the chart) is calculated by multiplying actual current-dollar GNP by the ratio of potential to actual 1958-dollar GNP. This potential GNP in current dollars is the denominator for the fiscal ratios.

The data for federal surplus (or deficit) and for taxes are from *NIPA* table 3.2, and are thus on a national-accounts basis (with corporate taxes as accrued rather than as paid). The surplus or deficit is taken directly from line 16 of this table. The tax figure (which *excludes* social security contributions) is the residual of "receipts" (line 1) less contributions for social insurance (line 5). Unemployment compensation (treated as a *negative item in federal operations* in this chart) is taken from *NIPA* table 2.1, which deals with personal income; the item used is line 17 of that table, which is described as "*state* unemployment insurance benefits" but of course represents the national program under which benefits are financed immediately by "withdrawals from the federal Unemployment Trust Fund."

security contributions, whose scale is reconsidered and changed so often that they have to be treated as "discretionary items") less unemployment compensation. (The numerous discontinuities and arrows on this bottom curve show the date and direction of major tax-rate changes which add discretionary to automatic changes; but from 1954 through 1961, tax rates were nearly enough constant to give a long stretch of highly comparable experience.) You will see that "automatic stabilizers" account for the swing in the federal budget as the realized percentage of GNP changes—in fact, the automatic elements actually "overexplain" the budget changes, which, as will be shown with more rigor in the third section of the chapter, often are inverse to those appropriate for economic stabilization.

Discretionary Fiscal Policy

Besides the standing arrangements which constitute automatic stabilizers, fiscal policy includes arrangements made year by year as to government expenditures and as to tax rates and structures. Stabilization policy may be carried on through these discretionary decisions which may also be determined in ways that contribute little to stabilization or even that destabilize the economy. It is important to sort out in the record these two aspects of fiscal policy—and not to let possible deficiencies of discretionary policy hide behind the automatic stabilizers.

Sorting out of automatic and discretionary aspects of the federal surplus or deficit. A general picture of the relation to economic activity of the automatic and discretionary sides of fiscal policy is offered in Chart 22-2 (and Table A in the Appendix to this chapter). Working with annual data, we estimate first the contribution to the federal surplus or deficit of the automatic stabilizers. Then starting from the surplus or deficit reported by the national accounts, we subtract the automatic contribution from the total surplus to arrive at a residual figure for the discretionary contribution. All the calculations are done taking as a unit 1 per cent of the level of GNP which apparently corresponds to full employment, called a "full-production level" for convenience.

The top curve of the chart shows the extent to which a federal deficit is generated by the fact that when activity is depressed taxes bring in less revenue and unemployment compensation leads to greater outpayments than when production is full. The second curve shows actual GNP as a percentage of its full-production level. As we would expect from the quarterly data presented in Chart 22-2, we find clear-cut evidence that these automatic stabilizers shift the budget toward the deficit side by a substantial fraction of any shortfall of

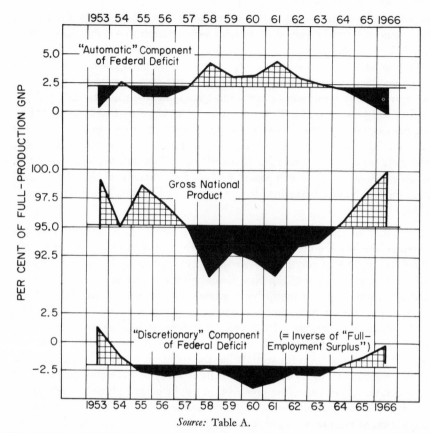

Source: Table A.

Chart 22-2: Deficit attributable to "automatic" and "discretionary," components of Federal budget, in relation to GNP, 1953–1966.

GNP below full-production levels.[20] We must, of course, see this movement of the "automatic" component of the deficit as the *result* rather than the cause of the movement of GNP—remembering naturally that in the absence of automatic stabilizers, the gyrations of GNP would probably have been considerably wider.

The bottom curve of Chart 22-2 shows the contribution to the federal deficit of discretionary policy. You will see that for every year shown except 1953, this contribution was *negative*. That is, the federal government ran what is called

---

[20]The figures used in Chart 22-2 are more refined than those of Chart 22-1 in that the procedures used in Table A include a correction for changes in tax rates. In exchange, we lose the detail of the quarterly figures used in Chart 22-1. The time span of Chart 22-2 (1953–1966) is shortened to improve comparability with the "investment-consumption" charts later in this chapter and with the monetary charts of the ensuing chapter. Data for 1947–52 are included however in Table A in appendix to this chapter.

a "full employment surplus." This expression (popularized by the Council of Economic Advisers) means that tax rates were so high that *if* they had applied to a full-production level of GNP, revenue would have exceeded actual government expenditures. It stands out conspicuously on the chart that during the years when production continuously ran below 95 per cent of potential (1958–63), the government continuously ran a full-employment surplus exceeding 2 per cent of full-production GNP. If discretionary fiscal policy had been guided by the prescriptions of the "New Economics" for stimulating the economy, the failure of the economy to come back to full production in 1959, 1960, 1961, and 1962 would surely have led to a shift toward deficit. We must infer that while the fiscal policy of this period was not fully dominated by old-fashioned doctrines of budget balancing, it was not guided by the "New Economics" either.[21]

Validity of the "New Economics" diagnosis. It is interesting to ask whether the government's apparent rejection during the 1950's and early 1960's of the "New Economics" *prescription* for a stabilizing fiscal policy showed a failure of the *diagnosis* of the New Economics. For practical men in Congress and the Administration might have learned by experience that the academic view of the "New Economics" was wrong and could not support such a policy.

In a nutshell, the New Economics diagnosis is that an economy which produces less than its potential output is showing an insufficiency of "investment." The prescription for stimulating the economy in slack times by a fiscal shift toward deficit looks upon such a shift as a way of increasing investment.[22] The diagnosis and hence the prescription might be inapplicable if experience showed that investment seemed to have nothing to do with activity. This is a question of fact; how do the facts look?

A first look at the relevant facts is offered by Chart 22-3. Here we look to see whether "investment" as conventionally measured seems to have the influence on "consumption" attributed to it by the New Economics.[23] Once more we

---

[21]Cynics about the American political process should take note that the "full-employment surplus" reached its peak value (almost 4 per cent) in the election year 1960.

[22]Strictly, what is at stake is the relation between *planned* investment and the saving which will eventuate at levels of activity corresponding to that investment. If we were being finicky, we might describe both taxes and transfer payments as influences in the first instance on saving rather than on investment. But for present purposes, it suffices to take the line that a shift toward deficit tends *either* to constitute an increase in investment or to constitute a subtraction from saving. In a complete analysis, one would consider also the effect of government expenditures and taxes on private investment incentives.

[23]This test is somewhat more solid than one which compares *total* GNP with "investment." Obviously total GNP consists in considerable part of items of investment (business plant and equipment, new houses, additions to inventories, excess of exports over imports), and these items account for a considerable part of the fluctuation of GNP. To compare GNP with investment is, therefore, uncomfortably close to comparing investment fluctuations with themselves. The comparisons of Charts 22-3 and 22-4 (following) are safeguarded by comparing with "investment" a total which *includes no elements included in investment*. Since it is obvious that non-"consumption" elements of GNP will show a strong parallelism with invest-

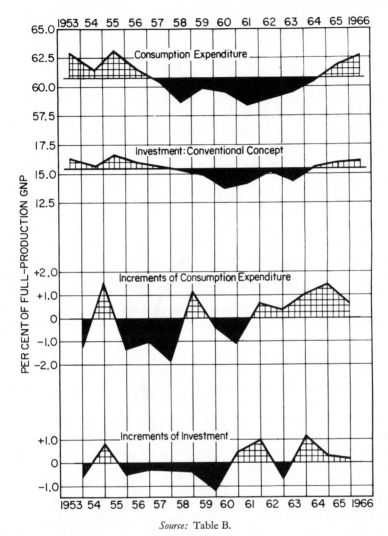

Source: Table B.

Chart 22-3: Consumption and investment, conventional concepts: levels and increments, 1953–1966 (unit: 1 per cent of apparent full-production GNP).

measure in per cents of full-production GNP. In the top half of the chart, we compare *rates of flow* of investment and consumption; in the bottom half, *increments* of these rates of flow. (The underlying data are shown in Table B in the Appendix to this chapter.)

ment (even though "investment" as calculated includes negative tax items and positive transfer-payment items which are not in themselves parts of GNP), we arrive at an argument *a fortiori* which says that if we know that "investment" swings consumption, we can be doubly sure that it swings GNP!

A glance at the top half of the chart will show that at least a rough general correspondence during the period of observation (1953–66) exists between levels of consumption and those of investment (taking "investment" as the sum of private domestic business investment, including housing, excess of exports over imports, and *deficits* of federal, state, and local governments). Both investment and consumption were high on the whole in 1953–56, low in 1958–63, and high again in 1964–66. This impression is confirmed by the lower half of the chart, which shows 1956–60 as a period when most of the time investment and consumption were registering declines from the previous year, and the 1960's as a period when most of the time both were registering expansion. In the expansion period, there is an interesting tendency for rates of growth of investment to move *sooner* than corresponding rates for consumption, which on the whole is consistent with viewing investment as the causal factor. We should note that there are a few discrepancies; in particular, the substantial gain in consumption (and in GNP) from 1958 to 1959 does not appear in "investment"; Table B shows that there were 1958–59 gains in private investment, offset by a sharp shift toward surplus in the federal government's budget. This discrepancy and other smaller ones indicate that the New Economics diagnosis does not cover all of the facts. Nevertheless, Chart 22-3 indicates that changes in consumption (hence in GNP) respond most of the time to changes in investment. Since the 1958–59 recovery was highly unsatisfactory (making up only 2.5 percentage points of full-production GNP, as compared with losses of 4.3 points from 1957 to 1958 or of 8.0 points from 1955 to 1958), this experience can scarcely be taken to show that a fiscal stimulus instead of fiscal restraint would have been a policy error!

The figures just examined are a rather imperfect representation of the forces at work. We have already seen that changes in the federal deficit are in good part effects of changes in activity. In addition, we must recognize that changes in inventory are largely induced by changes of activity, and that the same is true of changes in imports. We should, therefore, consider what happens to the "investment-consumption" picture if we remove the passive elements from the investment figures and make corresponding changes in the "consumption" figures. That is, we can regard "active investment" as including on the business side fixed capital formation (but not the growth of inventory), and the excess of exports over a *full-production level* of imports (rather than actual imports), and on the federal-government side the deficit corresponding to the full-employment surplus rather than the actual deficit. The noninvestment series to be examined for effects of investment then consists of consumption plus inventory-growth, adjusted for the difference between actual and full-employment levels of imports.[24] Figures on this basis are presented in Chart 22-4 (and Table C in the Appendix to this chapter).

---

[24]The import adjustment means that we try to arrive at a figure for *induced demand for domestic products*— considering that part of the demand for consumer goods and services plus inventories gets translated into a derived demand for imports, which will not stimulate *United States* activity.

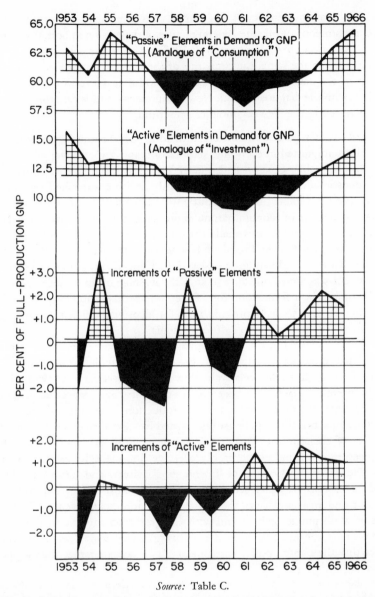

Source: Table C.

Chart 22-4: "Active" and "passive" elements in aggregate demand: levels and increments, 1953–1966 (unit: 1 per cent of apparent full-production).

This change in the presentation of the figures is clarifying, and on the whole makes the diagnosis of the New Economics seem more reasonable. Inclusion of the inventory swings on the "passive" side makes the fluctuations of consumption and the like sharper than in Chart 22-3. At the same time, measuring federal government on a "full-employment surplus" footing and offsetting exports against "full-employment levels" of imports gives us sharper movements of "active investment." While the general picture of depression in both investment and "consumption" from 1958 through 1963 and of better performance before and after is much the same, the similarity of the curves is improved by our refinement of the data.[25] Once more, we must find that the record is reasonably consistent with the diagnosis of the New Economics—and is far from giving a basis for rejecting the New Economics prescription.

Recent shifts in public and official attitudes. Great enthusiasm was aroused among those interested in economic stabilization and growth over an apparent major shift in public opinion and official attitudes in the United States early in the Johnson administration. The apparently decisive watershed was the tax cut (amounting in annual rate to about $10 billion) which was made effective in 1964 as a measure of economic stimulation. True, this was a seriously delayed response to recommendations made early in his term by President Kennedy; but partly as a reaction to President Kennedy's assassination, public opinion and official views rallied behind this part of the Kennedy program. The stimulus of the tax cut was aimed not only to stop the wastage of unproduced potential output, but to lay the foundation for a faster long-term economic growth of the United States, and to help provide jobs for deprived minority groups and people in the depressed region of Appalachia.

The tax cut of 1964 was a great immediate success in several ways. On the side of actual economic activity (as may be seen, for example, from the quarterly figures of Chart 22-1), the relatively slow pace of recovery in 1962–63 was replaced in late 1963 (when the tax cut was a certainty) by a marked acceleration, which brought the economy up to full-production levels toward the end of 1965. The impact of this experience (supported by careful analyses by a number of centers of economic studies) convinced many doubters that a stimulating fiscal measure could indeed be highly effective. President Johnson, Chairman Walter Heller of the Council of Economic Advisers, and Treasury officials offered interpretations which seemed to many economists a great improvement in candor and relevance over the policy pronouncements even of President Kennedy. With public opinion and with Congress, the curse seemed to have been taken off the identification of stabilizing policy with "deficit *spending*": the fact that the chosen policy instrument was a tax cut rather than a public

---

[25]The discrepancy in the change from 1958 to 1959 is much less bothersome on this footing: in Chart 22-4, there is at least a sharp deceleration in 1958–59 of the 1956–61 decline of "active investment."

Conspicuous in Chart 22-4 is a new discrepancy in the rate of expansion from 1954 to 1955 in investment— masked in Table B and Chart 22-3 by the inclusion there as "investment" of an unusually sharp rise in inventory. This 1955-expansion episode is an "exception which proves the rule": there was a most unusual expansion of "consumer investment in durable goods" in connection with the 1955 automobile models, which were the first to offer automatic transmissions as standard equipment in moderate-priced cars.

works program showed that fiscal policy could be used without any "extravagance" in public outlays.[26]

At this writing (mid-1968), we cannot yet judge whether a significant and durable change in public opinion and official views has really occurred. But there are many indications that the enthusiasm of 1964–65 over the "fiscal innovation" may have been premature. Both the Administration and Congress showed themselves in 1966–67 to be reluctant to carry through a tax increase when activity was high and rising military expenditures in connection with Vietnam threatened inflation. While certainly some room existed for argument about the urgency of the suggested tax increases, the character of the opposition suggested strongly that not much weight would ever be given to arguments for a tax increase on behalf of economic stabilization. If tax reduction is a one-way street, it becomes less possible to recommend tax cuts as a remedy for slack in the economy when it is quite possible that presently there will again be full employment and inflationary pressure.[27] The coupling of the tax boost eventually enacted in 1968 with expenditure cuts suggests conservative budget-politics rather than "New Economics" stabilization policy.

Possible improvements in discretionary fiscal policy. In this somewhat discouraging climate of opinion, to suggest improvements in discretionary fiscal policy from the stabilization standpoint may seem utopian. Yet one should not be a defeatist; and the need for fiscal reform can only be demonstrated by showing what rich possibilities lie open.

In the first place, a good deal of room still exists for developing useful expenditure programs that can be given *discretionary flexibility* in their timing. Economists have been interested for decades in a proposal to establish a systematic "shelf of public works projects," consisting of projects which have passed the stages of appropriation, engineering design, and provision of a site, but on which contracts have not been let. We have sometimes accumulated a backlog of such projects when inflation threats have induced the President to order a slowdown in the letting of contracts; but the backlog has tended to be worked off as soon as possible, and we have rarely entered a serious recession with a reserve of such projects that could permit acceleration of work. Besides the "heavy" projects with formidable engineering aspects of which one usually

---

[26]We teachers of economics may have something to answer for in our tendency to lump everything together as "investment," which has a tendency to increase aggregate demand. The normal use of the term (outside purely financial applications) would seem to carry implications that investment must be a process of *using present resources to provide a basis* (machinery, buildings, inventory, and the like) *for greater productivity in the future.* Some government spending is investment in this sense; much is not.

[27]The same objection may also lie against Walter Heller's attractive proposal to take advantage of the tendency of federal taxes at constant rates to outgrow the *federal* government's needs for revenue, by a systematic expansion of grants to states and to hard-pressed municipalities. If such changes are irreversible (as is probable) and if federal tax increases cannot be enacted, the situation becomes dangerous.

thinks in this connection, there are possibilities in "light" projects consisting largely of direct labor. Most of our urban parks, vacant lots, river banks, and the like need a "cleanup job" sometime within the next few years, but it may not matter very much for long-run purposes just when the work is done. Frank use of such jobs as "work-relief projects" (counting as benefits work experience for young men who might otherwise be unemployed, and the self-respect that goes with helping to correct some of the mess which surrounds slum-dwellers) would be defensible, permitting expansion when employment is slack.[28] The country is becoming more and more aware of a backlog of social needs in the fields of air pollution, water pollution, rubbish disposal, building maintenance, street maintenance, and so forth—calling for a mixture of "light" and "heavy" projects with many options as to timing. The social cost of such projects will be reduced to the extent that they can use manpower which otherwise would be unemployed. Consequently, the problem of good timing of such activities needs thorough re-examination.

As to the general course of government expenditures, great dissatisfaction exists with the traditional process of control through appropriations. There simply is too much slack in the timing of the process: to give government agencies the necessary freedom to make long-term contracts and commitments makes the appropriation process incapable of regulating the rate of flow of government outlays—even from year to year, let alone quarter-year by quarter-year as might be appropriate for economic stabilization. Recent Congressional attempts to control expenditures with a combination of pressures through tax legislation and the debt limit—referred to earlier in this chapter—seem likely to produce a highly arbitrary timing and composition of outlays, to the advantage neither of economic stabilization nor of the other objectives of public expenditures. Maybe improvements can be scored along the line of suggestions one hears in some quarters for a direct *rate-of-expenditure limit*—enacted by Congress, and throwing upon the President the responsibility for allocating the available sums. In case of a recession or an inflationary flurry, such a limit might be changed on fairly short notice for an oncoming quarter-year. In advance of experience, of course, it is hard to forecast what unexpected difficulties might crop up in such a program.

On the side of taxation, Congress is very jealous of its powers. There would be major Constitutional difficulties to any substantive delegation of taxing powers to the executive branch. But at least two major possibilities exist for tax flexibility. In the first place, Congress could provide a legislative framework within which "quickie legislation" would be feasible. It could be agreed in

---

[28]Perhaps one should say *when and where* employment is slack. The existence of unemployment which could staff such projects in one city may justify the projects, even though unemployment may be unusually low in other cities. There is enough difficulty finding economic policies which can help specifically with the recovery of "depressed areas" and "pockets of unemployment" so that the localization of such a program may be a major advantage.

advance that *if* tax changes were to be made, they would take the form of a rise or fall by so many percentage points in the individual income tax (or in some broadly based sales tax). The time-consuming process of legislative hearings and painstaking law-drafting could be applied to this framework; but the question which of (for example) three alternative rate structures should be applied could be decided on short notice—even for periods as short as a calendar quarter.[29] In the second place, Congress might possibly "give the taxpayer a suspended sentence"—deliberately enacting tax rates which are likely to prove higher than necessary, and delegating to the President the power to *abate* the statutory tax rates within limits. (Such Presidential power could be checked if desired by a "legislative veto"—with abatements going into effect only if not barred by a Congressional resolution within a stated notice-period.)

In short, the United States has not reached the end of the road as to flexibility in discretionary fiscal policy. Admittedly, we are in a worse position to organize such a flexible policy than a government such as that of Great Britain or Canada, which calls upon its Parliament to vote upon a year's budget (or occasionally an interim budget) as a whole rather than piecemeal, and which can make the budget a "question of confidence" so that it will not be distorted or delayed in the legislative process. But within our Constitution and general governmental framework, sufficient room still exists for adapting the timing both of expenditures and of taxes to the current and prospective economic situation. What is needed is the will to make such a reform—and above all, enough forethought to put *ad hoc* measures in a suitable framework, so that they can be effective without throwing government into disorder.

NOTES ON
ALTERNATIVE POINTS OF VIEW
AND SUPPLEMENTARY READINGS

On budget balancing and the role of public spending, see Francis Bator, *The Question of Government Spending* (New York: Harper & Row, Publishers, 1960). For a critical view of the balanced budget as a disciplinary measure, see Arthur Smithies, "The Balanced Budget," *American Economic Review*, Papers and Proceedings, May 1960.

On the "Swedish Budget," see G. Myrdal, "Fiscal Policy in the Business Cycle," *American Economic Review*, Papers and Proceedings, March 1939, pp. 183–93. For strong statements of the case for "compensatory" budgets, see A. P. Lerner, *Economics of Control* (New York: The Macmillan Company, 1944), pp. 302–22, and A. H. Hansen, "Stability and Expansion," in B. M. Anderson, J. M. Clark, *et al., Financing*

---

[29]We have several times had changes in *withholding rates* under the personal income tax within the calendar year. The emergency taxation of the Korean war, effective in October 1950 when the war broke out only in June, took the form of a rise in withholding coupled with changes in *level* which did not change *structure* for several key taxes.

American Prosperity (New York: 20th Century Fund, 1945), especially pp. 206–18. The Princeton statement referred to on page 450 was also printed in *American Economic Review,* December 1949. It should be noted that while it represented the unanimous sense of those present, the group was a middle-of-the-road one, and some competent economists of more extreme views might dissent.

On the postwar record of fiscal policy, see the testimony by A. G. Hart and others in Joint Economic Committee, *Hearings: Employment, Growth, and Price Levels,* Part 9A (Washington, D.C.: U.S. Government Printing Office, 1959).

For a statement of the merits of automatic stabilizers in view of forecasting difficulties, see Committee for Economic Development, Research and Policy Committee, *Taxes and the Budget* (New York: Committee for Economic Development, 1947), chap. i. For a discussion of automatic stabilizers in relation to other stabilization policies, see E. Hagen and A. G. Hart, "Timing and Administering Fiscal Policy," *American Economic Review,* Papers and Proceedings, May 1948.

A persuasive case for sole reliance on automatic stabilizers (including 100 per cent money) is made by Milton Friedman in his "Monetary and Fiscal Framework for Economic Stability" (*American Economic Review,* June 1948), reprinted in American Economic Association, *Readings in Monetary Theory* (New York: McGraw-Hill Book Company, Inc., 1951), pp. 369–93. For a full view of the issue of automaticity, ending with a much less optimistic view of its virtues, see Walter Egle, *Economic Stabilization* (Princeton: Princeton University Press, 1952), Part II.

For a review of recent fiscal history see Wilfred Lewis, Jr., *Federal Fiscal Policy in the Postwar Recessions* (Washington, D.C.: The Brookings Institute, 1962), pp. 12–24. More technical aspects of fiscal policy are examined in *Fiscal and Debt Management Policies,* research studies prepared for the Commission on Money and Credit (Englewood Cliffs, N.J.: Prentice-Hall, Inc., 1963).

TABLE A

AUTOMATIC AND DISCRETIONARY ELEMENTS IN FEDERAL BUDGET SURPLUS OR DEFICIT, NATIONAL ACCOUNTS BASIS, IN PER CENTS OF APPARENT FULL-PRODUCTION LEVEL OF GNP, ANNUALLY, 1953–66

	1953	1954	1955	1956	1957	1958	1959	1960	1961	1962	1963	1964	1965	1966
A. Estimate of shortfall in "automatic-stabilizer" budget elements from full-production levels														
Actual levels of automatic-stabilizer elements:														
1. Unemployment compensation	0.26	0.52	0.34	0.32	0.38	0.78	0.47	0.51	0.71	0.49	0.45	0.39	0.31	0.24
Taxes:														
2. Personal taxes and nontaxes	8.81	7.55	7.79	8.14	8.06	7.46	7.59	7.99	7.80	8.10	8.17	7.34	7.70	8.31
3. Corporate profits tax accruals	5.31	4.41	5.12	4.77	4.35	3.66	4.33	3.98	3.80	3.79	3.91	3.99	4.20	4.34
4. Indirect business tax accruals	2.98	2.53	2.65	2.60	2.54	2.33	2.42	2.46	2.37	2.43	2.43	2.44	2.37	2.14
Apparent full-production levels of automatic-stabilizer elements:														
11. Unemployment compensation	0.31	0.31	0.30	0.29	0.29	0.28	0.28	0.27	0.27	0.26	0.26	0.25	0.25	0.24
Taxes:														
12. Personal taxes and nontaxes	8.7	8.6	8.6	8.6	8.7	8.8	8.9	9.0	9.1	9.1	9.2	8.3	8.3	8.3
13. Corporate profits tax accruals	5.9	5.4	5.4	5.4	5.4	5.5	5.5	5.5	5.5	5.1	5.0	4.8	4.5	4.3
14. Indirect businesstax accruals	3.0	3.0	3.0	3.0	3.0	3.0	3.0	3.0	3.0	3.0	2.8	2.7	2.5	2.3
Contribution to surplus of automatic-stabilizer elements														
21. Actual level (2 + 3 + 4 − 1)	16.8	14.0	15.2	15.2	14.6	12.7	14.0	13.9	13.3	13.8	14.1	13.4	14.0	14.6
22. *Less* full-production level (12 + 13 + 14 − 11)	−17.3	−16.7	−16.7	−16.7	−16.8	−17.0	−17.1	−17.2	−17.3	−16.9	−16.7	−15.5	−15.0	−14.7
23. "Automatic" element in surplus	−0.5	−2.7	−1.5	−1.5	−2.2	−4.3	−3.1	−3.3	−4.0	−3.1	−2.6	−2.1	−1.0	−0.1
B. Estimate of "full-employment surplus" (= contribution to surplus of discretionary elements)														
31. Total federal revenues	19.1	16.6	17.9	18.0	17.6	16.0	17.3	17.7	17.3	17.7	18.3	17.4	17.9	19.3
32. *Less* total federal expenditures	−21.0	−18.1	−16.9	−16.6	−17.1	−18.0	−17.5	−17.0	−17.8	−18.4	−18.1	−17.8	−17.7	−19.2
33. Surplus, national-accounts basis	−1.9	−1.5	+1.0	+1.4	+0.5	−2.0	−0.2	+0.7	−0.5	−0.7	+0.2	−0.4	+0.2	+0.1
34. *Less* automatic element (item 23 with sign reversed)	+0.5	+2.7	+1.5	+1.5	+2.2	+4.3	+3.1	+3.3	+4.0	+3.1	+2.6	+2.1	+1.0	+0.1
35. Full-employment surplus	−1.4	+1.2	+2.5	+2.9	+2.7	+2.3	+2.9	+4.0	+3.5	+2.4	+2.9	+1.7	+1.2	+0.2

Source: Data for 1953–62 from *National Income and Product Accounts of the United States, 1929–65*; for 1963–66 from *Survey of Current Business*, July 1967. For calculation (by AGH) of apparent full-production levels of GNP, see Table D.

NOTE TO TABLE A:

Note: Since the sorting out of automatic and discretionary elements is so important for the analysis of fiscal policy, the methods underlying the estimates of Table A deserve some explanation.

To begin with, the estimates of "full-production level of GNP" which furnish the denominators for all the percentages of Table A may be taken as given; for their basis see Table D and its explanatory note. The data in lines 1–4 and 31–33 of Table A are simply the original information from the *National Accounts* table (number 3.1) on "Federal Government Receipts and Expenditures: Annually, 1929–65" reduced to percentages of full-production GNP, supplemented by payment of "state" unemployment insurance benefits (financed out of a federal trust fund) in the *National Accounts* table on "Personal Income" (number 2.1, line 17). The tax items given in lines 2–4 add up to less than "total federal revenues" (line 31) because revenues include social security contributions, on which rates and coverage changed so frequently that they must be regarded as discretionary elements in the budget.

The "apparent full-production levels" of unemployment compensation and federal taxes are estimated graphically, using scatter-charts of percentages of full-production GNP realized by actual GNP and by actual taxes or UEC. Drawing lines between points for adjacent years, it can be seen that taxes are higher and UEC lower as GNP is higher, with relationships which are fairly stable except at points (such as the end of 1953 and end of 1961 for corporate profits taxes and the end of 1963 for personal taxes) where there were sharp changes in rates of tax. Over stretches of years where there were not such major changes, freehand lines of apparent relationship are drawn and extended to the full-production level of GNP. In 1954–61, an upward drift is observable between early and late years in both personal and corporate taxes (related to the so-called "fiscal drag" of a progressive tax system). UEC shows a slight downward drift throughout the period 1953–66. While the resulting estimates of "full-production levels" are somewhat impressionistic, few of the entries in lines 12–14 of the table are likely to be in error by more than 0.1 per cent of full-production GNP, and there may be some compensation of errors. Changes in lines 1–4 are so much sharper than those in lines 11–14 that we can be sure of the significance of the differences in movement.

Given these underlying estimates, the logic of the table moves through two successive *residual calculations*. In the first place, the sum of actual taxes less UEC is entered in line 21. From this we subtract the sum (line 22) of the full-production-level estimates. The difference, which is a *negative* figure throughout, represents the contribution of the automatic-stabilizer elements of the budget to the government's surplus. (Or taken as a *positive* figure—line 22 minus line 21— it may be seen as a contribution to *deficit*, which corresponds to Chart 22-2.)

The second residual calculation is shown in Part *B* of the table. Here we enter in line 33 the actual surplus of the federal government (negative in 1953–54, 1958–59, 1961–62, and 1964, when there was a deficit on the national-accounts basis) as shown in the *National Income and Product Accounts*. The total surplus *less* the contribution to surplus of the automatic stabilizers must be the contribution to surplus of the discretionary elements in the budget (line 33). Since we are *subtracting negative figures* all across the table, every entry in line 35 lies higher than the corresponding entry in line 33, and all entries except that for 1953 turn out to be positive. That is, there was a continuous full-employment surplus in 1954–66.

NOTE TO TABLE B:

Source: Data for 1947–62 from *National Income and Product Accounts of the United States, 1929–65;* for 1963–66 from *Survey of Current Business,* July 1967.

*For calculation of "apparent full-production level" of GNP, used as denominator for the percentages, see Table D. Note that increments were calculated from figures rounded to nearest 0.01 per cent rather than to nearest 0.1 per cent.

TABLE B

RELATION OF "CONSUMPTION" TO "INVESTMENT":
CONVENTIONAL BASIS, ANNUALLY, 1947–56
(1 per cent of apparent full-production level of GNP)*

Year	Total GNP	"Investment" Private Domestic Fixed	Growth of Inventory	Private Foreign Exports	Imports	Government (deficit) State and Local	Federal	Total	Consumption Expenditure
A. Levels
1947	100.0	14.9	−0.2	8.5	−3.5	−0.4	−5.8	13.4	69.5
1948	99.0	15.9	+1.8	6.5	−4.0	−0.1	−3.2	16.9	66.7
1949	94.0	14.2	−1.1	5.8	−3.5	+0.3	+0.9	16.5	64.8
1950	97.7	16.2	+2.3	4.7	−4.1	+0.4	−3.1	16.5	65.6
1951	100.0	14.9	+3.1	5.7	−4.6	+0.1	−1.9	17.4	62.8
1952	98.8	13.9	+0.9	5.1	−4.5	+0.0	+1.1	16.6	62.0
1953	99.6	14.2	+0.1	4.6	−4.5	−0.0	+1.9	16.4	62.8
1954	95.0	13.9	−0.4	4.6	−4.2	+0.3	+1.5	15.8	61.5
1955	98.7	15.2	+1.5	4.9	−4.4	+0.3	−1.0	16.5	63.1
1956	97.0	15.1	+1.1	5.5	−4.5	+0.2	−1.3	16.0	61.7
1957	95.0	14.3	+0.3	5.7	−4.5	+0.3	−0.5	15.7	60.6
1958	90.7	12.6	−0.3	4.7	−4.2	+0.5	+2.1	15.3	58.8
1959	93.2	13.6	+0.9	4.5	−4.5	+0.2	+0.2	14.9	60.0
1960	92.2	13.0	+0.7	5.0	−4.3	−0.0	−0.6	13.8	59.5
1961	90.8	12.2	+0.3	5.0	−4.0	+0.1	+0.7	14.2	58.5
1962	93.4	12.8	+1.0	5.1	−4.2	−0.1	+0.6	15.2	59.2
1963	93.8	12.9	+0.9	5.1	−4.2	−0.2	−0.1	14.5	59.6
1964	95.5	13.3	+0.9	5.6	−4.3	−0.3	+0.5	15.7	60.6
1965	97.9	14.0	+1.4	5.6	−4.6	−0.2	−0.2	16.0	62.0
1966	100.0	14.1	+1.8	5.8	−5.1	−0.4	−0.1	17.1	62.7
B. Year-to-year increments
1947–48	−1.0	+1.0	+2.0	−2.1	−0.4	+0.4	+2.6	+3.4	−2.7
1948–49	−5.0	−1.7	−2.9	−0.6	+0.5	+0.3	+4.1	−0.4	−1.9
1949–50	+3.7	+2.0	+3.5	−1.0	−0.6	+0.1	−4.0	+0.0	+0.7
1950–51	+2.3	−1.3	+0.8	+1.0	−0.6	−0.3	+1.2	+0.9	−2.7
1951–52	−1.2	−1.0	−2.1	−0.6	+0.1	−0.1	+3.0	−0.8	−0.9
1952–53	+0.7	+0.3	−0.8	−0.5	−0.0	−0.1	+0.8	−0.2	+0.9
1953–54	−4.6	−0.4	−0.5	−0.0	+0.4	+0.3	−0.4	−0.6	−1.3
1954–55	+3.7	+1.4	+1.9	+0.3	−0.3	+0.0	−2.5	+0.8	+1.5
1955–56	−1.7	−0.1	−0.4	+0.5	−0.1	−0.1	−0.3	−0.5	−1.4
1956–57	−2.0	−0.8	−0.8	+0.2	+0.1	+0.1	+0.9	−0.3	−1.1
1957–58	−4.3	−1.7	−0.6	−1.0	+0.2	+0.2	+2.5	−0.4	−1.8
1958–59	+2.5	+0.9	+1.2	−0.1	−0.3	−0.3	−1.8	−0.4	+1.1
1959–60	−1.0	−0.6	−0.3	+0.5	+0.3	−0.2	−0.9	−1.2	−0.5
1960–61	−1.4	−0.9	−0.3	+0.0	−0.2	+0.1	+1.3	+0.5	−1.1
1961–62	+2.6	+0.7	+0.7	+0.1	−0.2	−0.2	−0.0	+0.9	+0.7
1962–63	+0.4	+0.1	−0.1	+0.1	−0.0	−0.0	−0.7	−0.7	+0.4
1963–64	+1.7	+0.4	−0.1	+0.5	−0.1	−0.1	+0.6	+1.2	+1.0
1964–65	+2.4	+0.7	+0.5	+0.0	−0.3	+0.1	−0.7	+0.3	+1.4
1965–66	+2.1	+0.0	+0.5	+0.2	−0.5	−0.2	+0.2	+0.2	+0.7

473

TABLE C

RELATION OF "CONSUMPTION" TO "INVESTMENT"; ADJUSTED BASIS WITH "PASSIVE" ITEMS OF DEMAND ON "CONSUMPTION" SIDE, ANNUALLY, 1947–66

(1 per cent of full-production level of GNP)*

| Year | "Investment" Excluding "Passive" Items | | | | | | "Passive" Elements of Demand for Domestic Product | | | |
| | Private Domestic Fixed | Private Foreign Adjusted | | Government (Deficit) | | Total | Consumption Expenditure | Growth of Inventory | Imports: Full Production Level—Actual | Total |
		Exports	Imports, Full Production Level	State and Local	Federal: Full Production Level					
A. Levels										
1947	14.9	8.5	−3.6	−0.4	−6.0	13.4	69.5	−0.2	−0.1	69.2
1948	15.9	6.5	−3.9	−0.1	−3.8	14.6	66.7	+1.8	+0.1	68.6
1949	14.2	5.8	−4.1	+0.3	−2.1	14.1	64.8	−1.1	−0.6	63.1
1950	16.2	4.7	−4.3	+0.4	−3.9	13.2	65.6	+2.3	−0.2	67.7
1951	14.9	5.7	−4.4	+0.1	−2.0	14.4	62.8	+3.1	+0.2	66.1
1952	13.9	5.1	−4.5	+0.0	+0.5	15.1	62.0	+0.9	+0.0	62.9
1953	14.2	4.6	−4.6	−0.0	+1.5	15.7	62.8	+0.1	−0.1	62.9
1954	13.9	4.6	−4.6	+0.3	−1.2	13.0	61.5	−0.4	−0.5	60.7
1955	15.2	4.9	−4.7	+0.3	−2.5	13.3	63.1	+1.5	−0.3	64.3
1956	15.1	5.5	−4.7	+0.2	−2.8	13.2	61.7	+1.1	−0.2	62.6
1957	14.3	5.7	−4.8	+0.3	−2.7	12.8	60.6	+0.3	−0.3	60.6
1958	12.7	4.7	−4.9	+0.5	−2.3	10.6	58.8	−0.3	−0.7	57.9
1959	13.6	4.5	−4.9	+0.2	−2.9	10.5	60.0	+0.9	−0.4	60.5
1960	13.0	5.0	−4.9	−0.0	−3.9	9.2	59.5	+0.7	−0.7	59.5
1961	12.2	5.0	−4.9	+0.1	−3.4	9.0	58.5	+0.3	−0.9	58.0
1962	12.8	5.1	−4.9	−0.2	−2.4	10.4	59.2	+1.0	−0.7	59.5
1963	12.9	5.1	−4.9	−0.2	−2.7	10.2	59.6	+0.9	−0.7	59.8
1964	13.3	5.6	−5.0	−0.3	−1.7	12.0	60.6	+0.9	−0.7	60.8
1965	14.0	5.6	−5.0	−0.2	−1.3	13.2	62.0	+1.4	−0.4	63.0
1966	14.1	5.8	−5.1	−0.4	−0.2	14.2	62.7	+1.8	−0.0	64.5

B. Year-to-year increments

Year										
1947–48	+1.0	−2.1	−0.3	+0.4	+2.1	+1.1	−2.7	+2.0	+0.1	−0.6
1948–49	−1.7	−0.6	−0.2	+0.3	+1.7	−0.5	−1.9	−2.9	−0.7	−5.5
1949–50	+2.0	−1.0	−0.2	+0.1	−1.8	−0.9	+0.7	+3.5	+0.4	+4.6
1950–51	−1.3	+1.0	−0.1	−0.3	+1.9	+1.2	−2.7	+0.8	+0.4	−1.6
1951–52	−1.0	−0.6	−0.1	−0.1	+2.5	+0.8	−0.9	−2.1	−0.2	−3.3
1952–53	+0.3	−0.5	−0.1	−0.1	+0.9	+0.6	+0.9	−0.8	−0.1	−0.0
1953–54	−0.4	−0.0	+0.0	+0.3	−2.6	−2.7	−1.3	−0.5	−0.4	−2.2
1954–55	+1.4	+0.3	+0.1	+0.0	−1.3	+0.3	+1.5	+1.9	+0.2	+3.6
1955–56	−0.1	+0.5	+0.0	−0.1	−0.4	−0.1	−1.4	−0.4	+0.1	−1.6
1956–57	−0.8	+0.2	−0.1	+0.1	+0.2	−0.4	−1.1	−0.8	−0.1	−2.0
1957–58	−1.7	−1.0	−0.1	+0.2	+0.4	−2.2	−1.8	−0.6	−0.3	−2.7
1958–59	+0.9	−0.1	−0.0	−0.3	−0.6	−0.2	+1.1	+1.2	+0.3	+2.6
1959–60	−0.6	+0.5	−0.0	−0.2	−1.0	−1.3	−0.5	−0.3	−0.2	−0.9
1960–61	−0.9	+0.1	−0.0	+0.1	+0.5	−0.2	−1.1	−0.3	−0.2	−1.6
1961–62	+0.7	+0.1	−0.0	−0.2	+0.9	+1.4	+0.7	+0.7	+0.2	+1.5
1962–63	+0.1	+0.1	−0.0	−0.0	−0.3	−0.2	+0.4	−0.1	+0.0	+0.3
1963–64	+0.4	+0.5	−0.1	−0.1	+1.1	+1.8	+1.0	−0.1	+0.0	+1.0
1964–65	+0.7	+0.0	−0.0	+0.1	+0.4	+1.2	+1.4	+0.5	+0.3	+2.2
1965–66	+0.0	+0.2	−0.1	−0.2	+1.1	+1.0	+0.7	+0.5	+0.4	+1.5

Source: Data for 1947–62 from *National Income and Product Accounts of the United States, 1929–65*; for 1963–66 from *Survey of Current Business*, July 1967.

*For calculation of "apparent full-production level" of GNP, used as denominator for the percentages, see Table D. Note that increments were calculated from figures rounded to nearest 0.01 per cent rather than to nearest 0.1 per cent.

TABLE D

ESTIMATION OF APPARENT FULL-PRODUCTION LEVEL OF GNP,

ANNUALLY, 1947–66

(dollar amounts in billions)

Year	Gross National Product in 1958 Dollars			Gross National Product in Current Dollars	
	Actual	*Apparent Full-Production Level*	*Ratio of Actual to Apparent Full-Production Level* (%)	*Actual*	*Apparent Full-Production Level*
1947*	309.9*	309.0	100.0*	231.3	231.3
1948	323.7	326.8	99.0	257.6	260.1
1949	324.1	344.7	94.0	256.5	272.8
1950	355.3	363.6	97.7	284.8	291.4
1951	383.4*	383.4	100.0*	328.4	328.4
1952	395.1	398.9	98.8	345.5	349.8
(1952–53*)	(406.9*)	(406.9*)	(100.0*)		
1953	412.8	414.1	99.6	364.6	366.1
1954	407.0	428.8	95.0	364.9	384.2
1955	438.0	444.4	98.7	398.0	403.4
1956	446.1	460.0	97.0	419.2	432.2
1957	452.5	476.4	95.0	441.1	464.2
1958	447.3	493.3	90.7	447.3	493.1
1959	475.9	510.9	93.2	483.7	519.0
1960	487.7	529.1	92.2	503.7	546.3
1961	497.2	547.9	90.8	520.1	573.0
1962	529.8	567.4	93.4	560.3	600.0
1963	551.0	587.6	93.8	590.5	629.7
1964	581.1	608.6	95.5	632.4	662.3
1965	616.7	630.2	97.9	683.9	698.5
1966	652.6*	652.6	100.0*	743.3	743.3

Source: National Income and Product Accounts of the United States, 1929–1965 for 1947–1962; *Survey of Current Business,* July 1967, for 1963–66.

*Actual 1958-dollar figures for 1947, 1951, 1966, and twelve months ended June 1953 are taken to represent "full-production level"; 1958-dollar full-production levels for intermediate years are interpolated on the assumption of uniform percentage growth at the following annual rates: for 1947–51, 5.469 per cent; from 1951 to 1952–53; 4.045 per cent; from 1952–53 to 1966, 3.560 per cent.

The ratio of the 1958-dollar actual and "full-production level" figures is then applied to the actual current-dollar figure to obtain a "full-production level" in current dollars, comparable to the current-dollar figures for taxes and unemployment compensation used to construct Table A.

Chapter 23

An Appraisal of Monetary Policy

The Importance of Monetary Policy

In recent years, economists and politicians both have given increased stress to monetary policy. This is partly the result of the difficulties with the politics of discretionary fiscal policy which we examined in the last chapter. By default of fiscal policy, the responsibility for economic stabilization (and especially for defense against inflation when the economy is operating at high levels) seems to fall upon the Federal Reserve System. The increased stress on monetary policy is also in part a compliment to its apparent success: on the whole, the economy has been remarkably stable since the Federal Reserve recovered its freedom of action after World War II in 1951–52. While (as will soon appear) considerable dispute exists as to *how* Federal Reserve policy affects economic activity, there seems to be much less doubt than formerly as to *whether* it does so. Economists and politicians who a few years ago were skeptics as to whether moderate shifts in monetary policy could exert any real influence are much more inclined today to take such shifts seriously.

The longer record of monetary policy. We could extend our review of monetary policy to the whole period of operation of the Federal Reserve System (since 1913); and in earlier editions of this book we did so. But there are many indications that monetary policy turned over a new leaf in 1952, and responsible criticism is best addressed to the way the Federal Reserve has operated since that time. A brief look at previous policies is called for only to put the recent period in perspective.

In large part, the record of Federal Reserve policy prior to World War II is one of policy blunders; and it is easy to make out a "score sheet" such as we presented in earlier editions, which will picture the Federal Reserve as moving in inappropriate directions most of the time. The worst experience of monetary policy was with the great deflation of 1929–33, which carried the economy into a depression so intense that the viability of the whole American way of life looked doubtful for some years. While there were certainly other factors than monetary policy at work (including a drastic disillusionment after the collapse of stock-market prices in 1929 and their renewed declines in ensuing years), it is hard to see how the Depression could have been so bad without deflationary monetary pressure. The Federal Reserve, after some attempts to ease money early in the Depression, went over to a policy of drastic restriction in 1931. Banks called loans right and left, and their attempts to liquidate bondholdings (compounded by the decline of earnings of railways and other issuers of bonds) brought bond prices far below par. Hundreds of banks failed, and billions of deposits of the public were tied up in these failed banks. We must thank the experience of the 1930's for a clear-cut demonstration of the power of sharp and long-continued monetary deflation to wreck an economy, and for showing the necessity (given our "unit banking system") of deposit insurance to make future monetary catastrophes impossible. But the lesson was dearly bought!

In World War I, the sharp inflation in the United States was clearly furthered by Federal Reserve policies of easy credit to business, and to those who wanted to be "patriotic" by buying bonds, but preferred to finance their purchases by borrowing rather than by saving. In World War II the Federal Reserve also showed a great deal of willingness to expand credit. Inflation was repressed by unexpectedly successful price-control measures; fiscal policy was much more successful than in World War I at diverting income from markets by taxation, and the public was persuaded to buy war bonds to a much greater extent out of their current flow of saving. The postwar inflation of 1946–48 was partly a retrospective adjustment to the "excess liquidity" piled up during the war, partly a response to the expansionary policy which the Federal Reserve found forced upon it by its commitments to support prices of United States government securities.

To a considerable degree, monetary policy had been discredited by its failure to exert a decisive influence in the period of incomplete recovery from the Great Depression, between 1933 and our entry into World War II. During most of this period, the Federal Reserve flooded the banks with excess reserves; monetary expansion was held back by a lack of "bankable loans." The stronger business firms (not especially needing funds, since activity was so slack that they had little wish to expand facilities and inventories) did not come to the banks for loans; those who came were in such a shaky business condition that banks shrank from the risk of lending. The Federal Reserve was widely held to have precipitated the depression-within-a-depression when recovery was broken off and reversed, far short of full employment, in 1937, at a time when the Federal Reserve had expressed fears of inflation and tightened up by increasing reserve requirements of member banks. But, in general, the period between 1933 and 1942 was one when the Federal Reserve was maintaining easy credit in hopes of contributing to economic recovery; and the experience was summed up by the aphorism: "You can't push on a string!" That is, the Federal Reserve was held to have power to *pull back* upon the economy through its "string" of credit control, but not to exert any real upward pressure.

The climate of monetary policy changed in the Korean war. The rather sharp inflation which began in June 1950 and ran into 1951 led to a sharp expansion of demands for credit. The Federal Reserve grew restive at being in the position of contributing to inflation because its bond-support commitments involved giving the commercial banks all the reserves they wanted; and strong support developed in Congress for a more restrictive policy. Early in 1951, as was noted in a previous chapter, Federal Reserve-Treasury relations were re-structured by an "Accord" which gave the Federal Reserve renewed power to use open-market operations for restriction; and after a few months devoted to weaning the market for government securities from its accustomed dependence on Federal Reserve support, the Federal Reserve began sometime in 1952 to have effective freedom of action. In the meantime the Korean-war inflation had run its course without the Federal Reserve being in a position to do much to combat it.[1]

The new Federal Reserve policy. Since 1952, the Federal Reserve has had a good deal of "independence" in the sense of being free to make decisions

---

[1] Congress did authorize the Federal Reserve to exercise "direct controls" over maturity and down payment of loan contracts for installment finance and home mortgages. But it seems likely that the inflationary effect of a race to arrange "commitments" for mortgages before restrictions went into effect outweighed the substantive effect of the mortgage controls. Installment credit controls probably helped postpone some demand for consumer durable goods from 1961 into 1962.

The momentum of the inflation died down after about the first quarter of 1951—despite the fact that the "cash surplus" of the federal government was replaced by a "cash deficit" as suppliers began to deliver large volume on contracts made in 1950. One must suspect that the force behind the inflation was in good part expectational. When war broke out, there were lively expectations of commodity shortages (hence hoarding especially of sugar and auto-mobile tires by consumers) and lively expectations of the imposition of "ceilings" on prices and wage rates. There seems to have been an effort to push wage rates and prices up before controls were established, for fear of being pinched by unfavorable decisions of the eventual price-control organization. Government officials and economists were inclined to postpone the onset of price control till "effective machinery" for rationing and for actual verification of prices could be set up. When at last with many misgivings the controls were announced (still without the "effective machinery"), businessmen and union leaders seem to have felt that their prices and wage rates were high enough, and to have exerted no real pressure against the rickety ceilings. The strong urge to build up inventories both of business and of households shifted at the same time to a sense that inventories were at least adequate, perhaps slightly excessive.

without formal directives from the White House or informal domination by the Treasury[2]—and with less direct influence from Congress, perhaps, than any other government agency in the economic field. In the course of the discussions of policy in 1951–52 and of the shift to the Eisenhower Administration—with its preference for more impersonal modes of economic policy, and with its strongly expressed fears of inflation—the Federal Reserve acquired a new position with public opinion. Previously, the Federal Reserve had seemed rather remote and technical; many people did not know it existed, and those who did were inclined to look upon it as of secondary importance. But at this time the Federal Reserve became much more visible, and came to be seen by a large and influential sector of public opinion as the focus of resistance to the widely feared inflationary tendencies of the economy.

Although "independent" in the sense just mentioned, the Federal Reserve has used its freedom of action to function as part of the general economic-stabilization machinery—taking seriously the Employment Act of 1946 as a replacement for the vague and possibly dangerous mandate of the original Federal Reserve Act to "accommodate commerce and industry."[3] The original standard might have been interpreted to require the Federal Reserve to expand credit in booms and contract it in recessions—thus reinforcing fluctuations of the economy. But since 1952–53, the Federal Reserve has considered itself called upon to "lean against the wind" and try to mitigate fluctuations. At the same time, the Federal Reserve has become much more open to outside intellectual influences, and has focused its analysis of current events much more upon the variables which economists deem relevant for tracing the effects of monetary policy. We have, thus, had rather favorable conditions for an effective contribution to economic stabilization from monetary policy. How far there has actually been such a contribution we shall consider in the next section of the chapter.

Effectiveness of Monetary Policy Since 1953

We come now to the question how monetary policy has actually behaved in recent years, and how far it seems actually to have exerted influence conducive

---

[2] At the time of the Accord, Mr. William McChesney Martin, who had been the negotiator on behalf of the Treasury, moved across and took the chairmanship of the Board of Governors of the Federal Reserve System. This might seem like a perfect formula for arranging an "informal domination." But in fact Mr. Martin seems to have been as little awed by Treasury authority as any leader in the history of the System—and knowing the Treasury from the inside, may have been less subject than others to being bluffed by Treasury contentions that new security flotations required the Federal Reserve to temper its policy.

[3] If the Federal Reserve maintained for a prolonged period a *constant* target-level of "free reserves," it might find itself reintroducing the standard of "accommodating commerce and industry." For if the banks in a boom depleted their free reserves by making loans which built up deposits and required reserves, the constant free-reserve target would call upon the Manager of the System Open-market Account to replenish free reserves by open-market purchases! Variations in free-reserve targets, of course, can cure this perverse tendency.

to economic stability and growth. The outcome on the whole confirms claims that the Federal Reserve has seriously attempted such a contribution and has been highly effective.

Federal Reserve policy as a response to "signals." One can demonstrate —not merely from Federal Reserve utterances but from the record of actual events—that Federal Reserve policy in its new incarnation has indeed acted as if it were much concerned with economic stabilization. A compact summary of the record from 1952 into 1967 is presented in Charts 23–1 and 23–2.

The first of these charts looks at the *level* of Federal Reserve policy variables as a response to the "signal" about economic conditions sent out by the level of unemployment. The percentage of civilian labor force unemployed is graphed in the middle curve. The top curve shows the ratio of the "free reserves" with which the Federal Reserve provided member banks to their required reserves; the bottom curve shows the discount rate of the Federal Reserve Bank of New York (graphed with an inverted scale, because a low discount rate, like a high level of free reserves, points toward monetary expansion). Horizontal lines are drawn through the unemployment and free-reserve curves at their average levels for the period. One can see at a glance that the high points of the free-reserve curve (tagged with numbers 2, 4, 6, 8) and its low points (tagged with numbers 1, 3, 5, 7) show a one-to-one correspondence with the high and low points of the unemployment curve. Furthermore, the dates at which the curves reach their high and low points, and the dates at which they pass through the average-level lines, match rather closely.[4] The same high and low points are visible also in the discount-rate curve; but the long stretches (especially in 1960–63) when the discount rate was unchanged make this a rather insensitive index of what the Federal Reserve is trying to do.

For a closer study, it is better to go over to the basis of Chart 23–2, where the variables are shown as *percentage rates of change*.[5] On this footing, we are looking at policy in terms of *intensification* (or relaxation) *of pressures,* and at the signals as *warnings that pressure should be intensified* (or relaxed). For example, a sharp rise in unemployment is treated as a signal which says: "For goodness sake intensify pressure for expansion or relax pressure toward restriction!"

The top curve ($\dot{Y}$-curve) of Chart 23-2 shows percentage changes from quarter to quarter in GNP, measured in 1958 dollars to make it a measure of physical activity. Since we are focusing on the direction of policy pressure, it is handy to show expansive policy in an upward direction and restrictive policy in a

---

[4] The vertical lines drawn across the chart represent dates (marked by *A*, *B*, *C*, and so forth) at which the *rate of growth* of real GNP reached its high and low points; the same set of dates is used in each of the charts of this chapter.

[5] This basis is better partly because it is more sensitive than a levels basis (making visible the shifts of several variables whose levels do not change at all dramatically) and partly because the school of economists who represent the "modern-quantity theory" assert that it is the *rate of growth of money stock* on which we should focus our attention; and to do so, we should state other variables in comparable form.

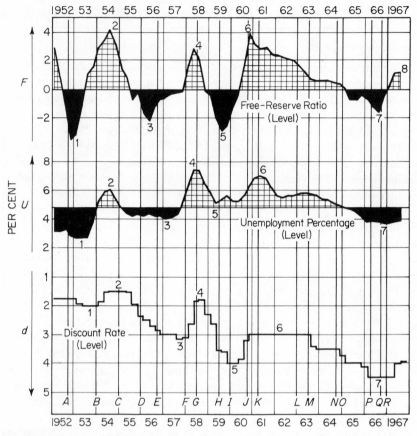

Chart 23-1: Levels of Federal Reserve policy variables seen as responses to "signal" offered by level of unemployment, quarterly, 1962–1967.

downward direction. But it is a *fall* in GNP which gives a signal for expansive pressure. Hence the GNP-scale is turned upside down. Maximum *rates of shrinkage* of GNP (intense expansion signals) are, therefore, registered by the high-points of the $\dot{Y}$-curve, tagged by letters B, D, F, and so forth; periods of declining GNP (or GNP expanding slower than the average rate of about 0.85 per cent per quarter-year) are shown by light shading above the average-growth line. Maximum *rates of expansion* of GNP (which permit if they do not require a shift of policy toward restriction) are shown by low points on the $\dot{Y}$-curve, tagged by letters A, C, E, and so forth; periods of more-than-average growth are shown by dark shading below the average-growth line. Note that if the signals given by fluctuations in the $\dot{Y}$-curve guided monetary policy, there would have been more than a dozen shifts (intensifications of expansive or restrictive pressures) in policy.

The next three curves on the chart register rates of change in the variables

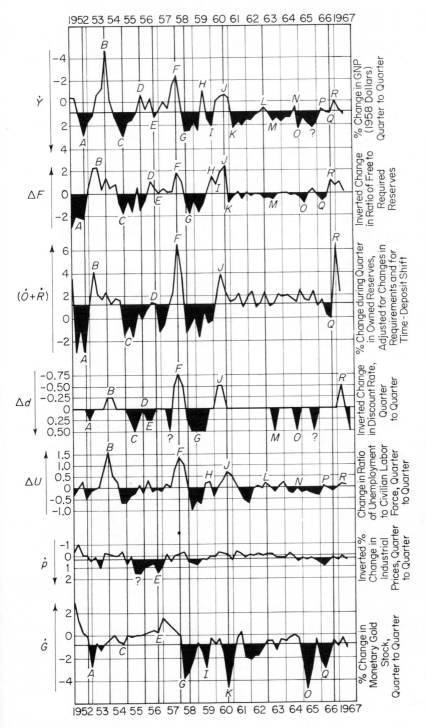

Chart 23-2: Changes in intensity of monetary policy as response to signals from changes in growth of GNP, employment, prices, and gold stock.

that directly record policy actions. The ΔF-curve shows changes from quarter to quarter in the ratio of free to required reserves at member banks. The $(\dot O + \dot R)$-curve shows percentage changes during successive quarters in the owned ("unborrowed") reserves of member banks, corrected for the release of reserves by the time-deposit shift—the same curve for growth of owned reserves which we used when we were studying "creation of deposits" in Chapter 5. The Δd-curve shows changes during successive quarters in the discount rate charged on member-bank borrowings at the Federal Reserve Bank of New York. Since a reduction of discount rates favors expansion, this scale also is inverted. Points of sharpest shifts toward restrictive pressure are tagged by letters B, D, F, and so forth, and periods when restrictive pressure was being intensified (in the case of owned reserves, when expansion adjusted for the time-deposit shift was less than the average rate of about 1.2 per cent per quarter-year) are shown by dark shading below the average-rate-of-change lines. Similarly, the sharpest shifts toward expansive pressure are tagged by letters A, C, E, and so forth, and periods when expansive policy was being intensified are shown by light shading above the line. To guide the eye, vertical lines are drawn through the highs and lows of the $\dot Y$-curve. You will see that it is rather easy to match up policy shifts with changes in the signals registered by the $\dot Y$-curve. After 1953 (that is, after post-Accord monetary policy had shaken down and both Federal Reserve and bankers were again used to operating the new line of monetary policy), the policy shifts indicated by the ΔF-curve, $(\dot O + \dot R)$-curve and Δd-curve come slightly later than the signals of the $\dot Y$-curve, and match rather well as to intensity. From 1961 into 1966, when growth of GNP was going at a fairly steady rate with only minor fluctuations, it is harder to match episodes; but note that the ΔF-curve and the $(\dot O + \dot R)$-curve agree with the $\dot Y$-curve in showing only minor fluctuations compared to those observed in 1953-60.[6]

This view of policy suggests that the Federal Reserve is sensitive to the state of the economy, and behaves very much as if it took its cue from signals offered by changes in GNP.[7] Since expansive pressure is intensified when GNP is declining and restrictive pressure tightened when GNP is gaining rapidly, this policy seems to be clearly of a stabilizing character. As Federal Reserve officials put it, they aim to "lean against the wind." Some interesting questions of timing

---

[6] The Δd-curve shows three moves in the direction of more restrictive pressure in 1963, 1964, and 1965. These are to be explained not out of the movement of the $\dot Y$-curve, but out of the worldwide "escalation" of interest rates and out of the gold-reserve shifts to be discussed in a moment.

[7] Note that we say "as if." It is known that the Federal Reserve authorities watch a number of indicators. In particular, they undoubtedly keep a close eye on the index number of industrial production which the Federal Reserve itself instituted by pioneer work in the 1920's, and in which it still takes well-warranted pride. The signals one would infer from changes in industrial production, however, would differ so little from those one would infer from changes in GNP that it would be hard to judge from Federal Reserve behavior whether one index or a combination was given more attention.

will be considered in a moment. But first we should consider one serious short-coming of this way of viewing the "signals"!

One can easily see that a decline of GNP suggests that policy should be more expansive or less restrictive; such a decline is clearly an evil that should be combated. But when the shift of GNP is upward, is that an evil? If an upward movement of GNP is taken as a signal for restriction, this must be because on the upswing GNP functions as a "proxy" for other variables whose behavior suggests that restriction is desirable. Since restriction is rather an evil than a good thing in itself, it must be adopted in order to avert some greater evil. When the Federal Reserve engages in restrictive measures, its public explanations run not in terms of the desirability of holding down output, but in terms of alleged inflationary price movements, "overheating of the economy" (which refers to the idea that inflation is in the making), or international monetary relations. Can our view of the "signals" be extended to take account of these influences?

The answer is to be seen in the lower part of Chart 23-2. Here we use three sets of signals. The ΔU-curve shows changes in unemployment. This is treated as capable of giving signals for expansion but not for restriction, so only the stretches above the average rate of change (essentially zero) are shaded.[8] The $\dot{P}$-curve shows changes in the index of "industrial" wholesale prices (excluding farm products and foods), with an inverted scale since it is rising prices that call for restriction. The $\dot{G}$-curve shows percentage changes in the monetary gold stock of the United States. The $\dot{P}$-curve and $\dot{G}$-curve are treated as capable of giving signals for restriction but not for expansion, so that only the stretches below the average-rate-of-change lines are dark-shaded. It will be plain that the major expansive-policy episodes (with high points B, F, J) are firmly based in the ΔU-curve. The major restrictive-policy episodes (with low points C, G, K, O, Q) are based *either* in the $\dot{P}$-curve or in the $\dot{G}$-curve or both.

This view of the signals, of course, makes it possible that the signals calling for restriction to resist an inflation or a gold loss might sound at the same time that other signals call for expansion to combat unemployment. This seems to have happened in 1956, when expansion leveled off and unemployment grew while prices were rising rather fast; and high-point D in the policy curves turns out to be a weak effort toward expansion. Furthermore, the combined price and situations seem to be the explanation of restrictive policy in 1966 (episode Q), when the leveling out of the rise in GNP might rather have suggested a balanced policy with no shift either toward restriction or toward expansion. In general, however, we find that the price-rise signal sounded only when output was showing a satisfactory rate of rise and could stand a slowdown.

---

[8] In a full-dress analysis along these lines, the level of unemployment should be taken into account along with its changes. No change in unemployment might call for an intensification of pressures toward expansion if the *level* of unemployment that refuses to budge is high enough to be serious.

It is not so easy to see why the gold-loss signal has not conflicted more often than it has with employment-and-production objectives; but one may guess that the international flow of funds is guided in good part by speculative judgments which are not likely to be adverse to the future of the dollar at times when the economy has slack to permit increases of demand to react on production rather than to inflate prices.

Economists tend to believe that the measures of monetary policy take time to act—a matter which we will examine shortly. To the extent that the Federal Reserve by changing the intensity of its monetary pressures is merely starting a lengthy process, the relation between signal and response which we have just examined, suggests that monetary action is always a jump behind events. It would even be possible to see the picture as that of a *monetary-policy cycle*. Suppose that the effects of monetary policy take between one and two years to work themselves out in the goods-and-services sphere. On this supposition, the recession of GNP (episode *B*) against which expansive monetary policy was directed in 1953–54 would be seen as the result of restrictive policy in 1952. The expansion with inflationary overtones which policy was trying to cool down by restrictive policy in 1955–56 would be seen as the result of expansive policy in 1953–54, and so forth. If we take the ΔF-curve as our main measure of policy, this view seems to work rather beautifully for 1953–60 and to break down completely thereafter: after the expansionary policy-push of 1959–60 (which according to the ΔF-curve was as strong as those of 1953–54 and 1956–58), we get not an explosive expansion but the remarkably steady and well-sustained upswing of 1961–66. If, however, we gauge the changes in intensity of policy by the $(\dot O + \dot R)$-curve, the policy-cycle view is easier to defend, since we find successive policy swings diminishing in intensity and could imagine that the policy-cycle damped itself out.

We should feel some skepticism, furthermore, as to whether *all* the effects of monetary-policy shifts take considerable time to work out. Remember that since 1953 the movements of the $(\dot O + \dot R)$-curve almost continuously show more-than-normal expansive pressure, just when the $\dot Y$-curve is showing less-than-normal growth. When we looked at the automatic fiscal stabilizers in the previous chapter, we argued that the fluctuations of GNP were held *smaller than they would otherwise have been* through the actions of the automatic stabilizers. If the decisions of monetary policy can be described as paralleling those of the automatic fiscal stabilizers (pushing upward as activity sags, and holding back as activity expands), we must conclude that the effect of any *quick* reactions of the goods-and-services sphere to monetary policy must reinforce the effects of the automatic stabilizers. The fact that the economy is fluctuating less than it otherwise would is not directly observable.[9] We will simply find ourselves say-

---

[9] *Analogue.* Our house in the country has an oil-burning furnace regulated by a thermostat. Suppose that the thermostat is set to cut in when the temperature falls to 69 degrees and cut out when it reaches 73.

ing: "Business cycles are mild these days, aren't they?"—and business cycles during the postwar period have been mild and apparently getting milder. Neither automatic nor discretionary fiscal policy seems to offer an adequate explanation for the apparent tendency of cycles to damp out, so that the experience is easier to explain if we suppose that monetary policy has had some quick-acting stabilizing effects.

Monetary-link variables. Since the Federal Reserve, as a "bankers' bank," has few direct dealings with the nonbank public, it is reasonable to suppose that monetary policy must be transmitted to the sphere of goods-and-services activity through "monetary-link variables"—for which one looks in the operations of the banking and credit system. The stock of money may be seen as such a link variable. In addition, the list of variables likely to act as monetary links includes various interest rates and quantities outstanding of various sorts of credit.[10] The controversy as to how monetary policy affects economic activity is largely an argument over the relative importance of various types of links, and over their interaction.

The behavior of a sample of monetary-link variables is shown in Chart 23-3. At the top of the chart, we reproduce from Chart 23-2 the $\dot{Y}$-curve and $(\dot{O} + \dot{I})$-curve, to give a frame of reference. Next come two curves—the $\dot{M}$-curve and $\dot{M}$-curve—which show percentage rates of growth in money stocks, with and without the inclusion of time deposits in commercial banks. (The series including these time deposits we call for convenience "Friedman Money," since emphasis on this series is associated for good reason with Milton Friedman.) Next comes the $\dot{L}$-curve, which traces per cent changes in the outstanding volume of loans at commercial banks. Near the bottom of the chart comes the "$\dot{R}_{FCP}$-curve," which shows percentage changes in the interest rate on short-term borrowings by finance companies. At the very bottom of the chart comes

---

If we set up automatic recordkeeping apparatus to chart the actual temperature in the house continuously and take twenty-four-hour averages, and also to record the oil consumption for each twenty-four-hour period, we will find that the average daily temperatures are almost constant and the oil consumption varies widely. If anything, the daily average temperatures will be a little lower when the oil consumption is highest; for on days when it is very cold outside, the furnace may run continuously without bringing the indoor temperature above 70.

An analysis based solely on oil consumption and indoor temperature will tend to "prove" that burning oil does not generate heat. If anything, it will seem that burning oil may make the house colder! Why have furnaces, anyway?

Plainly if we want a good analysis we must take account of the outside temperature. To get a *really* good analysis, we should station a caretaking couple in the house, so chosen that the husband is thin-blooded and always complains of the cold below 75 degrees, while the wife likes to spend all her time in the kitchen cooking, and finds things too hot if the furnace is going as well as the stove. By letting husband and wife change the thermostat settings on alternate days and taking account of the outside temperatures, we will be able to estimate rather accurately how burning oil heats the house.

[10]If we had the data, we might prefer to measure "credit availability" by some such index as the establishment of *lines of credit* which assure business firms or individuals that they can borrow up to a stated limit when they choose. But with the interesting exception of data on "commitments" to make mortgage loans, we lack statistics of this type for the United States.

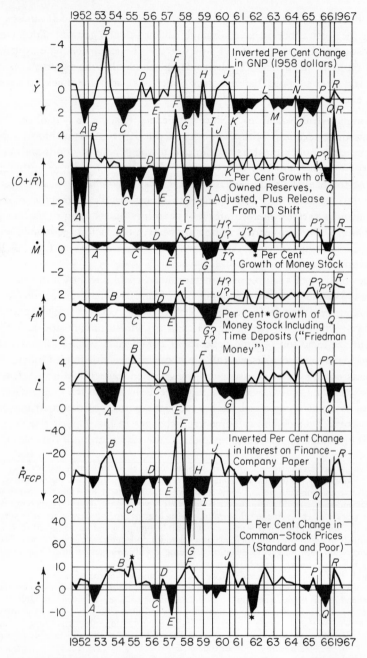

Source: Calculated by AGH from *Federal Reserve Bulletin* and *Survey of Current Business.*

Chart 23-3: Transmission of monetary pressures through "monetary link variables," 1953–1967.

the $\overset{*}{S}$-curve, which shows per cent changes from quarter to quarter of an index of prices of corporate common stocks. Although neither the Federal Reserve nor the commercial banks deal in common stocks, this index shows quarter-to-quarter changes very suggestive of the behavior of a "monetary-link variable"; and good reason exists to think that the movement of stock prices is a factor in the investment decisions of businessmen interested in plant and equipment and of householders interested in new houses.

If we look at the money-stock-change curves, they tend from 1954 onward to reproduce the general shape of the $(\dot{O} + \dot{R})$-curve. (This fact corresponds, of course, to our finding in Chapter 5 that deposit-creation at commercial banks conforms rather well to reserve-creation at the Federal Reserve.) The $_f\dot{M}$-curve in particular seems to follow the $(\dot{O} + \dot{R})$-curve very closely and with a slight lag; the relatively greater acceleration of the $_f\dot{M}$-curve as against the $(\dot{O} + \dot{R})$-curve from 1961 onward presumably shows a progressively greater willingness of commercial banks to operate with borrowed reserves. The $\dot{L}$-curve shows also a time-shape much like that of the $(\dot{O} + \dot{R})$-curve, but corresponding movements come well over a year later in the $\dot{L}$-curve. This fact suggests that loan-change is a relatively passive element in the process: when commercial banks change their rate of deposit-creation in response to monetary policy, the immediate impact must be on the banks' bond investments, which are a deferred adjustment of their loans. The $\dot{R}_{FCP}$-curve conforms to the $(\dot{O} + \dot{R})$-curve very well in its main outlines beginning with episode C (that is, from 1954 onward), and seems to show a very quick reaction. The $\overset{*}{S}$-curve, as might be expected, is more ideosyncratic; the two episodes tagged with stars (a sharp acceleration in 1955, and a considerable price break in 1962) seem to have no monetary counterparts. But the major changes shown by the $(\dot{O} + \dot{R})$-curve *do* have counterparts in the stock-price-growth curve—with stock prices moving in general a few months behind.

While we think of the monetary-link variables as transmitters of Federal Reserve policy pressures, changes in these variables do not reflect unilateral Federal Reserve actions but *interactions* between the Federal Reserve and the banks and or the nonbank public. The only elements in the monetary situation which are fully subject to unilateral Federal Reserve control are the reserve-requirement percentages applied to member banks and the discount rate. The course of owned reserves is *almost* fully subject to unilateral control—if we take for granted the availability of private holders of government securities who are willing to buy when the Federal Reserve sells and to sell when the Federal Reserve buys, and thus provide (motivated by prospects of profit) the collaboration necessary to make open-market operations feasible. The stock of money contains more elements of interaction: as we saw earlier, deposit-growth may move differently from owned-reserve growth if bankers choose to hold more excess reserves or to work more with borrowed reserves; and these differences of movement are great enough to meet the eye in such charts as we have been examining. The rates of interest on various types of credit (among which we must include the "yields" on outstanding marketable bonds) are set on markets which the Federal Reserve does not dominate—markets in fact which are to a great degree international, so that interest rates in New York, London, Toronto, Paris, and so forth make up a network.[11]

Students of monetary policy often proceed by asking what would happen if the Federal Reserve selected some one link-variable in which to frame its policy "targets"—and then set that variable either according to some arbitrary rule or as might seem appropriate according to a broader policy strategy such as economic stabilization. For example, one school of economists holds that the Federal Reserve could if it chose create an almost-uniform rate of money-stock growth, and that if it did so at a suitable growth-rate (say 3 per cent or 4 per cent per annum), it would be making its maximum contribution to economic stability and growth. Another school holds that the Federal Reserve could if it chose produce any desired pattern of interest-rate changes, and should exercise ingenuity so as to *forestall* recessions or inflationary spells and prevent them from happening. (From this standpoint one can also argue that the best the Federal Reserve can hope to do is to *mitigate* fluctuations, and that on the whole the high stability of recent years testifies that the interest-rate changes actually produced have been reasonably appropriate.) Federal Reserve utterances (including the archives of the Open-Market Committee, as these have been opened for public inspection) suggest strongly that at least much of the time the Federal Reserve has selected targets for free reserves. All schools agree that it is not possible simultaneously to control all these variables. If the stock of money is to follow a predetermined course, interest rates must be left to market determination, and free reserves (or owned reserves) must be handled in whatever way will induce banks to generate the desired money-stock expansion. If the rate of interest is to follow a predetermined course, money-stock expansion must be subordinated. But *one* target variable could probably be administered.[12]

---

[11]Even discount rates of central banks may be affected. While a central bank can if it chooses hold its discount rate constant although market rates are rising or falling, it "gets out of touch with the market" if it does so. Some central banks (notably in Canada) go so far as to observe market rates and set their discount rates to match, so that they give up unilateral control altogether. In the United States, the upward trend of discount rates since 1953 is better seen as an adaptation to a worldwide upward movement than as a unilateral Federal Reserve policy; though short-term movements reflect Federal Reserve freedom of action, and the Federal Reserve has sought policy strategies which would minimize the "escalation of interest rates," which arises out of the competition of various countries for the insufficient stock of international monetary reserves.

[12]Note that it would definitely not be feasible to carry out through thick and thin a monetary policy that would generate a predetermined rate of rise of common-stock prices. It would almost certainly be difficult if not impossible to use the standard instruments of monetary policy to bring about a predetermined movement of bank loans. (In the early 1950's there was consideration of the possibility of extending to other types of credit the pattern of "direct controls" applied in the Korean war to installment credit and mortgage credit; but both the authorities and the economists seem to have lost interest in such proposals.)

As to interest rates, one of the most pivotal is the rate on short-term Treasury bills; since it is precisely in such bills that the Federal Reserve carries out most of its open-market oper-

Which of the possible target variables should be regarded as best adapted to the purposes of monetary policy, of course, depends in good part on which comes closest to having predictable and definite effects in the goods-and-services sphere. It is not easy to analyze the record from this standpoint—partly because the economic relations are so complex that a full analysis calls for econometric tools at a level inappropriate for this book and partly because (as we saw above) some of the quick-acting effects of monetary-link variables may be masked by their very success.[13] But when we inspect the record, it does seem to be revealing.

A sketch of the record is offered in Chart 23-4. Of course, we cannot analyze in this manner the whole structure of the economy; but to study a few variables can give useful clues. We begin at the top of the chart with three curves. The $(\dot{O} + \dot{R})$-curve and $_f\dot{M}$-curve are carried forward from Chart 23-4. The first may be taken to represent a link variable very close to the basic policy decisions of the monetary authorities, the second a link closer to the goods-and-services

---

ations, it would seem clearly feasible to fix a bill rate and enforce it by standing ready to buy or sell bills on as large a scale as the market chose. Since the Federal Reserve has an enormous holding of such bills (and with the cooperation of the Treasury, more could be put out by refunding other types of government debt into bills as they matured), while purchases are financed by the "creation of Federal Reserve Bank credit," it would seem that the market could never offer to buy or sell more than the Federal Reserve could cope with. On the other hand, we must remember that the United States is not a closed economy, that interest rates in other centers are set independently, and that differences between centers set up flows of capital funds. Hence, the consequences of arbitrary selection of a bill rate may be unbearable.

Besides the rate on Treasury bills, there are other interest rates (such as those on long-term corporate bonds and on mortgage loans) which may be of more importance for economic activity. To some extent these other rates can rise or fall relative to the bill rate; and it may be possible by an "operation twist" to hold down such long-term rates at a time when bill rates are high. But except for rates on long-term government bonds, (and perhaps for "secondary mortgage rates" of the Federal National Mortgage Association, which is an autonomous government agency not under Federal Reserve control), the markets on which these rates are set are not subject to direct intervention by the monetary authorities; hence these rates, though they can clearly be influenced by monetary policy, cannot exactly be controlled.

[13]If monetary policy were: (a) completely capable of stabilizing the economy, and (b) perfectly administered, the fluctuations whose record could be studied would be purely the result of "random" disturbances which by hypothesis would be beyond the reach of policy measures to prevent (though, of course, their later consequences could by hypothesis be ironed out by policy). To be optimistic about the possibilities of gauging the effectiveness of policy from the record in the way we attempt in the next section of this chapter is, therefore, to be pessimistic about the extent to which policy has actually fulfilled its role! Specifically, the analysis may be taken to rest upon the following assumptions: (1) that much of the time, policy has set its tactical targets in terms of "free reserves"; (2) that these free-reserve targets have not been very precisely met; (3) that in any case, free reserves are not a very good measure of the monetary forces that act through our link variables, so that we can study the impact of the more effective link variables from a record which shows policy behavior that was less than optimal.

This view of the analytical problem, however, is not so pessimistic as it may sound. After all, we learn wisdom in any field largely by analyzing our mistakes. If these mistakes had been of the first magnitude, we might not have survived to make the analysis. But if we had not part of the time done things we are not sure now that we approve of, it would be hard to tell from experience what difference it makes to take one line rather than another.

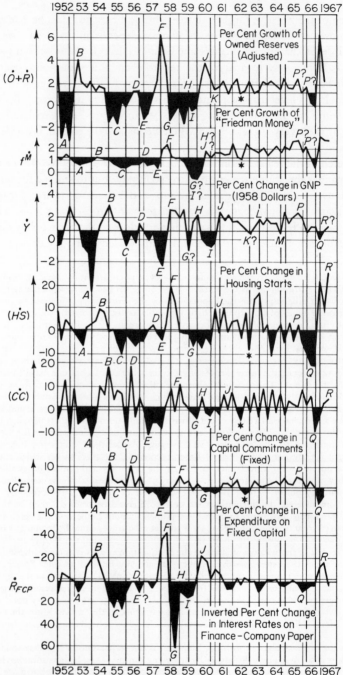

Source: Calculated by AGH from *Federal Reserve Bulletin, Survey of Current Business,* and *Business Cycle Developments.*

Chart 23-4: Apparent influence of monetary variables on major components of private investment, 1952–1967.

sphere. The $\dot{Y}$-curve in third position is the same as that we had at the top of Chart 23-3 *except* that we measure changes in GNP right-side up here, whereas before we measured them upside down. This change corresponds to the difference between looking at changes in GNP as they result from the changes in the policy variables and looking at them as signals that bring about those changes. (Consequently the letters which tag successive episodes along the $\dot{Y}$-curve are all displaced one phase to the right: episode A, for example, is now the GNP-shrinkage of 1953–54, seen as a possible effect of the check to money-stock growth which occurred somewhat earlier.) If we look at the $\dot{Y}$-curve in this manner, it again seems fairly easy to find counterparts between the different curves. Apparently, on the whole we get first a movement in the rate of creation of (adjusted) owned reserves; with a lag of one or two calendar quarter-years, a corresponding movement in the rate of creation of Friedman money; and with a further lag, a corresponding movement in GNP.[14]

An interesting test as to how much this apparent relation means can be made by trying to bring in some variables that represent *investment decisions,* as we do in the next three curves of the chart. Such a consideration of investment is necessary if we want to make any sense of the relationship between the "macroeconomic" approach that explains fluctuations as results of changes in fixed investment, government deficits, and the like and the "modern quantity theory" approach that presents fluctuations in activity and price levels as results of fluctuations in the creation of money. If the two views are reconcilable, we should be able to show: (a) that fluctuations in "investment" can be "explained" with monetary factors, and (b) that *investment decisions* (though not necessarily investment *expenditures*) move ahead of economic activity.[15]

The investment-activity curves in the middle of the diagram are designed to permit a rough test of this sort. The $(\dot{HS})$-curve in fourth position shows quarter to-quarter percentage changes in *housing starts.* The $(\dot{CC})$-curve shows percentage changes in what may be called "capital commitments."[16] The $(\dot{CE})$-curve

---

[14]The GNP-to-money relations would look stronger if we used *current-dollar* rather than 1958-dollar GNP figures.

If we used the $\dot{M}$-curve from Chart 23-3 instead of the $_f\dot{M}$-curve, the relation would seem weaker. Otherwise we would probably show less interest in "Friedman money." An uncharitable critic might accuse us (along with most monetary economists) of carrying along several alternative measures of certain variables, and then deciding which one we claimed was significant after we had "peeped" at the data to show which would make the best showing! But there really seems to be no mode of analysis which can avoid doing this "selection by peeping," since economics can have no real laboratory experiments.

[15]Adherents of the "new quantity theory" would claim that money stock and interest rates can influence consumption outlays as well as business investment. But it would seem plausible that effects on investment would be relatively more intense and would represent a quicker reaction if we measure in terms of *decisions.* Otherwise so strong a relation as we have shown above between the monetary curves and the $\dot{Y}$-curve would have to be interpreted— as it is interpreted by various schools of "monetary economists"—to show that the macroeconomic analysis via investment and a "consumption function" has no bearing on reality.

[16]These quarterly changes are calculated from the United States Census series called "contracts and orders for plant and equipment," published in the monthly *Business Cycle Developments* as series 10, on a monthly basis. The series we call "capital expenditures" has been put together to give an actual-expenditure counterpart to the "orders and contracts" series,

shows percentage changes in capital expenditures. These last two curves represent the same expenditures as seen when contracts are made and when the goods are delivered. Hence it is not surprising that movements of the $(\dot{CC})$-curve happen earlier in time than corresponding movements in the $(\dot{CE})$-curve.[17]

Examination of these curves shows that the two investment curves which register *decisions* (the start of construction on homes and apartments, and the commitment to acquire business fixed capital) do move a good part of the time ahead of the $\dot{Y}$-curve which shows the course of GNP. (The actual fixed-capital expenditures shown by the $\dot{CE}$-curve, on the other hand, seem, to move with or behind GNP.) Particularly interesting is that some of the movements in housing starts showed expansion at a time when GNP as a whole was still strongly declining. The hypothesis that monetary changes have a special influence in investment decisions thus survives handsomely this rough test. Note too that as between the two monetary-link variables at the top of the chart, the growth of owned reserves seems to match better with the growth of investment (at the point of decision) than does the growth of money stock. On the other hand, if we adopt as a monetary-link variable the rate of change of interest rates on finance-company borrowings—the $\dot{R}_{FCP}$-curve at the foot of the chart—it becomes very hard to obtain good matchings of the various fluctuations. The relative sharpness of the contraction-episodes tagged by letters C, E, and G, and the relative buoyance of expansion after 1960 both seem to match better as between the investment-decision curves and the $(\dot{O} + \dot{R})$-curve than as between the former and the $\dot{R}_{FCP}$-curve.

This sketch of an analysis would suggest—though it is certainly too incomplete to prove—that if we want to select a monetary-link variable that represents the effective transmission of monetary-policy pressure to the real sphere, we are probably best off either with the growth of owned reserves or with the growth of money stocks as our selected link variable, rather than with an interest-rate variable. A definitive study of this problem—if indeed it can be made from the kind of record which experience of the postwar period has left behind it—would call for careful interweaving of these monetary factors with evidence on the movement of other variables. In particular, the job should in principle

---

and is published in *BCD* (series 505) under the title "manufacturers' machinery and equipment sales and business construction expenditures (industrial and commercial construction) put in place." Both series correspond roughly to the item of the national accounts entitled "private fixed capital formation: nonresidential," except that both contracts-and-orders and sales presumably include a substantial amount of "hard goods" similar to industrial equipment that are bought by government— chiefly for military purposes.

[17]In addition, since the "contracts and orders" placed in a given quarter have varying durations to completion, the $(\dot{CE})$-curve tends to smooth out "double tops" and "double bottoms" to be seen in the $(\dot{CC})$-curve, and to fluctuate with less amplitude.

The fact that some of the strongest movements of the $(\dot{CC})$-curve (such as the peak-expansion rates tagged B and D) are matched by *simultaneous* moves of the $(\dot{CE})$-curve corresponds to the fact that some types of "fixed" capital (such as motor trucks) can be obtained within a few days or weeks of placing an order, even though others (such as turbines) take years from order to delivery.

weave in the effect of "exogenous" changes in exports, in government expenditures, and in the "discretionary" component of tax revenue. Since almost all studies to date have worked *either* with monetary variables exclusively or with "fiscal and investment" variables exclusively, this integration calls for careful and laborious study; the few synthetic efforts to date show chiefly how difficult the problem is.

A provisional summary. On the face of the record, apparently the variables which link monetary policy to the goods-and-services sphere can be identified, and their influence is strong enough to be visible to the naked eye even though many other influences are at work simultaneously to complicate the picture. Specifically, either the rate of expansion of owned reserves or the rate of expansion of money stock seemingly can be properly treated as influences on investment decisions. In view of the fact that investment decisions take some time to execute, it would seem also that shifts in monetary policy are apt to take hold on actual operations in the goods-and-services sphere with a "distributed lag"—some of the effects being almost immediate, but some deferred for several quarters or even as much as two years—with a concentration of the effects some two to four calendar quarters after the change of direction or intensity takes place in monetary policy. In view of the complexity of the problem of analyzing the evidence, some skepticism is in order in regard to the view just stated—still more in relation to the widely held view that interest rates are the crucial monetary link, which seems hard to reconcile with the record.

Proposals to Improve the Monetary System

Proposals to improve the monetary system are always in season. Presumably because the economic system as a whole and the monetary system in particular have performed rather satisfactorily for almost the whole postwar period, such proposals now before the public and the economic profession are rather less sensational than usual. The race of "money cranks" who propose to bring in the millenium on short notice by drastic monetary changes seems almost to have died out. It is true that influential economists are heard to declare publicly that the monetary system would work better if we abolished the Federal Reserve System and had no discretionary policy at all in the monetary field—only some sort of automatic machine to pump out a constant trickle of new reserves and bring about a steady rate of expansion in the money stock. But this should perhaps be read as a caution against the hazards of "oversteering" rather than taken literally.

Nevertheless, a number of suggestions need consideration. These may be classified roughly into (1) bank-structure reforms; (2) proposals for dealing with nonbank credit institutions; (3) governmental-structure proposals; (4) international monetary reforms; (5) proposals for changes in monetary strategy. These will be taken up in turn.

Bank-structure reforms.   Ever since the Federal Reserve System was established, economists have worried about the curious differentiation of banking rules for national banks, state-bank members of the Federal Reserve system, and other banks (perhaps sorted according to whether they are "insured" or not). Today one should perhaps mention a fourth category: overseas branches of United States banks, which seem to be able to operate in "Euro-dollars" in a way that gets outside the jurisdiction of all banking authorities in the United States without coming under the jurisdiction of the monetary authorities in any other country.

Concern about this differential treatment of groups of banks has turned largely on the danger of "erosion" of Federal Reserve controls because of the advantage enjoyed by nonmember banks in having more freedom of action than Federal Reserve rules would permit. So far as the scale of operations goes, such erosion would not seem to be an acute problem: the proportion of all commercial-bank deposits held by member banks has moved only from 86.6 per cent in 1941 to 85.0 per cent in 1947 and 82.5 per cent in 1967. Probably some tendency exists for the Federal Reserve authorities and for Congress to try to equalize conditions by relaxing controls (as during the 1960's when they have enabled national and other member banks to operate more freely in mortgages). But it is hard to feel that anything essential is being sacrificed. Some observers used to feel that there was danger in the relative decline of banks' capital funds relative to their deposits; the ratio of capital funds to deposits fell between 1941 and 1947 from 9.5 per cent to 6.9 per cent. But this ratio has been climbing in recent years, and stood in 1967 at 9.3 per cent. If anything, observers now have to worry as to whether the drive to build up capital funds of banks has led to undue complacency about their profitability.

The fact that the United States (almost alone in the world) has preserved a pattern of numerous "unit banks" instead of developing a few giant nationwide branch banks has always struck some observers as an anomaly. Even as branch banks have grown up (above all the Bank of California, which is one of the world's largest branch-bank systems), each bank has been confined to the state of its head office. It would appear that to some degree inefficiency is sheltering behind "state protectionism" and anti-branch-banking conservatism. Where branch banking is permitted, there has been a strong tendency toward mergers —rationalized largely as an effort to pool the scarce talent of lending officers. But again it is hard to get excited about unit banking versus branch banking as a national issue. The main drawback of unit banking was the vulnerability to failure of small unit banks; and the device of Federal Deposit Insurance has removed the catastrophe hazard on this side.

Perhaps economists and politicians should worry more than they do about the mushroom growth of the "Euro-dollar market," which represents operations that somehow fall outside all the recognized frameworks of monetary control. The "Euro-dollar" is not exactly the United States dollar, but certainly is not any other currency: genetically, it is a unit in which overseas branches of United States banks had a habit of accepting deposits and making loans. As we write, the possible weaknesses of the Euro-dollar have never been really tested: the Euro-dollar has worked rather smoothly under fair-weather conditions, but one could imagine conditions under which Euro-dollar credit would "freeze."[18] It would be comforting to be assured either that this is not a real possibility or that if it happened the inconveniences would be minor; but the whole situation is so undefined that it is hard to guess. It is in the nature of an operation, which falls between the jurisdictions of the various national monetary controls, that it does not generate enough public information to make its operations transparent. The problem is clearly one for international policy-making —perhaps in the first instance, a problem to be taken up by the International Monetary Fund. But the fact that branches of United States banks are nodal points in the network and that the currency unit involved is denominated a "dollar" suggests that any real solution would throw responsibilities on the United States government.

Important institutional changes have been going on in the *practices* of commercial banks and their customers. The business firms which have large current assets have become much more interested in managing these assets so as not to leave too much in noninterest-bearing demand deposits; they have learned to work with leaner demand balances, so that the velocity of circulation has risen enormously in recent years, as we saw in Chapter 8. Banks have been fertile in devices for enabling large depositors to hold funds in interest-bearing form while remaining able to cash them quickly without loss in case of need. "Time certificates of deposit" which may either be sold to another holder or redeemed ahead of schedule at the issuing bank have turned out to combine neatly for large holders the advantages of time and demand deposits, and have been treated by the Federal Reserve authorities as subject only to low time-deposit requirements.[19] A similar device which might have permitted an equivalent of demand deposits with no reserve requirements at all was tried out by a few banks which issued "capital notes" in round sums like certificates of deposit and with similar opportunities of marketability and redemption; but the Federal Reserve at least held the line by ruling that these were equivalent to time deposits. In general, it seems a doubtful practice to have a major difference in reserve re-

---

[18]To a large extent, the Euro-dollar market apparently represents Europeans dealing with each other outside the framework of their national monetary controls; an important element is borrowing by Communist governments of Eastern Europe. It would be interesting to know enough about the magnitudes involved to tell who would be left holding an "endorser's" or credit-middleman's liability if political conditions made it impossible or inexpedient for these governments to honor their Euro-dollar debts.

[19]Beginning in 1966, however, the Federal Reserve set up a separate reserve-requirement class of *time deposits in excess of* $5 *million* in a given bank, which covers about half of all time deposits and probably the great bulk of "CD's." The reserve requirement on such deposits stood in late 1967 at 6 per cent, compared with 3 per cent on savings deposits and other time deposits up to $5 million, and with 12 per cent or 16 per cent on demand deposits.

quirements against demand and time deposits unless there is a clear-cut difference (enforced either by tradition or by definite rules) between the two types. The remarkable complacency with which students of monetary policy have reacted to this problem is typified by the recommendations published in 1961 by the Commission on Money and Credit, which expressed satisfaction with the existing system of reserves on demand deposits and then (on two pages which face each other!) declared: "Time and savings deposits . . . both are tending to become more and more like demand deposits" and recommended "that existing statutory reserve requirements on time and savings deposits be repealed."[20] An earlier Federal Reserve proposal for basing reserve requirements on the activity of bank accounts (dismissed with faint praise by the Commission on Money and Credit) would seem to have real promise as a remedy for the tendency to homogenize deposits. In this case, what a bank gained in reducing reserve requirements by encouraging customers to disguise liquid funds as time deposits would be lost through the stronger reserve requirement against the remaining demand balance on which turnover would be concentrated. So long as the drift out of demand deposits was gradual, this issue was not important; but it would seem high time to do something about this phenomenon now that the evasion of reserve requirements has become so highly organized.

The problem of nonbank credit institutions. As we saw in Part I, a large and flourishing network of "nonbank credit institutions" tend to compete with banks both as holders of liquid funds and as lenders, and tend also to outgrow the banks. Funds held with mutual savings banks and with savings and loan associations are regarded by their holders as available on demand (though not directly usable for payments by check); yet such equivalents-to-commercial-bank-deposits are subject to no reserve requirements at all. The banks see this as an unfair advantage to their competitors; monetary economists are under obligation to consider it as a possible gap in the structure of controls over the creation of money.

The possible danger in mushroom growth of these institutions is accentuated by the fact that mutual savings banks to some extent and savings and loan associations almost entirely concentrate their assets in mortgage loans and in their own immediate geographical area. The credit squeeze of 1966 demonstrated that on mortgage markets which largely depend on these lenders, an acute spell of tight money can dry up the flow of funds and threaten to stop construction. Difficulties in California and Nevada savings and loan associations have demonstrated that their management may not always have been of the highest grade; and even if all were ideally managed, savings and loan associations could fall into acute difficulties in case of a decline of the market for real estate in their neighborhoods. (One of the bugbears of possible disarmament

---

[20]Commission on Money and Credit; *Money and Credit: Their Influence on Jobs, Prices, and Growth* (Englewood Cliffs, N.J.: Prentice-Hall, Inc., 1961), pp. 68, 168–69.

is the likelihood that it would cut back employment sharply in certain areas, and that homeowners there might find no buyers at acceptable prices as they tried to relocate elsewhere.)

If there is a weak spot in the financial system of the United States today, it probably lies in the savings and loan associations. In case of a real-estate crisis in even a few important areas of the United States, the government (through the Federal Savings and Loan Insurance Corporation) might find itself forced to choose between treating over $100 billion of "savings capital" in these associations as demand deposits subject to instant federal repayment if the association was unable to pay immediately, or else telling the holders that they must queue up and be paid off in the order in which they notified their associations they wanted to withdraw. Since the latter decision would produce a landslide of withdrawal notices, while the former would perhaps put the government into the mortgage business on a scale over $100 billion, this could be a very awkward dilemma. Logic suggests that it would be prudent either to prevent savings and loan associations from presenting themselves as offering perfect security and instant availability of funds to savers, or else to bring about a rapid transformation of these institutions into something more like commercial banks, with an asset structure not so subject to catastrophe hazards, and with reserve requirements and the like comparable to those that apply to Federal Reserve member banks on claims of comparable liquidity.

Life insurance companies provisionally seem to present no real monetary problem. While policy-holders have a claim to withdraw the "cash loan and surrender value" of their policies without notice, experience suggests that the rates of interest charged (and the habits of policy-holders) prevent active use of this potential liquid asset. Policy-holders often borrow on their policies at banks; but bank controls seem reasonably applicable. The insurance companies have such a powerful "cash flow" from the excess of premium receipts over benefits that there seems to be no appreciable danger of a drain of funds they could not meet.

Some potential monetary danger always exists in the stock market. Holders of stocks are apt to think of them as a delightful combination of instant availability of funds with strong prospects of capital gains. When stocks show a powerful upward tendency (as they have most of the time since World War II), their holders feel free to put part of their growing wealth into new houses and other forms of "capital consumption," and may feel largely emancipated from the need to set aside for saving a part of their salaries and dividends—for is the market not "doing their saving for them"?[21] The fact that the United States has

---

[21]"Flow of funds" statistics published in the *Federal Reserve Bulletin* show that for all recent years and for most recent quarter-years "individuals" have sold a larger amount of stocks than they bought. Funds put into stocks by pension funds outweigh funds obtained from the stock market by corporations selling new shares, so that the market has to be such as to persuade individual holders to realize and withdraw part of their "paper profits." But will this process go on working through all probable economic situations?

been able to run a fairly continuous high level of operations during a long period of rising stock prices does not prove that we could do equally well in a period when stock prices were stationary or declining. Admitting that there is an objective foundation for a secular rise of stock prices in the fact that corporations in most recent years have reinvested a larger share of profits than they have paid out as dividends, the stockmarket is a profoundly psychological phenomenon, and it would not seem like a safe reliance that it will go on rising at a steady rate. Neither is the rise of the real-estate market something to be counted on for every year. There are no promising policy proposals either for producing a bull market all the time or for keeping public psychology from getting unduly enthusiastic at some times. The likelihood of a disillusioning turn in markets for capital assets, however, has to be kept in mind as a factor that makes it probable we will some day have to cope with a more serious recession than any we have experienced since World War II. The upshot would seem to be that weak spots in the economy should not be ignored, and specifically that the growth of banks-not-regarded-as-banks in the field of savings and loans and the like should not continue to be accepted so complacently.

Structural relations within government.   Governmental authority in the monetary field would seem to be dangerously dispersed—to the point where responsibility becomes misty and coordinated action almost impossible. The presence of the fifty state banking authorities, and the fact that where federal institutions can be chartered (as with national banks and federal savings and loan associations), their activities are boxed up within one state is a problem some of whose aspects we have already examined. Within the federal government itself there is also dispersion of authority. One example is the division of bank supervision responsibility among the Controller of the Currency, the Federal Reserve, and the Federal Deposit Insurance Corporation—though overlapping is much reduced by giving each agency a distinct list of banks to supervise, and by having policy (which in this field need not change very fast) coordinated by the device of "conferences" among the examining agencies.

More important is the fact, to which we have referred several times above, that responsibility for "debt management" is divided between the Federal Reserve and the Treasury. The Treasury is responsible for paying off outstanding securities as they mature and for selling new securities—whether to refinance maturing debt or to cover deficits. The Federal Reserve is responsible for transactions in securities outstanding, which constitute its open-market operations.[22] In addition, certain "trust funds" under Treasury management have some scope

---

[22]Except in wartime, the Federal Reserve operates subject to a taboo on buying new issues direct from the Treasury. In many countries, where it is hard to find nonbank buyers for government securities, rules of this sort are effective barriers to deficit financing. But in the United States, where a large amount and variety of securities are always outstanding, the Federal Reserve can always find some outstanding issue whose terms and maturity are so much like that of the new issue that to buy this outstanding security is equivalent to buying the new issue.

for operations in government securities in the market; and a number of agencies (above all the Federal National Mortgage Association and the Commodity Credit Association) have assets they can throw on the market.

Since the Treasury obviously has an obligation to get the most favorable possible rate of interest, and likes to see its offerings safely "oversubscribed," the Treasury has a natural interest in "easy money" at times when new securities must be floated on a large scale. If the government is running a deficit because of a recession, this involves no conflict with the Federal Reserve, since in such a context it is appropriate to pull down interest rates in any event. But if the Treasury has to sell large amounts in a period of high activity (perhaps because of a cash deficit owing to military expenditures, as in 1952 and 1967, or perhaps because although the debt is not growing, there happen to be substantial maturities of long-term debt to face), the Treasury may want easy money at a time when the Federal Reserve feels restriction to be appropriate.

A different sort of conflict may arise (as it did in 1966) if the situation calls for restriction and the Treasury refuses to call for an appropriate tax increase (or having proposed one, fails to persuade Congress). In such a situation, the Federal Reserve may be forced to tighten credit although it feels it would be preferable to attack excess demand on the fiscal side. But though the Federal Reserve gets opportunities to testify before Congressional committees in favor of tax legislation the Treasury may have proposed, the Federal Reserve is not in a position to place its own tax proposals before Congress.

Various proposals have been offered for overcoming conflicts of interest and judgment between the Federal Reserve and the Treasury; for example, setting up some sort of "super-agency" with jurisdiction over both. If such a reorganization were part of a general restructuring around an "Assistant President for Economic Affairs," many economists would view it with favor; and puristic views about the "independence" of the Federal Reserve should not be weighted too heavily in this context. But if it meant merely that representatives of the Federal Reserve and the Treasury were locked up in a room together until they reached an agreement, many observers would expect the upshot to be that the traditional Treasury view would take primacy, and that the Federal Reserve would simply be debarred from putting its views to the public, to Congress, and into the channels most likely to impress the President.

An important factor in strategy toward the division of functions between the Federal Reserve and the Treasury is that as matters stand the Federal Reserve is often in a position to call for a change in the direction of policy ahead of the Treasury. As we have seen, hindsight often suggests that the Federal Reserve has shifted its policy stance too late rather than too early; but the Treasury regularly shifts later than the Federal Reserve. This difference is not unnatural, but has deep roots in the politics of economic policy. The Treasury cannot make an important new move without committing the President. The President may simply not be able to take time in the press of other emergencies to consider adequately the evidence that it is time for a shift toward more expansive or more restrictive policies. Besides, the President is likely to get into a wrangle with Congress if he proposes such a shift—particularly if a shift toward restriction calls for higher taxes. Furthermore, the Federal Reserve has policy instruments with which it is possible to feel the situation out; and it is able to slack off or reverse itself if it turns out that the need for action is not as strong as was felt. But the Treasury (particularly as regards tax legislation) has to stand still or take a long step. It follows that the greater flexibility of Federal Reserve policy is an advantage for the economic policy of the government at large; and to require a Treasury-type decision process over Federal Reserve actions would not be an improvement.

If it is not good strategy to put the Federal Reserve under the Treasury, or to put both under a super-agency, is it possible to let the Federal Reserve act for the Treasury as well as itself? This may seem an odd question, and there are areas (such as tax policy) where it is an obvious impossibility. But it would be entirely feasible to let the Federal Reserve act for the Treasury in debt management. To do this, policy should reverse the taboo on Federal Reserve purchase of new issues, and require on the contrary that all new Treasury issues should be sold to the Federal Reserve. Dealings with the public would then take the form of sale to the banks or the nonbank public either of Treasury securities out of the Federal Reserve portfolio or of Federal Reserve securities. If commercial banks can throw "CD's" on the open market, it is plainly feasible for the Federal Reserve if authorized to sell similar short-term securities—or to sell long-term bonds. Such a system could avoid the inconvenience of having to deal with changes of the public debt in large and possibly indigestible lumps of bonds and notes: the Federal Reserve could feed securities out onto the market more gradually. A natural counterpart to such a power would be to have the Federal Reserve rather than the Treasury manage the deposit balances at commercial banks now owned by the United States Treasury. These balances are built up by tax receipts and proceeds of security sales and drawn down by "calls" to transfer stated proportions of the balances into Treasury accounts with the Federal Reserve. If instead these accounts were owned by the Federal Reserve (which would credit Treasury working balances with equivalent amounts), a certain confusion of management could be avoided.

To have the Federal Reserve step in front of the Treasury in the field of debt management would, of course, not be feasible if it were deemed essential to restrict open-market operations to "bills only" as was done for several years in the 1950's and 1960's. Open-market operations in long-dated securities by the Federal Reserve can be avoided only by having such operations handled by the Treasury; for nobody would recommend transforming the whole mass of government debt in bank and private hands into short-term debt.[23] If such a limitation

---

[23]Many authorities consider that it should be a major element in debt-management strategy to "lengthen the debt." All long-term securities outstanding, of course, come twelve months closer to maturity every year. To prevent the average maturity of outstanding debt from getting

on Federal Reserve operations is to be accepted (even part of the time), the Treasury must obviously continue to operate in the long-term end of the market. One can appreciate the Federal Reserve's reluctance to get once again into a position where market speculation may be primarily a gamble on future Federal Reserve operations in long-term securities.[24] Consequently it is by no means obvious that the Treasury should step out of long-term debt management. But since the Federal Reserve is unavoidably engaged in managing the short-term debt, this part of debt management would work better if consolidated in Federal Reserve hands; and the merits and demerits of Federal Reserve management at the long-term end deserve careful consideration.

International monetary reforms.　As was made plain in Part III, the international monetary system poses serious problems for all major countries, and especially for the United States. Reliance on gold as the sole international reserve risks a chronic shortage of reserves. A gold-exchange standard (which means chiefly use of the United States dollar as reserve by other countries) is subject to hazards. To generate increased holdings abroad of the reserve currency (dollar), the reserve-currency country must be running a "deficit in its international balance of payments." But the continuance of such a deficit tends to weaken confidence in the reserve currency—particularly if, as in the case of the United States, there is an absolute as well as a relative fall of gold reserves while foreign liabilities keep growing. A "run" on the reserve currency may eventuate; so long as there is no obligation upon the other countries to hold at least a substantial share of their reserves in dollars rather than in gold, there exists a catastrophe hazard such as proved fatal to the previous gold-exchange standard structure in the early 1930's.[25]

---

shorter requires selling a large amount of securities with more-than-average maturity, or a moderate amount with very long maturity. Since the path of least resistance is to sell only short-dated securities (particularly at times when the debt is shrinking, but also when it is growing), the drift toward having only short-term debt needs a systematic corrective.

[24]It is very irksome for a public official to stand where if members of the public can figure out his future intentions (or if there is a "leak") somebody will make a lot of money. While, of course, every responsible man knows the distinction between confidential and public information, openness is part of the American folkways; and the Federal Reserve feels some obligation to guide the financial community by reasonably candid public talk about the economic situation and the reasons for policy measures. Since an expectation that the Federal Reserve would operate continuously in long-term securities would cause every Federal Reserve utterance to be studied for clues to future open-market moves, working conditions for Federal Reserve officials might be seriously impaired.

[25]American banking history contains an interesting analogy. Under the National Bank System before 1913, the downtown banks of New York and Chicago held reserve deposits for country banks; but the country banks had the option to hold a substantial part of their reserves in such deposits or to hold reserves entirely in currency in their own vaults. The threat of a financial panic, making it doubtful that the New York banks would be able to release currency if called upon, might realize itself by leading country banks to withdraw currency from New York while they still could. The Federal Reserve System was set up (after a disastrous panic in 1907) on a basis which *obligated* banks to keep reserves in Federal Reserve banks. Without any such obligation on the part of "members" of a gold-exchange standard to hold reserves in the central pool, the reserve-currency country gets into much the position in which the New York banks stood in 1907.

Furthermore, the countries whose currencies are used as international reserves may find that maintaining confidence in their currencies forces them into a monetary policy that imposes economic stagnation within the country. The dragging difficulties which eventually forced Britain to devalue the pound in November 1967 illustrate this danger. The United States as well ran through the early 1960's with levels of activity far below potential largely because of inhibitions on monetary policy from the international side (though we should note that when we measure monetary policy by the expansion of owned bank reserves it looks less restrictive than when we measure it by the course of interest rates). Since the United States dollar is the only candidate for the key currency role in the visible future—the pound being probably out of the running after the devaluation of 1967 demonstrated the reality of dangers the holders of sterling had feared—the inconveniences of being in the key currency business must be a factor in the larger strategic decisions of United States monetary policy.[26]

To build up international reserves without the hazards of a gold-exchange standard based on *dollar* exchange seems to call for reform of the International Monetary Fund. Amendments to the IMF Articles of Agreement which were agreed upon in 1967 permit "creation" of reserve funds by IMF, subject, however, to veto by any bloc of members with enough votes (meaning either "common Europe" if the six European countries involves all agree, or else the United States). Logic seems to call for reforms which make reserve-creation a reliable mechanism (reducing the prospects of a gold crisis, and thus the incentives to build up private hoards of gold in hopes that such a crisis will force an increase of the gold price above the official $35.00). It would be desirable also to fund the reserve-currency obligations of the United States—transforming a short-term United States obligation to individual countries into a long-term United States obligation to the IMF, thereby balancing IMF obligations to owners of reserves. What concessions the United States would have to offer to make it worthwhile for the other IMF members to accept such a funding is a matter for bargaining. In the large, let us say, that it is in nobody's interest to maintain the catastrophe hazard implicit in a dollar-exchange standard; therefore, the United States would not necessarily be asking its partners to accept inconveniences for which they must be paid. But there is another consideration in the background: its status as a reserve-currency country inhibits the United States against adjusting its foreign-trade position by devaluation of the dollar. A reform which transferred the reserve-currency obligations to the IMF (and which would entail clearly distinguishing the "IMF dollar" from the United States dollar) would give us more freedom of action, and might enhance the danger that the United

---

[26]Remember also that to the extent that other countries will finance a "deficit" by accumulating dollars, the United States can wield larger resources overseas for economic-development aid, military enterprises, and foreign investment than would otherwise be available. Concretely, the foreign-resources counterpart of the United States "deficit" in the 1950's and 1960's should probably be seen in the massive investments of United States companies in Europe.

States would shake up the trade situation of other countries by changing the parity of the dollar. Our partners in the IMF would have to weigh this risk against the risks they are involved in when United States trade difficulties in a reserve-currency role may force the United States into a recession—or may close off foreign export opportunities by a resurgence of U.S. protectionism, as was hinted by the powerful drive in 1967 for establishing a network of import quotas.

Monetary strategy in relation to fiscal policy.   Turning to internal monetary policy, plainly (as was indicated at the opening of this chapter) so long as fiscal policy shows itself incapable of well-timed "discretionary" actions for economic stabilization, monetary policy inherits a residual responsibility. The logic of macro-economics suggests that over a considerable range, monetary and fiscal policy are substitutes. If we consider a combination of monetary and fiscal policies which would be consistent with maintenence of full activity without an inflationary price drift and then shift fiscal policy in an expansive (inflationary) direction by a cut in tax rates or by an expansion of military outlays, a more restrictive monetary policy may be able to restore the balance. Similarly, it may be possible to offset the downward influence of a fiscal shift toward surplus by relaxing monetary restrictions. This sort of "policy-substitution" may not work if fiscal policy goes to extremes in either direction; but, in the range of fiscal action we have seen so far since the Korean war, it would seem to be possible.

The difficulty of flexible "discretionary" adjustments in fiscal policy suggests that monetary policy may have to be relied upon to compensate shifts in the response-patterns of households and business firms, as well as nonstabilizing shifts in fiscal policy and in foreign trade. Such a strategy would presumably imply that fiscal policy should move along not too far behind, taking up enough of the pressure toward inflation or toward recession so that monetary policy could revert to a more or less neutral stance pending the next disturbance. If fiscal policy shifts cumulatively toward stimulating or holding back activity, monetary policy may be forced into extremes. Too inflationary a fiscal policy may leave monetary policy with no way of being sufficiently restrictive short of threatening to bring on an old-fashioned "financial crisis"—to which we came uncomfortably close, for instance, in 1966. Too deflationary a fiscal policy may reduce monetary policy once more to "pushing on a string"; for monetary policy can only release, not generate, the driving power of business investment.

Excessive reliance on monetary policy is likely to mean concentrating the costs of economic stabilization unduly in a few sectors where monetary policy is especially effective. Spokesman of the construction industry complain that recent stabilization policies have been at the cost of creating gyrations in their industry; and this complaint is borne out to a considerable extent by the record of fluctuations in "housing starts" (Chart 23-4). Fiscal adjustments are more capable of spreading the adjustment over a number of sectors—including consumption—and of expressing national-policy choices as to the allocation of productive resources between consumption and investment. Particularly the types of investment which are not promising sources of private profit but are socially important—including much of what will be necessary to rehabilitate American cities or set up good substitutes for the urban way of life—can be stimulated only by fiscal measures. Hence the active use of monetary policy can never be a full substitute for flexibility of fiscal policy, though it may make it easier to live with the necessity of adjusting fiscal policy discontinuously and with something of a lag after the economic changes that require the adjustment.

Much can be said for trying to tune fiscal policy with a slight bias toward generating excess demand, and taking up the excess by monetary restriction. The reason we make this suggestion is that monetary restriction has a tendency toward *postponing* investment and thus setting up a backlog of private investment demand which is available to sustain activity in case of an unfavorable turn of events. It has been typical of postwar recessions that private, fixed-investment expenditure has held up well after total output and income have started to sag—though investment *decisions* as registered by corporate capital appropriations, orders and contracts for plant and equipment, and so forth have ordinarily turned down earlier. The momentum of private investment which was previously decided upon but could not immediately be carried out sustains activity in a recession, and gives stabilization policy a chance to adapt before total output falls to disastrous levels. Restrictive monetary policy at times of high activity creates incentives for businessmen with matured investment plans to accept places in the queue rather than try to "jump the queue" by offering fancy prices for quick delivery. The result is not merely to take the inflationary edge off a boom, but to provide in advance a defense against the next recession.

A major factor in the strategy of stabilization policy is to maintain the conviction of the business community that the government can and will prevent either major depressions or major inflations. Despite the sharp fluctuations we observe in *go-ahead decisions* for private investment (registered for example, in the capital commitments curve of Chart 23-4), we can realistically claim that business is planning much farther into the future than it used to do, and is already working on projects which will generate investment over the coming decade or two. If a recession cut so deep that business had to put all its planning effort into defensive action, and had to feel that the future of its markets were so uncertain that long-term planning was pointless, the underlying investment momentum which has made the two postwar decades the most sustained expansion period in the annals might be lost. Underlying business confidence makes the task of economic stabilization easier. But to sustain this underlying confidence, government must demonstrate over and over that it can in fact put the economy back on course before recession or inflation pulls it too far away. Both fiscal and monetary policy must show themselves adaptable and effective.

NOTES ON
ALTERNATIVE POINTS OF VIEW
AND SUPPLEMENTARY READINGS

On the role of economics and economists in stabilization policy, see E. A. Goldenweiser, "The Economist and the State," *American Economic Review,* March 1947, pp. 1–12, and E. G. Nourse, "Economics in the Public Service," *American Economic Review,* Papers and Proceedings, May 1947, pp. 21–30.

For contrasting views of postwar monetary policy, see the several essays in *United States Monetary Policy* (Frederick A. Praeger, Inc., 1964). For a critical appraisal of that policy, concentrating on the incidence of monetary policy, see the Staff Report on *Employment, Growth, and Price Levels* for the Joint Economic Committee (Washington, D.C.: U.S. Government Printing Office, 1960), chap. ix; also the paper by Warren L. Smith, mentioned in the text.

See also Giulio Pontecorvo, Robert P. Shay, and Albert G. Hart, eds., *Issues in Banking and Monetary Analysis* (New York: Holt, Rinehart & Winston, Inc., 1967).

A wide selection of readings on contemporary problems in monetary policy and theory is found in Alan D. Entine, ed., *Monetary Economics: A Book of Readings* (Belmont, California: Wadsworth Publishing Co., 1968).

A review of monetary institutions and policy was made by the privately financed Commission on Money and Credit. The Commissions rather bland conclusions and recommendations are set out in *Money and Credit,* A Report of the Commission on Money and Credit (Englewood Cliffs, N.J.: Prentice Hall, Inc., 1962).

The case for "automaticity" is examined critically by J. M. Culbertson in "Friedman on the Lag in Effect of Monetary Policy," *Journal of Political Economy,* December 1960.

Additional research on policy lags is found in A. Ando, E. C. Brown, R. M. Solow, and J. Kareken, "Lags in Fiscal and Monetary Policy," in *Stabilization Policies,* a series of research studies prepared for the Commission on Money and Credit (Englewood Cliffs, N.J.: Prentice-Hall, Inc., 1963).

For a more extensive discussion of the division of labor in debt management (and a slightly different solution to the problem), see A. G. Hart, *Defense and the Dollar* (New York: 20th Century Fund, 1953), chaps. v, vii, and x.

An excellent summary article of the various debt management theories is William E. Laird's "The Changing Views on Debt Management," *Quarterly Review of Economics and Business,* Autumn 1963, pp. 7–17.

Appendix

This appendix describes the derivation of the numbered series used in the charts of this book. Wherever possible, we have used series published in one of the major compilations. These volumes are designated by initials, as follows:

HS	U.S. Department of Commerce, *Historical Statistics of the United States, Colonial Times to 1957* (Washington, D.C.: U.S. Government Printing Office, 1960). Continued to 1962 and revised in *A Statistical Abstract Supplement to Historical Statistics* (Washington, D.C.: U.S. Government Printing Office, 1965).
BS	U.S. Department of Commerce, *Business Statistics,* 1965 edition (Washington, D.C.: U.S. Government Printing Office, 1965).
SCB	U.S. Department of Commerce, *Survey of Current Business* (monthly).
IO	U.S. Department of Commerce, *United States Income and Output* (Washington, D.C.: U.S. Government Printing Office, 1959).
NI	U.S. Department of Commerce, *National Income,* 1966 edition (Washington, D.C.: U.S. Government Printing Office, 1966).
SA	U.S. Department of Commerce, *Statistical Abstract of the United States* (annual).
FRB	Board of Governors of the Federal Reserve System, *Federal Reserve Bulletin* (monthly).

LTEG U.S. Department of Commerce, *Long-term Economic Growth, 1860–1965* (Washington, D.C.: U.S. Government Printing Office, 1966).

RWG Raymond W. Goldsmith, *et al.*, *A Study of Savings in the United States* (Princeton: Princeton University Press, 1955).

All data are annual, except as otherwise indicated.

Wealth Series

W-1 Total Reproducible Wealth in 1929 Dollars, 1897–1958. For 1897–1908, semidecadal averages of annual estimates; annual data from RWG, Vol. III, p. 20. Thereafter, LTEG (All Reproducible Capital Input Index). Both shifted to 1929 dollars. In billions of dollars.

W-2 Nonfarm Inventories in 1929 Dollars, 1896–1966. For 1896–1949, RWG, Vol. III, p. 21 (current-dollar data on p. 15); for 1950–66, Council of Economic Advisers, *Economic Indicators* (Washington, D.C., monthly), Total Business Inventories, converted into 1929 dollars. In billions of dollars.

Employment Series

E-1 Population of the United States, 1860–1966; decennial estimates. For 1860–1950, HS series A-20; thereafter SCB. Includes armed forces overseas. In millions of persons.

E-2 Work Force Outside of Farming and Government, 1870–1966; decennial estimates. For 1870–1930, Bureau of the Census, *Comparative Occupation Statistics for the United States* (Washington, D.C.: U.S. Government Printing Office, 1945); for 1940 and 1950, SA; thereafter, SCB. In millions of workers.

E-3 Manufacturing Employment, 1889–1914. From E. R. Frickey, *Economic Fluctuations in the United States* (Cambridge: Harvard University Press, 1942), diagram opposite p. 180. Presented as an index; 1899 = 100.

E-4 Number of Full-time Equivalent Employees and Entrepreneurs Outside Farming and Government, 1919–29. From Simon Kuznets, *National Income and Its Composition* (New York: National Bureau of Economic Research, 1941), pp. 314–17. In millions of workers.

E-5 Number of Full-time Equivalent Persons Engaged in Production Outside Farming and Government, 1929–66. From NI, IO, and SCB. In millions of workers.

E-6   Farm Employment, 1910–66. For 1910–59, BS, series K-73; thereafter, SA. In millions of workers.

Output Series

O-1   Capacity Output, 1872–1965. 1872–1908 developed from estimates of the annual rate of growth of total output as between peak years in actual output (1872, 1892, 1906, 1929); 1909–65 from LTEG, Potential Gross National Product, series A4 and A5. Presented as an index; 1929 = 100.

O-1A   Capacity Output in 1929 Dollars, 1872–1965. Series 0-1 converted into 1929 dollars by deflator implicit in LTEG series A4 and A5. In billions of 1929 dollars.

O-2   Gross National Product in Current Dollars, 1897–1966. From LTEG (1897–1908 series A7, thereafter series A8). In billions of dollars.

RO-2   Gross National Product in 1929 Dollars, 1897–1966. Series O-2 shifted to 1929 dollars using the Commerce Department price deflator for 1929. In billions of dollars, or as an index; 1929 = 100.

O-3   Gross Nonfarm Product in 1929 Dollars, 1889–1952. From John W. Kendrick, *Productivity Trends in the United States* (New York: National Bureau of Economic Research, 1961). Series A 17 in LTEG.

O-4   Manufacturing Output, Index: 1929 = 100, 1889–1956. From John W. Kendrick, *Productivity Trends in the United States* (New York: National Bureau of Economic Research, 1961). Series A-19 in LTEG.

O-5   Manufacturing Production, 1919–66. FRB, December 1959 and subsequent issues. 1947–49 = 100.

O-6   Industrial Production, 1899–1918. Based on annual averages of quarterly series O-22; linked to series O-5 using overlapping estimate by Solomon Fabricant as published in HS, series P-12. 1947–49 = 100.

O-7   Durable Manufactures Production, 1860–1914. From Edwin Frickey, *Production in the United States* (Cambridge: Harvard University Press, 1947), p. 64. 1899 = 100.

O-8   Nondurable Manufactures Production, 1860–1914. Same source as O-3, p. 64. 1899 = 100.

O-9   Durable Manufactures Production, 1919–66. Same source as O-5. 1947-49 = 100.

O-10   Nondurable Manufactures Production, 1919–66. Same source as O-5. 1947–49 = 100.

O-11   Gross Farm Product in 1929 Dollars, 1889–1953. From John W. Kendrick, *Productivity Trends in the United States* (New York: National Bureau of Economic Research, 1961). Series A21 in LTEG.

O-12   Gross Farm Product in 1939 Dollars, 1910–65. From LTEG, Gross Farm Product, series A22, converted to 1939 prices. Presented as an index; 1939 = 100.

O-13   Real Value of Building Permits, 1875–1933. Newman's series, as published in HS, series N-63. Series in 1913 prices, presented as an index; 1913 = 100.

O-14   Real Public and Private Construction Expenditure, 1915–62. From HS, series N-29 and N-29a. Series in 1947–49 dollars, presented as an index; 1939 = 100.

O-15   Steam-railroad Ton Miles, 1882–1962. HS series Q-29 and Q-82. Presented as an index; 1929 = 100.

O-16   Production of Electrical Energy, 1902–65. For 1902–62, HS series S-15; thereafter, SCB series converted from monthly to annual rates. Series in kilowatt hours, presented as an index; 1939 = 100.

O-17   Consumer Services Production, 1929–65. From NI, in 1958 prices. Presented as an index; 1958 = 100.

O-18   Minerals Production, 1899–1939. Barger and Schurr index as published in HS, series M-67. 1899 = 100.

O-19   Minerals Production, 1929–66. Federal Reserve index from FRB, December 1959 and subsequent issues. 1947–49 = 100.

O-20   Bituminous Coal Production, 1865–1929. From HS, series M-88. Presented as an index; 1899 = 100.

O-21   Industrial Production, 1919–66; monthly. Federal Reserve index of manufacturing, mining, and utilities output, from FRB, December 1959, and subsequent issues. 1947–49 = 100.

O-22   Industrial Production, 1899–1914: quarterly. From L. P. Ayres, *Turning Points in Business Cycles* (New York: The Macmillan Co., 1939), p. 203. 1899 = 100.

Price Series

P-1   Index of Wholesale Prices, All Commodities, 1860–1966. From LTEG, series B69, shifted to a 1926 base. 1926 = 100.

P-1A   Index of Wholesale Prices, Metals, and Metal Products, 1890–1945. From HS, series E-20. 1926 = 100.

P-1B   Index of Wholesale Prices, Farm Products, 1890–1966. For 1890–1951, HS, series E-15; thereafter, FRB series shifted to a 1926 base. 1926 = 100.

P-1C   Index of Wholesale Prices, All Commodities, 1899–1966: monthly. For 1899–1939, HS (1949 edition), series App-23; thereafter FRB. Data for 1899–1939, 1926 = 100; data for 1940–66, 1947–49 = 100.

P-2   Implicit Price Deflator for Gross National Product, 1897–1966. From LTEG, series B62 and B63 shifted to a 1929 base. 1929 = 100.

P-2A   Implicit Price Deflator for Consumer-durables Component of GNP, 1929–65. IO. 1958 = 100.

P-2B   Implicit Price Deflator for Consumer-nondurables Component of GNP, 1929–65. Same source and base as P-2A.

P-2C   Implicit Price Deflator for Consumer-services Component of GNP, 1929–65. Same source and base as P-2A.

P-2D   Implicit Price Deflator for Residential Structures Component of GNP, 1929–65. Same source and base as P-2A.

P-2E   Implicit Price Deflator for Producers-durables Component of GNP, 1929–65. Same source and base as P-2A.

P-3   Wholesale Prices, Farm Products, 1860–90. From Aldrich Report, as published in HS (1949 edition), series L-27. Linked to series P-1B; 1926 = 100.

Saving Series

S-1   Gross Private Saving, 1897–1949. From RWG, as in LTEG (personal and corporate saving plus capital consumption allowance). In billions of current dollars.

S-1A   Gross Private Saving, 1929–65. From LTEG (same coverage as in S-1). In billions of current dollars.

S-2   Gross Private Saving as a Per Cent of Gross National Product, 1897–1949. Series S-1 divided by series O-2.

S-2A   Gross Private Saving as a Per Cent of Gross National Product, 1929–65. Series S-1A divided by series O-2.

Money-stock Series

M-1   Commercial Bank Demand Deposits, 1896–1965: end of year. For 1896–1949, RWG (adjusted demand deposits *less* deposits of state and local governments and of other financial institutions),

Vol. I, p. 385; thereafter, FRB (adjusted demand deposits). In billions of dollars.

M-2 Money Stock, 1896–1965: end of year. Series M-1 *plus* currency outside of banks and the Treasury. For currency, 1896–1919, RWG, Vol. I, p. 382; thereafter, FRB. In billions of dollars. (Also presented in 1929 dollars as series RM-2.)

M-2A Money Stock, 1897–1966: average for year. Series M-2 centered on mid-year by averaging adjacent end-year estimates. In billions of dollars.

M-3 Cash Assets, 1896–1965: end of year. Series M-2 *plus* series L-1 and the net time deposits of commercial banks. Time deposits as in series L-4. In billions of dollars. (Also presented in 1929 dollars as series RM-3.)

M-3A Cash Assets, 1897–1966: average for year. Series M-3 centered on mid-year by averaging adjacent end-year estimates. In billions of dollars.

M-4 Cash Assets, 1941–65; end of year. Series M-3 *plus* Treasury bills in the hands of the public. For Treasury bills, FRB (holdings of "other investors"). In billions of dollars.

M-4A Cash Assets, 1941–65: average for year. Series M-4 centered on mid-year by averaging adjacent end-year estimates. In billions of dollars.

M-5 Cash Assets, 1873, 1875–92: average for year. Currency, demand and time deposits, as computed by AGH (*Money, Debt, and Economic Activity,* 2nd ed. [Englewood Cliffs, N.J.: Prentice-Hall, Inc., 1953], pp. 551–52]. In billions of dollars.

M-6 Cash Assets, 1892–1902: average for year. Same source as M-5. In billions of dollars.

M-7 Money Stock, 1982–1902: average for year. Currency and adjusted demand deposits. Same source as M-5. In billions of dollars.

M-8 Money Stock, 1919–41: semiannually. Currency outside banks and adjusted demand deposits. From Board of Governors of the Federal Reserve System, *Banking and Monetary Statistics* (Washington, D.C.: Federal Reserve Board, 1943), p. 34. In billions of dollars.

M-9 Money Stock, 1946–66: seasonally adjusted monthly estimates. Currency outside banks and adjusted demand deposits, from FRB, February 1960, and subsequent issues. In billions of dollars.

M-10 Individual Deposits in National Banks, 1899–1914: average of call dates. From A. A. Young, *An Analysis of Bank Statistics for the United States* (Cambridge: Harvard University Press, 1928), pp. 11–13. In billions of dollars.

M-11   Bank Loans to Business and Consumers, 1896–1927: total out-standing at end of year. From RWG, Vol. I, p. 410 (total non-farm, nonreal-estate loans, other than loans for purchasing securi-ties). In billions of dollars. (Also used as RM-11, deflated by price index implicit in Goldsmith deflation of series W-2; in billions of 1929 dollars.)

M-11A   Bank Loans to Business, 1923–66: total outstanding at end of year. For 1923–49, RWG, Vol. I, p. 410; total nonfarm, nonreal-estate loans, other than loans for purchasing securities and con-sumer loans; thereafter, FRB, similar coverage. In billions of dollars. (Also used as RM-11, deflated by same index as RM-11 and an extension of that index developed by deriving deflators for Commerce Department inventory investment estimates and transposing to a 1929 base; in billions of 1929 dollars.)

Liquid-assets Series

L-1   Mutual Savings Bank Deposits, 1896–1966: end of year. For 1896–1949, RWG, Vol. I, p. 413: thereafter, FRB. In billions of dollars.

L-2   Savings and Loan Shares, 1896–1966: end of year. For 1896–1949, RWG (private repurchaseable shares), Vol. I, p. 441; thereafter, FRB (savings capital). In billions of dollars.

L-3   Life Insurance Policyholders' Equity, 1896–1966: end of year. For 1896–1949, RWG, Vol. I, p. 450; thereafter, FRB (total assets *less* policy loans and other assets). In billions of dollars.

L-4   Total Deposit Liabilities of Commercial Banks, 1896–1965: end of year. Series M-1 *plus* net time deposits of commercial banks. For net time deposits, 1896–1949, RWG (time deposits other than U.S. government, *less* deposits of Postal Savings Sys-tem and state and local governments), Vol. I, p. 386; thereafter, FRB (same coverage). In billions of dollars.

L-5   Cash and Near-cash Assets of the Public (I), 1920–65: end of year. Sum of series M-1, L-1, L-2, and L-4. In billions of dollars.

L-5A   Cash and Near-cash Assets of the Public (II), 1920–65: end of year. Series L-5 *plus* United States Government Savings Bonds (zero before 1935); for Savings Bonds, FRB. In billions of dollars.

L-5B   Cash and Near-cash Assets of the Public (III), 1941–65: end of year. Series L-5A *plus* Treasury bills in the hands of the public. Treasury bills as in M-4 (assumed to be zero before 1941). In billions of dollars.

L-5C Cash and Near-cash Assets of the Public (II), 1921–65: average for year. Series L-5A centered on mid-year by averaging adjacent end-year estimates. In billions of dollars.

L-5D Cash and Near-cash Assets of the Public (III), 1942–65; average for year. Series L-5B centered on mid-year by averaging adjacent end-year estimates. In billions of dollars.

L-6 Liquid Assets of the Public (I), 1920–65: end of year. Series L-5A *plus* marketable United States government bonds. For marketable bonds, FRB (holdings of nonfinancial corporations and of other investors, *less* holdings of savings and loan associations; data prior to 1935 interpolated from June estimates and adjusted to exclude insurance company holdings). In billions of dollars.

L-7 Liquid Assets of the Public (II), 1920–65: end of year. Series L-6 *plus* series L-3. In billions of dollars.

Velocity Series

V-1 Money Stock Velocity. 1897–1965. GNP (series O-2) divided by money stock (series M-2A). In circuits per year.

V-2 Cash Assets Velocity (I), 1897–1965. GNP (series O-2) divided by cash assets (series M-3A). In circuits per year.

V-3 Cash Assets Velocity (II), 1945–65. GNP (series O-2) divided by cash assets *cum* Treasury bills (series M-4A). In circuits per year.

V-4 Liquid Assets Velocity (I), 1929–65. GNP (series O-2) divided by cash and near-cash assets (series L-5C). In circuits per year.

V-4A Liquid Assets Velocity (II), 1945–65. GNP (series O-2) divided by cash and near-cash assets *cum* Treasury bills (series L-5D). In circuits per year.

V-5 Demand Deposit Turnover Outside New York, 1919–51. Ratio of demand deposit debits to total demand deposits, from Board of Governors of the Federal Reserve System, *Banking and Monetary Statistics* (Washington, D.C.: Federal Reserve Board 1943) and FRB. In circuits per year.

V-5A Demand Deposit Turnover, Six Centers, 1951–64. Ratio of demand deposit debits to total demand deposits, six reporting centers outside New York, from FRB. In circuits per year.

V-5B Demand Deposit Turnover, All Centers Outside New York, 1951–64. Ratio of demand deposit debits to total demand deposits, 300-odd centers outside New York, and excluding V-5A, from FRB. In circuits per year.

V-5C Demand Deposit Turnover, Six Centers, 1965–66. Ratio of demand deposit debits to total demand deposits, six leading Standard Metropolitan Statistical Areas outside New York, from FRB. In circuits per year.

V-5D   Demand Deposit Turnover, All Centers Outside New York, 1965–66. Ratio of demand deposit debits to total demand deposits, 200-odd SMSA's outside New York, and excluding V-5C, from FRB. In circuits per year.

Interest-rate Series

B-1   Prime Commercial Paper (four to six months), 1890–1966: average in year. For 1890–1957, HS, series X-306; thereafter, FRB.

B-1A   Prime Commercial Paper (four to six months), 1890–1966: monthly. For 1890–1936, F. R. Macaulay, *Bond Yields, Interest Rates, and Stock Prices* (New York, National Bureau of Economic Research, 1938); thereafter, FRB. Also shown as bimonthly averages of monthly figures.

B-2   Yield on Long-term United States Government Bonds (Fully Taxable), 1946–56: monthly. From FRB.

B-2A   Yield on Long-term United States Government Bonds (Fully Taxable, New Series), 1953–66: monthly. From FRB. (This series includes a different collection of securities from that on which B-2 is based.)

Index